Books by Dan Kurzman

Kishi and Japan
Subversion of the Innocents
Santo Domingo: Revolt of the Damned
Genesis 1948: The First Arab-Israeli War
The Race for Rome

THE RACE FOR ROME

DAN KURZMAN

The Race for Rome

DOUBLEDAY & COMPANY, INC.
GARDEN CITY, NEW YORK
1975

Grateful acknowledgments are made for permission to include
copyrighted selections from the following:

General Mark W. Clark Collection, Archives-Museum, The
Citadel, Charleston, South Carolina.

CALCULATED RISK by General Mark W. Clark. Reprinted
by permission of Harper & Row, Inc.

THE ROME ESCAPE LINE by Sam Derry, published by
W. W. Norton & Company, Inc. Reprinted by permission
of the author.

ROMA CLANDESTINA by Fulvia Ripa di Meana, published by
Ramello-Editore-Corina. Reprinted by permission of the
author.

THE INTERPRETER by Eugen Dollmann, published by The
Hutchinson Publishing Group Ltd.

A SPY IN ROME by Peter Tompkins, Copyright © 1962 by
Peter Tompkins. Reprinted by permission of Simon and
Schuster, Inc.

BEFORE THE DAWN by Eugenio Zolli. Copyright, Sheed
and Ward, Inc., Publishers. Reprinted by permission of
the publisher.

Library of Congress Cataloging in Publication Data
Kurzman, Dan.
The race for Rome.
Bibliography: p. 447.
Includes index.
1. World War, 1939–1945—Italy—Rome (City)
2. Rome (City)—History—1870—   I. Title.
D763.I82R628   940.54′21
ISBN 0-385-06555-8

To Florence

Contents

I. BEFORE THE RACE

II. THE RACE

Acknowledgments

While working overseas on this book, I was particularly fortunate to have the assistance of Florence Knopf, whose brilliantly imaginative editorial advice proved invaluable. I cannot thank her enough.

Claire Knopf, her twin sister, also exhibited rare creativity and meticulous discrimination in the editing of this work.

In New York, Betty Prashker, my editor at Doubleday, offered exceptionally sound and sensitive counsel. And Berenice Hoffman contributed her profound literary wisdom.

I am also indebted to Ligia Chavez, Padrica Mendez, and Elizabeth Stace, who translated documents from Italian, interpreted, and assisted enormously in my research.

Others whom I wish to thank include my agent, Ruth Aley, who suffered with me throughout; Renato Loffredo, one of Italy's great journalists who helped me in numerous ways; Richard Deane Taylor, the world-renowned artist who drew the maps for this book; Diane Matthews of Doubleday who did much of the production work; Georgiana Remer who copy edited with great care and dedication; Shelly Sadeh who helped as an interpreter from Italian; Louise Montalto who aided in the research; and the following translators:

Rudolfo del Campio and Rolfe Chamness (from German and Italian); Nora Foster, Pat Kemp, Marie Molino, and Teresa Pase (from Italian); and Alfred Hiller, Alvaro Lopes, and Antonio Schras (from German).

Among those who furnished me background information or in other ways facilitated my research were:

FEDERICO ALESSANDRINI—*Vatican spokesman;* JOSEPH AVERY—*archivist, U.S. National Archives;* RICHARD BAUER—*archivist, U.S. National Archives;* FRITZ BECKER—*American Jewish leader;* PIETRO BOCCACCIO—*Italian priest who knew Zolli;* MRS. LOUIS B. BRANHAM—*technician, U.S. National Archives;* LUISA CAPO—*Administrative assistant, Comune di Roma;* GIORGIO CAPUTO—*Italian historian on liberation of Rome;* WILLIAM H. CUNLIFFE—*archivist, U.S. National Archives;* PROF. RENZO DE FELICE—*Italian author and expert on Roman Jewish community;* ETTORE DELL'ARICCIA—*Italian journalist, knew Zolli;* COL. DI PASQUALE—*Italian Defense Ministry official;* GABRIELE FRANZ—*German archivist, Bibliothek für Zeitgeschichte, Stuttgart;* JURGEN FINDEISEN—*West German Foreign Ministry official;* WILLY GEORGI—*West German Foreign Ministry official;* MSGR. ALBERTO GIOVANNETTI—*Vatican observer to United Nations;* FATHER ROBERT L. GRAHAM—*American-born Vatican historian;* WERNER HAUPT—*subchief, Bibliothek für Zeitgeschichte, Stuttgart;* HARRY HERSHENSON—*Chicago judge (formerly a U.S. Army officer in Rome);* PROF. LEONIDAS HILL—*Canadian biographer of Ambassador von Weizsäcker;* THOMAS E. HOHMANN—*archivist, U.S. National Archives;* DORA HOWARD—*technician, U.S. National Archives;* DR. JOSEPH LICHTEN—*American Jewish expert on Pope Pius XII;* MARIA GUZZUGLI MARINI—*administrative assistant, Comune di Roma;* FATHER ANGELO MARTINI—*Vatican historian;* WILLIAM BARRETT McGURN—*U.S. State Department official;* HERR MEYER—*Militärgeschichtliches Forschungsamt, Freiburg;* R. MOSSIN—*Polish journalist;* JOHN NORTH—*British biographer of General Alexander;* TOBIA PETTA—*custodian, Via Tasso Museum, Rome;* COL. MARIO PIZZUTI—*Italian Financial Police official;* ARMANDO RAVAGLIOLI—*official of Comune di Roma;* ELIO SAVELLONI—*chief of Il Messaggero archives;* FATHER BURKHART SCHNEIDER—*Vatican historian;* COL. DIONISIO SEPIELLI—*Italian Defense Ministry official;* MSGR. SILVESTRINI—*Vatican official;* GIOVANNI SLEITER—*Italian Defense Ministry official;* MAJOR RAY SMITH—*U.S. Army press officer, Pentagon;* BERNARD S. SOLOMON—*American who knew Chief Rabbi Zolli;* JOHN E. TAYLOR—*archivist, U.S. National Archives;* ELIO TOAFF—*present chief rabbi of Rome;* JOAN B. URBAN—*history professor, Catholic University, Washington, D.C.;* SAM WAAGENAAR—*American writer on Roman Jewish community;* GEORGE WAGNER—*technician, U.S. National Archives;* ROBERT L. WAGNER—*U.S. 36th Division historian;* MRS. FRED WALKER—*wife of 36th Division commander;*

FATHER WHALEN—*office of Apostolic Delegate, Washington, D.C.;*
ROBERT WOLFE—*specialist, modern European history, U.S. National
Archives.*

Characters in the drama of Rome's liberation who kindly agreed to
let me interview them include the following (identified by the positions
they held at the time, and by nationality *if* they are not Italian):

ERIC Y. ABE—*Nisei officer, U.S. 34th Division;* GIOVANNI AGNELLI—
member of Italian industrial family; SUSANNA AGNELLI (CONTESSA
PATTAZZI)—*sister of Virginia Agnelli;* CONRAD AHLERS—*German Army
officer, Cassino;* GIORGIO AMENDOLA—*Communist chief in Rome;*
ELLIOT W. AMICK—*U.S. 36th Division officer;* TADEUSZ ANDERS—
Polish Army officer (brother of General Anders); GEN. ERNESTO ARGEN-
ZIANO—*Financial Police commander;* RICHARD ARVAY—*French Jew in
Rome;* VAN T. BARFOOT—*U.S. 45th Division officer;* LUIGI BARZINI—
Italian writer; ETTORE BASEVI—*Centro X officer;* RICCARDO BAUER—
Action party partisan chief; COL. DIETRICH BEELITZ—*chief of operations
under Field Marshal Kesselring;* FATHER BENOÎT-MARIE DE BOURG D'IRE
—*French priest in Rome who helped Jews;* ROSARIO BENTIVEGNA—*a
Communist leader in Rome;* YOLANDA BERARDI—*Virginia Agnelli's maid;*
COL. HERMANN BERLIN—*German Tenth Army staff officer;* ALFREDO
BERNARDINI—*Clandestine Front officer;* LOUIS BERTEIL—*French Army
officer;* BRIG. GEN. ADAM BIELINSKI—*second in command, 5th Polish
Division;* JACQUES DE BLESSON—*French diplomat in Rome;* COL. WLADY-
SLAW BOBINSKI—*second in command, 2nd Polish Armored Brigade;* MAJ.
GEN. ZYMUNT BOHUSZ-SZYSZKO—*General Anders' second in command;*
CARLO BONCIANO—*Italian Army officer;* PAUL BONDIS—*French Army
officer;* COL. ALBERT BONHOURÉ—*aide to General Juin;* OTTORINO BORIN
—*Resistance officer;* FRANK BUONICORE—*U.S. 85th Division soldier;*
MARIO BUENTEMPI—*Clandestine Front officer;* RICHARD M. BURRAGE—
U.S. 36th Division officer; CARLA CAPPONI—*a Communist leader in
Rome;* MAJ. GEN. GIACOMO CARBONI—*officer charged by Marshal
Badoglio to defend Rome in Sept. 1943;* PROF. GIUSEPPE CARONIA—
partisan doctor, Rome; GEN. FILIPPO CARUSO—*commander of the carabi-
nieri in Rome;* ALDO CAVA—*Jewish refugee;* SOPHIA CAVALETTI—*secre-
tary to Chief Rabbi Zolli after his conversion;* FELICE CHILANTI—*Red
Flag partisan;* GLORIA CHILANTI—*Felice's daughter;* VIVIANA CHILANTI—
Felice's wife; MICHAEL CHINIGO—*American INS correspondent;* MSGR.
GIOVANNI CIGOGNANI—*Vatican representative in Washington;* HANS
G. CLAPPER—*U.S. Army intelligence officer;* LT. GEN. MARK W. CLARK

—commander, U.S. Fifth Army; ERNESTO COCCSTEIN—*German officer;* CARLA COLLI—*friend of Virginia Agnelli;* GIUSEPPE COSMELLI—*Italian government official;* MAJ. GEN. JOHN B. COULTER—*commander, U.S. 85th Division;* JEAN COURTOIS—*French Army officer;* COL. JOSEPH CRAWFORD—*U.S. 88th Division officer;* FEDELE D'AMICO—*editor, Catholic Communist newspaper;* YVES DEBROISE—*French diplomat in Rome;* LILLO DELLA SETA—*a Jewish leader in Rome;* PIERRE DELSOL— *French officer with Captain Planès;* MARIA DENISE (GUANI)—*Italian actress;* ERNEST H. DERVISIAN—*U.S. 34th Division officer;* FATHER DEZZA—*priest who knew Chief Rabbi Zolli;* GIOVANNI DI LORENZO— *Clandestine Front officer;* ELEANORA DI PORTO—*wife of Giacomo Di Porto;* GIACOMO DI PORTO—*Ghetto resident;* TOMASZ DOBROWOLSKI— *Polish Army soldier;* COL. EUGEN DOLLMANN—*SS officer in Rome;* GIUSEPPE DOSI—*Roman police officer and journalist;* RUDOLF DOUTH— *German officer, Cassino;* DONALD DOWNES—*American OSS agent;* PIERRE VICTOR DUBOIS—*French Army soldier;* GEN. BRONISLAW DUCH— *commander, 3rd Carpathian Division, II Polish Corps;* JANET DUNCAN— *wife of Stars and Stripes artist Gregory Duncan;* OLGA FERA—*Socialist partisan;* ADM. EMILIO FERRERI—*Italian naval officer;* MARIO FIORENTINI —*a Communist leader in Rome;* GUIDO GANELLA—*Vatican journalist;* ALDO GAROSCI—*Socialist partisan leader;* GEN. GABRIEL GASSIAT— *French Army officer;* COL. LEON GNATQWSKI—*Polish Army officer;* GIUSEPPE GRACCERA—*Socialist partisan leader;* PAUL S. GREEN—*Stars and Stripes reporter;* PIETRO GRIFFONI—*a Communist leader in Rome;* MAJ. GEN. ALFRED M. GRUENTHER—*General Clark's chief of staff;* MAJ. GEN. AUGUSTIN GUILLAUME—*commander of* goumiers; ROBERT GUILLAUMET—*French Army officer;* GERHARD GUMPERT—*German diplomat in Rome;* WALTER R. GUNTHARP—*U.S. 88th Division officer;* ROBERTO GUZZO—*Red Flag party officer;* WOLFGANG HAGEMANN—*Field Marshal Kesselring's interpreter;* LT. GEN. JOHN HARDING—*General Alexander's chief of staff;* GEN. FRIEDRICH-WILHELM HAUCK—*German task force commander;* GRAHAM HEILMAN—*U.S. 1st Special Service Force officer;* PIERRE HEITZMANN—*French soldier;* COL. JAMES W. HOLSINGER—*U.S. Fifth Army officer;* GRAHAM HOVEY—*American INS correspondent;* COL. HAMILTON HOWZE—*commander, U.S. Task Force Howze;* LEON HRYNKIEWICZ—*Polish officer, Cassino;* COL. ROBERT IVES —*U.S. 36th Division;* SISTER KATHARINE—*French nun in Notre Dame de Sion Convent, Rome;* BRIG. GEN. PAUL W. KENDALL—*second in command, U.S. 88th Division;* ALBRECHT VON KESSEL—*Ambassador von Weizsäcker's assistant;* COL. R. H. KILROE—*U.S. Fifth Army staff officer;* MAJ. GEN. SIDNEY C. KIRKMAN—*commander, XIII Corps, British Eighth Army;* COL. KARL-HEINRICH GRAF VON KLINCKOW-

STROEM—*chief of staff, German LI Mountain Corps;* UGO LA MALFA—*Action party leader;* LT. GEN. SIR OLIVER LEESE—*commander, British Eighth Army;* MAJ. GEN. LYMAN LEMNITZER—*U.S. officer on General Alexander's staff;* RENZO LEVI—*a Jewish leader in Rome;* EVA EPISCOPO-LIPINSKY—*Resistance supporter;* LINO LIPINSKY—*brother of Eva, Resistance supporter;* CHESTER LUBA—*Polish Army soldier;* EUGENE LUBOMIRSKI—*General Anders' aide;* RENZO LUCIDI—*member, O'Flaherty organization;* FALCONE LUCIFERO—*Italian government minister;* WALTER LULEY—*German Army officer, Cassino;* PIERRE LYAUTEY—*aide to General Guillaume;* COL. GEORGE E. LYNCH—*regimental commander, U.S. 36th Division;* FRANCO MALFATTI—*Socialist partisan;* DJILLALI MANSOUR—*Moroccan soldier in French Army;* LILY MARX—*assistant to Centro X officer Basevi;* JOZEF MINSKI—*Polish Army officer;* FATHER GIOVANNI BATTISTA MOCATA—*Roman priest;* ROBERT MODIGLIANI—*acquaintance of Chief Rabbi Zolli;* EITEL MÖLLHAUSEN—*German consul in Rome;* ORFEO MUCCI—*a Red Flag party leader;* JOSEF MÜLLER—*German diplomat;* MICHELE MULTEDO—*assistant to Colonel Montezemolo;* ARTURO MUSCO—*Roman police inspector;* COL. UGO MUSCO—*a Centro X leader;* PIETRO NENNI—*Left-wing Socialist party leader;* BERYL R. NEWMAN—*U.S. 34th Division officer;* GIORGIO NOVELLI—*Italian intelligence officer;* MARIOLINA ODONE (FAVORIT)—*daughter of General Odone;* NICOLA ONORATI—*Roman partisan;* MSGR. ALFREDO OTTAVIANI—*Vatican official;* REYNOLDS PACKARD—*American UP correspondent;* MSGR. PIETRO PALAZZINI—*Vatican official in San Giovanni in Laterano;* PRINCESS NINI PALLAVICINI—*member, O'Flaherty organization;* FRANÇOIS DE PANAFIEU—*French Army officer;* OLYMPIA PANCIERI —*sister of Rabbi Pancieri;* SANDRO PERTINI—*Socialist party leader;* LOMBARDO PERUGIA—*Jewish refugee;* PRINCESS ENZA PIGNATELLI ARAGONA—*friend of Pope Pius XII;* FERNANDO PIPERNO—*a Jewish leader in Rome;* COLETTE PLANÈS—*Free French ambulance driver, wife of Pierre Planès;* PIERRE PLANÈS—*French armored force commander;* HUMPHRY PLATT—*British Eighth Army officer;* LT. COL. JOHN PLATT—*British Eighth Army officer;* ANTONIO POCE—*commander, Red Flag partisans;* COL. ROBERT W. PORTER—*U.S. II Corps chief of staff;* GEN. O. POYDENOT—*French artillery commander;* DONALD PRYCE-JONES—*American OSS agent in Italy;* RUDOLF RAHN—*German ambassador to Mussolini's Salò government;* ALFREDO RAVENNA—*Roman rabbi;* JACK RAYMOND—*Stars and Stripes reporter;* LYDIA REDMOND (PRINCESS SAN FAUSTINO)—*sister of Virginia Agnelli;* CARLO RESIO—*officer under Admiral Maugeri;* FRANZ RIEHEMANN—*German officer, Cassino;* JOHN T. RIELLY—*sergeant, U.S. 88th Division;* MARCHESA FULVIA RIPA DI MEANA —*cousin of Colonel Montezemolo;* SALVATORE RISO—*Red Flag officer;* COL. PHILIPPE DES ROBERT—*chief of staff, 1st (Free French) Motorized*

Brigade; GOFFREDO ROCCAS—*Roman Jewish leader*; FRANCO RODANO
—*Catholic Communist party leader*; ANGELA MARIA ROMANO—*victim
of American bombing in Rome*; MARIE CELESTE (BIBI) ROSSI (*later
RUSPOLI*)—*Colonel Dollmann's secretary*; PRINCE FRANCESCO RUSPOLI
—*friend of Colonel Dollmann*; HANS ULRICH SCHROEDER—*German
General Staff officer*; CARLO SALINARI—*a Communist leader in Rome*;
FELICE SANTINI—*a Centro X leader*; AUGUSTO SEGRE—*a Jewish leader
in Rome*; ANGELO SERMONETA—*Jewish refugee*; ROBERTO SERMONETA—
Angelo's brother, Jewish refugee; CHARLES W. SHEA—*sergeant, U.S.
88th Division*; WILLIAM PHILIP SIDNEY—*British Eighth Army officer*;
ELENA SONNINO-FINZI—*Roman Jew*; SETTIMIO SORANI—*a Jewish leader
in Rome*; GIUSEPPE SPATARO—*a Christian Democratic party partisan
leader*; CERILO SPINELLI—*a Socialist partisan leader*; BRIG. GEN. ROBERT
STACK—*chief of staff, U.S. 36th Division*; MICHAEL STERN—*American
NANA correspondent*; COL. ORAN C. STOVALL—*U.S. 36th Division
officer*; COL. WILLIAM STRATTON—*British Eighth Army officer*; ELEA-
NORA (LIA) T.—*woman who saved Michele Multedo*; ERICH TIMM—
German Army captain; HAROLD TITTMANN—*U.S. representative to Vati-
can*; PETER TOMPKINS—*American OSS agent*; ANTONIO TRAVIA—*Monsi-
gnor Montini's secretary*; MAJ. GEN. HEINZ TRETTNER—*commander,
German 4th Parachute Division*; COL. PAUL MAURICE TRICOT-DUNOIS—
French Army officer; ANTONELLO TROMBADORI—*a Communist leader in
Rome*; ROBERT W. VAN DE VELDE—*U.S. Army intelligence officer*; GIU-
LIANO VASSALLI—*a Socialist party leader*; FRANÇOIS DE VIAL—*French
diplomat in Rome*; JOHN A. VITA—*U.S. Fifth Army sergeant*; HERMANN
VOELCK-UNSIN—*German officer*; FLORA VOLPINI—*Italian who helped Al-
lied POWs*; RICHARD WAKEFORD—*British Eighth Army officer*; COL. ED-
WIN A. WALKER—*U.S. 1st Special Service Force officer*; GEN. DUDLEY
WARD—*commander, 5th Division, British Eighth Army*; GEN. WALTER
WARLIMONT—*German General Staff officer*; REGINALD DE WARREN—
French Army officer; FATHER ANTON WEBER—*Vatican official*; HANS-
JOACHIM WECK—*German Army officer, Cassino*; ADELHEID VON WEIZ-
SÄCKER (GRÄFIN ZU EULENBURG)—*daughter of Ambassador von Wiez-
säcker*; MARIANNE VON WEIZSÄCKER—*wife of Ambassador von Weizsäcker*
RICHARD VON WEIZSÄCKER—*son of Ambassador von Weizsäcker*; LT.
GEN. SIEGFRIED WESTPHAL—*Field Marshal Kesselring's chief of staff*;
GEN. KARL WOLFF—*SS chief in Italy*; SIGNOR X—*Roman partisan*;
MIRIAM ZOLLI (DE BERNART)—*Chief Rabbi Zolli's younger daughter*.

The author warmly thanks all these people as well as all others who
contributed to the realization of this book but are not listed here.

Chronology

July 25, 1943   Mussolini is overthrown.

September 8, 1943   Italy signs armistice with Allies.

September 9, 1943   King Victor Emmanuel III and Prime Minister Badoglio flee Rome; Allies land at Salerno.

September 10, 1943   Germans occupy Rome.

September 12, 1943   Hitler orders SS General Wolff to prepare abduction of Pope Pius XII.

October 16, 1943   Germans round up Roman Jews.

January 17, 1944   British X Corps crosses Garigliano River.

January 20, 1944   U.S. 36th Division is smashed at Rapido River.

January 22, 1944   Allies land at Anzio.

January 24 to February 12, 1944   U.S. II Corps fights First Battle of Cassino.

February 16 to 20, 1944   Germans attack Anzio without success.

February 16 to 18, 1944   New Zealand Corps fights Second Battle of Cassino; Allies bomb Benedictine monastery.

February 22, 1944   General Alexander submits plan for Operation DIADEM to Allies for approval.

February 28, 1944   General Alexander explains DIADEM to his commanders.

February 29 to March 4, 1944   Germans attack Anzio unsuccessfully for second time.

March 15 to 23, 1944 New Zealand Corps fights Third Battle of Cassino.

March 23, 1944 Roman partisans kill 33 Germans on Via Rasella in Rome.

March 25, 1944 Germans shoot 335 hostages in Ardeatine Caves in retaliation.

April 2, 1944 General Alexander holds second conference with his commanders on DIADEM.

April 17, 1944 Germans and Fascists round up and deport 750 Romans.

April 24, 1944 First popular democratic government is formed in Italy.

May 1, 1944 General Alexander holds final conference with his commanders on DIADEM.

May 3, 1944 General strike in Rome fails.

May 10, 1944 Pope secretly receives SS General Wolff to discuss peace and the salvation of Rome.

May 11, 1944 Operation DIADEM starts.

May 12, 1944 French capture Monte Faito and Castelforte; British XIII Corps crosses Gari River; Poles fail to take Monte Cassino.

May 13, 1944 French capture Monte Majo.

May 14, 1944 German XIV Panzer Corps flees toward Adolf Hitler Line; U. S. II Corps captures Santa Maria Infante.

May 15, 1944 *Goumiers* capture Monte Petrella.

May 16, 1944 *Goumiers* capture Monte Revole.

May 17, 1944 Poles make second attack on Monte Cassino; British XIII Corps cuts Highway 6; French capture Esperia; U.S. II Corps captures Formia.

May 18, 1944 Poles capture Cassino.

May 22, 1944 French capture Pico.

May 23, 1944 U.S. VI Corps starts breakout from Anzio; Canadians crack Adolf Hitler Line.

May 24, 1944 U.S. II Corps captures Terracina; Canadians reach Melfa River.

May 25, 1944 U.S. 3rd Division captures Cisterna; U.S. II and VI Corps patrols link up at Borgo Grappa; General Clark orders change in direction toward Rome; British Eighth Army crosses Melfa River.

May 26, 1944 U.S. VI Corps changes direction toward Rome.

May 27, 1944 German Hermann Göring Panzer Division arrives at Valmontone in time to prevent cutting of Highway 6.

May 30, 1944 U.S. II Corps takes over attack on Valmontone.

May 31, 1944 U.S. 36th Division captures Monte Artemisio.

June 2, 1944 U.S. 36th Division captures Velletri.

June 3, 1944 U.S. 3rd Division captures Valmontone and cuts Highway 6; Hitler agrees not to defend or destroy Rome.

June 4, 1944 Allies liberate Rome.

Preface

The story of the Allied liberation of Nazi-occupied Rome in World War II has been largely untold up to now, except in technical military works, diaries, and memoirs that represent only individual threads in a complex tapestry.

This paucity of published material is apparently due in large measure to the timing of the event. It occurred on June 4, 1944—less than forty-eight hours before Allied troops landed in Normandy. D-Day obscured the liberation of Rome, relegating it to the fine print of history. Yet it was one of the most important and compelling stories of the war.

It is the story of a desperate, brutalized city—from the threatened Pope to the tortured partisan prisoner to the Jew in hiding to the Romans in general who faced cataclysmic punishment for "betraying" the Third Reich: mass deportation and even the destruction of their beloved city with its matchless art treasures.

It is also the story of an extraordinary final battle for Rome, Operation DIADEM, which began on May 11, 1944. Although in many ways brilliantly conducted by the Allies, it was flawed from conception with bitter Allied conflict and competition that shook the Atlantic Alliance and cost countless lives.

Prime Minister Winston Churchill, viewing Rome as a springboard into the Balkans, pushed a reluctant United States into this last battle. And the Allied commanders pushed each other off the roads to Rome in their hunger for the prestige of conquering the Eternal City. Americans, Britons, Frenchmen, and others all frantically scrambled for that glittering prize, almost ignoring the main objective of the battle— trapping the German army in Italy.

The Germans, just as obsessed with the prestige of Rome, had to decide whether to gamble their very existence as a defense force on a last-ditch battle inside the city or to escape the trap left open by the Allies in their feverish race for glory. Whether, if and when they did withdraw, to take the Pope with them and leave Rome a burned-out shell, perhaps under a Nazi-sponsored Communist regime that would presumably plague the Allied liberators.

The closer the Allies came to Rome, the more determined were the two sides to hold or seize it, the more intense was the Allied competition, and the more desperate were the Romans.

I first became interested in the story while visiting Rome in 1967 to research my book, *Genesis 1948: The First Arab-Israeli War*. In talks with Vatican officials and other clergy, former partisans, Jewish survivors, and, later, with soldiers who took part in the last battle for Rome, the story began to emerge, all the more meaningfully because Rome's fate is linked so intimately with the spiritual and cultural life of many people everywhere and because it is a city that is also a symbol.

I perceived in this last of Rome's numerous historical traumas a great epic of human courage and human frailty.

Researching and writing this book took more than three years. I interviewed over eight hundred people in the United States, Britain, France, Germany, and Italy, and read more than five hundred books, diaries, and memoirs, countless periodicals, and thousands of unpublished documents, a large number of them secret. Much of this documentation was not available in English, but only in Italian, French, German, Spanish, or Polish.

Many of the facts in this book have never been published before or are brought together for the first time to give a full-scale account of widely scattered material: facts about the Nazi plots to kidnap the Pope, burn down Rome, and set up a "Communist Republic" in the city before the Germans withdrew; about the Pope's reaction when he learned that the Roman Jews were being rounded up (the controversial subject of Rolf Hochhuth's play *The Deputy*); about the scheming of Allied commanders to beat each other into Rome; about the frictions dividing the Germans over Jewish, partisan, and military policy; and about the threat of civil war between rightist and leftist factions of the Roman Resistance.

I have not invented or fictionalized any of the material in this book, including dialogue and descriptive detail. The techniques of storytelling, of weaving facts together to make events both comprehensible and vivid, do not belong to fiction alone and cannot be dismissed merely as fictional devices. These techniques also belong to the honorable tradition of narrative history which can be traced as far back as Herodotus.

Whatever faults this book may contain, I take due responsibility as the author, but I stand by the authenticity of detail, all of which I have obtained from documentary material and first-hand interviews.

If a participant's memory of dialogue that had taken place years before could not be checked against the wording of recorded documents, I have, wherever possible, tried to substantiate the reconstruction by interviewing as well the other persons who took part in the original conversation.

Where statements of major historical figures could not be verified in documents, I have given the gist of what was told me. Sources of dialogue are indicated in the notes at the back of the book, and some are identified in the text itself.

When I lived in Rome from November 1971 to April 1973 while working on this book, I found few physical scars of the German occupation or of the fighting that had raged in the city. Miraculously, little of Rome was damaged during the war. It is today a highly urbanized area beset by the problems of all major cities and overwhelmed by the task of keeping its monuments intact.

Nevertheless, it remains the Eternal City, as magnetic now to visitors and tourists as it was to conquerors and would-be conquerors in the past. But for many of its inhabitants the memory of the war is still alive—a moment in their history that tested their mettle and marked their lives.

It is to them that I owe much of my feeling for the drama of the liberation of Rome, as well as to the major characters in the drama who inevitably occupy the center of the stage.

Dan Kurzman

Prologue

Rome was a symbol and an obsession to those trapped in its web of splendor when the Germans seized the city on September 10, 1943.

While awaiting liberation, Rome promised timeless glory to the conqueror, geopolitical advantage to the statesman, Caesarian power to the tyrant, political rebirth to the politician, redeemed honor to the partisan, ecclesiastic domination to the cleric, public respectability to the extremist, unlicensed liberty to the prisoner, social restoration to the aristocrat, instant prosperity to the pauper, sheer survival to the Jew, romantic gratification to the spy, *dolce vita* to the pleasure-seeker, and eternal changelessness to most Romans . . .

Seven months after the Germans stormed into Rome, on April 11, 1944, a United States Army Air Force plane touched down at Bolling Field across the Potomac River from Washington, D.C. It was 3 A.M., an hour when spies were presumably least observant. A tall, uniformed figure wearing a green neck scarf, the symbol of his army command, emerged into the predawn chill. After an absence of two years Lieutenant General Mark Wayne Clark was back from the Italian front to brief American leaders on an operation that would start exactly one month later—the conquest of Rome.

Two armies, Clark's Fifth and the British Eighth, had been inching up the Italian boot from hill to blood-drenched hill since September 9, 1943, when they had swept ashore at Salerno to gain the first Allied foothold in mainland Europe. Now, heavily reinforced and strung

A SALVATORIAN MONASTERY
B CASTEL SANT'ANGELO
C REGINA COELI
D S. MARIA IN TRASTEVERE
E PANTHEON
F THEATER OF MARCELLUS
G VITT. EMANUELE II MONUMENT
H MUNICIPIO
I VILLA MEDICI
J FONTANA DI TREVI
K ARCH OF CONSTANTINE
L COLOSSEUM
M QUIRINAL PALACE
N IL MESSAGGERO
O BARBERINI PALACE
P MINISTRY OF CORPORATIONS
Q HOTEL EXCELSIOR
R MACAO BARRACKS
S S. MARIA D'ANGELI
T KOCH'S HQ.
U GESTAPO HQ.
V SAN GIOVANNI IN LATERANO
W VILLA WOLKONSKY, GERMAN EMBASSY
X PORTA MAGGIORE
Y CHURCH OF SAN LORENZO
Z ISOLA TIBERINA

VILLA BORGHESE

PARIOLI

CORSO D'ITALIA

VIA VENETO

Q

VIA DEL 23 MARZO

VIA XX SETTEMBRE

R

PZZA BARBERINI

P

O

VIA QUATTRO FONTANE

S

Y

TRITONE

N

VIA RASELLA

PZZA ESEDRA

O

STAZ. TERMINI

T

M

VIA NAZIONALE

VIA CAVOUR

VIA PRINCIPE AMEDEO

TRAJAN'S FORUM

COLLE OPPIA

PZZA VITTORIO EMANUELE II

VIA DELL'IMPERO

ROMAN FORUM

L

K

VIA CLAUDIA

VIA MARCO AURELIO

U

VIA TASSO

VIA PRENESTINA

HWY 6

X

W

V

MAXIMUS

VIA D. TERME DI CARACALLA

VIA TARANTO

VIA APPIA NUOVA

VIA TUSCOLANA

PZZA D. RE DI ROMA

TERME DI CARACALLA

HWY 7

ROME 1943-44

MILES

0   ¼   ½   ¾   1

SAN PAOLO FUORI LE MURA

ARDEATINE CAVES →

R D TAYLOR

across the boot south of Rome from Monte Cassino to the Tyrrhenian Sea, they were about to make one last lunge for the Eternal City.

Since the Germans might suspect that a giant offensive was imminent if they knew of Clark's trip to the United States, his arrival was top secret. Even his mother was not informed in advance. His wife, Maurine ("Renie"), had received permission to meet him at the air field in a curtain-draped car, but he would not be allowed to go home with her.

When Clark walked over to the car and climbed in, his wife, she records in her memoirs, was "a little shocked. He looked so thin and tense and tired. And he looked haggard . . . His face was drawn tight and hard." Usually it was "full and handsome." But that was before Clark had led an army into battle; before he had seen thousands of his men die in the frozen, rocky wastes of southern Italy; before Rome had become the Promised Land.

Clark awkwardly embraced his wife and asked in a strained manner about the family. It had been so long. Gradually, however, the strangeness wore off and both began to feel relief from the long-accumulated tensions of war and separation. They drove directly to the home of General George C. Marshall, the United States Army Chief of Staff, where they stayed the night. And in the next few days Clark met with President Franklin D. Roosevelt, Marshall, and other national leaders.

When Clark described his plans for conquering Rome, both Roosevelt and Marshall stressed that capture of the city before General Dwight D. Eisenhower launched his invasion of France would nourish the morale of the D-Day troops while sapping that of the nervously waiting Germans.

Clark agreed. And he needed no encouragement. Conscious of his historic role and eager to maximize it, he was determined to beat the deadline—and the British. History would note Mark Clark as the modern-day conqueror of Rome.

During a short vacation in West Virginia with his wife, Clark tried to shut the war from his mind for a few days and rambled on wishfully about the distant future. How wonderful it would be to retire to some secluded place and spend all day fishing. And go on picnics with Renie. He often recalled their first meeting—at a picnic; she was his blind date.

Renie had found lanky Captain Clark rather dull; he would not talk or smile. And what a mess when the rains came and suddenly reduced the picnic to a car-bound lunch of damp, sticky sandwiches and cakes. Finally, Captain Clark spoke: "Got more of these what-you-call-'em sandwiches in here?"

As Renie moved to get them, she sat back and shrieked, then leaped out of the car and began jiggling and shaking and slapping herself. She had sat on a bee. The sullen captain was convulsed with laughter.

"I'll bet you're a good dancer," he said . . .

On their return from West Virginia to Washington, Clark was finally permitted to go home, where he felt almost like an intruder. He had to enter a basement door and use an elevator operated by a Secret Service agent. Still, he was home, and for a few more days Clark made an effort to relax.

But he, too, in a sense, had been stung by a bee—one that had nothing to do with picnics and bucolic scenes fondly remembered. There was a war on and he had a specific task, and if he could fulfill his mission as he saw it, he would be master of his destiny. The prize was Rome.

Finally it was time to leave. Carrying with him a bit of home—the family cocker spaniel Pal—Clark departed as secretly as he had come, his face once more hard and taut. Only in the Promised Land would he relax again—if he beat the British.[1]

To Adolf Hitler, Rome was the treacherous land. He had distrusted his Italian ally from the moment a dissident group of Fascists flung Benito Mussolini from power on July 25, 1943. And his suspicion was not misplaced. Simultaneously with the Salerno invasion on September 9, Marshal Pietro Badoglio, who had succeeded the Duce, signed a separate armistice agreement with the Allies, then fled south to the Allied lines together with King Victor Emmanuel III. In vengeful fury, Hitler ordered Rome occupied.

Fear gripped the Romans—anti-Fascists, royalists, Italian army deserters, the Vatican, and especially the Jews . . .

In the afternoon of September 10, as the Germans were entering Rome, the Chief Rabbi, Israel Zolli, rushed to see the regional commissioner of police, whom he knew was a secret anti-Fascist. Zolli relates in his memoirs that he anxiously asked him what he should do.

"If I have understood right," the commissioner replied, "one hour after entering Prague they killed off the chief rabbi of that city. In my opinion, you ought to leave your house for three or four days, until you see what system they will adopt here. After that you will be able to judge for yourself . . ."

When he returned home, Zolli had hardly shut the door when he heard cries from the street: "The Germans! The Germans!"

His daughter Miriam ran outside and came back pale and trembling.

"Away at once!" she exclaimed. "Here we are at the entrance of the Ghetto and everyone is fleeing."

She quickly packed some linen, then said: "I have put out the fire. Let us leave everything and go!"

"But I would like to take with me . . ."

"You will take nothing, Father, we must survive. Here we shall die!"

Zolli and his daughter and wife hurried out into the rainy evening and fearfully walked the deserted streets. The stout, white-goateed rabbi looked up as they passed the Palace of Justice and asked himself: Justice, where was justice? Would it not have been just for the Jewish leaders to meet and co-ordinate their plans as he had suggested? Why were they leaving the people in ignorance, without directions? Why had they summarily rejected his ideas and shown him so little respect?

Zolli's wife and daughter finally took refuge in the home of friends, but the rabbi, not wishing to overburden these people, sought shelter with another acquaintance.

"Let me spend the night here, I beg you!" he pleaded.

"It is impossible!" he was told. "I'll give you a note to . . ."

"Thank you, that's fine."

Zolli walked to the designated address, but soon realized that a telephone call had preceded him.

He said, "See, a chair is enough for me even in a dark corridor. I have some cigarettes with me and everything else I need."

But the man's expression spoke for itself, and once again Zolli found himself on the deserted streets, now after curfew. He decided to go home. But how ridiculous! He had no home. He was a wandering dog —Jew or dog, it was the same.

When he finally arrived at his house, he was unable to turn the key in the lock. Terror gripped him as a figure approached in the dark.

"Give me the key a moment, Professor. The Lord help you, Professor."

Zolli breathed a sigh of relief. It was the night guard.

"And you also; may He help us all!"

The rabbi, wet with perspiration, washed and changed his clothes in the dark and lay on his bed. His memoirs reflect his state of mind at that moment . . . He was regarded as a foreigner (having come from Austria). He was a Jew. He was the Chief Rabbi of Rome. What a prize catch!

He began to pray. Perhaps God would save him. Perhaps . . . even Jesus, whom he had seen, strangely enough, in several visions.

He waited for the ring of the bell, the knock on the door.[2]

Zolli's fear mirrored the fear of Rome. Not even Pope Pius XII was certain of his fate . . .

On September 12, two days after the occupation of Rome, Hitler summoned General Karl Wolff, the blond, playboy SS (Schutzstaffel) chief in Italy who was second only to Reichsführer Heinrich Himmler in the SS hierarchy, to a meeting at the Führer's headquarters, situated in a nest of fir trees near Rastenburg in East Prussia.

Wolff, whom Himmler had briefed in advance on the subject to be discussed, was nervous and disturbed on entering Hitler's office. According to notes that Wolff told the author he took during and immediately after the meeting, Hitler said to him:

"I have a special order for you, Wolff. It will be your duty not to discuss it with anyone before I give you permission to do so. Only the Reichsführer knows about it. Do you understand?"

When Wolff replied that he did, Hitler resumed: "I want you and your troops . . . to occupy Vatican City as soon as possible, secure its files and art treasures, and take the Pope and the Curia to the North. I do not want him to fall into the hands of the Allies or to be under their political pressure and influence. The Vatican is already a nest of spies and a center of anti-National Socialist propaganda."

Wolff apparently betrayed no hint of emotion as Hitler continued: "I shall arrange for the Pope to be brought either to Germany or to neutral Liechtenstein, depending on political and military developments. When is the soonest you think you shall be able to fulfill this mission?"

Wolff replied that he was unable to offer a firm schedule. He must transfer additional SS and police units to Italy, including some from Southern Tyrol, and that would take time. He would also need experienced specialists to secure the files and precious art treasures, men who knew Latin and Greek as well as Italian and other modern languages. He could not start the operation, Wolff concluded, for another four to six weeks, if that soon.

Hitler rejected Wolff's timetable. The Germans might be forced to leave Rome shortly, and the kidnaping, of course, had to take place while the city was still occupied.

"That's too long for me," Hitler growled. "Rush the most important preparations and report developments to me approximately every fortnight."

Wolff agreed and departed in a state of turmoil. He would willingly, and proudly, commit almost any act for the Führer, but abduction of the Pope seemed foolish. It would certainly complicate his police task in Italy. Moreover, the Pope could perhaps be useful to him in the future—if the worst happened and Germany lost the war.[8]

Pope Pius XII soon learned of the plot and regarded it seriously, whether Hitler did or not. The Catholic Church, he feared, faced disaster. He was determined to remain in Rome until forcibly removed, but he hesitated to take any action that might provoke the Führer to carry out his plan.

The Pope was deeply relieved when the Germans said they would not deport the Roman Jews, but would simply extort fifty kilograms of gold from them instead. He was pleased, of course, for humanitarian reasons. But also, it seems, because he might be forced to protest Jewish deportations—and thus trigger the kidnap scheme.

If blackmail was in fact Hitler's intent, the Führer played his cards impeccably. On October 16, with an order to round up the Jews, he flung his challenge at the Pope . . .

Princess Enza Pignatelli Aragona was sound asleep in her modest home in Rome when the telephone rang at about five that rainy morning. She lifted the receiver, she relates, and heard an excited voice cry:

"Princess, the Germans are arresting the Jews and taking them away in trucks!"

The princess, a tiny but dynamic woman, was shocked fully awake. She had hidden many Jewish friends in her house and in the homes of other Christian families, but she had never dreamed that the Germans would go this far.

"What can I do?" she asked the caller, a Christian friend who lived at the edge of the Ghetto.

"You know the Pope. Go and see him. Only he can save the Jews."

At first Princess Pignatelli considered this suggestion entirely unrealistic. Yes, she did know the Pope well. Of a noble Neapolitan family, she had been his student at a convent and her father had been a close friend. But even if the Pope would receive her at this hour, she could not get to the Vatican, for she did not have a car and no public transportation was operating this early.

Then she remembered her friend Gustav Wollenweber, a diplomat in the German Embassy to the Holy See who, she knew, opposed his government's anti-Semitic policies. She telephoned him.

"Please come and pick me up immediately," the princess urged. "I must go to the Vatican. I'll explain later."

When Wollenweber arrived and learned of her mission, he drove her first to the Ghetto to see if the report was true. They were halted at the edge of the quarter by SS police who refused to let even a German diplomat pass. However, the two saw people, many still in their pajamas, being marched down the street in the rain and thrown into black-canvased trucks. They saw frightened children clinging to their mothers' skirts and old women begging for mercy. They heard screams, pathetic wails of prayer, and the slap of leather on cobblestones as some Jews tried to flee.

While the couple sped to the Vatican, Princess Pignatelli reflected on the irony of her desperate undertaking; a German diplomat was helping her to frustrate official German policy. On arriving at the Vatican, she pleaded with an official:

"Please take me immediately to His Holiness!"

The startled official glanced at his watch and wondered if she were mad—coming at this hour to demand an audience with the Pope. But after she explained her mission, he guided her to the door of the papal chapel where the Pope was attending Mass.

When Pius XII emerged, he greeted the princess with a surprised smile, remarking on the hour, and suggested that they walk together to his study.

"Your Holiness," the princess urged, "you must act immediately. The Germans are arresting the Jews and taking them away. Only *you* can stop them."

The Pope halted and stared at the princess with a shocked expression. This was obviously the first word he had heard about the arrests.

"But they promised not to touch the Jews in Rome!" he exclaimed.

In his study, he urgently telephoned Cardinal Luigi Maglione, his Secretary of State, and asked him to make an immediate protest to the German ambassador.

As the Pope showed Princess Pignatelli to the door, he promised: "I'll do all I can."[4]

Reports of Hitler's plan to kidnap the Pope added to Mussolini's apprehension that the Führer expected to evacuate Rome soon. And to the Duce, abandonment of that city would be madness, since it was the heart and soul of the Italy he still claimed.

After his ouster and arrest on July 25, 1943, Nazi parachutists had freed him from confinement in a daring raid and Hitler had set him up as his puppet dictator over an "Italian Social Republic," comprising those parts of Italy still unoccupied by the Allies. His headquarters were now at Salò in the shadow of the Alps. But he *must* return to Rome . . .

Looking old, tired, and pallid, Mussolini, one day in early October 1943, rose behind a heavy baroque desk littered with papers to greet his visitor from Rome. When SS Colonel (Standartenführer) Eugen Dollmann, General Wolff's representative in the Eternal City, had congratulated him on his "return to power," the Duce immediately began discussing Rome. How exactly had Rome behaved after his removal and the subsequent German occupation of the city?

The Romans, Dollmann replied frankly, were happy about the *coup* and appalled by the occupation. Mussolini was silent for a moment, and his eyes reflected a deep inner wound. But then he asserted, with all the gusto he had once exuded while haranguing great crowds from his famous balcony:

"All the same, all the same, Rome must remain in our hands in spite of the Romans. Without Rome, the new Italian Social Republic is a mere trunk, a fragment without a base."

The Duce sat down, stared for a moment at the hills of his native Romagna framed in the window, and began jotting notes on a pad— a draft of a message to Hitler. As he watched Mussolini scribble, Dollmann had the uncomfortable feeling that the future of Rome was at stake. The Rome that Dollmann loved dearly for its artistic treasures and aristocratic tastes, for the power that it bestowed upon him and the pleasures that it proffered.

The Duce finally stopped writing, removed his glasses, and read aloud to his guest: While he was unacquainted with the plans of the German High Command, he wished to stress the vital necessity of holding Rome. Coming after the abandonment of Naples, the loss of Rome would have immense repercussions in Italy and the world at large. Prime consideration should be given to the political and psychological aspects of such a step. As for the military aspect, the fall of Rome would leave the enemy in possession of the thirty airfields in central Italy, facilitating not only the bombardment of central and southeast Germany but attacks on the Danube Basin and the Balkans.

Mussolini looked up at Dollmann with a glow in his eyes, like a child awaiting approval of a school recitation, and said that he would soon be sending Marshal Rodolfo Graziani, his Minister of National Defense, to see Hitler with this personal message on the question of Rome.

"And you, *caro* Dollmann, will go with him," he added. "Rome has become your home too, despite the Romans' behavior . . ."

Dollmann had to persuade Hitler to defend the city to the last house on the last street—to leave the Allies, if they could not be stopped, a burned-out shell.[5]

Colonel Dollmann and other Germans in Rome realized that defending the city, if Hitler decided to defend it, would not be easy. For one thing, the Roman Resistance was growing stronger and more daring daily and could take a terrible toll in an insurrection. As it was, however timid most of the Romans seemed, partisans were relentlessly attacking Nazis and Fascists on the streets and sabotaging German installations. The Communists seemed the most dangerous of all . . .

"This will be the most important occasion of your life," Viviana Chilanti assured her ten-year-old daughter Gloria one day in November 1943, "So be careful, and don't stop for anything."

"Yes, Mother," the little girl replied. "Will this be like one of Salgari's adventures?"

Viviana nodded with a smile, feeling pangs of guilt. Salgari was a famous writer of Italian tales in which children were the heroes in a world of fantasy.

Sometimes, it seemed to Viviana, the real world was actually the world of fantasy. Could Salgari imagine a child carrying fifty pounds of explosives through an enemy-occupied city to a rendezvous fifteen miles away? A child who was half starved and had only a pair of oversized, worn-through sandals to wear? Yet maternal concern must give way to the cruel demands of the struggle.

Earlier that day, Viviana, who commanded the women's section of the Communist Movement of Italy, a large, dissident Marxist organization known as the Bandiera Rossa, or Red Flag, party, had been ordered to send two people to deliver explosives that would be used to blow up a key bridge and disrupt German communications. She would go herself, but she needed a second woman and no other was available. It was too dangerous to send a man, for the Germans often stopped and arrested men on the street. So, as both recall the occasion, Viviana turned to her daughter, who commanded the children's section of the movement, called "Koba," Stalin's childhood nickname.

Gloria departed with a reinforced shopping bag cradled in each thin arm, each bag filled with explosives hidden under a thick layer of lettuce leaves. She walked swiftly despite her burden, looking straight ahead, as if nothing existed in any other direction. At Piazza Vittoria, as she passed a large market, several women came up and offered to carry the bags.

"No, I'm very strong," Gloria replied and continued on.

After a while, she longed to sit down and rest. Her feet hurt and she was so hungry that she even considered eating some of the lettuce hiding the explosives. It started to rain, and then, most disturbing of all, she had to go to the bathroom. But her mother had said that she could not stop for *anything*. In her misery, she started humming "Bandiera Rossa," the Red Flag song . . .

Eventually, Gloria reached the farmhouse where she was to leave the bags, and a peasant family greeted her. She rushed to the bathroom, then wolfed down an offering of bread and cheese.

Meanwhile, Viviana had delivered her bags of explosives to another contact even farther away and, utterly exhausted, began to wonder how her child could possibly accomplish a similar mission. Maybe she was lost. Maybe the police had stopped her. Maybe the explosives . . . On her way back, she stopped at a café and telephoned home. No answer. She drank down a whisky and frantically called several more times. Finally, about ten hours after they had departed on their separate missions, a child's voice answered.

"Dear, are you all right?" Viviana cried.

"Yes, Mama," the girl replied. "But my feet hurt. My shoes fell all to pieces."

Viviana hung up and ordered another whisky.

The next day she learned that something had gone wrong and the explosives had failed to work.

But there were still enough left for a revolution.[6]

Not all of the partisans were revolutionaries. Though linked with the leftists in the immediate common cause, many were rightists who supported and took orders from the King and Badoglio, now ruling from the Allied-controlled South. And one order was to prevent the leftists from sparking an insurrection in Rome as the Allied forces approached and possibly grabbing power before these forces arrived . . .

As General Filippo Caruso sat in the interrogation room of Via Tasso, the Gestapo prison in Rome, on May 30, 1944, a German soldier savagely punched him in the jaw. The general rose unsteadily and shouted:

"I am the commander of the *carabinieri* in Rome. I have nine thousand men under my command. I am a soldier and should be treated like one."

The *carabinieri* were members of a military police force traditionally loyal to the monarchy. And since the King had arrested Mussolini, fled

Rome, and gone over to the Allies, the *carabinieri* had switched sides, too, and, joining the Resistance, bitterly opposed the Nazi occupation of Rome. The Germans now feared that these policemen would help lead an insurrection against them if the Allies threatened Rome. And among the most fearful was Lieutenant Colonel (Obersturmbann-führer) Herbert Kappler, the Gestapo and SD chief in the city.*

"Are your men armed?" Kappler demanded.

"Yes," replied the general, "I could whistle on any *piazza* and they would come running to me. I am their leader. If you ask where the men and weapons are, I'll tell you nothing."

As Caruso describes his ordeal, two Germans tore off his shirt, stood him up against the wall, and lashed him with a bullwhip more than seventy times. Then they sat him down again and one of them beat him about one eye until his eyeball almost came out of the socket. They struck him on the head with a metal rod and kicked him, cracking his shinbone, breaking two ribs, and injuring his spine, then slowly pulled out thirteen of his teeth with a pair of pliers.

For six hours they tortured him, but they did not realize that the first powerful blow to his jaw had somehow numbed his whole body and that he was therefore able to stand the pain. Nor that this ability buttressed his feeling of superiority over his torturers, which, in turn, strengthened his powers of endurance.

Finally, as he sat limp in the chair, he groaned to the interrogator: "How can a young man like you perform such dirty tasks?"

Without expression, the German simply placed a cigarette between Caruso's swollen lips and lit it, acknowledging defeat.

The general was taken back to his cell, where he collapsed, his body bloody and broken. He had not talked—even to say, truthfully, that he was opposed to insurrection; that he had orders from the royal government to crush any leftist uprising, even if this meant civil war.

In Via Tasso there were no Communists or royalists, leftists or rightists—only Italians. And they did not like to think that, if they survived, they might have to kill each other.[7]

* The Schutzstaffel, or SS, was orginally a select group of bodyguards chosen to protect Hitler and other Nazi leaders, but Himmler, on taking it over in 1929, transformed it into a racial élite formation. He set up the Sicherheitsdienst, or SD, as the SS's exclusive intelligence service under Reinhard Heydrich. In 1939 the SD and the Secret State Police, or Gestapo, were united under the SS in a Security Office of the Reich. By the time Ernst Kaltenbrunner replaced Heydrich, who was assassinated in Prague on May 28, 1942, the SD and the Gestapo could hardly be distinguished from each other. In Italy, Colonel Kappler, as Rome's SD-Gestapo chief, was directly responsible to SS General Wilhelm Harster, the SD-Gestapo leader for Italy, with headquarters in Verona, and Harster took orders from General Wolff, who had overall responsibility for SS activities in that country.

Peace hovered strangely over the Italian front south of Rome on the night of May 11, 1944. Nightingales trilled, for once undisturbed by the uncouth belching of guns. Dogs barked at each other across the misty black meadows of the Liri Valley. And a haze of fireflies danced merrily over mine fields strewn with red poppies that swayed in the warm, death-scented air.

But soon, toward midnight, a full moon would bathe the charred patchwork of carnage in a soft spring glow—and guide fearful men, driven by pride and principle, vengeance and vanity, by bitter echoes from the past, in a new yet ageless race for Rome . . .

I

Before the Race

1

The Plans

Shortly before 11 P.M. on that night of May 11, the 2nd Battalion of the 4th Division's Somerset Regiment, British Eighth Army, stealthily marched toward the bank of the Gari River.* Its mission was to cross the swiftly flowing waterway which had already claimed thousands of Allied lives, skirt German-held Monte Cassino to the north, and dash up the Liri Valley to Rome.

Two men silently led the battalion through a maze of torn trees, shell craters, and the debris of interminable battle. They did not have to speak for each knew what the other was thinking. Lieutenant Colonel John Platt, the battalion commander, and Major Humphry Platt, the commander of the leading unit, A Company, were brothers.

How strange, they both thought, that the two of them, whose father and grandfather had served in the same regiment, should together be leading their father's battalion into its first big action of World War II. John, the elder, remembered how only a few years before he had returned home from an assignment in India bringing a tiger cub skin for his ecstatic little brother.

"Take care of Tuppy," their mother had only just written, referring to Humphry by his nickname.

* The Gari and Rapido rivers join just south of Cassino and the proper name of the combined waterway is "Gari," though during the war it became known as the "Rapido."

Suddenly John was seized with a horrifying thought—that, as his brother's superior officer, he might have to order him into certain death.

At a point near the bank the battalion divided up, with John splitting off from Humphry's company, and as Humphry started down the muddy incline toward the watery grave that sullenly awaited new victims, he smartly saluted his brother. John returned the salute and whispered:

"Cheerio, Tuppy. And jolly good luck."[1]

As Lieutenant Mahorowski, that same night, awaited the command to attack Monte Cassino with other soldiers of the II Polish Corps, part of the British Eighth Army, he dwelled in puzzlement on a dream he had had that morning. In the dream he was on his way to church with his sister when he slipped and fell into a puddle. Soaking wet and covered with mud, he refused, in his embarrassment, to continue on. But the sun came out and immediately dried—and cleaned—his clothes, and so he was able to attend church after all. Then he awoke with a strange premonition of disaster.

Unable to comprehend the dream, Mahorowski felt depressed despite his excitement at the prospect of battle. But whatever it meant, he was thankful that the moment had arrived when he could start toward home. He would fight his way to Poland regardless of obstacles, and soon he would be with his family, which he had last seen in Russia. The Russians, on entering Poland in 1939, had deported all members of his family to a labor camp but had finally freed them. Mahorowski had then gone off to fight with the Allies in the Polish force formed by Lieutenant General Wladyslaw Anders.

The task of Anders' II Polish Corps was now to capture the hills of Monte Cassino, including Monastery Hill upon which was perched the shattered Benedictine Monastery, a key stumbling block to Rome—and to Poland. It was proving to be one of the most formidable fortresses in the history of warfare, and Mahorowski was proud of the opportunity to succeed, in the name of his beloved homeland, where so many others had failed.

Like some hypnotic monster, the monastery in the past months had fatally drawn into its clutches soldiers from Britain, the United States, India, and New Zealand. Nor could anyone lurking in its shadow escape its burning gaze, its overpowering presence.

The order finally came for Mahorowski and his comrades to move forward. This would surely be the final reckoning with the craggy beast that blocked the road home.[2]

South of Monte Cassino, on the banks of the Garigliano River, Captain Pierre Planès, a tank destroyer commander in the 3rd Algerian Division of the French Expeditionary Corps (FEC), part of General Clark's Fifth Army, violently blew his nose and grunted "*Merde!*" to his petite blond wife, Colette, an ambulance driver with the division. What a time for his damned nasal condition to act up—when he was about to assault Rome on that night of May 11.

The couple were leaving the hospital tent where the doctor had advised Planès that unless he had an immediate operation to relieve the obstruction in his nose he could jeopardize his health. To think that he might be seriously endangered by a nasal obstruction while all around him, in the forbidding black hills, the Boches were waiting to kill him! Planès could barely keep from laughing.

He had been in such pain that morning that he had literally beaten his head against the wall, but he was not going to miss the battle, and Colette, knowing him all too well, did not even try to reason with him.

They listened silently to the nightingales—and to the hum of tanks warming up nearby. They would meet again in Rome. Rome wasn't Paris, of course, but it seemed a suitable place for a second honeymoon. Suddenly a motorcyclist screeched to a halt beside them and told Planès that he should proceed immediately to the take-off point.

The captain kissed his wife lightly on the lips and jumped into a waiting jeep. It was best that way before an attack. Parting from a comrade in arms was easier than parting from a wife in arms. As the vehicle pulled away, Planès shouted to the doctor:

"If I return wounded, please operate on my nose!"[8]

Further to the south, at Minturno near the Tyrrhenian coast, another medical case was waiting to attack with the Fifth Army's U.S. 88th Division.

Sergeant Charles W. Shea, a redhead from the Bronx, had been hawking hot dogs at a Dodger-Giant football game at the Polo Grounds on December 7, 1941, when he heard over the loudspeaker that Pearl Harbor had been bombed. Shea immediately tried to join the Navy, but was rejected because of punctured eardrums. He met the same response when he tried the other services.

Finally he was drafted, and the doctor said his eardrums were fine. But when he reached the port of embarkation, another asked in a shocked voice:

"How did you ever get into the Army? You'll never go overseas!"

Two weeks later, on a ship taking him to North Africa, still another doctor assured him: "This is a mistake. You'll certainly be sent home!"

In Casablanca, Shea's trip home was delayed until a replacement could be found and postponed again when he was sent to Oran, where still no one arrived to relieve him. He was then erroneously shipped to Italy, and when one of his ears started to run following a shellburst while he was on a patrol mission, his battalion surgeon exclaimed:

"Shea, we're going to send you home!"

On the evening of May 11, 1944, Shea was on the front line.

By one means or another, he—in league with fate—had tricked them all into letting him fight. But now, he was convinced, they were making one final effort to restrain him. He cursed as he sat in his dugout digesting the news that, when the attack started, his squad would be the reserve squad of the reserve platoon of the reserve company of the reserve battalion of the 350th Regiment.

At this rate, he would be in Rome without having lifted a rifle—a thought that almost made him wish he were back in New York selling hot dogs. This goddamned fucking army! To get this far on busted eardrums and then to be in the back seat when the action began . . .[4]

About ten that night, some thirty Germans, as they did every night, trudged up the rocky slopes of Monte Cassino carrying on their backs cartons of ammunition, food, water, and other supplies, which would be distributed to the posts from the monastery at the top.

They were greeted in the basement headquarters of the skeletal structure—which the Allies had intensively bombed during the previous battle of Cassino—by Second Lieutenant Hans-Joachim Weck, adjutant of the 1st Battalion, 4th Regiment, 1st Parachute Division.

"How are things down there?" Weck asked the commander of the porters as they started to stack the supplies.

"Calm. Very calm," the man replied. "Looks like we won't have much trouble tonight."

Yes, it was calm, eerily calm, thought Weck. For a while there had not even been any harassing fire by either side. Which was just as well. One battalion was being relieved, and the Germans had no desire to provoke enemy fire during the process. It was a good night to take some air.

Weck, helmetless, climbed the stairs from the basement and strolled outside amid the ruins. He stared into the starlit sky, listening to the nightingales and trying to ignore the overwhelming stench of the dead. He felt, with a sense of pride and importance, that he was standing not simply on a mountain, but on a symbol of German supremacy. The enemy, with all its power, with the finest soldiers of so many nations, could not budge the brave, dedicated defenders of his 1st Parachute Division. Whatever happened to the rest of the German army, the 1st Parachute Division would never leave *its* Monte Cassino.

What a splendid night![5]

❖   ❖   ❖

Throughout history, armies have carved bloody paths through the jagged hills and lush valleys surrounding Rome. According to legend, this tradition of violence stems from the seed of Mars, the God of War himself, who was, if not the father, the grandfather of Rome. The union of Mars and the vestal virgin Silvia produced Romulus and his twin brother Remus, who were abandoned by their mother following her indiscretion and left for suckling by a she-wolf.

Romulus later slew his brother, became the leader of a fierce band of shepherds and settled down with his followers in what is today central Rome. After this band had raped the Sabine women inhabiting the Quirinal and Viminal hills, the Sabine fathers felt it was only logical to unite their territory with the settlement of Romulus. Rome, according to this legend, was born.

Whatever the truth, Rome has been steeped in violence since about 500 B.C., when the Romans embarked on their quest to conquer the world. Carthage, across the sea on the African coast, was a formidable rival, but Hannibal, its leader, failed in an effort to take Rome from the south. The Romans later struck back, and, after three wars burned Carthage to the ground in 146 B.C. to emerge as the undisputed leader of the Western civilized world.

It was not until the fifth century A.D. that the great Roman Empire, rotting in corruption and decadence, finally collapsed under the sword of barbarians from the north. In 410 the Visigoths under Alaric sacked Rome and massacred the Romans; in 455 the Vandals under Gaiseric repeated the performance; and in 536 the Eastern Empire general Belisarius became the first warrior to take Rome from the south. Conqueror followed conqueror: the Lombards, the Saracens, the Normans.

In the midst of this perpetual chaos, the Church, by 755, had organized all of central Italy into papal states over which the Pope exerted political as well as spiritual authority. And, except for a brief period of sixty-three years when the French Pope Clement V transferred the seat of the papacy to Avignon, France, the popes remained rulers of Rome.

Their power, however, was often challenged. And, until the nine-teenth century, never more seriously than in 1527, when an imperial army of German Lutherans, Spanish Catholics, and Italian mercenaries scaled the walls of Rome, threw Pope Clement VII into prison, and sacked the city with savagery and rapine. They tortured people to extort money, kidnaped high prelates for ransom, raped even the nuns, de-stroyed or stole priceless art treasures, despoiled the churches of all precious objects, and even opened a papal tomb to rob the corpse of a ring.

And the Romans stood by helplessly, fearfully, fatalistically, in a traumatic state of paralysis, as they would time and again under French and Spanish attacks in the next three centuries—and still again during the Nazi occupation of World War II.

While the popes proved amazingly resilient throughout the ages, their political power gradually weakened, and in 1849 an Italian army under the patriot Giuseppe Garibaldi captured Rome—the second conqueror from the south—and ended papal rule. And though French troops soon afterward returned the Pope to power, the Italians, in 1870, ousted him again, this time for good, and established a united Italian kingdom with Rome its capital.

Fifty-two years later, in 1922, the stage was set for new bloodshed in the name of Rome when Benito Mussolini began his reign as dicta-tor of Italy. Dreaming of a new Roman Empire, Mussolini joined hands with Adolf Hitler in 1939 in a pact of conquest, which ended abruptly when the Duce was finally deposed on July 25, 1943.

Two months afterward, in the tradition of the northern barbarians, the Nazis occupied Rome, setting off an Allied controversy that would shake the Anglo-American alliance to is roots . . .

Prime Minister Winston Churchill, his cherubic face pale and wan, was utterly exhausted as he stepped into the car of General Eisenhower, Supreme Commander of the Allied Forces in the Western Mediter-ranean, on his arrival in Tunisia on December 11, 1943. He had just at-tended a grueling conference in Tehran with President Roosevelt and Marshal Stalin. As the car drove off toward the general's villa amid the ruins of ancient Carthage, Eisenhower's forward headquarters, Chur-chill, who was to leave the following day for a visit to the Italian front, said, he reports in his memoirs:

"I am afraid I shall have to stay with you longer than I had planned. I am completely at the end of my tether, and I cannot go on to the front until I have recovered some strength."

He slept all that day and on the next, the doctors found he had pneumonia. The Prime Minister deplored his luck. Just when great decisions had to be made, decisions that could determine the whole future of Europe. And the doctors, who tried to keep him from working in bed, were no help at all.

Finally, with grumpy resignation, he sat back in bed and listened while his daughter Sarah, sitting at the foot, read aloud to him from Jane Austen's *Pride and Prejudice*. What calm, simple, egoistic lives the characters led, he thought—as if the French Revolution or the Napoleonic Wars did not concern them. His efforts to relax were fruitless.

How could he relax when the Americans were about to relinquish all the advantages the Allies could enjoy in Italy, when his whole concept of how the war should be fought was being ignored?

He agreed with the Americans—and the Russians—outwardly, at least, that Operation OVERLORD, code name for the projected cross-channel invasion, should have first priority in Allied planning. But as he had told Roosevelt in Cairo just before they had left for the Tehran Conference with Stalin, while "OVERLORD remains top of the bill," it "should not be such a tyrant as to rule out every other activity in the Mediterranean."

Churchill had fought, pressed, and begged for approval of his plan to surge northward to Rome and beyond with powerful forces, arguing that "either they would gain Italy easily and immediately bite upon the German inner front, or they would draw large German forces" from the Channel front, which the Allies were to attack in May or June 1944. He invariably refrained from stressing what he meant by "bite upon the German inner front," for he knew the Americans would oppose him all the more—and the Russians doubly so.

However much lip service he gave to the importance of OVERLORD, Churchill, with Dunkirk still starkly engraved in his memory, was not at all sure the time would be ripe for it until the Germans were already on the run. Nor did the project make much political sense to him.

First, he felt, the Allies should strike toward Germany through the "soft underbelly of Europe," the Balkans, at once inducing neutral Turkey to join the Allies and preventing a Russian advance into Eastern Europe—while, incidentally, strengthening British influence in the Mediterranean area. War policy should be geared, he thought, more to future political benefits than to immediate military benefits, whatever the extra cost.

But President Roosevelt, General Marshall, and most other American leaders wanted, essentially, to put all their European eggs in one military basket—OVERLORD. A cross-channel invasion was the shortest route to Berlin, and the dispersion of forces elsewhere would simply reduce the power of that one great thrust. The Allies just did not have enough men or naval craft to conduct simultaneously, with maximum force, both a cross-channel operation and a sustained all-out offensive in Italy.

From the American point of view, Churchill was, therefore, jeopardizing OVERLORD by insisting that major Allied power be diverted to the Italian theater. And suspicion that he really wanted a Balkan adventure frightened the Americans all the more. For, aside from the threat to OVERLORD, the Balkans, they felt, were unsuitable for large-scale military operations.

And even if the Allies did capture the Balkans, Russia, which coveted this area, might conceivably make a separate peace with Hitler or, at the least, refuse to help the Western Powers fight Japan after Germany's fall. Geopolitics, the Americans felt, must wait until after the war.

Churchill had been forced at Tehran to "agree," but he would not abandon his own plans. Furthermore, he had no compunction about getting people angry, even his good friend Franklin Roosevelt. After all, the Americans had hesitated to invade North Africa and thus delay OVERLORD, but he had persuaded them that the Allies, not being ready yet for OVERLORD, had to attack somewhere. The Americans had also resisted an invasion of Sicily, but had gone along after he had led them to think this would be the final blow in the Mediterranean. And though they had opposed a landing on the Italian mainland, after Mussolini's fall they agreed to attack Salerno in a limited operation.

Churchill then prodded the Allied armies toward Rome until they became bogged down in the icy, muddy, bloody mountains south of the city—victims of a compromise that he considered better than nothing. At Tehran the Americans, backed by the Russians, tried once more to halt his creeping advance toward the Balkans. They decided that the troops should stop before reaching Rome; many would then be released for Operation ANVIL, a diversionary attack on southern France to be launched just after OVERLORD.†

Now Churchill, as he lay in bed deploring the "escapism" and "irresponsibility" of Jane Austen's provincial characters, vowed to force the Americans to give in again. He would never let them turn their backs on Rome and all that it implied.

"He who holds Rome," he had told Roosevelt in Cairo, "holds the title deeds of Italy."

And Churchill knew that he who held Italy held the key to the Balkans.

---

† As late as March 27, 1944, while Operation DIADEM was being planned, General Eisenhower opposed a drive to capture Rome as simply a drain on OVERLORD. An aide, Harry C. Butcher, writes in *My Three Years with Eisenhower* that on that day Ike indicated he was "delighted with the U.S. Chiefs of Staff decision to forget Rome." Churchill, however, was to persuade the Americans to support DIADEM.

It seemed appropriate that he had decided to take Rome while languishing in Carthage. He was confident that *he*, unlike Hannibal, would not fail.[6]

When British General Sir Harold Alexander, commander of the 15th Army Group fighting in Italy, moved into his headquarters in the magnificent royal palace at Caserta, about twenty miles north of Naples, he found himself faced with a problem which was to symbolize the larger one that would plague him when the race for Rome began.

Alexander enjoyed looking out of the huge window of his office at the beautiful gardens where once King Charles IV of the Two Sicilies had strolled with his wife. The King had built this palace for her, intending it to exceed even Versailles in grandeur. The general's staff, part British and part American, also enjoyed the view, but the two groups could not decide whether to do so through open or through closed windows. One day, Alexander writes in his memoirs, representatives of both came to him and said:

"We are in a great difficulty to which we can find no answer. The Americans, when they arrive at the office, like all the windows tightly shut and the British like all the windows open. Can you help us to find a solution?"

Alexander suggested that whoever arrived first at the office on a particular day have the right of decision for that day. His staff agreed and, after that, arrived not simply on time, but usually ahead of time.

The general was a master at smoothing out the inevitable frictions that disrupted relations among the various national forces composing his Army Group—British, American, French, Canadian, Indian, Polish, New Zealand, South African, and, later, others. Seldom, if ever before, had the soldiers of so many countries fought in a single battle under the orders of one commander. And it took a man like Alexander to coordinate such disparate forces, all of whom competed for headlines and glory.‡

For Alexander, unlike his more colorful compatriot, General Sir Bernard Law Montgomery, did not seek headlines and glory for himself, but was quite willing to let his subordinates struggle for their moment in history. A man of imperturbable temperament and dignified demeanor, he was an exquisite product of aristocratic upbringing. His

‡ General Alexander's desire to exhibit a united face to the world regardless of conflicting ambitions—and his fear that this conflict would show—was reflected in a message he sent to General Sir Henry Maitland Wilson on May 4, 1944, a week before the final drive on Rome was to start: "Relations between Fifth and Eighth Armies are excellent on all levels and it is essential that nothing is published that might cause friction."

Irish father and his father-in-law were both earls, and he had studied at Harrow and Sandhurst before becoming a courageous warrior who always fought according to the rules.

In World War I he had been wounded three times and won two high decorations. Earlier in World War II, at Dunkirk, he had coolly built sand castles on the beaches as he waited for ships to evacuate his British troops. In 1942 he led the British retreat in Burma, driving a jeep with one hand and gripping a pistol in the other while his aide peppered the jungles with machine-gun bullets. And later, in North Africa, he planned and mounted the attack in which Montgomery drove German General Erwin Rommel from the gates of Alexandria all the way back to Tripolitania.

In these battles Alexander seldom did more than "suggest" orders to his subordinates. And now that he was Commander of the Allied Forces in Italy and had to deal with non-British officers, this was his only way of commanding them. It was the best way, he thought, to harness their egos and win their co-operation—make them feel that whatever they were doing was their own idea.*

His civilized approach to war, no less than his courage, coolness, and tactical ability, made him Churchill's favorite commander. War to Churchill was a romantic calling, a gentleman's game, and Alexander played it with all the gentlemanly verve that Churchill himself had displayed in the Boer War.

"Nothing ever disturbed or rattled him," Churchill said of Alexander, "and duty was a full satisfaction in itself, especially if it seemed perilous and hard. But all this was combined with so gay and easy a manner that the pleasure and honour of his friendship were prized by all those who enjoyed it, among whom I could count myself . . ."

Furthermore, Alexander almost always agreed with Churchill, or at least listened quietly without contradicting him. How different from the Americans who were constantly interrupting the Prime Minister (if not often successfully), constantly telling him that he was wrong. Churchill liked the Americans, but he liked best those people who kept quiet while he told them how to do things.

And what he wanted to do now was to capture Rome, regardless of the Tehran ruling. He therefore called a meeting of Allied commanders on Christmas Day 1943, in Carthage, to tell them how to do it.

The wily, bullheaded Prime Minister had done a lot of thinking in

---

* General Eisenhower was so impressed with Alexander's ability to handle his commanders, among other qualities, that he wanted him to command the 21st Army Group that was to invade France. But Churchill rejected the appointment, feeling it was more important for Alexander to take Rome and lead the way into the Balkans. Thus Eisenhower settled for Montgomery, who was to become one of the heroes of OVERLORD.

bed. Since the Americans insisted on going through with Operation ANVIL, the diversionary attack on southern France, extra ships that would otherwise go to OVERLORD would, he found, be sitting idly in the Mediterranean waiting for ANVIL to begin. So why not use these craft meanwhile to land and supply two divisions on the Italian coast at Anzio, just south of Rome, and then race on to Rome before the Germans knew what was happening?

As Churchill sat in his bathrobe at the Christmas meeting in Eisenhower's villa, almost recovered from his illness, his pale cheeks flushed as he zealously put that question to the Allied generals, including Alexander, Eisenhower, who was about to take over as Supreme Commander of OVERLORD, and British General Sir Henry Maitland Wilson, called "Jumbo" because of his great bulk, who was replacing Eisenhower as Supreme Commander of the Allied Forces in the Western Mediterranean. The fate of Rome—and possibly of Europe—might be decided, the Prime Minister felt, in the next minutes.

Nor did Churchill appear discouraged when Eisenhower shrugged with skepticism. Alexander would certainly not oppose him—and he was the man who would lead the Anzio invasion. The Prime Minister was right—though Alexander's manner reflected little enthusiasm. Could a mere two divisions crash from the sea into Rome?

While Churchill was a gambler, Alexander was a deliberate and cautious man. But why try to bend a will that the general knew was unbendable? And Churchill *was* his patron. It wouldn't be gentlemanly to oppose him or even to disturb him with doubts. Thus, with the Americans compromising once again, it was agreed, in Churchill's words, "to land a wildcat that would tear out the bowels of the Boche . . ."

On January 22, 1944, the "wildcat" landed unopposed at Anzio, looked around at the threatening hills protecting Rome, and hesitated —just long enough for the Boches, their bowels still in good order, to seal off the Anzio beachhead.

Churchill was enraged. Why didn't the troops head for Rome, he demanded to know. Wilson replied on Alexander's behalf that "there was no lack of urging from above, and . . . both Alexander and Clark went to the beachhead during the first forty-eight hours to hasten the offensive."

Churchill replied tartly: "Senior commanders should not 'urge' but 'order.'"

Alexander could carry this business of "gentlemanliness" a little too far at times, he felt.

Alexander was distraught despite his quiet air of optimism, but he realized that the beachhead, even though contained, represented at least a partial victory for Churchill: the Americans could no longer call a halt to the Allied advance short of Rome. For the beachhead troops could only break out when the main Allied force, which was still crawling up the boot and had failed to capitalize on the landing, linked up with them. And this would mean the capture of Rome, for Anzio was on the city's doorstep.

Only one month after the landing, on February 22, Alexander submitted a plan to Allied leaders for just such a maneuver, called Operation DIADEM. It was a blueprint of the battle that must at last yield Rome.

The Allies, under an umbrella of bombers, would break through three main defensive belts: the Gustav Line, the current front; the Adolf Hitler Line, extending across the boot further north; and the Caesar Line, strung across the Alban Hills overlooking Rome.†

The British Eighth Army—composed of the II Polish Corps, the British XIII Corps, and the I Canadian Corps—would attack the German Tenth Army in the main assault on the Gustav Line. The II Polish Corps would capture Monte Cassino, which blocked Highway 6, the ancient Via Casilina, one of the two main roads that led to Rome. At the same time, the British XIII Corps was to cross the Gari River south of Cassino.

The way would then be open for the I Canadian Corps, held in reserve, to move forward, together with the other two corps. The whole British Eighth Army would thereupon streak north through the Liri Valley along Highway 6 toward Rome, crashing through the Adolf Hitler and Caesar lines before the retreating Germans could effectively man them.

Simultaneously, part of General Clark's U.S. Fifth Army—the French Expeditionary Corps (FEC) and the U.S. II Corps—would advance on the southern flank of the British Eighth Army against the German Fourteenth Army. While the French moved through the foothills south of the Liri Valley, the U.S. II Corps, still further south, would surge up the second main road to Rome, Highway 7, the coastal route known as the Appian Way. It would link up at Anzio with the rest of Clark's Fifth Army, the U.S. VI Corps that defended the beachhead.

These beachhead troops would then burst out of Anzio, race north-

† A heavy air effort called Operation STRANGLE was launched before Operation DIADEM and helped to destroy the routes over which German troops and supplies were sent to the north of Rome. Allied bombers attacked bridges, viaducts, and other communication bottlenecks for more than six weeks, with 50,000 planes dropping 26,000 tons of bombs. Although this air offensive was to slow up German military traffic, it would not have a decisive effect on the battle.

ward across the boot, and cut Highway 6 at Valmontone, southeast of Rome. The German Tenth Army being chased along this highway toward Rome by the British Eighth Army would presumably be trapped between the converging British and Anzio forces and annihilated, perhaps foreshadowing an end to the war in Italy.

The key to success, Alexander felt, was surprise. So he and his commanders drew up one of the most deceptive cover plans in military history. Although the attack would begin in early May, the Allies issued training and re-equipment programs for as late as May 21 and left some for the Germans to find.

Simultaneously, dummy signal traffic, which the Germans were certain to monitor, gave false hints that the main attack would come from the sea north of Rome. This "information" would presumably draw German reserves to the coastal sector and away from the Cassino zone. The misleading messages thus placed Canadian troops in Salerno training for an amphibious landing, though these troops were actually in the Cassino area. And the U.S. 36th Division, which was in the south on reserve, was falsely reported ready to participate as well.

Indeed, Alexander meticulously camouflaged the location and size of all formations in a masterful game of "musical chairs." He changed their battle positions and switched some from one army to the other.‡ No patrols were sent out for fear the Germans might learn the true situation from them if they were captured. The French, who would play a vital role in the attack, had to wear British-style helmets and false insignias to confuse possible German observers.

The big unanswered question was which Allied force would enter Rome first. Under Alexander's plan, the British Eighth Army would bypass Rome on Highway 6 while Clark's U.S. Fifth Army would move directly into the city along Highway 7—but only after the German Tenth Army was cut off. Clark and his commanders, however, strongly suspected that Alexander actually intended to get the British into Rome first.

Whatever his intention, Alexander's burden grew enormously after the Anzio fiasco, and he felt it was only proper that he repay his great patron, Winston Churchill, for his confidence with the jewel he had sought for so long.

Anzio had failed, but Carthage would yet yield Rome. And the

‡ The British Eighth Army was openly transferred from the inactive Adriatic coast to the Cassino zone since it would have been impossible to conceal so massive a movement. Furthermore, Allied leaders calculated that an open transfer would further persuade the Germans that the main attack would come from the sea and that any attack from Cassino would only be diversionary. The Germans would presumably be skeptical that the Allies would move so conspicuously otherwise.

British, as Churchill wished, would play the lead role—even if Mark Clark was planning to slam the window shut.[7]*

As he sat in his trailer headquarters behind the Caserta palace, surrounded by trees, ponds, and waterfalls, General Clark fumed as he read the wire that an aide had just handed him. Here it was May 5, only six days before Operation DIADEM was to start, and he had to worry not only about the Germans but also about the British.

The wire was from Lieutenant General Lucian K. Truscott, Jr., who in February had replaced Major General John P. Lucas as commander of the Anzio beachhead force after Lucas failed to move toward Rome. The day before, Truscott reported, General Alexander had visited his beachhead headquarters to discuss plans for the coming offensive.

Alexander wanted to make sure that the Anzio force would, on breaking out, head for Valmontone to trap the German Tenth Army, an operation code-named BUFFALO. The Briton suspected that Clark might send the beachhead troops directly to Rome along Highway 7 before they accomplished this task and thus let the Germans escape.

And Clark, in fact, had worked out three possible alternatives to BUFFALO, including a direct drive on Rome, and instructed Truscott to follow the plan that seemed best when the time came to break out. Truscott had described the three other plans to Alexander the previous day, but Alexander replied firmly that the "only worthwhile plan" was BUFFALO.

Truscott, regarding this comment as an order, then wired Clark, describing the conference with Alexander and adding: "In view of the above advise me if this meets with your approval . . . You know that I am with you all the way."

He should approve a plan forced on *his* subordinate from above? It was shocking, Clark felt, that Alexander should move in and try to run *his* army. He immediately telephoned Alexander, according to Clark's memoirs, and said with indignation that he was "surprised" by Truscott's message. Was it true, Clark wanted to know, that Alexander issued instructions contradicting his own order that Truscott was to prepare the alternate plans? Truscott, Clark said, was now confused and

---

* On May 9, 1944, two days before Operation DIADEM was to begin, General Alexander radioed a personal message to General Clark reflecting his fear that Clark might try to cut the British Eighth Army out of Rome by grabbing control of Highway 6: "I fully realise the difficulties but I must insist that Highway 6 . . . [is] sufficiently cleared at once for Eighth Army columns to get through and that all your traffic is off [Highway 6] as soon as is physically possible after. It is the only good road Eighth Army will have to maintain its forward columns whereas you will have all the roads into Rome south of Highway 6 and a much nearer base at Anzio . . ."

had asked for clarification. Alexander, somewhat flustered, assured Clark that he had not intended to interfere. Well, would Alexander please issue orders through *him* in the future and not directly to his subordinates, Clark replied.

Clark then grabbed his gold-braided overseas cap, dashed out to his Piper Cub, *Sans Culotte*, which was parked in a dry pond, and headed for the beachhead. Truscott notes in his memoirs that Clark, when he arrived, had a dour, angry expression on his lean face.

"The capture of Rome is the only important objective," Clark declared.

He did not think, Clark said, that a drive on Valmontone would trap many Germans. On the other hand, the quickest way into Rome was likely to be the shortest—straight up Highway 7. He would take no chances. The British were not going to beat him into Rome. Truscott was to be as fully prepared to take the alternative routes as the one desired by Alexander.

True, Alexander had assured Clark personally that the Fifth Army would enter Rome first. But the American did not trust him. And this distrust grew after Alexander's visit with Truscott. Clark remembered only too well what happened when his Fifth Army troops had stormed ashore at Salerno. A British force under General Montgomery that had landed further south was supposed to support them but, after what Clark regarded as a leisurely march, arrived too late to be of any help to the exhausted but victorious GI's. British public relations experts, however, announced to the world that Montgomery had raced up the peninsula and rescued him. Clark decided that the British were not playing cricket. There would be no such confusion over Rome.

Clark would be the conqueror of Rome—the first from the south, he liked to think, since Belisarius (he overlooks Garibaldi in his memoirs). Nor would the British publicists cheat him this time. His own would simply overwhelm them. Thus a public relations officer and a photographer—who was required to photograph only the "good side" of his face—became his constant companions and reporters attached to his headquarters were told to identify his troops as "General Mark Clark's Fifth Army."

Clark's ego had been easier to nourish before Rome. Once, in Morocco, he landed his Cub in a field that had been blocked by softball players in the middle of a game, and the soldiers, on seeing who he was, expected the worst.

"What's going on here?" Clark asked.

Just a game between headquarters officers and enlisted men, someone explained.

Clark smiled and proclaimed: "Well, I'm an officer of the Fifth Army Headquarters. I guess I can play, can't I?"

And he did—at first base. It is not certain how much he enjoyed playing, but he clearly enjoyed being accepted by his men.

That was in North Africa. Now he was in Italy. Here, his natural warmth and easy manner often gave way to shouts and ill temper. He could no longer relax. He was obsessed by Rome, forever fearful that the British were plotting to beat him there. He had been chosen to command ANVIL, the invasion of southern France to be launched after Rome fell, but he had virtually refused to start his new assignment until Rome was his.

Nor, it appears, could he block from his mind the big, black headlines that in previous months had announced Lieutenant General George S. Patton, Jr.'s victories in North Africa and Sicily. Patton had been a friend since childhood, but this relationship seemed only to stimulate Clark's competitive spirit.

Anyway, Clark showed no evidence of joy when he learned that Churchill and Eisenhower had agreed on Patton as the man to spark the drive from the Anzio beachhead to Rome after the initial failure. Patton, in London, had already packed his bags, ready to leave for Anzio and add Rome to his laurels. Clark, however, vetoed the assignment, choosing Truscott instead, a man who seemed to have all the virtues. Truscott was relatively unknown yet extremely capable, and, as he had stated in his wire, he was with Clark "all the way."

The fear, the tension, the uncertainty ironically served only to thwart Clark's ego all the more. During one trip to Anzio, after Clark had smilingly posed for a picture with a GI, both of them holding a K-ration they were supposedly to share, Clark returned the K-ration to the soldier, remarking: "Here, son, eat this."

Word soon got around, however unjustifiably, that the general did not consider GI food good enough for him.

And the closer Clark got to Rome, the more he resented playing second fiddle to a British general. Certainly, in his view, he deserved to be recognized as the real commander in Italy. He had been wounded as a fighting captain in World War I. He had helped to create new divisions for World War II. He had been General Eisenhower's deputy in 1942 when they had been sent to England to build up American forces in the European theater. He had helped bring the French in North Africa—then loyal to Marshal Henri Pétain's Vichy government—over to the Allied side after an incredible secret submarine voyage to the region, where he lost his pants while being chased by Vichy police. (He had removed them before leaping into a row boat that was to return him to the waiting submarine.)

He was the commander of the first United States army activated abroad in World War II—the Fifth Army. And he had mounted and executed the landing at Salerno, the first Allied foothold on the European continent. He was proud that, at forty-six, he was the youngest lieutenant general in the history of the United States Army.

Ambitious? Yes. General Marshall himself had asked Eisenhower to talk with Clark and "see what could be done about toning down" his ambition. Nevertheless, Clark knew that his close friend Ike thought very highly of him, though he did not know that Eisenhower had written a memorandum to himself calling Clark "the best organizer, planner and trainer of troops I have yet met in the American Army." Ambition was a good thing, Clark felt, because it forced a man to drive himself. And now he would drive himself ruthlessly.

He would be the first in Rome.[8]

The rosy-faced man with the star-spangled blue beret and leather flying jacket halted his pony and peered upward toward the gray peak of Monte Majo shimmering in the mists along the bank of the Garigliano River. As General Alphonse Juin, commander of the French Expeditionary Corps, squinted in the sunlight one day in late March 1944, he was sure that his men could make the treacherous climb and plant the Tricolor at the top of Majo, which guarded the entrance to the Liri Valley at its southern hinge as Monte Cassino did at the northern, across the valley.

Juin crossed the bridge over the river, escorted by Major General Richard L. McCreery of the British Eighth Army, and spurred his pony up the foothills, taking note of every ravine, cliff, and potential path. As Juin describes the scene in his memoirs, when they had climbed high enough along one precarious trail they halted again and stared into the distance, beyond Majo, where the rugged Aurunci range rolled northwestward toward Rome.

Most Americans and British commanders said it could not be done; no army could cross such a formidable chain of barriers. And one of them, General McCreery, saw no reason now to change his mind. But McCreery and the others, Juin was sure, did not know his corps, with its Moroccans, Algerians, Tunisians, and Frenchmen. They didn't appreciate that a mountain was as easy to maneuver as flatland for some of his troops, especially the Berbers from the hills of southern Morocco—his *goumiers*, as they were called.†

† The Allied Command's attitude toward the French was reflected in a message sent from the Chief of the British Imperial General Staff to General Eisenhower and General Wilson on March 15, 1944, while Operation DIADEM was being planned:

Nor did the Anglo-Saxons understand that a mountain was a small barrier to men determined to regain their pride—and their homeland. Beyond Rome lay France. Rome would symbolize the complete resurrection of the French spirit. His corps *must* take Rome or at least lead the way there—at any cost. For how could one gauge the cost of the French soul?

Juin had long been critical of the Anglo-Saxon tactics on the road to Rome. In October, shortly after Clark had captured Salerno, he told the American general, as their jeep threaded north through ponderous columns of armor and artillery, that such equipment, though ideal for the deserts of North Africa, would intolerably slow the Allied advance in Italy. It would take forever to plow through the river-furrowed valleys and gulleys that echoed with fire from enemy guns hidden, it seemed, behind every scrubby rock in the surrounding hills.

"*Bille en tête, non!*" he said, using a French billiard expression meaning "straight into the pocket, no." "*Par la bande, oui!*" he added. Pocket the ball "indirectly." Strike where the enemy least expected you and outflank bastions like Monte Cassino.

Clark listened politely, but Juin noted the skepticism in his eyes. A glance at the seemingly unconquerable hills stretching forever ahead was hardly persuasive evidence that this logic was valid. Clark had, in fact, heard this argument before—from Major General Geoffrey Keyes, commander of II Corps, one of the Fifth Army's two American corps. But after Keyes submitted a plan for outflanking Monte Cassino and was told that it was a "tactical monstrosity," he vigorously supported the head-on attacks sponsored by both Clark and Alexander.

Juin, on the other hand, had to be virtually forced to do what he had been preaching against. He had lost many men "unnecessarily" in such direct assaults, but he vowed never again. His men were not afraid to die, but they would not die uselessly as battering rams. Now, with Operation DIADEM soon to begin, he must try once more to convince his superiors that he was right.

As plans now stood, the French would take Monte Majo and then advance through the lower hills bordering the Liri Valley under the guns of Germans perched on the peaks. Not only would his men be cannon fodder, but they would not even enter Rome, for they were to be squeezed out northwest of Pico, by the Anzio British Eighth Army forces converging toward Valmontone on Highway 6.

This plan, Juin felt, was extremely unfair to the French and, more-

---

"The whole question of communicating information to French on future operations still under discussion. In the meantime you should tell [General Henri] Giraud [the French chief of armed forces] nothing about future operations without further instructions."

over, could not work, for it called for still another direct attack on Monte Cassino, this time by the II Polish Corps. Three previous attacks had failed, and he saw no reason why the next would fare better.

His French corps should be permitted to strike along the weakly defended center of the jagged, mountainous backbone separating Highways 6 and 7, from peak to peak, and thereby outflank Monte Cassino. The Germans on Monte Cassino would then be forced to retreat and the II Polish Corps would not have to charge up its corpse-strewn slopes in another suicide attack.

The irony of his plan was that success would place Juin's troops in front of the British Eighth Army, which was supposed to be making the main attack. Would Alexander, who, Juin was convinced, designed Operation DIADEM to get the British into Rome first, let the French lead the way—and risk *their* winning the race? And would Clark, who jealously wanted that honor for the Americans, be any more amenable?

Perhaps—if Clark were persuaded that the French, who, after all, belonged to his army, could help him beat the British.

More determined than ever after the reconnaissance tour, Juin returned to his headquarters on the opposite bank of the Garigliano and wrote a memorandum to Clark, pleading that his troops be permitted to strike *"par la bande"*—indirectly, across the mountains.

But a few days later, on April 1, Brigadier General Donald W. Brann, head of Clark's operations staff, visited Juin's headquarters and announced matter-of-factly that the original plan was final, and that was that. Juin argued eloquently but to no avail, though Brann, when he departed, was sympathetic and looked almost as crestfallen as Juin.

The Frenchman refused to give up—not with Rome the prize. He would appeal to Clark himself, though he recalled the American's cool response to his argument months earlier after Salerno had fallen.

Juin had first met Clark on the morning of November 10, 1942, in a small, stuffy room off the foyer of the St. George Hotel in Algiers, when Clark had been sent by General Eisenhower to force the Vichy French to stop firing at Allied troops who had invaded North Africa. Clark had stared with fury at the balding little man with watery blue eyes on his left, Admiral Jean-François Darlan, commander of the Vichy forces in North Africa. When Darlan, sweating and quivering, showed reluctance, Clark pounded the table repeatedly and shouted: "I will end this conference in thirty minutes . . . It will be necessary to retain you in protective custody . . . !"

Juin, Darlan's top general, winced at the table-pounding and blustering threats by this "big American." He himself was only too ready to obey; after all, the Allies were trying to liberate his beloved homeland.

He even called Darlan aside and lectured him on the senselessness of French resistance to the Allies, persuading him to at least compromise.

But Juin nevertheless felt that Clark's undiplomatic approach indicated that he did not comprehend the French military mentality. Clark evidently despised the French officers—perhaps understandably. Did not some despise themselves?

Many French officers, like himself, had fought hard against the Germans in 1940. Indeed, Juin, who had a paralyzed right arm from World War I wounds, was proud that he had resisted in Belgium against enormous odds and had retreated into France only after gallant rearguard fighting. He had then defended Lille and refused to surrender until 80 per cent of his troops had been knocked out, so impressing the victorious German general that he allowed Juin and his men to carry their arms through Lille while the Nazi troops presented arms.

When Vichy leader Marshal Henri Pétain negotiated Juin's release from a prisoner-of-war camp and sent him to his native North Africa to succeed General Maxime Weygand as commander of the Vichy French North African armies, Juin remained loyal to him. Pétain was his superior. And to most French officers, however plagued they were by a sense of shame and doubt, keeping a direct, unbroken chain of lawful command was traditionally more important than moral, national, or international considerations.‡

Yet, Juin was willing to abandon tradition—and Pétain—when the moment was ripe. And the Allied landings in North Africa seemed the moment.

Now, though Juin, under a provisional Free French government headed by Brigadier General Charles de Gaulle, had managed to unite the former Vichy troops with De Gaulle's Free French followers for this great drive on Rome, he realized that a mutual bitterness lingered. After all, each group had only recently regarded, or at least had felt the psychological need to regard, the other as traitorous. The Vichyites had considered the Free French traitors for turning against their superiors. And the Free French had thought the Vichyites traitors for collaborating with the Germans.

But Juin hoped that on the road to Rome the two groups would

‡ This attitude stemmed from the tradition of the *droit administratif*, which required every officer to obey his superior, regardless of circumstances, in return for complete immunity from subsequent punishment. France in its history had been convulsed by a succession of governments—monarchy, convention, directory, consulate, empire, monarchy, empire, and finally republic. The legalistic *droit administratif* was considered necessary to govern the action of French officers and officials in time of revolution and change; it was the only way to save the nation, to prevent anarchy.

learn to love each other again. And that Clark, who was now his good friend, would not pound the table when he, Juin, would insist on his own plan for taking Rome and restoring French honor.

With cool, compelling logic, Juin besought Clark to agree. But Clark's eyes reflected the same skepticism about such tactics that the Frenchman had noted when the two men discussed the subject after the Salerno landing. Yet . . . what if Juin were right? What if he *could* push swiftly across the mountains? Then the French, who were under Clark's command, would be leading the way to Rome—and the British would almost certainly lose the race. With a smile, Clark agreed.

Juin was overjoyed. He was sure that he had planted the seed of France's resurrection. The only problem now was Alexander. Would he approve this change of plans—when Juin's success could squeeze the British out of Rome?

At a meeting of Allied commanders on April 4, Clark supported Juin's plan, and Alexander hesitated. But finally the British general felt he could not challenge Clark and threaten the unity of his delicately balanced international command. He also agreed—but conditionally.

The French could attack across the mountains, but the British Eighth Army would still be the main striking force. The II Polish Corps would, as planned, charge up Monte Cassino. Thus, against Juin's advice, the British Eighth Army would not wait for the French to outflank Monte Cassino and force the German defenders to withdraw without bloody battle—a strategy which would make the U.S. Fifth Army the main striking force and virtually guarantee its entry into Rome first and perhaps exclusively. The French were still to halt their advance in the Pico area, even if they were ahead of the British Eighth Army when they arrived.

Having little choice, Juin agreed to the conditions. But on April 27, fifteen days before the attack, he wrote the defense committee of De Gaulle's provisional government: "I have a feeling that, once the breakthrough has been achieved, it will be the FEC [French Expeditionary Corps] that will set the pace."

Juin loved surprises—as the British, like the Germans, would perhaps learn.[9]

Lieutenant General Sir Oliver W. H. Leese, the British Eighth Army Commander, stared into the hazel eyes of the shaven-headed man sitting at the conference table, as if searching for the real answer to his question: "The responsibility is very great. Are you sure you understand what you are undertaking?"

Lieutenant General Wladyslaw Anders replied that he did. His II Polish Corps would storm the bastion of Monte Cassino—one of the most difficult missions any Allied unit in World War II was asked to achieve. It would do so though its heart was heavy with the knowledge that some of the best and bravest soldiers in the war had already tried and now lay dead at the rocky, weedy foot of what had become a symbol of military insanity.

In early February 1944 men of the American 34th Division had made an incredible, suicidal effort; when finally relieved, about fifty of the few survivors still at their guns had to be carried down the height on stretchers, too frozen and exhausted to move. About two weeks later, New Zealand and Indian troops also failed, even though the Allied air forces had dumped thousands of bombs on the ancient monastery.

Now, on March 24, it appeared that the New Zealanders and Indians would be stopped once more in an attack that had started nine days before. And the Poles were being asked to climb over the corpses that littered the mountainsides and try again.

Leese knew as he studied Anders' eyes that the Pole meant what he said, for here was a man, and a people, with nothing to lose. Psychologically, many had, in fact, come back from the dead and would prefer to be dead than to live without a country. The road to Rome was the road to Poland. And day in and day out, Anders, in talks with Leese, Clark, Alexander, Wilson, with visiting Allied politicians and diplomats and officers, had besought, argued, pleaded for a drive from Rome straight through to his homeland—so he could beat the Russians there.

The answer came, as reflected in Anders' memoirs, on that terrible day in December 1943, when he heard reports that the Big Three had discussed at the Tehran Conference a plan to let Russia absorb the eastern part of Poland. What were the Poles fighting for if not for Poland? It was difficult to quell his urge to pull his corps out of the war.

Still, he tried to reassure his men, to explain away the reports from Tehran. Did not Britain go to war in the first place when Germany invaded Poland? In appearing to agree with Stalin on the Polish question, Britain and the United States had simply been pursuing a "conciliatory" policy to assure military co-operation, but once Germany was crushed, their attitude would stiffen.

In any case, he would never let his two allies give away a square foot of Polish land. And to show the world that Poland would not die, his men would emblazon themselves in its conscience with glorious feats on the battlefield. Monte Cassino now offered the supreme opportunity. For what could be more glorious than to capture this very symbol of impregnability, this graveyard of hundreds who had failed—the doorway to Rome?

General Leese saw not only truth in Anders' eyes, but a deep sadness, for Anders felt that what he had told his men was false, that Tehran was betrayal. Now, as the Polish General saw it, Poland's only hope was Cassino. By opening the way to Rome, with all that Rome meant for the world, the Poles would put the world in their debt. Perhaps, by some miracle, Britain and America would place this dept above their pledge to Russia . . .

Russia . . . Russia to Anders was a word that meant hundreds of thousands of Polish slave laborers living under subhuman conditions. It meant a slice of black bread and a glass of groats each day. It meant dysentery, scurvy, tuberculosis; wet clothes that were frozen stiff when one awoke in a wooden bunk blanketed with bedbugs; rats that snatched at a crumb of dropped food. Russia meant deceit, murder, genocide. Russia was as evil as Germany.

Anders remembered that day, August 23, 1939, when he learned that the two countries had signed a pact. With Poland fighting for survival against the Germans, Russia had, in the words he would record in his memoirs, "flung herself like a hyena" against the rear of the bleeding Polish army, eager to devour what she could of the country.

After leading desperate battles against the Germans in Warsaw, he had fled south toward Romania and Hungary, determined to return one day with the Allies to throw out both invaders. He tried to pass with his men between the Soviet and German forces, but was finally captured by the Russians after being severely wounded.

At Lubianka Prison a guard trampled on a medal of the Blessed Virgin he had always carried with him, crying: "Let us see if this harlot can be of any help to you in a Soviet prison!" He was placed in an isolated, windowless cell where no sound penetrated. Even footsteps were silenced in the thickly carpeted corridors. There he was left to die, slowly, quietly.

Then, one day, in August 1941, the prison commander himself came for him and courteously led him to a huge room with windows and beautiful furniture. And through blurred eyes unaccustomed to the bright light, Anders saw two men rise behind their desks.

"How do you do?"

"Who am I addressing?"

"I am Beria," said one of them.

And he was free—free to lead his people out of the prisons and labor camps, free to fight his way back to Poland. For when Germany invaded Russia, the Poles had suddenly become Russian "allies" and were to be organized into an army under Anders' command. When Anders left the prison, his suitcase was carried out by the prison commander, and the car that drove him away belonged to Lavrenti Beria, head of the Soviet secret police.

Anders was taken to his new quarters, a luxurious four-room apartment complete with cook and maid, and awaiting him was a spread of caviar, champagne, fine wines. NKVD tailors arrived to fit him out with silver embroidered uniforms. He had hardly mentioned his love for dogs when he was presented two pure-bred police dogs. And a cement pavement was laid down outside in a few hours to make sure that he would not hurt his still-wounded leg on rough ground. Finally, he was treated to a cordial visit with Joseph Stalin himself to discuss future plans.

Within weeks a legion of human ghosts, barefooted and half starved, responded to Anders' call—men from 250 prison camps scattered in regions as distant as the Siberian steppes and the Caucasian plains. This army of recruits left for Iran and Iraq in 1942, then merged the following year with the Carpathian Brigade (later a division)—composed of Poles who had escaped both the Germans and the Russians and had already been fighting with the Allies in North Africa.

In Operation DIADEM, Anders realized, his corps would have certain advantages over the units that had assaulted Monte Cassino previously. Ten Allied divisions would be advancing simultaneously along the line instead of one or two as in the past, and the weather would be warm and the earth dry. Nor was he greatly worried, as his superiors seemed to be, that the Poles did not have enough men to replace their losses.

"But where will you get them?" Leese had asked.

"From the German side," Anders confidently replied. "The Poles who were forced to fight for the Germans will fight for us when they are taken prisoner."

With Tehran, Anders bitterly felt, Russia was again an enemy, and the world would now sanction its rape and plunder of Poland. At Cassino he would be fighting the Russians as well as the Germans, for the trophy would be Rome. And only Rome, it seemed, might save Poland from the Russians.[10]*

---

* Allied leaders received all kinds of suggestions for capturing Cassino. On March 30, 1944, a Pentagon general responded to the suggestion of one American citizen: "This is in reply to your letter . . . addressed to the chief of staff, in which you suggest that barrels of molasses be dropped into the ruins of . . . Cassino to stop enemy action. The patriotic motive which prompted your letter is appreciated. Your suggestion has been carefully noted and made a matter of official record in the War Department." The molasses was never dropped.

At five minutes before midnight on April 23, Field Marshal Albert Kesselring, German Commander in Chief of the Southwest Command and of Army Group C, comprising the Tenth and Fourteenth Armies, was about to retire to his quarters in Monte Soratte, north of Rome, when the telephone rang in his office. More speculation, he was sure. And he was exhausted after having spent the day with his Tenth Army commanders.

Major General Richard Heidrich, commander of the crack 1st Parachute Division holding Monte Cassino, had insisted that a new Allied attack on that stronghold was imminent. But Kesselring was just as certain that the Allies were not strong enough for such an assault. He had told his commanders that the enemy might, however, try to land on the coast at Leghorn to the north and cut off the German Tenth and Fourteenth Armies while driving up the boot to get as close to Germany as possible.†

Answering the telephone now, according to Tenth Army records, Kesselring heard the voice of Colonel General Heinrich von Vietinghoff, the Tenth Army commander, whose monocle, small brush mustache, and rigid bearing suggested a caricature of the unsmiling, heel-clicking Prussian general.

"Up here," Vietinghoff said, "we have a Moroccan deserter who claims that it [the big offensive] will start on April 25."

Kesselring was stunned. "Well! . . . The picture becomes still more uncertain!"

"It now seems," Vietinghoff continued, "that in addition to attacking on the coast he [the enemy] is going to do something between Cassino and Monte Cairo [northwest of Cassino]. Heidrich also feels that he is bringing up forces."

After the conversation, Kesselring immediately telephoned Hitler's headquarters in East Prussia and was ordered to prepare for an all-out enemy attack on April 25.

The news had overcome his fatigue, but he was calm, while Hitler, characteristically, was not. On April 13, on the basis of another unconfirmed report, the Führer had insisted that a new coastal landing

---

† Siegfried Westphal, Kesselring's chief of staff, writes in his book *The German Army in the West:* "It would probably have cost less blood in the end if, in September 1943, the Allies had landed not at Salerno but near Rome, and in January 1944, not at Anzio but near Leghorn, or if they had at least made good this omission in May 1944 . . . It is impossible to controvert the fact that a landing near Leghorn early in 1944 would almost certainly have cut off and annihilated Kesselring's Army Group." Westphal, however, does not take into account the Allied shortage of naval transport created by the demands of OVERLORD.

was about to take place, and now he believed the unsubstantiated claim of one Moroccan deserter. Yet what could a defender with no reliable information do except to take seriously every rumor? The situation seemed ludicrous to Kesselring; he had to build his whole defense plan around the questionable statement of one enemy soldier!

He reflected on the miserable state of his intelligence. Why couldn't his troops take more prisoners so he would know what was going on behind the smokescreen hiding the whole enemy line? He didn't even have any planes to reconnoiter the area. Before going to bed, he ordered an immediate alert and a strengthening of some positions in preparation for the "attack."

At 10:45 the next morning, April 24, Vietinghoff telephoned Lieutenant General Siegfried Westphal, Kesselring's brilliant young chief of staff: "Nothing has yet started here, but we expect big things to happen."

"Very good."

"We are scraping together everything, including the armored company, the pursuit company, and the education [political propaganda] company. If that isn't enough, there's nothing we can do about it."

At 5:30 that afternoon, the Tenth Army's XIV Panzer Corps radioed its subordinate formations: "Enemy large-scale offensive seems to be directly imminent. Highest degree of readiness as of 2400 [midnight], April 24."

But though the tension was great, Kesselring was, as usual, optimistic. Even Allied observers sensed his serene nature, calling him "Smiling Albert" because of the usual grin gracing his round, rather innocuous face that stretched to a high, evenly receding hairline. It was somehow disillusioning, even to them, when he removed his dashing, embroidered field marshal's hat and put on his horn-rimmed glasses to transform himself seemingly into a school teacher like his farm-bred father.

At 9:20 A.M., April 25, the tension eased when Vietinghoff phoned Kesselring: "The date wasn't correct. Everything is still calm here."

Vietinghoff and other high-ranking officers, who had packed their belongings the evening before and risen at an early hour "in order to be ready," felt rather sheepish. They had fallen for another false alarm.

The following day, April 26, there was a new disturbing report: the Canadians seemed to have replaced the Poles at the front.

"Then where would the Polacks go?" Westphal asked his informer. Who knew? Certainly not German intelligence.

Two days later, on April 28, Vietinghoff phoned Kesselring to tell him that perhaps he knew: "It seems that Polish uniforms have appeared near Castelforte [actually in the French-held sector]."

"What kind of uniforms?"

"They must be Poles. Reportedly our men saw them through binoculars . . . the insignia of the Poles were seen."

Kesselring was exasperated. Where the hell were those Polacks?

Not until April 30 was there what seemed to Kesselring the first important hint of Allied intentions. The following day he wired the Army General Staff:

"Intelligence service reports Headquarters 1 Cdn Inf Div at Nocera (10 km NW Salerno). Numerous Canadian troops and vehicles in Salerno area."

So the Canadians, and perhaps others, *were* preparing to land on the coast! His conclusion was strengthened when, on May 4, he received a report from his intelligence agents that "36 Am Inf Div said to have been moved to Averso [near Salerno] for exercises."

And the American 36th Division would also be in on it! Well, now at least he knew what to do with his mobile reserves—keep them along the coast. Any attack in the Cassino area would certainly be only diversionary, to keep his forces away from the landing zone.

Kesselring felt sure now that his optimism had been justified. That was the only way to fight a war—to look at the best side of the situation and wait for the opportunities, no matter how unfavorable things might seem. It was folly to give up territory on the theory that the enemy might or might not attack. Let him fight for every inch of earth. He was thankful that Hitler agreed with him and had not listened to General Rommel.

In November 1943 Hitler had been about to name Rommel Commander in Chief of the Southwest Command. Rommel was then commanding the German forces in northern Italy, while Kesselring was commanding in the south. Hitler favored Rommel not only because of his reputation, which Kesselring thought unjustified, but because Kesselring had guessed wrong about Italian intentions after Mussolini was ousted from power on July 25.

Kesselring had assured a highly skeptical Hitler that the new Italian leaders were sincere in professing continued loyalty to their German ally. When these leaders suddenly switched sides, Hitler began to think of the field marshal as weak, bumbling, and dangerously Italophile.

Even so, at the last minute, Hitler instinctively cancelled an order that he had already dispatched for Rommel's new appointment and selected Kesselring for the job. Kesselring's warning that Rommel's policy would spell disaster had rung a bell—all the louder after SS General Wolff, who feared that Rommel would interfere with his own authority in Italy, flew to see the Führer and to urge him to change his mind.

Rommel wanted to retreat to the Gothic Line in the Apennines, between Pisa and Rimini, which would be harder to outflank with coastal invasions than the more vulnerable lines further south.

But Kesselring, who scorned such conventional military thinking, as he had when Rommel wanted to retreat from North Africa "prematurely," was determined to keep his forces before Rome. His front was shorter than the one proposed by Rommel in the north, he argued. Moreover, the farther north the Allies got, the easier it would be for them to bomb southern Germany and invade the Balkans. Finally, Rome was a symbol of prestige, and no nation or army could honorably give it up without a fight. History would record that he was the defender of Rome—even if he were forced to destroy it against his will.

In the end, Rommel's tactical realism could not outweigh Kesselring's more heroic logic.‡ And as the months passed, Hitler's faith in Kesselring did not appear misplaced, for he forced the Allies to pay dearly for every foot they advanced. And Rome was still in German hands.

Yet, ironically, the Germans were not holding the Eternal City because they had correctly guessed Allied plans—Kesselring had, in fact, been surprised in Sicily, at Salerno, and at Anzio—but because the Allies did *not* have either the objectives or the capabilities he thought they had. The Allies had no plan, despite British urging, to push with maximum strength all the way up the Italian boot. Nor, in view of OVERLORD's "tyranny," were they capable of making more than one large-scale landing on the beaches of Italy—and that had been Anzio.

Kesselring's optimistic outlook had been nurtured by his success in helping to build the Luftwaffe, the German air force, into the first great *Blitzkrieg* air arm in history. His First Air Fleet had helped to bring Poland to her knees in a few days. So impressed was Hitler by his imaginative military mind that he appointed him, in November 1941, shortly before the United States entered the war, Commander in Chief of the Mediterranean Theatre.

An airman's aggressiveness, the Führer thought, was what was needed

‡ Hitler's original support of Rommel's view was reflected in a notation made by Propaganda Minister Josef Goebbels in his diary in September 1943: "Naturally we shall not be able to hold southern Italy. We must withdraw northward beyond Rome. We shall now establish ourselves in the defense line that the Führer always envisaged; namely, the line of the Apennine Mountains . . . It would of course be a fine thing if we could remain in Rome. But at Rome our flanks would be too long and too vulnerable. We would always be in danger there." But in the same notation, Goebbels also indicated the concern that finally helped swing Hitler to Kesselring's view: "Of course, if we permit the English and the Americans to go into Italy as far as the Apennines, this will constitute a steady threat to the Balkans, for Italy is the best springboard for the southeast.

on the ground as well as in the air. Ground officers, even Rommel, were too overcautious and overcalculating, too willing to retreat when the going was rough.

Kesselring himself was in constant conflict with his own commanders: General Eberhard von Mackensen, commander of his Fourteenth Army; General von Vietinghoff, commander of his Tenth Army; and Vietinghoff's subordinates, General Frido von Senger und Etterlin, who led the XIV Panzer Corps defending the area from the Liri Valley southward to the Tyrrhenian Sea, and General Valentin Feurstein, who commanded the LI Mountain Corps protecting the relatively inactive zone north of the Liri, from Cassino to the Adriatic Sea.

All too often, the field marshal felt, these commanders thought more about preparing for a retreat and strengthening rear lines of defense than about holding the front line. This attitude was defeatist and entirely contrary to the Führer's thinking—and his own. And he knew that his rigidity gave Hitler confidence in him.

Anyway, Kesselring could not oppose the man who was responsible for his meteoric rise. He was a soldier and that meant, above all, loyalty to his superiors. He only wished that *his* subordinates felt that way.

And although Kesselring viewed Nazism, he states in his memoirs, as a "brilliant and smooth-running organization" that had laudably created an ideal which men were willing to die for, the ideology itself mattered little to him. If political enemies and Jews were victimized by it, even unjustly—and it was not for him to judge—that was not his business. Hitler was his commander and benefactor, and that was the only thing that counted.

Kesselring's supreme optimism reflected the rather simplistic character that made him a perfect tool for Hitler.* Because of his unswerving loyalty to the Führer, he felt freer than more fearful, independent-minded commanders to state his opinions frankly, while Hitler followed most of his advice. At the same time, this exaggerated sense of loyalty permitted the field marshal to rationalize the enormous German casualties his strategy produced.

And also the ruthless suppression of the Italian people—tempered only by military considerations—whom he felt had committed the most odious possible crime: treachery against an ally. He could not forget that he had trusted them even after Mussolini had been deposed,

---

* General Walter Warlimont of Hitlers general staff told the author that officers of a more sophisticated nature like himself were often too frightened to tell Hitler what they really thought, but those of a rather simplistic character like Kesselring somehow didn't ponder as deeply the possible consequences of arousing the Führer's ire and, indeed, often ingratiated themselves with him because of their frankness.

when Hitler was convinced, rightly, that they would turn against Germany.

Still completely in the dark about enemy intentions on May 10, Kesselring demanded that his commanders furnish him intelligence reports "within twelve hours." Vietinghoff not only failed to do so, but was advised by General Feurstein of the LI Mountain Corps that the corps faced possible disaster and should withdraw to the Adolf Hitler Line even before the enemy attacked.

Sensing no immediate attack and knowing what Kesselring would say anyway, Vietinghoff flatly refused. He then lied to the field marshal, telling him on the phone the next morning, May 11, that "both corps commanders told me as one that they did not yet have the impression that anything was going to happen."

A few hours later, an aerial bomb wrecked Tenth Army headquarters at Massa d'Albe. But both Vietinghoff and Kesselring remained convinced that no major offensive could be expected before May 24— as the latest intelligence indicated.

So convinced were they that that very evening, just before the final battle for Rome would start, Vietinghoff left for Hitler's headquarters in East Prussia where, together with one of his corps commanders, General von Senger und Etterlin, he was to receive a decoration for military astuteness!

He would personally let Hitler know that Kesselring was prepared to defend Rome to the last drop of German blood.[11]

❖   ❖   ❖

At 10:45 that night of May 11, an officer of the 338th Field Artillery Battalion of the U.S. 88th Division, part of II Corps, ordered: "Battery adjust! Shell HE—charge 5—fuse quick."

Men quickly took their places at the gun and at the ammo racks.

"BDL 50—SI 295—on number four, close two—battery four rounds per minute for eight minutes—at my command, elevation 830!"

The breeches closed with sharp clicks.

At precisely 11:00 on a radio signal from the BBC, this officer, like hundreds of others at that moment, shouted: "Fire!"

And suddenly a deafening roar shattered the tranquil night and the nightingales could be heard no more. All along the front, from Cassino to the Tyrrhenian Sea, more than one thousand big guns choked forth their fury in the most thunderous bombardment of the war to date. Missiles streaked into the black depths of the enemy, tracers crisscrossed and bounced off naked cliffs, flares burst into mystically suspended red, green, and amber showers of light that cast giant shadows on a world bejeweled with burning trees.

The race for Rome had begun.[12]

2

The Plots

SS Colonel Eugen Dollmann felt uneasy on the evening of October 15, 1943, as he sat painstakingly translating into German a letter he had brought from Mussolini for Hitler. The letter pleaded with the Führer to defend Rome street by street if necessary.

Earlier that day, Dollmann had served as interpreter at a long conference in Hitler's East Prussian headquarters attended by the Führer and the Duce's Defense Minister, Marshal Graziani. The main subject of discussion was the planned build-up of a new Fascist army, but Graziani also brought up the question of Rome, though he personally opposed defending the city and risking its destruction.

Hitler had replied that he, like the Duce, was aware of the importance of Rome and would do his best to satisfy his friend, but that he could not make a decision immediately.

After the conference, Dollmann had retired to a special train, in which he would stay for the night, to translate the Duce's letter. He was to see Hitler later that evening to discuss the note and Rome's future, and he was disturbed that Mussolini expected him personally to press Hitler to defend Rome to the last.

Though Dollmann liked and admired the Duce and admits in his memoirs that he had fallen under his spell at their recent meeting in Salò, he unfortunately had to argue *against* his proposal. Dollmann could not agree with the Italian dictator that the Germans, for reasons of prestige, should, if necessary, destroy the city with all its treasures.

And Dollmann's attitude hardened as he translated the Duce's words, which called for even more drastic measures to hold Rome than the dictator had suggested at their meeting.

Dollman had fallen in love with Rome long before the war had so inextricably linked his fate with that of the city. He had come as a student in the late 1920s to relive the Renaissance and weave the fantasy of a new united Europe dedicated to the cherished values that had stimulated such creative achievement under the old monarchs and popes. On his arrival in Rome, as he stood on Monte Pincio and watched the clouds in the gathering twilight, he had recalled from *La Comédie Humaine* the thoughts of Balzac's student Baron Rastignac as he gazed upon Paris:

"Lights were beginning to twinkle here and there . . . There lay the splendid world he had hoped to gain. He eyed that humming hive with a look which foretold its despoliation, as if he already felt on his lips the sweetness of its honey . . ."

Dollmann first eyed his own splendid world as a child, when his mother, a close friend of His Imperial and Royal Majesty Franz Josef I of Austria-Hungary, took him along on a visit to the Emperor. While he listened to the low hum of conversation, he stared at the Emperor as if he were God, and as remote, until suddenly God spoke, beckoning to him:

"So that's the lad, is it? What's your name?"

"Eugen, Your Majesty."

"Well, Eugenio, be sure you grow up as fine a man as Eugenio of Savoy. He was a faithful servant of my house."

Yes, those had been regal days, days of gallantry and loyalty unto death.

And now he served Adolf Hitler.

Well, why not? It was a means to an end. And the end was to stay in Rome. For him, Rome was not simply there to be enjoyed; it implored him to accept its favors. He mingled with the social elite, the aristocracies, the artistic personalities of the time. Beautiful women vied for his attention, though he rather disdained women except as dispensers of gossip about the latest scandals.

Still, to maintain his reputation as a rather dashing figure, he often was accompanied to parties by the pretty daughter of the woman who operated Pensione Jaselli-Owen where he lived. He was fond of calling Marie Celeste Rossi, or Bibi, as she was known, his "girl friend," though he often preferred the company of Mario, his devoted Italian chauffeur, and Lupo, his giant Alsatian dog.

All the doors of Rome, at least those that counted, were open to Dollmann. And General Wolff, his superior, gave him almost complete freedom to do as he wished. His principal function was to serve as liaison between Wolff and Kesselring and between the field marshal and the Vatican.

But he was also to keep his hand on the pulse of Roman society, whose influence on the Vatican was powerful and whose political loyalties, geared to survival, could be dangerous. And with his sparkling wit, elegantly effeminate manners, and genteel appearance—ash-blond hair, expressive eyes, tapered hands, rosy complexion—he was the perfect man for this task. Dollmann and the Roman elite understood each other; both wanted to keep what they had at almost any cost.

But if Dollmann relished his job in part because of his entree into Roman society, he had soared swiftly in the SS hierarchy because of his remarkable ability to exploit this entree. He had first joined the Nazi party shortly after Hitler came to power because it was the thing to do among the German students in Rome.

After all, he had seen the anti-Nazi German ambassador, Ulrich von Hassell, showing the sights to the visiting SD chief, General Reinhard Heydrich, shortly after Hitler came to power in 1933. Hitler was a crude, rather boorish man, and even a bit mad, but this seemed to be the traditional mark of the German despot. And he might eventually unite Europe—the first step back to the old glorious Europe Dollmann pined for.

Dollmann's big break came in 1937 when he went to Germany as guide and interpreter for a group of Italian Fascist youth and served as Hitler's personal interpreter at a reception for them. The Führer commended him, and when Himmler visited Italy shortly afterward he used Dollmann as *his* interpreter. Charmed by Dollmann, Himmler enlisted him in the SS without the usual training, and Dollmann, with his intimate knowledge of the Italian scene, proved so valuable to the Nazis that he soon strutted the streets of Rome as a colonel, his finely tailored black uniform decorated with almost as much braid as Emperor Franz Josef had displayed.

Yes, he loved Rome, and now, as he prepared for his meeting with Hitler, he was quite persuaded that destiny had chosen him to save the city once more . . .

Many weeks earlier, on July 27, Dollmann had dined at Kesselring's quarters north of Rome and found himself sitting across from a huge, scar-faced figure in a fur-lined flying jacket—SS Lieutenant Colonel Otto Skorzeny, who had come from Germany on a secret mission.

After the meal, Dollmann relates, Kesselring and his officers adjourned immediately, leaving Dollmann alone with Skorzeny and SS Lieutenant Colonel Herbert Kappler, the Gestapo chief in Rome.

Skorzeny, after requesting that no one else be told the nature of his mission, informed Kappler and Dollmann that he was to free Mussolini, who had been ousted from power and arrested two days earlier— *and* to direct a *coup de main* to prevent Italy's anticipated defection from the Axis. This would mean arresting King Victor Emmanuel III, the royal family, the Cabinet, senior military officers, and the Fascists who had deposed the Duce.

"Although care must be taken not to kill or injure anyone while these persons are being taken into custody," Skorzeny said, "resistance must be broken."

Dollmann says he was troubled as Skorzeny spoke. This plan, conceived by Himmler, would mean a bloodbath and bitter street fighting in Rome, for the King's loyal troops would certainly resist. But who was he to oppose this powerful man and, indeed, Himmler himself? Dollmann showed Skorzeny the location of various ministries and royal palaces on a street map, pointing out the carelessly guarded entrances.

But he claims to have secretly warned the German ambassador's wife to make sure that the women and children of the royal family abandoned their palaces and left Rome immediately. Possibly as a result of this revelation, the Italian police chief, Carmine Senise, ironically called Dollmann to his office and informed him that he was aware of the German plan.

"I do not know what your intentions may be," he said, "but I must warn you that we have reinforced the guards at Villa Savoia [the King's residence] and the ministries. Furthermore, we are keeping a close watch on all your movements. Know, therefore, that we are prepared for all contingencies."

Dollmann—and Kesselring, who also opposed the plot, fearing military complications—were delighted. Now Dollmann could justify his opposition by saying that word had "unfortunately" leaked out, threatening the success of the whole venture. Dollmann says he then persuaded Kappler, who resented Skorzeny's "interference" in *his* sphere of activity, to urge Himmler to cancel the *coup de main*.

Finally, Dollmann claims to have worked on General Sepp Dietrich, the tough, squat commander of Hitler's mercenary SS Leibstandarte armored division, whose men would participate in the operation. He took him to a restaurant in the hills overlooking Rome for a feast of spaghetti and chicken served by pretty girls and washed down by the finest Frascati wine. And when his guest had fallen under the spell of sentimental music and the magnificent view of Rome, Dollmann told him how Emperor Nero had burned down the city to his everlasting shame.

Would Dietrich want to earn so infamous a niche in history? While the musicians played Puccini's "Inno di Roma," Dollmann relates Dietrich promised to entreat Hitler to cancel the project. And he kept his promise, adds Dollmann. Whatever the reason, the plan was never implemented . . .

Now Rome was in danger again, and Dollmann would himself appeal to Hitler. Before seeing the Führer on the evening of October 15, 1943, he informed Field Marshal Wilhelm Keitel, the German Chief of Staff, of his personal views, and Keitel seemed to concur.

Hitler finally received Dollmann, accompanied by Keitel, and cordially said:

"The field marshal [Keitel] has told me that you are doubtful about the possibility of staying in Rome and that you would prefer to evacuate the city. Why does an old Roman like yourself see it this way?"

Dollmann replied carefully—a misstatement, he feared, could bring the firing squad—with brief explanations interspersed with flashes of history. There were several reasons, he said. The Roman Resistance might cause trouble. The Vatican might, also. The Allies, who had already bombed outlying areas of the city, might continue such attacks. Priceless works of art would thus be endangered and the world might blame Germany for occupying the city. Furthermore, the problem of feeding Rome was great.

Unless military factors dictated occupation, he concluded, the Germans could well lose more prestige than they gained by staying in Rome.

With a look of some surprise and curiosity, Dollmann later reported, Hitler asked: "This evacuation which you advise, how do you suppose it can be carried out in practice? Undoubtedly you have thought about it. Or do you perhaps think that I should restitute Rome to the traitors from the south [where the King and his government had fled from Rome] as compensation for their violation of their agreements and their word of honor?"

The atmosphere was tense, and Dollmann noted the nervous expression on Keitel's face. There were two possibilities, Dollmann replied calmly, suppressing his own fear. One was to place the city under the International Red Cross, and the other was to extend the Vatican's control over the city. This second possibility, he added, would be a way to deliver a grave blow to the monarchy, which had traditionally opposed Vatican political power.*

Hitler asked suspiciously: "Have you spoken with Ambassador von Weizsäcker about this?"

He was referring to Baron Ernst von Weizsäcker, the German ambassador to the Holy See, who was regarded in high Nazi circles as having a "defeatist" mentality.

When Dollmann replied in the negative, the Führer said: "We are in Rome now and I think we shall stay in Rome."

As he departed, Dollmann wondered what Hitler's reaction had been to his suggestion that the Vatican assume control of Rome. He had offered it in the full knowledge that the Führer had a secret plan to kidnap Pope Pius XII and take over the Vatican.[1]

❖ ❖ ❖

SS General Wolff, whom Hitler had personally assigned, at their meeting on September 12, 1943, to carry out the papal abduction, immediately returned to his headquarters at Fasano, a resort town sprawled along the banks of Lake Garda southeast of neighboring Salò, the seat of Mussolini's republic. Once there, he set the machinery in motion, but, according to Wolff, only to make the Führer *think* he was seriously working on the project. The general maintains that he was, in fact, determined to sabotage it. And he felt this was possible because Hitler trusted him.

Himmler did, too, for Wolff was more the diplomat than the administrator and did not threaten his, Himmler's, position. On the other hand, Wolff, with his extroverted, easygoing charm, presented a civilized SS face to the world.

So valued was Wolff that he was given the unique title of "Highest SS and Police Leader" (*Höchster SS und Polizeiführer*), making him second only to Himmler himself in the SS hierarchy, though Ernst Kaltenbrunner, head of the Security Office of the Reich, was on an equal level. Before going to Italy in 1943, Wolff had been the chief of Himmler's personal staff and a liaison between Himmler and Hitler

* Colonel Dollmann's suggestion that the Vatican administer the city of Rome was in direct conflict with Mussolini's stand. Marshal Graziani said at his (Graziani's) trial after the war: "It was not Hitler who did not want Rome to be an open city, but Mussolini, who feared that in this way Rome could become the capital of a new papal state."

on the one hand and between Himmler and Foreign Minister Joachim von Ribbentrop on the other.

Wolff was so powerful that he dared on one occasion to go over Himmler's head to Hitler on a delicate personal matter. In early 1943, while still in Germany, he had wanted to marry a countess he had met and therefore requested permission from Himmler to divorce his current wife, since Himmler had to approve every marriage and divorce in the SS. When Himmler rejected the request, thinking that Wolff would set a poor example, Wolff went directly to Hitler, who extended permission. Wolff thus got divorced and married the countess.

Possibly because of this incident, Himmler "exiled" Wolff to Italy, though his job was indeed important—basically, to advise Mussolini on police matters and make sure that the Duce himself remained loyal.

Now Wolff had been given another mission—to raid the Vatican and abduct the Pope. This mission apparently was not a spur-of-the-moment whim on Hitler's part. Propaganda Minister Josef Goebbels recorded in his diary on July 26, 1943, the day after the Duce's overthrow, that the Führer assured his deputies:

"I will go right into the Vatican. Do you think that the Vatican disturbs me? We will take it immediately. It's all the same to me. That rabble is in there. We'll get that bunch of swine out of there. Later we can make apologies."

Goebbels reported on the following day, July 27, that although the Führer had intended to seize the Vatican—the diary does not specifically refer to a kidnaping of the Pope—he and Ribbentrop had dissuaded him. But apparently they did not, for two months later, on September 12, Hitler, spurred by the King's "treachery" and the Salerno landing, gave Wolff his new assignment.†

Wolff did not relish the task. He had enough trouble controlling the Italian partisans, who would certainly grow in number now that the King had "betrayed" Germany. An attack on the Vatican would turn the whole country against the Germans.

And though Wolff was apparently undisturbed by the linkage of his name with the deportation and death of hundreds of thousands of Jews‡ and political enemies, he dreaded the prospect of being associated for posterity with the kidnaping of the Pope.

† On October 10, 1943, an officer at Hitler's headquarters submitted a recommendation for an order to be used if the Germans had to flee Rome: key buildings and installations were to be destroyed, but the Vatican and the utilities feeding it should not be damaged. Hitler's chief of staff, Colonel General Alfred Jodl, scribbled a note at the bottom of this recommendation: "This is out of the question and not to be considered. Such an order creates instantly the supposition that even the top leadership doubts the ability of the [Gustav Line] to resist." Jodl makes no mention of the papal kidnap plot, but the order would not have been consistent with that plot.
‡ Shortly after the Germans captured Minsk (July 1941) in their invasion of the

Somehow he felt a strange awe before leaders like Hitler or the Pope, who were able, if in vastly different ways, to capture men's souls and mold their minds. Hitler, of course, was the god he still followed. Wolff even now was optimistic that Germany would win the war, that an enemy attack across the English Channel would be crushed. Even if it were not, he had heard of secret weapons that would soon be perfected. And he was hopeful that Britain and the United States might, in the end, join Germany in resisting a Soviet takeover of Europe, if it came to that.

Wolff, however, was prone to season his optimism with realism. If worse came to worst and Germany lost the war, it would be nice to have another god—the Pope—to serve as his protector.

Whatever his true feeling, Wolff, when he returned to Fasano after being ordered by Hitler to abduct Pius, worked hard on the plot. He ordered SS General Wilhelm Harster, his Gestapo chief for Italy, to recruit men from South Tyrol who could speak and write Latin, Greek, French, and English, and he drew up a plan based on guidelines provided by Himmler.

About two thousand of his men would seal off all exits from the Vatican, then occupy the Vatican radio station, arrest the Pope and the cardinals, and whisk them off in cars and police trucks to the north before the Italians or the Allies could intervene. The papal column would speed via Bozen and Munich into Liechtenstein, unless another destination was chosen.

Meanwhile, troops would search the Vatican for political refugees, German deserters, and Jews, and those who could not be found would

Soviet Union, Wolff accompanied Himmler to that city to witness the shooting of one hundred Jews, according to a German officer who was also present, Obergruppenführer Erich von dem Back-Zelewssky (*Aufbau*, New York, August 23, 1946). Some time later, on July 16, 1942, Wolff telephoned Staatssekretär Dr. Ganzenmüller of the German Transport Ministry for help when a railroad line to the death camp of Sobibor, on the Bug River, broke down. When Ganzenmüller replied that everything was all right—three hundred thousand Warsaw Jews had been diverted from Sobibor to Treblinka—Wolff wrote a letter of thanks: "For your letter of July 28, 1942, I thank you—also in the name of the Reichsführer [Himmler] . . . With particular joy I noted your assurance that for two weeks now a train has been carrying, every day, five thousand members of the chosen people to Treblinka, so that we are now in a position to carry through this population movement at an accelerated tempo. I, for my part, have contacted the participating agencies to assure the implementation of the process without friction. I thank you again for your efforts in this matter and, at the same time, I would be grateful if you would give to these things your continued personal attention." After the Warsaw Ghetto had been burned down in spring 1944 and almost all of its half-million residents murdered, Wolff welcomed Major General Jurgen Stroop, commander of the final operation, to Hitler's headquarters in East Prussia and praised him in the Führer's name. (Kazimierz Moczarski, "Rozmowy z Katem" ["Conversations with an Executioner"], in *Odra*, Wroclaw, Poland, Apr. 1972–Feb. 1974.)

be starved out. A special group of about fifty men would, at the same time, collect and pack the Vatican treasures—paintings, sculptures, gold, foreign currency, and records—including some 500,000 books, 60,000 pictures, and 7,000 incunabula, the Western world's first printed books.

Himmler and Martin Bormann, the head of the Nazi Chancellery —who originated the idea of the kidnaping in his fanatical hatred of the Vatican as a "spiritual" competitor of Nazism—particularly wanted to find the age-old runic papers, or scriptures, and other cultural documents showing that violence had been used by the Christians against the ancient inhabitants of Germany. They were also eager to find recent documents "proving" that the Vatican, in league with the monarchy, had plotted Mussolini's ouster. With such "evidence," the large Catholic population of Germany could perhaps be persuaded that Hitler was their only true spiritual leader.

Despite his pledge of secrecy to Hitler, Wolff described the plot to Ambassador Rudolf Rahn, the paunchy, bushy-browed emissary to Mussolini's new republic, and Rahn, shocked by the idea, apparently informed General Enno von Rintelen, the German military attaché in Rome. Rintelen, in turn, told Baron von Weizsäcker, the German ambassador to the Vatican.[2]

Weizsäcker, tall and taciturn with snow-white hair, had the mournful expression of a man facing instant doom, yet a hard, humorless glint in his eyes attested to his will to survive. He was probably the most disturbed German of all, although he tended to disbelieve the report of the kidnap plot at first. If it were true, all his own well-laid plans would be thwarted. For Weizsäcker was convinced that Germany could not possibly win the war and he had only one aim—to promote a negotiated peace when the time was ripe, with the Pope his instrument.

To abduct Pius, he felt, would be to kill the last hope for saving Germany from complete destruction, and the pillaging of Rome would be the first symbolic result. The Allies would certainly send in troops to save the Pope and the city would become a battlefield.*

Weizsäcker wanted peace because he was a realist, not because he necessarily disagreed with Hitler's demands. He had bitterly resented the provisions of the Versailles Treaty, and, belonging to a conserva-

---

* Whatever the Allies might have done if the Germans tried to kidnap the Pope, President Roosevelt told a White House meeting attended by Prime Minister Churchill and the Combined Chiefs of Staff on September 9, 1943, that a new slogan should be adopted: "Save the Pope."

tive family prominent in the old Kingdom of Württemberg—his father had been minister-president—he had deplored the chaos and liberal permissiveness of the democratic Weimar Republic that followed World War I. Originally a monarchist, he felt that some form of Prussian authoritarianism was desirable, but not the rabble-rousing dictatorship of Adolf Hitler, an emotionalist without manners.

Like most traditional German diplomats and bureaucrats, Weizsäcker had wanted Germany to get back what it lost in World War I and annex Austria as well, but through dynamic diplomacy, not unwinnable war. Of course, if the realities were different and Germany *could* win a war, that might be another story. Realism, not moralism, was Weizsäcker's forte.

Thus, the very quality that made him dread war kept him in his job under a man he despised. Hitler had come to power whether he liked it or not, and he could either retreat to the sidelines or remain and perhaps influence events.

To choose the second course, as he did, would mean that he would be living a lie—if, indeed, he lived at all. He would give the *impression* that he was serving Hitler's policies while unobtrusively working to defeat or limit them.†

Weizsäcker was not the only high-level German "saboteur." Other diplomats and bureaucrats and even military officers were similarly engaged, but probably none were more influential, durable, or subtle. A naval officer during World War I, Weizsäcker joined the foreign service in 1920 and swiftly rose in rank as he brought his extraordinary diplomatic talents to posts in Basel, Copenhagen, Geneva, Oslo, and Berne, before being called to Berlin in 1936 as head of the Foreign Office Political Department.

In 1938 the vain and arrogant Joachim von Ribbentrop became Hitler's Foreign Minister and, to avoid choosing a high Nazi party functionary—and possible rival—as his State Secretary, named Weizsäcker, the highest ranking department officer, to the post. He had been told by Erich Kordt, the head of his ministerial bureau and also a leader of the conspirators for peace, that Weizsäcker would be more

† Although Weizsäcker despised Hitler, he was willing to accept the Führer as long as he didn't go to war. In his memoirs, Weizsäcker writes: "Peace with Hitler? Is that what the opposition within Germany wanted? To preserve Hitler—and in addition to let him have the glory of a victorious war? To me all this presented no problem, and I had no hesitations. I was for peace, no matter on what basis it was concluded . . . My view was that both must be made an end of, the war as well as Hitler's rule, but Hitler must not be removed by means of war and by the incalculable sacrifices which war would demand . . . I should never have approved—I should have found it absolutely inexcusable—to promote the catastrophe, to bring on war, in order to lose it, and thus to get rid of Hitler."

than "merely a subordinate," that, as a former naval officer, he "would know how to obey."

"So he can obey," replied Ribbentrop. "Then ask him to please have lunch with me today."

Weizsäcker accepted the post with mixed feelings. On the one hand, he would now be in an excellent position to influence German policy, but on the other, Ribbentrop was not only personally repulsive to him but was perhaps even more war-minded than Hitler. Still more disturbing was the psychological trap in which he was caught. He must sabotage his government's war policies, but where was the dividing line between sabotage and treason? He was, after all, still a rigid national-ist who wanted most of what Hitler wanted, if without war.

Finally, a few months after taking over his new post, Weizsäcker decided he must step over the line on the question of Hitler's designs on Sudetenland. He conspired with Kordt to warn British Prime Min-ister Neville Chamberlain of Hitler's intentions. The two Germans urged the British to continue pressing for a peaceful settlement of the Sudetenland issue, but simultaneously to make clear that they would oppose any use of force. Hitler would then back down, they assured the British.

Weizsäcker was able to rationalize this flirtation with treason when Hitler met with Chamberlain in Munich in September 1938. On the basis of a discussion plan which Weizsäcker had helped to draft, Chamberlain agreed to let Hitler swallow up Sudetenland. Weizsäcker was ecstatic.

"The Munich Agreement," Weizsäcker later wrote, "was one of the rare examples in modern history of important territorial changes being brought about by negotiation."

He had helped to obtain what he wanted without resort to the sword; the *threat* of the sword had been enough. It was not morality but what one could get away with that was important. Later, Weiz-säcker—and the British—learned the price of appeasement when a new crisis arose: Poland. Certainly, he was convinced, Britain would take up the sword if Hitler and Ribbentrop carried through plans to invade that country.

Again he urged Hitler to talk, not fight, and, in June 1939, warned Britain of a possible German pact with Russia, in the vain hope that London would make a deal with Moscow before the Führer could. In the end everything failed. On August 25, 1939, Weizsäcker recorded in his diary:

"It is an appalling idea that my name should be associated with this event, to say nothing of the unforeseeable results for the existence of Germany and of my own family."

Even when war seemed inevitable, Weizsäcker desperately appealed one last time to Hitler and Ribbentrop at a meeting with them on August 30. In his pocket was a pistol loaded with two bullets. When his entreaties were spurned, Weizsäcker departed in a nervous sweat —the pistol still in his pocket. He had been unable to bring himself to use it.

On September 5 he wrote: "And now the struggle has begun. God grant that not everything that is good and valuable will be utterly destroyed in it. The shorter it lasts, the better. But one must remember that the enemy will never conclude peace with Adolf Hitler and Herr von Ribbentrop. What does that mean? As if anyone could fail to see what that means!"

Almost simultaneously, he received the first agonizing hint of what it meant. A stark telegram informed him that his son Heinrich had been killed in Poland on the second day of the war.

Weizsäcker, nevertheless, did not give up hope of ending the war swiftly, and if the only way was to get rid of Hitler, he was ready to co-operate. He appears to have been involved in a plot to oust the Führer, though he would play no direct role, only a diplomatic one. The plot culminated in Rome in December 1939, when some German generals made contact with Pope Pius XII.

Francis D'Arcy Godolphin Osborne, British Minister Plenipotentiary to the Holy See, cabled the Foreign Office after an audience with the Pope on January 12, 1940:

> If the German generals could be assured of a peace with Great Britain . . . they were prepared to replace the present German government by a . . . government with which it was possible to negotiate— and then to reach a settlement in Eastern Europe with the British government . . .
> [The Pope felt that] his conscience would not be quite easy unless he sent for me. He wished to pass the communication on to me purely for information. He did not wish in the slightest degree to endorse or recommend it.

Nothing ever came of this peace feeler, for the British were suspicious of its vagueness and the apparent desire of the conspirators that Germany keep most of the territory, particularly Austria, that Germany had swallowed up. But Weizsäcker was still hopeful. The Pope *had* relayed the message. He was the only man in the world now who could serve as an effective instrument of negotiated peace. Perhaps if he, Weizsäcker, were sent to Rome . . .

Anyway, what was the purpose of staying in Berlin, now that war had broken out? And Ribbentrop, who reciprocated Weizsäcker's hostility, appeared only too willing to send him off to some distant post where he could utilize his considerable diplomatic talent without being able to affect Nazi policy greatly.

Unmentioned, and unmentionable, was the possibility that, if the worst happened, Weizsäcker might be useful in persuading the Pope to mediate some kind of peace that would save the Nazi regime from complete disaster.

In early 1943 Weizsäcker was thus transferred to Rome as ambassador to the Holy See. Almost immediately he managed to exact a promise from the papal Secretary of State, Cardinal Luigi Maglione, that he would be given a sign as soon as any chance for peace occurred . . . And now came this report that Hitler was planning to raid the Vatican and kidnap the Pope!

Soon after Weizsäcker had learned of the plan, Monsignor Giovanni Battista Montini (later Pope Paul VI), one of Pius' two Assistant Secretaries of State, summoned him to say that the Pope wished to see him about the report of the kidnap plot, which had reached his ears. It had, indeed, reached many ears, for on the previous day, October 7, a Salò government broadcast had unexplicably hinted at Hitler's "secret" by declaring that "quarters are being prepared in Germany for the Pope." An audience was set for the following day, October 9.

As he entered Pius' study, Weizsäcker was impressed as always by the serene manner and august bearing of the man sitting behind the large, neat papal desk. The visitor bowed stiffly, but with grace, and sat down, with the light coming from his back illuminating the Pope's thin, ash-gray countenance, so furrowed, despite the tight, parchmentlike skin, with the worries of the world.

Here was a man, Weizsäcker reflected, more powerful in a sense than Adolf Hitler—and yet so gentle. Nor was the perfect calm that was mirrored in the Pope's bright, bespectacled eyes the least disturbed when he brought up the question of the rumor. He had heard it, Pius said, from "serious Italians" who had been informed by high-placed Germans. He stated that he was determined to remain in Rome . . .[3]

Actually, the Pope was not quite sure that he would. After all, in 1798 Napoleon Bonaparte's French Troops removed Pope Pius VI from Rome and he died in their hands. And in 1809 Napoleon had Pius VII taken prisoner and brought to Fontainbleau, near Paris. Was Hitler any less fanatical—or irrational—than Napoleon?

Pius XII had been concerned about the Führer's intentions since April 25, 1941, when he heard that Ribbentrop had asked his Italian counterpart, Foreign Minister Count Galeazzo Ciano, to oust the Pope from Rome. Ciano had reportedly replied that he favored simply isolating and controlling the Pontiff within the Vatican.

When Vatican officials inquired about that report, the Italian leaders denied it. However, the officials were so worried that on May 8, 1941, at a meeting of cardinals, Cardinal Maglione revealed that special powers would be given to papal representatives abroad in case the Pope would "not be able to communicate" with them. Anxieties grew when, subsequently, several German officers and diplomats secretly informed the Vatican of rumored plans being worked out in Berlin.‡

Further fueling fears was the arrival in Rome in 1943, shortly after Weizsäcker had come, of Ludwig Wemmer, an official of Bormann's National Socialist party chancellery. As Bormann's religious affairs adviser, Wemmer would be just the man to help carry out a papal abduction. Though it could only be surmised at the time, Wemmer's main job was to spy on Weizsäcker to make sure he was not conspiring with the Pope against Nazi interests.

The Vatican took the mounting reports seriously, so seriously that the Pope ordered his personal archives sealed up in false floors and documents of the Secretariat of State scattered in obscure corners.

At one point some papal assistants in the Secretariat were given orders to stand by with bags packed ready to accompany the Pope on short notice. And Allied diplomats living in Vatican City decided to burn their official papers on the advice of Cardinal Maglione and to follow the Pope into exile. On August 4, 1943, Maglione told a special meeting of cardinals:

"The Italian government fears that there will be a German strike against Rome. In such a case, they foresee also an invasion of the Vatican. This cannot be excluded, as German threats against the Vatican have been growing for the last few years."

Alarm reached a peak on September 10 with the German occupation of Rome, and Maglione desperately appealed to Weizsäcker for help in sparing the Vatican. The ambassador tried to reach Kesselring for some forty-eight hours, but without success. As it turned out, the Vatican was subject to no immediate raid . . .[4]

Now the Pope himself was conferring with Weizsäcker, seeking to elicit some hint of what might lie in store for him. Should his cardinals and assistants keep their bags packed indefinitely?

If the Pontiff probed very delicately, Weizsäcker was equally cautious in his reply, neither knowing the answer firsthand nor wishing to con-

‡ Monsignor Mella Di Santella writes in *Istantaneo inedite degli ultimi 4 papi* that a colonel in Hitler's High Command came to a papal audience one day and, taking the Pope aside, told him about the kidnap plot. Pius replied: "I will not move from Rome. Here I was placed by the will of God and therefore by my own will or with my consent I shall not leave my Seat. They would have to tie me up and carry me out, because I intend to remain here!"

firm that Germany, even under a man like Hitler, would be capable of such a crime. He simply asked the Pope if he wished him to make use of the rumors to discourage any such possibility.

The Pope replied no, but he was clearly hoping that Weizsäcker would use his influence in the affair. And behind the Pope's vague smile was the awareness of a family history that made the prospect of leaving Rome all the more agonizing . . .[5]

More than a century earlier, Pius' grandfather Marcantonio Pacelli had been the solicitor of Pope Pius IX. When, in 1848, anticlerical rebels attacked the Vatican, Marcantonio fled with the Pope to the sea fortress of Gaeta. But he returned with Pius two years later under the protection of French bayonets and was appointed Secretary of the Interior for all the papal dominions—a position he held until rebels attacked again in 1870 and this time permanently relieved the Vatican of all political power.

Pope Pius IX locked himself inside the Vatican as a voluntary prisoner, while the "Black aristocracy," the families of the popes, kept the front doors of their palaces in Rome partially shut as a sign of mourning. In this same defiant spirit, Marcantonio disdainfully rejected a position as state councilor, and instead founded the *Osservatore Romano,* the influential Vatican newspaper that today still voices the papal views.

Pope Pius XII could well understand the deep chagrin of his grandfather. He was himself a prisoner of sorts, if an involuntary one. And soon the remaining remnant of Vatican authority, recognized by the Lateran Treaty with Italy in 1929 that established the sovereignty of Vatican City, might be squashed.

Yet, the Pope did not seem greatly concerned about his personal safety. He had proved his physical courage in the past. When he had served as Vatican representative in Munich in 1919, the Communists, who had temporarily taken over the city in the chaotic wake of World War I, raided his nunciature armed with guns, butcher knives, and other weapons. But the thin, black-robed figure of Archbishop Pacelli confronted them like an apparition and held them at bay.

"You must leave here," he said calmly. "This house does not belong to the Bavarian government but to the Holy See. It is inviolable under international law."

Over the muttering of the mob, someone yelled: "What do we care for the Holy See? We'll leave if you show us your secret store of money and food."

"I have neither money nor food," Pacelli replied. "For, as you know, I have given all I had to the poor of the city."

"That's a lie!" someone shouted.

"No, it's true," another agreed. "Let us go."

And the leader, in frustration, threw his Luger pistol at the archbishop, hitting him on the chest and denting the jeweled cross that hung from his neck. Pacelli did not move but put his hand on the damaged cross and stared into the angry faces with sorrow and pity.

But at the same time, Pacelli, now the Pope, appeared little inclined to suffer the martyrdom that the cross symbolized. When, as a child, he had been told by his uncle the heroic story of a missionary priest who was crucified by pagans, the boy replied:

"I think that I, too, would like to be a martyr."

But then he added with thoughtful discretion: "Yes, I would like to be a martyr—but without nails!"[6]

Weizsäcker, after leaving the Pope, pondered how to remove the nails from Hitler's Vatican policy. He must discourage his superiors from going ahead with the kidnap plot without appearing to oppose Hitler's will or, indeed, to be mixing in business that was supposedly to be kept secret even from him.

On the following day, October 10, he was helped by a BBC commentator who quoted the Salò government broadcast suggesting that the Pope might be seized and taken to Germany. Since the British announcement had linked this statement to Weizsäcker's audience with the Pope, the ambassador, in a dispatch to Berlin on October 12, observed that it might be useful for Berlin to deny the report.

Two days later, on October 14, the Foreign Minister replied that "no public denial of the rumors is envisaged."

Further alarmed by this response, Weizsäcker sent a second cable, indirectly ridiculing the idea of removing the Pope by recalling an anecdote from Napoleonic days: if Napoleon wished to seize the Pope he would have in hand "no Pope but only [a] poor monk."

During this period, Ambassador Rahn, who had just moved his embassy from Rome to Fasano, where General Wolff was also based, telephoned Berlin and suggested that he report personally to Hitler on the "general situation" in Italy. He left immediately for the Führer's headquarters in East Prussia, where he addressed a meeting of top Nazis. Without directly referring to the kidnap plot, he spoke ironically of the "foolish" rumors and emphasized the importance of good relations with the Vatican in maintaining order in Italy. He said that he had managed to reach a kind of "miniature concordat" with the Vatican that would prevent Communist partisans from becoming too trouble-some.

Hitler and his henchmen seemed noncommittal—all except Martin Bormann, whose face, according to Rahn, was red with anger.

Unlike Weizsäcker, Rahn was known to his superiors as a "good Nazi." What they did not realize was that as Germany faced defeat, Rahn's enthusiasm for Nazism cooled. A diplomat's job was to win diplomatic victories, but Hitler's rash and intemperate decisions had made this impossible. And as the German adviser of the Duce, he could not be optimistic about the durability of totalitarianism after seeing the once-proud and powerful dictator disintegrating daily into a pathetic, helpless puppet.

Now the "harebrained" kidnap plot—which would turn the whole world into one great Resistance front—made Rahn question the rationality of Nazism all the more. He could only try to hold Hitler in check.*

Hitler's ultimate intention was, in fact, not clear—though Wolff, perhaps to make himself look like the heroic savior of the Pope, told the author he was convinced that the Führer really meant to invade the Vatican and abduct Pius. But blackmail, it appears, was a primary motive, as suggested by the Salò radio hint.

In any case, the Pope's susceptibility to the threat would be severely tested within days after the broadcast. The question was whether the Pope would interfere with Nazi racial atrocities committed under his "very eyes."[7]

* According to the German Consul in Rome, Eitel Möllhausen, Ambassador Rahn, before leaving for Fasano, asked him to remove from a wall of the Embassy in Rome a portrait of Hitler with his hands at his belt. "I cannot bear to see that adventurer's face," Rahn said.

3

The Jews

Although Israel Zolli, the Chief Rabbi of Rome, was frightened and anxious as he set out on his desperate mission early on September 28, 1943, a prosaic self-consciousness strangely dominated his emotions. He was on his way to the Vatican wearing a shabby suit!

"I am dressed like a beggar," he lamented to his friend Giorgio Fiorentini, a lawyer, who was driving him.

But Zolli had no other suit. In his rush to escape the Germans when they had occupied Rome eighteen days earlier, he had left almost all his belongings in his apartment. After staying the first fear-filled night there, he had spent the next three moving from one "friend's" home to another's until finally Amedeo Pierantoni, a Catholic whose son Luigi worked for the Resistance, gave him refuge. But now he had to come out of hiding and risk capture. He would try to save his people whether they appreciated it or not.

"We shall go in by one of the back doors," Fiorentini said. "The Vatican is always guarded by the Gestapo. A friendly person will be waiting for you, and so that you can avoid showing personal documents stamped 'Hebrew Race,' you will be presented as an engineer, called to examine some walls that are being constructed."

"The art of examining walls has always interested me," Zolli wryly replied.

At the Vatican, the builders greeted the plump, bespectacled "engineer," who, after thoughtfully inspecting their construction plans, nodded his approval. The two visitors then nonchalantly walked to the office of the Vatican Treasurer, who welcomed them warmly. As the Treasurer left to see the Pope on Zolli's behalf, the Chief Rabbi pleaded:

"The New Testament does not abandon the Old. Please help me. As for repayment, I myself shall stand as surety, and since I am poor, the Hebrews of the whole world will contribute to pay the debt."[1]

The debt would be for Vatican gold to buy Jewish lives. Two days before, on September 26, the two top Jewish lay leaders, Dante Almansi, president of the Union of Italian Jewish Communities, and Ugo Foa, president of the Jewish Community of Rome, had been summoned to Colonel Kappler's headquarters on Via Lasso. The blond Gestapo chief had greeted them courteously, even expressing regret for any inconvenience he might have caused. But then his tone suddenly changed and his angular face hardened, accentuating the long, thin scar that crossed his left cheek.

"You and your coreligionists," he said quietly, "are Italian nationals, but that is of minor importance to me. We Germans consider you only as Jews and therefore our enemy. Rather, to be more precise, we consider you a distinct group, but not completely apart from the worst enemies we are fighting. And we will treat you accordingly."

Almansi and Foa listened with dread.

"It is not your lives or the lives of your children that we will take—if you agree to our demands. It is your gold we want, in order to buy new arms for our country. Within thirty-six hours you must pay fifty kilograms of gold. If you pay, you will not be harmed. If you do not, two hundred of your Jews will be arrested and deported to Germany, where they will be sent to the Russian frontier or otherwise rendered harmless."

The shocked Jewish leaders persuaded Kappler to extend the deadline by more than four hours and pridefully turned down an offer of men and vehicles to help them collect the gold. As they were leaving, Kappler warned:

"Keep in mind that I have conducted a number of operations like this in the past, and all ended well. I failed only once, and a few hundred of your brothers paid with their lives."

Kappler felt rather proud of himself, for the Jews-for-gold idea was his own. He would just as soon deport the Jews, but he was a policeman responsible for German security in Rome, and the treacherous, soft-hearted Italians would only cause him more trouble—especially if the Pope reacted with vigor.

And after all, the Jews of Rome numbered only about eight thousand and were not really a great danger. Perhaps the Führer would be satisfied with their gold.[2]

Almansi and Foa, who had both held high positions in the Fascist Hierarchy before Mussolini had cracked down on the Jews in 1938, visited their former colleagues and argued that Fascist sovereignty would suffer if the extortion were permitted. Failing in this effort, they called a meeting of the Community Council, the most influential Jews in Rome, to decide how to meet the deadline.

The meeting opened in the great temple, or synagogue, on the right bank of the Tiber River at 10:30 the following morning, September 27, and a half hour later the gold collection campaign began. A jeweler and two goldsmiths, equipped with a scale, sat behind a table in a hall of the temple and waited for the Jews of Rome, who had learned of the ultimatum by word of mouth, to come with all their gold jewelry and trinkets.

An atmosphere of desperation permeated the hall as the leaders waited for their brethren to respond. Since most of the rich Jews had already fled the city, it would be up to the poor ones to save the community. Most of them lived in the slums of Trastevere just across the Tiber River from the traditional Ghetto—the rag-peddlers and laborers traditionally disdained by the wealthier Jews.

And as the hours flew by, few showed up . . .[3]

Chief Rabbi Zolli was the one important Jewish leader who had not come to the meeting in the temple that morning. He writes in his memoirs that he remained in his hideout, the home of Amedeo Pierantoni, a Catholic, and sent word through his friend Fiorentino that his presence would "not be in the least helpful, since the discussion would be of financial matters." If he could do anything useful, however, the community could count on him. He contributed his gold chain and five thousand lire, and instructed his younger daughter Miriam—his elder, Dora, was living elsewhere in Rome with her husband and child—to collect gold rings.

At seven the next morning, after learning that the community had managed to gather only about thirty-five kilograms of gold, fifteen short of the requirement, he agreed to Fiorentino's suggestion that he ask the Vatican for the balance . . .

Zolli waited prayerfully while the Vatican Treasurer spoke with the Pope. Yes, the New Testament, as he had remarked, did not abandon the Old. And no one, he felt, knew this better than himself, for his knowledge of the New was almost as profound as that of the Old.

He had first sensed the meaning of Christianity when, as a boy in Austria (in a section that a few years earlier had been part of Poland), he would spend afternoons at the home of his friend Stanislaus, where they would do their homework together in a large white-walled room. On one of those walls hung a crucifix of plain wood, with the branch of an olive tree over it.

The youth wondered why he kept raising his eyes to stare at the crucifix, why he felt so strange in its presence. As strange as he had felt when, as a very young child, he would take his father's Bible and read it line by line, page by page, fearful of missing the thread of the story, while other children frolicked in the sun.

In the white-walled room, as in his father's library, he had yearned, he writes, for "something infinite and indefinable." And somehow linked with this longing was a vision he had seen, much later, in 1917, as a young, learned rabbi: a vision of Jesus, who appeared as if in a large, frameless picture in a dark corner of his study while he had been working on a religious treatise.

Now, when he was much older, there seemed something symbolic also in his mission to the Vatican. In a way, this thought made him rejoice in what he felt was his boundless love for mankind. Still, he was saddened and puzzled by the attitude of his fellow Jews. They seemed somehow immune to his protestations of love. They refused his embrace and his advice.

When Zolli had been Chief Rabbi in Trieste, before being transferred to Rome, he read many documents and spoke with many Jewish refugees from Germany and Eastern Europe about Nazi atrocities. He knew that when the Germans occupied Rome they would attempt to destroy the Jews there, too.

But his flock would not believe him, preferring the more comforting advice of Foa and Almansi—that there was no need to leave their homes and hide, that this was, after all, Italy, where little anti-Semitism existed. Why, even Mussolini himself, after decreeing anti-Jewish laws in 1938 to satisfy Hitler, did little to enforce them.

The trouble was, thought Zolli, that Foa and Almansi had fooled themselves into thinking that their Fascist friends would come to their aid in the crunch. But Zolli was convinced that these "friends" would —or could—not. Zolli had always opposed Fascism and had even argued against it with his own daughter Miriam, who, as a student, had been an ardent Fascist herself. But now Fascism was more dangerous than ever, at least for the Jews, for it offered false hope to those who, after having served the system for so long, still could not believe that it would betray them so ruthlessly.

And, of course, Zolli knew that he, as Chief Rabbi, would be the first on the Nazi list to be sacrificed on the altar of their "stupidity."[4]

Late on September 9, some hours before the Germans had entered Rome, Zolli telephoned Almansi from the temple and warned: "They are about to enter. Tomorrow they will be here. Let us meet with [Foa]. Do invite him to be at your office tomorrow at seven. I shall tell you what I think must be done to protect the Jewish population. If you follow me, I will take upon myself the greater part of the responsibility for the transformation and the adaptation. If only you agree and act at once."

According to Zolli, Almansi, who had been a regional prefect, or governor, under Mussolini, laughed and replied: "How can a mind as clear as yours think of interrupting the regular functioning of offices and the regular conduct of Hebrew life? As recently as yesterday, I went to the minister and received quite reassuring information. Do not worry."

"But you see . . ."

"No, I repeat that you can keep quite calm. And, moreover, you must communicate absolute confidence to the people. Don't worry, and have a good night. Good night."

Zolli hung up and said to Gemma Contardi, an usher in the synagogue who was standing nearby: "Remember, in Rome there will be a bloodbath. Who knows how many Jews will pay with their life!"

Four days later, on September 13, after Zolli and his family had fled into hiding, the Chief Rabbi went to the synagogue for a talk with Foa. It would not be easy, for Foa, who came from a renowned Jewish family and had won a medal for military valor in World War I, was a proud and tough man, and the very idea of running, for whatever reason, was contrary to his nature.

He had studied law, then, like most of his countrymen, joined the Fascist party in 1932 as a matter of form. The Ministry of Justice appointed him a magistrate in 1936, and for two years—until the anti-Jewish laws of 1938 forced him out of the government—he administered Fascist justice without harboring the least suspicion that one day this justice would be fused with a Nazi attempt to obliterate his community.

"Listen, Mr. President," Zolli claims he urged his white-haired listener, "give orders that the temple and all the oratories be closed. Send all the employees home and close the offices. Let the secretary . . . draw one million lire, or even two, from the bank; and give all the employees three months' advance pay.

"All this will give a little alarm to these thousands of people who are going about the streets of the Ghetto ignorant of the danger. Give to a committee of three whom you trust a large sum of money to subsidize the exodus of the poorest. You will see that the first ten families will be a good example to the others."

Hardly taking a breath, he continued: "Solemn funerals must be handed over to Aryans of the city. The prayers can be said at home; the same for other functions. Let everyone pray where he is; after all, God is everywhere. All this is absolutely necessary, especially now in the fall, when there are so many great solemnities. We have thousands of Roman Jews and thousands from other cities who have taken refuge here. The Germans can surround the synagogue and the oratories with their cannons and guns exactly at the hour when those places are jammed with people."

As Zolli paused, he searched Foa's wrinkled face for a response until the president rang a little bell summoning the secretary of the temple. By some miracle, the Chief Rabbi concluded, he had convinced Foa.

"Is Miss —— in the office?" Foa asked the secretary.

"No, she is afraid."

"Notify her that she is fired."

"Yes, sir."

The secretary then left, and the president said stiffly: "You should be giving courage instead of spreading discouragement. I have received assurances . . . As to your proposals, I shall keep the temple and all the oratories *open*."[5]

Now, on September 28, the Vatican Treasurer finally returned from his talk with the Pope about the request for gold and told Zolli: "Come back shortly before one o'clock. The offices will be deserted, but two or three employees will be here waiting for you and will give you the package. You may leave a receipt in the form of a simple note. There will be no difficulty."

"Please give my thanks to His Holiness," Zolli said.

And he felt the kind of exhilaration he had experienced when, as a young student, he had stared at the simple wooden cross in the white-walled room of his school chum.[6]

Apparently unknown to Chief Rabbi Zolli, the Jewish Community Council had, on the previous afternoon, sent two other representatives on an identical mission. Renzo Levi and a fellow Jew had visited Father Borsarelli, the vice abbot of the Sacred Heart Monastery, to request that he obtain the gold from the Vatican. The priest said he would ask the Vatican and advised them to return two hours later, at 4 P.M., for a reply.

But by the time the two Jews got back to the temple, many people had gathered at the entrance waiting to contribute to the collection. Most were poor Jews dressed in tattered, patched clothing who had come pathetically with wedding rings, lockets, bracelets, and whatever other gold trinkets they possessed. But some were wealthier Jews and a few, rather self-conscious non-Jews who seemed, strangely enough, unsure whether *their* contributions would be accepted. Some "contributors" agreed only to *sell* their gold—and received four hundred lire per gram, paid with cash donations from others.

More and more people joined the crowd, ready to add their bit to Hitler's store of loot. And as each item was placed on the scale and its weight duly recorded, it appeared that the total might reach the required fifty kilograms after all.

Renzo Levi was therefore elated when he returned to Sacred Heart Monastery, where additional good news awaited him. Father Borsarelli reported that the Vatican had agreed to the request for gold.

"Yes," the priest said, "we are ready to lend you any quantity of gold you may need. But it is obvious we want it back."

The loan, which the Pope himself had approved, could be repaid in installments, with no time limit for the final payment.

Levi was slightly surprised by the priest's emphasis that the gold was to be a loan rather than a gift, though the Jewish community would certainly have repaid the Vatican in any case. Still, he was appreciative and thanked the priest for the offer, though he added:

"Now we are more confident that we will reach our goal. If I don't return here by 6 P.M., that will mean that we will not need the loan."

He never returned. Thus, when Zolli went to the Vatican the next morning, September 28, also to ask for gold, the Vatican apparently thought his visit was connected with Levi's request. In any event, Zolli learned that the Vatican gold would not be needed after all when he sent Miriam to Foa with a note about the Vatican offer and with a verbal message saying that he would volunteer to be the first on the list if hostages were demanded.[7]

Foa was scornful of Zolli's efforts and offers, and his scorn had grown when the Chief Rabbi failed to appear at the Community Council meeting on September 27 to discuss the demand for gold, whatever his excuse. It was shameful, he told his colleagues, that the community should have as its Chief Rabbi a "cowardly" man who, instead of nourishing the spirit of his people, worried only about saving his own skin.

Foa decided to fire Zolli. The community, he felt, needed a man of courage and faith—a man like Rabbi David Pancieri, Zolli's assistant, who, day in and day out, led services in the synagogue, attended funerals, visited the sick and the needy. A man who served as an example for the community, not one who fled into hiding and, to justify his own cowardice, urged others to do the same.

Why, Foa argued, should people leave their homes? It was not practical. In these hard times, it took money to move in with other families. Only the relatively wealthy could afford so drastic a solution, one which he considered unnecessary anyway. And how could one burden the Catholic institutions with thousands of refugees on the basis of questionable fears? Besides, Jews must show that they are a brave people.

The thing to do now, thought Foa, was to reassure the Jews, not to create panic, as Zolli would do, by warning them of possible Nazi actions—which his friends in the Fascist government had told him would never come.

Many other Jews shared Foa's hostility to Zolli. Though Zolli always spoke of love and brotherhood, his words, they sensed, had only a cold, mystical meaning to him, abstract words that fitted neatly into his brilliant theological sermons and treatises but which he was unable to transform into feelings of the heart.

Actually, Zolli appears to have been at once too mystical and too rational for his flock—tendencies which were in constant conflict within himself. His mysticism led to a fatalistic dependence on prayer, which the rabbi claimed gave rise in him to emotional ecstasy. But his rationalism tempered this ecstasy with infusions of reality—the reality, in particular, of a possible Nazi crackdown.

Though Foa's feelings reflected the sentiment of many Jews, they were colored by a personal antagonism. For Zolli was constantly reminding the community that Foa—and Almansi—had been high officials in the Fascist hierarchy before they were ignominiously dismissed under the racial laws. The two men now argued that they had been merely functionaries who had to make a living, not convinced Fascists; that everyone, in some way or another, had to work for the Fascist regime to survive.

But the question persisted: could they have risen to such high positions within the government—Almansi had been a prefect, Foa a magistrate—without having compromised themselves completely with

Fascism? And in this question lay the poisoned root of a conflict that had torn the community apart.[8]

Most Italian Jews, like their Catholic countrymen, found Mussolini and his Fascist system acceptable when he came to power in 1922. After all, since the unification of Italy in 1870, no government had demonstrated any degree of anti-Semitism, and there was little reason to believe the Fascists would be different. The official Fascist attitude up to about 1937 was expressed in the oft-used phrase: "The Jewish problem does not exist in Italy."

And since many of the Jews were strong nationalists precisely because they had been treated without prejudice for so long, they were attracted by the Duce's promise of a great and powerful Italian empire. Many thus followed in the tradition of their fathers who, like Foa, had fought bravely in World War I and were among the most enthusiastic soldiers to invade Ethiopia in 1936.

Mussolini himself had no special feelings toward the Jews. Always the political opportunist, he supported them as long as they proved useful—even after Hitler came to power in 1933. At that time, wishing to show the world that "humanistic" Italian Fascism was superior to Nazi "barbarism," he authorized the Italian Jews to render aid to their persecuted brothers in Germany. But when he wanted to reduce Nazi influence in Austria, he advised Austrian Chancellor Engelbert Dollfuss to add "a dash of anti-Semitism" to his program so he could compete for popularity with Hitler.

Therefore, when the Duce decided to throw in his lot with the Führer, he had few compunctions about pleasing his partner with so cheap a concession as a set of racial laws restricting the Jews in all fields of endeavor.

Even before these laws were passed in 1938, many Jewish leaders reacted with fear at the first sign of Fascist attack about a year earlier. They vehemently protested their loyalty to Fascism and, for good measure, declared their violent opposition to Zionism, which Mussolini then saw as a British threat to his imperial ambitions.

In 1937, when a group of rabbis, including Zolli, issued a declaration defying a Fascist order that the Italian Jews cut their ties with world Jewry, other Jews, some convinced Fascists, were horrified by this defiance. The community found itself bitterly split.

Almansi, Foa, and most other Jews occupying high places had no intention of voluntarily rejecting their source of bread and butter. Or of giving up hope in a system they had so loyally served, one they had simply accepted as a way of life, whatever its merits or defects.

When they were finally forced out, they felt like children who had been abandoned by their mother. Yet, despite their disillusion, they blamed Hitler more than Mussolini. The Duce, they were sure, would still come to their aid if the Germans proved too overbearing.[9]

Even the Nazi demand for gold did not dampen the optimism of Foa and Almansi; on the contrary, the gold was buying protection. Was that not what Kappler had said? And so it was with enormous relief that the two men and their delegates, in a convoy of taxis, automobiles, and police motorcycles, arrived with the gold on September 28 at Gestapo headquarters on Via Tasso, where SS Captain Kurt Schutz brusquely received them.

After an SS man had removed the gold items from large cartons and placed them on a weighing pan, Schutz snarled that he was being cheated, that the Jews had brought not fifty but only 45.3 kilograms. The two Jewish leaders asked for a reweighing, and an argument ensued that resembled the haggling that might take place at the fruit market over the price of bananas. Finally, Schutz agreed to repeat the lengthy process.

In the temple, the Jews of Rome waited anxiously for the delegation to return, and, as each hour passed, their anxiety grew. Perhaps the delegation had been arrested. Had the community been tricked? People telephoned each other frantically, exchanging the latest rumors. Should they flee after all?

It was not until late evening, several hours after they had departed, that the delegation came back. The second weighing had proved that the full fifty kilograms had been delivered, though Schutz even then refused to give a receipt.

Word soon spread through the Ghetto, and the Jews rejoiced. They had bought their lives and were safe, they would not have to abandon their homes.[10]

❖　❖　❖

The Ghetto bustled with life on the rainy Friday afternoon of October 15.* It was the usual pre-Sabbath rush. Kerchiefed housewives

* Guarding the Ghetto is the Porticus of Octavia, where one day almost two thousand years ago the ancient echoes of festive pomp heralded the start of the great triumphal march, led by Titus and the Emperor Vespasian in their purple robes and

laden with umbrellas and shopping bags cried "Good *Shabbath*" to each other as they darted along the winding, cobblestoned alleys from store to store, pushcart to pushcart, sometimes forced to wait in long lines for some precious item.

Although little food was available, such staples as spaghetti could go a long way, and tomorrow shops would distribute one egg to each ration card holder. Even more important to some people, tomorrow the weekly tobacco ration would be sold—at least, to those willing to spend half the night waiting in line to make sure the supply did not run out before they reached the counter.

Despite the hard times and gloomy weather, the atmosphere was cautiously cheerful. The payment of gold to the Germans about two weeks before had made the Ghetto residents feel secure. And many of the men who had gone to live with relatives and friends when the Nazis had come, to avoid forced labor, were drifting home.

Actually, the Germans had continued to harass the community even after collecting their ransom. The very next day, September 29, Kappler's men burst into the temple to search for "evidence" that the Jews had been helping the anti-Fascists. The intruders wrecked everything and even threw the sacred Torahs to the floor before leaving with truckloads of files.

A few days later German experts came and removed the temple's priceless collection of rare books after they had, with delicate, caressing fingers, leafed through the yellowed pages with the care, skill, and passion that only a true art lover could show.

But the Ghetto Jews were not unduly alarmed. For had not their leaders assured them that the looting of books by no means presaged the round-up of people? To some Ghetto residents the books were not really that important, for they could not read. If President Foa was not afraid and refused to hide, what was there to fear?

They were not aware that Almansi and some other Jewish leaders had switched apartments in the past week. Nor did they know that the only complete and up-to-date address files of the community had fallen into German hands, a disaster that Zolli and many other Jews later attributed to Foa's decision to hide rather than destroy these files. Such knowledge might not have alarmed most Jews anyway. After all, the ransom had been paid.

---

crowning laurel, to celebrate the destruction of Jerusalem. Actually, the ancient leaders, particularly before the final fall of Jerusalem, had, in general, been good to the Jews, and even the slaves gradually became freedmen. Julius Caesar had treated them so well that when he was assassinated they wept for him and chanted dirges. And they bewailed for a whole week the death of Augustus, who had enriched the Temple of Jerusalem with costly gifts and had encouraged the Jews to observe their Sabbath with strictness. They did—refusing to lose their identity whoever sat on the conqueror's throne in Rome.

As sundown approached, the streets began to empty and the sound of iron shutters grinding down over the store fronts echoed through the Ghetto. As she locked the door of the small clothing store that belonged to her in-laws, Eleanora Di Porto did not share the good spirits of many other Ghetto residents. This would be another sad and lonely Sabbath eve, for her husband Giacomo and all the other men in her family were still hiding in the home of an aunt who lived outside the Ghetto.

A slim, striking brunette who looked older than her sixteen years, Eleanora recalled those exquisite Friday nights before Italy went to war when her family and that of Giacomo would crowd into her mother's house for a sumptuous meal and joyful moments of song, chatter, and laughter. After dinner, while she played the accordion and two cousins accompanied with a guitar and a harmonica, her little sister would sing nostalgic Jewish and Italian songs, and the whole neighborhood, leaning out of windows all along the street, would listen and then cheer and applaud. Eleanora and Giacomo had been engaged then, and how wonderful the future had looked.

Suddenly the gaiety ended, and there seemed no future at all. The anti-Jewish laws forbade Eleanora to attend public high school, kept Giacomo's family from obtaining quality goods, and threatened to force Giacomo to work on defense projects. The Jews were no longer Italians; they were Jews. Eleanora never played the accordion again and the neighbors kept their windows closed. She now wondered whether Giacomo would be with her when she gave birth to their baby in the spring.

Eleanora started across the small *piazza* separating the store from the home of her parents where she would stay that night, a solitary figure in the deserted streets. Suddenly she saw a group of people approaching, waving and shouting in the distance. She stopped and gazed and her face lit up as she saw running toward her a short, swarthy young man—Giacomo.

In a minute, she found herself clasped in his arms while the women in her family and their children ran out into the *piazza* to welcome the other men. All the men had come home for the Sabbath, convinced that the danger had passed, and for ecstatic moments there were kisses, tears, embraces, sweet words.

As Eleanora and Giacomo started off toward their own home, which they shared with his parents, the girl's mother kissed her on the cheek and said:

"Didn't I tell you, dear? There is no reason to fear, because God is watching over us, and He is good. Good *Shabbath,* my children."

That night, October 15, the Di Porto family—Eleanora, Giacomo, and his parents—went to bed early. They were exhausted from the excitement of the homecoming and depressed by thoughts of the future. The Germans remained in Rome and it was still dangerous for Giacomo to be in the streets, for he might be grabbed at any moment for forced labor—like any other Italian male.

The young couple, as they lay in bed unable to sleep, pondered the kind of world their baby would enter. Would the child also be kept out of school, prevented from earning a decent living, forced to pay a ransom in order to survive?

They finally dropped off to sleep, when at about 4 A.M. they were suddenly awakened by loud knocks on the door and a familiar voice shouting: "Run! Run! Escape while it's possible!"

Giacomo jumped out of bed and let in his grandfather, who lived nearby.

"What are you screaming about, Grandfather?" he asked.

"The Germans are coming in trucks! They're surrounding the Ghetto! I was standing in line waiting for my cigarette ration and I saw them! Run before it's too late!"

Within minutes, the whole family had hurriedly dressed and run out into the rainy night. They decided to seek refuge in a nearby garage owned by a non-Jewish friend, and while the Germans burst into home after home in the Ghetto and Trastevere, dragging out everybody they could find and piling them into trucks, the Di Porto family hid in rented cars in the garage, which was to be their home for two days.[11]

❖   ❖   ❖

In the morning of October 16, shortly after Princess Enza Pignatelli Aragona had informed the Pope of the round-up, Ambassador von Weizsäcker left his Embassy for a hastily scheduled conference with Cardinal Maglione, the Vatican Secretary of State. He was alarmed. Never had he been in a situation requiring greater diplomatic tact. His whole mission in Rome, as he conceived it, now teetered in the balance.

He must keep the Pope from protesting publicly against the arrests.

Despite his anxiety, Weizsäcker was apparently confident that he would succeed. The Pope, after all, had not protested openly against the deportations and reports of mass murder in other parts of Europe. The ambassador could not know that the Pope had, indeed, defied the advice of Allied diplomats and even one of his own cardinals.

Harold Tittmann, assistant to President Roosevelt's personal representative to the Holy See, Myron Taylor,† had told the Pope in July 1942 that his silence was "endangering [the Vatican's] moral prestige and is undermining faith both in the Church and in the Holy Father himself." But the Vatican replied that it was doing its best for the Jews and that it could not confirm the atrocity reports anyway, though they were flowing in.‡

The Pope had also ignored the advice of French Cardinal Eugène Tisserant to issue an encyclical instructing Catholics, including, of course, German soldiers, to follow the dictates of their conscience rather than "criminal" government orders—an attitude that moved Tisserant to express the fear "that history will reproach the Holy See with having practiced a policy of selfish convenience and not much else."

Pius, Weizsäcker felt, was a realist like himself. They both thought that a public protest would not only fail to save a single Jew, but might provoke Hitler to go through with his kidnap plan and make the Allies more reluctant than ever to negotiate peace with *any* German group.

A negotiated peace was, in fact, as important to the Pope as to Weizsäcker, for the only alternative was the total destruction of Germany. And Pius, like the ambassador, dreaded this prospect. Not only did he have a great affection for the German people—he had spent many years in Germany as the Vatican representative—but the country was a necessary barrier to the spread of Soviet Communism in Europe.*

† Taylor worked out of Washington, leaving Tittmann alone in the Vatican. Like diplomats in all Allied missions to the Holy See, Tittmann was a kind of prisoner within the Vatican walls, unable, of course, to set foot in Axis-controlled Rome proper. When the Allies arrived in Rome, many Allied diplomats moved their Vatican missions into the city while Axis diplomats, including Ambassador von Weizsäcker, became the "prisoners."

‡ Vatican claims in late 1943 and afterward that reports of mass Jewish killings could not be confirmed are not easily understandable in view of the many eyewitness accounts of such genocide available at that time to the Holy See. For example, Monsignor Antoni Czarnecki, now head of St. Catherine's church in Warsaw, told the author that before and during the Warsaw Ghetto uprising of April–May 1943, when he was vicar of a church in the area, he and other priests sent details of mass deportations and gassings in Treblinka and other death camps through their superiors in Poland to the Vatican. "Confirmation," not conjecture, was sent, according to Monsignor Czarnecki.

* When Germany invaded the Soviet Union in 1941, Berlin was surprised by the Vatican's lack of encouragement. According to German diplomatic records, Fritz Menshausen, the counselor at the German Embassy in Rome, explained that the Vatican feared "that after the defeat of Bolshevism the Catholic Church, and indeed

Weizsäcker sent many dispatches to Berlin emphasizing the papal fear of Russia, and though these reports were apparently exaggerated in order to convince Berlin that the Pope could be trusted, Pius' fear was real enough.† He seems, indeed, to have feared Communism even more than Nazism. Whatever his ultimate intention, Hitler had given the Church considerable freedom in the areas under his control, whereas Stalin had not. And in long-range terms, after the war Communism would be stronger than ever while Nazism would no longer exist.

In short, Pius appears to have been persuaded, a public protest against the Jewish arrests might at once trigger an immediate Nazi raid on the Vatican and, by precluding a negotiated peace, set the stage for a future Communist threat.

There was another related menace as well—an erosion of the power of the German Church, one of the largest in Europe. The Pope, while serving in Germany, had signed concordats with the various German states and later with the Third Reich. These treaties had helped the German Church to survive. But they had also encouraged Catholics to support Nazism without moral qualms—to the extent, ironically, that the Pope could barely compete with the Führer for Catholic loyalty.

If the Pope, therefore, protested on behalf of the Jews he might force many pro-Nazi German Catholics into a crisis of conscience. They might have to choose between Hitler and God.

All these dangers appeared to militate against a loud Vatican protest. Pius felt that his principal function was to protect the Church as an institution so that it might continue to save souls. He would not readily imperil the institution to save lives—even the lives of Romans who had traditionally been under the personal protection of the Pope in his capacity as the Bishop of Rome . . .[12]‡

---

all Christianity, would, so to speak, go from the frying pan into the fire. If the Pope should now speak against Bolshevism, against which the Holy See had after all spoken repeatedly in principle, he would also have to take a position against 'the anticlerical measures and tendencies hostile to Christianity in Germany'; the reports 'continually received' at the Vatican on this subject provided 'overwhelming material' to justify such a step; the Pope's silence was the best proof that he would like to avoid everything that would injure Germany."

† Weizsäcker sent this typical report to Berlin on August 4, 1943: "To the Church, the archenemy, at home and abroad, is Communism and so it will remain."

‡ In support of the Pope's attitude, the following considerations were usually cited by high Vatican officials: (1) Since it would be difficult to distinguish degrees of violation against the moral and natural laws by either side, if the Pope protested one atrocity, he would have to protest all, great or small. (2) The Holy See could not spend all of its time determining the facts and adjudging the guilty. (3) The danger of error in descending to the particular in the heat of war would be great. (4) The Pope already condemned major offenses against morality in war time, if in general terms without identifying the victims. (5) Clergymen speaking out do so with the

There had been Paul II, who, in 1468, laughed heartily as Jews, stuffed with food, were forced to race each other between jeering, taunting lines of spectators in what would become a regular event at public festivals—until horses finally replaced the humans.

There had been Paul IV, whose Bull of 1555 required the Jews to live in ghettos, placed them under a curfew, forbade them to engage in any occupations except garbage collecting and second-hand trade, prohibited them from owning property or associating with Christians, and restricted them in their religious life.

There had been Pius V, whose Bull of 1569 claimed that the Jews were "fences for robbers and thieves," lustful men who stole "into the houses of respectable women where they incite many to abysmal lewdness" with "satanic jugglery, with fortune-telling, wizardry, magic arts, and witchcraft."

There had been Innocent III, who ordered the Jews to wear a badge of shame, and John XXII, who banned the Talmud and had it publicly burned.

And then there had been Pius IX, the patron of Marcantonio Pacelli, Pius XII's grandfather. Pius IX had started out as a friend of the Jews and had not complained when non-Jewish Roman citizens tore down the walls of the Ghetto in 1848. But after his return from an exile imposed on him that year by Italian rebels, he blamed the Jews for supporting the short-lived revolt, and anti-Jewish restrictions soon rivaled the worst in Italian history, ending only with the revolution of 1870 that overthrew papal rule permanently.

Many popes, however, had been good to the Jews—by traditional standards. Some had followed the teachings of St. Thomas Aquinas, whom Pope Pius XII greatly admired (though it is not known what he thought of St. Thomas' attitude toward the Jews). In *Summa Theologica*, St. Thomas said that the Jews should be tolerated but banned from public office and permitted to enter universities and the liberal professions only on a strict quota basis.

Even the worst popes, after all, treated the Jews with some humanity. They did not sponsor pogroms or try to drive them out of Rome. Nor would such a policy have succeeded. Unlike the ghettos and "pales" of northern and Eastern Europe, the Ghetto of Rome was neither a symbol of popular hatred nor a means of protecting the Jews against violence,

---

approval of the Pope. (6) Any papal protest would not do any good, but would greatly worsen the already precarious situation of Catholics obliged to reside in German-controlled areas.

for the Italian Christians never rejected the Jews. On the contrary, under papal rule the Italian Christians were to be protected *from* the Jews or at least from their unholy influence.

At the same time, little effort was made to convert more than a handful. The Jews of Rome had come from Jerusalem, many as slaves of their Roman conquerors, more than two thousand years ago, and formed the oldest Jewish community in the Diaspora.* They were to serve as eternal witnesses to the truth of the Christian revelation. Indeed, they were a part of Christian ritual.

A newly elected pope, after his crowning in St. Peter's, would mount a white palfrey and, on the way to take possession of his cathedral, the Basilica of San Giovanni in Laterano, pause to receive the Pentateuch from the Chief Rabbi of Rome. The pope would hold the book for a few moments and then return it upside down, and the rabbi would bow his head and extend his hand. The camerlingo (papal chamberlain) would then place twenty pieces of gold in the hand, supposedly making the rebuke tolerable, though actually adding to the humiliation.

The pope's flock was to observe in unmistakable terms the degradation of those who blinded themselves to the revelation they had themselves witnessed. No, the Jews were not to be physically attacked, driven out, or even converted. They were needed—as Jews.

The trouble was that some students of the Church had observed too well and were getting out of hand. They ignored the paternalistic and charitable spirit of papal bigotry and tried to change the character of anti-Semitism.

In 1934 the Jesuit magazine *Civiltà Cattolica*, published in Rome and traditionally close to Vatican thinking (though there is no evidence that Pius XII, then a monsignor, agreed in this case), observed regretfully that Nazi anti-Semitism "did not stem from the religious convictions nor the Christian conscience . . . but from [the Nazis'] desire to upset the order of religion and society." It added that "we could understand them, or even praise them, if their policy were restricted within acceptable bounds of defense against the Jewish organizations and institutions . . ."

In 1936 the same publication clarified its viewpoint: Opposition to

* According to Jewish legend, it was not the union of Mars and the Vestal Virgin Silvia but the union of King Solomon and Pharaoh's daughter that produced Rome. After their marriage, an angel fixed a long reed in the sea, marking the place where the Eternal City would one day rise. An island gradually formed at this spot, and a forest grew on the island. The first inhabitants built two huts of rushes, but the sage Abba Kolon then appeared and, seeing the huts collapsing, proclaimed that no hut could endure unless the earth had been moistened with the water of the Euphrates River. He thereupon undertook the long, hazardous journey to the Euphrates and returned with the water, and, on the dampened earth, he erected new huts, which now stood firm. Rome was born, to await the coming of the Messiah.

Nazi racialism should not be interpreted as a rejection of anti-Semitism based on religious grounds. The Christian world, without un-Christian hatred, must defend itself against the Jews by suspending their civic rights and returning them to the ghettos.

Certainly not by sending them to the gas chamber . . .[13]

Ambassador von Weizsäcker looked grim as Cardinal Maglione greeted him in his antechamber and immediately broached the subject of their meeting. The Pope, said Maglione, according to secret Vatican documents, was profoundly distressed that poor and innocent people should have to suffer simply because they belonged to a particular race, especially "under his very eyes."

The ambassador listened attentively to the protest and carefully composed his response. He must ask the cardinal to grant a highly irregular request—to permit him to keep the protest a secret from his own government!

"I think of the consequences that a protest of the Holy See may precipitate," Weizsäcker said. "The order for the action comes from the highest level. Will Your Eminence leave me free not to take account of this official conversation?"

When Maglione expressed surprise at this request, Weizsäcker assured him he would do everything possible at the local level to save the Jews but said that he did not want to take the responsibility for telling his superiors of the papal protest. He knew their mentality, he asserted, and they would react with even greater violence, not only against the Jews but against the Church.

Clearly, the word "kidnap" was on both their minds.

The cardinal tentatively consented and Weizsäcker departed, deeply relieved. The Pope did not override Maglione, apparently trusting in Weizsäcker's good faith and feeling that the ambassador's warning about the dangers of even a *private* protest only confirmed what he himself had felt—that a public protest would not only fail to save a single Jew, but would threaten the very existence of the Vatican.

No one can say what the Pope might have done if Weizsäcker had offered contrary advice. Perhaps not even Pius himself could have known without actually being faced with so clear a challenge to his natural inclination.[14]

Weizsäcker's feeling of relief after his talk with Cardinal Maglione soon gave way to new concern, for if the SS really deported the Jews, the Pope might decide that he had no choice. He might protest after all. Somehow, the Jews must be saved.

The ambassador was perhaps not more anti-Semitic than the average Christian living in an atmosphere poisoned with bigotry—even though, when in Berlin, he had been part of the deportation machinery.†

He had initialed a copy of the minutes taken at the secret Wannsee Conference in January 1942 that blueprinted the "Final Solution" to the Jewish problem.

He had sent Ribbentrop—it is not clear whether on request—the first proposal to get the Italian Fascist regime to "bring about a final solution . . . also on their part."

When Sweden offered to absorb the Jews deported from Norway to Auschwitz, he told Ribbentrop that he had refused even to discuss the question.

He pressed Hungary to "resettle" in Eastern Europe the Hungarian Jews who might "stir panic."

One cable bearing his name was sent to the German mission in Slovakia stating, in answer to a complaint by Slovakian Nazis about the lack of transportation to deport Jews: "The suspension of transportation of Jews was a surprise in Germany, especially because Slovakia's co-operation regarding the Jewish problem has been estimated highly here."

In the face of this grisly record, Weizsäcker argues in his memoirs that as early as 1941 he "appealed to Ribbentrop . . . to take energetic action against these atrocities in general. I never learned what his reactions to this were."

According to Weizsäcker's professed logic, if he refused to approve formally any measure regarding the Jews or failed to reply "appropriately" to anti-Jewish pressures, he would not save any Jews but would certainly be expelled from the government, imprisoned, or even executed. On the other hand, by exercising extreme subtlety he would remain in a position to at least *limit* these inevitable crimes.

In the final analysis, the Jews, he writes, could be saved only by the overthrow of Nazism, and his central goal was a negotiated peace that would achieve precisely this. Whatever the moral, or practical, aspects

† Weizsäcker's brand of anti-Semitism, nonviolent but conventionally arrogant, is perhaps reflected in this observation he makes in his memoirs about an attack on Jewish shops in Germany after Hitler came to power: "The first victims were the 'non-Aryans.' Intelligent Jews had admitted before 1933 that with the great opportunities they had had in the Weimar Republic they had overdrawn their account. But nevertheless, the danger which now threatened them could not have been foreseen. Anti-Semitism was really not a German characteristic; but now it had become a weapon of revolutionary agitation, however little the middle classes and the State officials might like it."

of his argument, he was prepared to sign—or do—almost anything to reach this goal.

It does appear that when the Germans occupied Rome, Weizsäcker tried to save the Jews from the Final Solution proposed by the document he had earlier sent to Ribbentrop. And it seems he was encouraged by his closest friend and collaborator, Embassy Secretary Albrecht von Kessel, who apparently, with Weizsäcker's knowledge though not his assistance, was actively plotting Hitler's assassination.

On the evening of September 10, 1943, a few hours after the Germans arrived in Rome, Weizsäcker and Kessel discussed the situation and agreed that the worst was to come and would certainly engulf the Jews. They decided, according to Kessel, to warn the Jews to hide.

That same evening Kessel visited his friend Alfred Fahrener, the Swiss general secretary of the Institute for International Law, who knew some of the Jewish leaders, and asked him to spread the word that the Jews should leave their homes immediately and seek shelter elsewhere.

Kessel says he went home convinced that he had prevented a catastrophe—until he heard, three weeks later, of the gold ransom deal. Instead of fleeing, the Jews, who he felt must be harboring a "death wish," were bargaining with those who would murder them.

Kessel returned to Fahrener, who had apparently contacted some Jews, but not the heads of the community. There was nothing to worry about, Fahrener told him. After all, calm and order had been restored, and the Germans has been behaving correctly. Kessel maintains that he was aghast. This man, he later wrote, thought that "terror is identical with chaos and flourishes only in the midst of chaos, whereas the exact opposite is usually the case." He warned Fahrener that if the Jews didn't "vanish" at once, every last one of them would be deported, adding, he says:

"If they are killed, their blood will be on my head and on the heads of my friends—and we don't deserve that. I implore you to take my advice seriously and use all your influence with the Jews in Rome!"[15]

Kessel had good reason for concern—although he apparently did not know that just about that time, on September 25, Colonel Kappler received a highly secret message from Himmler telling him of a plan to arrest all Jews and deport them to "the north."

The message did not directly order Kappler to take action, but he knew it meant that he should prepare to act. And though he felt a round-up would be impractical, he was no man to disobey orders, whether he approved of them or not. Hardly had he read the implied order, however, when he was advised of a discreet way to evade it—by Eitel Friedrich Möllhausen, the German consul.

At the age of thirty, Möllhausen had just taken over direction of the Embassy in Mussolini's republic, temporarily replacing Ambassador Rahn who had been hurt in an automobile accident. (Rahn would soon move the Embassy, now located in the elegant, park-surrounded Villa Wolkonsky in south Rome, to Fasano, leaving Möllhausen in Rome, and then fly to see Hitler in an effort to discourage a raid on the Vatican.) Möllhausen had learned of Himmler's message earlier that day from General Rainer Stahel, the German commandant of Rome, who had surreptitiously read it, though it was intended for Kappler's eyes only.

> It is known [said the message] that this nucleus of Jews has actively collaborated with the Badoglio movement and therefore its swift removal will represent, among other things, a necessary security measure guaranteeing the indispensable tranquillity of the immediate rear of the southern front. The success of this effort will be assured by means of a surprise action, and for this reason it is absolutely essential to suspend the application of any anti-Jewish measures in the way of individual acts in order not to arouse any suspicions among the population of an imminent *Judenaktion*.

"I don't want to have anything to do with such *Schweinerei*," said Stahel, a Wehrmacht soldier without strong ideological convictions.

"All right," Möllhausen says he answered, "then you should have no difficulty sabotaging the plan."

"I came to you precisely because there is nothing I can do," Stahel responded. "The order was sent directly to Kappler, and unless he informs us, we will have to pretend that we are ignorant of it. But I thought you could perhaps do something through the Foreign Office."

"How? I'm only a second-grade diplomat. And the Jewish question concerns only the SS."

Möllhausen reflected for a moment and added: "Let me think about it overnight. I don't know what I can do, but let me think about it."

"I know you well enough. I know you will do something," concluded Stahel.

Möllhausen had done something about the Tunisian Jews when he had been stationed in North Africa. He had saved them from deportation by persuading the Luftwaffe commander to claim that no planes could be spared for such a venture. The Jews were used for local labor instead—and survived.

Möllhausen, who was half French, had a swarthy Mediterranean complexion that seemed entirely in harmony with his excitable, nonconformist nature. He had lived in Marseilles until shortly before the war, then returned to Germany where the Foreign Ministry hired him because of his command of languages. He was sent to Paris, developed a friendship with Rahn, who was also based there, and, as Rahn's protégé, followed him to North Africa and then to Rome.

Through this combination of luck and connections Möllhausen now found himself in a position of considerable power—an extraordinary rise for a man so young and so adamantly opposed to joining the Nazi party. Influenced by such people as Rahn, he had become an intense nationalist, but he could not swallow the Nazi ideology. He decided simply to compromise by goose-stepping with nationalist fervor while ignoring, evading, or frustrating any Hitlerian policy repugnant to him. But though he would try to bend the system with enough zeal to ease his conscience, he would not risk his career—and his life—trying to eliminate the source of evil.‡

Now Möllhausen would try to work for another "Tunisian" solution. But would Kappler co-operate? . . .

"How did you know about this order?" Kappler demanded when Möllhausen had mentioned the secret cable.

"What is the difference? The order exists and I would like to know what you are going to do."

"I have been given an order and there is nothing I can do about it."

"You can pretend you never received it."

Möllhausen paused, adding cautiously: "You received the order from Berlin. But you also accept orders from Field Marshal Kesselring, don't you?" . . .

The two men immediately drove to Kesselring's headquarters outside of Rome, and Möllhausen, reminding the field marshal that he (Kesselring) had approved the "Jewish solution" adopted in Tunisia, said that the deportation of the Roman Jews would have "damaging consequences" for Germany. Would Kesselring agree to a "Tunisian" solution for Rome? The two men exchanged long stares, and the field marshal asked Kappler the one question that mattered to him:

"How many men will you need to carry out this operation?"

‡ Möllhausen told the author that in early 1944 Ambassador von Weizsäcker's assistant, Albrecht von Kessel, and another German official, Adam von Trott zu Solz, had visited him to propose that he join in a plot being prepared by military dissidents to assassinate Hitler. Möllhausen declined, arguing that any such plot was doomed to failure. Whatever the consul's real motives for refusing, the plot, of course, did fail when Hitler escaped alive after a bomb exploded at a military staff conference he was attending on July 20, 1944.

A motorized battalion in addition to his own men, was the answer. Kesselring replied:

"Under those circumstances, I regret to say that I cannot give my approval . . . I need all available forces for the defense of the city."

But the Jews, he added, could be used to build fortifications around Rome.

Möllhausen and Kappler then departed. That was all they had wanted to hear, if for different reasons.[16]

Although Kappler now had an excuse for ignoring orders, he had no intention of letting his SS superiors think that he was being soft on the Jews. And so overnight he conjured the idea of extorting gold from them as an alternative to deportation and, on September 26, demanded such ransom.

One Nazi leader who was unimpressed by Kappler's "pragmatism" was Adolf Eichmann, chief of the Gestapo Jewish affairs bureau. He decided to send to Rome his most experienced "Jewish expert," Theodor Dannecker, who had made a name for himself rounding up the Jews of Paris. If Kappler was reluctant to deport the Roman Jews, Dannecker who had a facial tic, was grateful for this new opportunity to ease his tensions.

On hearing of Dannecker's arrival in early October, Weizsäcker, Kessel, and Möllhausen met and, after conferring with General Stahel, drew up a counterplan. As decided under this plan, Möllhausen sent a cable to Ribbentrop on October 6 referring to the message about deportation that Kappler had received before the gold collection. The aim of the cable was to make Berlin think that word of the deportation had leaked out and that it could not, therefore, be implemented. Marked "very very urgent" (though no official classification existed with more than one "very"), the cable read:

> For Herr Reichsminister personally. Obersturmbannführer Kappler has received orders from Berlin to seize the eight thousand Jews resident in Rome and transport them to Northern Italy, where they are to be liquidated. Commandant of Rome General Stahel informs me he will permit this action only on approval of the Herr Reichsminister for Foreign Affairs. In my personal opinion it would be better business to employ the Jews for fortification work, as was done in Tunis, and together with Kappler, I will propose this to Field Marshal Kesselring. Please advise. Möllhausen.

Kesselring, of course, had already supported this view, but Möllhausen did not wish to indicate that he had conferred with him without notifying Berlin.

On the following day, October 7, Möllhausen sent another "very very urgent" cable to Ribbentrop:

> In connection with telegram of the 6th, no. 192. Field Marshal Kesselring has asked Obersturmbannführer Kappler to postpone planned *Judenaktion* for the present time. If however it is necessary that something be done, he would prefer to utilize the able-bodied Roman Jews in fortification work near here. Möllhausen.

These cables only enraged Ribbentrop, partly because Himmler found out about them and asked what the Foreign Office was doing interfering in Gestapo affairs, but mostly because Möllhausen had used the word "liquidated" in an official document for the first time. And no one, other than top Nazi officials, was supposed to know what ultimately happened to the Jews—the reason why Himmler's cable of September 25, addressed to Kappler, indicated only that the Jews were to be deported to "the north."

Ribbentrop furiously complained to Ambassador Rahn about Möllhausen's cables. Rahn, who had recovered from his injuries and had by now established his Embassy in Fasano, leaving Möllhausen as his representative in Rome, called Möllhausen in turn and demanded that he come to see him immediately to explain the unauthorized cables.

According to Möllhausen, he had deliberately used the forbidden word in the hope of frightening his superiors into calling off the round-up. But instead, Rahn severely reprimanded Möllhausen, and a cable from Berlin ordered the consul to "keep out of all questions concerning Jews."*

Weizsäcker, Kessel, and Möllhausen had played their last card. The round-up would take place . . .[17]

In mid-morning October 16, about the time Weizsäcker was speaking with Cardinal Maglione, Kessel, in desperation, rushed to Möllhausen's Embassy, but found that the consul had left for Fasano to explain his "blunder" to Rahn. Standing in for him was Gerhard Gumpert, the economic secretary, whose principal function was to obtain Italian goods for Germany.

Kessel insisted that Gumpert act to stop the arrests and imminent

---

* According to Möllhausen in his memoirs, he received the reprimand from Rahn while he was discussing the situation with Kessel. He quotes Kessel as saying: "Those gentlemen in Berlin can boast of losing the last bit of sympathy Germany enjoyed in the Vatican . . . Those gentlemen think it is enough simply to pay tribute to the Church. But they are wrong. And now, they must win the war totally and swiftly if they don't wish many other disappointments, because no one will ever be able to forgive them for the persecution of the Jews and for the fate of all those unhappy people who suffer and die in the concentration camps . . ."

deportations, arguing that if his own Embassy became directly involved Hitler might react against the Vatican.

"But Kessel," replied Gumpert, a frustrated lawyer with an ulcer, "what can I do? If you asked me for some barrels of potatoes or sacks of grain, I could help you. But I don't know about these things."

"Well . . . well," Kessel stuttered in his strong nasal tone, "something must be done."

Finally, Gumpert argued that the only answer was to tap the Vatican's influence—indirectly. The two men then conceived a complicated plan whereby a high Vatican official would write a letter to General Stahel requesting that the arrests be halted. When the letter was delivered to Stahel, Gumpert would propose that it be turned over to him as a diplomatic matter and then cable its contents to Berlin without anybody suspecting that he played any role other than to act as a transmission link.

Kessel and Gumpert requested Bishop Alois Hudal, rector of the German Catholic church in Rome, Santa Maria dell'Anima, to sign the letter and Father Pankratius Pfeiffer, Superior of the Salvatorian Order in Rome and the Holy See's liaison with the Germans, to deliver it. Hudal agreed—it is unclear whether with Vatican approval—provided he acted in an unofficial capacity, using his own letterhead. Kessel and Gumpert then composed the letter for him:

> I must speak to you of a matter of great urgency. An authoritative Vatican dignitary, who is close to the Holy Father, has just told me that this morning a series of arrests of Jews of Italian nationality has been initiated. In the interest of the good relations that have existed until now between the Vatican and the High Command of the German Armed Forces—above all thanks to the political wisdom and magnanimity of Your Excellency, which will one day go down in the history of Rome—I earnestly request that you order the immediate suspension of these arrests both in Rome and its environs. Otherwise, I fear that the Pope will take a position in public as being against this action, one which would undoubtedly be used by the anti-German propagandists as a weapon against us Germans.

As soon as Father Pfeiffer delivered the note to Stahel late that afternoon, Gumpert called at Stahel's office and, as anticipated, was told about it. When Gumpert suggested that this was a diplomatic not a military matter, Stahel seemed only too glad to give it to him for disposition. Gumpert immediately cabled the contents of the letter to Berlin, pointing out that it had been addressed to Stahel.

Several hours later Weizsäcker, who had been briefed on the scheme by Kessel, sent a follow-up message:

I can confirm that this represents the Vatican's reaction to the deportation of the Jews of Rome. The Curia is especially upset considering that the action took place, in a manner of speaking, under the Pope's own window. The reaction could be dampened somewhat if the Jews were to be employed in labor service here in Italy. Hostile circles in Rome are using this event as a means of pressuring the Vatican to drop its reserve.

It is being said that when analogous incidents took place in French cities, the bishops there took a clear stand. Thus, the Pope, as the supreme leader of the Church and as Bishop of Rome, cannot but do the same. The Pope is also being compared with his predecessor, Pius XI, a man of a more spontaneous temperament. Enemy propaganda abroad will certainly view this event in the same way, in order to disturb the friendly relations between the Curia and ourselves.

Weizsäcker thus conveniently used the Hudal letter to convey the sense of Cardinal Maglione's protest that morning, but without specifically indicating that a formal protest had already been made or by whom. Such a message, he apparently felt, would not be strong enough to provoke a violent reaction against the Vatican, but might be strong enough to give Berlin second thoughts about continuing the arrests and deporting those who had already been arrested.[18]

It was too late. On October 18 a line of freight cars pulled out of the Tiburtina suburban railway station packed with more than one thousand men, women, and children, among them Eleanora Di Porto's mother and ten other members of her family. They were calm, resigned, unsuspecting.

In the rubbish left behind on the platform, a sweeper found a crumpled, unaddressed message, whose author, a well-known businessman, Lionello Alatri, apparently trusted that the finder would guess his identity and take it to his company:

> We are going to Germany! I, my wife, my father-in-law, and Anita. Notify our traveling salesman Mieli. Give 600 lire to my *portiere* at the end of every month and 250 lire to Irma, whom you must also reimburse for the gas and electric bills . . .
>
> I don't know whether the merchandise will remain requisitioned. If we will be able to sell it, remember that the prices in the first block must be sold proportionately to the type of merchandise. If you can make currency exchanges at the Bank of Sicily, do so . . .
>
> We face our departure with fortitude, though of course the presence of my father-in-law in his poor condition alarms me. Try to be brave, as we ourselves are. I embrace you all. Lionello.†

† Alatri scribbled the following pathetic postscript under his signature: "Tell the

And on the following Sabbath, October 23, the first several hundred Roman Jews met their death in the gas chambers of Auschwitz.

On that same day, Ribbentrop leisurely referred the Rome cables to Adolf Eichmann, who, in turn, asked his superior for instructions he apparently was never to receive.

Now the Jews knew—even President Foa, who temporarily fled to Leghorn on the day part of his community was being shipped to oblivion. Miraculously, most of the eight thousand Jews of Rome had escaped the rather haphazard Nazi dragnet. Some had gone into hiding earlier, but most, like the Di Portos, had been warned just before the Germans could close their trap.

Many crowded into Roman monasteries, churches, and convents, all declared by the Vatican to be open to refugees, though only a handful of the richest and most influential were permitted in the Vatican itself. Raids on any of these individual shelters outside the Vatican walls would not greatly menace the Church as an institution.[19]

"New demands come to increase the number of families already welcomed, and there is beginning to be a lack of space. But how can we refuse any of the distressed?"

A sister in the Convent of Notre Dame de Sion scribbled this notation in the convent diary on October 18 after nearly one hundred Jews had arrived in the two days since the round-up. And among the newcomers that day were the Di Portos, who had finally fled from the garage where they had hidden in automobiles.

They *were* welcomed, despite the crowded, chaotic conditions, for the sisters were not only of pure heart but felt a special affinity toward Jews. The order had been founded by a converted French Jew, Father Théodor Ratisbonne, a century earlier.

While visiting a small church in Rome one day in 1842, his brother Alphonse had suddenly perceived, in a burst of brilliant light, a vision of the Virgin Mary. Alphonse felt that she wanted him to convert to Catholicism and to induce his fellow Jews to follow suit. Both brothers

---

baron that Ettore and Elda and her cousin Lella are with us. Tell sales representative Riccardelli that his wife and children are with us and are fine. Tell Bucellato that Vito of Via Flavia is with us and fine. Notify the *portiere* at Via Po, no. 42, that sister and sister-in-law with us and fine. Notify *portiere* Via Po 162 Lello and Silvia with us and fine. Notify *portiere* Via Vicenza 42 that the furrier is with us and fine. Notify *portiere* Corso Italia 106 the Di Veroli family with us and fine. Raoul with us and fine. Notify the *portiere* Via Sicilia 154 Clara with us and fine."

thereupon converted and Alphonse asked Théodor to start an order dedicated to fulfillment of Mary's wish. Now, suddenly, one hundred years later, God had filled this convent with Jews.

"If only we could reach some of these souls and make them see the light," a nun recorded in the diary on October 25.‡

But clearly this was of secondary importance to the sisters, who viewed as their main task the saving of lives, regardless of religion. They invited the Jews to Bible discussion meetings, but though some priests urged that they should take this opportunity to cure the refugees of their spiritual "blindness," the nuns relied mainly on the example of Christian charity and kindness.

They doubled up in their own quarters to make space for the Jews and helped the harried, frightened mothers diaper and put the children to bed. The women did their own cooking in the kitchen with food they riskily purchased outside while disguising their Jewish identity with Christian medallions. And Giacomo's mother showed the convent's regular cook, Sister Katherine, how to prepare a delicious kosher chicken.

Giacomo and Eleanora spent most of their time together, roaming the green gardens that were hidden from the street winding past the convent by trees and shrubbery and making love in some secluded corner when night had fallen. They attended Jewish services on Saturday and, to make the sisters happy, Mass on Sunday, like most of the other Jews. Their faith, however, sprang mainly not from prayer but from a desperate will to survive so that they might build a saner world for their unborn baby.

Eleanora was tormented by thoughts of her family, whose fate she did not know. And both feared that the Germans might break into the convent at any moment and drag them off, though an alarm system had been set up and a hiding place prepared behind a false wall in the basement in case of emergency.

Their fear grew as mysterious telephone calls warned of an imminent raid and was not dissipated even when the mother superior obtained a certificate, approved by Ambassador Weizsäcker, which she hung on the front gate, designating the convent as Vatican territory beyond the reach of the police.[20]

On October 25, two days after the first deportees were dead, Weizsäcker read with concern a commentary in the Vatican newspaper, *Osservatore Romano:*

‡ Shortly after World War II Notre Dame de Sion, according to convent officials, abandoned its original mission of converting Jews to Christianity.

Persistent and pitiful echoes of calamities . . . continue more than ever to reach the Holy Father. The August Pontiff . . . has not desisted for one moment in employing all the means in his power to alleviate the suffering, which, whatever form it may take, is the consequence of [the] cruel conflagration. With the augmenting of so much evil, the universal and paternal charity of the Pontiff has become, it could be said, ever more active; it knows neither boundaries nor nationality, *neither religion nor race . . .**

A master of subtlety himself, Weizsäcker, his supporters say, viewed this complaint about the deportations, however veiled, as jeopardizing the Vatican, especially in light of Berlin's failure to answer the cables from Rome. This failure, he is said to have felt, showed that he had been right in the first place. If his superiors could regard the *threat* of a public papal protest so casually—not even worthy of a reply—it was not likely that an *actual* protest, even so vague a one as that which appeared in the Vatican organ that morning, would move them either, except perhaps to retaliate against the Pope.

The only thing he could do now, argue his supporters, was to give his superiors the *impression* that the job was completed and that there were not enough survivors to make a new round-up worth while. He must also convince them that the Vatican was quite harmless and that the little help it gave the Jews was insignificant. If Hitler thought there was not much to gain, perhaps he would ignore the remaining Jews rather than provoke the Pope.

Weizsäcker, in any event, cabled Berlin a subtly worded message that has often been used as evidence that he had approved the round-up:

The Pope, although under pressure from all sides, has not permitted himself to be pushed into a demonstrative censure of the deportation of the Jews of Rome. Although he must know that such an attitude will be used against him by our adversaries and will be exploited by Protestant circles in the Anglo-Saxon countries for the purposes of anti-

---

* On October 31, 1943, fifteen days after the round-up of Jews, Osborne, the British minister to the Vatican, cabled to the Foreign Office, as indicated in British diplomatic records, a message which he said was "of particular secrecy and should be retained by the authorised recipient and not passed on": "Most Confidential—As soon as he heard of the arrests of Jews in Rome Cardinal Secretary of State sent for the German Ambassador and formulated some [sort?] of protest. The Ambassador took immediate action with the result that large numbers were released. It appears that only German and Italian Jews were retained and that those who had one Aryan parent or were themselves parents of children were released. Vatican intervention thus seems to have been effective in saving a number of these unfortunate people. I enquired whether I might report this and was told that I might do so but strictly for your information and on no account for publicity, since any publication of information would probably lead to renewed persecution." Actually, about 250 persons were released, but, except for several Jewish spouses of non-Jews, all were gentiles, or at least convinced the Germans they were.

Catholic propaganda, he has nonetheless done everything possible even in this delicate matter in order not to strain relations with the German government and the German authorities in Rome. *As there apparently will be no further German action taken on the Jewish question here, it may be said that this matter, so unpleasant as it regards German-Vatican relations, has been liquidated.*

In any event, there is one definite sign of this from the Vatican. *L'Osservatore Romano*, of October 25–26, gives prominence to a semi-official communiqué on the loving kindness of the Pope, which is written in the typical roundabout and muddled style of this Vatican newspaper, declaring that the Pope bestows his fatherly care on all people without regard to nationality, religion, and race. The manifold and growing activities of Pius XII have in recent times further increased because of the great sufferings of so many unfortunate people. *No objections need be raised against this statement, inasmuch as its text . . . will be understood by only a very few as alluding in any particular way to the Jewish question.*

Whether this apparent attempt to make the Pope look "reasonable" in Nazi eyes actually helped the Jews by encouraging Berlin not to provoke the Pope unnecessarily, whether it hurt them by making Berlin think the Pope would not take a strong stand, or whether it had no effect at all is open to debate.

Over one thousand more Jews were deported in the next seven months, and others were killed in Rome. They were captured, however, not in organized round-ups but in individual arrests, many by Italian Fascists seeking reward money.

In any case, the Pope was more trusted now in Nazi circles and less likely to be abducted; he even asked the occupiers to bring *more* police forces into the city to protect Romans from "Communist" disorders that he apparently felt might stem from the deportations.

According to a dispatch cabled by Harold Tittmann, the United States representative at the Vatican, to the State Department on October 19, three days after the round-up, the Pope "seemed preoccupied that, in the absence of sufficient police protection, irresponsible elements might commit violence in the city . . ."

The Pope further secured his position when he authorized Cardinal Maglione to accept Weizsäcker's request to publish in the *Osservatore Romano* a communiqué expressing gratitude to the German troops for respecting the Vatican and the Pope, the protector of all Romans. In return, the Germans promised to maintain the same respectful attitude in the future.

The communiqué appeared within a week after most of the captured Jews of Rome, among the most deeply rooted Romans, had been turned into ash in Nazi incinerators.

So improved were Vatican-German relations that, on October 25, Tittmann could assure the State Department:

> The anxiety displayed by Holy See with regard to possible violation of Vatican City neutrality during first days of German occupation of Rome would appear to have been progressively allayed to such an extent that at present moment atmosphere in Vatican can be described as optimistic.
>
> Vatican seems to be convinced Germans realize they would have more to lose by removing the Pope than by allowing him to remain here even though he may fall eventually under exclusive influence of Allies and to feel that for time being only danger is that a sudden outburst of anger against the Church on part of Hitler himself might overrule the wiser counsels of those who have the long-term interests of Germany at heart . . .[21]

Hitler's anger had, in fact, subsided. SS General Wolff, visiting the Führer in mid-December to report on his preparations for the raid on the Vatican, told him, as indicated in the general's notes, that in his opinion the Church, the only indisputable authority in Italy, should not be molested; that the operation would lead to "extremely negative effects at home and at the front." On the other hand, Wolff said, the Pope could be "very useful for us in the future" in helping to establish the new order in Europe.

Wolff felt relieved when Hitler calmly absorbed what he said, seeming at last to understand.

"All right, Wolff," he replied. "Act as you, an expert, think best. But do not forget that I shall hold you responsible in case you fail to fulfill your optimistic guarantees."

The general departed with a sense of satisfaction, yet with trepidation. For if the Pope should suddenly act against Hitler's interests, Wolff, as well as the Pope, would feel his whip of wrath.

And the Führer could be gratified with the apparent results of a mere threat to the Church. He had neutralized Vatican hostility for the time being, and there was no longer any need to rush the plot since he had decided to reject Rommel's proposal to withdraw from Rome immediately and to support Kesselring's plan to hold the city.

He could always carry out the raid later.[22]

4

The Escapers

Pope Pius XII was chatting with foreign diplomats on the morning of July 19, 1943, when suddenly the sharp crack of antiaircraft guns interrupted the conversation. After a short, startled silence, explosions shook the earth. The Pope rose from his desk and hurried to a rattling window of his study. The diplomats saw him grow pale as he observed columns of black smoke rise like huge, grasping fingers and converge into a fist that thrust into the summer sky.

The war had come to Rome as Allied planes bombed the marshaling yards in the district of San Lorenzo, a poor workers' area on the eastern edge of the city.

For two hours Pius stood at the window watching the tarnished heavens, mumbling prayers, removing his spectacles occasionally to wipe the moisture from his eyes. Finally, he went to his desk and called Monsignor Montini.

"How much cash is there in the Vatican Bank?" he asked.

"About two million lire, Your Holiness."

"Draw it immediately and take the first car you find in San Damaso courtyard. We will join you."

The Pope and Montini climbed into a small car and set off swiftly through the streets of Rome until they reached barricades blocking the way to the flaming railroad station. The two passengers descended, and officials, astonished to see the Pope, informed him that bombs had partly destroyed the ancient Basilica of San Lorenzo and had struck the cemetery where the Pacelli dead were buried, scattering the remains of his own father and mother.

The Pope plodded through the smoking rubble of charred houses where more than five hundred dead victims were strewn, while survivors struggled to touch his white cassock. Then a laborer spread his jacket on the cobblestones and the Pope knelt upon it to pray. Before departing, he cradled a dead infant in his arms and ordered Montini to distribute alms from the bag the monsignor was carrying.

To Pius, Rome lay in the Vatican's embrace spiritually and traditionally. He was the Bishop of Rome and his papal predecessors had once ruled the city. Its people were his flock, and its churches and other Catholic institutions an integral part of the Vatican. His devotion was all the stronger because he was himself a native Roman, full of the exquisite memories of growing up in this sacred city. At his ordination in 1899 Father Pacelli had chosen to read his first Mass in the Borghese Chapel of the Basilica of Santa Maria Maggiore because over its altar hung the painting of the Virgin Mary, "Salvation of the Romans" . . .

And now his beloved Rome had been bombed.

On his return to the Vatican that day, the Pope immediately penned an emotional protest to President Roosevelt. He had "had to witness the harrowing scene of death leaping from the skies and stalking pitilessly through unsuspecting homes striking down women and children; and [to contemplate] the gaping ruins of that ancient and priceless papal Basilica of San Lorenzo . . ."

Roosevelt, however, could hardly have felt that the bombing was a mistake when six days later, on July 25, Mussolini was ousted from office partly as a result of this attack, which dramatically underscored the failure of his policy. The Pope besought Mussolini's successor, Marshal Pietro Badoglio, to demobilize the city as the Allies demanded, but before the new Premier could act, planes struck once more, on August 13, barely missing the Basilica of San Giovanni in Laterano.

Pius again rushed to the scene to comfort the injured, pray for the dead, and distribute alms to the homeless, returning to the Vatican this time with a blood-stained cassock. Nor did the raids stop when the Germans occupied Rome on September 10. They, too, ignored the Pope. All roads led to Rome, and the Germans had to send troops and supplies from the north through the city.

In desperation, the Pope suggested to Harold Tittmann, the American representative to the Holy See, that the advancing Allied forces bypass Rome and, presumably, force the Germans to retire without battle. He pleaded for an open city. Tittmann rejected the plea, telling the Pope that "the President had said . . . the Germans alone would be responsible for any destruction wrought in Rome."

But Pius was adamant and contrasted the Allied bombings with the German attitude toward Vatican property. He observed, according to Tittmann's report on the audience, "that so far the Germans had respected the Vatican City and the Holy See's property in Rome . . ."

This was the audience that took place on October 19, three days after the Germans had rounded up the Roman Jews.

And the Pope's frustration did not diminish when one of his own shepherds threatened his neutralist policy—and thus whatever chance remained of turning Rome into an open city . . .[1]

❖   ❖   ❖

"I'm afraid this is it, Hugh," said Prince Filipo Doria Pamphili one day in October 1943 as he glanced out of the window toward Via del Corso where squads of Gestapo men were pouring out of cars that had just pulled up all along the street. "There is no point in resisting. There is no way to escape this time."

Monsignor Hugh O'Flaherty seemed unperturbed. His blue eyes, behind steel-rimmed glasses, somehow retained their ironic glint and his thin lips curved in a humorous smile.

"Don't you believe it!" he replied in a strong Irish brogue, stuffing his pockets with 300,000 lire that the prince had just given him. "Bye . . . God bless you."

And with giant strides, he dashed out and downstairs toward the cellar.

This was not the first time Monsignor O'Flaherty had been cornered and he knew it would not be the last, for Kappler was determined to crush his organization. Its function was to help escaped Allied prisoners of war in Rome hide from the Germans, and since his headquarters lay in Vatican territory, Kappler could not go in and flush him out—at least, not until Hitler gave the word to invade the area. The Gestapo chief therefore set traps for the monsignor at all places he was thought to frequent outside such territory.

One of these places was the home of Prince Pamphili, a known anti-Fascist who gave O'Flaherty funds for the billeting of escapers with Italian families, black-market food, and bribery of Italian officials.

Escaped prisoners poured into Rome as the Allied armies drew nearer, adding their numbers to those who had been freed by their Italian guards when the Italian government switched its allegiance to the Allies on September 8. The 300,000 lire that Prince Pamphili contributed would go a long way toward keeping the escapers hidden until they could join up with their units again.

O'Flaherty had first involved himself with Allied prisoners in 1941, when the Vatican sent him to prisoner-of-war camps in North Italy to gather news for their families. He not only traveled back to Rome every day to make sure the families were contacted without delay, but, on his own initiative, speeded the delivery of Red Cross packages and distributed thousands of books. So effective was he in cutting through Italian red tape—infuriating the Nazi-Fascist bureaucrats and camp commanders in the process—that he was finally recalled to the Vatican.

Most Vatican officials did not celebrate the return of this maverick monsignor who refused to gear himself to neutral Vatican policy. In their view, he disobeyed almost every regulation and jeopardized the dignity of the Church. He met for bridge with princesses and duchesses and played golf, a game at which he excelled, though the rules of the Diocese of Rome forbade a priest to engage in this unseemly sport. At one time he had even been an amateur boxer.

Yet, to the resentment of many colleagues, he worked for the Holy Office, the most inflexible and powerful arm of the Church, the secret office that examined challenges to the Faith, arguments on morals, the veracity of claimed visions and miracles, the acceptability of books, and the problems of marriage. His superiors, however irked by his independent attitude, realized that Monsignor O'Flaherty was a remarkable human being.

No sooner had the Vatican slapped his wrist for excessive zeal in helping Allied prisoners of war than he was helping them again—this time from the Vatican itself. He even dared to hide refugees in his own residence at the Collegio Teutonicum, or German College, located on extraterritorial ground but just outside the Vatican walls.

It was the Vatican's obsession with neutralism, its fear of provoking the Germans, that gave O'Flaherty his real start in the prisoner-of-war business. So many escapers were seeking refuge in the Vatican that Vatican officials ordered the Swiss Guards to forcibly turn them away at the gates if necessary. And the Guards did, manhandling those who persisted. O'Flaherty quietly began finding places for the escapers outside the Vatican.

A fierce Irish nationalist, the monsignor sometimes wondered why he was helping the British who he believed had so cruelly treated his people. But every time he saw the Germans perform a brutal act, like making elderly Jews get on their knees and scrub the roads, he realized that he knew why.

He would have to undertake himself, mainly with the help of simple priests, the duty that the institution he served would not, or could not, undertake. His troublemaking activities, after all, had already made him so unpopular at the Vatican that he would never become pope anyway . . .

Now, as he made his way in the dark through a cellar passage in Prince Pamphili's house, O'Flaherty began to wonder if he would ever serve again even as a monsignor. Suddenly he saw a ray of light. Coal—the prince's winter fuel supply—was sliding down a chute from an open trapdoor in the courtyard. He crawled up the hill of black rocks just as a coalman approached with a sack he was about to unload.

"Hold it!" O'Flaherty whispered. "Stay exactly as you are and listen. I'm a priest . . . The Germans are after me. Leave that sack on the side there and come down here a moment!"

The shocked coalman obeyed, and in a few minutes the monsignor, his face and clothes smeared with coal dust and his clerical robe stuffed into the sack slung over his shoulder, climbed to the surface and casually walked through the lines of SS troops guarding the courtyard and out the front gate. He washed up in the bathroom of a church nearby and returned to the Vatican, an immaculately gowned prelate.[2]

Soon after he launched his clandestine organization in the fall of 1943, Monsignor O'Flaherty realized that the Gestapo was by no means his only worry. The job of finding accommodations for the increasing numbers of escapers was getting out of hand, and he did not have enough people trained in such work to help him. The organization was headed by a Council of Three—Count Sarsfield Salazar of the neutral Swiss Legation; John May, the cook-butler of the British minister to the Holy See; and himself.

But a senior military officer was needed who knew more about running an underground organization. None, however, was available—until a tall, square-jawed British major, Sam I. Derry, suddenly appeared.

An Italian Resistance contact man had helped Derry, an escaped prisoner, to infiltrate into St. Peter's Square at a moment when that splendid *piazza* was seething with German soldiers. In the shadow of the colonnade that curved around both sides of the *piazza*, Derry and his contact saw a tall, lone, black-robed figure with his hands folded in front of him and his head slightly bowed as if in prayer. As the two men approached, the cleric said quietly:

"Follow me—a short distance behind."

The clergyman led the visitors through a wide-arched entrance into a sunny square and then to a great doorway with an inscription over it that read "Collegio Teutonicum." Derry shuddered at the thought of voluntarily entering a German establishment, but was soon put at ease as the stranger, after sending the contact man away, ushered him into a small study and said, while offering him biscuits:

"Now you'll be all right—you can talk here."

But Derry was too busy munching on the biscuits to talk much, for he had eaten little in the past few days. And the sight of a bathroom further reduced his powers of speech; he hadn't taken a bath since he had been on leave in Cairo, nearly a year and a half earlier!

Only a few days before he had been on a prisoner-of-war train taking him to Germany—the second time he had been captured. After his capture in North Africa in early 1942, he had escaped while being herded through the desert, but then, five months later, he was caught again, oddly enough, by the same unit he had escaped from.

He then planned to flee the prison camp where he was confined, but before he could act the Germans sent him to Italy en route to Germany. They lost him once more, however, when, while returning from the train toilet, he sidestepped a guard, pulled open the door, and leaped into the Italian sunshine, bouncing off the ground a free man.

Badly cut and bruised but elated over his good luck, Derry hobbled through the countryside to a farmhouse and, in pidgin Italian, convinced a peasant couple terrified by the sudden appearance of this unshaven, unkempt figure in torn, blood-stained clothes that he was not a German agent but a British officer. He slept in a haystack and awakened the next morning to peer into the shimmering distance at a strange yet familiar sight—the glittering dome of St. Peter's. He realized that he was in the hills only about fifteen miles northwest of Rome.

Derry's hosts put him in contact with other British soldiers hiding in caves deeper in the hills, and he soon found himself the leader of a small army of about fifty escapers. Determined to guide them through the German positions to the Allied lines in the south but needing funds to pay for food and protection, he asked a local priest to solicit money in Rome from British diplomats whom he knew were lodged in the Vatican. The priest returned not only with money but with an invitation for Derry to come himself.

He set out in the pony cart of a trusted peasant, burying himself in a mass of cabbages, and after passing through several German checkpoints bumped over the Tiber into Rome. The cart finally halted in

front of a dilapidated apartment building and the peasant led Derry
up to the first floor, where two shifty looking men whom the Briton
instinctively distrusted greeted them. One, disguised as a priest, introduced himself as Pasqualino Perfetti.

Derry exchanged his tattered shirt, blue-dyed battle trousers, and
cut-down desert boots for conventional working clothes and left with
Perfetti's comrade for the Vatican, traveling by trolley.

And so he met the person who had sent the money—Monsignor
O'Flaherty.

When he had bathed, changed into clothes the monsignor provided
him, and settled down in a "guest" room of the German College,
Derry was visited by a stocky, dark-haired man wearing a black coat
and pin-striped trousers and carrying a small black-leather briefcase under one arm. The man grinned and, removing from his briefcase a
package of cigarettes and a bottle of whisky, said with a London ac-
cent:

"We've been expecting you. I thought you would be glad to have
these to celebrate your safe arrival."

O'Flaherty then entered the room and introduced John May, the
cook-butler of Sir D'Arcy Osborne (newly knighted), the British minister to the Holy See. The minister, said May, requested that Derry and
the monsignor dine with him that evening.

"It is easy enough to get into the Vatican without being captured by
the Germans," O'Flaherty assured the major, "but the difficulty is we
want to get you out again. If you are caught by the Vatican guards or
gendarmes you will either be interned for the duration or immediately
expelled into the arms of the Germans."

"You know," said May, glancing with a smile at the two men, first
at one, then at the other, "it is surprising how alike you two are in size
and shape."

That evening, two men over six feet tall, identically dressed in low-
crowned black hats, long black cloaks with scarlet buttons down the
front, bright scarlet sashes, and silver-buckled black shoes, walked in
measured steps across St. Peter's Square. They then zigzagged through
passages and little *piazze*, heads bowed, eyes lowered, lips mumbling
in prayer, while guards and gendarmes respectfully made way for them.
When they finally reached the British minister's residence, John May
ushered them into a world that overwhelmed Derry with its Victorian
grace and elegance.

After a sumptuous dinner, the host and his guests moved to the
drawing room for coffee and dessert.

"Your note signed 'S. I. Derry, major,' was the first contact we had made with a senior British officer," said Osborne, a trim young sixty, who seemed to Derry the perfect movie conception of a British diplomat—courtly, suave, utterly unflappable.

The minister continued: "I must tell you that I consider the monsignor's efforts absolutely wonderful, but he feels, and I agree, that the time has come now when we must appoint somebody to co-ordinate all the work . . . Are you prepared to take command?"

Osborne's keen interest in O'Flaherty's organization did not stem entirely from a wish to protect a few thousand Allied escapers. He saw it as an excellent instrument for obtaining military intelligence that would guide the Allies into Rome. The priests and other agents working for the monsignor, he felt, might as well gather useful information while they went about their humanitarian business.

Osborne therefore contributed sizable funds to the operation, using John May to distribute the money to the *padroni*, or landlords, who were hiding the escapers and to introduce them to black-market contacts whom May, in his capacity as cook, had himself cultivated so that he could prepare the gourmet dishes to which his boss was accustomed.

By giving a British officer practical control of the organization, Osborne was also giving O'Flaherty an excuse to remain "ignorant" of the intelligence activities, which could compromise the officially neutralist policy of the Vatican as well as the monsignor's own position. O'Flaherty, for his part, did not ask what Derry was doing, except in matters of billeting.

The Vatican—while not offering assistance—did not, for the time being at least, crack down on the organization. In a sense, the Vatican was merely confirming its own neutrality, since it was equally passive about Axis spies—mainly German priests—who used the floor just below O'Flaherty to carry out espionage for the Nazis.

"How can we work out of here," an assistant asked the monsignor, "when those spies know everything we're doing?"

O'Flaherty laughed, replying: "Well, we know everything *they're* doing, don't we?"

Derry began his "co-ordinating" task on November 1, 1943, and within a month the number of escapers and evaders on his books had exceeded two thousand, most of them hidden in villages outside Rome where—when possible—they were helped to infiltrate to the Allied lines. It was difficult, dangerous work but the operation somehow managed to keep going with the help of priests and other amateurs—such as Princess Nini Pallavicini.[3]

The attractive blond princess, daughter of a former Fascist minister, the Marchese Medici del Vascello, headed a committee to provide food, money, and false papers for the escapers in hiding. She had been, like her father and most Italians, a loyal Fascist until the mid-1930s, when freedom was greatly curtailed and Mussolini headed toward war. Though she and her husband had strongly opposed Italy's entry in the war, he served as a pilot until killed over Sicily.

Nini was shocked into actively supporting the Allies by the round-up of Jews on October 16. Awakened by the cries of victims, she rushed into the street and hid many Jews in her great palace, a labyrinth of grandly furnished rooms and twisting passages. She was accustomed to the risk, for she had also given refuge to a number of high Italian military officers, some of whom were hiding in a sealed-off room, nourished by food lowered to their window by ropes. After the round-up of Jews, she permitted these officers to operate a secret radio that transmitted military information to the Fifth Army.

But one day, the *portiere* rang the alarm signal. The Gestapo was raiding the palace. The refugees hid in various concealed corners and Nini leaped through a kitchen window and ran to a nearby theater. It was locked, but the manager had given her the key for use on just such an occasion. As she sat breathlessly in a cushioned seat, she felt in the vast emptiness like a phantom come to haunt a vanished world. She could almost hear the laughter and applause and feel the warmth of her husband's hand clasping her own.

Finally, she returned home, converted her palace into a convent protected by the Church, and went to work for Monsignor O'Flaherty, taking with her the precious radio, which would now transmit messages from the Vatican.[4]

Derry received much-needed additional help when he was joined by three fellow Britons who had escaped from a prison camp about eighty miles east of Rome. Derry knew all three personally since he had been in the same camp with them in North Africa. He was a good friend of two, Lieutenants John Furman and William Simpson, but he had never trusted the third, Joe Pollak.

Derry had long thought that Pollak, a small, sallow Cypriot who spoke perfect Italian, had denounced prisoners planning to escape. Thus, when Pollak was directed to him through the organization's secret network, Derry initially feared that the whole enterprise might be compromised. He grew particularly suspicious when Pollak said that he had slipped into Rome with six other escapers and two helpful Italian girls. Such a large party would find it difficult indeed passing checkpoints and avoiding capture.

But Derry's fear receded when Pollak told him that Furman and Simpson were among his companions, and it finally dissolved when those two, at a reunion with Derry, explained that Pollak had, in fact, led the group into Rome with extraordinary courage and ingenuity.

The three newcomers moved into the comfortable apartment of an Italian film director, Renzo Lucidi, and his family, from where they directed billeting and intelligence operations. Like most of the Allied soldiers they assisted, they were not immune to the seductive pleasures of Rome. Often they met during the day at expensive restaurants and bars, sometimes in the same room with German officers, to sort out details of their work.

A favorite haunt was the bar in the Osteria dell'Orso restaurant, where the bartender, Felix, aware that they were British, would signal them when danger approached by reaching up toward one particular bottle of liqueur on a high shelf. So many Allied escapers "lived it up" while miraculously avoiding arrest that one Fascist newspaper expressed resentment that enemy officers were dining in the finest restaurants, dressed in the most elegant clothes anti-Fascist tailors could make, while most Romans went hungry.

Nor were Derry's three assistants inclined to let the Gestapo interfere with their cultural life. One evening they stood arguing about seats with the clerk at the opera booking office when a German officer waiting behind them asked in perfect English:

"Are you going to be much longer?"

"No," replied Pollak, also in English.

And they left!

But they returned another night with the Lucidis—and found themselves occupying a box that adjoined one containing, it seemed, the whole German general staff. They were nervously considering what to do when they noted that one officer frequently turned away from the stage, where Italian singers were in full voice, to glance at the lovely profile of Lucidi's French wife, Adrienne. She smiled at him and, leaning over, asked if she could borrow his opera glasses, which he gallantly offered her. One of the Britons then suggested:

"You've made a conquest. Why don't you ask for his autograph?"

"But of course," Adrienne replied, arching her eyebrows slightly.

When the performance had ended, she leaned over once more and asked the officer to sign her program.

"I will do better than that," the German said, beaming. "I will get the general to autograph it for you."

And the enemy watched while the general signed his name. The signature was that of General Kurt Mälzer, who had just replaced General Stahel, thought "too soft" by Berlin, as the Commandant of Rome.

Aghast, the Britons and their protectors departed, wondering if they were not perhaps pushing their luck a little too far.

Their luck, in any event, took a turn for the worse. One of the Italian girls who had accompanied the three Britons to Rome, Iride, telephoned Pollak on January 8, 1944, and said it was "vital" that he come to her at once. Pollak consulted with Derry.

"It looks like a damn trap," Derry said. "Joe, I don't think we dare let you keep that date with Iride."

"But supposing it really is something vital to our people . . . ?" Pollak argued. "We can't just ignore it."

And so Pollak went to see Iride while his three comrades and O'Flaherty nervously paced the floor in the monsignor's office waiting for a telephone call from him confirming that he was safe.

The call never came, but a note from Iride did. She had indeed lured Pollak into a trap—in order, she explained, to save the rest of them.*

Two days later the Gestapo, tipped off by the servant of a *padrone* who was billeting some escapers, captured Furman while he was visiting their apartment. When Simpson later came to the same place, he escaped arrest only because the doorbell failed to work, giving the *portiere* time to warn him that the Germans were in the apartment.

O'Flaherty and Derry feared that their whole organization might collapse, and they were by no means reassured when the monsignor recklessly attended a reception at the Hungarian Embassy and met Ambassador von Weizsäcker. Drawing O'Flaherty aside, the diplomat cautioned:

* Iride's note to Derry read: "Yesterday at midday I was arrested . . . They are looking for Giuseppe [Pollak's code name] and at all costs must take him. I begged Giuseppe to come to me because I am very sick, but I am guarded. I think the arrest of Giuseppe will be the saving of us all. I won't talk unless threatened that I endanger the life of my baby by not doing so, in which case I shall poison myself . . . You must not believe if they take Giuseppe that it is a betrayal. He is of no interest to them—they only want to know who supplies the money, and I repeat they will never know from me—I prefer death. I am only afraid that Giuseppe may talk if he believes himself betrayed. Iride."

"It has gone on too long. In the future you must stay where you belong. If you leave the area of the Vatican, you will be arrested on sight. This is a final warning. Think carefully about what I have said."

"Oh, to be sure I will," O'Flaherty answered irrepressibly. "Sometimes."

He wasn't afraid of the Germans, but how would the Vatican respond to the increased pressure that it would certainly feel—at a time when the fate of thousands was in the balance?[5]

❖ ❖ ❖

Among these thousands were many Frenchmen—escaped prisoners of war from General Juin's corps, Vichyite deserters from the German army, and Jews who had fled from southern France. They were being helped by a French Mutual Aid Commitee directed from the Vichy French Embassy to the Holy See. Though Ambassador Léon Bérard himself was a loyal supporter of Marshal Pétain, First Secretary Jacques de Blesson and Vice Consul François de Vial secretly sabotaged Pétain's policies.

Both met frequently with O'Flaherty and Derry to co-ordinate their clandestine activities and collect British Embassy funds. And the two groups often shared their workers, including Pasqualino Perfetti, the greasy, shifty-eyed, but highly effective agent in priest's clothing whom Derry had met when he first arrived in Rome en route to the Vatican —and still did not trust.

The French Mutual Aid Committee had its clerical counterpart of Monsignor O'Flaherty: Father Benoît-Marie de Bourg d'Ire, known to Italians as "Father Benedetto," who headed a branch dealing exclusively with French and other foreign Jews. A Capuchin priest from Marseilles, Father Benoît had, in 1942, saved from deportation many of the fifty thousand Jews of foreign origin whom the Vichy government had promised to deliver to the Germans.

When southeastern France was occupied by Italian Fascist troops, he persuaded the Italian police chief in Nice to ignore the deportation order and manufactured in his Marseilles monastery every type of false document—passports, identity cards, baptism certificates, employers' letters of recommendation. The monastery became a way station for Jews being smuggled into Spain and Switzerland.

But when Italy defected to the Allies, German troops swept into the

Italian-occupied zone of France, and thousands of Jews fled in panic across the Alps into Italy—accompanied by Father Benoît.

With all Jewish survivors in Rome forced into hiding by the October round-up, Jewish leaders appointed Benoît director of the Rome-based Delegation for Assistance to Jewish Emigrants (DELASEM), which became affiliated with the French Mutual Aid Committee.

Foreign Jews now streamed into secret DELASEM headquarters in the International College of Capuchins in Rome, where Benoît personally welcomed them with biblical authority, his squat form draped imposingly in a brown robe, his bald pate, flowing black beard, and gently tough countenance lending him saintly dignity. The Jews were immediately assigned billets and given money and false identity documents.

Among the people who came were two raggedly garbed but unusually healthy-looking young men.

"We are Jews," one of them told the *portiere*, an elderly monk.

"Ah, then, God's blessing upon you, my friends."

"We need help," the second man said. "We need passports."

The *portiere* stared at them warily and responded sympathetically: "Ah, then, you have come to the wrong place. You must be looking for the government offices, though I don't expect that they will be open this late at night. Nonetheless, I will give you directions. You must go down . . ."

"You old fool!" shouted one of the men. "We are not looking for government offices. We are looking for the priests who take care of Jews!"

"Oh, my friends, then you are indeed in the wrong place," said the *portiere*, who had suspected the visitors immediately. "What would we have to do with Jews? We are only poor monks who know nothing of such matters. I regret that I cannot help you, but I will ask the fathers to pray for you. Good night, and go with God."

Shocked, the callers—Gestapo agents—departed, but Father Benoît now knew that the Germans were closing in.

And his troubles multiplied when other German agents reportedly captured red-handed a messenger who was smuggling DELASEM funds into Rome from the north. At any rate, the funds disappeared before reaching Benoît. Suddenly left with only a trickle of financial support from the French Mutual Aid Committee, Benoît, in desperation, turned to the Vatican for aid.

He was not very hopeful. A few months earlier, in July 1943, he had personally gone to the Pope with a plan to help Jews emigrate from France to other countries, explaining the grave peril to Jews posed by the Vichyites.

"I would never have thought that of France!" Pius exclaimed, according to Benoît.

The Pope commended Benoît for his plan, but offered no financial or other assistance. (The Vatican was already sponsoring an emigration program but almost exclusively for Jews who had converted to Catholicism.) Benoît heard no more from the Vatican—except through another monk, who received a note from a church official saying, in reference to Benoît:

"If we need him we'll contact. But doesn't seem we will."

Benoît was devastated. But now he would knock on the Vatican's door once more. This time, he sadly reports, his request yielded three hundred kilograms of flour!

Finally, through the good offices of British Minister Osborne and American Representative Tittmann, Benoît obtained funds from Italian businessmen and American Jewish sources.

But the Gestapo danger grew. And among the threatened victims was Richard Arvay . . .[6]

Arvay, a French Jew who had escaped from a Vichy concentration camp, had precariously made his way to Rome and stopped the first Catholic priest he saw to ask for help. The priest immediately guided him to Father Benoît.

"You must go to police headquarters and register," Arvay was told. "Don't worry. You'll be perfectly safe."

Astonished and afraid, Arvay entered the station and a police official sitting behind the registration desk said without preamble: "You are French, Catholic, Aryan, are you not?"

Before Arvay could reply, the official issued him a registration card. Like many Roman policeman, this one co-operated with the Resistance.

As soon as he was billeted with an Italian family, Arvay started working for Father Benoît, helping others in need—even two soldiers in German uniform who had come and explained:

"We were forced into the German army. We are French. Here are our papers. We want to desert. Please help!"

The papers were genuine. They spoke French as only Frenchmen could. And so Arvay recommended that the two deserters be helped. They were given civilian clothing, money, false papers, living quarters, and, when one fell ill with jaundice, the wife of a Jewish leader nursed him.

The two Frenchmen soon expressed their gratitude. They sent notes to several Jews demanding money—more than the Gestapo was offering them.

And the deserters knew Arvay's identity and that of almost everyone else working for Father Benoît . . . [7]

❖ ❖ ❖

Under increasing German pressure, the Vatican finally closed the street door leading to the German College, jeopardizing Monsignor O'Flaherty's lifeline to escapers. No one could now enter from Rome proper without passing through a checkpoint guarded by zealously obedient Swiss Guards.

Then, one day, the monsignor entered Major Derry's office, grim-faced, and told him his Church superior had ordered that Derry leave the premises. O'Flaherty, who was himself to be severely reprimanded by Vatican officials, explained:

"It seems the Germans now know that Patrick [the major's underground name] Derry is the lad who has been issuing all the help to escaped prisoners. If you stay here, they may pay you an unwelcome call within hours, but if you go to a billet, you'll have to make up your mind to remain there. They'll pounce as soon as you show your face anywhere round here."

"But that's impossible, Monsignor!" Derry exclaimed. "How can we keep the work going if I can't remain in touch?"

In despair, he paid a visit to Minister Osborne to see if there were a way around the edict. There was none. In fact, Derry was forced to move in with the minister and "disappear" altogether.

Major Sam Derry thus "ceased to exist," chased so far underground that he became a ghost known in secret messages only as "Toni." The Vatican had succeeded in cutting down the life-saving activities of a monsignor who did not understand that if the Church was to continue saving souls, it could not afford, under the circumstances, the moral luxury of taking sides against evil.[8]

5

The Partisans

With the Nazi threat diminishing because of his "realistic" attitude, Pope Pius XII turned his attention to another menace—the Communists. The Nazi occupation of Rome could only be temporary, but the Communists would remain, and there would be no Mussolini to jail or exile them. Moreover, they would enjoy the backing of the Soviet Union, which would probably emerge from the war more powerful than ever.

At his meeting with American diplomat Harold Tittmann on October 19, three days after the round-up of Jews, the Pope, while praising German respect for the Vatican, expressed his fear of "irresponsible elements"—"little Communist bands" who, he said, were stationed around Rome. They might commit violence in the period between German evacuation and Allied arrival. Pius said he hoped that the Allies would take necessary measures in time . . .[1]

A frail young woman with flowing titian hair waited in a doorway on Via del 23 Marzo, her green eyes expectant as she played with the metal object in her jacket pocket.

She was about to perform her first assassination.

In a few minutes a German soldier, as he did every day, would leave military headquarters at Hotel Excelsior carrying a leather bag full of

documents. He would head down Via del 23 Marzo and walk toward
another headquarters at Piazza Barberini.

Today he would not arrive. Today—March 1, 1944—Carla Capponi,
a rebel contessa, would pass her final test, an ordeal she had been preparing for since she was fourteen, eight years earlier. Since the summer
of 1935 when she had found the key to a forbidden drawer . . .

Carla's family, of noble Florentine origin, had rented a house outside
Rome from an anti-Fascist friend, and in a bedroom drawer she discovered many old newspaper clippings and documents describing how
Mussolini's blackshirts had murdered Socialist Deputy Giacomo Mat-
teotti in 1924 shortly after the Duce had come to power. Carla read
all the material, horrified by the details of this tale of evil. Until then
she had had no interest in politics, even though her father, a mining
engineer, had spent some time in Albanian exile for refusing to join
the Fascist party.

Carla took some of the papers back to Rome with her and distributed
copies to her friends at school. When her father was informed of her
"indiscretion" by a school official, he rushed to the school and silently
brought her home, broaching the subject only on arrival:

"Carla, I should have spoken to you before. What you have done
could hurt me very much. Fascism is strong. It can destroy us. And
there is nothing we can do. Do you understand?"

She understood. And her understanding grew when at school a
British student gave her a book about women in the Soviet Union, the
first material she had ever seen on Communism. She then persuaded
the librarian at the National Library to lend her a copy of a book by
Trotsky on revolution, which was supposed to be seen only by pro-
fessional researchers. It was apparently the only book on Communism
in the library. The Fascist government reasoned that since Trotsky had
been an enemy of Stalin, his works could be useful in dividing the
Communist movement.

Having learned the rudiments of Marxism, Carla searched Rome for
the Communist party, but it had gone so far underground that she
could find no trace of it. Biding her time, she often gazed from the
window of her home on Piazza Foro Traiano, across Trojan's Forum,
at the brown, fifteenth-century building on Piazza di Venezia that had
been constructed with stones from the Colosseum, the building that
housed Benito Mussolini. One well-aimed bullet . . . Carla's thoughts
came to naught, for on July 25, 1943, Mussolini was driven from power.

That night Carla celebrated with thousands of her countrymen at
Piazza di Venezia, where the Duce, from his balcony, had so often

promised glory and greatness to other cheering crowds. She waved a red handkerchief and shouted gleefully at the top of her voice:

"I am a Communist! I am a Communist!"

A young man in the crowd edged up to her and introduced himself as a "fellow Communist."

"Come with me and I'll introduce you to some more," he said.

Within a few days Carla's house, when her parents were absent, became a meeting place for Italian Communist leaders, who found the bourgeois surroundings very inviting after years of living in cellars and hiding in closets. Here plans were made for the future. And here Carla met Rosario Bentivegna.

Bentivegna was a scholarly medical student, with a slender build and a mercurial Sicilian temperament, who somehow seemed to brood even when he smiled. His father had been an anti-Fascist when Mussolini came to power—until Fascists sprayed his house one day with machine-gun fire.

In fear, the elder Bentivegna embraced Fascism and was appointed a commercial attaché in Bulgaria. Later he headed an organization of Fascist merchants. But in 1933, after an agonizing struggle with his conscience, he bolted Fascism and joined the anti-Fascist underground. When arrest seemed imminent, he fired a bullet into his head.

His son Rosario was spared a struggle of conscience. As a student, after reading Trotsky and seeing one of his best friends, a Jew, kill himself because he had been expelled from school under the anti-Jewish laws, he became a Trotskyite and the leader of a secret student Marxist "discussion group."

Carla and Rosario, whose code names were "Elena" and "Paolo," had much in common. They had both discovered Marxism by themselves, knowing little about the ideology except that it promised to wash away every trace of Fascist iniquity. They had not been the victims of Communist party propaganda; they had sought out the party.

It was not surprising, therefore, that their initiative should carry them beyond the bounds of normal party service. If they were to fight for justice, they would truly fight. In October 1943 they both joined the Patriotic Action Group (GAP), the activist arm of the party, the arm that wielded the bomb and the gun.

Bentivegna was chosen to lead one of four GAP groups operating in Rome, with Carla to assist him. Their task at first was to terrorize only the Fascists and discourage their collaboration with the Nazi occupiers. Thus, in October Bentivegna killed a Fascist policeman in a campaign to force Fascists to discard their uniforms. But in November a bitter struggle broke out within the party over the wisdom of striking at the Germans as well.

The question arose when it became clear that most Romans—bureaucrats, clerks, shopkeepers with little revolutionary bent—were passive toward the Resistance, an attitude that had permitted the Germans to occupy Rome so easily in the first place.

The Romans traditionally were skeptics, who trusted more in fate than in themselves; and their skepticism had only grown when, after celebrating the "demise" of Fascism, they found themselves under the Nazi as well as the Fascist boot—left in the lurch by their King and Premier, who had fled to safety.

To the Romans, their city was Eternal, as the Church had taught. Armies could come and go; dictators could rule and perish; revolutionaries could revolt and vanish; but Rome would remain Rome, changeless in its grandeur, its opportunism, its ability to remain unchanged in a changing world.

With the advent of Fascism, they had shrugged their shoulders and hoped for the best. In the golden days after the conquest of Ethiopia, the Romans took pride in their new imperial status, acquired so cheaply. However, when the cost began rising during the Spanish Civil War, with long casualty lists, the gold began to tarnish. And as the Duce bowed ever lower before Hitler, finally flinging the nation into World War II, the Romans shrugged their shoulders again and waited for destiny to save them, as it always had.

Communist leaders, however, were determined to shape destiny, not to be shaped by it. Now, in the fall of 1943, some wanted to terrorize the Fascists alone, on the theory that attacks on the Germans would, by inviting retaliation against the Romans, make them even *less* willing to co-operate with the partisans.

Others argued that, on the contrary, retaliation would so fuel Roman hatred of the Germans that the Romans would be *more* willing to co-operate. Nor did any people blackmailed into passivity deserve liberation, these Communists felt.

Finally it was decided at a meeting of national Communist leaders led by Luigi Longo, at Monchiero in Piedmont, that the most effective way to enhance partisan power and influence would be to incite the Germans to take reprisals against the Italian people. Rosario and Carla accepted this order without reservation—though Rosario had argued in favor of attacks on the Fascists exclusively—and started attacking the Germans. Carla was not expected—yet—to personally gun anyone down, but Rosario, with Carla guarding him, assassinated individual enemy soldiers and also threw bombs at Nazis and Fascists from a speeding bicycle. On one occasion both placed bombs in German trucks, which blew up when officers emerging from the Teatro dell'Opera climbed in.

The immediate reply to such terrorism was disappointing. Instead of retaliating massively, the Nazis remained relatively quiet, trying, in fact, to keep the incidents concealed from the people so that the occupiers would not appear vulnerable to attack.

Soon, however, German soldiers were ordered to carry their firearms wherever they went and not to walk the streets alone; the use of bicycles was banned to avoid hit-and-run bombings; rewards were offered for information leading to the capture of terrorists; and warnings were posted threatening to execute ten Italians for every German killed.

Still there was no notable retaliation, beyond the normal arrests of Jews, partisans, Italian army deserters, and draft dodgers. The Communists would have to be satisfied with making life miserable for the Nazis and Fascists. And indeed, no German or Italian Fascist could feel safe on the streets . . .

Carla Capponi would now, on March 1, 1944, further contribute to the occupiers' anxiety by shooting her first victim—a far more severe test of her will, conviction, and idealism than the placing of bombs that would explode after she was long out of sight. Nearby stood Rosario and two other members of the execution squad. But she would pull the trigger.

Carla finally saw a figure in German uniform, leather bag in hand, approaching on Via del 23 Marzo from the direction of Hotel Excelsior. She stared at the man, who was blond and young. In a few moments, she heard the sound of his boots on the sidewalk, and then he passed her.

She stepped out of the doorway and for a second considered calling to him. A warning seemed only fair. But then she thought of her three comrades, who she knew were following her at discreet intervals. She couldn't endanger them.

Carla removed the pistol from her pocket and fired a bullet into the German's back. She heard a loud gasp, and the man crumpled to the ground. Grabbing his leather bag, Carla dashed to Piazza Barberini and then slowed to a walk. She began to weep as she continued on toward Piazza Colonna, where she entered a building and walked down to the cellar, which had been converted into a bomb shelter. She sat down on a bench, still crying.

A minute later Rosario, who had followed, was sitting down beside her.

"The struggle is very hard," he said softly, drawing her to him and kissing her. "We're not killers. We are trying to liberate the people."

Yes, soon Rome would be free, then Italy, then the world . . . But the German soldier had been so young . . .[2]

In speaking of "irresponsible elements," the Pope made little distinction between genuine Communists and members of other leftist, or even centrist, political parties, however well-meaning he felt some might be. For he feared that the Communists, more dedicated and politically sophisticated than the other groups, would, in any case, dominate them, especially during periods of chaos—to the detriment of the Church.

Italian democracy, after all, had crushed Vatican temporal power in the revolution of 1870, victimizing Pius XII's grandfather in the process. Moreover, relations between the Vatican and the succeeding Italian governments remained strained—until Mussolini took power and set up an authoritarian hierarchy that the Church, with a similar power structure, could at least understand. Only when the Vatican signed a Concordat and Lateran Treaty with the Duce in 1929, establishing the sovereignty of Vatican City, did the Church feel secure again in Italy.

True, Fascism eventually became overbearing, and even menacing, when Mussolini began drawing too close to Hitler, who influenced him to view the Church as a dangerous competitor for men's souls. But if Fascism had outworn its usefulness, it did not necessarily follow that complete political freedom, which the Communists would only exploit, was an appropriate alternative.

Actually, a number of anti-Fascist parties, in addition to the Communists, sprang from underground, indeed from the grave, after Mussolini fell on July 25, 1943. Dazed and uncertain after years in prison, in exile, or in silent isolation, their leaders suddenly found themselves heroes to a population intoxicated with their new freedom.

The six leading parties immediately formed a loose alliance, comprising three center-rightist parties—Christian Democratic, Liberal, and Democracy of Labor—and three leftist or left-leaning parties—Action, Socialist, and Communist.* None of these parties could dominate the

---

* The Christian Democratic party was a kind of Vatican agent, and, presumably, an informant, within the six-party alliance—and the Pope's main hope for preventing a Communist take-over in a democratic era. Although it was a heterogeneous party embracing extreme conservatives as well as quasi collectivists, members were bound by a common desire to give a Catholic character to the Italian state. The conservative Liberal party looked to the great anti-Fascist philosopher Benedetto Croce for intellectual guidance, and the tiny conservative Democracy of Labor party, to Ivanoe Bonomi, who was to become the president of the Committee of National Liberation (CLN). The only party with any real understanding of modern democracy was the Action party, which stood for basic agrarian, educational, and economic reforms—a leftist program in Italian terms. Influenced by Roosevelt's New Deal policies in the

others, for none had a large following. The Communists had the largest, but still could boast no more than five thousand throughout Italy and only several hundred in Rome.

While embracing the anti-Fascist leaders as individuals, the Italians did not necessarily accept their ideology. They were still too sluggish from the Fascist narcotic to grasp *any* unfamiliar ideology, including Marxism. And the Communists realized, as the Pope apparently did not, that for this reason they would have an exceedingly hard time coming to power.

Indeed, it would be hard enough setting up any kind of party regime. For the King and Badoglio, fearing the Communists—and democracy —as much as the Pope, would not allow even the more conservative politicians into the government, which they restricted to their own followers.

Nevertheless, these two leaders, by abandoning the Romans just before the Germans occupied Rome, ironically generated a Resistance movement that would eventually discard them.[3]

King Victor Emmanuel III was a pathetic product of his heritage. The House of Savoy, which he headed, had started in 1003 when a young bandit called Humbert the White-handed pillaged his way to eminence in the northern region of Piedmont. The Piedmontese dynasty that took root was the one that Garibaldi, in 1861, was to place on the throne of a united Italy. Victor Emmanuel II, the first King of Italy, was succeeded by Humbert I, who was assassinated in 1900 by an anarchist after a corrupt, ineffectual reign.

Victor Emmanuel III ascended the throne and became the puppet of a series of premiers. In 1915, hoping to acquire new territory, he followed one into World War I on the Allied side. After that war, with agitation against the monarchy mounting, he found the answer to royal survival: Benito Mussolini. The King refused to sign a decree banning the Duce's followers from marching on Rome in 1922, and Mussolini took power after promising to support the monarchy.

Thenceforth, the King never refused to sign a Fascist decree, whatever his personal views. In 1938 he even approved, if reluctantly, the Fascist anti-Semitic laws and greeted Hitler with pomp and smiles on the Führer's visit to Rome.† Only on July 25, 1943, after the Fascist

United States, it had a devoted but small following. The spirit behind the party, Count Carlo Sforza, a rigid anti-Communist, was constantly frustrated in his effort to apply in tradition-bound Italy what he had learned in American exile.
† On November 28, 1938, shortly after Mussolini decreed the anti-Jewish laws, Count Galeazzo Ciano, the Duce's Foreign Minister—and son-in-law—wrote in his

Grand Council, shaken by the Allied invasion of Sicily and the first bombing of Rome, had demanded Mussolini's resignation, did the King summon the courage to stand up to the Duce . . .

Dressed in a dark blue suit, his face haggard after a sleepless night, Mussolini, though bitter, had arrived hopefully at Villa Savoia, the royal residence, for the encounter. He seemed less contemptuous than usual of the dwarfish little man with the large white mustache as he challenged the legality of the Grand Council's action. The King, his usually darting, indifferent blue eyes fixed relentlessly on his visitor, replied:

"My dear Duce, it is no longer any good. Italy is in pieces. Army morale is at rock bottom. The soldiers don't want to fight any more. The Grand Council's vote is overwhelming . . . At this moment, you are the most hated man in Italy. You can no longer count on more than one friend. But one you have left: I am he. That is why I tell you that you need have no fears for your personal safety, for which I will ensure protection. I have been thinking that the man for the job is Marshal Badoglio . . ."

The King escorted the shocked Duce to the entrance of the villa, smiled weakly, and shook hands with him. Minutes later a group of *carabinieri* policemen suddenly grabbed the dictator and propelled him into an ambulance under arrest.

Marshal Badoglio, the conqueror of Ethiopia,‡ was the King's next guest—not surprisingly, considering his record of resilience. In World War I his troops had been crushed, but he nevertheless became chief of staff a few years later. In December 1940 Mussolini forced him to resign from the army after a near military disaster in Greece, and now once more he bounced back—as Premier.

With Fascism swept away, at least formally, the same fear and opportunism that had once made the King and Badoglio grovel before Mussolini now made them hesitate to break away from the Axis. They

diary: "I found the Duce in a state of indignation against the King. Three times in the course of their conversation this morning the King said to him that he feels an 'infinite pity for the Jews.' He cited cases of persecution . . . The Duce said that there are 20,000 spineless people in Italy who are moved by the fate of the Jews. The King replied that he is one of them."

‡ The army of Badoglio that invaded Ethiopia in 1936 was heading toward defeat until his Military Intelligence Service (SIM) intercepted Haile Selassie's telephone calls and informed Badoglio of Ethiopian plans and positions. Finally subduing the Ethiopians with the help of poison gas, Badoglio triumphantly entered Addis Ababa, had himself named viceroy, and confiscated all the furnishings in the imperial palace, selling part of them and sending the rest to his villa in Rome, including the imperial throne for use as a couch for his poodle.

assured the Germans that "the war continues" and simultaneously negotiated an armistice with the Allies.

They could not bolt the Axis, they told the Allies, until the Allies guaranteed that fifteen divisions would land to protect Rome—and themselves. The Allies agreed to parachute *one* airborne division into Rome, an operation to be followed immediately by a landing at Salerno in the south.

On September 7, 1943, the night before the scheduled air drop, Badoglio was visited in Rome by two Americans, Brigadier General Maxwell Taylor and another officer,* who had daringly smuggled themselves ashore from an Italian naval craft and had driven to the capital hidden in an ambulance. Their objective was to determine conditions for the airborne landing.

Badoglio, dressed in pajamas and bathrobe, was about to greet them in his study when Major General Giacomo Carboni, whose task would be to defend Rome against the Germans, expressed shock at his appearance. He found the Premier "a demoralizing sight, with his bald cranium, long wrinkled yellow neck, glassy eyebrowless eyes . . . a weird featherless bird."

"Excellency," the general said, "you cannot show yourself thus to two unknown American officers. You are still a marshal of Italy. Please dress and freshen up."

Badoglio agreed, but elegant clothes could not cloak his fear. The Italian forces, he told the Americans, were not yet ready to guarantee the security of the three airfields where the division was to land. Nor, it seemed, would they ever be. To Badoglio and his fellow Italian leaders, it would be tragic enough to turn their beloved Rome, the seat of their fortunes, the source of their power, the root of their culture, into a ravaged battleground. But worse, what revenge would the Germans wreak on them if the operation failed?

When Taylor reluctantly agreed to recommend cancellation (some military experts think that such a surprise assault would have saved Rome from German occupation and forced the Nazis to flee northward), Badoglio begged him to postpone announcement of the armistice agreement, also scheduled for the next day, until he *was* ready to receive Allied forces.

"If I announce the armistice and the Americans don't send sufficient reinforcements and don't land near Rome," he said almost tearfully as he sat surrounded by the mementos of a glorious military career, "the Germans will seize the city and put in a puppet Fascist government."

* The officer accompanying General Taylor was Colonel William Tudor Gardiner of the Troop Carrier Command who had been twice elected Governor of Maine.

Drawing his hand across his neck, he added: "It is my throat the Germans will cut!"

Nevertheless, the Allies went ahead with the announcement as planned, since it had to coincide with the landing at Salerno (the time and place of the landing had been kept a secret from Badoglio for security reasons, though he had learned about Allied plans from his own intelligence sources) to insure that Italian troops would not help the Germans resist the invasion.

Badoglio, after hesitating, delivered a radio address in a depressed, subdued voice, confirming that Italy had surrendered to the Allies and asking the people to cease resisting the victors but to resist "any attack which might come from another quarter."†

In the early hours of September 9, 1943, Badoglio, afraid for his life, awakened the King and urged that they both flee to the Allied lines in the south.

"I'm an old man," the monarch muttered. "What could they do to me?"

But he did not wait to find out. Wearing a light raincoat over his uniform and carrying an old fiber suitcase, he climbed into his Fiat limousine and left the sleeping Romans to their fate.

A general then said to Badoglio: "I'm going to give some orders before I leave. You'll want to do the same, I suppose."

Badoglio replied: "No, I'm going to leave right away."

And he, too, abandoned the Romans.[4]

As all governmental and military authority melted away and Italy sank into deadly chaos, the alliance of six political parties, unable even to contact the King, that very day set up the Committee of National Liberation (CLN) as a revolutionary authority, with its center in Rome—which the Germans would occupy the following day, September 10, 1943—and with branches in other major cities. A white-bearded, conservative anti-Fascist, Ivanoe Bonomi, was chosen president.

The CLN, in turn, formed a military committee composed of the partisan counterparts of the parties to fight the Germans and their Fascist agents, who had now raised their heads again.

Politically, the CLN demanded that the King abdicate and that Badoglio resign to make way for a democratic party regime which, once in power, would decide on whether to keep a monarchical system.

† At the last minute Badoglio deleted from his message a specific order to take action against the Germans, an order he felt he could not honorably issue after years of Italian partnership with the Nazis—nor issue without provoking Hitler to take even more merciless vengeance than he might otherwise take.

The King and Badoglio, however, replied—once they were safely behind Allied lines—by trying to suppress the parties, and they enjoyed the support of Prime Minister Churchill, who wanted to keep in power a puppet government he thought Britain, with its vital Mediterranean interests, could and should control after the war. But since Roosevelt favored the CLN, the King was finally pressured, in February 1944, to accept a formula whereby, without formally abdicating, he would turn over his powers to his son Humbert as soon as Rome was liberated, though the CLN distrusted the crown prince almost as much as his father.

Meanwhile, the three leftist parties—Communist, Socialist, and Action—set themselves up as a "subcommittee" within the CLN and secretly pledged to seize Rome in an insurrection when the Germans were forced to retreat from the city. If possible, they would, as the Pope feared, present the arriving Allies with a *fait accompli*—a leftist regime.

How far left remained to be seen. The Socialist and Action parties were convinced that they could control the Communists. But the Communists, who realized they would be unable to establish a Soviet-type government during an Anglo-American occupation (some questioned whether such a regime would work in Italy anyway), were equally convinced that they could control a coalition government, since they had a stronger popular base than the other two groups.

After the war the Communist party would be in a position, its leaders calculated, to dominate completely—through the polls or through violent revolution, as circumstances, and Stalin, dictated.

To good Communists like Carla Capponi and Rosario Bentivegna, the future looked bright indeed—especially when they learned that the inspirational Communist and former Comintern leader, Palmiro Togliatti, known in the underground as "Ercole Ercoli," was returning home from exile in Moscow.

He would command the Communist partisans in their struggle to seize Rome.[5]

While the Communist party felt considerable pressure on the right, it had to contend also with an important force on its left.‡ For the Communist Movement of Italy, or Red Flag party (Bandiera Rossa),

‡ Still another Marxist group was the small Catholic Communist party, which called for communism with Christianity and without the conventional materialistic approach. The party dissolved after the war when Pope Pius XII condemned it, maintaining that Catholicism was incompatible with Marxism. Most members joined the regular Communist party or other leftist groups.

had a following in Rome probably larger than the regular party, if one far less disciplined.

It was led principally by Marxists leaning toward Trotskyism, but also embraced anarchists and various other leftist and intellectual ideologists. Its rank and file consisted mainly of poor, uneducated workers, artisans, and small shopkeepers, in contrast to the Communist party proper, whose members came mainly, at this time, from relatively prosperous, well-educated middle-class families. The traditional distrust of these two social groups for each other was carried over into Marxism and compounded by their strong disagreement over Stalinism. The Red Flags deplored the Communists' absolute dependence on Soviet policy, while the latter viewed the Red Flags as unrealistic adventurers.

The "adventure" that the Red Flags were planning most fervently —with the assistance of several splinter leftist groups—was the "capture" of Rome as soon as the Germans departed, with or without the collaboration of the Communist party. The Red Flag leaders themselves were divided and could not agree on an ultimate tactic. Some wanted to set up a Communist government immediately, others wanted to share power with non-Communist leftists—at least until a full-scale revolution was possible.

The leaders reasoned that the Allies, fully occupied battling the Nazis, would not divert their resources, even to root out an extreme leftist government. Nor would they dare to antagonize people whose aid they needed. At any rate, the time for revolution was now! Once a bourgeois government was in the saddle, the chance might be gone forever.

Yet the movement, however revolutionary, was sharply at odds with the Communist party's cynical decision to terrorize the Germans in Rome in order to provoke reprisals that would presumably win the co-operation of the Romans. Such a policy, the Red Flag leaders felt, would result in severe damage to the Resistance while yielding no compensatory advantage. Not indiscriminate terrorism, but sabotage and eventually military action, the Red Flags believed, would hasten Nazi withdrawal without weakening the forces of revolution.

Red Flag members were effective saboteurs. Typically, by infiltrating key ministries and services they were able to "censor" spy messages intended for the Nazis, create chaos in telephone communications, and falsify the census to thwart Mussolini's military draft. An official report they prepared indicated that 90 per cent of the Romans were female and the rest mainly people under sixteen and over eighty!

Their daring actions, undertaken without tight discipline, resulted in a large number of arrests, though some members, among them Felice and Viviana Chilanti and their ten-year-old daughter Gloria (who had walked fifteen miles to deliver a bag of explosives), often managed to make hairbreadth escapes . . .

Viviana, though the head of the women's section, was not a typical Red Flag leader, for she came from a wealthy landowning family in Tuscany. She remembered from her earliest years how her father, a military officer like many wealthy landowners in those days, had treated their shriveled old gardener with disrespect, and even cruelty, because he worked "too slowly." How her mother, a Jewess, was afraid to interfere.

Viviana revolted early against the pride and arrogance of her father —and her class. She gave away all her jewelry to poor children and, at fourteen, ran away to Rome. There, two years later, she met a young extreme leftist journalist named Felice Chilanti who came from an impoverished peasant family. Both started working for the anti-Fascist movement, but were arrested in 1941 and exiled to the Lipari Islands until the Duce fell.

When Viviana married Felice in 1933, her father disowned her, and she saw him again only years later, in late 1943, when they met by chance in a café in Milan while she was on a partisan mission. Resplendent in Fascist military uniform, he said coldly:

"It's nice to see you . . . But watch out, they kill people like you."

If only her father knew that three Russian soldiers—prisoners of war who had escaped from a German labor camp—were hiding in her attic!

Yes, they killed people like her. And she expected to be killed at any moment. Her luck couldn't last forever . . .

Just before Christmas 1943 Fascist police had stopped a truck in which she, accompanied by Gloria, was delivering copies of her husband's clandestine newssheet to her comrades. Fortunately she was giving a ride to several peasants, who had climbed into the truck with flour they intended to sell on the black market.

A policeman glanced into a sack containing the flour and, assuming that the contents of all the sacks were identical, did not bother to look into the ones containing the forbidden newssheets. Mother and daughter were jailed, ironically for black market activities, but were released on Christmas Eve.

One night, some weeks later, the Chilanti family was awakened by an ominous ring of the doorbell. When Felice and two other partisans hiding in the apartment had climbed to the roof, Viviana calmly answered the door and was blinded by a flashlight.

"We are looking for Chilanti," announced a stranger in civilian clothes, showing a police badge. One of three men, he was short and olive-skinned and had an ascetic face.

"I live here alone with my daughter," Viviana said. "My husband has gone north and I haven't seen him for weeks."

Without bothering to turn on the lights, the men then searched the house with flashlights and found three beds. Gloria was asleep in one, but the others were unoccupied—and mussed.

"You must come with us," the leader said to Viviana.

She replied with an embarrassed smile that she had a lover. He had left just before they came.

The short, dark man studied the woman caught in the glare of his flashlight, the long, blond locks, the teasing blue eyes.

"I see," he said. "Would you like to go back to sleep? I could keep you company."

Before Viviana could reply, he said that first he had to make a phone call. As he dialed a number, Viviana watched and mentally noted it. He winked at her while talking with his superior and she pondered the price she might have to pay in the service of mankind. After explaining that Viviana's husband was not home, the man received instructions and hung up.

"I'm afraid we must go now," he said, gallantly kissing her hand. "But tomorrow you must dine with me. My name is Walter."

When the three men had gone, Viviana whistled and the three on the roof came down. They checked with their contacts at the telephone exchange on the number that Walter had called and learned that it was that of the headquarters of a new Fascist police gang led by one Pietro Koch. This was an unusual opportunity to learn what the enemy was doing.

The next day, Viviana met Walter for lunch.

"Let's go to your apartment," he suggested.

"Oh, no, the neighbors would talk."

"Yes, we must find a little place."

But they never did find an appropriate "little place," and meanwhile Viviana learned a great deal about Koch and his gang. They held some of the "best" prisoners. Walter, whose last name was Di Franco, did not reveal that Koch considered him his finest torturer.[6]

❖   ❖   ❖

While the political parties, though split ideologically, agreed that the King and Badoglio must go, Italian military officers in the Resistance disagreed. True, these officers, like the politicians, deplored the royal flight from Rome, which left them without orders and at German mercy, but they nevertheless remained unshakably loyal to the King. They had served Fascism because the King had; now they would serve the Allies because the King did.

But whatever their initial reservations, their devotion to the Allied cause grew with every Nazi atrocity committed against the Romans. They were even willing to co-operate with the CLN leaders, who had been their enemies under Fascist rule, though they feared the CLN wanted to destroy Italian tradition, promote drastic social change, and perhaps set up a Communist government.

Most of these officers, though the cynical and opportunistic products of Fascism, were brave men; men who were suddenly to discover, often to their own amazement, that there were things of genuine value worth fighting and dying for.

The reorientation of many had begun when German forces started marching into Rome on September 10, 1943. Although left behind in Rome by the King and Badoglio without even the benefit of instructions, some Italian officers had tried to defend the city with a few disorganized troops, but they finally surrendered when Field Marshal Kesselring threatened to bomb Rome with seven hundred planes.

The Italians accepted terms which permitted them, once disarmed, to go free and which designated the center of Rome an open city to be commanded by the King's son-in-law, General Count Giorgio Calvi di Bergolo.

On September 12, two days after the surrender, Major Felice Santini, an air force intelligence officer, visited the open-city headquarters at the War Ministry and met with Colonel Ugo Musco, one of General Calvi's officers. Musco and Santini had known each other for many years and shared a mutual trust—to the extent possible in this traumatic period of military turnabout.

The two men agreed that the Germans were not likely to let Calvi retain his position for long. They would hardly trust the King's brother-in-law to do their bidding.

"Well, then," suggested Santini, "why not continue the battle? Why not help the Allies and the King from Rome?"

"How will we communicate with the Allies?" Musco asked dubiously.

That was the very question, Santini replied, that he wanted to discuss with Calvi's chief of staff, Colonel Giuseppe Lanza Cordero di Montezemolo. The two men then went to Montezemolo's office and Santini reported that he was in radio contact with Badoglio's headquarters in the southern city of Brindisi, now behind the Allied lines.

Montezemolo was highly skeptical that Santini had managed such a feat and asked that two test messages be transmitted. But the problem was that no useful messages could be sent without a code system. How was Brindisi to get a copy of the code?

"Very simple," Santini replied.

He had hidden a small reconnaissance plane a few miles outside Rome.

The following day Musco and Santini drove to Urbe Air Field, where the plane stood in an obscure corner behind a wall. They fired at German guards to divert them while five crewmen taking part in the plot dashed to the plane, rolled it onto the runway, and took off for the south.

On their arrival in Brindisi, the crewmen were arrested by the Allies, and their protestations that they had come on behalf of pro-Allied officers were distrusted. The request for a code system could be an enemy trap. But a few days later, on September 18, the Allies sent Giuseppe Baldanza, an Italian army radio engineer, to Rome with a radio and a code. He investigated the officers and satisfied the Allies that they could be trusted.

Equipped with the means of transmitting military information to the Allies—through Badoglio's Military Intelligence Service (SIM)— Musco and Santini immediately formed an underground radio unit called "Centro X," with two stations—one in Villa Savoia, the King's abandoned private residence, and the other in the home of a relative of Baldanza.

Musco, whom the Germans distrusted, resigned from the open-city government, and Santini entered it, feigning loyalty to the Germans. And also joining it in the service of Centro X was a young officer, Lieutenant Ottorino Borin, who, because of his fluent knowledge of German, had access to classified German military information.[7]

On September 23, at 11:45 A.M., German armored cars blocked off all exits from the War Ministry and General Stahel, the Commandant of Rome, accompanied by SS Colonel Dollmann, entered and marched to the office of General Calvi, who was conferring with his chief of staff, Colonel Montezemolo. Stahel saluted and, on behalf of Field Marshal Kesselring, informed the Italians through Dollmann, who served as his interpreter, that in fifteen minutes Mussolini would be proclaimed the head of the "Italian Social Republic."

"Are you prepared to recognize and co-operate with the new government?" Stahel asked, fully realizing that he was requesting Calvi to repudiate the status of the King—his father-in-law—as supreme military commander.

Calvi replied, as expected, that he was not, and Stahel responded that Calvi, in that case, must be interned in Germany under "honorable conditions."

Calvi was allowed to keep his sword, but he handed his pistol to Stahel, though it was later returned to him. When he requested time to pack, Stahel replied that he must be ready within an hour and that he could take with him an officer and an orderly. The Germans then left the office and Calvi said to Montezemolo, who was also to be arrested:

"Come with me." But then he immediately added: "No, stay and try to save yourself. You are the only one who can convince His Majesty that you did not betray him but served him loyally until the end."

The two soldiers embraced and Montezemolo, who had prepared for this moment, returned to his own office past two Germans guarding the door. He entered a small room at the rear, changed to civilian clothing, carefully knotted his tie, put a pistol and some documents in his pocket, and calmly walked out of the office past the guards, who did not recognize the tall, blond man in the gray suit as the uniformed officer who had entered a few minutes earlier.

As he wound his way through the War Ministry corridors toward the exit, Montezemolo suddenly recognized a German colleague approaching. He doubled back and, with the help of an Italian officer, found a basement passage that led to an unguarded exit and escaped, looking back with an air of unconcern at the display of military might around the ministry.

Montezemolo rushed to the home of his cousin, Marchesa Fulvia Ripa di Meana, where that night he developed plans for leading a military Resistance in Rome until the Allies arrived. Certainly, he was convinced, they would come within a month.

He turned on the radio and listened to Marshal Graziani, the Duce's Minister of National Defense, vilify Badoglio for his "betrayal." As related in his cousin's memoirs, Montezemolo switched off the radio and "shook his head from side to side." What had happened to Italy since those brave days when Fascism was honorable, before the Italians had to lick German boots, before the King had been forced to flee Rome? He had worked hard for the King, whom he would support under any political system. He had tried to live up to his family tradition. Ever since the thirteenth century, the Montezemolos had been faithful servants of the Piedmontese dynasty which now ruled Italy. All of their sons served in the army or navy, and all of their daughters married military men.

Montezemolo had been on delicate missions in North Africa with the Germans. He had won two medals for action in Africa, where he had repeatedly asked to remain and fight. His argument had not been with Mussolini's objectives, but with the Duce's reluctance to demand more military aid from Hitler—a show of weakness that Montezemolo had personally witnessed when he had served as interpreter between the two dictators at a meeting in Feltre in July 1943, a few days before Mussolini's overthrow.

Instead of sending the necessary help, Germany, after the Duce's fall, deployed divisions in northern and central Italy in order to grab control of the country. To Montezemolo, *this* was the betrayal—and completely justified the King's switch to the Allied side. And, of course, his own.[8]

Montezemolo immediately started organizing a "Clandestine Front" around Centro X, helped by Michele Multedo, a young painter of noble birth, who contacted many top officers in hiding and brought them into the organization. Dissident Roman policemen, mainly *carabinieri*, who were traditionally loyal to the Crown, became the Front's activist arm.

The *carabinieri* had begun sabotaging the Germans as soon as Kesselring occupied Rome. They disobeyed orders to confiscate arms. They helped Italian deserters and draft dodgers to escape capture. They warned factories in advance that they would be coming to round up labor for Germany. The Germans planned to transfer the untrustworthy *carabinieri* to the north, but its members fled into hiding and some nine thousand joined the Clandestine Front under the command of *carabiniere* General Filippo Caruso.

One of Caruso's best men was a priest, the son of a *carabiniere*—Father Giuseppe Morosini. A former military chaplain in Mussolini's army, Morosini started his partisan career by conducting mass for the *carabinieri*. But he was soon providing them with clothes, food, weapons, and military information, including the German battle plan for the Cassino front, which he apparently obtained from an Austrian officer he had befriended. But Father Morosini made friends too easily. He was too trusting in a city where no one could be trusted.

In addition to the *carabinieri*, some four thousand armed treasury and customs agents of the Guardia di Finanza, or Financial Police, a uniformed relic from Napoleonic times, secretly supported the Clandestine Front. And so did the regular police force, which dealt mainly with minor crimes, street traffic, food rationing, and other "nonpolitical" activities. Its co-operation was guaranteed by the force's inspector-general, Arturo Musco, the dynamic, roly-poly elder brother of Centro X's Colonel Ugo Musco.

Still another element in the military Resistance was the Italian navy. The naval underground commander was Rear Admiral Franco Maugeri, who had been chief of naval intelligence before deserting to the Allies. Maugeri had helped to arrange for the transfer of the Italian fleet to the Allies before the Germans could seize it, hoping that such action would win for Italy, he writes in his memoirs, "something better than unconditional surrender."

But if Maugeri, like many other Italian leaders, initially viewed a possible switch in loyalty with an opportunistic eye, the German jackboot in Rome crushed underfoot this traditional Italian formula for survival.

After the armistice, the Germans had confronted Maugeri, as they had Calvi, Montezemolo, and other senior military officers, with a simple choice: collaborate or go to a concentration camp. He could, of course, hide. But he was an officer, and Italy was at war. He had to fight for someone, for something. And Rome showed him for whom, and for what, to fight. He thus called a secret meeting of naval commanders and started a naval Resistance he called "Rome Underground."

The main purpose of this group was to furnish the Allies with German military intelligence, especially on naval matters. But Maugeri had a problem. He possessed no radio to communicate this information. He learned, however, that an army underground had also been formed and, through a series of contacts, arranged to meet the army leader on a street corner. The leader, identified by the black tie he was wearing, turned out to be his old friend "Bepo" Montezemolo, who readily agreed to let Maugeri use Centro X to relay his messages.

As the Clandestine Front grew, conflict developed when Musco and Santini refused to reveal their radio code to Montezemolo.

"But I am the commander of the Clandestine Front," Montezemolo argued with injured dignity.

"Yes," Musco replied bluntly, "but the fewer people who know the code the better."

Musco and Santini were in direct contact with the Allies in the south through Badoglio's SIM, and they saw no reason to share their privileged position with anyone else. Moreover, Montezemolo "recklessly" exposed himself to arrest on the streets of Rome, personally making contacts and even issuing money. He carried false papers identifying him as an engineer and disguised himself with dark glasses and a darkly dyed mustache, but his tall, ramrod-straight physique, long neck, and sharply chiseled features would make him easily recognizable to any German or Fascist who had ever met him.

Sooner or later Montezemolo was bound to be picked up, and who could say what a man would divulge under torture?

But most Clandestine Front leaders agreed on one thing: they must make sure they did not exchange Nazi suppression for the Communist brand—and some regarded even moderate social change as communistic. Thus, while the Front's paramilitary role was to gather arms, conduct sabotage, and fight the Germans if the latter decided to defend Rome, it was also to maintain "law and order" from the moment of German departure to the moment of Allied arrival.

For Montezemolo and the others, like the Pope, suspected that the leftists would try to seize power in Rome before the Allies came and, whether Communist or not, they would certainly try to overthrow the monarchy and set up a republic with all kinds of dangerous programs. And the Crown and the traditional class structure were as inviolate to many Front leaders as the Church was to the Pope.

To reduce the danger of a leftist coup, Badoglio, whom the Front faithfully served, tried to unify all Resistance groups in Rome under a single commander responsible to him. But the CLN refused to accept the commander he selected—General Quirino Armellini. It pointed out that Armellini, while serving as Badoglio's police chief after Mussolini's ouster, had tried to suppress political party activities.

The Clandestine Front was not discouraged. It had, after all, built up large arsenals, one of them—with the apparent collusion of priests—in the Basilica of San Paolo fuori le Mura, which was, by treaty, Vatican territory!

These arms could be used to fight the Germans—or the leftists.[9]

＊＊＊ ＊＊＊ ＊＊＊

While political and social frictions threatened to rip the Roman Resistance apart, German brutality helped to keep it together. Indeed, this brutality strengthened both the CLN and the Clandestine Front, driving new members into each.

Recruitment especially soared in December 1943, when the Nazis began masive labor round-ups. Thousands of men, afraid of being picked up on a blocked-off street and forced to work on local defense projects or in Germany, fled to refuge in the Resistance. Those of conscription age were the most frightened by the round-ups since they could be arrested for draft evasion.

So tight was the Nazi police net that, on one occasion, it trapped the new chief of the regular Fascist police force, General Pietro Caruso (not to be confused with General Filippo Caruso, the *carabinieri* chief), on the very day he arrived in Rome. Intervention by a Fascist general was required to save him from deportation. The Germans thus made many Roman men feel safer as partisans than as passive citizens minding their own business.

The round-ups had begun shortly after Fritz Sauckel, a high German Labor Ministry official, came to Rome and told Kesselring that Germany urgently needed Roman labor for its armament program.

"If the Italians are allies," Sauckel heatedly argued, "they should volunteer for work, and if they are enemies, why should they not be treated as such?"

Kesselring nodded. He was impressed with this argument.

Consul Möllhausen was not, realizing that the Resistance would benefit enormously from a forced labor policy. And from a human point of view, he claims in his memoirs, he considered such a policy abhorrent. He had been shocked, he says, on witnessing a street scene in which husbands, fathers, and sons were literally torn from their families and thrown into trucks while women screamed and children wept.

Möllhausen went to the new Commandant of Rome, General Kurt Mälzer, who had replaced General Stahel in late 1943. If Mälzer agreed to cancel the round-ups, the consul was sure, Kesselring would also agree. But Möllhausen was not very hopeful, since he considered Mälzer not only vulgar and repugnant but utterly irrational.

An old regimental comrade of Kesselring, Mälzer, who liked to call himself the "King of Rome," looked older than his fifty-five years, despite efforts to hide his bald pate with a beret boldly slanted over his right ear. A heavy-set man, he dressed untidily, walked inelegantly, and talked unintelligently. But he still imagined himself irresistible to women—even to a tasteful woman like Adrienne Lucidi of Monsignor O'Flaherty's organization, for whom he had gallantly autographed an opera program.

Besides being a "fool," Mälzer was an undisciplined drunkard and, allegedly, a black-marketeer—not at all the staid Möllhausen's cup of tea.

Pessimistic though he was, Möllhausen says he told Mälzer: "For those four or five hundred people taken, there are tens of thousands who are hiding in fear in their houses, who run away in terror at the sight of a German uniform . . . [They] have disappeared [presumably into the Resistance] . . . and have decided not to show up again until they are certain that the manhunt is over."

Mälzer's face turned red.

" 'Manhunt'!" he exclaimed, "I shall report this expression to Monte Soratte [Kesselring's headquarters]."

Möllhausen himself went directly to Kesselring and repeated that the forced labor policy was swelling the ranks of the Resistance. He pointed out that forced labor was, in any event, a matter for the Fascist government to handle.

"You're right," the field marshal agreed, hesitating no longer than he had when Sauckel had argued *his* case. "The game is not worth the candle."

Kesselring telephoned Mälzer and ordered him to call off the round-ups. Möllhausen rejoiced. And from that time on, the Fascists, rather than the Nazis, rounded up men for labor. Wives and children continued to scream and weep, but Möllhausen could now listen with a clear conscience—and Romans, he felt, would be less inclined to blame the Germans and join the Resistance. Once again, he had found a way to round off the rough edges of evil.[10]

Round or rough, this evil not only sent young men swarming into the CLN and the Clandestine Front but posed, as a result, a growing challenge to these organizations. New members needed advice, help, and hope.

Providing such support in large doses was Ettore Basevi, who, with the aid of a young German-Jewish refugee, Lily Marx, gave Centro X a new dimension—a press and forgery service, financed largely with British Legation funds distributed by Monsignor O'Flaherty.

Basevi edited a news bulletin with information gathered mainly from Allied radio reports and from his own informers planted in governmental agencies and in German circles, telling the people what was happening in the outside world, on the war fronts, in German and Fascist offices and drawing rooms. Some thirty other underground publications drew from this information for their own readership. Young people, mostly girls, risked their lives distributing the news bulletins in churches, on streetcars, in theaters, and on street corners.

More significantly, Basevi helped to save tens of thousands of people from imprisonment and death, as well as from hunger, with a daring operation that provided them with false identity and ration cards. The various political parties, Monsignor O'Flaherty's organization, the

Jewish community, the *carabinieri*, Italian army deserters, draft dodgers, forced labor escapers, and other hunted groups all turned in to him photographs and false names. In a few days they were furnished with splendidly forged documents—identity cards, residence permits, declarations of unfitness for military service, labor cards, and other necessary papers.

The hardest document to forge was the ration card, without which food was unobtainable, except at exorbitant black-market prices. Even card holders were issued only 150 grams of bread per day (reduced to 100 in late March 1944)—a small bun containing a smattering of elm-tree pitch, rye, dried chick peas, maize flour, and mulberry leaves. Hungry people were scrawling on the walls such slogans as BREAD! BREAD! BREAD!—DEATH TO THE PEOPLE WHO ARE STARVING US!

And the food situation worsened as the Allies bombed supply trains and truck convoys and as the Germans invalidated the cards of every male who failed to register voluntarily for defense work, meaning almost all eligible young men.

Since the ration card had special watermarks that could not be duplicated, Centro X had to steal the special paper from the State Polygraphic Institute where the cards were manufactured.

One night Basevi and four of his agents parked a truck in front of the Institute and, carrying large bundles, entered through a small door deliberately left open by an officer of the Guardia di Finanza with access to the building. Inside, they exchanged their bundles, which contained waste paper, for others they found and departed with enough of the special paper to produce 500,000 food ration cards.

A few days later Basevi and a colleague were directing production of the card in a printing shop when the telephone rang. It was Colonel Ugo Musco's brother Arturo, the inspector-general of the regular nonpolitical police:

"The police are going to raid the place within the hour," he warned Basevi. "Get the paper out as fast as you can!"

Within minutes the paper was loaded on a truck and taken to the home of a partisan. Basevi and his comrade stayed behind in the shop, thinking they now had nothing to fear. They wanted to learn if the police suspected anything—and found, when they arrived, that they did. The police, explained an officer, had picked up a youth selling scrap metal; the scrap included lead slugs from this printing house and the words these slugs produced were not flattering to the Germans. The two partisans humbly protested their innocence, but the police arrested them and the typographer and took them to the police station.

When the police chief tried to find the evidence, however, he discovered that it had disappeared—thanks again to Arturo Musco.

Basevi was permitted to leave and soon was busy at another printing shop. In a few days a half-million hungry people of all political complexions were eating again—to the utter dismay of the Germans, who wondered why the queues in front of the food stores were growing so long.[11]

In their mutual struggle to survive German cruelty, the political left and right, even while plotting against each other, developed a mutual respect. And this attitude was reflected in their reaction to a German effort to divide and conquer them.

In late 1943 a German officer called on Filippo Grenet, an Italian diplomat whom the Germans suspected—correctly—of supporting the Clandestine Front, and asked him to convey a proposal to Montezemolo.

"We will not seek out or arrest the *carabinieri* if the Clandestine Front co-operates in the capture of Communists and other CLN partisans," the officer promised.

The Germans, he said, simply wanted to make sure that the leftists would not grab control of Rome after their departure.

Montezemolo never did reply.

Almost simultaneously, a German officer sent a message to Carla Capponi promising that the Germans would leave the Communists alone if they collaborated in the capture of the *carabinieri*. Carla kept the officer on a string—until she could arrange for his assassination.

Common products of the strange Italian ethos, neither side would betray the other—even as they headed toward civil war upon the liberation of Rome.[12]

❊   ❊   ❊

"Think of it, if all goes well, in a couple of days I'll see my dog again!"

Major Peter Tompkins felt a certain cynical reassurance on hearing this incongruous remark in the cabin of the torpedo boat taking him and several other Allied agents from Corsica on the night of January 20, 1944, to a point on the Italian coast about one hundred kilometers north of Rome. The remark, made by a woman who was going to Milan, indicated to him that she really did not intend to spy for the Allies after all, but simply posed as an agent so that she could rejoin her family in German-held territory. With such idiotic friendly agents, who needed enemy ones?

Tompkins pondered the "insanity" of the whole operation. In his boat and in a second one following sat a total of six spies assigned to three different missions. With a single sweep, the enemy could abort all three. That, he lamented, was what came of depending on men like Captain André Bourgouin, who now sat across from him. Bourgouin had arranged this mass invasion by the U.S. Office of Strategic Services (OSS).

Yet, Tompkins, exuberant as a child playing cowboy, enjoyed his role of spy and felt proud that he would help to liberate his beloved Rome. Although his mother, a painter, and his father, a sculptor, were Americans, they had settled in Bohemian Rome when Peter was a small child. He had spent his vacations in Italy while attending school in England and in 1939 began working as a newsman in Rome. He joined the OSS when the United States entered the war, and now, at the age of twenty-four—a beard fringing his tense, dramatic face made him look older—he was undertaking the most important assignment yet given him by OSS director Major General William ("Wild Bill") Donovan.

With his intimate knowledge of Rome and perfect command of the Italian language, Tompkins seemed the ideal man for his new task —to pave the way into Rome for soldiers who would land at Anzio two days later, on the morning of January 22. He would set up an intelligence and sabotage network in the city, direct paramilitary operations, and prevent a disastrous civil war between the CLN and the Clandestine Front in the wake of German evacuation. He would arrange for a *united* insurrection in Rome.

Tompkins was hopeful that he could play a role in setting up a democratic Italy. A Fabian socialist himself, he had long deplored the pro-Badoglio policies of American and British intelligence. Badoglio's intelligence agency, SIM, and its creature, the Clandestine Front, were, he felt, still rooted in Fascism, whereas Italy's future lay in the political parties of the CLN.

Tompkins faced many difficulties—and Captain Bourgouin, in his view, was one of them. Bourgouin, a stocky, rosy-cheeked Alsatian, had been drafted into the German army in 1914, but deserted to the French and served as a spy behind the German lines. In World War II, when the Allies landed in North Africa, he helped the OSS plot the killing of pro-Vichyite officers. Though other OSS officers respected his work, Tompkins suspected that he was a double agent who wanted only to make sure that the "Monarchist-Fascists" in Italy remained in power.

Once in Rome, Peter Tompkins was determined to build his own
espionage service . . .

The engines of the torpedo boat suddenly stopped, and the craft
drifted noiselessly toward the coast. Tompkins and the others climbed
up on deck and, when they saw a green light flashing in the distance,
slipped into a yellow rubber boat, while the passengers in the second
torpedo boat followed. The two rubber craft rode the waves to shore,
where several silhouetted figures stood like phantoms in the sand. The
agents debarked and, after a silent exchange of greetings, the "phantoms" climbed aboard the two rubber craft to be taken south in the
torpedo boats.

As Bourgouin, who would return to his base, was about to leave with
them, he assured Tompkins in a nervous, staccato voice that he had
nothing to worry about. A peasant would come with a cart to take the
party to a nearby house where someone would be waiting with a car
to drive him into Rome.

On arriving at the house in the peasant's cart, Tompkins and his
companions discovered that the several other agents they found casually drinking coffee knew nothing about arrangements to get them
to their ultimate destinations. Tompkins began to suspect that Bourgouin had laid a trap. Then he learned that two of the men in the
house had chauffeured the limousine that had brought the departing
group from Rome. Although they had received no orders regarding
Tompkins, they agreed, for a large consideration, to take him and four
other agents back with them.

As the limousine zoomed off loaded down with spies, guns, and
bombs, Tompkins felt like a character in a comic gangster film. He
could only hope that if the Germans stopped the car they would simply not believe that a carload of seven spies would be speeding down a
major highway armed to the teeth.

From his earliest days, Peter had learned to concoct some kind of
story, some excuse, however ridiculous, in case he were caught in the
middle of a forbidden escapade. But he could think of nothing to
cover the present absurdity. He began to wonder if the two drivers
were German agents, feeling relieved only when the assistant driver
and one of the passengers shouted with glee on recognizing each other
as former army comrades.

Suddenly, two German soldiers waving red lanterns signaled the
limousine to stop, but the car speeded up and drove straight through
without a shot being fired. Tompkins shuddered. How many hours he
had spent learning the subtleties of infiltration!

Just before Rome, the car came to another roadblock. The chauffeur stopped this time, descended, and exhibited his papers, while a helmeted German flashed a light inside. Tompkins showed his papers, and apparently the guard was satisfied. Let's move! he wanted to cry. But one of the agents got out and casually urinated on the road.

By the time the spies crossed the Tiber into Rome, Peter Tompkins, muttering something about the "crazy Italians," was a nervous wreck.[13]

Later that morning of January 21, Tompkins suddenly awakened from a short siesta to find himself face to face with a police lieutenant. From his armchair, he stared in panic at the polished boots, arm band, and revolver.

"Don't jump!" cried the wife of the partisan whose home he was in. "It's one of our friends."

When he had recovered his composure, Tompkins was introduced to four men who had come to meet him. The OSS had infiltrated this team of Italian agents into Rome some months earlier with a radio transmitter code-named "Vittoria." It was over this radio that Tompkins would send information to Anzio after the landing, due to take place the following morning.

Tompkins sized up the four men quickly and decided he trusted only two of them: the pale young police officer, Maurizio Giglio, code-named "Cervo" (stag), who was in charge of the radio, and Franco Malfatti, a debonair man with a well-cut overcoat and expensive doeskin gloves, who gathered the intelligence for transmission.

Tompkins felt a certain distrust, however, when he looked into the dark, burrowing eyes of Mino Menicanti, code-named "Coniglio" (rabbit), who led the team and reported to Captain André Bourgouin. Nor was he favorably impressed by the fourth man. His impressions seemed confirmed when he learned that Giglio and Malfatti belonged to the Socialist party Resistance, which he respected, and that the other two worked for Badoglio's SIM, which he did not.

Giglio's father was a high Fascist police official, but the son had rebelled against him.

"For a long time," Giglio had written a friend, "I was trying to find the truth in myself, seeking feverishly where and what was the right road . . ."

He finally found it in the OSS.

Tompkins informed the team that the Allies would land "somewhere along the coast soon," and he discussed its task. Menicanti then agreed to arrange a meeting for him the following morning with the various Resistance chiefs to co-ordinate activities, and Giglio suggested that he hide in his house.

"Who," he asked, grinning, "would expect to find an American OSS agent in a Fascist policeman's bed?"

Tompkins' fear returned, and he fantasized that the whole incredible venture might simply be a cynical OSS trick to have him captured and tortured into revealing the date and place of landing—which would actually take place at another time, elsewhere. He could just see his "buddies" sitting around laughing.[14]

❖ ❖ ❖

Major Wolfgang Hagemann, Kesselring's interpreter, was fast asleep on a cot at the field marshal's headquarters in Monte Soratte early on January 22, 1944, when the telephone rang. He reached for it and his master's voice boomed:

"Wolfgang, come immediately to my office!"

"Yes, sir," replied Hagemann, who was the officer on duty. "I'll shave and come right over."

"Never mind shaving. Come now!"

Hagemann rushed down the corridor to Kesselring's office, where he found the field marshal behind his desk poring over a large map.

"Hagemann," he said without looking up, "where the hell is Aprilia? I can't find it on the map."

"Oh, it wouldn't be, sir," the interpreter responded. "It's a new town the Duce founded—near Nettuno."

As he stood behind Kesselring pointing to the approximate location, he asked, noting his commander's tense manner: "Is there anything wrong, sir?"

Kesselring, still studying the map, replied cogently: "An enemy force landed at Nettuno a couple of hours ago and there's a report they've reached Aprilia."

He added matter-of-factly: "You better pack your bags. We have no troops between Rome and Nettuno . . ."[15]

The Germans thus learned with shock that the Allies had landed at Anzio, an area they referred to as Nettuno. The Resistance had been informed about the invasion plan some hours before the landing when news of it was reported over Centro X radio and also over the radio in Monsignor O'Flaherty's quarters at the German College. The Allies declared that they would be in Rome soon and instructed the underground to rise up.

Colonel Ugo Musco, the commander of Centro X, sent word by messenger to all Clandestine Front leaders to mobilize their forces. However, General Armellini, whom Badoglio had named supreme commander of the Roman Resistance despite CLN opposition, immediately called a meeting at a Front member's house and, amid shouts, curses, pleas, and applause, flatly prohibited an insurrection. Brusquely calling for silence, he declared:

"Such action will cause useless bloodshed. I will not permit it."

Musco was furious. "But we have received orders from the Allies," he argued. "We must attack the Germans. It is our duty."

But his protest was ignored.

Actually, Armellini and his followers feared not only "useless bloodshed," but also the possibility that the leftists would gain control of an insurrection and set up their own government—even though the Allies had warned against any political activity before they arrived.*

The Front, Armellini made it clear, would move only to prevent a "Communist revolution"—unless the Germans tried to destroy Rome.

A few hours later, soon after the landing, Musco and three deputies rushed to meet an American patrol, as instructed by radio, at a village near Anzio. They stopped their car as a convoy of jeeps drew up on the road and got out to greet the Americans in the first vehicle.

"What is the situation in Rome?" asked an Italian-speaking American officer. "Will the Resistance rise up against the Germans?"

"We issued orders for an insurrection to all Resistance groups," Musco replied, too embarrassed to add that these orders had been cancelled. "But we can't guarantee that they will respond. The situation is very dangerous because the Germans are in a state of alarm and everybody is afraid."

* An American diplomat attached to Allied headquarters in Algiers reported to the State Department on January 27, 1944, that on January 22, the day of the Anzio landing, the Action party had adopted a resolution "affirming its intention of expressing the will of national resurgence (in other words, of setting up a republican leftist government) at the moment of enemy evacuation." Noting that General Armellini had requested instructions to be made known to the political leaders, the diplomat reported that the Allies proposed that "Badoglio send Armellini a telegram repeating that Allied authorities will not tolerate any open activity after German evacuation of Rome until authorized by the Allied military commander in Rome [Alexander] . . . Badoglio suggested that the message be sent by the Allied Commander-in-Chief [apparently Eisenhower] rather than by himself (apparently) due to some apprehension on Badoglio's part that it might not be obeyed." But the Allies insisted that the telegram go in Badoglio's name "rather than run the risk of disobedience of an order directly from the Commander-in-Chief."

Then Musco added: "Much depends on when your troops arrive in Rome. When can we expect them?"

The American, according to Musco, did not reply.[16]

As the Germans and Fascists frantically prepared to leave Rome, the leftists tried to harangue the Romans into a rebellious mood, ironically in accordance with Allied orders. They still planned to take over the city before the Allies arrived and set up a leftist regime if possible, despite Allied warnings against political activity.

The Communist party openly held four public meetings. Rosario Bentivegna, addressing about three hundred people at Piazza dei Mirti, shouted:

"Comrades, now is the time to kill the Germans, to chase them out of Rome! . . ."

A few Fascists suddenly appeared and, as the crowd scattered, tried to arrest Bentivegna and other Communist leaders. Firing broke out and in the ensuing battle Rosario killed two of the Fascists.

At another meeting, in Piazza Tassoni, Carla Capponi sat calmly with a pistol in hand as the speaker here, too, pleaded for an uprising. The crowd applauded—and spies scribbled names.

In general, there was little violence on either side. The Germans and the Fascists were too busy packing, and most Romans preferred cheering to chasing.[17]

The Germans might have to leave Rome "momentarily," confided Colonel Kappler to students at the Gestapo sabotage school on the morning of January 22, "but we shall not let the Allies have it to themselves, just for the asking."

The Gestapo, he revealed, was setting up huge ammunition dumps in key spots scattered around Rome, and after the evacuation, sabotage teams remaining behind would blow up the dumps and destroy at least part of the city.

That night, they would start with a dump in the park atop Pincian Hill where, in ancient times, blossomed the gardens of Lucullus, the scene of Messalina's rollicking orgies. On the nights to follow they would explode dumps on Via Stoppani, on a street in the Magliana district, and at other appropriate places.

Kappler was obeying Hitler's standing order in the event of a necessary evacuation—in fact, overdoing it a bit. The order had been to destroy specific utilities, bridges, buildings, et cetera, but there was no time to be fussy now. The Germans had been caught with their bridges and buildings down. They would now simply destroy what they could.

The Allies, if they moved swiftly, as expected, would find little opposition between Anzio and Rome, and in Rome itself the Germans had few defenders. Kappler commanded less than one hundred Gestapo men, and General Mälzer, a skeleton company composed of his office staff and hospital patients.

The Germans were nervous, even panicky. At lunch that day, Consul Möllhausen assured Colonel Dollmann that Sherman tanks were about to crash into Rome. And later Kesselring expressed the same fear. Furthermore, the field marshal thought, the Resistance was about to strike and would massacre the few Germans in and around the city; and the Allied tanks would come to their aid. Dollmann, who felt he understood the Roman character, argued otherwise.

"The Romans will never rise up," he maintained. "They like to talk but not to fight."

"Only a miracle and your faith can save us," Kesselring replied.

And he continued packing . . . while Kappler laid plans for blowing up Rome.

Kappler selected three trainees for that night's work. One of them was a one-armed young man named Michele Coppola, who was considered by the Gestapo instructor, Major Aars, one of his brightest pupils. And so he was. That was why Admiral Maugeri, the commander of the naval Resistance, was hopeful that Coppola, one of his agents, could sabotage the sabotage operation.

Coppola, a Tunisian-born Italian, had joined Maugeri's organization several weeks earlier. A former pilot, he had lost his arm in combat fighting for a cause he had gradually come to despise. Maugeri had placed Coppola in the Roman telephone exchange at first; Coppola determined which partisan numbers were being tapped and listened in to conversations of the Gestapo, the German armed forces, the police, and various enemy headquarters.

One day, a fellow boarder in his *pensione* began to talk with him about working for the Gestapo, and Coppola encouraged him until he could get instructions from Maugeri. The admiral was reluctant at first, feeling that Coppola, still inexperienced in intelligence work, might make a mistake that could doom the whole organization.

But he finally agreed, and Coppola enrolled in the Gestapo sabotage training school. Within three weeks, he had become an expert in the manufacture of bombs, fuses, time clocks, and booby traps.

And now he was ready for his final examination—the destruction of Rome![18]

"If anyone stops you, just say, 'Police!'" Maurizio Giglio whispered to Peter Tompkins a few hours after the Anzio landing as they sped through Rome on a police motorcycle to the meeting with Resistance leaders that Mino Menicanti had arranged.

Wearing an old, gray police overcoat and a battered Borsalino over his eyes, Tompkins, certain that every German they passed recognized him, could only mumble through chattering teeth: "*Sicuro!*" ("Sure!").

They finally arrived at the meeting place, and Tompkins followed Giglio up a dark stairway to a cold, dusty, unfurnished apartment where they found a motley group of overcoated men waiting for them. As Tompkins explained his mission, he noted that they showed little interest. Only one man, Giuliano Vassalli, seemed to care.

Tompkins was depressed. Except for Vassalli, these men clearly were not eager for military action or anything resembling insurrection. After the meeting he learned that Vassalli was a partisan leader of the Socialist party and the only CLN representative present. The others were not partisans, but a "*camarilla* of agents" for industrial complexes who offered useful information, according to Tompkins, either to the Germans so they would not sabotage their investments or to the Allies so they would not bomb these investments.

Peter was sure that Menicanti had arranged the meeting to deceive him into thinking that these were the real Resistance leaders. Menicanti apparently wanted to prevent him from helping the CLN to launch an insurrection.

Civil war now seemed a greater threat than ever, and Tompkins' anxiety grew when he learned that Colonel Montezemolo, without consulting the CLN, had assigned his officers various targets to be occupied the moment the Germans began to retreat.

Nor did tension diminish when General Presti, who, at least theoretically, was chief of all Italian police forces in Rome, reportedly said that his men would crush an insurrection. His most important force, the Italian African Police (PAI), which had served in North Africa before the Allies arrived, ostensibly supported Nazi "law and order," though many members acted against the partisans with great reluctance and even helped them in some cases. The Allies would presumably thank Presti for stopping a "Communist revolution."

CLN president Bonomi pleaded with the CLN forces not to risk a clash with the Clandestine Front. But the CLN leftists were determined to carry through an insurrection against all opposition and despite the apparent apathy of most Romans. And the Red Flag party was prepared to join them.

Tompkins felt that the only way to avert a civil conflict at this stage was to have everyone attack the Germans at once, but a catalyst action was necessary for such an operation. The answer, he decided, would be an Allied paratroop landing in the city.

He immediately started planning one. The drop would take place in Villa Borghese, Rome's public park, at the head of Via Veneto, and would be protected by Giglio's mounted police squadron, which regularly patrolled and drilled in this area. The remaining partisan forces would then join in the assault. If the operation went well, not only would Rome be liberated in a single coup, but the entire German defense in southern Italy might collapse. He hopefully radioed his plan to Anzio headquarters.

Vassalli then arranged with the CLN military committee, headed by Riccardo Bauer of the Action party, to meet with Tompkins in Giglio's house. As the group sat around the dining room table smoking cheap Italian cigarettes, they discussed plans for an insurrection and the protection of Rome. But Tompkins decided not to reveal his proposal for a paratroop drop until he received approval from the base.

Giglio then entered with a message—from the base. The Resistance was not to move on any account. The liberation of Rome was temporarily postponed. The paratroop drop would be held in abeyance.

The Resistance leaders were shocked at the news. What was holding the Allies up? How long would they have to postpone their insurrection?

The word came back: Indefinitely! Hesitating too long on the beachhead, the Allied forces were being hemmed in by the Germans. Kesselring unpacked his bags, and Kappler canceled the destruction of Rome.

The Romans shrugged their shoulders once again. Whatever happened, Rome was, after all, Eternal.

And so life in Rome continued as before—except for the Resistance. Too many spies had identified too many partisans who had come out from underground in the euphoria of imminent liberation.[19]

6

The Traps

Michele Coppola, Admiral Maugeri's one-armed agent, who had been slated to assist in the destruction of Rome, was called to the German Embassy on February 27 for assignment to another daring mission. The Germans, explained Major Aars, his Gestapo boss, were preparing a massive offensive against the Anzio beachhead that would throw the Allies into the sea, and Coppola would take part in a diversionary operation behind the Allied lines.

With three other saboteurs, he would go by boat from Fossa Incastro, a village about twelve miles from Rome on the right flank of the German line, circle around the no-man's land between the two sides, and sail to the mouth of the narrow Moletta River, only about seven hundred yards from the tip of the Allied left flank.

Their first objective was to destroy by dynamite the tank repair facility that was operating near the beach. The second, and more important, objective was to blow up the advance Allied headquarters. The action would take place when, according to intelligence reports, Generals Alexander and Clark were in the headquarters.

Coppola could hardly wait to report the news of his mission to Admiral Maugeri, but his instructions required that he and the three other members of his team remain in the Embassy until they left Rome three days later. Coppola was frantic. He must alert Maugeri.

Fortunately, the Germans had neglected to provide flashlights in the equipment issued to him and the other saboteurs, giving Coppola an excuse to ask Major Aars for permission to leave.

"*Jawohl*," Aars replied. "Go and get them."

But another saboteur must accompany him.

Coppola desperately argued that every man was needed to process and pack the equipment.

"After all, you know, I can manage to carry four flashlights by myself."

Aars considered the question for several moments while Coppola held his breath. Finally, the German agreed. Coppola rushed directly to the home of another agent, who telephoned Coppola's contact with Maugeri. Coppola then dashed out to buy the flashlights and returned by the time his contact had arrived. As no time remained to ask Maugeri for a decision, the contact, a man named Sandrelli, instructed Coppola:

"Go ahead with it and do everything you can to wreck it once you get out to sea."

Sandrelli reported the sabotage plans to Maugeri, who, in turn, was able to send a message to the Fifth Army through Centro X radio. The message gave details of the plot, including the date, time, and place. A few hours later the Fifth Army replied:

FOR FRANCO [Maugeri's first name] STOP SPECIFY EXACT POSITIONS STOP POINTS INDICATED BY YOU ALL BEHIND PRESENT GERMAN LINES STOP

Maugeri was dismayed. Had the Germans given the saboteurs false information for security reasons? There was no longer any way to check the facts with Coppola. The admiral responded:

IMPOSSIBLE CHECK FURTHER STOP DETAILS PLACE, DATE, TIME MAY BE IN ERROR STOP BUT ATTACK DEFINITELY PLANNED STOP YOU ARE NOW ALERTED STOP FRANCO

Now he would simply have to wait for the prearranged signal over the BBC to know what happened. If Coppola succeeded in aborting the attack, BBC would announce:

"Francesco and Francesca have arrived."

The sabotage team left Rome on February 29 for Ardea, headquarters of the German zonal command, and that evening set out on foot for the beach, carrying their boat and equipment. On arrival, they found the sea raging in strong winds and a driving rain.

"With such a sea and that wind," Coppola said, trying to gain time, "we'll all drown."

Two of the saboteurs, Bianconi and Cattani, seemed undecided. But the remaining one, Franco, the most dedicated Fascist among them, wanted to sail regardless, though he finally relented after Bianconi supported Coppola. The team hid the boat and equipment in some bushes and went back to Ardea.

The next evening they returned to the beach and found the sea still very rough, though the wind had calmed and the rain had ceased. Coppola urged a further postponement until the sea was smoother, but this time he was overruled. The four embarked in their small boat and were buffeted from wave to wave while Franco urged them ahead with the reminder that "Italy's honor" was at stake. The craft simply plowed around in circles.

Coppola argued that at this rate they would arrive at their destination after daylight, when it would be impossible to carry out their mission.

"Besides," he added, "even if we should get there before dawn, all our equipment will be useless. The powder, fuses and detonators are soaked already."

The boat was returned to shore. But sooner or later, Coppola realized, conditions would permit the boat to sail.

Only on March 9, ten days later, did the weather finally clear, and now Coppola had no further excuse to delay the operation. He was able to assume the job of steering the boat, however, and instead of following the preconceived plan of sailing south close to the shoreline, he swung the craft in a wide arc hoping to meet Allied patrol vessels further out to sea. None happened by and Franco began asking what time it was and when they would land. At 11 P.M., Coppola felt he could stall no longer.

He released the tiller, took a grenade from a pile of ammunition, and, in a steady voice, told his fellow passengers that he was an agent of the King and the Allies and that he was going to head for shore and surrender to the Allies.

When the shock had dissipated, Franco roared: "Not while I'm in this boat!"

And as he started toward Coppola, the one-armed agent tightened the fingers of his one hand on the firing pin and warned: "One more step, Franco, and I'll blow all of us to bits!"

Franco hesitated for a moment, perhaps because of the deadly calmness of Coppola's voice. Then he sat down, cursing.

"Now, my friends," said Coppola, as he laid the grenade beside him and reached for the tiller again, "you'll row for all you're worth while I make for shore."

An hour later, about midnight, the boat ground into the sandy shore and, with the grenade in hand again, Coppola instructed Cattani to unload the explosives. When Cattani had done so, Coppola ordered him back into the craft while he himself got out. He then pulled the pin on the grenade and raised his arm to throw it. The three men in the

Left, Lt. Gen. Mark W. Clark
and his dog Pal
near front line south of Rome.

Below, General Clark,
Gen. Sir Harold Alexander,
Lt. Gen. John Harding
(behind Alexander),
Lt. Gen. Joseph T. McNarney
(Deputy Supreme Allied Commander
of the Mediterranean Theater),
and Maj. Gen. Lyman L. Lemnitzer
confer in Clark's hut.

French Gen. Alphonse Juin (in beret) with Gen. Charles de Gaulle.

Lt. Gen. Sir Oliver Leese and Gen. Wladyslaw Anders relax between battles.

Maj. Gen. Lucian K. Truscott before his hut.

2nd Lt. Charles W. Shea wearing Congressional Medal of Honor.

Monte Cassino as seen from Hills 593 and 569.

British soldiers in Cassino town use sketch of Hitler to draw German fire.

French Capt. Pierre Planès.

French Ambulance Driver Colette Planès.

The *goumiers* on the attack.

French Maj. Gen. Augustin Guillaume, commander of the *goumiers*.

French troops advance through the mountains.

German Field Marshal Albert Kesselring (facing), with Hitler and Mussolini.

Above, German War Crimes defendants Gen. Kurt Mälzer (second row right) and Gen. Eberhard von Mackensen (second row center) in courtroom during trial in Rome after the war.

Left, SS Gen. Karl Wolff.

boat gasped, but the missile sailed over their heads and landed in the sea with a great explosion that sent a wall of water into the black sky.

Suddenly, machine guns crackled in the distance, and Coppola and his fellows, soaked in the spray, fell flat on their stomachs. Shortly, a dozen shadowy figures emerged from inland with rifles drawn . . .

In Rome, Admiral Maugeri anxiously listened to the BBC, waiting for the words that would signal Coppola's success. Each day he searched the newspapers for a clue. What could have happened? It had been so long, yet not a word. The German offensive against the Anzio beachhead had already failed, though only after a desperate Allied stand. Then, one afternoon, he read an item vaguely referring to an "attempt" on General Clark's life, but the details and the outcome were not indicated.

Some days later, as he sat by his radio, a BBC announcer, to Maugeri's great joy, declared: "Francesco and Francesca have arrived."[1]

※   ※   ※

Daisy Marchi, her voluptuous, bronzed body almost completely nude, reclined luxuriously in the lap of her lover, Pietro Koch, her face flushed and her dark eyes shining, as she watched and listened to the screams of the man being tortured. Daisy, or Dusnella, was not always present when Koch, head of the Special Department of the Police of the Republic, observed his men at work beating and kicking their victim, burning delicate parts of the body, pulling out hair, tearing off fingernails, sticking pins in bruised flesh. After all, Daisy, an exotic dancer, was only Koch's second mistress, a girl he had recently met. His first, Tamara Cerri, had priority for the seat of honor Daisy now occupied.

No less enthralled by the sadistic entertainment in the former *pensione* that served as Koch's headquarters, was one of his secretaries, Marcella Stoppani, who found in it poetic inspiration. In fact, she wrote a poem, often read, like a benediction, at dinner in honor of the men she so faithfully served, body and soul:

> *Those . . . who defy the Duce . . .*
> *Must reckon with a band.*
> *Pietro Koch commands it.*
> *He carefully makes a plan,*
> *And Tela gives him a hand . . .*

> There's no cure for Mase's punch,
> But Giorgio . . . isn't joking either . . .
>   Di Franco's heart flutters with love . . .
> And the man next door rejoices, too.
>   What are those shrieks?
> Is Brilli at work again?
>   Or Pallon with his large fists? . . .
> The Communist, his face sad . . .
>   Says what he must,
> The certain result . . .
>   This band belongs to Koch,
> And I, like all of you, shout
>   "The Duce for us!"

Koch's band was one big happy family. There were those who loved, like Walter Di Franco, who had just met the pretty young wife of a Red Flag partisan, Viviana Chilanti. There was the pious priest, the jolly *portiere*, the endearing cook. And there was Pietro Koch himself, a suave, gentle-mannered man, only twenty-six, with brilliantined black hair, a short, trim mustache, and a refined vocabulary who would not even touch his victims—without gloves.

Koch had set up shop in Rome at a most opportune time—just before the Anzio landing. Many of the underground leaders had surfaced in expectation of an imminent Allied capture of Rome. It would now be simple to trap them one by one and torture them into talking. Giulio Tamburini, Mussolini's national police chief, would not be sorry for assigning him a task which others had bungled.

The Duce was a proud leader. True, the Germans had occupied Italy, but as his ally. They had no right, he felt, to monopolize the police function. He had to admit, however, that his regular Fascist police force in Rome lacked the ideological militancy to handle this function with the necessary ardor. And, of course, the Italian African Police (PAI) was utterly useless, even treacherous. Ruthless men were needed, men who would not hesitate to use any means to obtain information, men who could show the Nazis a thing or two about dealing with the enemy.

When the Nazis occupied Rome, Tamburini had thus set up a "special police department" in Braschi Palace, Fascist party headquarters, under the supervision of three reputed hoodlums and killers—Pollastrini, Bardi, and Franquinet. The trouble was that they often arrested people on false charges so that they could steal their possessions and obtain ransoms for their release. Soon the palace became not only a torture house, but a storehouse—for stolen goods that included clothes, foodstuffs, cigarettes, and even a live cow!

Colonel Dollmann and Consul Möllhausen, among other Germans, were scandalized. What right did the Italian Fascists have to behave like the German Nazis—torturing people and stealing their wealth? Right or wrong, the Nazis at least acted in defense of an ideal. And they tortured only legitimate suspects and stole only from the guilty—except, of course, for the Jews. The Italians, however, were simply gangsters.

Dollmann even moralized about the "scandal" to Kappler, whose own torture chambers at his headquarters on Via Tasso were among the most efficiently operated in Nazi Europe, and Kappler agreed that a "cleanup" was necessary. No opportunistic Italians were going to compete with him!

Dollmann summoned Möllhausen, Kappler, and Tamburini to a meeting at which the Germans ordered Tamburini to eliminate the "disgrace." Finally, in late November 1943, Tamburini agreed, after great pressure was exerted on the Salò government.

While the Fascist police chief disarmed his "special policemen" and sent them north, Kappler inspected the store of goods that the Fascists had accumulated, and the sight only confirmed to him the crudity of the Italian people. While he collected art treasures from his victims, they collected cows!

The Duce and Tamburini were not inclined to suffer this humiliation for long. They decided to establish another "special police department" in Rome, and this one would be led by a fanatical ideologist paid enough so that he would not be tempted to steal from just anyone. He would be a man the Germans could respect, a man with polish and perhaps some culture. And Pietro Koch, who liked to call himself "Doctor," seemed to fill the bill.

Actually, Koch did not even have a secondary school diploma, for he had been expelled at fifteen after he had unblushingly masturbated in front of the girls in his class. Always a winner at poker, always a "lady-killer," he harbored a supreme sense of self-confidence and domination over others that gradually manifested itself in the sadism that he would come to relish.

"Hate is a feeling," he once confided to a friend, "that makes me vibrate far more than love. Even that of women."

And the armistice between Italy and the Allies gave Koch an ideal outlet for his hate. For though his mother was Italian, his father was German, and he would never forget the words of his father when he,

Pietro, had left Rome, where his parents and estranged wife lived, to fight on the German side:

"Convince yourself that the Germans are a strong nation. Even if they don't win the war, they will fight it like victors. Behave like them."

When Italy "betrayed" Germany by signing the armistice, Koch took his father's advice and went to see Tamburini, pleading that he wanted to avenge the Italian betrayal. He started out as a member of a police group in Florence and proved so brutally competent that Tamburini sent him to Rome in January 1944 to run his own group.

The Nazis resented him despite his German blood and militant belief in Fascism, but found him useful, especially after the Anzio landing. Many Jews and Communists were now locked up in what Koch humorously called his "sad room," a chamber that could hold any number of maimed and groaning victims.

Indeed, Koch's band was a model of efficiency compared to its predecessors. Walter Di Franco had even managed to infiltrate the Action party. And Daisy Marchi could be helpful, too, though it is not clear that Koch realized how helpful. Her former boy friend belonged to the Clandestine Front . . .[2]

Nicola Onorati first met Daisy a few days after the armistice when he had fled to Rome from Verona, where he had been stationed as an Italian army lieutenant. His unit had surrendered to the Germans, but he had managed to escape from his barracks by obtaining permission from a German guard to let him visit his "pregnant wife." He then vanished into the home of his mistress who lived nearby and finally left to stay with his parents in Rome.

Onorati immediately found work with his good friend Rudi Clair, a famous tap dancer and show business impresario, who hired him as a publicity man for a new variety show. One of the stars of the show was Daisy Marchi, a beautiful brunette dancer of modest origin and simple mind, for whom Rudi had obtained special permission from his police friends to perform virtually in the nude.

Onorati often visited her apartment, but secretly spent most of his time in his father's printing shop, which published propaganda material for the Resistance. Soon he found himself working for the Clandestine Front. Among the documents he printed were copies of a German labor contract which permitted the holders to collect wages from the War Ministry. Thus, hundreds of Resistance members were able to collect salaries without actually working.

One day Onorati returned to Verona to see his other mistress, and the police, searching for him, arrested her as a hostage while Onorati escaped. He tried to obtain the girl's freedom through army friends intimidated into working with the Germans but was told that she would be released only if he gave himself up.

"And if you do," warned an army friend, "they will shoot you. They know you are working for the Resistance."

Onorati was stunned. How would the police in Verona know that? Who could have talked? He had kept his activities secret even from Daisy . . .

He rushed back to Rome and found that the police had closed his father's printing house and that his father had gone into hiding. Onorati then moved in with Daisy and, fully trusting her, told her the whole story—except for the part about his other mistress.

For good luck, she gave him a gold religious medal. He would need it, since Pietro Koch was attending Daisy's show at the Galleria di Roma Theater ever more frequently.

One night, during a performance applauded by high-ranking Germans and Fascists sitting in the front stalls, the police arrested Rudi Clair for having publicly exhibited a "defeatist" attitude. Daisy intervened with Koch, and soon Onorati moved out of her apartment. Daisy had found a new love—and life.

And now, on many nights after work, she emerged from the stage door laden with jewelry and furs, to be taken by chauffeur-driven car to Koch's quarters. In scanty attire, apparently to add to the excitement, *she* would now be the spectator, with some of Onorati's partisan comrades the involuntary performers.

The "sad room," from which they emerged like bulls to the *corrida*, contained some distinguished names, any one of whom might have left the bloody imprint of a pleading hand that stained one of its walls like a grotesque seal of death. One occupant was Luchino Visconti, the film director, who had hidden weapons in his house. Another was Ferruccio P., nephew of a high-ranking Vatican official, whom Koch had arrested for making advances to Daisy but had been forced to release after powerful intervention.

Nicola Onorati, who suspected that Daisy had denounced him, doubted that he would be that lucky if Koch ever laid his hands on him. He managed, despite a number of close calls, to elude him.[3]

❖   ❖   ❖

Denunciations were far from a rarity in the wake of Anzio, or even earlier. The Nazis and Fascists had begun a serious clamp down on the Resistance about three weeks before the landing. The arrest of several members of Monsignor O'Flaherty's organization, including John Furman and Joe Pollak, early in January 1944, was followed by that of Father Morosini, who had given weapons and military information to the *carabinieri*.

A youth named Dante Bruna, whom Morosini had befriended, had planted an automatic pistol in the priest's linen trunk. The police then came, "found" the pistol, and arrested Morosini and a fellow partisan, Lieutenant Marcello Bucchi. While Bruna collected a 70,000-lire reward, the police took the cleric and Bucchi to the station and tried—unsuccessfully—to beat information out of them. When one German inquisitor, hoping for an excuse to free the young priest, asked him what he would do if liberated, he replied without hesitation:

"I would continue to do what I did before."

The two partisans were taken to Regina Coeli prison, and Morosini composed a "pastoral fantasy" dedicated to his "unforgettable comrade of ideals and of imprisonment, Marcello Bucchi," a piece of music full of joy and delicacy culminating in a triumphal hymn. In the evening he would recite the rosary in his warm, resonant voice, and the prisoners in neighboring cells would respond:

"*Sancta Maria, mater Dei, ora pro nobis peccatoribus nunc et in ora mortis nostrae.*" (Holy Mary, Mother of God, pray for us sinners now and at the hour of our death.)

And the hour of death was near for Father Morosini. His execution was set for March 20, and everything was ready—the execution squad, the coffin, the grave dug at Verano cemetery. Only the Pope could possibly save him.[4]

❋   ❋   ❋

Disaster also threatened Admiral Maugeri's underground network in early January. The hunters in this case were the men of Captain Valerio Borghese, Pietro Koch's naval counterpart and his bitter foe. Borghese, supported by the Germans, was believed by Mussolini to be plotting against some members of his government, and the Duce had charged Koch with keeping an eye on him. But Borghese and Koch had much in common; both were fanatical Fascists determined to stamp out every spark of anti-Fascism.

Borghese belonged to one of Italy's noblest and most famous families, a family that had given Italy popes, statesmen, princes, and generals.

And Maugeri had long admired the husky captain as a courageous born leader, dominating, yet charming and gracious, but since September 8, Boghese's charm and grace had dissolved in hatred, vengeance, and brutality. He had turned his organization, the Tenth MAS Flotilla, which he still commanded, if without ships, into a bloodthirsty machine to trap, torture, and murder his enemies. And his principal enemy was Admiral Maugeri.

One day, Borghese's men stormed into one of Maugeri's hideouts, but found only the admiral's orderly, Seaman Salvatore Russo. They kept him there as bait in the hope that other partisans would return, and indeed, one of Maugeri's deputies, Giuseppe Libotti, did stop by. As Libotti waited for the elevator to take him to the apartment, Russo and his guards, returning from an interrogation in Borghese's head-quarters, entered from outside and everybody crowded into the elevator together, with Russo and Libotti giving no sign of recognition. Russo and his guards got off on the fourth floor, but Libotti continued on to the sixth, then raced downstairs and over to the apartment where he and Maugeri were now staying.

The admiral and his men now could avoid the trap, but would Russo, a sly, lazy, sentimental Neapolitan, who knew much about the organization, talk? Two days later Libotti answered the phone and Russo was on the line. Only one sailor was guarding him now, Russo said, and he had been "working on" that guard. The sailor periodically went out to buy food, cigarettes, newspapers, and wine for him.

"That's why I'm able to call you now," he explained. "I just sent the idiot to fetch me a bottle of wine."

Libotti asked why Russo didn't just run off, since he was left un-guarded.

"Ah," retorted Russo, "but you forget our friend the *portiere!* Be-sides, they may have some guards posted downstairs, by the elevator."

Russo hung up abruptly, and Libotti reported the conversation to Maugeri, suggesting that they rescue Russo. After all, if he talked . . . The admiral agreed.

A plan was then drawn up calling for a half dozen men to enter the building in which Russo was being held at different times within a half hour period, then at the appointed time to converge upon the apartment, let themselves in with Maugeri's key, and overwhelm Russo's single guard. Maugeri and Libotti then warned Russo through a bribed employee in the building that they were "thinking of him" and that he would be hearing from them within three days.

They were welcomed warmly—by the Fascists. Russo had betrayed them, after being threatened with torture and death.

The naval Resistance, with an informer in Fascist hands and some of its best men arrested, was seriously compromised.

Then came the army's turn . . .[5]

❖   ❖   ❖

On January 25, three days after the Anzio landing, Colonel Montezemolo, who had joined other military refugees in Princess Nini Pallavicini's huge palace (he had moved out of the home of his cousin, Marchesa Ripa di Meana), rose early. He was to attend several meetings that day to arrange for the triumphal entry of the Allied beachhead forces, which, he was certain, would arrive in a few days. As soon as the Germans departed, his Clandestine Front would move immediately to take over the utilities, ministries, and other public buildings, making sure that the CLN forces did not occupy them first. He was aware that the very existence of the monarchy and the traditional social system was at stake.

Montezemolo's paramilitary troops would co-operate with the CLN groups to prevent the Germans from destroying Rome as they left. After all, they were fighting a common enemy, a brutal enemy that had aroused in his people, of whatever political shading, a sense of national pride they had seldom felt in the recent past. But the Communists and other leftists could not be permitted to rule the nation. Montezemolo was sure the Allies would understand why General Armellini and he were not supporting an insurrection, despite instructions to the contrary.

At breakfast that morning, the princess recalls, she tried to dissuade Montezemolo from leaving the palace.

"It is too dangerous to leave," she pleaded. "You are easy to recognize and they are looking for you."

"It's my duty," the colonel replied calmly.

Montezemolo put on his dark glasses, picked up a briefcase, and walked to the door.

"Don't worry," he again reassured the princess. "I'll be back before five o'clock."

Montezemolo's first meeting that morning was with the Clandestine Front leaders at an apartment on Via Sant' Agata dei Goti to discuss the missions that various groups would undertake to grab control of the city.

In the afternoon he met with General Armellini, Michele Multedo, the painter who had helped to bring important people into the Front, and Filippo Grenet, the Italian diplomat in whose home the group had gathered.

At about 3 P.M., after they had agreed, in an atmosphere heavy with tension and excitement, on last-minute preparations for saving Rome and greeting the Allies, the four men drained their coffee cups and left the house. As Armellini and Multedo descended the stairs, they saw three SS cars parked down the street.

"Don't turn!" Multedo recalls Armellini muttering. "Walk straight ahead!"

While they crossed the street with calculated casualness and escaped, Montezemolo and Grenet came down the stairs and were greeted by SS men at the bottom.[6]

❖   ❖   ❖

Pietro Koch was disgruntled. More than a week had passed since the Anzio landing, and he had failed to catch the biggest fish. His archfoe, naval Captain Borghese, had captured many of Admiral Maugeri's men, and the Germans had arrested Colonel Montezemolo.

Now Koch would have to come through with a coup or the Duce and Tamburini, the national police chief, might think his (Koch's) police gang was ineffectual. And he was already under German pressure to disband. He had to capture more men to torture into betraying still others.

The answer, he decided, lay in a sensational strike against one of the religious institutions harboring traitors and Jews. He was experienced at such an operation. About six weeks earlier, on December 21, 1943, his men had surrounded a group of papal buildings at Piazza Santa Maria Maggiore and invaded some of them, notably the Lombardo Seminary, bagging forty-seven refugees whom they beat mercilessly before dragging them off to Koch's torture house.

Now his gang must invade a bigger, more important institution, but for such an operation he would need the co-operation of the regular Rome Fascist police. He therefore discussed the question with the new head of this force, General Pietro Caruso, and the two men contacted

Tamburini, who, apparently after speaking with Mussolini, indicated such an operation would be useful.

Together Koch and Caruso laid plans to invade the Basilica of San Paolo fuori le Mura and the adjoining Benedictine monastery, which, they suspected, were bulging with military refugees, Jews, weapons, and loot.

At 11:40 P.M., on February 3, 1943, the night bell of the monastery began to ring. An old monk on guard duty peered out of the window and saw in the moonlight two robed friars standing at a side door beside their car.

"What do you wish?" the doorkeeper called out.

In pronounced Tuscan accents, the two strangers replied that they had just arrived from a monastery in Florence and would like shelter for the night.

"Very well," said the doorkeeper. "I'll be right down."

While the old monk went to open the door, a palatine guard in the garden of the monastery saw several figures climbing over the wall.

"Who goes there?" he shouted.

When no reply came, he cried: "Halt!"

But still to no avail. He then fired into the air the single bullet in his 1891 model rifle and ran into the monastery to inform the other guards. On his way he met the old monk heading toward the side door and excitedly told him what happened. The monk, seeing no connection between the transgressors and the two friars requesting entry, continued on, accompanied by the palatine guard.

The monk pulled back the bolt of the door and was nearly knocked over as the door swung wide open and the two "friars," followed by four other men in black shirts decorated with skulls, femurs, and other macabre symbols, pushed their way in waving pistols and submachine guns. They disarmed the palatine guard, then dashed into the doorkeeper's room and cut the telephone wires. Simultaneously, while Caruso and about three hundred of his Fascist police surrounded the grounds, dozens of other black-shirted members of the Koch band, led by Koch himself, stormed into both the monastery and the basilica and disarmed the remaining palatine guards, blocked off the corridors, and broke into room after room searching for prey and booty and scattering copies of clandestine newspapers as "evidence" of subversion.

Refugees—Jews, military officers, draft-dodgers—staying in the monastery were herded into a large room on the ground floor and ordered to stand against the wall. Koch and several of his men walked down the line of people, stopping to ask questions and beat people with pistol butts and fists, kick them, and spit in their faces. They accused the monks of plotting against the government and, confronting them with the planted "evidence," forced them to sign a "confession" that they were in possession of subversive literature.

Meanwhile, a representative of the Pope, Count Enrico Galeazzi, arrived and demanded that the transgressors leave the prisoners alone and depart, stressing that the building and grounds were extraterritorial property under Vatican jurisdiction.

"I am acting on orders from my government," Caruso replied.

"Tell your government," Galeazzi answered, "that even the Bolsheviks, against whom you say you want to defend Europe, respected all the Apostolic Nunciates during the occupation of the Baltic countries!"

Caruso then revealed that his men had found weapons hidden in the monastery—the weapons placed there by the Clandestine Front for use against either the Germans or the leftists.

"They can keep even tanks here if they like!" Galeazzi replied. "And you know that perfectly well."

Caruso started to waver, but Koch remained adamant, loudly insisting that they could not disobey orders from above. In the end, strangely enough, Caruso and Koch agreed to leave the weapons in place, but they refused to free the prisoners or force their men to give up the loot they had already divided up in the courtyard.

Caruso and Koch had harvested a rich crop: sixty-seven persons, including a general, Adriano Monti, who was dressed as a priest, ten other officers, twenty noncommissioned officers, and the rest Jews and young draft dodgers. And the loot, including more than a million lire in cash, as well as jewelry and other valuables, would keep the Fascist police viable for some time.[7]

The Vatican lodged a strong protest with Ambassador von Weizsäcker, and Weizsäcker's assistant, Albrecht von Kessel, rushed to the office of Consul Möllhausen and with a nervous stutter asked him to read the text. Möllhausen took it and perused it gravely.

"From the tone of this," he said, "I don't think the Vatican will accept any further infringement of its sovereignty."

Kessel agreed. The Church, they realized, regarded the daily capture, torture, deportation, and murder of individuals as bad; but the Pope had not spoken out against these actions. However, it appeared from this protest that the Pope viewed the violation of Church property as intolerable. It might just be the act, they feared, that would end his silence.

When Kessel had left, Möllhausen called General Caruso to the German Embassy and communicated the Vatican's protest to him. Weizsäcker, the consul reminded him, had countersigned the letters of protection conferred on the religious institutions, and the Italian police must honor these commitments.

"These observations are incomprehensible," Caruso replied, his face expressionless. "I reported by telephone to the Duce, and he told me: 'Excellent, continue!'"

Möllhausen called Ambassador Rahn in Fasano, and Rahn requested guidance from Ribbentrop in Berlin, suggesting German intervention. But Ribbentrop replied that the Germans should not "in such circumstances . . . obstruct the Italian government."

However, when the Spanish government complained to the Germans that the San Paolo attack was bitterly resented in Catholic Spain, Ribbentrop, not wishing trouble with Spain during this critical period in the war, changed his mind. He killed Fascist plans to "clean out" the religious institutions, at least temporarily.

Near panic, nevertheless, gripped the thousands of refugees hiding in churches, monasteries, convents, and other Catholic establishments throughout Rome, who expected to be arrested at any moment. In the Convent of Notre Dame de Sion, Giacomo Di Porto and his pregnant wife Eleanora considered trying to find refuge elsewhere. Their baby would be born in April; and what if they were in prison then? But where would they go? Where would it be safer? Where, indeed, for any of the refugees?[8]

Among the most fearful refugees were some of the top uncaptured leaders of the Resistance, whom the Fascists might now put out of business. The Seminary of San Giovanni in Laterano, where they were hiding, had been, in fact, the next target on the Fascist list—until Ribbentrop intervened.

In one section of the seminary compound lived the principal political chiefs of the CLN, including its president, Ivanoe Bonomi, who was constantly conferring with his colleagues over the question of how the CLN would rule the nation after Rome's liberation.

Especially at home there was Alcide De Gasperi of the theocratic Christian Democratic party, who knelt in prayer at every Mass. Left-wing Socialist Pietro Nenni, on the other hand, sometimes attended out of respect for his benefactors, but in a cynically erect posture. He felt that if there were a God, He could hardly, under the circumstances, save one politician without saving them all.

In another area were the most important surviving leaders of the Clandestine Front: General Armellini, who had managed to escape the Gestapo when it arrested Colonel Montezemolo, and Ugo Musco and Felice Santini, the Centro X chiefs. Centro X headquarters had moved from Villa Savoia, the King's abandoned residence, after the Anzio landing, and now Musco and Santini operated one of their two radios here.

They transmitted information brought by their agents with the secret approval of a Vatican official in San Giovanni, Monsignor Pietro Palazzini, though it is not clear that his superior, Monsignor Roberto Ronca, who was directly responsible to the Vatican, was even aware of the radio's presence until much later—when the Vatican would exert great pressure for its removal. Needless to say, the danger of a raid grew with every radio signal transmitted.

The concentration of Clandestine Front leaders in one confined area did not make for harmony. Friction had already developed between Armellini and Musco on the morning of the Anzio landing, when Musco opposed Armellini's order to halt plans for an insurrection. Now, with the Fascists raiding even religious institutions, frayed nerves, aggravated by the cramped quarters, produced new conflicts.

The explosion came at dinnertime a few days after the San Paolo transgression, when a priest burst in with an alarm that Fascists were about to storm San Giovanni. Everybody jumped to their feet, sending cups of barley soup (which substituted for coffee) spinning through the air, and arguments began anew.

"Destroy the radio!" Armellini shouted.

Three times he yelled this order, but Musco and Santini refused to obey.

"It's our only weapon!" cried Musco.

Meanwhile, two radio technicians ran out, took the transmitter apart, and hid the pieces behind the altar in the basilica and in other preassigned places.

Finally, after guards fired several times, the prowlers, apparently a small group of Fascists, vanished, everyone calmed down, and the radio, if not the Clandestine Front, was put together again.

The San Paolo raid, coming after the Allied failure to break out of Anzio and the capture of some top partisan leaders, terrified the Romans—the Resistance and the passive majority alike. If even the Vatican was powerless before the Germans and Fascists, what would happen to the people of Rome? Fewer of them shrugged their shoulders now, as more were arrested each day.[9]

❖   ❖   ❖

"That bastard Perfetti has gone over to the Boche!"

French Vice Consul François de Vial of the French Mutual Aid

Committee spat these words with a mixed expression of shock and fury as he sat with Major Sam Derry, the Vatican "ghost," in the apartment of British Minister Osborne, where the major was now secretly living.

Derry was not really surprised. He had never trusted the sleazy Pasqualino Perfetti, the man who had worn priest's clothing at their meeting when he had entered Rome on his way to the Vatican. That was why he had let Perfetti gradually slip out of Monsignor O'Flaherty's organization, although Perfetti had continued to find billets for French escapers.

"We knew Perfetti had been arrested," De Vial said, "but we were not too worried. We thought it was all routine. Then we heard that he was about again, limping heavily, and obviously badly battered about the head and face. And, *mon Dieu*, he was not alone. He was with the Gestapo. Sometimes in a car, sometimes on foot, he was guiding them from place to place. We lost a dozen billets before we could do anything, and a lot of our men have been taken in by that Fascist gang and badly beaten up."

Perfetti was now working for Koch, whose agents threatened the whole Rome escape line with their arrests. The traitor had denounced not only Frenchmen, but British and American escapers as well.

Derry, however, was able at first to keep these arrests to a minimum with the help of Bill Simpson, as well as John Furman and Joe Pollak, who had both turned up again after miraculously escaping from German captivity a few weeks earlier . . .

Furman had already climbed into the boxcar of the waiting train that was to take him to Germany when he saw a rusty iron bar on the tracks. Pleading a severe case of dysentery, he debarked, carelessly threw his jacket over the iron bar, and squatted while several guards looked on. He then picked up the coat—and the bar—and climbed back into the boxcar, and within a few hours he and his comrades had hacked a hole in the side of the car and jumped off the train.

Pollak, whom the Italian girl Iride had betrayed, had been mistaken at first for a Jewish spy and brutally beaten. On his way to be tried by a court that inevitably would have sentenced him to death, he passed a group of British prisoners of war being marched to his jail and recognized an officer he had known.

Thus able to establish his identity as a prisoner of war, he was merely sentenced to be returned to a prison camp in Germany. But the RAF conveniently bombed the train station from which he was to leave, and in the confusion, he, too, escaped . . .

Now, Pollak and Furman, together with Simpson, kept shifting the escapers from one house to another—for they knew when they would be raided. A Resistance spy in Pietro Caruso's Fascist police headquarters known only as "Giuseppe" gave them lists of the areas to be raided within the next two or three nights, making it possible for them to clear the threatened billets in time. Nevertheless, unexplainably, some arrests were made.

Shortly after De Vial's talk with Derry, Giuseppe verified the Frenchman's story in one of his reports: "I have been informed that one Pasqualino Perfetti had been collaborating with the Fascists and German police . . . It has been confirmed that he has given much information."[10]

Among those endangered were Renzo Lucidi and his French wife, Adrienne, who had given shelter to Furman, Simpson, and Pollak when they had first arrived in Rome. The Lucidis had felt so secure, as we have seen, that they had even attended the opera—and sat in the box adjoining that of General Mälzer, whose autograph Adrienne obtained. Yet in January the Gestapo had raided their home and taken Renzo and his stepson, Geraldo, to Via Tasso. The Germans, however, had been seeking only Geraldo—his name appeared in the address book of a captured Communist philosophy professor—and suspected nothing of Renzo's underground activities.

Father and son were both released, but Renzo now feared that the Germans and Fascists would soon be back, especially with Perfetti talking. And this fear did not seem unjustified when one day he heard shots in the street nearby and then, some minutes later, a violent pounding on his door. Holding his breath, Lucidi opened the door and saw before him a wild-eyed British escaper, Wing Commander E. Garrad-Cole . . .

Garry, as he was called, had leaped out of a POW train en route to Germany a few months before, made his way to Rome, and, through a priest he had stopped on the street, contacted Monsignor O'Flaherty's organization. He hid for a while in the abandoned British Embassy, but soon met a tall, blond marchesa, who introduced him to friends who were happy to put him up under more comfortable conditions.

Dressed in a finely tailored Italian suit and disguising himself with glasses and a mustache, Garry, accompanied by his marchesa, spent much of his time in the more exclusive hotels, cafés, and bars, amid German officers and Fascists, "hoping to pick up information of value."

One day, the couple lunched at the Osteria dell'Orso restaurant, topping off an excellent meal with double scotches served at the bar by

Felix, the man who specialized in making life bearable for Allied escapers. They departed contentedly, boarded a crowded streetcar, and
found themselves pressed against two German SS men, who kept eyeing them suspiciously. Garry decided to alight alone at the next stop,
hoping at least to draw the two soldiers away from the marchesa.

As he had aticipated, the SS men followed him off the streetcar
and down Via Flaminia. When he stopped to look in a shop window,
they did likewise. Garry then turned down a narrow street and, within
moments, the two Germans pulled up on either side of him.

"Your papers, please," said one in broken Italian.

"Certainly, here is my identity card," Garry replied, presenting a
forged document.

The German studied it carefully, then slid it slowly and deliberately
into his pocket.

"This," he said, "is false. Come with us."

Forced to accompany them, Garry thought of the torture that probably awaited him and noted that the two Germans, though hefty, did
not look particularly bright. Suddenly, he swung at one of them, hitting
him behind the ear, and simultaneously tripped him with his leg. The
spinning German grabbed onto the second to break his fall, and in the
confusion Garry raced down the street, with bullets whistling past him.

It suddenly occurred to him that the Lucidis, who had earlier helped
him, lived nearby, and he ran to their apartment building, rushed up
five flights of stairs, and pounded on the door . . .

"We heard the shooting," Lucidi said when he saw Garry. "You cannot remain here. They will search the block and we are suspect already.
Come—quickly!"

The two men raced up to the roof. Garry, seeing a small hut housing
the machinery at the top of the elevator shaft, told Lucidi: "Go and
bring the lift up to the very top."

The Briton then followed Lucidi down the first flight of stairs to
the top floor landing and, when the elevator arrived, climbed to the
roof of the cage, on which he sprawled full length.

In minutes, as he lay sweating and praying, he heard shouting, stamping, the slamming of doors. Finally, after about ten minutes—Lucidi's
voice:

"Garry, are you okay?"

"Yes."

"Then listen. The Germans have gone but they will be back to search
again when they fail elsewhere. You must get out of this building at

once. I've sent little Maurice out to see what's going on in the streets. Come down to the flat until he gets back."

Maurice, Lucidi's eleven-year-old son, returned with a report that German soldiers had asked if he had seen an American wearing a light-colored raincoat and black trilby hat. Lucidi gave Garry a brown hat and overcoat, then talked the reluctant Briton into walking out hand in hand with Maurice to allay suspicion, arguing that the family was in danger anyway.

Garry and Maurice then departed, their hands locked, and walked casually past knots of Germans to the Tiber, where Maurice smiled goodbye and cheerfully returned home.

And soon Garry was back with his marchesa, though no longer so eager to "pick up information of value" while dawdling over the finest Italian veal and scotch whisky.[11]

The heat on Monsignor O'Flaherty's organization intensified when another Italian helper, named Grossi, was arrested and began talking. After being released, Grossi visited O'Flaherty and told him about some escapers:

"They tell me there are a half a dozen more hiding near Fara Sabina [some thirty miles from Rome] but I myself can't get them into the city. One of the men is sick but I could soon get him well again. I have plenty of *pasta* and *vino*."

Could the monsignor himself perhaps bring them into the city?

"Well," replied O'Flaherty, "I will have to be rather careful. The Germans are very keen to entertain me, you know. But I think I can arrange to go out there to say Mass next Sunday, the Feast of St. Joseph, and we can bring in the sick man at least and the others later, God willing."

But a few days later, on St. Patrick's day, March 17, O'Flaherty interrupted a holiday party in his room to answer the telephone, and his smile suddenly disappeared as he listened.

"All right, I understand," he said. "God forgive him."

When he returned to the party, John May, the British minister's butler, asked: "Everything all right, Monsignor?"

"Oh, yes, John," O'Flaherty replied. "Yes, indeed. Our little friend [an unidentified contact] was just after telling me not to go to Fara Sabina on Sunday. Apparently the Germans know all about our plan. Grossi . . . Grossi is working with them. You had better tell Major Derry. There will be things he has to do."

But Derry couldn't do them before several more escapers and their helpers were captured as the result of Grossi's betrayal.

Neither Perfetti nor Grossi, however, were responsible for the arrest of Derry's assistant, Lieutenant Bill Simpson. Simpson spent one night with an American escaper, Lieutenant Dukate, in the home of two Italian black-marketeers, and Dukate's girl friend, Carla, knew about it. She also knew that her American lover had taken a sudden interest in another girl. In a jealous tantrum, she went to see Pietro Koch and told him where Dukate could be found. Koch was delighted. Sooner or later the trail would lead to Monsignor O'Flaherty himself, and he had sworn to his colleagues that "I'll have the nails off his fingers before shooting him."

Thus Simpson, as well as Dukate, fell into Koch's gloved hands.[12]

※ ※ ※

Nor did the Jews who had survived the October 16 round-up fare much better—partly because of the treachery of the two French deserters from the German army who had been helped by Jews working for Father Benoît's operation to save foreign Jewish refugees. The Frenchmen had written letters to several Jewish leaders demanding five thousand lire ($50) for every Jew they refrained from denouncing to the Gestapo, and the Jewish community was forced to pay them—through a leader of the French Mutual Aid Committee. But not before many Jews were captured.

Richard Arvay, the Jew who had fled to Rome from France and then worked with Father Benoît, was among those denounced. No sooner had Italian police officials, who co-operated with Benoît, tipped Arvay off than his doorbell rang—once! That meant danger, as friends would have rung twice. Arvay, who was entertaining a visitor, did not answer the door. But the bell rang again, this time longer. Finally, someone knocked. While the visitor went to open the door, Arvay stood at a window ready to climb out.

Suddenly he heard a familiar shout: "Nobody is to leave the apartment!"

It was one of the French traitors!

As horrified cries and the stamping of heavy boots reached his ears, Arvay climbed out of the window and balanced himself precariously on the smooth rim of a small cornice. He looked five floors down and saw a man casually sweeping the street. A half-dressed woman stared at him in disbelief from the window of a neighboring house.

His mind paralyzed, Arvay edged his way along the cornice, preferring instant death to deportation. He began to lose his footing as the cornice sloped, then ended—about ten inches from, and slightly higher than, a ledge on the next building. Only ten inches. But the cornice was smooth—and he was five stories up! He thought of what the famous Austrian architect Adolf Loos had once said:

"If I ever go to heaven, I will find that the houses there have smooth façades."

Arvay was about to advance but found himself glued to the wall. He finally moved one foot, but then drew it back and, looking up at the sky, prayed:

"Dear God . . . only ten inches . . . please help me once more!"

Then he jumped—and landed on the ledge.

He climbed onto a balcony, opened a glass door, and entered. An old man sitting at a desk gasped as Arvay rushed past him and down the stairs to the street and freedom.[13]

As deadly to the Jews as the two Frenchmen was a buxom girl of eighteen with long black hair and an alluring smile—Celeste Di Porto,* who was called Stella ("star" in Italian) by her family and friends in tribute to her beauty. Only the coldness in her black eyes betrayed the meaning of the second nickname by which she was to become known: the Black Panther.

Celeste was a Jew who made a living denouncing other Jews—for the usual five thousand lire per head.

On October 16 she had barely escaped the Gestapo round-up after the Germans had entered her tenement in the slum of Trastevere. Fearing the hunters and craving a "better" life, she thereafter betrayed the hunted. The Fascist band of Luigi Rosselli welcomed her. Rosselli's band and other small, independent gangs were more acceptable to the Germans than the larger police groups, such as Koch's, which took orders from Mussolini's Salò government, not from the SS. Rosselli worked directly for the Gestapo and let the Nazis do the torturing and at least share the plunder.

And Rosselli's band was particularly useful. Specializing in the capture of Jews who had evaded the October 16 dragnet, it had the finest con-

---

* Celeste was not related to Giacomo Di Porto, who had taken refuge in the convent of Notre Dame de Sion. So inbred are the Jews of Rome after two thousand years of ghetto life that their family names number hardly more than a score, many identifiable as the names of towns in Italy.

tacts. Rosselli's wife, Filomena Mastrani, had successfully infiltrated Jewish circles and would fix appointments, extort money and jewels with the promise of obtaining the release of captured Jews, and then denounce the blackmailed people.

But Celeste Di Porto, being Jewish herself, was even more valuable. And Rosselli's gang had much to offer her, too. Not only physical security, but physical pleasure with many of its members—a pleasure she could never enjoy under the influence of her religious parents. Moreover, she no longer had to live in a rat-infested slum. She lived well, even luxuriously. And all she had to do in return for this new and exciting life was to walk down the street, flash her lovely smile, and greet every Jew she recognized with a few warm words, such as "So nice to see you, Mr. So-and-so."

Then she would continue on, and several comrades following her would arrest the man who had been greeted and deliver him to Gestapo headquarters at Via Tasso. And in case the victim denied he was a Jew, as he usually did, Celeste would come to testify and, to the laughter of her Fascist friends, personally pull down the victim's trousers to show that he was circumcised.

Nor did Celeste play favorites. She denounced her cousin and childhood playmate Armando Di Segni, and when his wife begged for mercy, she replied serenely:

"Don't worry, he's fine. He was cold, and so I gave him a blanket."

Celeste denounced another cousin, too—Silvia Di Segni. And when this cousin's husband went to the Germans to offer himself in exchange, he was deported together with his wife.

Even her own father was not safe. Crushed with shame by his daughter's bestial behavior, he had, on meeting her one day, struck her.

"If you do that again," Celeste said, "I'll have you arrested, too!"

The Jewish community, to sustain its spirits, began to recite a new "psalm":

> Star of the Port, Star of the Orient,
> You have made so many weep,
> You are the spy of Piazza Giudia!†
> I want to sing this serenade
> Until Stella Di Porto is killed.
> Star of the Port, Star of the Orient,
> The dead ask for vengeance,
> Yes, vengeance on that spy . . .

But the cries for vengeance had not yet reached their crescendo.[14]

† "Piazza Giudia" means "Jewish Square," located just outside the western gate of the Ghetto.

Peter Tompkins, the OSS agent, was roused from a restless sleep in his new secret hideout (he had moved from Giglio's) by an insistent pounding sound. He stumbled to the door, prepared to stare into cold Nazi eyes, but the caller, to his relief, was Giglio, who was in charge of the OSS radio that was code-named "Vittoria." Giglio was excited.

"The Vittoria operator hasn't been seen since last night," he reported. "We're worried something has happened to him."

"How the devil could anything happen to him," Tompkins asked, "if he's been sitting in his apartment as ordered?"

The operator, code-named Enzo, had disobeyed orders, Giglio explained. He had gone down to a bar and simply disappeared.

Tompkins was alarmed. He had warned Enzo to take no chances after Enzo had told him a frightening story. Another Italian working for the OSS had, a few weeks earlier, introduced Enzo to a man named Walter Di Franco. Shortly afterward Di Franco had met Enzo on the street and asked if he was still transmitting with a secret radio!

Finally, Di Franco had left a note in the bar frequented by Enzo requesting an urgent appointment. But the bartender, when passing on the note, warned Enzo that "Walter," who posed as a leftist—he had, in fact, joined the Action party—was actually a Fascist agent. He was, of course, Pietro Koch's chief torturer, who so admired Viviana Chilanti of the Red Flag party. And the OSS agent who had introduced Di Franco to Enzo turned out to be a double agent.

This was the result, thought Tompkins, of dealing with such politically questionable agents as Captain Bourgouin and his protégé Mino Menicanti, whose only interest was, Tompkins was persuaded, to sabotage the CLN for Badoglio. Tompkins was sure that many of the people the CLN hired or worked through were double agents. Menicanti had given him much trouble indeed. He had weakened the whole OSS network in Italy by claiming to his underground contacts that he was the OSS chief in Italy.

If people believed Menicanti, Tompkins felt, his own influence would be compromised. And even when he, Tompkins, complained to the base at Anzio and the base ordered Menicanti to operate only in northern Italy, the Italian ignored the order.

Menicanti, Tompkins thought, was also sabotaging OSS activities in another way. While the American and his own men ground out daily

military reports based on information obtained by the extensive Socialist party intelligence network—information that, indeed, helped save
the Anzio beachhead from being overrun—Menicanti was sending
mainly political information. He seemed interested, Tompkins believed,
only in evidence "confirming" the claims of the King and Badoglio
that they were far more popular in Italy than the CLN parties.

When Tompkins deleted all political material from Menicanti's re-
ports passed on to him for transmission, Menicanti was enraged, and the
American gravely feared that the Italian agent might betray the whole
OSS operation.

With the apparent capture of Enzo, Giglio, too, was in danger, for
he was in charge of the radio and Enzo knew his true identity, though
not that of other members of the OSS network. But Giglio's first concern was to move the radio, which he said would be set up in a Tiber
river boat operated by a partisan. Tompkins warned Giglio to be especially careful, and they arranged for a "conventional phrase" to be telephoned to the American by Giglio's sister if something went seriously
wrong.

Accompanied by his orderly, Giovanni Scottu, Lieutenant Giglio
drove his motorcycle to the river bank, then ordered Scottu to watch
the vehicle while he descended to the boat for a few minutes. But
when Giglio failed to reappear after more than an hour, Scottu grew
worried and approached the craft.

At that moment, two men emerged from the boat and invited him
in. Inside, he saw Enzo and a slim, silky-haired man with a striped
brown suit who introduced himself as the "Commissioner of Public
Security"—Dr. Pietro Koch.

"Now we must be gay and pretend that nothing in the world is
wrong," Franco Malfatti urged Peter Tompkins on the night of March
18. "Here come the girls."

Malfatti had convinced Tompkins, with not too much difficulty, that
the whole OSS operation might be seriously jeopardized if they continued to neglect their sex lives. For an agent had to be able to account for a normal everyday life when questioned by the police, and
any Italian who had not slept with a girl for six weeks was regarded as
either "queer" or subversive.

So, for the sake of the Allies, Rome, and the reputation of the Italian
male, it was essential for Tompkins to throw a party—which would be
an all-night affair since no one could leave during the curfew.

Tompkins had little enthusiasm for a party since Giglio's sister had just telephoned him and spoken the "conventional phrase"—"Have you bought me any honey?"—warning him of her brother's arrest. But Malfatti argued that with all of them in greater danger than ever, a display of "gaiety" was even more necessary than before. Therefore, the party would go on—in the apartment of one of Tompkins' assistants, a young man known as Baldo.

Tompkins looked the part of the Italian playboy. Luckily, an underground tailor had arrived the day before with a new sport jacket and a pair of gray flannels, and his Capri shoes were still in good condition. The girls, accompanied by two of Baldo's friends, arrived in a gay mood. They were attractive and well-dressed, wearing sheer stockings and scented with French perfumes. The party got off to a roaring start, with everyone sitting around the fire emptying bottle after bottle of good English gin, straight.

Tompkins, who was trying his best to block out thoughts of Giglio, finally retired to the kitchen where he prepared mountains of crisp bread, ham, and omelettes. Then the dancing started, and, Malfatti, discovering that there was one girl short, decided to go out and fetch another, using his false curfew pass.

One of the girls then rang a friend at another party being held in a house nearby and announced to the guests that this friend wanted to come—with a German captain. Tompkins felt he could not refuse without arousing suspicion.

"What sort of a German captain is it?" he asked.

"An SS captain."

Tompkins nearly choked on his gin.

At about that time, Walter Di Franco was working over Giglio and Scottu at Koch's headquarters. He beat them, pulled out whiskers, attached two steel points to their temples drawn together by a band of steel. Bleeding profusely, Giglio was taken back to his cell by his torturer, and there, Enzo, the radio operator, tried to comfort him. After talking with him, Enzo left for a while to report to Walter on the conversation, then returned with a cigarette and food. He had apparently cracked.

But neither Giglio nor Scottu "talked."

With a girl friend, L., and one of his male agents, Lele, accompanying him, Peter Tompkins left his party and walked the short distance to the house where he was to pick up the German captain and his friend. He tried not to think as the elevator rose toward what he felt might be his doom. They entered a large living room filled with people, and, at the far end, Tompkins saw a blond woman lying on a sofa wrapped in furs while a snake-eyed German officer sitting beside her held her hand. As he approached, he could see from the woman's glassy eyes that she was doped.

Lele introduced Tompkins to the loudly dressed host as "Roberto Berlingieri," and Tompkins immediately recognized the man—a famous racketeer. When the host smiled in greeting, Lele said to him:

"Funny you don't know my friend Berlingieri. Known him all my life. Sure you don't know him? Must have seen him around . . ."

"Brother of Antonio?" the host asked Tompkins, offering him a cigarette.

"No . . . no . . . cousin," Tompkins stammered.

The German captain then came up, introduced himself, and stared into Tompkins' eyes. Tompkins was petrified. What must the German think, this stranger bursting in after curfew curiously dressed in Baldo's camel's hair coat and an open shirt collar. When the host went to the telephone, Tompkins was convinced the end had come. He grabbed his girl and danced her around the room, not stopping until he saw the opportunity to follow some people out. But the host, his actress wife, and the German captain, minus his doped girl friend, were right behind him.

At Tompkins' party a card game, *chemin de fer*, got underway, while the German, when he wasn't fondling the breasts of the racketeer's wife, chatted about the Anzio beachhead with Malfatti, who had just returned from his nocturnal search with a girl on each arm. Meanwhile Tompkins danced with a pretty young woman he had never met before, who gigglingly insisted that his rhythm was more American than Italian. With a nervous laugh, he replied boldly, within a few feet of the German, who was, fortunately, preoccupied with the actress' breasts:

"But of course! Can't you see? I *am* an American!"

The girl, as he had hopefully anticipated, begged him not to tease her, and Baldo, dancing by at that moment, wondered if Tompkins had lost his mind and fully expected to nurse his hangover on the torture rack.

Finally, the German, accompanied by the racketeer and the actress, departed, after clicking his heels and bowing slightly. The party now grew wilder. The lights gradually went off, and couples cuddled in every corner. Soon there was nothing but the flickering fire, the soft music of the record-player, and the groans of people laboriously establishing an alibi for the police . . .

At Koch's headquarters Giglio was being tortured for the fourth time.

"How do you think it went off?" Tompkins asked Baldo on the morning after the party, his head pounding.

"As a party," asked Baldo, "or otherwise?"

"As a party there isn't any question about it," Lele interrupted. "It was fine. The only trouble is that when you get full of gin you not only look, but dance and behave in a manner so patently American that you might as well have a sign on your back: USA! Luckily our [SS] friend Erich wanted to make the girl so badly and was so busy grabbing at her breasts that I don't think he noticed very much."

"The hell he didn't!" Baldo said. "The last thing he did before leaving was ask me who you really were. Luckily, Franco [Malfatti] was nearby and described—with great speed and fascinating detail—what a no-good playboy you were, that he had known you for years, and that the only things you cared about were gambling and women!"

Suddenly, as Tompkins' mind cleared, it all came back in horror. Malfatti, as he was leaving the party that morning, had asked him:

"Do you know who that SS captain is?"

"No. Who?"

"Hauptmann Erich Priebke."

"Well?"

"He's the Sicherheitsdienst [SD] officer at Via Tasso in charge of uncovering and eliminating enemy agents and key partisan leaders!"[15]

❖ ❖ ❖

"Make an attempt through the Pope . . . I will try to last as long as I can."

Marchesa Fulvia Ripa di Meana was distraught on reading this secret message from her dear cousin Bepo—Colonel Giuseppe di Montezemolo. The message, the marchesa says, had been smuggled out of Via Tasso written with invisible ink—lemon juice—on a small emptied plate returned with the tray that had been sent to the prison with food for a privileged prisoner. (A pen and a slice of lemon had been smuggled into Via Tasso in a bottle of red wine that the Germans, in a generous moment, had let pass.)

The message, emerging on the plate after the application of a hot iron, seemed to indicate that Montezemolo was sinking. And the marchesa learned from the messages of other prisoners that her cousin, who knew more about the Resistance than any other man, had been tortured pitilessly. The Germans had broken his jaw and did not relent even when he suffered a violent attack of mastoiditis. But Montezemolo had not talked.

Unable to reach the Pope immediately, the marchesa arranged to see SS Colonel Dollmann through his friend Prince Francesco Ruspoli, in the hope that Dollmann would intervene to get Montezemolo transferred to a hospital, where at least he would no longer undergo torture.

Accompanied on March 3 to Dollmann's *pensione*, the marchesa was greeted by Bibi Rossi, the beautiful young daughter of the owner who served as the colonel's "girl friend" at social functions and as his secretary during working hours. (Perhaps her most memorable task had been to conduct Himmler on a Christmas shopping tour in 1942.)

The marchesa placed great hope in Bibi for, despite her friendliness toward the Germans, the girl had helped to save a number of partisans and Jews (she and Dollmann both told the author that, with his knowledge, she hid two Jews in the *pensione*). And she was very influential with Dollmann, who had lived at the *pensione* for a decade watching her grow up. She had even been engaged to his nephew.

As recalled in the marchesa's memoirs, Dollmann kissed her hand with characteristic grace and sat down beside her on a sofa.

"Ruspoli has told me," he said, "that you wished to speak to me about Colonel Montezemolo."

"Yes. As his only relative in Rome, I feel it is my duty to intervene on his behalf, since I know for certain that he is gravely ill . . . [His family is] in southern Italy and it is impossible to communicate the news to them."

"The poor things. I'm sorry for them. And how many children does he have?"

"Five. Therefore, you can see why his welfare is so close to my heart . . ."

"Oh, I understand very well. But unfortunately that's the way things go."

Dollmann then launched into a harangue, stressing that Montezemolo was the most tragic and important case in hand.

"We Germans know him well," he said, "and I perhaps more than the others, and we have great esteem for him. He is the only intelligent officer in the Italian army. He was the one who made the other idiot generals, who don't understand anything, move and talk. In fact, no other Italian officer was treated by us with equal respect; we gave him our highest decoration."

Dollmann paused, then continued in a tone of regret: "But in exchange for our friendship he became our most ferocious adversary and fought us in every way possible . . . We have absolute proof . . ."

He paused again, lowered his eyes sadly, and went on: "This is all very painful for us . . . but . . . under these conditions, we arrested him with displeasure and now he must be judged by a German military court."

Finally, Marchesa Ripa di Meana was given an opportunity to reply: "Colonel . . . I assure you that you are completely wrong."

As Dollmann lifted his eyebrows in surprise and irritation, she continued, suggesting a community of interest: ". . . It is true that he was active, but only in assuring that there will be public order when the Germans leave Rome. He had the power to do this. And he would have it again if he were liberated because he effectively controls all the elements that pose the greatest threat to you Germans . . . I am sure that under the same circumstances, you would have acted as Montezemolo did."

Dollmann replied curtly: "That is of no importance. You Italians don't know how to run your republic!"

"Colonel," the marchesa resumed, ready to play her final card, ". . . certainly the German military court will act with justice and he will be absolved. But in the meantime, he is ill, as you must know."

Dollmann angrily interrupted: "And how do you know this?"

"From the medicine he has asked for and from some indiscretions that have leaked out of Via Tasso . . . Anyway he is very ill and . . . I beg you to see that he recovers in a clinic."

Dollmann replied that he had no direct power over this decision, but that he would keep her request in mind and do his best.

The marchesa thanked him profusely and departed with renewed hope. Bibi, waiting at the entrance, reassured her:

"Don't worry, Marchesa, you will see, if he promised you! He is so kind, Colonel Dollmann!"

When Marchesa Ripa di Meana had departed, Dollmann informed Colonel Kappler that news of the torture was leaking out. Whether he intended this information as a deterrent to further torture or as a warning to cut off the leak is not known, but Kappler immediately tightened the surveillance of his victims.[16]

Marchesa Ripa di Meana heard nothing more from Dollmann, but her spirits rose again when some two weeks after her talk with him, on March 19, she finally obtained an audience with the Pope. The timing seemed favorable. Pius was desperately concerned about the continuing Allied bombing of Rome and of religious shrines in neighboring areas.

On February 10, the Americans had bombed Castel Gandolfo, the Pope's country residence, believing that it had been converted into a Nazi stronghold, and had killed about five hundred refugees hiding there. Three days later, the Allies partially destroyed the monastery atop Monte Cassino with a saturation bombing. And on March 10, 14, and 18—the day before the marchesa's meeting with the Pope—planes had bombed various sections of Rome.

On March 12, the fifth anniversary of his coronation, the Pope, appearing on his balcony for the first time since the occupation began, had told a huge crowd overflowing St. Peter's Square:

"How could we believe that anyone would dare to turn Rome, this noble city which belongs to all times and all places . . . into a field of battle, perpetrating an act as inglorious militarily as it is abominable in the eyes of God and to a humanity conscious of the highest spiritual and moral values . . ."

On March 18 the sooty smell of destruction from the previous day's raid still permeated the city and the Communists threatened disorder. Marchesa Ripa di Meana therefore felt confident that the Pope would agree to use his influence to secure the liberation of her prestigious cousin who could then persuade the Allies to halt the bombings and keep order when the Germans departed. If this argument had not impressed Dollmann, it would surely move the Pope.

The marchesa said after she had knelt before the pontiff and seated herself: "I have come to implore you for a grace which, if accorded, would not only save a person's life and give joy to his family, but would have important consequences for retaining order in Rome."

When Montezemolo had been free, she pointed out, Rome was not continuously bombed as it was now, nor were raids as indiscriminate, because he had radioed orders where the planes should drop their bombs. Furthermore, she said, he had controlled all the military groups in Rome and the various political parties had obeyed him.

"Now, from his prison," she said, "he begs for your help and we Romans unite with him to implore your help. You, our Holy Father, who have done so much for our beloved city and will continue to do so, please listen to our prayer and help us. Save at least his life, I beg you, eventually having him interned in the Vatican until the end of the war."

The Pope seemed less than enthusiastic about this request for internment but promised he would try to help Montezemolo.

When the marchesa had left, the Pope called in Monsignor Montini and instructed him to occupy himself immediately with Montezemolo's case. But what could the Vicar of Christ do if the Germans refused to listen to his quiet, private entreaties? Condemn their actions from his balcony in St. Peter's Square?[17]

❖ ❖ ❖

"Now listen, Gloria, do exactly as I say. Take the three books and bring them by streetcar to Acqua Acetosa. You must come immediately. Do you understand?"

Ten-year-old Gloria Chilanti replied to her father, Felice, that she did, then put down the telephone. Koch's men were closing in on the Red Flags that evening of March 21, and as the leader of Koba, the children's section of the Red Flag party, Gloria undertook this new dangerous assignment with the coolness of a veteran. Since her mother, Viviana, was on a mission in Milan, it was up to her to save the three "books." . . .

The "books" were three Soviet prisoners of war who had been hiding for weeks in the attic located over the terrace of the Chilanti apartment. They were among the Soviet prisoners of war whom the Germans had brought to Italy to work on defense projects. The Communist and Red Flag parties had helped about four hundred to escape from work camps and factories in and around Rome, and individual members sheltered them with financial aid from Monsignor O'Flaherty's organization.

The Vatican, apparently without the Pope's knowledge, was thus helping not only the local Communists but the Soviets it so feared!

The chief organizer of this Russian escape line was Aleksej Nikolaevich Flejsher, the son of a noble family who had fought with the White Russians during the 1917 Revolution and then had been sent abroad. In Rome, influenced by the Italian Communists, Alessio, as the partisans called him, converted to Communism, and now he was helping Soviet prisoners to escape, hide, and fight with the Italian guerrillas. It was Alessio who had sent the three Soviet soldiers to hide in the Chilanti apartment.

The situation for the Red Flags was now highly dangerous because a spy among them had brought about the round-up of many leading members. On December 6, 1943, the Red Flags had simultaneously entered dozens of movie theaters and scattered anti-Fascist leaflets, but sixteen members were captured either at the theaters or later in their homes.

When torture had failed to make the victims talk, a trial, the first for Roman partisans, was held and eleven members were condemned to death and five given prison sentences. The condemned leader, Ezio Malatesta, a young journalist, spat in the prosecutor's face. And when, at dawn on February 2, 1944, the condemned men were taken to Forte Bravetta near Rome for the mass execution, another leader, Colonel Gino Rossi, looked at the PAI policemen who were about to shoot them and said:

"I am sorry only that I am to be shot by you, Italians, and not by Germans. May God forgive you!"

The execution squad fired into the ground or at the victims' legs, and a German medical officer had to finish them off with a pistol.

The executions were followed by a new wave of arrests, and the surviving Red Flags decided this time to attack Regina Coeli, the fortresslike main Nazi-Fascist prison, where most of their comrades were being held, and liberate as many prisoners as possible. Partisans disguised as German officers would enter the prison and receive the cell keys from guards who had agreed to co-operate.

Outside the gate, two fire brigade vehicles driven by Red Flag members would be waiting, ready to speed off, sirens screaming, with the prisoners. Meanwhile, Red Flags working at the central telephone exchange would prevent all telephone communications between Regina Coeli and the rest of Rome, and armed squads would hide near the prison ready to occupy Germans or Fascists with an exchange of shots while the fire engines roared off.

The escape was to take place on March 18, but was postponed for further preparations. On March 20 several Red Flags met with partisans of the Action party in a joint effort to sabotage some telephone lines near the prison and walked into a trap—apparently set by Koch's lieutenant, Walter Di Franco, who had infiltrated the Action party. A little book with the names and addresses of many Red Flag members was found on one of the prisoners.

Now, the following night, Koch's men were sweeping down on the Red Flags, and Walter Di Franco would regretfully have to arrest his seductive blond friend, Viviana Chilanti, among other Red Flag leaders. (He could not know that she was safely out of Rome.) When her husband Felice, who was out on a mission, had been warned of the round-up, he immediately telephoned home to Gloria . . .

The little girl signaled for her guests to come down from the attic and three giants jumped to the terrace. Nobody, she was sure, would ever take them for Italians, especially the two Mongolians with the slightly slanted eyes. And all three were ridiculously clothed, wearing sweaters several sizes too small over their Russian uniforms. She could not even give them proper instructions since they knew no Italian at all. As they put on raincoats too tight to button, she put a finger to her lips; they should keep their mouths shut.

Gloria's father had instructed her to take the streetcar since the danger of being picked up appeared to be greater if they walked, and so they boarded one and Gloria bought four tickets. All eyes turned to the strange-looking men, including the eyes of a Fascist officer, who asked Gloria, as the Russian sitting next to her caressed her hand in a fatherly manner:

"Who are these men, little girl?"

"They're my uncles," she replied.

The Fascist stared at her, then at the three giants, incredulous.

And before the conversation could resume, Gloria rose and her three "uncles" followed her off the streetcar, one stop before they were supposed to descend. They ran the rest of the way and met Felice at the designated meeting place by the Tiber, where a small boat was waiting to take the Russians to fight with the guerrillas.

"Here are the 'books', Daddy," said Gloria breathlessly. "I told everybody they were my uncles, but I don't think they believed me."

With thirteen Red Flag leaders crowding into Koch's torture house that night, the attack on Regina Coeli had to be postponed again until the party could reorganize.[18]

❖ ❖ ❖

On the morning of March 23 Franco Malfatti reported to Peter Tompkins that his men had located the place where Giglio was imprisoned—a *pensione* being used as a torture house by the Koch gang. They had seen what looked like three corpses being carried from the building, and neighbors had reported hearing screams and shots throughout the night.

Tompkins was horrified. And tired. Tired from running. After the party a few nights before, he and his agents had moved again, this time into a temporarily inoperative brothel appropriately furnished with an enormous bed surrounded by mirrors placed at every salacious angle. In the freezing cold, he, Baldo, and Lele sat on the bed with their hats and coats on, playing cutthroat bridge and warming themselves with a bottle of cognac.

Tompkins was nervous indeed. When he lit a match to burn some jotted notes, he set fire to a pink celluloid lampshade and panicked at the sight of the reflection in the mirrors, which gave the impression that the whole room was going up in flames. When the fire had finally been put out, a new worry cropped up. The lady who lived and worked here did not know that she had guests. What would she say when she returned? But Lele assured him that she was in the hospital—for treatment, Tompkins surmised, of an illness contracted in the very bed on which they sat playing bridge.

But tired and worried as he was, Tompkins plotted with his men to attack Koch's headquarters and liberate Giglio. And he owed it to Giglio, he felt, to be there personally when the attack was launched.[19]

❖　❖　❖

With time running out for him, Colonel Montezemolo, in his small Via Tasso cell, decided to act on his own. He approached a sympathetic Croatian guard named Paolo, and they worked out an escape plan. During the changing of the guard each night, a section of the street running past the prison was left unguarded for a few minutes. Just before the switch took place, Paolo would unlock Montezemolo's cell on the second floor of the five-story former apartment building, and the colonel would immediately rush downstairs and take the key to a main-floor room from a guard's desk drawer. He would enter the room and jump out of an open window to the street.

Montezemolo, his body torn and broken, was not sure he would be strong enough to succeed, but he wanted to try. Death, in any event, was preferable to further torture. Before he embarked on this desperate attempt, he scribbled a message to his wife asking her to tell his sons how painful it was to part from them and how he had performed his duty to the end, leaving them a respectable name.

He did not want his family to mourn him. Death for a cause was not a reason for sadness but for pride; therefore, there should be no sign of external pain.

At 2:20 one morning, Paolo's heavy tread approached his cell. Then the footsteps ceased and a key turned in the lock. In exactly ten minutes Montezemolo would open the unlocked door and go downstairs.

The minutes ticked by slowly—and suddenly there were voices in the corridor! Never since his arrest had there been a night inspection. But tonight . . . there was one! They were trying all the cell doors on his floor. Finally, his. The door gave way, and an officer threatened Paolo, who was accompanying him, with severe punishment for such laxity. Leaving a prison door unlocked!

The team then continued inspecting and left the prison only at 3 A.M., marching past the new guards.

Montezemolo, his messages indicated, knew that his end was near, but he could not guess its nature—or that all Rome would bleed with him.[20]

7

The Corpses

"Be sure to leave the windows open tomorrow," Rosario Bentivegna advised Dr. Giuseppe Caronia at Polyclinico Hospital in the center of Rome.

Rosario had known Caronia, the hospital director and a friend of his family, since childhood, and although he had never told him that he belonged to a Communist party GAP group, he made no secret of his rather active partisan role. He sometimes hid in the hospital after taking part in a terrorist raid.

During a recent dynamite attack on a German army truck, some windows in the hospital had shattered and the doctor had asked Bentivegna kindly to inform him in advance of any new attacks in the vicinity, to allow him time to open the windows.

Accordingly, Rosario, on March 22, obliged. But for Caronia the warning was now almost laughable. As if there were many windows left to shatter! Four days earlier, American planes had unloaded bombs nearby, hitting three wards and injuring a number of patients.

A conservative anti-Fascist, Caronia hid dozens of refugees in his infectious-disease department, which Nazi and Fascist policemen were loath to inspect.

"Don't try anything against the Germans," the doctor counseled Bentivegna. "They've been promising to kill ten Italians for every German killed."

"Don't worry," Rosario responded. "We're only going to attack the Fascists."[1]

Colonel Dollmann rolled his eyes until his pupils almost disappeared under the lids, mocking the emotional speech being delivered by Mussolini's Undersecretary of Aviation, Carlo Borsani, who had been blinded in the war with Albania. On this memorable day, March 23, the twenty-fifth anniversary of the Fascist party, who at this great gathering of Fascists in the Ministry of Corporations could appeal more to Roman sentimentality than a blind war hero?

Dollmann, though a cultural romanticist, was not sentimental, especially, it seems, when he saw some of his own questionable qualities reflected in others. Most of these Fascist hangers-on, he appears to have felt, were detestable opportunists with no real commitment to the Fascism they served and profited from, but too compromised to switch camps now as most Italians had done.

". . . The spring that renews the warmth of the heavens and of the earth, and the hopes of men of good will, reawakens from the sleep of the unrecognized and the outraged the memory of our past only because our future will be greater and more joyful . . ."

Consul Möllhausen was rather moved by Borsani's well-meaning if pompous oratory. But he was constantly distracted by Dollmann and his Fascist friend Minister of Interior Guido Buffarini-Guidi, who joked with each other like schoolboys, and by one particular man in the audience who applauded at the wrong times and smacked his lips in an apparent expression of approval.

Finally the speech ended and, while the great hall echoed with thunderous applause, Möllhausen rose and went out on the balcony to enjoy the brilliant hues of Rome at mid-afternoon. As far as Möllhausen was concerned, he and Dollmann had been right in forcing cancellation of a dangerously provocative parade that Giuseppe Pizzirano, vice secretary of the Fascist party, had wanted to stage.

The Resistance might have played havoc along all those streets. And it was a good thing, too, that this meeting, which had substituted for the parade, was over before dark. The chances for a successful partisan strike had been minimized. Möllhausen's reflections on the matter were interrupted by a powerful explosion several blocks away.

A few minutes later, a German soldier ran toward the ministry shouting breathlessly that bombs had decimated his unit as it had marched up Via Rasella.[2]

Until this moment, Rosario Bentivegna, Carla Capponi, and other Communist party leaders had been discouraged. They had tried their best to provoke the Germans. On March 1 Carla had assassinated the soldier carrying documents from German headquarters in the Excelsior Hotel. On March 8 she had bombed a German army gasoline truck near the Colosseum, starting a fire that lasted all morning.

Her comrades had committed similar acts of terrorism and sabotage. The Germans and Fascists, however, had reacted not with wild reprisals, but with cool, cruel, silent efficiency, arresting and torturing individual partisan leaders without substantially raising the public temperature. As more and more Resistance leaders were being captured in the wake of the Anzio failure, the chances for insurrection when the Allies would finally arrive dwindled accordingly. The Romans appeared more apathetic than ever, and the Resistance, partly because of the demoralizing arrests, was disintegrating.

CLN President Bonomi was about to resign because the most extreme antimonarchist group, the Action party, refused as a matter of principle to accept a monarchist system even until the end of the war—a stand that even the Communists would not take, at least publicly, for fear of fatally weakening the Resistance.

Moreover, the Clandestine Front still posed a threat to insurrection. True, Badoglio agreed to name General Roberto Bencivenga, an old, conservative anti-Fascist who was acceptable to the CLN, to replace the divisive General Armellini as the over-all leader of the Roman Resistance and the man who would rule Rome in the period between German departure and Allied arrival.

But Bencivenga was a cautious soldier with no understanding of modern political trends and techniques, at least in Communist eyes. He would certainly try to stifle an insurrection. The Romans had to take matters into their own hands. They had to be roused to the boiling point of revolt. For their own good, some would have to die.

And so, German blood must flow in the gutters of Via Rasella.

Via Rasella seemed the ideal place for a bombing that would at once seriously wound the enemy and detonate a reaction powerful enough to set off a rebellion. It was a narrow street, near Piazza Barberini in the center of Rome's shopping area, that echoed with the tramp of heavy boots and the rhythm of marching songs every day at about 2 P.M. The sounds came from the men of the 11th Company, 3rd Battalion, SS Polizeiregiment Bozen, mostly over-age recruits from

South Tyrol who had just been brought to Rome to help wipe out the Resistance.

Because the street was narrow, the troops had to march in close files and the partisans could more easily bomb them. And as the route led up a hill, the marchers had to slow their pace, making them still easier targets.

An attack on this force was originally suggested by a Communist GAP officer, Mario Fiorentini, who lived nearby and noted that the troops took this route at the same time each day. His commander, Carlo Salinari, at first approved the attack as one of many pinprick terrorist actions scheduled; one or two small bombs would kill or injure a few Germans. But then Salinari discussed the attack with the top Communist military commander in Rome, Giorgio Amendola, and they decided that this would be no routine operation.

The possibility for a massive assault at just the right psychological moment—during the celebration of Fascism's twenty-fifth anniversary —was simply too good to pass up. For the first time, all four GAP groups operating in Rome would work together.

The Via Rasella operation would be no pinprick.[3]

"You better be careful," said the street cleaner to one of his colleagues, who had parked his rubbish cart in front of Tittoni Palace on Via Rasella. "An inspector from the Sanitation Department is checking around here. Get busy or you may be fined."

The man who had been warned nodded and started sweeping the area around him, but when his fellow street cleaner had gone away, he stopped his work and looked at his watch. Almost 3:30 P.M. An hour and a half late. Would those Germans never come?

A youth casually sauntered by and mumbled as he passed the sweeper. "Give them ten minutes more. Then leave."

The sweeper—Rosario Bentivegna—was disgusted. He had dragged his rubbish cart, which resembled a baby stroller, halfway across Rome, and now, if the Germans didn't come, he would have to drag it all the way back—together with the forty pounds of TNT it contained!

At the top of Via Rasella, which ended at Viadelle Quattro Fontane, Carla Capponi, whose long titian hair had been cut and dyed black, waited in front of Barberini Palace. Nervous and apprehensive, she had already bungled one aspect of the plan. She was to have waited down the hill around the corner from Via Rasella in front of the *Il Messaggero* building, then, on receiving a signal from another partisan that the troops were approaching, to have turned up Via Rasella and walked past Bentivegna to the top. Her advance would be the signal to Rosario that the Germans were coming. However, she had misinterpreted the signal *she* had received and had moved ahead prematurely, giving a false alarm.

Now she could not return from Barberini Palace to *Il Messaggero*, as two Fascist policemen guarding the newspaper building had already become suspicious and had followed her, remaining about a block away. She would simply wait in front of Barberini Palace and cover Bentivegna when he headed up the hill after lighting the fuse. Actually, another partisan, Guglielmo Blasi, was supposed to be there, but he had disappeared. Carla would have to cover Rosario's escape alone.

Suddenly she was horrified to see several children playing in the garden behind the gates of the palace.

"Go home, children," she urged. "Hurry!"

But they simply moved further into the garden.

Finally the sound of marching men could be heard. The Germans were coming up Via Rasella! The pounding of their boots on the cobbles sounded like a gathering storm, almost drowning out the vigorous military rhythm of 156 voices. Carla waited . . . and as she would later recall in a poem:

> *Long pain marked the minutes,*
> *Quivering like struck blades of steel about to*
> *descend on us,*
> *We who were trapped in the narrow street*
> *Our hearts compressed in our breast . . .*
> *Under the pounding heels,*
> *A cadence sounded on the pavement,*
> *Echoing in the heart (only the brain left the*
> *vow intact) . . .*
> *Eyes upon us at every corner*
> *Watching, waiting . . ."*

Franco Calamandrei, who stood near the bottom of Via Rasella, walked across the street in front of the troops and lifted his cap. With this signal, Rosario lit a long fuse snaking from the rubbish cart and placed his own cap on the cart, the signal that everything was in order.

He walked up the hill to Via Quattro Fontane and turned the corner to the right, where he met Carla. And as the two of them started running down the street, the earth shook under a tremendous explosion, then three more from shells hurled by partisans from behind the troops.

> *. . . And it passed, swept away with fear,*
> *The timidity of youth,*
> *Of our twenty years . . .*[4]

"Revenge! Revenge for my poor *kameraden!*"

General Mälzer, the Commandant of Rome, was beside himself with rage and grief when he arrived at Via Rasella shortly after the explosions. And the extraordinary quantity of alcohol he had consumed at lunch with Colonel Kappler fed his wild, incoherent emotionalism as he saw the bodies of German soldiers, many of them dismembered, lying in pools of blood amid the wreckage and listened to the groans and cries of the wounded.

"I am going to blow up the entire block of houses!" he raved. "I have already issued the necessary orders. I'm going to blow the whole thing up. I swear it. And nobody is going to stop me!"

Dollmann and Möllhausen, who had arrived shortly after Mälzer, tried their best to stop him. Soldiers were already breaking into every house along the street, dragging out the occupants, men, women, and children, and lining them up in front of Barberini Palace.

"*Herr General,*" Möllhausen pleaded, "I beg you not to do it. Try to calm yourself. This is a matter of Germany's good name as well as your own. Since it is we who have been attacked, we have a psychological advantage . . ."

Mälzer started to weep. "My soldiers!" he sobbed. "My poor soldiers! I'm going to blow up the whole neighborhood, with whoever might be in the houses. And you, Möllhausen, with your face of a Byzantine Christ, I'm going to dump you into jail at once!"

Mälzer then ordered an aide to contact Kesselring.

"Telephone the field marshal immediately," he shouted. "Explain the situation. Tell him that I request full powers and tell him, also, that the *Herr Konsul* disagrees with my orders."

"Wait a moment," Möllhausen told the officer. "If you use my name, tell the field marshall why I disagree."

"I remind you again," Mälzer shouted to the consul, "this is my business and I am the commander here. Anyway, no one asked you to come here!"

With a mocking salute Mälzer walked away, and Möllhausen angrily jumped into his car. The consul was driving toward his Embassy, hoping to call Kesselring before Mälzer did, when suddenly he saw Kappler's car speeding toward Via Rasella. Möllhausen and Kappler stopped their vehicles, got out, and discussed the situation.

"That fool Mälzer wants to blow up all the houses here," Möllhausen ranted. "He must be stopped at any cost!"

After some minutes, Kappler returned to his car and continued on to Via Rasella, where Dollmann confronted him and repeated what the consul had said, but in a calmer manner. Both men knew that a far-reaching decision would have to be made on the spot . . .

Dollmann seldom went out of his way to commit evil, but he was usually willing to go along with it—after all, was he not enjoying the fruit of such collaboration? Kappler did not collaborate with evil; he was part of its machinery. This distinction in commitment and role created friction between them, and this friction was exacerbated by social differences. Dollmann's aristocratic snobbery clashed sharply with Kappler's small-town policeman's mentality.

Recently, there had been a certain improvement in their relations because of an attempt by Kappler's estranged wife to use Dollmann to damage her husband's reputation in revenge for his flagrant infidelity. Frau Kappler had offered Dollmann copies of reports that Kappler had made about him to his superiors. Dollmann informed Kappler of his wife's machinations—thus putting the Gestapo chief in Dollmann's debt. As it turned out, Kappler's wife solicited help elsewhere and almost had her husband recalled from Rome.

Kappler could not afford any more scandals. He was an ambitious man. He had even adopted a son through the Lebensborn society for fatherless SS children since he knew that he would not get much further in the SS without a child, and he was prepared to carry out the orders of his superiors to the last comma.

But Dollmann remained a threat. He knew many things about Kappler's private life aside from what his wife had told him—for example, that Kappler was having an affair with a mysterious Dutch girl whom Dollmann deeply distrusted. And Dollmann *was* a protégé of Himmler and Wolff.

The decision as to what to do next in the affair of Via Rasella was not a simple one . . .

"You see, Kappler?" Mälzer said, greeting the Gestapo chief. "You see what they have done to my boys? Now I am going to blow up all these houses."

Kappler stared at the row of bodies that the survivors had laid along the street, then quietly persuaded Mälzer to return to his headquarters, promising to take care of everything. As Kappler helped him into his car, Mälzer, glancing at the civilians lined up in front of Barberini Palace, issued one more order:

"They are all to be shot!"

But the cold and methodical Kappler decided to defy Mälzer's unstable show of authority. Although technically Mälzer, as the Commandant of Rome, was his superior, Kappler had really to obey only his SS bosses.

Now if only he could keep that gossipy Dollmann out of his hair.

Consul Möllhausen arrived at the German Embassy about an hour after the incident, still in a state of fury. He kicked aside a chair in his path, picked up the telephone, and called Kesselring, only to learn that he was at the front and could not be reached. He then spoke with Kesselring's chief of operations, Colonel Dietrich Beelitz, who immediately called Hitler's headquarters in East Prussia. A Hitler aide, General Treusch von Buttlar, went to report the Via Rasella incident to the Führer and returned to the telephone a half hour later, about 4:30. He told Beelitz:

"He is in an uproar and wants an entire quarter of the city blown up together with all those who live there, and he wants an exceptionally high number of Italians to be shot. For every German policeman shot he wants from thirty to fifty Italians shot."

That night Möllhausen, after learning of Hitler's order from Beelitz, rushed to see Kappler at Via Tasso and a scene took place reminiscent of their encounter months before when an order had come to round up the Jews for deportation.

"I do not have to tell you," the consul reports he said, "that I would do nothing to aid or favor the enemy. I do not forget that we are at war. But what you plan to do goes beyond war and the Fatherland . . ."

Kappler listened patiently, his small, lead-gray eyes expressionless. What might one expect to hear from a weepy diplomat?

"All those picked," he calmly replied, "will be, or already have been, sentenced to death. Or else they are guilty of at least being *Todeskandidaten* [candidates for death] . . . For each name that I write, I shall think three times."

Kappler would do considerable thinking that night, for he would have to compile a death list of 320 men—ten for each of the thirty-two Germans killed on Via Rasella. General Eberhard von Mackensen, commander of the Fourteenth Army, to whom Mälzer was responsible, first set that figure on his own in discussing a reprisal with Kappler. Mackensen also approved the idea of executing only *Todeskandidaten* —persons already in prison and condemned to death or life imprisonment, and detainees who had not yet been judged but were accused of crimes punishable by death.

What if there were not enough Italians in these categories to make up the full required list? Never mind, said Mackensen. The full figure could be publicized even if fewer were actually shot. Now all that was needed to implement this reprisal plan was the approval of Kesselring and Hitler.

When Kesselring returned from the front that evening and learned with shock what had happened, he agreed to the plan and telephoned Hitler's headquarters. The chief of staff, Colonel General Alfred Jodl, after conferring with the Führer, relayed final approval. The reprisal Hitler ordered must be carried out within twenty-four hours. Kesselring was relieved. After all, people who deserved to die would die. He did not question Kappler's apparent assurances that only men in the prescribed categories would be shot—though he was aware that there were few such men. The less he knew about the details of the operation, the better.

But the details *did* greatly interest Kappler, who had to compose the list of men who would die. The number of *Todeskandidaten* available in Via Tasso, Regina Coeli, and Koch's torture house was insignificant indeed compared to the total figure needed—only four prisoners were actually under sentence of death. He would thus have to add many "less guilty" people to the list.

But Kappler did not dare tell anyone, especially not Dollmann, who might resort to blackmail and would certainly ask General Wolff to order Kappler to cut down the list and then lie about it publicly—as General Mackensen had instructed. Wolff had already ordered Kappler to delay all reprisal plans until he, Wolff, arrived from Fasano the following day, March 24, but Kappler would go ahead anyway, as Hitler had commanded.

After working through the night and conferring with Caruso and Koch, Kappler found that he could not complete his list even by including the vaguest suspects in hand. But his immediate SS superior, General Wilhelm Harster, made a helpful suggestion by phone from his headquarters in Verona:

"If you can't reach the right figure, take as many Jews as you need."

Kappler thought this was a fine idea, but found that he did not have enough Jews to make up the required number. He would have to collect a new batch.[5]

Luigi Rosselli, whose Fascist band specialized in capturing Jews for money, had a new assignment for his Jewish agent, Celeste (Stella) Di Porto. The Germans needed fifty Jews urgently.

On the night of March 23 she went prowling for Jews with other members of the gang.

One victim was twenty-two-year-old Pacifico Di Segni, who was captured in the home of a friend. As was her custom, Celeste, immediately after the young man's arrest, went to see his mother, feeling that it was only fair to break the news to loved ones personally. The elderly woman grew hysterical. Celeste had already taken two other sons from her—Giacomo and Angelo—who had both been deported. This was the girl's third visit of death. Noting that this time she looked more prosperous, wearing several gold bracelets, the mother begged:

"My Celeste, I will give you a bracelet that weighs twice as much as all those put together, but give my son back to me."

"Don't worry," Celeste replied sympathetically. "He's fine where he is. I've given him a mess tin so that he can eat."

During the rest of the night, Celeste led her companions to other victims. But she was still short of her quota. Then, after daylight . . . what luck! There, walking down Via Arenula, was Lazzaro Anticoli, known as Bucefalo the Boxer, who had been a famous prize fighter before Mussolini's racial laws excluded Jews from even that activity.

As he strolled along, Anticoli suddenly saw Celeste approaching, accompanied by three men. Before he could flee, the men were upon him, but he had not forgotten how to fight and with several punches laid them out, one by one. However, six more men then ran up and though he threw punches wildly, they finally overcame him.

They first dragged him to Celeste's apartment, where they beat him into a pulpy mess while the hostess serenely looked on, then to Regina Coeli. On arriving, Celeste learned that one of the Jews picked up was her own brother, Angelo. Whether she cared very much one cannot know, but there seemed to be more than enough Jews now to complete the death list anyway. A prison secretary typed the name "Lazzaro Anticoli" on a narrow strip of paper and pasted it over the name "Angelo Di Porto."

And in cell number 386 of the third block, Anticoli scratched on the wall the inscription: "I am Lazzaro Anticoli known as Bucefalo the Boxer—if I don't see my family again it is the fault of that traitor Celeste Di Porto. Avenge me!"

Meanwhile, Celeste's father was seen sitting on a curbstone with his face in his hands, sobbing convulsively. He had just been approached by a victim's mother who besought him to intervene with Celeste for her son. He had looked at the woman with a black stare, helpless in his agony, and she had cursed him in her own agony. Nor was his wife around to comfort him. She was begging in the streets with her youngest children.

And so Celeste's father presented himself to the Germans as a way to expiate what he regarded as his share of the responsibility for his daughter's crimes—though too late for inclusion on the death list that Celeste had helped to round out.[6]

"Mamma, Mamma, they've killed me!"

Lieutenant Giglio was barely able to utter these words on the night of March 23, several hours after the Via Rasella incident, when Walter Di Franco, Koch's master torturer—and an old acquaintance of Giglio —had kicked him violently in the groin. Peter Tompkins' agent had been sitting on a bed in the torture room, wiping blood from his mouth after a beating, while weakly calling out to his mother when Di Franco delivered the blow. As he tried to turn on his side, Walter kicked him again, this time between the kidneys and the sacroiliac.

Di Franco was in a frenzy. Not only did Giglio refuse to talk, but earlier in the day, when Di Franco had offered the Lieutenant a cigarette, chocolate, and verbal regrets for the pain he had caused him, hoping to soften him up, Giglio had groaned contemptuously:

"Walter, you are like Judas!'"

At about 2:30 P.M. on March 24, Di Franco informed those in Giglio's cell that they would be turned over to the Gestapo and that each of them might send a last note to his family. Giglio was immediately taken to Regina Coeli.

At about that time, Peter Tompkins was hosting a tea party in Baldo's apartment surrounded by the same girls and agents who had been at the previous party. Franco Malfatti arranged this one to establish whether it was safe to reoccupy Baldo's flat. As the guests sat around a fire consuming tea, cakes, and good French brandy, Tompkins began to forget his fears.

The following day, a partisan locksmith would enter a vacant apartment just below Koch's headquarters and plant enough dynamite to blow a hole in his floor. In the ensuing confusion, Tompkins and his agents would attack the guards and free Giglio and the other prisoners. But now Tompkins was preoccupied with the girl called L., who was eyeing him curiously—the girl who had gone with him that night to fetch the German SS officer, Captain Priebke.

The American could not know that at that moment Priebke was at the caves on Via Ardeatine, a network of tunnels that had been excavated about forty years earlier, where the hostages would be killed. Priebke's job was to make sure that everyone on Kappler's death list— including Lieutenant Giglio—was actually executed that day.[7]

The sun streamed through the window of Colonel Kappler's office in Via Tasso on the morning of March 24, and the Gestapo chief, though exhausted from the long night's work, was cheered as usual by the view of the lovely Roman garden behind the building, the evergreens, magnolias, myrtles, and fine cypresses, the gaily colored flowers. But today he would have no time to linger in the garden as he often did when following the narrow gravel path that curved around a spouting fountain to the seventeenth-century villa at its far end.

Today in the villa the torture scenes would be limited to those portrayed in the frescoes covering its walls and ceilings, scenes from Dante's *Inferno* that featured Lucifer and his devils at work . . .

Almost every day Kappler would make the short trip through the garden to watch his own devils at work—prying information out of men whose agony was the greater for the scent of roses still clinging to their nostrils from their own garden walk. Immaculately dressed in civilian clothes, his trousers sharply creased, his tie in perfect harmony with his suit, Kappler would enter a small room with walled-up windows, sit down, and observe the illumined face of the prisoner tied to a chair and blinded by the glare of a high-powered lamp. A quiet, friendly voice would break the silence:

"If you give the names of your companions, you will have ten thousand lire and your immediate freedom."

"I don't know anything."

"You will have twenty thousand lire if you speak. Come on, don't be foolish. We know that you are a good boy. It's only your bad friends who have misguided you. Speak and you will be saved."

"I have nothing to say."

"Speak! Speak for your own good . . . *Schnell*, quickly . . . the names of your companions."

Silence.

The voice, belonging to Kappler, issues an order to two soldiers at his side, and they take off one of the prisoner's shoes and insert his toes between the cylindrical drum and the base plate of a mimeograph machine where paper is normally fed in.

"Will you speak now?"

"No . . . Murderers!"

A soldier turns the handle of the machine.

"Now do you want to tell me the names?"

Hidden in the shadows, Kappler gives a sign and the handle is tightened further.

A piercing cry, a pathetic whimper . . .

Another turn. The man's pupils disappear beneath his eyelids. A stream of saliva snakes from his mouth. His head falls back. Kappler orders his toes removed from the machine. Blackish blood drips to the floor.

Kappler looks at his watch. Time to go. His girl friend is waiting. He is disappointed, but his men stood up well. He is proud of them . . .[8]

Yes, they were well trained, conditioned . . . But so many prisoners must die; so many hours were needed. How long at one stretch could a man, even an SS man, remain dehumanized? Even Major Hellmuth Dobbrick, commander of the battalion that had been attacked on Via Rasella, had refused to order his soldiers to avenge their own comrades. It was up to Kappler. And although the Gestapo chief had faith in his own men, he was nevertheless concerned.

With renewed energy, Kappler now called for his officers and, as they sat before him in his office, told them that they must be the first to shoot the hostages and thereby set an example for their men. Anyone— officer or enlisted man—who refused to fire would be court-martialed!

But Kappler's heart was really softer than his death lists suggested . . .

"Would you feel better if I were at your side when you fired?" Kappler gently asked one of his young officers, SS Obersturmführer Wetjen.

The doomed men in Via Tasso had all been brought to the Ardeatine Caves in a convoy of trucks, ignorant of their fate until the last minute. Wetjen had refused to join in the killing, which had been going on for a few hours already, telling Kappler that he felt a "revulsion." Well, Kappler thought, that was understandable. Wetjen was just a boy who meant well but still lacked experience. And Kappler had to agree that this assignment was not simple, especially since he had decided to shoot the victims individually to make sure they were dead and to ease the problem of hiding the bodies.

He had himself killed a victim already—each soldier had to choose one, force him to his knees, and fire a bullet into his neck—and he well realized that it was a messy, tedious business. And it was getting messier and more tedious by the hour. After the victims were shot inside the caves, the bodies had to be stacked up neatly to leave room for others, and the stacking job was becoming ever more difficult as the pyramids of corpses grew higher.

Nor was the situation at the caves Kappler's only problem. The Via Tasso prisoners were now being killed, but those from Regina Coeli had not even left the prison yet. Caruso was not performing efficiently. Kappler had sent an officer to Regina Coeli to impose a deadline; Caruso had until 4:30 P.M. to process the release of the fifty men on his list.

When the deadline passed, Kappler's officer simply grabbed at random all the prisoners he could find and threw them on a truck, creating even greater delays, since Caruso, now in a panic, had to cross off the list a corresponding number of names in order not to exceed his quota.

Who should he cross off? He picked names indiscriminately, though concentrating on the Jews, since—at least to an Italian—they seemed less guilty than the political suspects. After all, ten of the Jews on the list, mostly brought in that morning by Celeste Di Porto and other members of the Rosselli gang, had been added only a few hours earlier after a thirty-third German victim of the Via Rasella attack had died— since Hitler had ordered ten deaths for one—and so it seemed logical to give the Jews a break.

Caruso was not particular which ones. Nor, at this point, did Kappler care who was on the list. He wanted corpses. At 8 P.M., Hitler's twenty-four-hour deadline would be up, and the last victim had to be dead by then.

Kappler's principal problem at the moment was morale. His men were getting tired and despondent, sloppy in their shooting. It was one thing to machine-gun a mass of people, but somehow quite another to shoot person after person at close range. A man, even an SS man, could be disturbed when he had time to note that he was murdering another human being.

Kappler had to maintain discipline. He tried to explain this to Wetjen in the calm, rational way a father might tell the facts of life to his adolescent son. Wetjen finally agreed, and Kappler put his arm around the youth's waist as they entered the caves together. Each then fired into the neck of a prisoner, and Captain Priebke, Peter Tompkins' party guest, who kept tabs, marked off two more names on his list. Wetjen had learned the facts of life—and death.

Kappler finally solved the stacking problem, too. When the grisly pyramids grew too high for his men to pile additional bodies upon, the victims were forced to climb atop their dead comrades so that when they were shot their bodies would not have to be moved.

Thus did 335 men perish—actually five more than called for under the ten-to-one ratio plan approved by Hitler. A miscalculation had been made, but since the extra five were already there—and could be dangerous witnesses if they lived—it seemed foolish not to kill them, too. When the operation was finally completed, the Nazis sealed the caves by dynamiting the entrance and went home to get drunk as thoughtfully ordered by Kappler.*

Among those buried in the mountains of flesh were Colonel Montezemolo; his diplomatic collaborator, Filippo Grenet; Lieutenant Giglio; Luigi Pierantoni, the partisan son of Amedeo Pierantoni, in whose home Chief Rabbi Zolli had hidden; and, of seventy Jews, twenty-six who had been betrayed by Celeste Di Porto, including her cousin Armando Di Segni, Pacifico Di Segni (no relation to Armando), and Lazzaro Anticoli, the boxer.

One prisoner spared—at least temporarily—was Father Morosini, who had remained on his knees in prayer while Nazi soldiers flung open the cell doors in Regina Coeli and dragged out those whose names were on the list, tying their hands behind them and kicking and pushing them down the stairs in their furious effort to meet Kappler's deadline. After the Pope had personally intervened in the priest's behalf, Kesselring referred his case to Hitler himself and was still awaiting a reply.[9]

While rumors of massive retaliation against the Resistance for the Via Rasella killings ricocheted across Rome, the Nazis remained cruelly silent throughout the next day, March 25. On the morning of March 26, Rosario Bentivegna and Carla Capponi were among many Romans anxiously waiting at the entrance to the *Il Messaggero* building for the noon edition of the newspaper to come out.

Finally, someone placed an unfolded copy behind the glass of a display case and the small crowd pushed forward, straining to read it. All eyes focused on a two-column box in bold type halfway down the page. After a few moments Rosario and Carla stared at each other in anguish. A Nazi communiqué read:

> On the afternoon of March 23, 1944, criminal elements executed a bomb attack against a column of German police in transit through Via Rasella. As a result of this ambush, thirty-two men of the German police were killed and several wounded.

* A German noncommissioned officer has left a description of the massacre: "The prisoners had their hands bound behind their backs. Their feet too were tied so that they could move only with very short steps or jumps. They were picked up and thrown into the lorries like baggage. Many of them had signs of ill treatment on their faces and some had lost their teeth. Out of curiosity, I went into the caves and watched the execution of about sixty hostages. They were made to kneel in a row of from five to ten, one behind the other. SS men, stepping behind the rows, discharged their guns into the necks of the victims. They died quietly, some crying 'Long live Italy!' Most of them were praying . . . An old man, whom I learned to be General Simoni, was speaking words of encouragement to all the rest . . . I came away because I felt I was going to be sick."

Above, SS Col. Eugen Dollmann chats with Hitler.

Left, Col. Gen. Heinrich von Vietinghoff, General Wolff, and Colonel Dollmann, left to right.

Left, General von Vietinghoff being questioned after his capture by the Allies.

Below, General Mälzer politicking in Rome in 1944.

Above,
SS Col. Herbert Kappler
after his capture
by the Allies.

Left,
German Ambassador
Ernst von Weizsäcker.

Mussolini is briefed by an officer in Field Marshal Kesselring's headquarters.

Left, Fascist Special Police Chief Pietro Koch.

Below, Fascist Police Chief Gen. Pietro Caruso (left foreground) after his capture by the Allies.

Pope Pius XII blesses crowd after Allied bombing near San Giovanni in Laterano in August 1943.

Monsignor Giovanni Battista Montini (now Pope Paul VI) stands beside Pius XII.

Cardinal Luigi Maglione, Vatican Secretary of State.

The vile ambush was carried out by Communisti-Badogliani. An investigation is still being made to clarify the extent to which this criminal deed is attributable to Anglo-American involvement.

The German Command has decided to terminate the activities of these villainous bandits. No one will be allowed to sabotage with impunity the newly affirmed Italo-German co-operation. The German Command has therefore ordered that for every murdered German ten Communisti-Badogliani criminals be shot. This order has already been executed.

The communiqué understated the extent of reprisal by declaring that thirty-two rather than thirty-three Germans had been killed on Via Rasella, thereby implying that only 320 Italians were shot in retaliation when, in reality, 335 were executed. Not only did the Germans wish to hide the fact that Kappler had killed five more men than the ten-to-one ratio order required, but Kappler's colleagues, looking to possible postwar repercussions, were far from sure that it was "legal" to shoot the ten extra hostages shot for the German who died *after* the order was issued.

The Romans were shocked and paralyzed by the German communiqué, and none more so than Rosario and Carla. They and their fellow Communist leaders had expected a reprisal—one large enough to move the Romans to revolt, but not this large. Suddenly they realized that some of the top Resistance leaders, the people on whom they had depended to help lead the revolt—once they had somehow got out of prison—had probably been killed. Had the Communists defeated their own purpose? Who *were* the victims? The Germans remained silent while Rome mourned for unknown martyred sons.

To learn the fate of loved ones, relatives of prisoners lined up in front of Regina Coeli carrying packages of linen or food wrapped in brown paper, calculating that if the guards accepted a package the prisoner was still alive, and if they rejected it he was dead. In almost unbearable anxiety, the visitors waited for the "reply." Most visitors departed with their packages.

Finally, after many days, in some cases, weeks, the relatives of the dead were notified. By this time, a terrible stench had begun to pervade the area around the Ardeatine Caves.[10]

On the morning of March 25, before the German communiqué was issued, Peter Tompkins was waiting in his apartment for Franco Malfatti to arrive with news of the hour and final arrangements for the raid they were to stage on Koch's headquarters that day. The rumor that the Germans had killed many hostages had not eased his hangover from the "tea party" he had hosted the day before, though he did not guess that Giglio was among the victims. It was Malfatti who informed him.

"They have shot Cervo [Giglio's code name] and eleven of our men."

Only then did Tompkins notice Malfatti's paleness and bloodshot eyes.

"We will kill a lot of guilty Fascists," Malfatti said, gripping Tompkins' arm.

"All who are guilty," replied Tompkins.

Nevertheless, Tompkins did not feel sad or depressed. He was, in a strange way, relieved. Giglio's death had ended for him what must have been horrible torture, and for Tompkins, the terrible fear that Giglio might be forced to talk. At the same time, he writes in his memoirs, there "was the warm, glowing realization that a human being had achieved one of the highest peaks within his limits." And the peak was especially high, since Giglio, if he had given his comrades away, might have saved himself. As his father worked for the Fascist secret police, he might easily have passed off the story that he had been a double agent all along.

Tompkins suddenly realized that at the very moment Giglio was being shot, he himself had probably been guzzling brandy while cuddling in the arms of a girl. But even if he had known the moment Giglio was to die, he thought, "we might have but drunk deeper, danced later into the night."[11]

SS General Wolff was enraged when he learned on his arrival in Rome at 3 P.M., March 24, that the Ardeatine massacre was in progress. Not because he disapproved of the action, but because Kappler had not waited for authority from him to proceed.

Colonel Dollmann, who, after meeting Wolff at Viterbo Airport two hours earlier, had accompanied him to Kesselring's headquarters in Monte Soratte, claims in his memoirs that he was also irate, but for a different reason. He had surmised that Kappler was planning some kind of reprisal for Via Rasella, but had not been informed of the details and had felt sure anyway that Kappler would not act before Wolff arrived. And Dollmann had hoped, he writes, to persuade Wolff, whom he considered a reasonable man, to prevent any killings.

He says that he had a plan of his own: Fly the families of the men killed on Via Rasella to Rome and parade them through the streets in a solemn funeral procession to win the sympathy of the Romans. Simultaneously, the Germans would threaten drastic action if terrorism continued. According to Dollmann, he had actually discussed this plan elements," the occupier, need only be "aware" of their responsibility toward human life. After all, the "irresponsible elements" *had* provoked the "responsible." And had not the Pope himself asked the Germans to increase their police force in Rome in order to maintain law and order? It would be difficult now to tell them how to run their business.

And so, on the very day the article appeared, the Vatican reached an agreement with the Germans for an open city. The Germans did remove some troops and equipment from the city: by no means all but enough to keep the Allies from making any further air raids on Rome. Pius had at once appeased the Nazis and the Allies, justifying in his eyes the Vatican's neutralist policy . . .[18]

Monsignor Bonaldi, the chaplain at Regina Coeli prison, quietly entered Father Morosini's cell and stared at the man sleeping peacefully on the floor. It was 4 A.M., April 3.

"My God! My God!" he whispered to himself.

He gently prodded the priest, calling out his name. Morosini shook himself awake.

"Monsignor, you here . . . at this time?" he muttered.

Bonaldi did not answer, but simply looked at him tenderly. After a moment's silence, the priest started to get up.

"I understand," he said calmly.

Hitler had replied to the Pope's appeal for clemency, transmitted through Kesselring, with a harshly worded refusal. Father Morosini must die.

"Be brave," Bonaldi murmured.

Morosini replied with a smile: "Monsignor, it takes more courage to live than to die."

When Bonaldi had heard his confession and had given him absolution, Morosini exclaimed: "What a beautiful day this is, and how full of peace I feel!"

The two clerics then went to the prison chapel to celebrate Mass with the condemned man's relatives and other priests. Before the communion, Morosini pardoned the man who had betrayed him and the judges who had condemned him and prayed for peace and prosperity for Italy. Then he was taken in an open truck to Forte Bravetta, where he faced the Italian firing squad and said:

"I am the victim of the love of my country, for which I offer my last thoughts."

And he pardoned those who must kill him.

Still dressed in his clerical robes, he was tied to a chair, blindfolded, with his back to the firing squad. The commander gave the order to fire, but most of the executioners fired into the ground, and the priest was only wounded. An Italian officer came up and delivered a *coup de grace*, but, strangely, his bullet was not fatal either. Then someone fired a burst from a submachine gun, finally killing the prisoner.

In his last words, Father Morosini had asked the attending monsignor to thank the Pope for trying to save him and to tell the Holy Father that he was offering his life for him.[14]

❖   ❖   ❖

Dollmann had been surprised when he learned from Father Pfeiffer that the Pope had ignored his plan for avoiding a reprisal, but he saw some virtue in this demonstration of Vatican deference to the Germans. It could perhaps help Dollmann frustrate the plan to deport a good part of the Roman population.

On the night of the Via Rasella reprisal, Dollmann met with several colleagues, including Wolff, Kappler, and Möllhausen, in Wolff's suite in the Excelsior Hotel to discuss the executions and the deportation plan. When Kappler, his eyes flaming in dark sockets, his face gray and haggard, reported on the killings, Wolff, according to Möllhausen, said that the Romans did not "merit favored treatment." They must suffer more.

Wolff then detailed plans for deporting them, but Dollmann and Möllhausen pointed out the technical difficulties and the terrible world-wide reaction that would follow. In this case, Dollmann said, he was sure the Pope would not remain silent. And had not the Pope been most co-operative so far? Even Kappler showed no enthusiasm for the plan, which would only create new, massive problems for him as the local Gestapo chief. Especially so if the Pope protested.

At about one in the morning of March 25, Dollmann telephoned Himmler, after persuading Wolff to let him explain the need for Ambassador von Weizsäcker to discuss the matter with the Pope to make sure the pontiff would not publicly condemn the deportation. Dollmann argued, in his call to Himmler, that nothing could be gained and much could be lost by provoking the Pope with these deportations. Himmler reluctantly agreed to Dollmann's suggestion that they be postponed on condition that "in the judgment of the influential people in Rome it is absolutely essential."

The next day, Wolff and Dollmann went back to see Kesselring, who seemed more opposed to the plan than ever after listening to all the arguments. Möllhausen reports that he had visited Kesselring that morning and had drawn a verbal picture for him: "Hundreds of thousands of persons marching north on foot . . . carrying their possessions, with the weaker ones falling along the way . . . The supply roads blocked, the troops endangered."

Most persuasive of all was the unsentimental military rationale of General von Mackensen. His Fourteenth Army was planning a new attempt to throw the Allied forces at Anzio into the sea, and he could not spare troops for a nonmilitary purpose. As for the Tenth Army, it was at that moment fighting off an Allied assault on Monte Cassino.

Wolff, who had already been authorized by Himmler to postpone the operation until the Pope could be persuaded to remain silent, now advised Himmler that he would hold off until the Fourteenth Army could spare the troops needed—presumably after the new attack on the Anzio beachhead (the planned attack, in the end, was cancelled). Meanwhile, Kappler prepared a plan for the deportation operation.

This assignment, perhaps because it was so challenging, kindled Kappler's enthusiasm, especially after new, if minor, terrorist attacks cast doubt on the deterrent value of the Ardeatine massacre. He decided to test the plan with a relatively small round-up. At dawn on April 17, his men and those of Caruso surrounded the Quadraro quarter, considered a dangerous refuge for Communists and other partisans, entered each house methodically, and dragged off every man they could find, young or old. About 750 people were thus deported to German concentration or labor camps.[15]

❖ ❖ ❖

The prospect of another, vastly larger round-up added to Dollmann's growing conviction that perhaps only the Pope's influence could save Rome, the Romans, the Vatican, and, incidentally, Germans like himself. He had told Weizsäcker about Himmler's deportation plan and the ambassador, shocked by its brutal audacity and, playing for time, apparently informed the Pope of it. This time, Dollmann says he felt, should be used to help Pius extend his influence for the salvation of Rome.

Dollmann apparently felt that he could not afford to fail in this effort. Aside from his love for the city and its artistic beauty, he knew that Germany was losing the war. It was just a matter of time. And what better way was there to protect himself than to demonstrate to the victors—with the support of the Vatican—that *he* had made it possible to save the Eternal City?

Not only was the mass deportation being planned, but, as the Allies approached, the papal kidnap plot might be revived, for Hitler was still reluctant to let the Pope fall under Allied control or influence. Furthermore, Mussolini was continuing to pressure the Germans to fight for every street and building in Rome, while coolly calculating that such battle would produce 200,000 dead and 20,000 destroyed houses.

In mid-March, about a week before Via Rasella, a top assistant of the Duce, Prefect Zerbino, had arrived in Rome and asked Dollmann to arrange a meeting with Kesselring. He said that Mussolini was extremely worried about rumors that Kesselring might evacuate Rome without defending it—and the Duce did not exclude the possibility that Dollmann had induced the field marshal to make such a decision for mistaken psychological and moral reasons.

Dollmann claims to have asked Zerbino whether the people in Salò had lost their heads. Didn't they realize what the destruction of Rome, even if only partial, would mean to the world at large? What was the Pope to do—emulate his Medici forerunner, Clement VII, by taking refuge in the Castel Sant'Angelo at dead of night and calling on the Swiss Guards to defend him and the Vatican?

Zerbino replied indignantly: "The Duce's view is that the war cannot be run like a museum tour if it is to be won at all. Besides, if need be, he has agreed to concentrate his defense on the Tiber bridges—which he trusts have all been mined long ago."

Dollmann would not arrange the interview with Kesselring but conferred himself with the field marshal. After exacting the reply he wanted—though the field marshal was actually not yet sure of his plans—Dollmann told Zerbino with straight-faced cynicism that Mussolini must state how many armed divisions he had available for a battle in Rome and agree to command them personally. Zerbino, ignoring Dollmann's mocking tone, replied that Kesselring should confine himself to following Mussolini's instructions.

Mussolini, in any event, did not give up his campaign for the defense of Rome. At a conference between Hitler and the Duce on April 22 near Salzburg, the Fascist leader pleaded his case directly to the Führer, arguing again that since Rome was the spiritual center of Italy, its loss would be disastrous politically as well as militarily. Hitler, apparently agreed, but left his options open.†

† Mussolini's bitterness toward the Romans was reflected in a conversation he had with Consul Möllhausen during a visit by Möllhausen to Salò. When the consul suggested that the Duce visit Rome, the dictator replied: "I do not want to come to

At this critical juncture, Dollmann felt that he must arrange a secret meeting immediately between the Pope and a high German military figure to co-ordinate a plan for blocking any demand by Hitler to fight in Rome, destroy the city, kidnap the Pontiff, or deport the Romans. Kesselring would never do anything behind Hitler's back. But Wolff? . . . After all, he had already resisted the kidnap plot. Was he not, like himself, looking to the future? A little religion might do him—and thus Rome—some good.

Actually, Wolff's sense of realism, together with his vanity and ego, had already calmed his Nazi fury. Though he had demanded terrible punishment for all Romans, he would save the life of one of the most "dangerous"—at once assuring a useful future reference and impressing his gallantry upon a beautiful young woman . . .[16]

"Have courage," urged the sister of Michele Multedo, the aristocratic young painter who had worked with Colonel Montezemolo. "We're lifting heaven and earth to help you."

Multedo had been arrested on April 17 after living what seemed like a charmed life. Not only had he barely escaped the Gestapo when it had trapped and arrested Montezemolo, but he had almost been caught one day when, dressed like a priest, he had entered a church to meet a Resistance contact. As the police followed, he hid in a confessional booth and escaped only after reluctantly rejecting the efforts of a woman in the adjoining booth to confess her sins to him.

Shortly afterward he was finally captured on the street and imprisoned in Via Tasso. Despite his importance in the Resistance movement, he was given better treatment than the other prisoners because, as an artist, he was held in unusual respect by the cultured German torturers and killers at the prison. He was even permitted to receive members of his family and friends.

Multedo's sister had come, accompanied by a stunning young woman with dark hair and blue eyes, Eleanora, or Lia T. Multedo, who expected to be shot soon by his respectful wardens, realized that his only hope lay in Lia. She was a close friend of the father of his col-

---

Rome until, side by side with the Germans, Italian troops are fighting on the front. I shall come to Rome when the city is defended by my own people." There was a risk, Möllhausen persisted, that the Romans "might place a different interpretation on your absence"—that he was apparently afraid of his own people. Mussolini replied: "And who says the Romans will applaud me if I come?" "Experience . . . teaches that they will," said the consul. "And if that is so," responded the Duce, "why did they throw my photo out of the window on July 25 [when he was deposed]?" Möllhausen: "Nations are like schoolboys: When the teacher has been in class too long and then goes out, they feel the need to kick up a row." Mussolini smiled: "That is an original thought." But he never returned to Rome.

laborator, Ettore Basevi, who directed Centro X's underground press and forgery service, and she often used her German contacts to help the Resistance.

Her principal contact was SS Captain Ludwig Wemmer, the man whom Martin Bormann had sent to the German Embassy to the Holy See to spy on Ambassador von Weizsäcker. Apparently through Wemmer, who, if he was not hoodwinked, was being cleverly opportunistic in the face of certain German defeat, Lia had obtained, among other things, special identity documents signed by Weizsäcker for the Basevis and other partisans. The supreme irony was that the elder Basevi was half Jewish.

Multedo was nevertheless doubtful that even Lia could help him. After all, some of the most important people in Italy had been massacred in the Ardeatine Caves. Would he fare better, especially with the Germans aware that he had been a close associate of Montezemolo? His only consolation was that he had managed to save others. By sheer ingenuity he had kept the Nazis from finding his little notebook so packed with names and addresses.

As soon as Multedo had been thrust into an already crowded cell, a tiny, bare room with boarded-up windows and almost no ventilation, he offered to sketch his guard, who readily agreed. Multedo removed the notebook from his pocket, sat on a plank bed, and began drawing, but after several minutes he studied the sketch and shook his head, then started again on the next page. Somehow he was still dissatisfied and kept turning pages. Finally, he completed a good likeness on the last leaf, which he tore out and presented to the delighted guard—who did not suspect that Multedo had blacked out the information on all the other pages!

Multedo had wondered whether he could endure torture; whether he had the courage and character of Montezemolo, who would not speak though he had suffered the most horrible agony. The interrogations began. Where were the secret radios? Who was operating them? Who had replaced Montezemolo? Claiming mistaken identity, Multedo played the madman. He replied to questions with dissertations on philosophy and religion. He recited poems and finally asked for a piano!

"If you answer our questions," replied the frustrated interrogator, "we will give you a piano."

When several sessions still yielded no information, Multedo was taken to a room that featured bloodstains on the wall and a table with belts in the center. He desperately argued that he had a heart disease, breathing heavily as he spoke. If they wanted to keep him alive in the hope of eventually extracting information from him, they would have to treat him gently.

The guards called an Italian doctor and Multedo was sure his scheme had failed—when suddenly the Germans were distracted by a noise on the street. As they rushed to the window, Multedo muttered to the doctor:

"Invent something or they will torture me!"

The doctor then examined him and told the Germans: "Yes, he has a very serious heart condition. He needs rest and care."

So now he was being given injections each day, and between non-violent interrogations spent his time sketching prison officials, hoping to survive as long as there were still some to be sketched. But from the way these officials were talking, time was running out, and it now seemed that Lia T. was his last hope. But did she have enough influence with the Germans? . . .

Lia thought she might. A few weeks earlier she had been dining in a restaurant with the elder Basevi when a handsome blond gentleman at a neighboring table sent a waiter to her with his card. He would grant her any three favors within his power to dispense. Would she please phone him? The card was signed "General Karl Wolff."

Lia's table companion immediately saw the possibilities of using the SS chief in Italy to help the Resistance. When Multedo was arrested, he asked Lia to call Wolff, and, after visiting Multedo in prison, she did. Reminding him of his offer, she requested the three favors: an increased milk ration for her child, *laissez-passers* for her "family"—and Multedo's release.

"I can assure you," she said, "that they have arrested the wrong man."

Wolff courteously agreed to all three requests, but he soon called her back.

"I have checked," he reported, "and the prisoner *is* the right man. He has committed serious crimes."

She had deceived him, he charged in a hurt manner.

However, Lia, with feminine wile, managed to regain his confidence and he came to visit her.

"You did give your word of honor," Lia persisted. "The word of a German officer."

Multedo was too compromised, Wolff still argued. No, he could not order his release . . . But he would cancel his planned execution.

Lia smiled. He was so kind. So chivalrous . . . Now about the milk and *laissez-passers* . . .[17]

Colonel Dollmann also had a beautiful woman on his mind. He disdained most women for their deviousness and duplicity, though many of his acquaintances perceived these very qualities in him. But

Dollmann trusted implicitly this particular woman. She might be the only person who could bring together Pius, the Vicar of Christ and Wolff, the protégé of Hitler.

Ambassador von Weizsäcker, who normally would arrange such an audience, was not even to be told about the meeting in advance, since no German official other than the ambassador was supposed to see the Pope without Berlin's approval.

Dollmann thus went to see his old friend Donna Virginia Agnelli, forty-four-year-old widow of Edoardo, the Turin Fiat heir, née Princess Parma del Monte. Wearing a Venetian lace bed jacket, Virginia greeted him from her bed in the clinic where she was recovering—under police guard—from a tonsillectomy. Shortly, another woman arrived. Dollmann rose to kiss the hand of Princess San Faustino, the patient's sister, who appeared shocked and frightened on seeing this officer with an SS insignia on his collar.

"It's quite all right," said Virginia, smiling. "Colonel Dollmann has arranged for my release." . . .

In early January 1943 two Fascist policemen in mufti had come to Virginia's magnificent old mansion, Villa del Bosco Parrasio, at the foot of Janiculum Hill in Trastevere, and asked to see her. Though she was in bed suffering from a sore throat and fever, she came downstairs and was whisked away to San Gregorio Convent, which the Fascists had converted into a relatively comfortable prison for ladies of rank and breeding but with dangerous political inclinations.

Virginia, whose mother was American (and whose son Giovanni, or Giani, is the present president of Fiat), was largely apolitical, as befitted members of industrial families that could never be sure for whom they might have to produce their products in the future. She had entertained Crown Prince Humbert, Colonel Dollmann, and many Fascist figures in her stunningly furnished drawing rooms in the preceding years.

But her heart was with the British, and she was not at all unhappy when Mussolini had been overthrown. Nor did she keep these sentiments to herself. She often conducted her cocktail chatter and telephone conversations in English rather than in Italian, providing considerable material for Fascist police diaries. Her arrest followed.

When even the most important Fascist generals and diplomats failed to obtain her release, Virginia remembered Colonel Dollmann, who had secured the freedom of other socially prominent prisoners. Dollmann had always treated Virginia with great deference, and his charm and wit had brightened many of her soirées during the golden days of Fascism. Dollmann recalls in his memoirs that he had joked about her

Anglophile tendencies and offered friendly warnings that she speak Italian rather than English to avoid arousing police suspicions. She had smiled and asked Dollmann, he relates, if he had suddenly joined the neo-Fascists.

While under detention, Virginia wrote Dollmann asking for his help. He recalls that shortly after the Germans had occupied Rome, she had, over champagne cocktails, expressed concern that when the Germans would eventually leave—and, after all, she gently pointed out, international opinion was predicting that they would—Rome might be destroyed in battle or by sabotage. She had felt that only the Pope's influence could save her beloved city.

Now here was Virginia, who knew Pius well, asking for help—at the very moment he, Dollmann, was trying to reach Pius. After receiving the approval of Wolff, who, "thinking to the future," agreed to meet with the pontiff if an audience could be arranged, Dollmann rushed to San Gregorio Convent. He advised Virginia to pretend that her sore throat had developed into a serious infection, permitting him to have her transferred to a clinic. Virginia fell gravely "ill" at once and was duly transferred. A serious case of tonsillitis, her Italian doctor falsely reported, intending to simulate a tonsillectomy and thus give his patient time to "recover" from the "operation."

But with a German doctor and nurse looking on at the operating table and Fascist guards standing outside the room, the surgeon had little choice; he would have to remove Virginia's tonsils, necessary or not. And he did, while Princess San Faustino—who did not know of Dollmann's role in the plot—stood by dressed as a nurse to silence her sister if she protested . . .

Now, Colonel Dollmann was visiting Virginia in the recovery room to tell her how she could help save Rome.

Virginia's recovery period gave Dollmann a chance to pull a few wires and, shortly after his visit, he returned to the clinic with Kesselring's own medical officer. Awed by the sight of the beribboned officer, the police, sympathizing with Virginia anyway, permitted the two Germans to leave with the patient. Still attired in lace, but with a silk scarf around her neck, Virginia found herself some minutes later in a suite of the Excelsior Hotel, German military headquarters.

But she did not stay long. Seeing her miraculous deliverance, in Dollmann's rhetoric, as a sign from heaven that she was destined to save Rome, she left for Fasano to see General Wolff. On her return to Rome, she and Dollmann pressed Father Pfeiffer, the Vatican liaison with the Germans, and he interested Cardinal Caccia Dominioni in their enterprise.

In early May, the cardinal arranged a papal audience for Virginia and she went to see Pius. He agreed to receive Wolff.

Dollmann decided to break the good news to Wolff at a dinner party to be held on May 9 during one of the general's visits to Rome. A papal audience had been scheduled, in fact, for the following day. Wolff would be surprised, since he had doubted that the man whom he was supposed to kidnap would ever receive him.

The general arrived at the party in good humor, his fair Aryan face alight, a mood perhaps stimulated by the company of an attractive blond woman he was ardently courting and who appeared to be most receptive. When Dollmann informed him of the audience, he seemed even happier and more relaxed.

In the past weeks, as reflected in his intervention on behalf of Multedo, Wolff had lost much of his lust for revenge on the people of Rome for Via Rasella. The end was drawing near and he perceived the value of cultivating personally the confidence of a man who might someday replace Adolf Hitler in his private, protective pantheon; a godly patron who could attest to his humanitarianism, his efforts to save the historic bricks and stones of Rome. And if Wolff had to save the rabble of Rome in the process—Communists, traitors, Jews—well, so be it . . .[18]

Giacomo and Eleanora Di Porto had not eaten as well since they had taken refuge in the Convent of Notre Dame de Sion. It was April 17, the birthday of Giacomo's father, and everybody in the convent, including the nuns, contributed rations for a birthday dinner that at least looked sumptuous by normal standards, including kosher food prepared jointly by Giacomo's mother and Sister Katharine, the regular cook, and such rare delicacies as chocolate—and a birthday cake!

The people sitting at the many tables seemed hopeful, even gay, as they gossiped and joked and remarked on the fine quality of the *cuisine*, and they could hardly wait for the honored guest to blow out the birthday candles so that the cake could be served. But before they tasted the cake, Eleanora cried out in sudden pain. Sister Katharine rushed over to her as she lay in Giacomo's arms and knew that the time had come. Eleanora was in labor.

The nun immediately telephoned an obstetrician who lived nearby, and Eleanora, accompanied by her mother-in-law (the danger was far greater for men violating the curfew than for women), walked in the deserted darkness to the doctor's house about five hundred yards away. Early the next morning Eleanora gave birth to a boy.

The following day she had company. Giacomo's sister Rosa, who was hiding with her husband in a private home, arrived and also gave birth to a son. The problem now was how to perform a circumcision on the two infants, for, according to Jewish tradition, all male children must be circumcised within eight days of birth. A Jewish doctor and a rabbi were finally found and, at considerable risk to themselves, emerged from hiding to come to the obstetrician's house for the double *brith* ceremony, in which the two operations were performed.

Some days later Eleanora and her baby returned to the convent and Giacomo rushed to embrace his wife and hold the child while everyone gathered around smiling and complimenting the couple on the baby's exceptional beauty. But Giacomo did not listen. He silently thanked God as he held the child before finally giving the sisters a chance to cuddle it.

His wife and baby had come through in good health, but what now? They had no home, no business, no future. And Giacomo had heard a rumor that Eleanora's whole family had been deported. They were living from day to day, in constant fear. And they had brought a son into this horrifying world . . .

Hardly had Giacomo welcomed his wife and child when a friend telephoned him: "Leave the convent at once! The Germans are coming!" . . .[19]

With his tall, broad physique almost bursting the seams of the ill-fitting civilian suit provided him by the smaller Dollmann to avoid recognition, General Wolff sat listening to the Pope with all the reverential attention he usually reserved for the Führer. According to accounts by Wolff and Dollmann, Pius said that he had heard rumors of certain goings-on at Via Tasso and asked that Wolff do something about it. Wolff promised to speak to Kappler.

Could not Wolff help to end the horrors of war by using his influence for peace? If the Germans compromised, the Pope said, maybe the Allies would, too. The Allied call for unconditional surrender, he added, was, at best, likely to prolong the war. Wolff agreed with this view and said he would do his utmost to help terminate the war.

Pius then dwelled on the immediate danger to Rome, referring to the threats of destruction and mass deportation, as well as to the papal kidnap plot.

"Whatever happens," he said, "I will not leave Rome voluntarily. My place is here and I will fight to the end for the Christian commandments of humanity and peace."

Wolff apparently promised that he would try to frustrate all plots and to avoid fighting, bloodshed, and sabotage in Rome.

The Pope was impressed. Even before the audience, Wolff, to show his good faith, had agreed to a papal request for the release from Via Tasso of Giuliano Vassalli, the Socialist party activist who had met Peter Tompkins at the meeting with the false Resistance leaders. The Pope was a personal friend of Vassalli's conservative father, who had pleaded for his intervention after Giuliano was arrested in early April.

With deep feeling, Pius told Wolff: "How many injustices, how many crimes, how many offenses against the Christian spirit of love for his fellow man, how many misunderstandings could have been avoided if you had come to me first of all."

And he warmly added: "You have a hard road to travel, General Wolff. Will you allow me to give you my blessing as you tread this perilous road—you and the members of your family?"

After the blessing, Wolff rose, clicked his heels, and stiffly raised his arm in the Nazi salute!

Father Pfeiffer, who was waiting at the open door, could hardly believe his eyes. But Pope Pius XII smiled forbearingly. Wolff, in his enthrallment, had simply confused his gods.

The following day, May 11, the Allies began the drive that would finally settle the fate of Rome, its people, and its Pope.[20]

II

The Race

8

The Rippers

In the cellar of the monastery atop Monte Cassino, the bell on St. Benedict's finger jingled furiously. The Germans headquartered in the ruins of the great edifice were sharing the cellar with a statue of the saint, who held a book in one hand while pointing in emphasis with the other as he silently preached.

Ironically, Benedict had preached the principles of a new civilizing movement in this embattled monastery, which he had built in the sixth century upon the ruins of a pagan shrine to house his Benedictine order. Constructed in the form of a trapezium around five cloistered courtyards, the original abbey reached four stories high and had thick, cream-colored walls pocked with small windows reminiscent of eyes— eyes that stared at the world either with benevolence or with majestic cruelty.

Time and again armies surging to and from Rome had manipulated or attacked this shining monument to human progress, turning it into a dark symbol of death. Finally, in February 1944, Allied bombs reduced it to a scorched, skeletal structure with great open wounds, a grotesque monster that seemed deadlier and more vicious for its brutal deface- ment.

"Benedict is sounding the alarm," Lieutenant Hans-Joachim Weck noted as the bell rang once again.

Actually, the bell was hardly needed to let the Germans know that a shell had landed nearby. The earth shook and the walls trembled,

and dust billowed into every gutted room, requiring the defenders to wear gas masks. No one could see or breathe without one, and Weck felt that he had been entombed alive, along with the dead, who were sprawled everywhere in the jagged debris.

"What's happening?" Weck asked his companies over the radio.

"Strong artillery fire!" came the answer each time.

No one knew if this artillery barrage signaled the start of the long-awaited big Allied offensive.

Weck could not call Tenth Army headquarters for information and instructions since it had been knocked out. And Field Marshal Kesselring's headquarters at Monte Soratte had also been bombed, forcing the field marshal and his staff to take refuge in nearby mountain caves. Later, Kesselring did manage to communicate orders from these make-shift quarters.

"The attack has begun! Hold your positions!"

A shell suddenly burrowed through the monastery walls to the cellar room where ammunition was stored, exploding and starting a fire, and Weck and his men were barely able to extinguish the blaze with sand and blankets before the flames reached the explosives.

Monte Cassino was simply a diversionary target, a sideshow, Weck had been assured. The main attack would come from the sea.

Perhaps. But if the bell on St. Benedict's finger did not stop tinkling soon, there might be no one left for the enemy to divert.[1]

Before the attack began on the night of May 11, General Alexander, in his order of the day, subtly tried to stress the connection between the blow about to be delivered in Italy and the long-awaited assault across the English Channel. The Combined Chiefs of Staff had directed that, for security reasons, the connection could not be specifically mentioned, but Washington and London had agreed he could say:

"From the East and the West, from the North and the South, blows are about to fall which will result in the final destruction of the Nazis and bring freedom once again to Europe, and hasten peace for us all."

And proudly he added: "To us in Italy has been given the honor to strike the first blow."

❖ ❖ ❖

Major Humphry Platt, commander of A Company, 2nd Battalion, Somerset Light Infantry Regiment, was full of optimism when, after

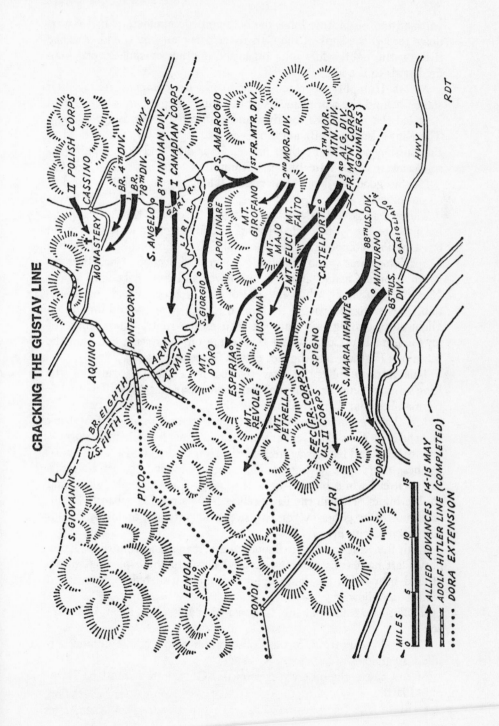

CRACKING THE GUSTAV LINE

II POLISH CORPS
CASSINO
MONASTERY
HWY 6
BR. 4TH DIV.
BR. 78TH DIV.
8TH INDIAN DIV.
I CANADIAN CORPS
S. ANGELO
S. AMBROGIO
1ST FR. MTR. DIV.
4TH MOR. MTN. DIV.
2ND MOR. DIV.
3RD ALG. DIV.
FR. MTN. CORPS (GOUMIERS)
HWY 7
RDT
S. APOLLINARE
MT. GIROFANO
MT. MAJO
MT. FEUCI
MT. FAITO
CASTELFORTE
88TH U.S. DIV.
85TH U.S. DIV.
GARIGLIANO
GARI R.
LIRI R.
S. GIORGIO
S. D'ORO
AUSONIA
ESPERIA
MT. REVOLE
MT. PETRELLA
SPIGNO
MINTURNO
FORMIA
PONTECORVO
AQUINO
ARMY
ARMY
EIGHTH
BR.
U.S. FIFTH
MT. D'ORO
EEC (FR. CORPS)
U.S. II CORPS
S. MARIA INFANTE
S. GIOVANNI
PICO
ITRI
LENOLA
FONDI

MILES
0   5   10   15

ALLIED ADVANCES 14-15 MAY
ADOLF HITLER LINE (COMPLETED)
DORA EXTENSION

parting from his brother John, the battalion commander, he had started down toward the bank of the Gari River. His company would cross the river on the right, while John organized another crossing several hundred yards to the left.

But as Humphry approached the bank, his company found itself stalled behind the rear elements of the King's Regiment, which should have led the way across the river and completed its crossings by now. The King's leading battalion, however, had lost its way and arrived at the crossing points more than half an hour late, and now some of its soldiers were wildly retreating past Humphry's company.

"It's no good up there!" one cried. "Things are too hot! We've lost all our officers!"

Things had gone badly indeed. The Somerset and King's Regiments belonged to the British 4th Division, which, together with the Indian 8th Division, composed Major General Sidney Kirkman's XIII British Corps. This corps would establish a bridgehead over the Gari River between Monte Cassino and the Liri River and swerve behind Monte Cassino, isolating it, while the II Polish Corps conquered the mountain. The two corps, part of the British Eighth Army, would link up on Highway 6, cutting this main German escape route. The Eighth Army's I Canadian Corps would then come out of reserve and lead the way along Highway 6 to the area east of Rome.

This intricate blueprint now seemed in jeopardy because of the King's initial blunder. The bombardment that was to soften up the German-held far bank had already lifted, since the artillerymen assumed that the infantry had crossed the river and occupied that bank on schedule. Thus the Germans could now emerge from their dugouts and foxholes and blast away freely at the river-fording units.

These units were having trouble enough paddling against a deadly-swift current while blinded by a thick fog of mist, smoke, dust, and cordite fumes. Though the flat, keelless boats struggled valiantly to survive, most were either overturned, swept downstream, or hit by mortar and machine-gun fire.

With the King's survivors floundering in panic and confusion, Humphry Platt halted his men and crawled down to the exploding corpse-littered near bank. He came upon another British officer operating a radio in a hollow.

"Hello!" he said. "Thank God somebody is alive here! Who are you?"

"Major John Pearson, forward observation officer of the Gunner Artillery Regiment."

After a pause, the observer exclaimed: "Good lord, it must be Humphry Platt!"

The two men had not seen each other since student days at Wellington.

"What's going on here," Humphry asked. "It seems to me we're the only ones alive."

"Only about two or three of the King's, one of them an officer, got across." said Pearson. "Strictly speaking, there's nobody on the other side to form a bridgehead."

Deeply discouraged, Humphry made his way back to his company and decided that he must radio his commander . . . his brother. What would John think if his younger brother sounded pessimistic? And Humphry had been so happy when he first learned that he was to join his brother's battalion . . .

"I understand, sir, that I am being sent as a reinforcement to the 2nd Battalion, Somerset Light Infantry."

"Yes."

"I would like to know, sir, who is commanding it?"

"A chap, oddly enough, with the same name as yours."

"Is he a tall, lean, sandy-haired chap?"

"Yes, that's right."

"Well, he must be my elder brother!" . . .

Bloody awkward!

"The shelling is extremely heavy here," Humphry shouted on his radiophone to Lieutenant Colonel John Platt. "The King's failed to get across, and only a few boats are left. I'm not sure we can make it. Perhaps I should divert my men to your crossing."

As John could hardly hear over the roar of battle, the time required for repetition permitted him to ponder his dilemma. His answer might determine the outcome of the battle—and mean life or death for his brother. The fact was that the situation was no better on the left than it was on the right. All the assault boats on the left had been smashed and he was now trying to transport some men in two reserve boats. Yet his younger brother, a courageous, even reckless, man, was telling him that to cross on the right would be suicide.

"I'm afraid, Tuppy, you've got to try it," he finally said, calling his brother by his nickname. "The situation over here is just as bad, maybe worse. So carry on!"

"Very good, sir," Humphry replied.

Humphry decided to lead one squad across the river first to reconnoiter the opposite bank before committing his whole company. With his orderly, Private James Read, and two other men, he climbed into a boat and Read, in the face of heavy fire, virtually pulled it across the rushing current by jerking at a wire rope that suicide swimmers had stretched from bank to bank. When, after a second trip, the whole squad was across, Humphry led his men forward until he spotted in the moonlight a German machine gun some distance ahead. That, thought Humphry, was the gun causing most of the trouble.

"We're going to take that post!" he whispered to his men.

"Sh . . . sh!" sounded one.

Humphry froze. A German patrol was passing only a few yards away. Platt fired his submachine gun, then suddenly felt numb and dropped the weapon. He grabbed a grenade and pulled the pin, but slumped to earth before he could throw it . . .

John Platt, in the midst of chaos, managed to send some units across the river on the left and at another point as well. When he joined one of the boatloads, bursting shrapnel wounded him lightly in the head and face, and he returned to the near bank. But shortly he received orders to go back again and push forward from the small bridgehead that had now been formed. And, despite his wounds, he returned, together with the King's commanding officer, who was killed by a mortar burst as soon as the boat reached the opposite bank.

John began crawling toward bridgehead headquarters when he heard the shriek of another approaching shell. He almost lost consciousness in the wake of the explosion and found himself unable to move, with gaping wounds in both legs, one hip, and one arm. And with the terrible glow of day laying bare the battlefield, German mortars blanketing the area would not encourage his comrades to emerge into the open to search for him.

He thought of his mother. To lose, perhaps, two sons at once—and he was responsible.[2]

❖   ❖   ❖

Daylight cast a grim shadow over units of the British 4th Division that clung to a bare foothold on the German-held bank of the Gari River. Intense enemy fire had foiled all attempts to build bridges for tanks to rumble across, and now it was up to the Indian 8th Division, which was crossing the river further south on both sides of the key village of Sant'Angelo, to ease the pressure on the British force.

But the Indians were running into the same problems as the British. They had arrived late at their crossing points after running into an unrecorded American mine field laid months earlier and lost most of their men and boats during the attempted crossings. And those who did get across were, like the British, barely able to hang on.

Menaced in particular were units of the 3/8 Punjab Regiment, which were pinned down by heavy machine-gun fire from four posts. The commander of the Indian units called for a volunteer to get around the rear of the right-hand enemy post and silence it.

A young olive-skinned youth named Kamal Ram, who looked about fifteen, immediately volunteered, convinced that this assignment on his first day at the front would be fun. He crawled forward, attacked the post, and shot the first gunner. A second German tried to seize his weapon but Ram bayoneted him, then shot a German officer who was about to fire a pistol.

Without pause, Ram attacked the second machine-gun post, shooting one gunner and throwing a grenade that induced the other Germans to surrender. He then joined an Indian comrade in assaulting and destroying the third post.

Ram's rampage, in large degree, enabled the Indians to establish a firm bridgehead and to complete two bridges—on which the life of the whole British XIII Corps seemed to depend. During the day of May 12, four squadrons of Canadian tanks were thus able to cross and temporarily relieve the pressure on the British.

Kamal Ram, a peasant boy from a small Indian village, had single-handedly dealt a powerful blow to the enemy (and was later rewarded with the Victoria Cross, Britain's highest decoration). His first day in combat, however, was to be his last. For his superiors suspected that he had lied about his age when he had enlisted and sent him back to India.[3]

❖   ❖   ❖

While the British XIII Corps struggled to hold its tiny bridgeheads on the far bank of the Gari River, the II Polish Corps attacked Monte Cassino, just north of the British zone of attack. The two corps were to link up on Highway 6 behind Monte Cassino to trap its defenders before they could flee and then surge toward Rome.

As men of the 3rd Carpathian Division crawled and scratched their way up the rocky slopes of Hill 593, southeast of Monastery Hill, Lieutenant Mahorowski wondered if he would ever make it to the top. Perhaps the answer was locked in the dream he had had that morning. What did it mean? He had slipped and fallen into a puddle on his way to church with his sister, and refused to continue on because his trousers were wet and dirty. But the sun then dried his trousers and he became clean again and was able to attend church after all.

Mahorowski returned the mocking stare of the monastery silhouetted against the moonlit sky as the monster flashed its fury in the night. First, Hill 593, then Hill 569, and finally that dark prize. Yes, he was on his way to church. After the monastery would come Rome. And then . . . Poland. At last he would rejoin his family, which he had left in Russia when he departed with General Anders' army. They, like many Poles, had been deported to forced labor camps by the Russians, and then freed. But he remembered the premonition of disaster that afflicted him when he awoke that morning.

Disaster had, in fact, already struck. Before the attack Mahorowski had decided that the two youngest soldiers in his platoon, both from Lvov, should not accompany his unit into action. But when he so informed them, they wept and begged to go.

"Are we not good soldiers?" one, named Barabas, asked. "We want to fight the Germans."

"Of course you are good soldiers," Mahorowski had assured them. "You can prove it later. There will certainly be plenty of other opportunities."

"But we want to fight now!"

Finally, the lieutenant had yielded, though he sensed that he should not have.

Indeed, almost immediately poor Barabas was fatally wounded. But before he died he told his comrades:

"My dear friends, you don't know how dreadful death can be. Now I shall have to miss the rest of the battle."

The other youth had had a leg blown off.

Everything had gone sour. The units had lost their bearings and no one was certain of his whereabouts. Telephone lines had been cut and only one was working. All the radio operators had been killed or their radios knocked out. Most of the officers were dead. And the shelling grew more and more deadly. Finally, the most deadly shell of all . . .

Mahorowski and twelve of his men fell screaming to earth. The lieutenant had been hit in both legs and he was sure that one of them had been severed. He could see but not feel it. Medics came and, with their help, he dragged himself upright and started to hop toward an aid station. But after a few yards, he collapsed unconscious in a puddle of blood.

And the sun would not rise for hours.

Some men arrived at the summit of Hill 593 and continued on toward the next hill, 569, but soon there were few left to hold on to these gains. The company on the southern slopes of 593 dwindled to one officer and seven men. And tanks, thwarted by mines and heavy fire, could offer little aid. Nor could the tank-led troops of the 5th Kresawa Division hold on to Phantom Ridge, east of 593, after reaching the top.

Thus, with daylight approaching, the Poles found themselves exposed on the open slopes and unable to move or receive reinforcements and supplies. Every position was vulnerable to fire from every enemy position, while the eyes of the monster on Monte Cassino gazed cynically upon the new sacrifices falling at its feet.

At 2 P.M., May 12, General Anders, after losing about half his force, ordered a general withdrawal of all his troops back to their original defense line.

Poland was as far away as ever.[4]

❖   ❖   ❖

The first thing Major Humphry Platt saw when he regained consciousness during the day of May 12 was the monastery, lit up in flashes. The fighting was still in progress. He drifted back into unconsciousness and awoke again that night to see two rifles pointed at him—and the silhouettes of two German helmets.

Sometime later he found himself lying on a straw mat on the floor of a German aid station that was crammed with both German and British wounded. And next to him lay Jim Read! His orderly had been wounded in the hand.

"Don't worry," Read assured him. "Our lads will be here soon."

And the Germans apparently thought so, too. The middle-aged doctor in charge spruced himself up and pinned his Iron Cross on his jacket. He would surrender with dignity. But Read would not defer to his dignity.

"You bloody bastard!" he yelled. "Get my officer a cup of coffee!"

And the doctor obeyed, acknowledging his new masters.

Humphry lost consciousness again just as his comrades arrived to liberate him and the other prisoners.

A few days later, as he lay in a hospital in Naples, another patient on a stretcher was carried into his ward and placed on the bed next to his. Humphry could hardly believe his eyes.

"Good heavens!" he exclaimed, trying to sit up. "John! How terribly kind of you to come! Jolly decent of you!"

John had finally been picked up after lying on the bridgehead for thirty hours. He had been operated on for multiple wounds at another hospital and then, when he heard that his brother was at this one, had asked to visit with him before being flown to England.

"Hello, Tuppy!" said John with a smile. "Just dropped by for news to bring the family."

The news would not be good. They wanted to amputate Humphry's leg as there were signs of gangrene.

"Should I let them do it?" Humphry asked calmly.

Poor Tuppy. And he had been a rugby and boxing star at school.

"You really haven't much choice, have you?"

"No, I suppose not."

After a while John was carried out on his stretcher.

"Good luck, Tuppy," he said as he departed.

"Thank you, sir. My love to Mother."[5]

After General Anders had ordered his force to withdraw to their original defense line, General Leese, commander of the British Eighth Army, drove by jeep to Anders' headquarters trailer. He dreaded the meeting. Anders had been so confident, so passionate about succeeding. Somehow the whole future of Poland seemed, in the Polish general's eyes, bound up with this battle. And he had instilled an almost super-human will in his men. They were fighting not for a mountain, not for a city, but for their very souls—and the soul of Poland.

And now so many of these men had died in a battle which, though diverting a large German force from the Gari River front, had been futile in itself, with the survivors back where they had started. Anders had wanted to attack again immediately and had asked Leese for the necessary artillery support. But the artillery was needed to save the XIII Corps bridgeheads and Leese had been forced to reject the request.

Leese found the shaven-headed Pole sitting alone in his trailer, red-eyed, stubble-faced, disheveled. He had never seen him look so discouraged. Normally, Anders was impeccably groomed and constantly flashing a gold-toothed smile.

"What are you doing sitting here alone like this?" Leese asked, his rather droopy eyes feigning good humor.

"Nothing."

"Then wouldn't you be better off in bed?"

Staring into nowhere, Anders asked: "What do we do now?"

"Stay where you are, but hang on to what you have. Don't lose that whatever happens."

"But we must attack again."

Before visiting Anders, Leese had conferred with General Kirkman, commander of the XIII Corps, who had urged: "Please don't let Anders attack again until we are ready for him or there won't be any Poles left."

Leese now explained to Anders that the XIII Corps was also behind schedule. It had not broken out of its bridgeheads yet. The Poles should remain quiet, he said, until the XIII Corps was ready to cut Highway 6 behind Monte Cassino. That would be the time for the Poles to attack again, link up with the British, and trap the Germans defending Cassino.

Leese sensed that Anders was relieved, since he would now have a chance to reorganize his badly battered units. The Briton knew, however, that Anders was wondering how his men would accept the delay. They didn't want to lose a day, an hour, a minute.

The next morning, General Alexander, after conferring with Leese, radioed General Wilson:

"The Poles have lost all their previous gains and are now back where they started. They were very depressed last night but are in better spirits today and are now reorganizing for further effort . . ."

But the British commanders themselves were not at all sure when their own men would be ready to cut Highway 6 and head for Rome.

If the Poles had to depend on the British, were the British to depend, humiliatingly, on the French?[6]

❖　❖　❖

French fighters of the Army of Italy, a great battle whose outcome can hasten final victory and the liberation of our homeland begins today. The struggle will be general, implacable, and pursued with the utmost energy. Having the honor of carrying our colors, you will win, as you have already won, while thinking of martyred France which awaits and watches you. Forward!

No one took General Juin's simple, stirring order of the day more seriously than Captain Pierre Planès, commander of the 7th Chasseurs d'Afrique, a special tank destroyer unit of Major General Goisland de Monsabert's 3rd Algerian Division, one of the four French divisions in Clark's Fifth Army. Starting from the Garigliano River—the French had won both banks in an earlier battle—Planès advanced in front of his tanks and half-tracks armed only with a cane to encourage them forward, too preoccupied blowing his obstructed nose even to hear the missiles whistling by. With each shell burst he would merely shout "*Merde!*" blow his nose once more, and wave the leading vehicle on with his cane.

Finally, when Planès had led his unit through a mine field, some of his men grabbed him and gently deposited him in his tank, though they were not sure which was worse: the shell bursts outside or the nose-blowing inside. Planès was furious. He must provide an example to speed up the advance. During the morning of May 12, almost all his tanks and half-tracks had been hit, but that was no excuse. His men were taking too long to repair them. At this rate, they would never reach Castelforte . . .

Castelforte was the gateway to the Ausente Valley, which wove northwestward through a formidable chain of mountains, dominated by Monte Majo, that extended from the Liri River to the Tyrrhenian Sea. Captain Planès' armor would help the 4th Moroccan Mountain Division attack Castelforte in the south while other French forces scaled the mountains to the north, first, those flanking Majo—mainly Monte Faito and Monte Feuci—and then Majo itself.

Once both Castelforte and Majo fell, the Gustav Line would be irreparably broken, Monte Cassino to the north would be outflanked, and the Germans would have to flee to the next fortified defense belt before Rome, the Adolf Hitler Line. But so confident were the Nazis that the great mountainous zone between Castelforte and Majo was impenetrable that they felt no uneasiness about defending it with only one division—the 71st Infantry. And *it* was inexperienced in mountain fighting . . .

Planès knew that Castelforte lived up to its name—"strong fort." Since it lay in the foothills and was therefore far more accessible than the towering heights north of the town, it had to be powerfully fortified. Castelforte was, in fact, a jumble of cement block houses, many connected by underground passages, and all protected by vast mine fields and jungles of barbed wire.

After struggling ahead yard by yard for hours, Planès' force, at dusk, May 12, nosed through the powdery debris of southern Castelforte under withering fire while the 4th Moroccan Mountain Division helped to close the circle around the town. Planès decided that it was too dangerous to move further through this stronghold in the dark and lay down in his tank to sleep. Soon the firing tapered off and the night resounded mainly, it seemed, with Planès' nasal explosions.

At dawn Planès awakened, stretched, and listened for signs of enemy activity. All was quiet. It was safe for him to go outside and urinate. He lifted the turret cap, crawled through, and stood atop his tank in the cool morning air. As he started to relieve himself a German soldier suddenly sprang from behind a tree in front of him and put up his hands, crying: "*Kamerad!*"

Without flinching, Planès raised his free hand, palm out, and called out in French: "First let me finish pissing!"

Finally, after emitting what must have seemed to the German like an endless stream, the Frenchman shook off the last few drops, slowly began the careful process of buttoning his fly, deliberately took a handkerchief out of his pocket, and loudly blew his nose. Then, beckoning to his prisoner, he cried:

"*Alors*, now you may advance!"

And thus did Castelforte fall to the French.[7]

At about 1 A.M., May 12, Commander Foucaucourt of the 1st Company, 1st Battalion, 8th Regiment, 2nd Moroccan Division, reached out his hand as he lay stomach-down on the crest of Monte Faito.

"Is that you, Foucaucourt?" whispered the man who grasped his hand.

"Is that you, *mon Commandant?*" replied Foucaucourt. "It has been very hard, you know . . . I have lost my whole command group . . . I have no more rifles, no more radio. I had to abandon the wounded. I lost the Lecompte squad . . . I am here all alone with one man . . ."

If only the French could have softened up the enemy with an artillery barrage. But the French lines had been too close to the German.

Foucaucourt had climbed to the summit a half hour earlier, and now Major Jannot, his battalion commander, had just arrived with more men. They wanted to push ahead to Monte Feuci, the next height en route to Monte Majo, but the French forces on both of their flanks were unable to reach their targets and were falling back. The conquerors of Faito, isolated, formed an arrow extending into the enemy domain. All they could do was to stay where they were and try to ward off inevitable counterattacks.

And so they waited all through the morning of May 12, taking refuge from mortar and machine-gun fire behind boulders or simply by hugging the hard, stony ground. And then, at 1:30 P.M. that same day, the Germans attacked. Foucaucourt led his men against them, personally knocking out a machine-gun post with a grenade. The fighting was ferocious. While Foucaucourt and Jannot took cover together behind rocks, a soldier approached Jannot calmly, halted before him, saluted, and cried:

"*Vive la France, mon Commandant!*"

The two commanders were startled. The man, Sergeant Cadene, looked pale and his eyes were closed.

"*Vive la France, mon Commandant!*" he repeated.

"But yes, my brave friend, *ça va! Vive la France!*" said Jannot. "But for the love of heaven, get down!"

"*Viva la France, mon Commandant!*" the sergeant repeated again.

And he fell dead from a bullet that had pierced his chest some minutes earlier.

The handful of French survivors grimly held. But Monte Majo, its peak provocatively veiled by the mist of war, still seemed a million miles away, except when the valleys echoed with its screeching, deadly rage.[8]

General Juin gazed at Monte Majo from the window of his headquarters in the medieval, ivy-covered Sessa Aurunci castle behind his line. The tricolor should have been waving atop Monte Majo by now. But it was not and perhaps never would be. At least according to the reports Juin had been receiving all morning. Except at Castelforte and Monte Faito, his men had failed everywhere with astronomical losses. And every time he saw a geyser of smoke spiral over Monte Faito, he knew the casualties were rising.

Perhaps he had been overconfident. If he did not succeed, the Anglo-Americans, whom he had been imploring to make a wide turning movement around Cassino, would certainly gloat at his failure to achieve such a maneuver in his own zone of operation. The French, they would say, did not really understand modern warfare.

Juin dejectedly received some officers he had called to a conference and one of them assured him:

"A simple halt, I think, my General, before continuing our advance."

The general reflected on his position . . . When he had been a boy in Algeria, he had once been confronted in a forest by a black panther, and though he had a gun, it contained only one bullet. He decided it was best to stand frozen, and the beast, after contemplating him for several moments, walked away peacefully. When he told his grandfather of this frightening experience, the old man, while congratulating him on his escape, blamed him for entering the forest without sufficient protection.

"If one day you become an officer," he admonished, "never send your men into battle with insufficient arms, inferior to those of the enemy, and never let them fight under bad conditions. Remember that, my boy!" . . .

And Juin now did. Slowly, deliberately removing a cigarette from his lips, he said in reply to the optimistic officer:

"In saying that, do you know what it's like attacking a fortified line? After the first attack, you either pass or you crash. If you pass, good, it's a success. But if you crash, it's folly to want to go on regardless. It costs too much. As for me, I don't want all my men killed uselessly. We will renew the attack, but under better circumstances."

Then he added, exuding supreme confidence: "You can be sure that we have all that is necessary to pass. We shall pass!"

He stared through the window once more at Monte Majo. The mist was lifting, and he could see the gray, snub-nosed peak. And beyond, in his mind's eye, Rome—and France.[9]

❖   ❖   ❖

"What the hell do we do now, Chuck?"

Sergeant Charles W. Shea didn't know, but he was going to do something. His squad had finally been called from reserve near Minturno at dawn, May 12, to fill a gap in the line, and as a member of F Company, 350th Regiment, 88th Division, he would lead his men in an attack on Hill 316.

This hill was the northernmost nose of Mount Damiano, the first regimental objective, which lay southwest of Castelforte. Shea's men would help to protect the southern flank of the French attacking Castelforte, and then as part of General Keyes's II Corps—which also embraced the 85th Division—head west and up the Tyrrhenian coast to a link-up with the isolated Anzio beachhead force.*

But his platoon leader had been hit, and in the confusion of battle no one knew exactly where they were or what the platoon objective

* The 85th and 88th Divisions were the first all-Selective Service divisions to go into the front lines in World War II. Both were to prove that draftees could be trained to be superior fighters.

was. When one of Shea's fellow squad leaders therefore asked him if he knew what to do, he could only look around and guess. Were they perhaps to take that house on the hill? Anyway, it was a place to attack, and after all the trouble he had getting to the front with his broken eardrums he wasn't going to let a mere question of objectives stop him.

"Follow me!" he cried.

And though he was only a squad leader, it seemed that every unit in the area followed him, Pied Piper-style, in a great confused mob. He led the mob to the base of the hill, which luckily turned out to be 316, the right objective, through a mine field, and up a series of terraces.

Suddenly a machine gun opened up on the men to his rear. Considerably ahead of the others, Shea began running toward the gun, about fifty yards away, and threw himself behind a low stone wall. He then peered over the wall, saw the machine-gun emplacement, and killed two members of the crew with gunfire and grenades. The third machine gunner fired back and ran behind another wall, and Shea and his adversary kept popping their heads up alternately like targets at a carnival shooting gallery, each firing at the other.

Instinctively, Shea turned around and noticed that three terraces below another German was aiming a submachine gun at him. In his excitement, Shea neglected to fire, but charged toward the German with bayonet pointed, leaping from terrace to terrace in the style of Douglas Fairbanks, Sr. As the German threw down his gun and raised his hands, Shea halted.

At that moment, two other Germans emerged from a second machine-gun nest camouflaged behind some bushes. Shea disarmed the three, motioned them toward the Allied lines, and advanced uphill again when he heard still another machine gun firing. He crawled behind it and, seeing two men by the weapon, extended his bayonet between their heads, tapping one helmet, then the other. The two Germans stared at each other. Shea sent them down the hill, too.

Not satisfied, he felt he still had some unfinished business. The third German in the first machine-gun nest, who had exchanged shots with him, was apparently still loose and was probably sniping at his men right now. He ran back to the first emplacement and found two men sprawled dead and one in a kneeling position apparently holding rosary beads in his hands and praying. Shea sneaked up behind this German and kicked him in the buttocks. The man fell over dead.

Poor guy, thought Shea, a devout Irish Catholic himself. The German was a good Catholic saying his prayers when he had killed him. The sergeant felt better, however, when he found that the "rosary" was actually a chain to clean rifles. Probably wasn't even a Catholic!

With the three machine guns thus knocked out, Shea then led his "mob" to the house at the top of the hill. But he still worried that another idiot doctor would find him unfit for combat because of his broken eardrums and send him home to sell hot dogs at the ball game again.[10]

Just south of Hill 316, the humpbacked village of Santa Maria Infante crowned the bleak hills overlooking the Ausente Valley, solidly blocking the Allied advance northward. The village was powerfully defended by soldiers of the German 71st and 94th Divisions, perched on twin heights known as the "Tits" and, further on, just before the town, on a ridge called the "Spur." Units of the U.S. 88th Division grabbed the left and right Tits after bitter, confused fighting, but the Germans clung to the Spur doggedly.

Lieutenant Colonel Ray Kendall, commander of the 88th Division's 2nd Battalion, 351st Regiment, was dogged, too. At any moment a soldier might expect to feel on his helmet the tap of the colonel's stick, meaning: "Move your ass!" But even the dreaded tap could not budge the men of E Company, who were to capture the Spur, when they reached the forward slope and were greeted by at least a dozen machine guns. Kendall sent a squad to wipe out one nest, but the Germans mowed down nine of the twelve men.

That did not stop Kendall. He had to take a particular house on the crest from which the heaviest fire was coming. Exchanging his stick for a Browning automatic rifle (BAR), he fired at the house until he ran out of ammunition. Then, successively, he used a carbine, an M-1 rifle, antitank rifle grenades, and a bazooka. Feeling the house had now been softened up, he sent several men to encircle it, but they were pinned down at the crest.

There was only one way left—rush the house. The colonel personally led his remaining men forward, all firing and throwing grenades as they ran. The Germans inside the house scrambled out and fled. Kendall's daring charge had worked. But before he could complete his victory, bullets struck him in the face as he was about to throw a grenade. The grenade exploded against his own body, and he fell dead.

Whether he was accidentally killed by his own men cannot be determined. But those with him were fired on by their comrades, who mistook them for Germans. The survivors now had the house but they were surrounded by enemy machine-gun nests. Tanks failed in an effort to break through, and one entire company which outflanked the Spur was encircled and captured after being tricked by Germans who had approached with hands raised shouting, *"Kamerad!"*

But thanks mainly to Colonel Kendall, the Americans had reached the crest of the Spur—the key to Santa Maria Infante.[11]

❖ ❖ ❖

Late on May 12, after a full night and day of fighting, General Alexander slumped exhaustedly at his desk, shuffling through the latest battle reports. He remained outwardly unshaken, but his aides could perceive disappointment in his eyes. The situation was grim almost everywhere. The Poles were back at their starting line. The British XIII Corps had gained only about half of its initial objectives, and most of its boats had been sunk. And the Americans had been stopped before Santa Maria Infante.

The best news came from the French front—the capture of Castelforte and Monte Faito. But even the French were in a precarious position, for Monte Faito was isolated and the occupying troops could easily be cut off.

General Clark and General Leese were also worried, and Clark's concern was not relieved by the dejected mood of Major General John E. Sloan, the 88th Division commander, whose men had suffered terrible casualties. Even so, Alexander, Leese, and Clark clearly had no intention of letting the world think that the battle was not going smoothly. After they conferred at Alexander's headquarters, Alexander optimistically radioed General Wilson:

> The offensive was launched according to plan . . . On the whole the battle has gone fairly well considering the stubbornness of the opposition . . . I saw both Army commanders . . . and they are reasonably satisfied with the opening stages of the battle but there is no doubt that the Germans intend to fight for every yard and that the next few days will see some extremely bitter and severe fighting.

What had gone wrong? All intelligence reports indicated that the Germans had not expected an attack at this time—they were, in fact, regrouping at the moment of attack—and did not even know which Allied troops occupied which sector. Yet the Germans were defending powerfully, and if Field Marshal Kesselring brought up his reserves in time, he might well frustrate Operation DIADEM completely.

The Allied generals were filled with gloom. After all the planning, all the hope and optimism. Would Rome, the memesis of Hannibal and so many other ambitious conquerors, subdue the Allies as well?

Everything now depended, it seemed, on how completely Kesselring had grasped the situation and how quickly he would react.[12]

❖   ❖   ❖

Kesselring had never been faced with a greater dilemma. As reports of Allied attacks poured into his primitive headquarters in the cave he now occupied near Monte Soratte, it was clear to him that the enemy had launched its long-awaited assault on Rome. What was unclear was whether these attacks were simply the prelude to new landings along the coast.

Whether, indeed, the enemy would commit all his free Western Mediterranean forces against Italy, a move that might signify that the cross-channel invasion plan had been scrapped in favor of one to make Italy the real "second front."

Until he knew the answers, Kesselring felt he could not intelligently deploy his reserves.

The inexperienced 92nd Division stood ready to crush a landing at the port of Civitaveccia, north of Rome. The Hermann Göring Panzer Division waited at Leghorn, far to the north, to throw back a similar attack. The 26th and 29th Panzer Grenadier Divisions guarded Anzio, prepared to smash either a fresh landing or a breakout from the beachhead. And the 90th Panzer Grenadier Division was at Frosinone, between Cassino and Rome, coiled to spring at Allied airborne troops expected in that area.

Could Kesselring afford to send any of these reserve units to the Gustav Line to help shatter the enemy offensive if this meant leaving the probable landing sites and his defenses at Anzio critically vulnerable? Was that not what the Allies were hoping he would do?

Kesselring's dilemma grew as he read the reports from his commanders. The intelligence diary of the Tenth Army's XIV Panzer Corps noted on May 12:

"The Corps expects an expansion of the battle through a landing operation. It is believed that the enemy will carry out such an operation once he believes that the coastal forces [Kesselring's reserves] have been moved to the focal points of the land front."

And the daily intelligence reports of the Fourteenth Army, which hemmed in the beachhead, said:

"Now that the enemy has launched his attack on the southern part of the land front, an attack from the bridgehead [Anzio] must be expected at any moment . . ."

Kesselring was not only ignorant of the probable Allied strategy, he could not yet judge the strength of the enemy forces attacking the Gustav Line. He calculated that the enemy had six divisions in line between Cassino and the Tyrrhenian Sea and that his four would be adequate to hold them, considering the ruggedness of the terrain. (The Allies actually had the equivalent of over *thirteen* divisions.)

He was worried, however, about reports of the French advance. His intelligence still indicated that only *one* French division was involved (though actually four were). But how could one division make such progress in virtually impassable country?

Kesselring demanded that his commanders let him know who they were fighting against. What a time for Generals von Vietinghoff and von Senger und Etterlin to be receiving decorations from Hitler! Even Senger's chief of staff was on leave, and his own, General Westphal, was in the hospital ill.

Kesselring decided that he must keep his reserves where they were until he could better judge how the Allied attacks would develop.[13]

❖   ❖   ❖

Wearing his traditional open-necked khaki shirt and blue beret decorated with five stars, General Juin visited the front of the afternoon of May 12 and immediately understood how bitter the resistance had been. As he climbed captured Monte Faito, easing his way with a cane, he saw Germans lying dead behind their guns and in their dugouts and pillboxes. They had not retreated. And passing him along the trail were stretcher parties carrying down his own casualties, with Foucaucourt and Jannot, who had led the way to the crest of Monte Faito, among the wounded.

Juin finally reached the command post of Major General François Sevez, commander of the 4th Moroccan Mountain Division.

"Tomorrow morning we will resume the attack and continue to the end," he told Savez. "We have before us a solid curtain, but, if we tear it, it will rip apart."

And this time he would start ripping it with an intensive artillery barrage before the attack. This time the German lines were now far enough from the French base to permit a bombardment. He was taking the advice his grandfather had given him when, as a boy, he had encountered the panther in the forest. He would not let his men fight "under bad conditions."

Juin then told Sevez, paraphrasing a proverb that Marshal Foch had used at Marais de Saint-Gond in World War I: "When everything seems to be going badly, it is really going well!"

Juin continued on his tour of the front, climbing rocky paths that would in the end, he was sure, wind to victory. He finally reached the cave which served as headquarters for Major General André W. Dody, commander of the 2nd Moroccan Division which was to lead the attack on Monte Feuci and Monte Majo. Embracing Dody, Juin said:

"You understand, Dody, we hold in our hands the fate of the battle. It is here, at Feuci and Majo, that the die will be cast . . . We must succeed at any cost!"

At 11:30 A.M., May 13, Dody's troops reached the summit of Monte Feuci without firing a shot, after Monte Girofano and another flanking hill had been captured in hard fighting earlier in the day. Juin had apparently been right. An artillery bombardment had churned the German defenses into dust, and the enemy had fled. And now there was only one more mountain to go—Majo!

As Dody's men were about to assault this bastion at about 1 P.M., a French officer rushed into Juin's headquarters to hand him a German order that had just been intercepted:

AS FEUCI CAPTURED, ORDER GENERAL RETREAT

The order had come through uncoded. Were the Germans in so great a panic? Within minutes the message was relayed to all French units, electrifying the atmosphere. The Germans were retreating! Did that mean they had abandoned Majo?

Commander Pons prepared to lead his battalion toward the crest to find out. From Feuci he peered through his binoculars, searching for some sign of life, or even death, on Majo. But all he saw was naked sunlit rock. He decided to send first a patrol under Adjutant Vella to make sure the battalion would not walk into a trap.

From rock to rock the patrol climbed, ready to fall flat with the first burst of machine-gun fire, but there was still no sound, no hint of human presence. Finally, at about 3 P.M., the men below saw the tiny silhouette of Vella against the clear blue sky. He was on the summit waving his carbine!

And shortly, General Juin observed from his window the Tricolor fluttering at the top of Monte Majo. It was visible in the bright sunlight for miles around, signaling to the world that Juin had been right. And that Rome would redeem French honor.[14]

The fall of Monte Majo so panicked the leaders of the Tenth Army's XIV Panzer Corps defending against Clark's Fifth Army that, over the few lines of communication still open, they neglected to inform their superiors what was happening. On the morning of May 14, shortly after the disaster, Kesselring wired the Tenth Army:

> I must demand of the divisions that they obtain a clear picture of their own situation and that of the enemy. It is an intolerable condition when a division remains in the dark for one and a half days about the events in its own sector. It is equally intolerable for a division to be in fighting contact with the enemy for two days without knowing whom they are fighting. I demand a clear picture by 1200 hrs . . .

But the only thing clear was that the two divisions of the XIV Panzer Corps—the 71st and the 94th—were hastily retreating northward toward the Adolf Hitler Line. As Juin had predicted, the curtain was ripping apart.

Indeed, hardly had Monte Majo fallen than the 1st (Free French) Motorized Division cleared the whole west bank of the Garigliano River to its junction with the Liri. The following morning, May 14, the U.S. 88th Division finally bulldozed into Santa Maria Infante as resistance disintegrated there also.

Nor did the terrain favor the fleeing Germans. For their path of retreat, on a front from the Tyrrhenian coast to Esperia on the Adolf Hitler Line, was split by the great Aurunci mountain crests—the Petrella, the Revole, the Fammera. Thus, the two German divisions would have open flanks on either side of these mountains. But their leaders were not too concerned, feeling that these trackless heights would be as inaccessible to the Allies as to their own troops. No army could cross *those* mountains!

And so the farther north the Nazis fled, the wider became the gap in the center of the XIV Panzer Corps front, with the Americans chasing the 94th Division up the coast along Highway 7 and the French dogging the 71st Division through the Ausente Valley toward Esperia.

It was now time for General Juin's master play—to pass through the impassable gap and come up behind the enemy.[15]

"Forward! Forward! *Zidou l'gouddam!*"

Major General Augustin Guillaume, his short, powerful body planted firmly on a mountain-trained Moroccan horse, urged his men on. His *goumiers*. This was the day Guillaume, commander of the French Mountain Corps, had been waiting for these last three years. The day he had been planning for. The brown-skinned *goumiers*, his devoutly loyal Berber mountain warriors—who were willing to fight and die, not for a country, but for a leader they loved—would show the modern world what they could do. The spearhead of his corps, they used mules instead of tanks, and often *koumias*, ten-inch knives thrust into the belt, instead of guns, but they would win Rome and lead the way to France.

"*La Allah! Moulay Zeroual . . . la Allah! Moulay Zeroual . . .*"

And onward they marched beside their supply-laden mules, bare-chested or in their native dark-striped, hooded gowns, or *djellabas*, through the hills west of Castelforte toward the foot of the massive Petrella, which rose hazily in the distance. They were bearded and fierce-eyed, with gleaming white teeth and plaited pigtails on their heads so that Allah could more easily pull them into heaven if they were killed. They were constantly smiling, singing native songs, wanting to fight and, between battles, to fornicate with any female, of whatever age or inclination, who happened to be around.

To reduce the rape rate, General Clark had approved the transport by the U.S. Navy of Berber women to Italy, provided they came disguised in men's uniforms so that respectable people back home would not raise a clamor over the "immoral" use of American fighting vessels. But the uniforms proved too small for their chubby Berber figures and they arrived with their trousers slit down the side and their underwear showing.

General Guillaume had trained the *goumiers* in secret when he had been responsible for interior security in Morocco under the German occupation. The Germans had thought that these primitive warriors, who inhabited the Atlas Mountains in the south, were simply serving as policemen, but Guillaume had taught them military tactics and the use of mortars, artillery, and other army weapons.

When the Americans landed in Morocco in November 1942, General Patton had been so impressed with Guillaume that he (Patton) told his interpreter after their first meeting:

"This man is worth three divisions!"

And now Guillaume would prove that he was. For who else could provide the means for leaping over the mountains into Rome?

He had not had an easy time, Guillaume says, convincing General Clark that he was capable of this miracle. On May 8, three days before Operation DIADEM started, he had stood on the bank of the Garigliano River with Clark, Juin, and other officers to observe the mountains in the distance and decide on the feasibility of such a miracle. It was late afternoon and the Petrella, more rugged and inaccessible than Majo, lay silhouetted against the sky like a solid black wall sealing off Rome from the world. Clark asked skeptically:

"Do you really think you can jump over such a barrier?"

"I prefer a hundred times to attack in the mountains than before tanks and artillery in the valleys," Guillaume answered. "I know that we can do it, but only under certain conditions."

"And what are they?"

"First, I need double the number of radio sets normally issued to keep contact with the men. Second, you must drop food for the men and the mules by plane. Third, you Americans must capture Spigno. Give me the key to Spigno and I will give you the key to Rome."

Clark laughed at this reference to a strategic village at the foot of the Petrella. Yes, Guillaume would have his radios and his food.

"And you, Geoff," he said to General Keyes, the commander of II Corps, "will take Spigno." . . .

And in the early morning of May 15, Guillaume's liaison officer met Brigadier General Paul W. Kendall, second in command of the U.S. 88th Division, near the foothills of Monte Petrella. Kendall's men were covering Guillaume's left flank along the coast, en route to a link-up with the Anzio force.

"I gave you Spigno at seven o'clock this morning," Kendall said, smiling.

"Mon general!" the liaison officer replied casually, "asked me to tell you that we will be on Petrella at three o'clock."

The goumiers were ready to forge a path over the pathless Petrella.

Guillaume had split his Mountain Corps of nine thousand men into three groups, each containing a regular Moroccan infantry battalion and a tabor, or unit, of goumiers who would lead the way. One group had already raced through the Ausente Valley and was now attacking Monte Fammera, north of Monte Petrella. Guillaume himself would lead his other two groups over Petrella, and then across Monte Revole, just to the north. From Monte Revole, he would storm down the northern slopes to cut the road from Pico to Itri behind the Adolf Hitler Line and make it impossible for the retreating Germans to re-form adequately in this long-prepared system of fortifications.

In single file, Guillaume led his men up Monte Petrella on his spirited horse, feeling his way ahead between boulders and along sheer cliffs.

"Forward!" he cried. "Zidou l'gouddam!"

Meanwhile, Field Marshal Kesselring, finally learning the approximate strength of the French forces after three days of intelligence failure, decided in his desperation to send a battalion of the 15th Panzer Grenadiers to climb Monte Revole, north of Petrella, or at least make the attempt—just in case the enemy did likewise.[16]

9

The Squabbles

The nostalgic melody of "Lili Marlene," partially smothered under a roof of rubble, sounded like a ghostly wail in a cemetery. The Germans in the town of Cassino, which lay prostrate in the shadow of the monastery, were serenading the British during an artillery lull after the British had earlier sung a homely English song.

First Lieutenant Hermann Voelck-Unsin, a company commander in the 4th Regiment of the 1st Parachute Division, joined the chorus. He rather liked the British, even though they were the enemy, finding them a civilized people with a traditional respect for Christian values. The British prisoners he had taken were gentlemen and had even said "thank you" when he gave them cigarettes or water. Besides, one became used to one's neighbors and they were close neighbors indeed.

Cassino had once been a prosperous town of neat stone houses where, since ancient Roman days, travelers, on their way to Rome or Naples, stopped to take a thermal bath. Mark Antony had kept a villa here, apparently finding the quiet, country atmosphere conducive to recovery from the exertions of nightly orgies. Now, as a result of systematic leveling by artillery and bombs, Cassino seemed on the surface to be utterly lifeless, a wilderness of crumbled masonry, blocks of stone, rusting metal, and water-filled craters. Here and there a wrenched skeleton of a house was visible.

Nevertheless, the town supported a great deal of life. In the cellars under the desert of steel and stone, Britons and Germans—soldiers like

Voelck-Unsin—sat helplessly entombed, in some cases separated by little more than a wall, sharing the ruins of the town, each side waiting for the other to raise a head that could be targeted.

One German who had failed to duck in time lay dead in a narrow rubble-carpeted street and had become the object of a grim kind of game. The British wanted the body in order to identify the dead man's unit, and the Germans were just as determined to keep it from them. Over a period of several days, ingenious Tommies managed to reach the corpse with a long, hooked stick and dragged it forward inch by inch under heavy sniper fire until it had been recovered.

The British had won that game. But sooner or later one of *them* would get curious, and then . . . Meanwhile, they might as well sing to each other to while away the time. Voelck-Unsin agreed that it was the neighborly thing to do.[1]

❋   ❋   ❋

The breakthrough on the Fifth Army front at first had little effect on the British Eighth Army front in the Liri Valley. The Germans staunchly held on to every inch of ground against the British and Indian troops of the XIII Corps trying to cross the Gari River. Nor did the Germans have to do much fighting at Monte Cassino since the Poles were under orders not to attack that stronghold again before the XIII Corps broke out of its precariously held bridgeheads.

With few boats left to carry troops and equipment to the German-held bank of the Gari, both the British and the Indians had depended at first almost entirely on the two bridges that the Indians had managed to build in their sector. But these bridges were not enough to maintain the British bridgeheads for long. Another bridge had to be constructed in the British zone—even though the builders would be more vulnerable to enemy fire here than they had been in the Indian sector. The order went out that a Bailey bridge had to be built "at all costs."

At 5:45 P.M., May 12, two field squadrons of the British 4th Division, under a thick smoke screen, began the formidable task of building Amazon Bridge. Whenever the smoke thinned the sappers came under murderous sniper and machine-gun fire. As one fell, another would replace him. And many fell, for each man was a perfect target. After eighty-three of the two hundred sappers had been hit, the bridge stood—a miracle that seemed to rival the biblical parting of the Red Sea.

And one that marked the turning point in the battle of the Liri Valley as troops and tanks of the XIII Corps poured over the bridge toward Highway 6, the main enemy escape route, and Rome.[2]

The time was now ripe for attacking Monte Cassino again. While two British divisions—the 4th and 78th—crossed the Gari River and cut Highway 6 south of Monte Cassino, the Poles would attack the mountain strongholds again from the north and capture the monastery. They would then rush down the southern slopes to link up with the British on the highway and trap the surviving Germans.

By the night of May 13, however, some Allied officers had begun to question the need for another bloody attack on Monte Cassino. For with the wild retreat of the Germans before the Fifth Army, the southern flank of Monte Cassino suddenly lay exposed. And as General Juin had argued, why expend lives assaulting such a powerfully defended bastion when the French would outflank it anyway and force the defenders to retreat or risk encirclement?

General Kirkman, the XIII Corps commander, told the author that he had also opposed a new Polish attack, feeling that the Poles would suffer unnecessary casualties. And General Montgomery, who was in England preparing for D-Day, vigorously concurred, writing General Leese—Leese informed the author—that another assault would be "madness." Nor did the Germans, in their later appraisals, disagree.

"The enemy had no need to attack Cassino," General von Senger und Etterlin writes in his memoirs.

But General Alexander wanted the British to lead the way to Rome, whether they actually entered the city or not. Monte Cassino had to fall immediately if the British were to catch up with the Fifth Army, and a new Polish attack was therefore necessary.

Certainly he would not wait for the French to circle northward, cross Highway 6 behind Cassino, and cut off its defenders. He would not permit the French to "invade" the British zone of advance. For what could then stop them from continuing along Highway 6 to Rome —in front of the British?

The Poles, already weakened by 50 per cent casualties, would storm Monte Cassino once again, even though Juin's promise of a bloodless victory seemed near fulfillment.[3]

"We are short of antitank weapons. Heidrich [the 1st Parachute Division commander at Cassino] needs tanks . . ."

General von Vietinghoff, having returned from his visit with Hitler in East Prussia, was pleading with Field Marshal Kesselring for help over the telephone at 6 P.M., May 15.

"No, I cannot help you," Kesslring replied. "Only passive defense is possible."

Vietinghoff felt betrayed. On the one hand, Kesselring refused to release enough reserves to plug the holes at Cassino. And on the other, the field marshal prohibited a retreat to the Adolf Hitler Line though the troops at Cassino might soon be cut off. True, Kesselring had finally released the 90th Panzer Grenadier Division to him, but too late to be of much help. Half the division had to be diverted to the crumbling front facing the French. Kesselring still stingily held on to his other reserves, convinced even at this late date that the Allies were about to land forces on the coast.

In their desperation, Vietinghoff and his deputies secretly plotted to retreat to the Adolf Hitler Line in defiance of Kesselring's "unreasonable" demand that Monte Cassino be held. General Bruno Ortner, commander of the Austrian 44th Division holding the eastern slopes of the mountain, sparked the plot by sending a note to General Feurstein, the LI Mountain Corps commander, saying that "the situation requires either the commitment of strong reserves in close formation, or the withdrawal to the Senger Line [Adolf Hitler Line] during the night 15/16 May at the latest."*

Feurstein agreed, and told Vietinghoff that Monte Cassino "could not be held indefinitely." Immediately after this talk, Feurstein began ordering some rear echelon units to the Adolf Hitler Line. Vietinghoff had approved a gradual retreat without informing Kesselring, persuaded that, if manned too late, this line could not be held at all.

And General Feurstein fully co-operated, even sending his chief of staff, Colonel Karl-Heinrich von Klinckowstroem, to General Heidrich's headquarters to solicit his support for a withdrawal of the 1st Parachute Division. But Heidrich, Klinckowstroem told the author, agreed with Kesselring. His brave men who had defended Monte Cassino again and again against the best Allied troops—retreat? The very suggestion was obscene. They would hold on to Monte Cassino whether cut off or not.

Klinckowstroem was aghast, as were Vietinghoff and Feurstein. The whole Tenth Army faced annihilation, it seemed, because of Kesselring's optimism and Heidrich's pride.[4]

---

* The Germans changed the name of the Adolf Hitler Line to the Senger Line, in honor of General von Senger und Etterlin who helped to plan it, when it appeared that the line might be pierced by the Allies. The commanders did not want it said that a defense line named after the Führer could possibly fall.

A little after midnight, on May 13, motorcycles careened into 78th British Division bivouac areas and dispatch riders handed company commanders an urgent message:

"Battalion will be ready to move from present area by 0400 hrs. Company Commanders conference Battalion Headquarters immediately."

Sleepy company commanders, swearing under their breath, put their coats on over their pajamas, hazily stumbled to their jeeps, and zoomed off to their respective meetings chilled to the bone. The 78th was to cross the Gari River as soon as possible, they were told. There wasn't a minute to lose! The listeners grunted. Somehow there was something too melodramatic about this midnight meeting in pajamas to stir their souls. Nevertheless, by 4 A.M. the whole division had packed up and was ready for battle.

Trouble was, the battle was not ready for the division. The 78th was supposed to cross over three bridges, but two of them—Congo and London—had not even been built yet! Work on London Bridge, to span the river from Sant'Angelo, had to await the town's capture, which would take place only that afternoon. And work on Congo had not started because no one had bothered to tell the engineers that the bridge was needed that morning. And there was too much traffic on the other bridges to accommodate the 78th.

So the troops lounged in some vineyards and waited for the bridges to be built, catching up meanwhile with London newspaper headlines that finally told them what was going on. The most informative one announced:

REINFORCEMENTS STREAMING ACROSS RAPIDO BRIDGES

This headline clearly did not apply to the 78th, though it was supposed to. And because it did not, the attempt to surround and crush the defenders of Monte Cassino had to be postponed again. Finally, on May 15, the troops "streamed across" the two new wooden-planked bridges—and ran into further delays. Bogged down in soft, makeshift approaches, held up by uncleared mine fields, the traffic on the bridgehead side resembled Piccadilly Circus at rush hour.

General Juin was right again. The British Eighth Army was defeating itself. While primitive soldiers who preferred knives to guns were pushing forward from mountain to mountain in the French sector, a completely modernized and mechanized British army had virtually ground to a halt in a level valley, stopped primarily not by the enemy, but by the sheer weight of its equipment and staff blunders.

At 7 A.M., May 17, three days late, the 78th Divison—and the 4th—began marching northwestward to cut Highway 6 and help lay the monster to rest at last, while the II Polish Corps charged it frontally . . .[5]

❖   ❖   ❖

"Give your situation," Major General Bronislaw Duch, commander of the Polish 3rd Carpathian Division, ordered over the radio.

"The situation is not clear," replied Captain Drelicharz of the tank company attacking Phantom Ridge, east of the monastery. "We are still here. The sappers will not clear the mines."

"Order them forward!"

"They say they will not move."

"If they do not obey orders, shoot them!"

Captain Drelicharz was distraught. Shoot his own men? Of course, he felt, the sappers *should* move forward, even though this would surely be suicide. His tanks were to squeeze through a pass on the southern slope of Phantom Ridge to the crest, from where they would give fire support to 3rd Carpathian infantry units attacking Hill 593, just southeast of the monastery. It was on Hill 593 that, in the earlier battle of May 12, Lieutenant Mahorowski, who had dreamed of falling into a puddle on his way to church, had been cut down with so many of his comrades.

As in the first battle, the 3rd Carpathian Division was to capture, after Hill 593, Hill 569 and finally the monastery, while the 5th Kresawa Division took Phantom Ridge and other flanking heights. The tanks of Captain Drelicharz had managed to reach a point on Phantom Ridge about a hundred yards below its summit, but had been stopped by mines. And the sappers refused to remove them since enemy machine-gun fire was raking the mined area, which was entirely exposed.

But no assignment was too dangerous, thought Captain Drelicharz and General Duch. The whole battle was at stake. Perhaps the very future of Poland. The tanks had to move.

Desperately seeking a solution short of shooting his comrades, Drelicharz radiophoned his immediate superior, Colonel Wladyslaw Bobinski, second in command of the 2nd Polish Armored Brigade: "General Duch has ordered me to shoot the sappers if they do not obey."

"Hold everything," Bobinski replied. "I'm coming."

Bobinski arrived on foot and crawled to the first stalled tank, ac-

Former Chief Rabbi Israel Zolli after his conversion to Catholicism.

Fascists force Jews to work on banks of Tiber River.

Giacomo Di Porto,
who took refuge in
Convent of Notre Dame de Sion.

Eleanora Di Porto,
Giacomo's wife.

Father Benoît-Marie de Bourg d'Ire,
who saved thousands of Jews.

Celeste (Stella) Di Porto,
the "Black Panther," who denounced many Jews.

IL MESSAGGERO

King Victor Emmanuel III.

IL MESSAGGERO

Premier Pietro Badoglio.

A scene in Via Tasso SS prison as sketched by Michele Multedo.

Rosario Bentivegna and Carla Capponi.

Germans line up Italian civilians after Via Rasella killings.

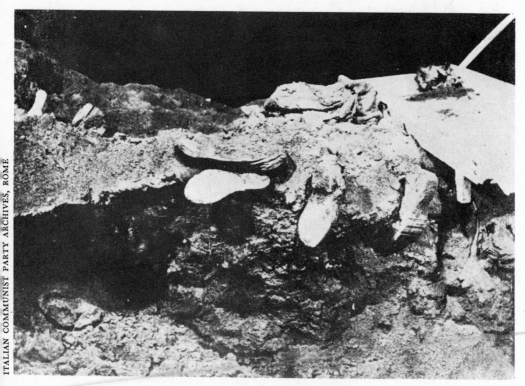

A corpse unearthed in Ardeatine Caves.

Communist Resistance leaders in Italy: Secchia, Togliatti, Longo,
Scoccimarro, Amendola.

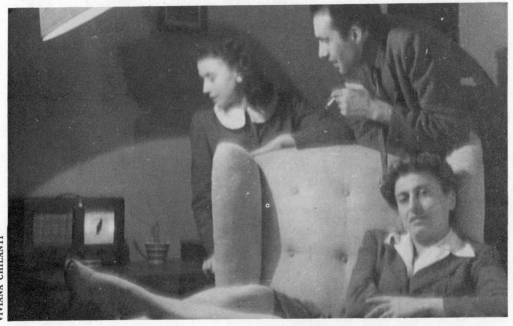

Ten-year-old Gloria Chilanti, her mother, Viviana,
and another Roman partisan listen to BBC while in hiding.

companied by the sapper officer who had refused to order his men forward. An enemy machine gun began firing, and Bobinski soon realized it was impossible to move beyond the first tank. He rushed to the rear and proposed a new plan to his superiors. With his finger on a map, he said:

"Instead of advancing along this exposed road, why not have the tanks move along the pathless slopes of Phantom Ridge—completely hidden from enemy observation."

His superiors looked up from the map in astonishment. Tanks could never maneuver along the rocky slopes. But Bobinski insisted that they could and finally urged:

"Let me at least try."

They did, and Bobinski immediately ordered three tanks to move off the road and advance below the crest, hidden from enemy eyes. Soon Germans were standing face to face with tanks they never imagined would be crawling over such rough terrain. They surrendered by the dozen.

The tanks then swung up to the crest in a dazzling triumph of armored strategy and from there were able to cover infantry troops climbing Hill 593.[6]

Lance Corporal Tomasz Dobrowolski plucked a bright red poppy from the stony earth where he lay while his battalion paused on the slopes of Hill 593. He stared at the flower. So delicate and ephemeral. Yet how many men would die before the poppies faded? Forward again. The fire from Bobinski's tanks was helping to clear the way.

It was a hot day and the going was difficult up the steep grade. And all the more because the air was redolent with the stench of men killed in past battles. Dobrowolski looked around. The weakest soldiers could no longer keep pace and his company was scattered. No squads, no platoons. Total confusion. Everyone would have to act on his own.

Finally the crest! And just across the valley to the southwest, the shattered monastery, the wounded monster, reaching into the hazy sky with giant charred claws. They beckoned to him.

Dobrowolski peeked over a low stone wall on the crest and saw the shadows of helmets on the slope leading into the valley. At that moment, the valley echoed with gunfire, and many Poles fell dead, some hanging over the wall after having thrown grenades. Earlier, another battalion had almost been wiped out at this position. Now a half hour after the arrival of Dobrowolski's company, about 60 of its 110 men had fallen.

As Dobrowolski hurled grenades, he suddenly felt as if a giant fist had smashed into his back, and he collapsed—wounded by a German grenade that had burst against his pack. A cushion of chocolate, iron rations, and towels had saved his life. He struggled to his knees and raised his head above the wall. The monastery was shimmering in a smoky mist, teasing, taunting. He looked around. He was alone at the wall with the dead.

"You sons of bitches!" Dobrowolski cried out, looking to his rear. "Do you expect me to take Monte Cassino all by myself?"

He leaned over the wall, and while bullets zinged around him, began throwing grenades wildly. Then he called back to his comrades to bring him more. Finally, several came up and pulled him away by the legs before he fell unconscious amid the fragile red poppies that also graced, with indifferent splendor, the ground where lay his many victims.[7]

Thanks in part to the valor and initiative of such men as Lance Corporal Dobrowolski and Colonel Bobinski, by evening, May 17, the 3rd Carpathian Division was in control of Hill 593. And the 5th Kresawa Division had finally captured Phantom Ridge and other key hills. But soldiers clinging to forward positions on one of these hills, after running out of ammunition, could do nothing more than hurl stones at the enemy—while singing the Polish national anthem.

The Poles had done better than in the first attack, but after again suffering enormous casualties they had been stopped.

Important hills remained unconquered, among them the central objective—Monastery Hill. The Poles, despite their hard-won gains, were not in a position to link up with the British on Highway 6.

The irony was that the monster had exacted the new tragic sacrifice frivolously—when its doom was certain.

"I've nothing else to throw in," General Rudnicki, the deputy commander of the 5th Kresawa Division desperately radioed General Anders as he awaited a counterattack on one hill.

But Anders, oddly, did not seem greatly concerned. "Don't worry, my dear fellow," he replied calmly. "I know the situation on the whole front. The Germans are beaten!"

Anders knew, of course, that the Germans were fleeing before the U.S. Fifth Army to the south, leaving the defenders at Cassino isolated with an open southern flank. And now he had just learned what the Germans on Monte Cassino were planning to do . . .

At about 2 P.M. that day, May 17, a Polish signalman in the corps communications trailer had intercepted a radio message sent by German Tenth Army headquarters to the monastery and routinely handed

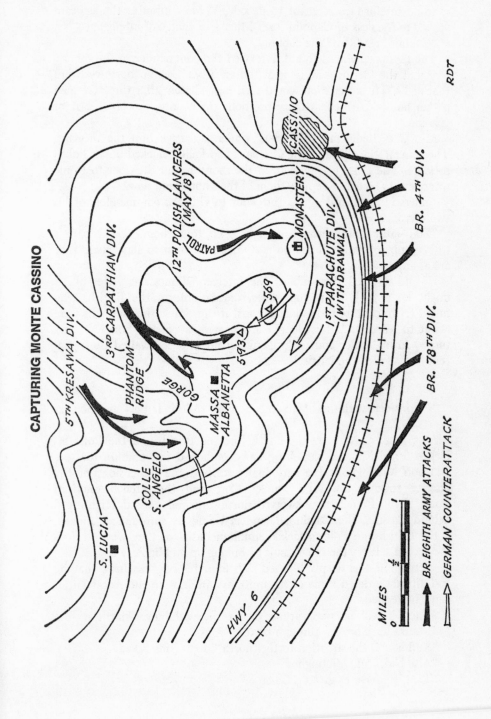

CAPTURING MONTE CASSINO

S. LUCIA

5TH KRESAWA DIV.

3RD CARPATHIAN DIV.

PHANTOM RIDGE

COLLE S. ANGELO

GORGE

MASSA ALBANETTA

593

569

12TH POLISH LANCERS (MAY 18)

PATROL

MONASTERY

CASSINO

1ST PARACHUTE DIV. (WITH DRAWAL)

BR. 4TH DIV.

BR. 78TH DIV.

HWY 6

MILES

0   ½   1

→ BR. EIGHTH ARMY ATTACKS

⇨ GERMAN COUNTERATTACK

RDT

it to an intelligence sergeant to decode. Within minutes the sergeant rushed to the desk of Captain Jozef Minski, in charge of intelligence.

"Captain, read this!" he shouted.

The message, Minski found, informed the commander in the monastery that the Germans were to withdraw from Cassino northwestward that night. The evacuation would start immediately after three German planes bombed Allied artillery positions on Monte Trocchio, east of Cassino.

Minski excitedly ran to Anders' trailer and gave him the message. The general's face lit up. The Germans had finally cracked under Polish pressure. The Poles had pulverized the monster and the door to Rome was open. Who could deprive them of their homeland now?

Anders jumped into a jeep and went to visit the commanders of his two divisions.

"You must hold through tonight," he told them. "Send patrols to keep up spirits at all the posts. Order your men to stay where they are at any cost."

He did not tell them about the intercepted message. After all, it might be a trick. Nor, apparently, did he inform the British, who might try to capture the monastery first if they knew the Germans were about to leave, and thus deprive his own men of that honor. He returned to his trailer and with agonizing impatience awaited the signal that he had won the battle.[8]

"I consider withdrawal to the Senger [Adolf Hitler] position as necessary."

At 5:25 P.M., May 16, the day before the British and the Poles attacked, Field Marshal Kesselring had telephoned this opinion to General von Vietinghoff. He had finally realized the dimensions of the disaster striking the XIV Panzer Corps on the French-American front. If the French now swerved northward and crossed Highway 6 behind Cassino, the Cassino defenders would be surrounded. Indeed, if the British and Poles attacked simultaneously—as they were to do—they could achieve the same result by linking up on Highway 6.

Vietinghoff was deeply relieved. Without telling Kesselring that he had already ordered some of his units to withdraw to the Adolf Hitler Line, he replied:

"Then it will be necessary to begin the withdrawal north of the Liri; tanks have broken through there."

"And how is the situation further north?" Kesselring asked.

"Also bad," said Vietinghoff.

"Then we have to give up Cassino."

"Yes."

Kesselring then authorized Vietinghoff's troops to withdraw to the Adolf Hitler Line where they could perhaps halt the Allied advance. Shortly after 8 P.M., Vietinghoff sent an order to General Feurstein, commander of the LI Mountain Corps:

"The Army will carry out a fighting withdrawal to the Senger support line, beginning tonight. 51st Mountain Corps must prevent the enemy from breaking through to the Via Casilina [Highway 6]."

Thus, the corps' 1st Parachute Division, which held Monte Cassino, would have to keep the British and Poles from encircling the mountain until the Germans had withdrawn. With this withdrawal order, it looked on the night of May 16—though the Allies, could not know—as if another bloody battle for Monte Cassino might be avoided after all.

But General Heidrich defiantly gave his own order that the 1st Parachute Division hold its position at any cost. And the next morning, May 17, when the British and Poles attacked, the defenders fanatically obeyed, unaware that Kesselring had ordered them to start withdrawing the previous night. Even when Feurstein, late that afternoon, repeated his order to Heidrich, demanding that the delayed retreat take place that night (the order apparently intercepted by the Poles), Heidrich was adamant.

His men would *not* retreat from Monte Cassino.[9]

"General Anders! The planes just dropped the bombs!"

The general leaped from his trailer and his eyes, peering upward, reflected the brightness of the flare-lit night sky. It was about 9 P.M., May 17. Anders immediately contacted his artillery commander and ordered him to direct all his fire toward the rear of the monastery to catch the Germans as they withdrew.

Anders then told his aide, Major Eugene Lubomirski: "Lubo, I'm going to take a little nap. Wake me up at five-thirty."

He lay down on his cot, relaxed for the first time in days, and went to sleep.[10]

With aching heart, Lieutenant Weck watched from the entrance of the monastery as the men defending Monte Cassino groped their way toward Highway 6. They could not cross the road, for the British had already cut it, but stealthily walked and crawled over the rocks and through the bushes along the slopes parallel with the road. Since the

Poles had not reached the highway, the escape route was open along these slopes—for those who evaded the Polish shells peppering the way.

Movement MUNICH had begun at last. Field Marshal Kesselring, furious at Heidrich's insubordination, had personally ordered the general to withdraw his men. Thus, after enduring so many months of horror and heroism, after repelling the cream of the Allied armies, the 1st Parachute Division finally had to retreat, though still unconquered. It seemed that all the sacrifices had been in vain. Weck felt like weeping as he watched shadowy figures leave their posts and disappear into the bitter night.

Only the battalion based in the monastery itself remained behind. But not for long. At about 2 A.M., May 18, it was ordered to destroy all ammunition and supply stores and to depart as well. About two hours later, Weck, his commanding officer, Captain Beyer, and their troops were ready to go, leaving behind only two medics and several seriously wounded men who could not be moved. The men advanced in small groups along the slopes. Those in Weck's group, mainly staff officers, were suddenly caught in a heavy barrage and dived into a cave where they remained for several hours.

At about dawn, Weck noted that firing on the monastery had slackened, probably meaning that the Poles were about to charge it. And then they would certainly find the cave.

"We should leave now, or the enemy may capture us," Weck advised Beyer, one of his companions.

But Beyer felt that the firing was still too heavy to risk leaving.

"If you want to go now, you may go," he told Weck.

Hobbling on sticks to make the enemy think they were wounded in case they were sighted, Weck and another officer then made their way to the Adolf Hitler Line.[11]

Shortly after the three German planes had bombed Monte Trocchio, Lieutenant Voelck-Unsin gathered his forty-odd men and, one by one, they crawled from the stinking, debris-matted cellar where they had lived for weeks in the ruins of Cassino town. They picked their way through the ashen desolation, freezing like shadows between artillery bursts to blend in with the grotesque silhouettes of carnage. After reaching the lower slope of Monte Cassino, they plodded on to Highway 6.

As Voelck-Unsin led his men along a ditch at the side of the road, the cry in English, "Germans!" pierced the air.

The men fell on their stomachs as bullets whistled overhead. After several minutes Voelck-Unsin was about to rise when, to his shock, a machine-gun barrel resting on the trunk of a tree that had fallen across the ditch hardly two yards in front of him began spitting flame. The machine gunner knew Germans were somewhere in the shadows, but they were out of his line of sight. Someone threw a grenade and the machine gun fell silent.

Unable to move forward, Voelck-Unsin led his men off the road and up the hill, with the enemy on their heels shouting:

"Come down! You're surrounded!"

"You come up if you want us!" Voelck-Unsin cried back, throwing two grenades for punctuation.

As he had defended the monastery for months, he knew every path intimately, including one along the rocky hillside that led between the Poles atop Monte Cassino and the British on Highway 6.

He would rather miss his British neighbors in the cellars of Cassino, though they would never learn to carry a tune—or close a trap.[12]

Awakened at 5:30 A.M., General Anders, sleepy-eyed but bursting with energy, immediately radioed General Kirkman, the XIII Corps commander. Without mentioning the intercepted German message, he asked Kirkman to leave to the Poles the honor of capturing the monastery. He felt that he could not take a chance on the British seeking that honor for themselves. Kirkman, whose headquarters had also intercepted a German message indicating a withdrawal from Monte Cassino, apparently a later one, replied:

"Delighted to leave your gallant troops honor of occupying the monastery."

Anders then ordered his aide, Lubomirski: "Telephone General Leese and ask him for permission to send a patrol to the monastery to put up the Polish flag."

Leese was angry on picking up the phone: "What the devil are you waking me at this hour for?"

When Lubomirski relayed Anders' request, Leese seemed surprised. "All right, Lubo," he said, "If he thinks he can do it, let him try."

Lubomirski was careful not to mention the intercepted message, nor did Leese tell him that the British had also intercepted a similar message.

Anders then ordered his aide: "Now connect me immediately with Colonel Bittner."

Lubomirski called Bittner, the commander of the 12th Polish Lancers, and Anders ordered him: "Send a patrol immediately with a flag and place it on top of the monastery!"[13]

The British 4th and 78th Divisions had fought their way to Highway 6 the previous day, May 17, and waited for the Poles to swing over
the crest of Monte Cassino for a link-up on the highway.

Throughout the night, small-arms fire, hoarse shouts of "Halt!" and
the tramping of hobnailed boots on the rocky mountainside signaled
the capture of Germans trying to flee. "Another couple coming down,
sir," seemed to be the night's password. Meanwhile, 4th Division troops
stormed the town of Cassino, and human moles, British and German,
emerged from their cellar prisons, the Germans no longer singing.

At about the same time, Major W. I. Thomas of the 4th Division's
Royal Fusiliers, who had led the division's assault on Highway 6 the
previous day, stared up at the monastery and wondered if any Germans were left up there. Of if the Poles had already occupied it. Why
leave such a prize abandoned?

With one of his men, he began the tortuous climb toward the monastery to investigate. On the way he found a German sergeant major
sleeping behind a rock—he rudely awakened him and sent him down
the hill to British headquarters. Higher on the slope he surprised six
more Germans, and his companion escorted them down.

As he inched ahead to within a hundred yards of the monastery,
Thomas saw a steel helmet in the mouth of a cave and shouted for its
wearer to come out. The helmet disappeared and was replaced by a
white tablecloth at the end of a pole.

"Come out!" shouted Thomas again.

And suddenly the standard bearer emerged, followed by nineteen
comrades, just as another British soldier arrived. When the Germans
had lined up with their hands raised, one of them exclaimed with embarrassment:

"Only two?"

Thomas took one of the prisoners as a guide and continued climbing
toward the silent monastery. He could hardly believe his luck. After all
the months of savage battle it looked as if he would capture it all by
himself. But as he finally arrived at the entrance of the battered structure he saw several soldiers in British-style helmets.

The Poles had beaten him to it.[14]

A unit of the 12th Polish Lancers had just arrived at the monastery,
finally linking up with the British, though too late to trap most of the
Germans. The Poles were now planting atop the ruins of the structure
a hastily made regimental banner cut from a Red Cross flag. Later the
Polish and British national flags would flutter in its place.

What happened inside the monastery in the first minutes after their arrival is disputed. The Poles say that they treated well all the Germans they caught—only two orderlies and a few wounded actually emerged —despite German cruelty to Polish prisoners.

Some Germans claim differently. In his book Von Himmel zu Hölle (From Heaven to Hell), Wilhelm Berthold says that the Poles fired wildly in the courtyard before descending to the cellar of the monastery where the wounded were waiting.

"They should stop this nonsense!" an old medic muttered as he went upstairs to turn over the wounded.

The helpless men, according to Berthold, "looked after him and saw in the dim candlelight his bent back. How tired he was as he mounted the stone steps; a man who had to fulfill his last bitter duty on Monte Cassino."

The men then heard a shot, Berthold maintains. The Poles had killed the old medic. The Poles then came down the stairs shouting in broken German:

"Where be? . . . Where be? . . . Pigs!"

They then ordered the wounded to rise, writes Berthold, and those unable to obey were immediately shot.

"The shots resounded through the vaults. The wounded parachutists died with surprised, unbelieving expressions on their faces."

Berthold's claim that "dozens" of seriously wounded were left behind in the monastery appears to conflict with a statement made by Lieutenant Weck to the author that "several" wounded were left. Correspondents who arrived shortly after the monastery was captured reported, in any event, that three wounded were taken prisoner.

Whatever the truth, the monastery reeked with the smell of death. Corpses, many days or weeks old, lay everywhere amid the rubble and trash. Some were stuffed in huge drawers normally used for the storing of liturgical clothes.

A number of the Germans found hiding in nearby caves were only half alive—among them Captain Beyer, who had lost his leg in an artillery barrage after refusing to flee with Lieutenant Weck during the night because of the heavy firing.

With the monster finally subdued, the tinkling of the bell on St. Benedict's finger gave way again to the delicate voice of the nightingale singing odes to the dead dotting the hills where Benedict had preached peace and brotherhood.

About a thousand soldiers would be buried in a Polish military cemetery at the foot of Monte Cassino—the Poles had suffered more than four thousand casualties in their two attacks—while at the summit a simple marble spire would proclaim to a world that would crush their dreams:

We Polish soldiers,
For our freedom and yours,
Have given our souls to God,
Our bodies to the soil of Italy,
And our hearts to Poland.[15]

❖   ❖   ❖

"The situation doesn't look too good," groaned Lieutenant General Fritz Wentzell, the Tenth Army's chief of staff.

He was phoning a report on the French advance to Colonel Dietrich Beelitz, Kesselring's chief of operations, on May 16. The French troops, Wentzell said, were slashing through the mountains and overrunning German positions with incredible speed.

Uttering a low whistle, Beelitz exclaimed: "Jesus Christ! I didn't think the enemy would be that strong!"

"You don't know the French colonial troops," Wentzell told him. "They are a fierce bunch. Life means nothing to them." . . .[16]†

The following day, May 17, General Guillaume demonstrated how fierce his *goumiers* could be.

"What did you see?" he asked when several of his men had returned from a reconnaissance tour of Monte Revole.

"It looks like at least a battalion of men."

A mysterious column, still distant below them, was slowly winding its way up the lower slopes of the mountain.

Guillaume, keeping his promise, had, on May 15, led his *goumiers* to the summit of Monte Petrella just a few hours after the Americans had taken Spigno at its foot. They had then continued on to Monte Revole, a four-thousand-foot-high keystone of the Dora Line, which was actually a two-pronged southern extension of the Adolf Hitler Line that blocked the Liri Valley. The Dora stretched from the southern banks of the Liri through the Aurunci Mountains to the Tyrrhenian Sea. The *goumiers* were now, in the afternoon of May 17, about to descend the relatively gentle western slope of Revole to cut the Itri-Pico road behind the defense belt.

† Hitler apparently considered Juin's troops the best of the Allied forces in Italy. At a staff meeting in his headquarters on May 18, 1944, General Jodl reported: "The English have suffered the heaviest losses, the Americans a little less, and the French have had the smallest losses." Hitler replied: "Because they are the best!"

But who were the men climbing this steep, treeless mountain toward them—friend or enemy? They were still too far away to identify. Maybe they were the American paratroops General Clark had promised to send if Guillaume asked for them. He had not asked for them, but Clark, who earlier that day had dispatched thirty-six bombers to drop some forty tons of supplies to feed and equip the *goumiers*, might have sent these men anyway.

"Have they any vehicles with them?" Guillaume asked one observer.

"Yes, five tanks."

That settled it. Paratroops would not be coming with tanks. Realizing that they must be Germans trying to occupy the Dora Line, Guillaume radioed his officers that the *goumiers* should prepare to attack.

"Don't fire a shot!" he ordered. "Let them walk into a trap. Do you understand? I'll give the order to fire myself."

Guillaume then deployed his men on the heights overlooking the advancing soldiers, who moved leisurely, smoking cigarettes, and singing —the language was now clear: *"Ich hatt' ein' Kameraden. . . ."*

The general watched from behind a large rock as they approached. They stopped singing as the grade grew steeper and their breath shorter.

"If you fire without my order," repeated Guillaume in his radiophone, "I'll have you court-martialed. You still have five minutes!"

The five minutes passed slowly as the sound of stones rolling and metal and boots grinding on gravel echoed through the valley. Then Guillaume shouted over the radio:

"Allez-y! Zidou l' Gouddam!"

A rain of steel and lead suddenly poured into the advancing force from almost every direction. The surprised Germans, a battalion of the 15th Panzer Grenadiers, whom Kesselring had sent to occupy this mountainous zone "just in case," scrambled behind rocks and down the slopes, but they could not escape the trap. Within minutes, all but a few had been killed by bullets or mortar shells and the rest taken prisoner.

On maps the Germans carried, the area where the battle took place was marked: "Impracticable for combat."

Guillaume then sent part of his force northwestward toward Pico. Under Alexander's battle plan, this was the place where the French would halt and go into reserve, squeezed out between the Americans and the British. The rest of Guillaume's men swept down the western slopes of Monte Revole to cut the Itri-Pico road behind the Adolf Hitler Line even before the fleeing Germans were able to man this line.[17]‡

‡ Some hours after he conquered Monte Revole, General Guillaume sent a patrol led by a young artillery officer, Second Lieutenant de Kerautem, across the Itri-Pico road

Nor were the Americans on their southern flank along the coast far behind. The German 94th Division facing them steadily disintegrated. When Kesselring learned on May 17 that one regiment of the 94th had been ordered to scatter, with the men to make their way to the rear as best they could, he complained in a phone conversation with General Wentzell, the Tenth Army chief of staff:

"I can tell you quite frankly, I can't call anything like that 'tactics.' "18

"Tonight I am not here," fantasized the vivacious French girl as she waltzed around the garlic-smelling room with an imaginary sweetheart in her arms to the tune scratched out by an ancient Italian victrola. "Tonight I am in Paris, wearing a long red evening gown and silk stockings and satin shoes and a beautiful white flower in my hair."

But when the record was played out, she would be "here" again—in a ramshackle farmhouse that served as medical headquarters. She would be dressed in fatigues, leggings, and muddy boots, with the dust of battle in her hair. And she would be sent to pick up the wounded, together with the other French women who had volunteered to drive ambulances—among them Colette Planès . . .

Colette's husband, Captain Pierre Planès, was happily surprised to see his pretty blond wife step out of the ambulance. They had been separated since Operation DIADEM had begun, when they had listened together to the nightingales. The captain had then led his men into the enemy-infested mountains, and somehow it had seemed improbable that they would meet again on the battlefield.

Colette ran to him and they kissed and embraced.

"Ça va, cherie?" Pierre asked. "Is everything okay?"

"Ça va. But I haven't been able to undress, even to sleep, since the attack started."

"Neither have I."

And that prosaic fact seemed to sum up all the horror and misery they had endured in those few days.

Their meeting took place at a French aid station in the hills above

behind the German lines. When the unit had scaled Monte Velle on the west side of the road and overpowered the German defenders, De Kerautem directed French batteries throughout the following day onto German concentrations below. Practically surrounded by Germans at nightfall, the patrol slipped once more through the enemy lines, returning to Guillaume with a bag of prisoners including the commander of a tank battalion.

the village of Monticelli, northwest of Esperia, after the French had nearly wiped out the retreating German 71st Division. The 3rd Algerian Division, spearheaded by Planès' tanks, had plowed its way from Castelforte through the Ausente Valley and had taken Esperia on May 17 after a stiff fight with the 90th Panzer Grenadier Division, which Kesselring had finally sent from reserve to stop the French.

Meanwhile, north of Esperia, units of the 3rd Algerian swept down the slopes leading to the Liri Valley to make contact with the 1st Free French Motorized Division, which was speeding up the southern bank of the Liri ahead of the British Eighth Army crawling forward on the other side of the river. As the commander of the 3rd Algerian force met General Diego Brosset, commander of the 1st Free French, the two men searched each other's eyes and embraced, kissing each other on both cheeks.

The French Army of Africa that had earlier supported Vichy and the Free French force created by General de Gaulle had agreed to fight jointly under General Juin, but until this moment they had remained cool to each other, harboring bitter memories of fratricidal battle. Now, as representatives of the two groups met in the euphoria of victory, they were simply Frenchmen. As Juin had hoped, they had learned to love each other again on the road to Rome.

When Esperia and several key heights nearby had fallen, Planès' tanks had helped to capture the hill town of Monticelli. Now his men were resting on the way to Pico, where they would link up with other French forces and, presumably, be squeezed out of action.

As Planès led his wife toward the wounded, who lay grouped nearby, she asked who they were. Her green eyes reflected her grief when he told her. Colette knew all the men on the list, some like brothers. And now they might die in her arms.

When all the wounded had been placed in the ambulance, a machine gun suddenly rattled a deadly message. The Germans were counterattacking. Colette jumped into the driver's seat next to another nurse, feebly waved to her husband, and raced the ambulance down the narrow, rocky road toward Esperia in the rear.

Almost immediately, German planes appeared in the clear sky and bombs exploded on all sides of the speeding vehicle. The other nurse clamped a helmet on Colette's head and, to calm the wounded and themselves, the two girls burst into the drinking song, "Chevalier de la Table Rond." As the ambulance trembled under the explosions, however, Colette's courage began to wilt. She wanted to slam on the brakes and run for cover, but suddenly she saw before her a vision of her husband—the demanding eyes, the strong chin, the large nose, the thin, stubborn lips.

They had met in 1940, after the Germans had occupied Colette's native Lyon, on a boat taking them to Algiers, she to join her family, he to join the Army of Africa to avenge France's humiliation. When they had married she insisted on sharing in this mission . . . And now she heard him repeat what he had said then:

"Very well. But if there is a bullet, a shell, or a mine with the name 'Colette Planès' on it, I ask you to die the wife of a French officer."

Colette raced through the lethal storm and finally arrived safely in Esperia.[19]

Francesco F. stepped outside his hillside farmhouse near Itri, on the border between the American and French fronts, to greet the group of dark-skinned soldiers who were approaching. It was Sunday, May 20. The day before, the first American troops had marched by after capturing Itri, asked for water from his well, and continued on. They had been polite and even patted the children on the head.

About seventy relatives and friends had crowded into Francesco's large house after their own homes had been destroyed by bombs and shells or ransacked by retreating Germans, feeling a certain safety in numbers. Francesco's village had been cruelly caught in the web of war. But it looked now as if the worst was over. The Germans were gone and the Americans had been kind. Soon those villagers whose homes were still habitable would scatter and Francesco could start working in the fields again.

But he soon learned that the worst was not over. The new group of soldiers, goumiers, pushed him inside his house, threatened the terrified occupants with their guns and knives, then grabbed Francesco's twenty-year-old sister-in-law and dragged her away screaming to a hayloft. There, four soldiers raped her, and then a second woman as well.

Outside, five or six goumiers caught a niece, twenty-three, while she was trying to escape with some goats and attacked her. Seven others grabbed another niece the same age and began to rape her in the fields, letting her go only when an American happening by in a jeep threatened to shoot the rapists. Two goumiers attacked another young woman living in Francesco's house while she was on a stroll some distance away.

The goumiers then departed with all the cattle and cash they could find.

Later that same day, a family living in a neighboring village, hearing about the atrocities, fled toward Spigno, but was stopped by two goumiers and a soldier they later claimed was a white Frenchman. The three ordered one of the daughters, nineteen, to come with them, but she pretended to be ill and finally dissuaded them.

They then turned to another daughter, sixteen, who cried in terror that she was ill, too. Now infuriated, the men kicked and beat the whole family—the mother, an eighty-two-year-old grandmother, three daughters, a son, and even a crying baby. In desperation, the mother, Margherita G., offered them seven thousand lire from her shabby purse to leave the family in peace, but the soldiers, while taking the money, still demanded physical satisfaction.

"You have a choice," one said. "Give yourself to us or we'll take your daughters."

And so Margherita yielded to them to save the honor of her daughters.

In the coming days, hundreds of Italian women, from twelve to seventy, and even some men, were to be outraged if their villages lay in the path of the advancing *goumiers*, who viewed rape and robbery, and even murder, as no worse than killing people on orders and, indeed, the natural privilege of the conqueror. They held no grudge against their civilian victims, but they also held none against the Germans. What was war without spoils?

When reports of the atrocities reached General Clark, he wrote General Juin asking that he immediately discipline the *goumiers*.

On May 27 Juin, deeply disturbed by this blemish on the honor of the force he hoped would become the liberating army of France, sent, in turn, a memorandum to his commanders demanding that "an example be made of those guilty by exercising punishment without mercy." Juin said he relied "on the sense of duty and honor among his officers and NCO's to put an immediate stop to these acts which are unworthy of a strong and victorious army and are such that may seriously compromise the French cause."

Many of the rapists were then shot on the spot by their commanders and some were even hanged in village squares. Nevertheless, officers insisted that they could not control the *goumiers*, who, in leading the way to Rome—and France—were leaving in their wake a trail of horror and hate.

The curse of Rome had seized even the conqueror.[20]

❖ ❖ ❖

With Allied forces storming up the boot toward Rome, the time was near for the troops isolated on the Anzio beachhead, the U.S. VI Corps, to break out and link up with them. Therefore, on May 17, General Alexander visited Clark to discuss once more the delicate question of the direction the VI Corps troops should take when they broke out.

Alexander had not changed his mind since he told General Truscott, the VI Corps commander, shortly before Operation DIADEM that he wanted the corps to head not northwest toward Rome, but northeast to Valmontone on Highway 6—Operation BUFFALO. By cutting this road, Alexander still insisted, the breakout force could trap the Germans fleeing from the British Eighth Army.

Clark had not changed his views either. He still doubted, Clark told Alexander, that such a maneuver would work. Since several secondary roads wound through the hills beyond Valmontone, he argued, the Germans did not *have* to retreat down Highway 6. He spread a map on his desk and drew a circle around the high ground that Truscott would occupy when and if he reached Valmontone.

"Where will Truscott go from there?" he asked, according to his memoirs.

Alexander replied that fast, mobile patrols could cut the German routes beyond Valmontone, but Clark insisted this could not be done.

"There will be no roads and only footpaths over which to move from [Valmontone]," Clark argued, "and the enemy still will hold the Alban Hills [through which ran the Caesar Line, the last defensive belt before Rome; it overlooked the route from Anzio to Valmontone] and its dominant observation. It seems to me that we should keep ourselves in a position to evaluate the situation when the time comes, and it may prove then that the . . . Valmontone direction is the wrong one."

Yes, the "wrong one," thought Alexander. It didn't lead to Rome.

Alexander departed and wishfully informed Prime Minister Churchill that he would soon have the Americans at Anzio "punch out [to Valmontone] to get astride the enemy's communications to Rome." Simultaneously, Clark pondered how he could head for Rome without overtly disobeying orders. He finally found a "solution."

The following day, May 18, he summoned Truscott to his headquarters to discuss a new alternative to BUFFALO. Under his "compromise" plan, he explained to Truscott the next morning, he would strike northeast, as BUFFALO prescribed, and advance to Cisterna on the way to Valmontone. But then, only *one* unit, the 1st Special Service Force, would continue on to Valmontone. The rest of Truscott's force would change direction at Cisterna and head directly for Rome.

Truscott was amused by, but extremely wary of, this "compromise." It was clever. Who could say that Clark disobeyed Alexander as long as he *technically* complied with his order by sending *one* unit to Valmontone.

Clark, Truscott writes in his memoirs, "was obviously still fearful that the British might beat him into Rome."

Though Truscott was loyal to Clark, he was not as excited by the race for Rome. Unlike his superior, he was a man of extreme modesty who shunned rather than courted publicity. He was a soldier with a job to do, and, in his view, the main job was to destroy the German armies. Rome's capture would obviously have great psychological value, but from a strictly military viewpoint it was of secondary importance. This was also Alexander's argument, though it is not as evident that Rome was really secondary to him.

Truscott's modesty and reasoned approach, which suited the Oklahoma schoolmaster he had been as a very young man, contrasted sharply with the flamboyant and eccentric aspects of his outward personality. He wore a luminous, enameled helmet and a white scarf around his neck and sometimes, for luck, a treasured pair of faded pink cavalry breeches and high brown cavalry boots.

He was, moreover, extraordinarily finicky about food, trusting only Chinese-American cooks. And his angry gravel-voice, damaged by poison he had accidentally swallowed as a child, could be heard throughout Anzio when his orderly neglected to decorate his tent with fresh flowers.

It was not simply his voice that established a rather ferocious authority. His jutting jaw, fierce scowl, and squinting gray eyes suggested the kind of protective toughness that made men follow him resolutely into the most suicidal battles. In North Africa, he had molded the 3rd Division, which he then commanded, into one of the most aggressive in the United States Army, and, since taking over from General Lucas at Anzio in February 1944, he had sharpened his VI Corps to razor edge.

And now it was ready to go—though he was not sure where.

At their meeting, Truscott insisted to Clark that the 1st Special Service Force, a slashing, commando-type unit composed of Americans and Canadians, would not alone be strong enough to capture Valmontone and cut Highway 6. Clark, finally persuaded, glumly abandoned the plan—at least temporarily.

Alexander, meanwhile, did some planning of his own. On May 20 he called in Major General Lyman L. Lemnitzer, a member of his staff, and requested him to relay an order to Clark. Although Lemnitzer was American, he supported the Briton's view that Truscott's force should head for Valmontone. Alexander was now ordering Clark to have Truscott break out in that direction the following night, May 21.

Lemnitzer personally drove to Clark's headquarters and handed him the order. Clark's eyes glared with fury as he read it. How could Alexander issue such an order without consulting him? Looking up, he told Lemnitzer that Truscott could not possibly attack out of the beachhead with such little notice. Nor did it make sense to send Truscott forward until the Germans had been driven into a position from which they would have to fall back beyond Rome. Was it his fault if the British Eighth Army had not yet driven the enemy into such a position?

When Lemnitzer returned to Alexander with Clark's reply, it was now Alexander who was furious—in part, it seemed, because he knew Clark had a point. Unfortunately, the Eighth Army was creeping at a snail's pace through the Liri Valley. It probably could not link up with the breakout troops at Valmontone—and close the trap on the Germans— for some time.

The British Eighth Army was still the victim of its own mechanized power and complicated staff planning. Traffic jams were constantly holding up its advance, and tanks and other vehicles could hardly cross the bridgeless streams or maneuver along the rough, tree-strewn terrain of the charred valley, especially in the teeth of strong German rear-guard resistance.

Alexander's hope that the Eighth Army would, as the French had done in their sector, burst through the Adolf Hitler Line before the retreating Germans could firmly man it had thus proved vain. The Eighth now would have to mount a full-scale attack against this powerfully fortified line, and suffer all the attendant casualties, before reaching Valmontone.

Alexander carefully pondered his battle strategy. Under the circumstances, it would be terribly nice if the Fifth Army cleared the way for the Eighth Army—even though the Eighth was supposed to be the main striking force. Yes, he would, after all, let the French, upon reaching Pico, turn north and come in behind the enemy facing the Eighth Army—though he would only permit them to advance to Highway 6, not beyond it. Nor would he let them use the road, even if they arrived before the Eighth Army.

Highway 6 would still be reserved for the Eighth Army. And the French would still be squeezed out before reaching Rome, though somewhat closer to the city than originally planned.

Suppressing his irritation, Alexander drove to see Clark again and rather sheepishly asked him whether the Fifth Army would not outflank the German positions to make it unnecessary for the Eighth Army to attack the Adolf Hitler Line. The Eighth Army would thus be able to conserve losses—ironically, the same argument that Juin had advanced before the terrible bloodbaths at Cassino. But Clark thought little of this idea, apparently feeling that Alexander was mainly interested in keeping the Fifth Army from getting to Rome before the British—this chicanery to be achieved with Clark's help.

Clark replied that to conserve losses in the Eighth Army would mean to increase losses in the Fifth Army. No, he said, both armies should attack with maximum effort at the same time. He added:

"I believe that it will be necessary to delay the attack from Anzio at least twenty-four hours and possibly forty-eight hours . . ."

Alexander found himself overruled even on the timing of the breakout. The date was finally set for 6:30 A.M., May 23. And what direction would the Anzio troops take? Neither man apparently brought this delicate subject up again. Alexander had little reason to think now that his ambitious subordinate would follow orders. Nor were his spirits nourished by a cable he received from Winston Churchill on May 23, the day of the breakout:

> . . . Owing to the enemy pivoting backwards on his left, the advances of the French and the Americans are naturally filling the headlines . . . At Cabinet yesterday some queries were made as to whether the part played by the British troops was receiving proportionate notice . . . We do not want anything said that is not justified, but reading the current press one might well doubt if we were making any serious contribution. I know of course what the facts are, but the public may be upset. Could you therefore bring them a little more into the communiqués, presuming of course that such mentions are deserved?

Alexander replied with a glowing over-all report on Allied progress, pointing out that "British troops have played a conspicuous part in very bitter fighting . . ."

"I will see," he added, "that they have their share of publicity in the communiqués."[21]

※   ※   ※

"Everything seems to be too late," General Wentzell lamented to Colonel Beelitz over the phone on May 18. " . . . We can no longer contain the enemy."

Even Kesselring, the eternal optimist, had begun to view the situation with alarm. The German Tenth Army was scrambling toward the Adolf Hitler Line, which the French had already pierced. And the Fourteenth Army, which was massed around the Anzio beachhead to prevent an enemy breakout or new landing, might be wiped out if the Americans marching up the coast linked up with the beachhead troops.

Kesselring's problems, moreover, were complicated by bitter squabbles with his two top commanders, General von Vietinghoff of the Tenth Army and General von Mackensen of the Fourteenth Army. Both thought he was basing his decisions not on military reality but on sheer optimism.

Vietinghoff felt that Kesselring had jeopardized the very survival of his army by waiting so long before permitting it to withdraw to the Adolf Hitler Line. What could have been an orderly movement had turned into a chaotic rout. And once his army started retreating, the field marshal refused to send him reserves to stem the tide until it was too late.

Mackensen, a monocled Prussian aristocrat, while agreeing that Kesselring should have ordered an earlier withdrawal, felt that the field marshal had compounded his blunder by giving Vietinghoff the reserves he finally did send. Almost the only reserves in central Italy had been based around the beachhead under Mackensen's command ready to crush a breakout or a new landing. By transferring some of them to the Tenth Army Kesselring might have doomed the Fourteenth Army. And the proud Mackensen was determined not to blemish his family name with an ignominious defeat.

Both Vietinghoff and Mackensen tried to sabotage Kesselring's plans. Vietinghoff had ordered a gradual withdrawal of his troops to the Adolf Hitler Line without the field marshal's knowledge. And Mackensen delayed obeying orders to transfer his reserves to Vietinghoff.

When Kesselring, on May 16, ordered Mackensen to release the 26th Panzer Division so it could help the Tenth Army halt the French in the Pico area, Mackensen delayed so long that the division arrived in piecemeal confusion and too late to assist anyway.

Mackensen stalled again when Kesselring ordered him to send the 29th Panzer Grenadier Division to the Tenth Army zone south of the beachhead to help Vietinghoff prevent a link-up between the two American corps at Anzio.

This was too much for Kesselring, who vowed to punish him. Didn't Mackensen realize that he was stabbing his own army in the back? That because of the delay the Americans storming up the coast toward Anzio could probably not be stopped?

But the literal tug of war between the two army commanders continued. Each pulled at Kesselring relentlessly, predicting dire consequences if the other won. On May 22 Vietinghoff, after the 29th Panzer Grenadiers had arrived too late to halt the Americans, pleaded for still more reinforcements.

"If we don't get reinforcements," he warned by phone, "the people above shouldn't be surprised if we can't hold out here."

But the harried, helpless field marshal this time alibied: "The Führer insists that men are loafing about in the rear areas. Until everything has been combed out ruthlessly . . . no reinforcements."

Actually, Kesselring still did not know *where* to deploy his reserves, and one reason was that he could not be sure which direction Truscott's beachhead troops would take when they tried to break out. Mackensen was almost certain than they would head directly northwest for Rome, and he therefore blocked that route with his best divisions. But Kesselring was not so sure. If he were in Alexander's shoes, he would strike northeast toward Valmontone to cut off the Tenth Army. Mackensen, however, was guarding that route with only light forces.

With a new storm about to break, catastrophe appeared almost inevitable—and the German commanders blamed each other. They might have been more hopeful if they had known about the squabbles on the Allied side.[22]

❖ ❖ ❖

" '*Ten*shun!*'"

The rasping voice of the colonel echoed through the illuminated cellar beneath the Villa Borghese at Anzio, and the correspondents wearily, reluctantly got to their feet. They normally rose when a general entered at a press conference, but not, as they did now, at the bellowed order of a staff officer. The scene seemed almost rehearsed to some, especially when General Clark strode in and said in a kingly if almost apologetic tone:

"Sit down, gentlemen!"

It was the night before the breakout, May 22, and General Clark, who had that day moved his headquarters from Caserta to Anzio, had called the conference to brief the correspondents on the operation. The breakout force would head northeast to take Cisterna, Clark said with sweeping gestures, as he stood before a large war map. From there, it would advance north to cut Highway 6 at Valmontone and continue on to sever other roads further north, thus trapping most of German troops being chased up the Liri Valley by the British Eighth Army. He outlined Alexander's plan down to the last detail.

And then Clark spoke of the importance of Rome . . .

After four months of savage fighting and brutal isolation on the Anzio beachhead, the men of General Truscott's VI Corps were finally poised to crash out. They had fought and lived in a tiny, in-hospitable prison-land—a patchwork of sandy beaches, stingy pasture-land, low scrub, impassable swamps, and forests of cork oak matted together by tangled undergrowth.

The Germans had attacked with their best forces and had rained tons of shells on them day after day. But the defenders had held in one of history's greatest sieges, waiting for tomorrow, whenever that might be. And now tomorrow had arrived.

In a strange way, some would miss the unique challenge of improvis-ing life under unlivable conditions in the middle of a battlefield pocked and furrowed by foxholes, trenches, dugouts, barricades, and barbed wire. Not a few had burrowed themselves into caves, dug, according to legend, in the time of Nero, an Anzian himself. Persecuted Chris-tians are thought to have hidden in them, followed by people fleeing with all their worldly wealth from the Barbary Coast pirates.

Later, these caves were used as wine cellars, and, in the past four months, they had often echoed the harsh rhythms of the drunken bull session, with frustrated officers sometimes no more successful in finding their men than had been the Barbary pirates in seeking their wealthy prey.

Nor did the soldiers wine, dine—or even die—in needless discom-fort. They installed electric lights, heating units, telephones, office equipment, radios, direction charts, and sleeping quarters in these caves, as well as in the cellars of farmhouses and other wrecked buildings that dotted the depressing landscape outside.

They paid the few local Italian peasants—before the peasants were finally evacuated to Naples—to do their laundry. They bought cows from them to obtain meat and milk. And there was plenty of im-provised entertainment when they were not listening to "Axis Sally," the Nazi radio propagandist, who always put on a good show with her sultry voice and nostalgic recordings.

They shot pheasants with sawed-off shotguns used for guarding prisoners. They went fishing in Mussolini Canal. They rode mules in "Anzio Derbys" in which betting was heavy. Shells often interrupted their games, but sometimes even the Germans joined in the Allied revelry. One intoxicated American soldier, wearing a tall, silk hat he had found in an Italian villa, stumbled right through the enemy lines, but the Germans simply adjusted the hat, turned him around, and sent him back unharmed.

But it is unlikely that anyone settled into Anzio quite as elegantly, or as profitably, as First Lieutenant Graham (Gus) Heilman, who commanded B Company of the 1st Regiment, 1st Special Service Force. When his company captured the village of Borgo Sabatino in an advanced sector of the beachhead, the men simply moved in, renamed the hamlet "Gusville," and elected Gus mayor.

He turned out to be a good one. Soon the village issued a newspaper, the Gusville *Herald-Tribune*, and had new street names such as "Tank Street," commemorating a thoroughfare down which enemy tank shells frequently whizzed. It also boasted a fine collection of stolen livestock —cows, pigs, horses, chickens.

Gus even opened a bar, supplying it with captured German stocks. It wasn't as plush as the one he operated in Charlottesville, Virginia, but it was much livelier, especially after the Germans zeroed in on it.

But now it was time to close down the bar, the town, the beachhead. On the morning of May 23 the whole front would erupt. While VI Corps broke out of Anzio, the II Corps, rushing up the coast, would link up with it, and the British Eighth Army would smash through the Adolf Hitler Line with French help. It seemed not impossible, least of all to the Germans, that the concerted Allied attacks would trap, slice up, and destroy both German armies, with the exquisite plum of Rome to be plucked at leisure.

Still, at his Anzio press conference on the eve of the showdown, Mark Clark did not sound like a man who could wait for the plum to ripen while picking less appetizing fruit. It was perhaps the way he said:

"We're going to take Rome!"[23]

10

The Survivors

On a warm morning in early May, a few days before Operation DIADEM began, two planes swept down toward two lonely figures walking along a railroad track east of Rome. Hastily the strollers—a man and a woman—threw themselves into the high grass beside the track as a rain of bullets swept over them, sprinkling the earth only yards away.

Rosario Bentivegna and Carla Capponi were horrified to discover that they were being attacked by Allied planes. Apparently the pilots had mistaken them for Germans—and they were maneuvering for another pass . . .[1]

Ironically, Rosario and Carla were hiking from Rome to the green hills around Palestrina, a town north of Valmontone, where they were to lead guerrilla attacks on German troops who would, if Allied plans went well, soon be retreating from Cassino. The partisans would ambush these Nazis as they tried to escape over a narrow, dusty road that ran through Palestrina roughly parallel with Highway 6. (This was one of the roads that Clark argued could not be cut by the Anzio troops, but which Alexander insisted *could* be.)

The Allies had requested such help at a most appropriate moment for the Roman partisans, whom the Nazis were relentlessly tracking down in the wake of the Via Rasella explosion. Many of these partisans had fled to the countryside, hoping to return shortly before the Allies arrived to spark an insurrection.

The Communists had quite simply miscalculated the likely popular reaction to reprisals for Via Rasella—at least in Rome. In industrial northern Italy, where the Resistance was far more influential, the Ardeatine massacre had spurred the guerrillas to greater activity, which, in turn, yielded new savage reprisals.

In Rome, though a few explosions and assassinations of Germans occurred, most people had been intimidated into nursing their deeper hatred of the occupier in passive silence. What would be gained, they asked, by killing a few Germans when the Allies would soon liberate them anyway? Unlike the relatively few activists, most Romans did not view insurrection as the road to resurrection, nor did they wish redemption nourished by *their* blood. And the Ardeatine massacre only solidified this attitude. The Germans now ruled Rome even more ruthlessly than before, and fear was growing that they might even deport most of the people.

To many Romans the perpetrators of Via Rasella were not heroic figures but practically as blameworthy as the Germans for the killing of so many sons, husbands, fathers, and friends. Sensitive to this negative popular reaction, the CLN leadership at first planned to publicly disclaim responsibility for Via Rasella. Even the Red Flag party condemned the attack, saying in its bulletin that a distinction should be made between acts of terrorism carried out in areas where the population was solidly behind the partisans, as in the working class sections, and in areas where it was not.

"We cannot know what the [regular Communist party] would do just for the sake of being mentioned on Radio London," declared the Red Flag bulletin.

But the Communists, backed by the other leftist parties in the CLN, finally persuaded the rightist parties—apparently as the price of leftist co-operation in the future—that the CLN should publicly take responsibility for Via Rasella. It did—to the detriment of its public image.*

Hunted by the enemy, scorned by the people, the Communists tried their best to continue the battle. But somehow, nothing worked any more.

* The Communists persuaded the other parties not only to take responsibility for Via Rasella, but to use the German reprisal to spur the population to resistance, the main reason for the attack in the first place. A shrill official CLN proclamation—to the embarrassment of many members—declared: "The blood of our martyrs must not have flowed in vain. From the graves where the 320 Italians [the actual figure, 335, was not known yet]—of every social class, of every political creed—lie united for all time in their sacrifice, a solemn call is raised to each of you: All for the liberation of the fatherland from the Nazi invader! All for the reconstruction of an Italy worthy of its fallen sons!"

In early April, Carla Capponi led three men on a mission to assassinate Giuseppe Pizzirano, the vice secretary of the Fascist party. She was to flag down his car as it left his home while the others poured bullets into the vehicle. But though she succeeded in slowing down the car by standing in its path, when the three men tried to fire not one of their pistols worked!

A few days later Carla and Rosario were plotting the assassination of General Mälzer, the Commandant of Rome. A partisan was to shoot a certain Fascist militia chief at whose funeral, it was calculated, Mälzer would certainly appear. A bomb would go off during the funeral procession, timed to hit Mälzer's car. The Fascist chief was duly shot and the bomb was hidden in a flower pot in a florist's stall beside the road leading to the cemetery. But Mälzer did not attend the funeral. Nor was there even a procession. Only the car with the Fascist passed the flower stall, and he was already dead.

Disaster then struck. In mid-April, during a routine round-up, Pietro Koch arrested Guglielmo Blasi, the conspirator in the Via Rasella operation who, for some reason, had failed to stand guard as ordered in front of Barberini Palace. Faced with torture, Blasi, an old-time Communist who had been completely trusted, talked, naming almost all the plotters, though he knew them only by their underground names. Koch was determined to learn of any meetings these partisans had scheduled . . .

On April 27 a man slouched toward two persons who had just met on a street corner near the Colosseum and from the rear tapped one on the shoulder.

"Spartaco?"

Carlo Salinari, who had directed the Via Rasella operation, turned around on hearing his code name and stared into a pistol barrel.

A car drove up, and Salinari and his companion, Franco Carlmandrei, another Via Rasella conspirator, were pushed in. When they arrived at Koch's headquarters, Carlmandrei, pleading illness, asked to go to the lavatory and received permission. After considerable time had passed, his captors began to wonder if he could be *that* sick. They went to investigate—and found the lavatory vacant. Carlmandrei had wriggled through a tiny window and escaped.

Salinari, meanwhile, was taken to an office where Koch sat dressed in elegant civilian clothes in front of a large red flag pinned on the wall.

"Don't be surprised," Koch said with a smile. "I happen to be a Communist, but a dissident one. Your leaders are nothing but agents of Russia, but *I* am an Italian Communist."

Before Salinari could recover from the shock of finding that Koch apparently considered him stupid enough to believe this, Koch went on: "As long as the Allies occupy Italy, we must fight them. *Then* we'll fight the Germans as well. I know you're a GAP [Patriotic Action Group] commander here in Rome. Tell me who your leaders are."

When Salinari insisted he was a simple soldier and knew nothing, Koch's men went to work. They tortured Salinari for ten days, then transferred him to Via Tasso prison.

Many other partisans suffered the same fate, among them most top Socialist leaders, including Giuliano Vassalli, for whom the Pope would intervene with SS General Wolff, and Bruno Buozzi, Italy's chief labor leader.

This string of arrests assured the failure of a general strike that the partisans had called for May 3—especially since Salinari and Buozzi were two of the main organizers. To fend off the strike, the Germans kept public transport workers locked in the garages all night and were able to force them to operate their vehicles in the morning. Virtually alone in striking were the printers at *Il Messaggero*, the Fascist newspaper. They were deported.

Though General Alexander stated in a war communiqué on May 22 that Italian partisans, including those in Rome, were keeping six German divisions tied up, the arrests and the failure of the strike proved the near futility of partisan activity in the city until the Allies drew closer.

And with the police searching for the two of them, the time seemed ripe for Rosario and Carla to fight in Palestrina where they could help the Allies achieve that goal—if Allied aircraft did not kill them first . . .[2]

As the planes swept down once more, Rosario and Carla clung to each other in the grass. It seemed strange to Carla that death should strike from a sky so blue and bright. And before the last bullets had whined by, they were gently, rhythmically, moving in each other's arms, trying to compress a lifetime into what might be their last moment alive. Carla would later poetically recall . . .

> *Sun in my eyes,*
> *Stinging, tears—*
> *The eyes weep*
> *But the flesh rejoices,*
> *And in the air the warm*
> *Scent of grass.*
> *And the cricket is singing,*
> *Who knows where?*

Here, between myself and my heart,
The dialogue of love has grown closer.
I hope to pierce through it
With the sweetness
Of your loving,
Which gives no rest
To my blood, gives no rest
To my mouth; shaking
This person I am,
I, so small, I, a child,
And tears away under the sun
Of your kisses all resistance,
To the last drop,
Which now—do you hear it?—falls
Trembling on the clear glass
Of the consciousness of this woman,
Who is just now born
Into love.

The planes passed over and vanished, leaving only the hidden cricket to witness the sweetly desperate dialogue.[3]

❖   ❖   ❖

The nerve-wracking blast of a bugle shocked Peter Tompkins partially awake. He wanted to turn over on his straw mattress that smelled of brilliantine and urine and go back to sleep, but he was too patriotically stirred by the sound of a United States Army reveille call. What a beautiful sound. Still, how in the world had he joined the army? Had he been *that* drunk? Then, as his mind cleared, he realized that he was in an Italian African Police (PAI) barracks, and that the reveille had emanated from Axis Sally's radio propaganda program, hooked into the police public address system.

Yes, he was now an Italian policeman! . . .

It had been Franco Malfatti's idea. Malfatti had asked a pro-Allied lieutenant in the PAI to enroll a certain "Italian Air Force major" as a noncommissioned officer in his company. He explained that the Allies needed the major for the development of guided aircraft rockets. The Germans, however, were looking for him, and he needed temporary refuge. The lieutenant agreed but wanted the approval of the colonel commanding the whole PAI outfit. Malfatti talked with the colonel, introducing himself as an Allied agent, and the colonel, wishing to be on the right side when the Allies arrived, stood at attention, saluted, and approved.

And so, after another drunken party, highlighted by mixed bathing in the bathtub, Tompkins, together with two of his agents, Primo and Vito, went in early April 1944 to enlist in the PAI.

Tompkins was delighted by this chance to work under cover within the Fascist system, complete with uniform and credentials, especially since the alternative could well mean arrest. The Nazi-Fascist crackdown had already so depleted the Socialist party, whose underground network was Peter's main source of intelligence, that Malfatti was virtually the only Socialist partisan leader still at large. One morning Baldo came to Tompkins with particularly frightening information.

"Good morning," Baldo had said casually. "Have you heard the news?"

"No, what news?"

"Ah, well, in that case you'll be amused."

Drawing up a chair, Baldo continued: "Ottorino has discovered that both the German and Italian police are busy looking for a young man by the name of Peter Tompkins who used to be in Rome as a newspaperman and is now back as an officer in the intelligence service! It would appear they know about you in some detail!"

Lieutenant Ottorino Borin was the Resistance spy who had infiltrated the German-controlled open-city government and worked for the Clandestine Front—though also for Tompkins. Peter was *not* amused. In fact, he could almost see the torture table with the spikes and the belts. And this vision seemed especially vivid when he thought of Mino Menicanti, the Italian OSS agent who was claiming that he and not Tompkins was the chief OSS representative in Rome. Peter wondered how far Menicanti—and his French boss, Captain Bourgouin —would go to get rid of him.

As Tompkins had been out of contact with his base since Koch arrested Giglio and confiscated his radio, he was infuriated most of all by Menicanti's refusal to give him the radio equipment he needed— crystals and a signal plan—for another radio he had obtained. Menicanti possessed this equipment but could not use it, since he did not have an operator, while Tompkins had several operators—none of whom wanted to work for Menicanti. Meanwhile, vital intelligence was piling up on Peter's untidy desk.

In desperation, Tompkins tried to request instructions from his base in Anzio through a British agent who had a radio. But unknown to Peter, British intelligence in the south had ordered its man in Rome not to relay any messages from Tompkins—perhaps because it had received false information that Peter was a fraud, because it trusted intelligence only from pro-Badoglio sources, or because it considered itself in competition with the OSS.

And while Tompkins nervously waited for word from his base, he figured that the PAI would offer him just the cover he needed for continuing his activities without serious danger of arrest and torture . . .

Tompkins' main problem after enlisting in the PAI was to find ways to goldbrick until the pro-Allied lieutenant who had recruited him and his two cronies could get them assigned to his company. Only then would the agents enjoy freedom to pursue their own activities. The three, still in civilian clothes, thus spent as much time as possible at a camp kiosk where an old man sold them black-market wine and doughnuts. But often, before they could get high on the wine, their commander, a *brigadiere* (sergeant) seven feet tall—according to Tompkins—would find them and roar his indignation.

When on one occasion he ordered them instantly into uniform, Tompkins, fearful that, once out of civilian clothes, they would be unable to leave the barbed-wire-surrounded camp, pleaded that their uniforms were still at the tailor.

"Then wear your summer drills!" shouted the *brigadiere*.

Left without choice, the three agents did.

But they were saved when in the mess hall an officer complained that their leggings were not regulation tint and ordered the three to dye them darker. So they changed back into their civvies, and while Tompkins and Vito dyed the leggings Primo sneaked out of the camp to learn from Malfatti what was happening.

Primo returned after some hours, pale and nervous.

"They've caught the PAI lieutenant," he announced. "He's at Via Tasso. The SS came for him last night!"

"What is he in for?" Tompkins asked.

"For aiding subversive elements."

"Not us!"

Primo grimaced.

Tompkins' heart sank as he realized that they were trapped for the night without possible exit. His apprehension grew when the corporal of the day entered the barracks and ordered him and his two assistants to report to the *brigadiere*. As they lined up in the orderly room, Tompkins thought that he would collapse.

"You're the new recruits . . ." the *brigadiere* snarled.

Then he dug into the drawer of his desk. He was reaching for an automatic, Tompkins was sure. But instead, the *brigadiere* drew out six green packages of cigarettes.

"Here," he said, distributing two to each man. "Your weekly ration! Sixty a man. Not bad!"

The next day Primo went once more to see Malfatti while Tompkins and Vito tried to goldbrick behind an evergreen hedge. But the two were again discovered by the giant *brigadiere* who now ordered Tompkins to "get his ass" immediately to the company barber to have the back of his head shaved clean. Peter procrastinated, weighing his vanity against the terror evoked by the *brigadiere*'s vicious scowl. He went to the barber.

Primo eventually returned from his meeting with Malfatti and breathlessly reported that the PAI colonel who had approved their "enlistment" was being watched by the SS. They would have to hold everything and wait. However, their efforts to goldbrick anew while waiting failed once more.

"Where the devil have you been?" demanded the corporal of the day on finding them. "The *brigadiere* wants you at the stadium, this minute, and fully armed. He wants to know what the devil you mean by skipping drill!"

As soon as the *brigadiere* saw them he swore incoherently. Then, examining Tompkins' capped head, he demanded to know why he hadn't had his hair cut. When the frightened agent insisted that he *had* had it cut, the officer screamed:

"What do you mean you've had it cut!"

Tompkins then removed his cap and repeated: "I had it cut."

"Oh, so you've had it cut! Right! You'll have it shaved to nothing after drill. Corporal! Take their names. They are all confined to quarters!"

But not until they had been drilled into utter exhaustion by an officer who could not understand how these men, who had records showing them to be veterans of so many bloody campaigns, could be ignorant of even the simplest drill procedures.

Enough was enough! And besides, Primo had brought information that Menicanti had cancelled all of Peter's orders to other OSS agents. Tompkins went to see the PAI colonel, clicking his heels and performing an almost perfect Fascist salute. The colonel, still thinking that Tompkins was an Italian Air Force major in hiding, suggested with some alarm that he and the two other "recruits" leave immediately since the arrested lieutenant, if he talked, could get "everybody" in trouble. Perhaps they could return if all went well; with luck, the Germans might shoot the lieutenant before he talked.

Tompkins heartily agreed with the suggestion, executed another snappy salute, clicked his heels, and strode out. Orders for the demobilization of the three men followed immediately, and so did their departure. The last thing Tompkins saw on his way out of the camp was the seven-foot *brigadiere* glaring at the still unshaven back of his head.

And now he would deal with that "treacherous" Menicanti.[4]

❖ ❖ ❖

Chief Rabbi Zolli was miserable as he struggled to survive the German occupation. The small room he had occupied in Amedeo Pierantoni's house during the winter of 1943–44 was like a refrigerator. He was always hungry, and the future looked bleak, even if he managed to escape the clutches of the Gestapo.

The Germans had broken into his abandoned house and searched in vain for documents of a political character, then had left the doors open, inviting hoodlums to carry away everything, down to the last towel and handkerchief. His bitter foe, President Foa of the Jewish Community of Rome, had cut off his salary, charging that he had deserted his post. Nor could Zolli relieve his anguish with the biblical and other literature that he so loved. The Pierantoni library consisted of only an algebra manual and a dilapidated English grammar.

Zolli's anxiety grew when Pierantoni's son Luigi, a physician, was arrested in a Red Cross hospital for partisan activities, and then shot in the Ardeatine Caves in March. The rabbi personally burned all messages he could find in the Pierantoni house dealing with the Resistance and scoured the premises for weapons or explosives which might have been hidden by Fascist spies so that they could be found by Nazi search parties and used as evidence against his host—a trick often used by the Germans.

Finally, it had become too dangerous to stay at the Pierantonis'. Zolli's eldest daughter, Dora, asked him to live with her and her husband, Victor, and their child. They had false papers showing them to be Catholics.

"Come to us, Father, for a few days," Dora said.

"No," he replied, "you are safe, you are young. I am an old rag."

"I am going to repeat all this to Victor, then you will see," she threatened.

She left, but returned within an hour and took his baggage—a briefcase.

"I shall carry this," she said. "We shall not know each other in the trolley. When I leave the car, you get off too and follow some way behind me. When I arrive at my house, I shall go in, but you walk up and down the street. Victor will presently join you. You must wait for the moment when the *portiere* goes off duty to eat before you can come in."

Victor met Zolli as planned, and they kept moving, returning at intervals to a point from which they could see the house. But an hour and fifteen minutes passed and they still had not received their cues. The rabbi's grandson would play ball and watch the movements of the *portiere*, and when she left for lunch he would chase the ball toward the two men while Dora would pull in a red carpet hanging out of the window.

"It is evident," the rabbi told Victor, "that the *portiere's* last meal was very substantial."

"Yes," Victor agreed. "Had I known, I would have given her some pills to stimulate her appetite."

But a second later he said: "There! Dora has taken in the red carpet. The coast is clear!"

And at the same moment the young boy came toward them in pursuit of his ball, as planned, and the two men entered the building.

Still, with the Gestapo intensifying its searches after the Ardeatine massacre, the danger of Zolli's being found at his daughter's home seemed to grow. Dora and her husband were particularly worried about their son. One day Dora returned from shopping and said:

"You know, Father, I have met a friend of mine, a certain Emilia Falconieri, and she is coming here to visit us. When she comes you need not lock yourself up in the other room."

The next day the bell rang and Emilia entered. She placed her hand on Zolli's shoulder and said smilingly, referring to him by his future alias: "Listen, Giovanni, I have lost my father, and my husband, Gino, has lost his, so tomorrow you must come to us. You will be Papa Giovanni. You will be good to us, and love us, won't you?"

"Why not," replied Zolli, a bit shocked, yet amused, at her instant familiarity. "If you are good and obedient."

"Most obedient, Papa Giovanni."

Zolli moved in with the Catholic Falconieri family and was now more comfortable, physically and psychologically. He had a small room, but it was neat and shining, and there was even a book on the history of art to read. And Gino, by some miracle, would sometimes bring him a package of cigarettes.

This greater comfort permitted him to relax and he meditated a great deal on the meaning of his agony. Why did the Jewish community want to crush him? Well, he would not oppose them. It was no longer a battle of justice against injustice, but between conscience and conscience. He struggled to determine the pattern of his own conscience, so different from that of other Jews.

Comparing the Old and New Testaments, Zolli recalled the teachings of St. Paul. The Jews had only a law written in cold ink on cold parchment, but the gentiles of whom Paul spoke lived by natural law springing from faith and love. Perhaps, Zolli thought, this difference explained why he was unloved by his own people yet loved by gentiles like the Pierantonis and the Falconieris. (Zolli's Jewish foes say that he apparently did not ask himself how his people, if they had only a scroll of "cold parchment" to sustain them, managed to survive centuries of persecution and even genocide.)

As the conscience of Paul grew within Zolli, so did the conflict between his mystical and rational tendencies. The greater spiritual strength he felt did not reinforce his physical courage. Rationally enough, Zolli still hesitated to set foot out of the house to perform his duties. After all, the Germans had deported and killed the chief rabbis of Modena, Bologna, and Genoa. Why should he, too, suffer and die unnecessarily? Or set a fatal example for his people? So many had already perished because of what he viewed as the misplaced courage of men like Foa.

If his people "ungratefully" rejected his love for them and refused to reciprocate it, he must seek love elsewhere. He would learn more about how another dissident Jew had earned the love of others—to the woe, incidentally, of his own people. Zolli pondered Paul's words: "I speak the truth in Christ. I wish myself to be anathema from Christ for my brethren!"[5]

Unlike his former chief, Rabbi David Pancieri, who had replaced Zolli, had little time for meditation in this period of catastrophe. To this thin little man with a goatee and white hair, the law on the "cold parchment" was absolute, a godly guarantee that his people would survive whatever happened.

"Do you see that tree they're uprooting?" he said to a friend as they strolled beside the Tiber. "They're taking it away to plant it elsewhere. When it is planted again, it will grow even stronger. They have taken many of us away, too. But we, too, shall only grow stronger."

Pancieri thus did not seem overly alarmed when one morning in early May three men in civilian clothes called at his house—he had refused to go into hiding—and told his sister: "We've come to take the rabbi away."

This was not the first time Fascist policemen had visited him. A few weeks earlier another three had come, questioned him, examined his books, and then departed. Now they had come to arrest him. Rabbi Pancieri had defied fate too long.

Although the temple had finally closed after the October 16 round-up of Jews, he had continued to conduct services every day at the Jewish old people's home on Isola Tiberina (Tiber Island), which, for some reason, the Germans never raided. He trudged from house to house carrying out circumcision ceremonies, visiting the sick, performing marriages. He went to the Jewish cemetery to hold services for the dead. God would care for the Jews. It said so on the "cold parchment."

In panic, Rabbi Pancieri's sister ran to his room to wake him. He got up, dressed, and went to meet the callers in his small living room. He was very calm.

"Good day," he said, smiling.

"We're sorry," one of them said. "But you'll have to come with us."

"*Va bene,* very well," the rabbi replied. "But first let me say my prayers."

While his sister served the callers coffee, Pancieri put on his prayer shawl and began to pray, bobbing his skull-capped head slightly.

The three visitors gazed at the rabbi in wonder, barely touching their coffee.

When Pancieri had mumbled his last "amen," he removed his shawl and said: "Well, gentlemen, if you have finished your coffee, I am ready."

But the men rose, shook the rabbi's hand, and, without saying a word, departed.

The tree remained that much stronger—paradoxically raising the question in the minds of many Roman Jews after the war of how strong it would have been if more Jewish leaders, however personally courageous, had abandoned ceremony and tradition to lead their people into hiding.[6]

Almost immediately after Eleanora Di Porto returned to the Convent of Notre Dame de Sion with her newborn baby, her husband, Giacomo, frightened by a telephoned warning that the convent was about to be raided, sent them back to the obstetrician and went himself to stay with a relative.

They departed just in time. For a few days later the alarm bell in the convent rang. Fascist police had surrounded the grounds. According to plan, the women ran to the third floor to hide while the men crowded into a small, almost airless room in the cellar, its entrance hidden behind sacks of potatoes and other vegetables. Several of the men, however, sought to escape over the wall, and two were caught—Aldo Cava and Angelo Di Veroli.

Cava found his path blocked by several men in civilian clothes.

"You are a Jew!" one of them snarled.

Cava insisted he was not, but changed his story when he was taken to Via Tasso and saw Di Veroli beaten until he "confessed" he was Jewish.

Both men were then taken to an Italian army barracks where Jews were being collected for deportation to Germany. And though it was late May and the Allies were closing in, they were sure that it was too late for them to be saved.[7]

✿   ✿   ✿

The Allied advance was, in fact, already saving lives in Rome, since many Fascists were afraid of what might happen to them when the city finally fell. This fear helped to explain why the PAI colonel permitted Peter Tompkins, disguised as a refugee Italian major, to join his police force. And also why the three policemen who had come to arrest Rabbi Pancieri—however moved they were by his courage—left without him.

Such Fascists, expecting to remain in Rome, were looking for people who would vouch for their "kindness" and underlying "pro-Allied" sympathies.

Monsignor O'Flaherty and Major Derry decided to exploit this trend fully—especially in trying to free Derry's assistant, Bill Simpson, whom Koch had captured. They feared that the Germans, when they left Rome, might take Simpson and other prisoners with them—or even shoot them before quitting the city.

Adrienne Lucidi, the French wife of Renzo Lucidi, the Allied agent, offered what seemed the best plan for liberating Simpson. She would go to see a certain Dr. Ubaldo Cipolla, who had worked with the organization until Derry discovered he was a double agent, and ask him to present the Germans an ingenious proposal: Release two of the British officers held in Regina Coeli prison—Simpson and a Captain John Armstrong who had recently been captured—and let it be known that Cipolla was responsible for the release so that he could ingratiate himself with the British. Then, when the Germans left Rome, he would remain behind as an invaluable agent for the Germans.

"Cipolla is frightened by his prospects when the Allies arrive," Adrienne said. "He will jump at this chance to help us."

O'Flaherty and Derry approved the idea, though rather overwhelmed by the complexity of Cipolla's role. Already a double agent, he would now pretend to be a German agent pretending to be a British agent in order to obtain information for the Germans! If this scheme worked, perhaps their luck would change. Recent enemy crackdowns, stimulated by the betrayal of the false priest, Perfetti, had greatly weakened their organization.

And compounding their troubles was the decision of the Swiss Legation, which had been furnishing the prisoners of war with Red Cross parcels and other aid, to halt these "unneutral" activities. Ambassador von Weizsäcker had warned the Swiss minister that the Legation officer who was in contact with the O'Flaherty organization might be arrested if such aid continued. Besides, Weizsäcker had cynically inquired, why should the Swiss help the prisoners when the British Legation to the Holy See was financing the prisoners so generously that British officers were often seen dining at the finest Roman restaurants?

Cipolla gladly agreed to Adrienne Lucidi's proposal, since it would improve his standing with both the Allies and the Germans, an ideal situation for a double agent. He conferred with his German contact, who also viewed the plan favorably, since Cipolla seemed to make sense when he argued that he could be a valuable German agent when the Allies arrived. The German gave him a list of all the British prisoners in Regina Coeli, but Cipolla could not find the two names he sought. Finally, rather than raise suspicions by asking to return another time, he chose two names at random for release.

What had gone wrong? Both Simpson and Armstrong, Derry soon realized, were listed under false names. And worse, he discovered, the Germans had learned that Simpson was using an alias, though they did not know his real name.

But soon another opportunity arose. A Roman nobleman called on Monsignor O'Flaherty—the brother of a girl the organization had helped to save. The girl, daughter of Duchessa Colerina Cesaro, had been sought by Koch for her anti-Fascist activities, and her brother had asked O'Flaherty to give her sanctuary in the Vatican, though all unauthorized people were to be kept out of this center of spiritual—if not physical—salvation.

John May, the British minister's butler, then "borrowed" a Swiss Guard's uniform, smuggled it out to her, and the girl, disguised as a guard, unobtrusively tagged on the end of a troop during a guard change one night. As the guards marched past a particular corner, a black-sleeved arm reached out, grabbed the imposter by the shoulder, and pulled her into the shadows—where she was greeted by O'Flaherty, Derry, and May.

Now the girl's brother had come on a new mission—for Pietro Koch!

"I think he has no illusions," the emissary said. "He wants to make a bargain with you. He says that if the monsignor will arrange to place his wife and mother (who still lived in Rome) in hiding in a religious house when he goes, he, in exchange, will insure that the monsignor's friends are left in Regina Coeli instead of being transported to Germany."

O'Flaherty was startled. The brutal Koch, who, incidentally, had vowed to capture him, had a touch of decency in him after all. The monsignor immediately saw a new opportunity for liberating Simpson and Armstrong.

"Tell Koch I agree to his suggestion on one condition," he replied. "As evidence of his good faith, he must first deliver safely to me the two British officers who are in Regina Coeli—Lieutenant Simpson and Captain Armstrong. If he does that I shall make the arrangements he desires for his wife and mother."

The nobleman went back to Koch with O'Flaherty's reply, and the Fascist immediately agreed to free the two officers.

Shortly, Regina Coeli's loudspeaker called out: "Lieutenant Simpson! Captain Armstrong!"

But no response was forthcoming. Both Simpson and Armstrong thought the announcement was a trap and so remained silent.

Monsignor O'Flaherty found himself in a painful dilemma. If he told Koch that "William O'Flynn" was really William Simpson, Koch would have proof that the lieutenant was working with O'Flaherty's organization, perhaps assuring Simpson's deportation or even execution —and Koch might be laying a trap. If Simpson were not released immediately, however, the Germans might kill him anyway before they left Rome since they already knew he was using an alias, even though they were ignorant of his true identity.

After weighing every factor, the monsignor finally decided to tell Koch that Simpson could be found under the name of "O'Flynn," though he did not know what name Armstrong was using.

Then he knelt and prayed that he had made the right decision.[8]

※   ※   ※

The aroma of perfume still clung to Peter Tompkins as he entered an apartment building on the evening of April 18 for a meeting with Mino Menicanti. Peter's girl friend L.—the young woman who had accompanied him to the party where he had met SS Captain Priebke—

had spent the morning with him in Baldo's flat. Now Tompkins wondered whether he would ever see her again; whether, by agreeing to see Menicanti in Menicanti's apartment, he was not entering a trap. Still, he, Tompkins, had sought the meeting and he had to take the risk. He must obtain the radio equipment Menicanti possessed so that he could renew contact with his base.

As soon as he entered the building he found himself surrounded by a group of silent, rough-mannered men, two of whom led him into the elevator. At the fourth floor they motioned him out, leaving him alone on the landing. He could hear movement on the floors above and below. Was it indeed a trap? Was Menicanti planning to dispose of him with a silenced automatic? Is that why Menicanti had agreed to this meeting?

A door opened onto the landing and Menicanti stood squinting behind his glasses, his lips stretched in what Tompkins considered a cynical smile. As the Italian emerged, he extended his hand in an outward show of cordiality, and Peter, deeply relieved that the trap had not closed, gripped it weakly and came right to the point:

"Look, Coniglio [Menicanti's code name], I am an American citizen employed by the U.S. Department of State and the OSS. I am a close personal friend of the British minister and the American representative to the Vatican. I have already filed a report with them of all my activities. [He had, in fact, left a report with a Vatican contact which, in an emergency, would reach the two diplomats.] If you try to kill me, you won't get away with it."

Tompkins paused and wondered for a moment why he should not start shooting first. But then he thought of the men on the floors above and below and continued:

"When the Allies arrive, you're going to have to answer for your actions. Now I'll give you access to our radio and a radio operator. You may send any messages you wish back to the base. All I want from you are the crystals and signal plan that will enable me to contact the base. I shall only file military intelligence. If you wish to file political intelligence, you are free to do so."

Menicanti smiled again and, instead of replying, began speaking about what had happened to Giglio and other irrelevant matters. But when Tompkins cut him off, he finally agreed to send an assistant with the equipment to a rendezvous the next day with Peter's chief operator, Eugenio. Then he hinted that he was already in contact with the base.

"In that case," Tompkins said, "ask them for orders and see what you get for an answer."

But from Menicanti's reaction, Peter deduced that he was bluffing to make it appear that *he*, Menicanti, was the man the base was depending on.

The two spies shook hands frigidly and Tompkins rushed down the stairs, fearing that he would not reach the bottom alive. Even when he walked out the door he took no chances. He changed trolleys four times to avoid being followed.

The next day, Eugenio, the radio operator, went to meet Menicanti— who failed to show up but later sent Eugenio word that he wanted a written order from Tompkins before delivering the equipment. Peter was convinced that Menicanti was stalling, that he was out to destroy his organization. He wrote Menicanti a brusque note stating that he had told the base through the British agent (who had been ordered by his superiors not to relay Tompkins' messages) that if communications were not re-established within three days, Menicanti could be held responsible.

The following day, Primo brought Menicanti's reply to Tompkins: "The crystals and the rest of the equipment are not in my possession . . . If Eugenio had maintained contact with me, he would have had everything by now."

Dismissing this statement as a patent lie, Tompkins read on: "I have advised the base that I decline all responsibility for the service in Rome. This was necessary because, as you well know, the whole organization depends on me as far as Italy is concerned, and, naturally, had you acted in accord with me and not tried to make me lose prestige, the service would have been resumed long ago."

So Menicanti considered his "prestige" more important than getting vital information to the Allies. And he even had a channel open to the base—or so he still boasted. This was treachery, Tompkins thought.

Menicanti, however, did reveal in his message who now had the equipment—one of the agents, it turned out, who had driven into Rome with Tompkins. Tompkins contacted this agent, who agreed to turn over the equipment to him. The American was ecstatic. At last he would be able to contact his base again. But before he could start operating his new radio, Malfatti rushed in with news that the Germans had learned about the whole OSS operation and were about to pounce.

Tompkins felt ill—though not too ill to move with the speed of lightning. He and his three assistants, Malfatti, Lele, and Baldo, jumped in a car and raced toward the Adriatic to find a boat that would take them south to the Allied lines, where they would remain until things cooled off in Rome. Eugenio remained to direct the radio operation.

But after a nerve-wracking drive through the Nazi-controlled mountains to the sea, the fleeing agents were unable to obtain a boat and were forced to return to their hideout in Rome—only to find that Eugenio had been captured and taken to Via Tasso. The radio, too, had fallen into Nazi hands.

Tompkins wondered if he would go mad. He went outside, sat on the ground, and tried to calm his nerves by watching an ant, muttering to himself: "If that ant walks all the way along that piece of wood without turning off, everything will be all right."[9]

❖ ❖ ❖

The bitter, if rather melodramatic, struggle between Peter Tompkins and Mino Menicanti reflected the ideological conflict that continued to simmer in the anti-Fascist camp. The rightists and leftists in March 1944 were still on a collision course that could lead to civil war. And both sides, oddly enough, were working out their military plans in the same place—the Seminary of San Giovanni in Laterano, in which many top leaders of almost all parties and other anti-Fascist groups had been embarrassingly flung together for their mutual safety.

One newcomer was General Roberto Bencivenga, who replaced General Quirino Armellini as the nominal supreme commander of the Roman Resistance on March 22. Like the Pope and many upper-class Italians, he trembled at the thought of "Communist revolution," though he was considered more moderate than Armellini. Issuing orders from his bedside after he had broken his leg in a fall, he vehemently announced to his followers that an insurrection must be prevented.

Rightist concern grew as the "insidious" Communist influence spread. In January 1944 the Allies approved the return to Italy of Palmiro Togliatti, the veteran Italian Communist chief who had long been in Russian exile. And on March 13 came an astonishing announcement that Italy and the Soviet Union—which had until then sneered at the King and Badoglio as Fascists—would resume diplomatic relations. Even Badoglio, it seemed to the rightists, had been taken in.

It seemed so to the Allies, too, and Churchill, in particular, was aghast. *Their* puppet had made a deal with Russia without consulting them, permitting the Russians to move in on *their* territory. Washington and London finally persuaded Moscow to grant the Badoglio government simply *de facto* rather than *de jure* recognition and then had little choice themselves but to follow suit.

The new twist in Soviet policy was reinforced—and clarified—when Togliatti, alias "Ercole Ercoli," finally disembarked at Naples from an American warship on March 28, a broad smile on his professorial face and a look of inflexible purpose in his bespectacled eyes. He had come directly from conferences with Stalin carrying a startling blueprint for Communist strategy that would set a new political course for Italy.

Togliatti had long been close to Stalin. In 1921 he helped to split the left wing from the Italian Socialist party and convert it into the Communist party. Five years later, with Mussolini's police cracking down, he fled to France. Stalin then gave him an order that was brutally to test his Communist soul; he obeyed, sending to the Fascist police a secret list of Socialist leaders who were thought to be "sabotaging" the Communist movement.

Stalin never forgot his quiet, affable protégé for this act of blind obedience and promoted him rapidly in the Comintern—which was finally dissolved in 1943 as a step toward making Communism internationally "respectable." And now, in Italy, Togliatti would take another step . . .

The day after he arrived in Naples Togliatti disavowed the declared policy of his own party, telling a stunned Communist gathering in his calm but resolute manner:

"It is impossible to give any guarantee of freedom to the Italian people until the Nazis have been driven from our native soil. We must, therefore, redouble our war effort in order to liberate our country. Let us then form a national government; in doing so we shall be taking an immense step forward."

The Communists would henceforth support the Badoglio government and the monarchy, he said, because national unity was necessary to win the war swiftly. After the war the people could decide whether to retain the monarchy. Togliatti called, in effect, for a national front like the one he had helped to form as a Kremlin agent in Spain during the Spanish Civil War. He even ordered his followers to abandon the red flag and to display only the red, green, and white national colors.

Of course, he added, the Communists would be glad to join Badoglio's government immediately.

The conservative Ivanoe Bonomi, who had resigned as president of the CLN because the leftists, including the Communists, had refused to enter the Badoglio government, called Togliatti a "prodigious knight, a Lohengrin back from the dead," and took over the reins of the CLN again. But the Socialists and Actionists were shocked, and so were many Communists who had for so long condemned the King and Badoglio as unreconstructed Fascists.

The leftist coalition that was to lead an insurrection against the Germans and seize power in Rome suddenly disintegrated.

Why did the Communists reverse course?

First, the Big Three at the Tehran Conference in late 1943 apparently agreed tacitly to divide postwar Europe into eastern and western spheres of influence, and Italy fell into the western sphere. Moreover, Stalin, by backing a government that Churchill strongly favored, may have been reciprocating a speech Churchill had delivered to Parliament on February 22, 1944, in which the British leader suggested support of Soviet demands for "secure" borders with Poland and Tito's leadership in Yugoslavia.

Second, Stalin apparently did not want to risk failure in Italy. If the Communists grabbed power in Rome, even allied with more moderate leftists, how long would they keep it after the Anglo-Americans arrived? On the other hand, by joining a government led by weak, compromised former Fascists, the Communists might be able to take it over through democratic means—or otherwise—when the war ended.

Third, and probably most important, Stalin, as Togliatti's statement implied, was more concerned at the moment with Soviet survival than with world revolution and wanted to keep as many German divisions as possible tied down in Italy so that they could not be sent to the Russian front. Therefore, national unity, even under "reactionaries," was necessary and took precedence over divisive revolution.

The King and Badoglio found themselves stronger than ever, backed by both Britain and Russia—though for different reasons. The United States, however, did not revel in this twin-pillared support. Any new Italian government under those two leaders might consist almost entirely of men from the extreme right and extreme left, since the moderates—mainly the Action and Socialist parties—still refused to join such a cabinet. And a polarized government was certainly what Togliatti and Stalin wanted. They could far more easily take over a government they shared only with rightists than one in which moderates diluted Communist power.

Roosevelt ordered Robert Murphy, the American representative on the Allied Advisory Council directing Italian policy, to force the King to give up his powers immediately so that a broader, more stable government could be formed.

With cool dignity, Victor Emmanuel received Murphy and a British representative—who had gone along without asking Churchill's approval—on April 10, 1944, standing before a large wall map of Italy. He held his stunted body erect and remained standing while Murphy explained his mission. Suddenly, as Murphy recalls in his memoirs, the King, his chin quivering and his pale blue eyes tearing, spoke pridefully of the thousand-year history of the House of Savoy.

"A republican form of government is not suited to the Italian people," he said mournfully, though Murphy had demanded only that Crown Prince Humbert replace him, if at once. "They are not prepared for it either temperamentally or historically. In a republic every Italian would insist upon being President, and the result would be chaos. The only people who would profit would be the Communists."

When Murphy refused to modify the virtual ultimatum from President Roosevelt, the King finally agreed—or so Murphy thought—to announce the immediate transfer of his powers to his son.

Shaking with indignation, he said: "Gentlemen, your coercion has no precedent in history. I am prepared to sign immediately the proclamation you demand, but stating at its head that I sign only under the pressure of your governments. [He did not know that, despite the presence of the British representative, Churchill had nothing to do with this effort to pressure him.] And now I ask you to leave, for your presence has already vexed me enough."

But the King was tenacious. His proclamation, while leaving out the threatened charge of coercion, concluded: "I have decided to withdraw from public affairs by appointing my son, the Prince of Piedmont, Lieutenant General of the Realm. This appointment will become effective by the formal transfer of powers on the day on which the Allied troops enter Rome. This decision, which I firmly believe furthers national unity, is final and irrevocable."

The King, ironically supported by the Communists he had claimed would benefit from his resignation, thus refused to step down immediately, defying Roosevelt and Murphy, who would not press the monarch further.

The Americans now transferred their pressure to the Action and Socialist parties and both finally agreed to join a new government under Badoglio and the King. On April 24 this government, in which Togliatti held the post of Minister Without Portfolio, took the oath of allegiance to the King.

Victor Emmanuel was joyous. Twenty years earlier, Mussolini had saved his tottering throne and now Stalin had come to his rescue. And here he had been worrying about the Communists throwing him out! But neither he nor Badoglio was confident that the Communists would not betray them when the Germans fled Rome. And they trusted even less now the Socialists and the Actionists, who had only joined the government with the greatest reluctance. And then there was the undisciplined, fanatical Red Flag party that scorned the new government. It was still openly bent on revolution.[10]

�֎   ✖   ✖

In late May a group of Soviet escapers, carrying rifles and pistols, stood outside a mountain cave near Palestrina, their faces taut with rage.

"We want to kill them," one of them shouted in Russian.

A thin, unshaven youth stood at the entrance of the cave, a rifle in hand, and shook his head, understanding their intention if not their words.

"You'll have to kill me first," said Rosario Bentivegna.

He hated the Germans as much as the Russians did, but he would not let the forty-seven prisoners jammed into the cave be slaughtered. Partisan squads led by Bentivegna and Carla Capponi and including a group of Russian escapers had captured these Nazis in the hills of Palestrina during the German retreat from Cassino. The Russians, many of whom had lost their families in the brutal German invasion of their homeland, now sought revenge. But Rosario—and Carla—saw no ideological purpose in killing for killing's sake.

Until shortly before this confrontation, they had gotten along well with the Russians, including the three whom the Chilantis of the Red Flag party had hidden in their home before ten-year-old Gloria guided them to safety. The two Italians had been on many operations with them since arriving in the Palestrina area and found them to be formidable guerrilla fighters. Many had been killed in battle, for they seldom retreated, even before superior forces. And they were willing to take orders from Rosario and Carla, who knew the land and the language.

On May 5, a few days after the two leaders arrived in Palestrina, Carla had led a group of Italians and Russians in a successful raid on the town's archives to burn the military call-up lists, frustrating Fascist efforts to capture draft dodgers.

Three days later Carla and Rosario, leading another group of about thirty Italians and Russians, set out to ambush a unit of German soldiers who had established a camp near Palestrina in a little valley surrounded by woods. Hiding in the brush, the partisans captured two Germans who had gone to fetch water from a spring, disarmed them, and ordered them to advance toward the camp. About a hundred yards away, the two Germans were forced to shout to their comrades that they must all surrender because the camp was completely surrounded by partisans, and, in panic, Germans scrambled from their tents and raised their hands.

The partisans then entered the camp, disarmed some hundred soldiers, burned vehicles and fuel supplies, and departed with an arsenal of weapons, medicine, and food, leaving the Germans, who were too numerous to take prisoner, to their fate.

The relative bloodlessness of such raids and the disposition of the loot, however, began to upset the Russians. They did not believe in taking prisoners or letting Germans go free. They argued with Carla, who communicated to their leader in French, that they were not being given a large enough share of the captured medicine and food. They were particularly indignant that, while the scarcity of food was seriously affecting their ability to fight, the little being snatched *from* the Germans was, in part, going back *to* the Germans. Rosario and Carla were even feeding their prisoners before themselves.

This rather gallant behavior only nourished the Russians' lust for revenge and so they planned to kill the prisoners on their own—until Rosario defiantly stood before the cave. The Russians backed off, but they were in an ugly mood, some wondering whether the Italians were just posing as partisans while actually serving the Germans.

One afternoon as Carla sat on the ground negotiating with the Russian leaders on how to distribute some captured medicine, a badly wounded Russian named Boris demanded that his men get the lion's share. But Carla rejected this demand, arguing that the Italians also needed medicine.

Later that day Carla and Rosario went off to a meeting of guerrilla leaders some distance away, leaving one Italian partisan to guard the cave with the prisoners. As he stood by helplessly, the Russians deserted with all the food and medicine and most of the weapons in the camp—apparently too concerned about a getaway to bother forcing the issue and killing the German prisoners before they left.

When Carla and Rosario returned they found themselves in a desperate situation, trapped in an isolated mountainside wood without food and with only a few pistols for protection. They sent Italian members of their band to search for the Russians and seek help from Italian partisans in other sectors and went themselves to look for food. They managed to obtain two sheep from a peasant—the only animals in the area, it seemed, not yet taken by the Germans or the partisans—though, after the forty-seven prisoners were fed, virtually nothing remained for the two lovers, who had eaten little enough even before the Russians had deserted.

After three days without food—and without word that help was coming—Rosario collapsed, leaving Carla alone with the prisoners. The plans to slow down the German retreat through Palestrina until the troops from Anzio arrived seemed to have collapsed as well.[11]

11

The Breakthroughs

Under a leaden dawn sky pierced here and there by starlight that promised a clear day, Generals Clark and Truscott sat on the damp earth of an artillery observation post at Anzio, silently contemplating the faint outlines of the Alban Hills. Just beyond those hills, through which ran the Caesar Line, lay Rome. It was May 23, and if all went well, that was where they would be in a few days. The two men kept glancing at their watches. It was almost 5:45 A.M.—zero hour.

Not a sound could be heard nor a living thing seen in the gray shadows that cloaked the surrounding prairies. Yet lying in the high grass amid the daisies and flowering thistle were 150,000 men prepared to break out of the beachhead, destroy the German Fourteenth Army, and close the trap on the German Tenth Army—or, if they failed, at least to taste the frosting of Rome.

All was ready. The Germans had already been thrown off balance by Truscott's two British divisions, the 1st and 5th, which, though slated to play only a minor role in Clark's strategy, had launched a fierce feinting attack in the direction of Rome some hours earlier. After the usual morning shelling, to which the enemy had become accustomed and seldom reacted, the main assault would begin—an uphill thrust across the ditches and canals furrowing the face of Anzio and northward along the front of the Caesar Line.

The U.S. 3rd Division would lead the attack on the first objective, the stronghold of Cisterna, supported on its left flank by the U.S. 1st

Ivanoe Bonomi, leader of the CLN.

Col. Giuseppe Lanza Cordero di Montezemolo,
leader of the Clandestine Front, disguised for
a false identity card as an engineer.

Above, Monsignor Hugh O'Flaherty is presented
a medal by an American officer
for his Resistance activities.

Left, Gen. Roberto Bencivenga,
chief of the Roman Resistance.

Left, Col. Ugo Musco, leader of Centro X.

Below, Ettore Basevi working on the Resistance *Bulletin*.

Above left, Gen. Angelo Odone,
deputy to Resistance leader
General Bencivenga.

Above right, Mariolina Odone,
General Odone's daughter,
who was active in the Resistance.

Left, Rear Adm. Franco Maugeri,
head of Rome Underground,
the Naval Resistance.

Princess Nini Pallavicini at her wedding.

Gen. Filippo Caruso, the *carabinieri* leader, in uniform and in disguise as a partisan.

Michele Multedo,
painter-partisan.

MICHELE MULTEDO

Father Giuseppe Morosini,
who was executed
for his Resistance activities.

Above, Peter Tompkins (second from left) in hiding, with
Ottorino Borin (on Tompkins' right), Lele, Mario, and
Franco Malfatti (left to right on Tompkins' left).

Left, Maurizio Giglio (Cervo), another Tompkins agent,
in the uniform of a police lieutenant.

Below, a painting of Donna Virginia Agnelli.

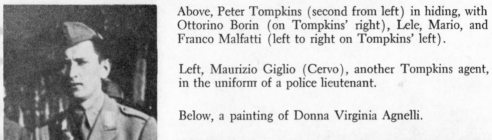

EUGEN DOLLMANN

German soldiers captured in battle for Cisterna.

Armored Division and on its right by the U.S.-Canadian 1st Special Service Force. From Cisterna, under Alexander's plan, Truscott's whole VI Corps would storm to Valmontone and cut off the German retreat on Highway 6. Then at least some units would continue on into the Palestrina hills to trap more Nazis.

Suddenly, at 5:45, a thunderous roar pulverized the quiet world of Anzio and lightning flashes illuminated the clouds. This first crash settled into a steady rumble and the earth trembled for about forty minutes while a great wall of smoke and dust rose to seal off the two armies from each other. Clark and Truscott looked up to see the silvery wings of Allied bombers vanish into the haze. The attack had started.

Meanwhile, troops of the German LXXVI Panzer Corps holding the eastern sector of the Fourteenth Army front went about their morning business in their dugouts, trenches, and houses, some of the men still only partly dressed. Just another bombardment, if a fiercer one than usual, by the wasteful Americans.

And then tanks, nosing through the fog like phantom ships, were suddenly upon them en route to Cisterna.[1]

As American troops swarmed toward Cisterna, they were assaulted by the smell of flesh rotting in the poppy fields—the remains of Colonel William Darby's Rangers who had fallen almost to the last man in another, bygone, battle . . .

In January 1944, shortly after the landing at Anzio, the Rangers had set out to capture Cisterna and had reached its edge when the Germans started firing. Pinned down, the Rangers suddenly saw a tank behind them and cheered—until they found out it wasn't theirs. When the tank opened up on them, they attacked it, set it afire, and killed the crew as the Germans tried to climb out of the turret.

Ten tanks soon replaced this one, followed by infantry. The Rangers leaped on the tanks, threw themselves on the turrets, and blew apart the vehicles—and, in some cases, themselves—with grenades. The tanks and infantry kept coming, however, and the last words Colonel Darby heard over his radio were those of a sergeant reporting:

"I'm destroying the radio, sir. They're closing in, but they won't get us cheap." . . .

Nor would the Germans now get their vengeful comrades cheap . . .

In this new attack on Cisterna, when the Nazis belatedly realized what was happening they poured artillery and mortar shells into the Allied troops, knocking out entire units. On the 3rd Division front, one mortar shell landed in the midst of a platoon, killing and wounding all but four men just as they had begun to advance. Another company lost

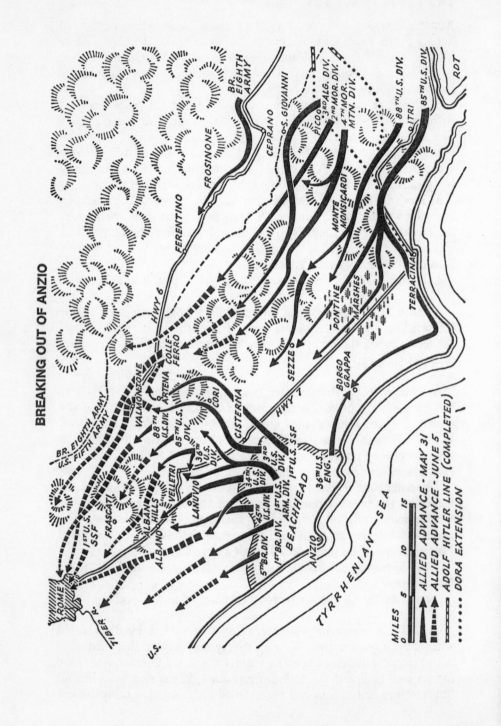

BREAKING OUT OF ANZIO

fifty men within minutes. The survivors marched ahead to the sound of the screams of their fallen comrades.

Presently the screams were drowned out by fire from a German 88-mm gun, protected by three machine guns. Private First Class John Dutko, carrying a BAR, jumped up from an abandoned enemy trench and charged toward the guns about a hundred yards away while bullets and shrapnel kicked up dirt around him. He halted about thirty yards away from the first machine gun and hurled a grenade, killing both gunners.

Bullets from the second machine gun knocked him to the ground, but he got to his feet and rushed toward the 88-mm gun, firing his BAR from the hip, and with one long burst killed its five-man crew from ten yards away. Then he turned on the machine gun that had wounded him and killed its gunner and his assistant. Running in a crouch toward the third machine gun, he was wounded a second time but continued on, shot dead both members of the crew, and died himself as he leaped upon his victims with his last breath.

Dutko's comrades surged ahead and soon reached the railroad that passed in front of Cisterna and led northwestward to Rome. Just beyond, the Germans, entrenched in high ground, again held up the 3rd Division. Another soldier now broke the impasse.

Sergeant Sylvester Antolak, after conferring with Staff Sergeant Audie Murphy (who was himself to become the most decorated Allied soldier in Italy), shouted for his men to follow him and charged across the bare terrain in short rushes toward the enemy stronghold, keeping about thirty yards ahead of his squad. Though automatic fire wounded him in the shoulder, he stumbled on, falling only when struck a second time. He then rose and resumed his grim charge.

Audie Murphy, as he watched, was aghast. The Germans were firing a machine gun, "spit" pistols, and rifles as fast as they could squeeze the triggers. They sensed, he was sure, that Antolak was sparking the advance. They had to knock him out.

About fifty yards from the stronghold, Antolak was hit again and thrown to earth, his right arm shattered. He wedged his submachine gun into his left armpit, got to his feet, and staggered ahead once more. When he got to within fifteen yards of the strongpoint, he killed the two machine gunners with a single burst and the remaining ten Germans surrendered to him.

When the rest of his squad caught up with Antolak, another German machine gun a hundred yards away opened fire. Corporal William Harrison, as he treated Antolak's wounds, urged him to take cover in the post he had just captured.

"You're too weak to keep going," he said.

"No, I'm okay," Antolak replied.

And he moved on toward the new strongpoint with his men behind him until, after about sixty yards, he was hit a fourth time. He reeled forward another ten yards and collapsed while his squad overran the German position. When the men returned to Sergeant Antolak, he was dead.

By the end of the first day of battle, such extraordinary performances had helped to bring the 3rd Division to the outskirts of Cisterna, while the 1st Armored Division and the 1st Special Service Force, after cutting the railroad, were threatening to outflank the town. The 3rd Division alone had 995 battle casualties, probably the largest number suffered by any single American division in one day during World War II.

On the second day, May 24, the Allies repulsed innumerable counterattacks before they broke through the final beachhead defense perimeter, with the 1st Armored Division cutting Highway 7 north of Cisterna and the 1st Special Service Force severing it south of the town.[2]

The German defenders of Cisterna, remnants of the 362nd Infantry Division, continued, despite their relatively poor reputation, to resist the U.S. 3rd Division fanatically, after being ordered by General von Mackensen to fight to the last man. Mackensen, finally realizing that he had stationed his best divisions, comprising the I Parachute Corps, in the wrong place, desperately sought to save his own reputation.

During the previous night, May 24, Mackensen had begun switching elements of that corps—which was manning the coastal sector of the Caesar Line to block an Allied thrust up Highway 7, the direct route to Rome—to the Cisterna-Valmontone zone. Mackensen's whole future seemed to be riding on the ability of these troops to arrive in time to save Cisterna.

Kesselring, meanwhile, boiled in fury. He had warned Mackensen about the light defenses along the road to Valmontone, but the general had ignored him. At 8 P.M., May 23, after the first day's disaster, the field marshal telephoned General von Vietinghoff at Tenth Army headquarters and said with remarkable restraint:

"For your information I wish to say that, contrary to all expectations, things do not look good on Mackensen's front."

He added, as if afraid that the Allies might find out: "Keep this to yourself!"[3]

Late in the afternoon of May 24 General Truscott, after touring the VI Corps front, returned to his command post, a partially shattered house in the village of Conca, to meet General Clark. After exchanging pleasantries, the two men sat down and Clark casually asked: Had Truscott considered changing the direction of the attack from the northeast to the northwest, down Highway 7 toward Rome, when Cisterna had fallen?

Truscott pondered the question for a few seconds, trying also to be "casual." He replied delicately that, in his opinion, a switch toward Rome would be justified *only* if Mackensen transferred to the Valmontone area the bulk of the powerful I Parachute Corps still manning the Caesar Line in the Alban Hills overlooking Highway 7.

If Mackensen kept most of the I Parachute Corps where it now was, Truscott felt, the Germans might be able to halt Allied troops on this direct route to Rome. In that case, the road to Valmontone would probably be lightly defended and would therefore be the logical one for him to take.

Truscott apparently agreed with Alexander that a good part of the retreating German Tenth Army could be trapped at Valmontone. Clark, on the other hand, still felt that most of the Germans would escape over the secondary roads beyond Valmontone and that, because of the mountainous terrain, Allied troops could not effectively cut these roads.

Nor was Clark concerned only with military logic, of course. He was thinking of Rome. Yet, ironically, some military experts say that by capturing Valmontone, a relatively easy objective, Clark would probably have gotten to Rome faster than by taking the strongly defended direct route. From Valmontone, Truscott's troops could wheel northwest up Highway 6 through the weakest part of the Caesar Line and then have smooth going to Rome.

The trouble with this longer, if perhaps swifter, route was that the Eighth Army coming up Highway 6 *might* beat the Fifth Army to Valmontone and be in a position to monopolize this road from there to Rome.

If Truscott did not sound eager to switch directions at Cisterna, he diplomatically pointed out to Clark that his staff was already preparing plans for a possible switch—just in case circumstances favored it.

Clark, Truscott writes in his memoirs, agreed with his analysis and asked him to keep the plans up to date.[4]

Sergeant Samuel Pollard of the 3rd Division's F Company, 7th Infantry Regiment, decided that his comrades were not moving fast

enough through the demolished town of Cisterna on the morning of
May 25. On his own initiative he pulled together a nine-man patrol
and decided to clean out every shattered house along the main street
with or without the rest of his regiment.

He led his men over piles of rubble and through a lunar landscape of
craters, each mound and depression the remains of a recent strongpoint reduced to debris by a storm of shells and aerial bombs. Muti-
lated chunks of flesh lay beside machine guns poking from the dust.
Instructing his men to cover him, Pollard assaulted the first house with
a submachine gun and emerged with four prisoners, then proceeded to
search every house on the street, taking more prisoners as he went.
Now there was only the last house, a bastion from which heavy fire was
sweeping the street.

Pollard charged across twenty yards of open space toward the house,
firing as he ran while enemy bullets whizzed past him. He dived through
a large hole in the house wall and wounded three Germans on the
ground floor, then mounted a stairway and took more than twenty
prisoners.

As he emerged from the house, he saw three Germans run into a
ditch and vanish in a large tunnel dug in the far bank. He ran to the
mouth of the tunnel alone, fired into it, and shouted for the occupants
to surrender. To his shock, 107 soldiers meekly filed out and gave themselves up, bringing Sergeant Pollard's grand total of prisoners to 134.

A German garrison holed up in the remains of an old castle dominating the town continued to hold out even though Allied tanks and
artillery had pulverized the building. Major General Heinrich Greiner,
commander of the young and inexperienced 362nd Infantry Division
defending the area, had ordered scattered reserve units he had scrounged
up to counterattack that afternoon in order to relieve pressure on the
castle garrison. When he realized that the relief thrust would fail, he
asked permission from General von Mackensen to abandon Cisterna
and order the garrison to fight its way out.

Mackensen, however, refused, determined to tie up the enemy in
Cisterna until his expected reinforcements arrived from the area overlooking Highway 7, the direct route to Rome. But Allied troops blocked
the path of these reinforcements, and Mackensen, crushed by his failure,
finally, at 4 P.M., granted Greiner's request. It was too late. Radio communication with the garrison had been cut, and there was no way to
order it to flee.

While Greiner was desperately trying to contact the castle garrison,
U.S. Technical Sergeant Earl Swanson led his platoon in three successive
assaults against the castle. In the final attack, he charged a hundred
yards over ground swept by machine-gun fire and battered his way

into the massive stronghold, killing two Germans and capturing forty. Then he opened the cellar door, flung several grenades, and seized about a hundred more.

An Allied tank now roared through the entrance to the castle grounds followed by troops, who routed about 250 Germans from a cave beneath the castle—including the commander of the defending regiment and his staff.

Cisterna, the hinge pin of the German beachhead defense system, had fallen and the time for decision had come. A decision that could determine the fate of Rome and the whole German army in Italy.[5]

Shortly before 10 A.M., May 25, while the battle in Cisterna still raged, General Clark, driving in his jeep, heard on the radio that elements of General Keyes's II Corps, pushing toward Anzio along the coast, had finally linked up with elements of General Truscott's VI Corps. Clark was exuberant. He ordered his driver to the link-up site near the village of Borgo Grappa . . .

Determined to break through to the beachhead, red-headed Lieutenant Francis Xavier Buckley had left Terracina, the last important town south of Anzio, at noon the previous day with a reconnaissance party of armored cars. The column had gone about twenty miles by sundown, then bivouacked near Borgo Grappa.

Buckley could not sleep. He kept thinking of a meeting like that of Stanley and Livingstone: "VI Corps, I presume!" Still, he feared that his large column might be held up by the Germans. One jeep, however, could probably infiltrate through.

He awakened one of his men and the pair sneaked out of camp and headed in a jeep for the beachhead. Halting at a blown bridge, they parked the vehicle and strode northward, accompanied by a curious crowd of Italians on bicycles.

Suddenly, in the distance they saw several figures approaching along the road, then heard a voice shout:

"Where in hell do you think you're going?"

"Anzio!" Buckley yelled back.

"Boy, you've made it," said the stranger.

A minute later, "Stanley"—Buckley—shook hands with "Livingstone"—Captain Benjamin Harrison Sousa—who led a unit of engineers. The men sat down and, instead of jungle fruit, consumed a box of candy that Buckley had received a few days earlier from his wife.

Shortly, a fleet of jeeps rumbled into view from the northwest and ground to a halt. General Clark descended, followed by an army of reporters and photographers. Buckley and Sousa swallowed their candy, rose, and smartly saluted.

"Lieutenant Buckley, Company B, 48th Engineers, making contact with the beachhead."

"You are the first one in," Clark said, smiling. "Well, this is a great day, isn't it?"

"Goddam," said Buckley, "I've been waiting for it for a long time, sir."

"We sure have all been waiting for you to get here," the general replied. "It's a fine day."

It was a fine day; the day of decision. A decision that would show General Alexander and the rather sluggish British Eighth Army the folly of challenging Mark Clark's rightful claim to everlasting glory.[6]

❖   ❖   ❖

"Surrender, you English gentlemen—you are surrounded and will only die."

A voice cried back: "We ain't English. We ain't gentlemen—and be goddamned if we'll surrender!"

This exchange took place between a German officer under cover of a white flag and a Canadian soldier amid the fortifications of the Adolf Hitler Line, which extended from Piedimonte on the slopes of Monte Cairo through Pontecorvo to the southern bank of the Liri River. (The Dora extension, as indicated earlier, continued the line in two prongs through the Aurunci Mountains to the Tyrrhenian Sea.)

It was only through such personal contact that Lieutenant Voelck-Unsin of the 1st Parachute Division, who had managed to escape from Cassino town before the British and Poles could close their trap, realized that he was facing yet another country's army. On the morning of May 23, while the Americans bolted from Anzio, the I Canadian Corps launched an assault against a northern section of the Adolf Hitler Line, between Pontecorvo and Aquino, that blocked the path of the British Eighth Army struggling toward Valmontone for a link-up with Truscott's force.

But the Canadians, facing soldiers of the crack 1st Parachute Division and of strong reserve units, found the going even rougher than the Americans, though their casualties were no greater. The trouble was that the British Eighth Army had marched so leisurely through the Liri

Valley after Cassino's fall that the Germans had had ample time to man and strengthen the northern segment of the Adolf Hitler Line.

The Germans had worked feverishly. They embedded Panther tank turrets with long snoutlike guns in concrete emplacements, tunneled connecting bunkers deep in the ground, dug more antitank ditches, and laid more mines and belts of wire.

And yet, because of the narrowness of the front and the difficulty in moving troops forward, the Eighth Army was attacking with only one division—the Canadian 1st Infantry; the Canadian 5th Armored would follow through once the Adolf Hitler Line were cracked. This plan had been sharply criticized by General Clark, who thought several divisions should attack simultaneously.

Try as it might, the Eighth Army could not move any faster. Tanks and other vehicles still clogged the way and the shallowest creek seemed enough to hold up the whole army, while the Germans added to their troubles with skillful rear-guard action. Only the day before, May 22, the Canadians had tested, and tasted, the fury of German resistance at the new line. A token Canadian attack had been repulsed with great losses.

Now, on May 23, a bigger attack was underway, and both the Allied and German commanders were aware of the high stakes. If the Eighth Army broke through to Valmontone and linked up there with the U.S. VI Corps fighting its way from Anzio, the trap would close on the Germans.

As Voelck-Unsin fired round after round at the Canadians from his dugout, he felt confident that he and his comrades could hold. Could any force break through these fortifications, this wall of steel and concrete? But then he began to wonder, having seen his comrades at Cassino survive the explosion of tons of bombs and shells. The most powerful weapons man produced had not, at Cassino, destroyed man.

And were not the targets he saw in his sight also men? In fact, they were his courageous singing neighbors—Englishmen, or people just like them.

Voelck-Unsin would try to resolve his doubts by counterattacking. With two tanks and forty men he assaulted units of the Canadian 1st Division and stopped them on his front. And all along the line, other defenders were stopping them as well—until, in the center, unknown to Voelck-Unsin, a group of Canadian tanks finally plowed through the defenses while other squadrons followed to keep the hole open.

Early next morning, May 24, Voelck-Unsin's force suddenly found itself under fire from the rear. The Canadian tanks that had broken through the line had wheeled around and were attacking his men. Why hadn't anyone told him the enemy had pierced the steel and concrete wall? From his dugout he ordered his men by radio to fire their antitank guns, and they hit the lead tank, which exploded into flame. Others that were following then withdrew.

Voelck-Unsin rejoiced—until a runner dashed in to tell him that the men had only a few shells left. The lieutenant was shattered. At that moment, he somehow felt that the war was lost. He gazed out of his lookout window and was stunned to see an endless line of enemy tanks maneuvering for another attack from the rear. He had escaped at Cassino. He would escape this time, too. But to where? To another "invincible" fortress?

Grabbing an antitank gun, he ordered his men to follow him northward. But the tanks were closing in. In desperation Voelck-Unsin leaped into a foxhole while his men scattered to find other cover, and within minutes he stared into the underside of a tank, and then another and another. Fifty-four tanks crawled over his dank abode, all following in a line to avoid mines.

When the last tank had passed over him, Voelck-Unsin peeked out and aimed his antitank gun at it. But it jammed. Then, in the distance, he saw Allied infantry tracing the tracks of the tanks. He lay flat in the foxhole, playing dead, and listened to the pounding of footsteps on soft earth grow louder.

Suddenly, Voelck-Unsin felt something poking at his buttocks, and he looked up into the eyes of a soldier who was casually aiming a rifle at him. Slowly the German rose and climbed out, throwing down his own gun.

"*La guerre est finie*," he said.

His captor laughed. And Voelck-Unsin laughed, too. Then other soldiers came up and searched him, and one offered him a cigarette.

"Thank you," he said. "That makes us even. I've given cigarettes to my prisoners, too."

And as Voelck-Unsin started toward the rear he laughed again.[7]

The tanks and troops that had overtaken Lieutenant Voelck-Unsin were thrusting toward the Melfa River where General Feurstein, commander of the LI Mountain Corps, directed his men to make a last stand. Feurstein had dared order them to withdraw from the Adolf Hitler Line to the river without approval from his superiors. He must save them from encirclement and annihilation. He must prevent a complete breakthrough toward Valmontone and Rome. Even if this meant his career—or his life.

He had pleaded by telephone with Tenth Army headquarters for permission to withdraw before it was too late but was constantly put off, apparently because Vietinghoff himself could not obtain permission

CRACKING THE ADOLF HITLER LINE

TO ROME

VALMONTONE

HWY 6

FROSINONE

APENNINES

5TH MTN. DIV.

MONTE CAIRO

44TH INF. DIV.

PIEDIMONTE

BR. X CORPS

II POLISH CORPS

BR. XIII CORPS

I CANADIAN CORPS

LI MTN CORPS

CEPRANO

1ST PARA. DIV.

90TH PZ. GR.

AQUINO

26TH PZ. DIV.

PONTECORVO

FEC (FR. CORPS)

U.S. II CORPS

PICO

XIV PZ CORPS

LEPINI MTNS.

71ST DIV.

ITRI

FONDI

94TH DIV.

TERRACINA

CISTERNA

362ND DIV.

LXXVI PZ CORPS

29TH PZ. DIV.

HWY 7

715TH DIV.

I PARACHUTE CORPS

CORI

U.S. VI CORPS

BEACHHEAD

ANZIO

TYRRHENIAN SEA

RDT

MILES
0 5 10 15

ALLIED ATTACKS

GERMAN COUNTERATTACK

ADOLF HITLER LINE (COMPLETED)

DORA EXTENSION

from Kesselring and preferred that his subordinate take responsibility for a withdrawal. Feurstein was prepared to accept this responsibility. But his men would have to hold at the Melfa . . .

On that morning of May 24, Lieutenant E. J. Perkins of the Canadian 5th Armored Division swiftly led a reconnaissance troop riding three tanks to the bank of the Melfa to pave the way for a crossing by the rest of the division. After finding a likely crossing point, he helped his men blow up obstructions while under fire from the opposite bank. Then, with pick and shovel, they built a retaining wall of tree trunks and dirt and their three tanks slithered across the river.

Perkins crept along the far bank until he came to a house where he saw eight German paratroopers staring out of the windows. He crawled to the rear of the house and abruptly entered through a back door.

"Drop it!" he shouted, and the men let their rifles fall.

Perkins sent one man back with the prisoners, leaving only thirteen to hold the bridgehead until tank reinforcements arrived, but when they did, a German barrage from the opposite bank prevented them from crossing.

The Germans now concentrated on wiping out the bridgehead, and Perkins thought they would—unless he could trick them. He ordered his men to fire as heavily as possible to confuse the Germans as to their strength, a tactic that worked for a while. But then about a hundred Germans began closing in, supported by three Panther tanks, two 88-mm self-propelled guns, and a battery of antiaircraft guns, mortars, and machine guns.[8]

At about this time, in midafternoon of May 24, Kesselring's chief of staff, General Westphal, telephoned General von Vietinghoff and sternly reported:

"Only a short while ago [General] Jodl rang up. The Führer absolutely demands that any withdrawal be carried out step by step and with the consent of Army Group [Kesselring]. If at all possible, no withdrawal is to be made without the personal concurrence of the Führer."[9]

At 3:30 P.M., May 24, a company under Major John Mahoney crossed the Melfa just in time to save Perkins' men, beating off the Germans with PIATs (antitank guns), mortars, and grenades. Mahoney himself, though wounded, as were most of his men and all but one of his platoon officers, shouted encouragement and even crawled forward to the position of a squad that had been pinned down and guided it to safety.

After five hours of battle, with his company in shreds, new reinforcements finally arrived. Only then did Mahoney agree to have his wounds treated.[10]

At 7:50 P.M., just before these reinforcements came, General Wentzell, Vietinghoff's chief of staff, telephoned Westphal: "I have been in communication with [Colonel] Klinckowstroem [General Feurstein's chief of staff]; he tells me that the enemy has attacked with over a hundred tanks and has passed the Melfa. Several battalions have been destroyed . . . All our antitank artillery is there!"

"Well," Westphal replied laconically, "all I want is that you should defend yourself in that sector."

Kesselring would not be swayed by military reality. Rome must be held regardless. It was, after all, the very symbol of German tenacity. Germany's prestige—and his own—were at stake. Besides, the Führer himself had demanded an end to all withdrawals, whatever the circumstances. Nor did Kesselring doubt that his commanders, so steeped in pessimism, *could* hold if they were willing to take more casualties. At 2:28 A.M., May 25, a few hours after the Canadians had crossed the Melfa River in force, he radioed Vietinghoff and Mackensen:

> With the beginning of the enemy attack from the [Anzio] beachhead the current battle has entered its decisive phase. The main goal must be to paralyze the offensive spirit of the enemy by the infliction of very heavy casualties. This can only be done by fanatical defense of the designated main defense lines. I therefore forbid the withdrawal of any division and the giving up of any strongpoint without my prior explicit consent.

At midday Vietinghoff, with this cable in hand, instructed Feurstein: "I would like to emphasize once more that according to the Führer's orders the Melfa line must be held for several days. An early withdrawal is out of the question. Enemy elements that have crossed the river must be thrown back . . ."

Incredulous, Feurstein replied that he would issue the order but did not believe it could be carried out with the troops available.

"I report as a matter of duty," he said, "that we will not bring back many men if we have to hold at all costs."

"We must accept that risk," Vietinghoff replied, silently sympathizing with Feurstein. "Army Group [Kesselring] has given explicit orders to hold the line for several days."

"I report to the Colonel General [Vietinghoff]," Feurstein responded sadly, "that the enemy has already crossed the Melfa in two places and that no forces are available to rectify the situation."[11]

Feurstein might have been cheered slightly had he realized that the confusion and congestion behind the Canadian advance would not permit the British Eighth Army to exploit the breakthrough engineered by Lieutenant Perkins and Major Mahoney. The artillery lagged too far behind to support the Canadians pouring into the bridgehead, and tanks, bridging vehicles, and bulldozers lingered uselessly on pitted roads and at stream crossings.

Meanwhile, despite the Canadian surge through the Adolf Hitler Line between Pontecorvo and Aquino (which had trapped Lieutenant Voelck-Unsin's unit), the British 78th Division could not break the German 1st Parachute Division's hold on Aquino itself. Nor, despite new suicide assaults, could the remnants of the II Polish Corps that had fought at Cassino snap that division's grip on Piedimonte, the northernmost stronghold of the Adolf Hitler Line. General Heidrich, the 1st Parachute Division commander, ignored Feurstein's order to withdraw from the two towns, as he had ignored his order to abandon Cassino.

Thus, on May 24, though most Germans were retreating in near panic, the British Eighth Army, except for the Canadian spearhead, was unable to move!

It was not until the following day, May 25, that Heidrich relented. Under mounting pressure from both the enemy and his superiors, he finally withdrew from Aquino and Piedimonte, again, as at Cassino, barely in time to prevent the encirclement and destruction of his troops.

Eighth Army traffic then began to move again—only to grind to a halt once more when the British 6th Armored Division—slated to be one of the first to catch up with the lonely Canadians—was held up, ironically, by a huge mine field that had previously halted the Canadians, who had changed direction without bothering to inform the British about its existence.

Without the necessary support, even the Canadians started to lose momentum.[12]

Kesselring felt that the British Eighth Army's failure to exploit the Canadian breakthrough justified his optimism, while his commanders, though embarrassed by their pessimistic predictions of imminent destruction, continued to plot ways of circumventing his orders. Attributing the Eighth Army's sluggishness to the tenacity of his own routed forces, which he thought his generals vastly underestimated, Kesselring admonished Vietinghoff on the morning of May 26:

"It is the Führer's explicit order and also my belief that we must bleed the enemy to exhaustion by hard fighting . . ."

He added almost cheerfully:

"You have always been optimistic; why has your attitude changed?"

Because, it seemed, saving the German army was more important to Kesselring's commanders than saving Rome.[13]

❖   ❖   ❖

General Truscott's leathery face reflected his jubilance as he returned from the front late in the afternoon of May 25. The U.S. 3rd Division had captured Cisterna as well as Cori further north. Other troops were pushing on toward Valmontone, where little resistance was expected. By the following morning, he was sure, his troops would be astride Highway 6 ready to annihilate the retreating German Tenth Army.

As he entered his command post he saw a familiar figure waiting for him—Brigadier General Donald Brann, Clark's operations officer. Hardly had the two men greeted each other when Brann told Truscott:

"The Boss wants you to leave the 3rd Division and the Special Force to block Highway 6 and mount that assault you discussed with him to the northwest as soon as you can."

Truscott's jubilance suddenly dissolved in shock. Clark was ordering him to split his VI Corps, thus technically "obeying" Alexander's order that the corps advance to Valmontone, but actually sending the bulk of it northwest, through the Caesar Line, directly to Rome. Truscott says in his memoirs that he was appalled by this decision. His whole corps was probably capable of either pushing swiftly to Valmontone and cutting Highway 6 or of breaking through the powerful Caesar Line defenses blocking Highway 7. But divided between the two objectives, his men might fail to achieve either.

Truscott protested to Brann that the conditions he had stressed to Clark had not been fulfilled. There was no evidence of any significant German withdrawal from the hills overlooking Highway 7—the Caesar Line—nor of any German concentration in the Valmontone area. Surely this was no time for a truncated force to drive northwest toward Rome where the enemy was still strong. Maximum power should be poured into the assault on Valmontone, as Alexander wished, in order to cut off and destroy the retreating German Tenth Army.

Truscott went on to say that he would not comply with the order without first talking to General Clark in person. Brann replied that Clark was not in the beachhead. He could not be reached even by radio. Clark, he repeated stiffly, as if irked by Truscott's attitude, had ordered the attack toward Rome.

Brann has disputed Truscott's version of the conversation. Truscott's only objection, according to him, was against a suicide frontal attack on one of the strongpoints to the northwest—Velletri—which straddled Highway 7. At any rate, after the talk, at 3:55 P.M., Brann radioed Clark at his southern command post on the II Corps front—though, according to Truscott, he had said that Clark could not be reached— where Clark had flown to explain his new plan to his chief of staff, Major General Alfred Gruenther. Truscott, Brann reported to Clark, was "entirely in accord" with the switch. Two hours later, at 5:55 P.M., according to Brann, Truscott telephoned him, saying:

"I feel very strongly we should do this thing. We should do it tomorrow."

What was Truscott's real reaction? Did he favor Clark's new plan or oppose it? He was a man known for his frankness and honesty, though some observers suggest that his postwar claim of disapproval may have been motivated by the way Clark was to treat him before reaching Rome. It could be, however, that the reports of Truscott and Brann are reconcilable in the context of Truscott's statement in his memoirs that "there was nothing to do except to begin preparations."

Whatever he thought of Clark's plan, Truscott had no choice but to accept it. So why not do so with "enthusiasm"—at least until the war was over? Indeed, that evening Truscott presented the plan to his division commanders as if it were his own—meeting considerable resistance, particularly from Major General E. N. Harmon, commander of the 1st Armored Division that was to spearhead the strike toward Rome.

"The Boche," Truscott insisted, "is badly disorganized, has a hodgepodge of units, and if we can drive as hard tomorrow as we have done the last three days, a great victory is in our grasp."

Clark returned to his Anzio headquarters that same evening and worked out details of the new strategy with Truscott.

He had not yet consulted with his own boss, General Alexander.[14]

While visiting General Gruenther that afternoon, Clark had prepared the way for breaking the news to Alexander. Gruenther was to explain it to the Briton the following day—when the decision had become irrevocable! That night, after his meeting with Truscott, Clark radioed Gruenther:

"I am launching this new attack with all speed possible in order to take advantage of the impetus of our advance and in order to overwhelm the enemy in what may be a demoralized condition at the present time. You can assure General Alexander this is an all-out attack. We are shooting the works!"

At 11:15 A.M. the next day, May 26, almost twenty-four hours after Truscott had been informed of Clark's decision and fifteen minutes after the attack toward Rome had already begun, General Gruenther welcomed General Alexander at the Fifth Army's southern command post. He broke the news casually.

Alexander, always the gentleman—and the realist—appeared "well pleased with the entire situation and was most complimentary in his reference to the Fifth Army" and to Clark, according to Gruenther. Far from objecting to the shift of the main axis, Alexander agreed that the plan "is a good one."

"I am for any line," Gruenther quotes him as saying, "which the army commander believes will offer a chance to continue his present success."

But then Alexander asked Gruenther, still according to Gruenther: "I am sure the army commander will continue to push toward Valmontone, won't he?"

Gruenther reported to Clark afterward: "I assured him that you had the situation thoroughly in mind and that he could depend on you to execute a vigorous plan with all the push in the world!"

He was convinced, Gruenther added, that Alexander "left with no mental reservations as to the wisdom" of Clark's decision.

But, true to character, Alexander, it seems, was, in reality, simply avoiding unpleasant confrontations with subordinates and one which, at this point, would not change the situation anyway. In his memoirs, he complains:

"Mark Clark switched his point of attack north to the Alban Hills, in the direction of Rome . . . I can only assume that the immediate lure of Rome for its publicity value persuaded him to switch the direction of his advance."[15]

While General Clark decided to attack Valmontone with only a limited force so that the larger force could push directly to Rome, Field Marshal Kesselring decided to defend Valmontone with only a limited force so that he might halt the enemy as far from Rome as possible. And in reaching his decision, Kesselring, like Clark, ignored the advice of other commanders. He, too, was obsessed with Rome . . .

General von Senger und Etterlin who, like his superior, Vietinghoff, had returned newly decorated to the front from his most untimely visit with Hitler, was appalled to find his XIV Panzer Corps shattered and in wild retreat before the French. Many of his troops were desperately seeking to escape northeastward toward the Liri Valley where they could fuse with General Feurstein's LI Mountain Corps that was staving off the British Eighth Army and race up Highway 6 past Valmontone to the powerfully fortified Caesar Line.

Senger, who felt a sense of guilt for having been away at a crucial time, was determined to save his troops. A former Rhodes scholar and an Anglophile, he had opposed the war, he writes in his memoirs, but fought because he was a soldier. He asserts that he despised Hitler, and his meeting with the Führer, to accept a medal, had utterly depressed him. Hitler's complexion was flabby and yellowish. His blue eyes were watery; Senger thought he might be taking drugs. His handshake was soft and his left arm hung limp and trembling. Even his yellow military blouse with yellow tie, white collar, and black trousers had repelled Senger. And he had been disgusted by the confidence the young officers at the ceremony still showed in this man "to whose fiendish tenacity and nihilistic will the German people were committed."

Even so, Senger accepted the medal, a medal for fighting men he liked who were trying to depose the "fiend" he hated. In the name of this "nihilist" he had even defended the Benedictine monastery at Cassino, though he himself was a lay member of this order that stood for love and peace. And every day he saw young boys die trying to keep this "nihilist" in power—following orders from himself.

He almost envied people like Kesselring who fought with conviction, who were ready to die for a cause, even a lost cause. What a tragedy to die without one. To die a dishonest man. To die at all when there was so much beauty to enjoy in the world. The art of Rome itself would take years to absorb. He dreamed of visiting Rome again—before it fell.

Senger's ascetic, birdlike face, with bony beak and drooping, furry-browed eyes, reflected his torment as he stood for long periods by a window in his headquarters, which was situated in a fine old country house near Frosinone, off Highway 6 between Cassino and Valmontone. He gazed with deep foreboding at the black clouds of war curling over the distant hills that enclosed his private world of peace. He must save his men from what seemed at the time this onslaught by Truscott's whole VI Corps on Valmontone.

On May 26 Senger advised Vietinghoff to take several divisions out of the XIV Panzer Corps and send them to stop the Americans at Valmontone. It was clear, Senger stressed, that if Valmontone fell and Highway 6 were cut, Senger's troops, who were retreating before the French, as well as Feurstein's men, who were fleeing the British Eighth Army, would be trapped. While the force at Valmontone held, Senger went on, the rest of the Tenth Army could escape through the town and swing into the Caesar Line to the northwest. (His anxiety might have been less if he had realized that that very day Truscott's main forces would change direction toward Rome, leaving only a small element to attack Valmontone.)

Vietinghoff approved Senger's suggestion and asked Kesselring for permission to send two of his divisions to Valmontone—though the town was actually in Mackensen's Fourteenth Army defense sector. Kesselring refused. The Hermann Göring Panzer Division, plus other scattered units, would be strong enough to defend Valmontone, he insisted.

Several days earlier the Hermann Göring, which had been in reserve near Leghorn in northern Italy, was about to embark for France when Kesselring, desperately needing reinforcements, ordered it to rush to Valmontone. After all, Field Marshal Göring's own pet division had proved to be a formidable force in North Africa, even though finally beaten. It could hold Valmontone almost alone. It must.

Nor would Kesselring change his mind even when this division, as it sped southward along Highway 6 in broad daylight, had been gravely depleted by Allied air attacks. On May 26, the day Vietinghoff pleaded for a stronger defense at Valmontone, only one battalion of the division had so far arrived in the town to meet an imminent attack by Truscott's "whole corps."

Though Kesselring was enraged, convinced that the delay and the heavy losses could have been avoided, he felt that he could not afford to transfer to Valmontone other troops needed to "bleed" and slow up the French and the British Eighth Army further south.

In despair, Senger suggested to Vietinghoff what seemed the only alternative to almost certain entrapment of the German Tenth Army. As many troops as possible must be herded up a mountain road leading northward from Highway 6 at Frosinone. Some men would follow a branch of this road that wound through Palestrina and the rest would continue north through Subiaco. Allied planes or troops could, of course, easily block these twisting, pitted pathways, Senger realized, but at least the Germans would stand a chance—*if* they could only switch onto the roads from Highway 6 before the British reached Frosinone to cut the lifeline.

Vietinghoff concurred with this plan and persuaded Kesselring to approve it. Senger then supervised the operation, and when the mountain routes were jammed with Tenth Army soldiers, he prepared to depart himself, since the British Eighth Army was now approaching Frosinone. His house, the scene of so many pleasant tea parties for the local gentry, had become quite inhospitable anyway; only he and his orderly remained.

As Senger was about to go, another general visited him with a British airman who had been shot down, and the three men sat in the beautiful garden amid blossoming flowers and chatted amiably over a last cup of tea.

The tea was bitter. Truscott's force had begun its advance from Cori, just north of Cisterna, on Valmontone, while the bulk of the Hermann Göring Panzer Division still had not arrived to oppose it. If Truscott got to Valmontone first, all would be lost. Not only would he have cut off that part of the German Tenth Army retreating on Highway 6, but he could send his men forward into the northern hills to trap those Germans who were packed like cattle on dusty ribbons of mountain road.[16]

Colonel Hamilton Howze was furious as he crouched in his tank watching his armored task force lead the way down the road toward Artena and, about two miles beyond, Valmontone.

He had been asleep in a ditch early that morning, May 25, when he was cruelly awakened and forced to drag his exhausted body to the command post of his 1st Armored Division. There, General Harmon had given him the bad news. His battalion plus other units, designated as Task Force Howze, would be attached to the U.S. 3rd Division for an attack the following day, May 26, on Artena and Valmontone while the rest of the 1st Armored Division swung northwest toward Rome.

It was idiotic to split the VI Corps, Howze—like Harmon—thought. The way to fight a war was to reinforce success, not gamble with failure. The whole VI Corps was in full stride. It could easily take Valmontone and then head for Rome. And with a little bit of luck, Howze felt, he might just lead the first Allied unit into that town.

Rome would be a nice feather in the family cap. His father had commanded the 38th Division in World War I and had won the Congressional Medal of Honor fighting the Apaches. His brother and uncle had been generals, his grandfather and great-grandfather high army officers, and his wife's grandfather a general who had also won the Medal of Honor in the Indian wars. Now Rome offered him an opportunity to uphold the family tradition. But he wondered whether, alone, either segment of the VI Corps would be strong enough to break through to

Rome, a painful doubt reflected in the gray scowl masking his collegiate good looks.

Nor did reports that Valmontone was occupied by only a few troops and tanks calm him. He knew the Germans. They would put up a hell of a fight. And besides his own battalion, there was only the 3rd Division and the 1st Special Service Force to crack the nut.

The going was easy as the attack began in the morning of May 26 out of Cori. Virtually no opposition developed—until, shortly after noon, some planes dived out of the sky, bombing and strafing the advancing columns. When the smoke and dust cleared, more than a hundred men of the 3rd Division lay dead or wounded—the unintended victims of five United States P-40 fighter-bombers. The pilots were apparently overeager after meting out the same punishment to the Hermann Göring Panzer Division that was on its way south the day before to fight these very troops.

Howze's fury turned to agony. As if the attack force were not small enough, *American* planes had to whittle it further. Later, German aircraft swooped down and did additional damage. Still, the force wheezed and hobbled on, stopping for brief fire fights with small groups of Germans and taking some prisoners along the way.

Late in the day Howze's tank coughed to a halt. The engine, as well as the tank radio, had gone dead. Howze tinkered with the engine, and because it occasionally restarted and chugged along for a few yards, he remained hopeful that he could bring it to life.

Meanwhile, Howze was out of communication with his force and by the time he gave up on the tank, shanghaied another one, and caught up with his second in command near Artena, new disaster had struck. He saw three of his tanks burning nearby while artillery and small arms fire poured into the area. Other tanks then returned from a forward position.

"What the hell's going on here?" Howze shouted at his subordinate.

The latter, who apparently did not realize that his superior force faced only light opposition, explained that his tanks had passed Artena and advanced to within six hundred yards of Valmontone and Highway 6 when they met "powerful" resistance. He had then repeatedly tried to radio Howze to request instructions, but in vain. Finally, a forward artillery observer "relayed" an order from Howze to withdraw the tanks to a railroad track some distance to the rear, and they had been mauled during the retreat.

Howze's agony turned to horror. Six hundred yards from cutting off the German Tenth Army!

"I never gave any such order!" Howze gasped.

Who had told the artillery observer that he had? No one ever found out, for the following day, May 27, the observer was among those killed when American, as well as German, artillery ripped one of Howze's battalions apart in a double-barreled bombardment!

The following day, also, the tardy bulk of the Hermann Göring Panzer Division finally arrived in Valmontone. Partly because of a stalled U.S. tank engine, the Germans won the race to that key town.[17]

About the time that Howze's tanks were retreating from Valmontone, at 6:25 P.M., May 26, General Wentzell, Vietinghoff's chief of operations, phoned Colonel Beelitz, Kesselring's chief of operations:

"We have to get out of here as fast as possible or we will lose the whole XIV Panzer Corps."

Beelitz, who sympathized with this view, daringly replied that the Armed Forces High Command—which took orders directly from Hitler—was the source of all the trouble.

At 7:15, Wentzell spoke with General von Altenstadt, chief of staff of the XIV Panzer Corps, and the two men agreed that they were on the brink of a "catastrophe"—which would begin the following day. How could the Armed Forces High Command refuse to permit a swift retreat? The decision could only be based on ignorance of the situation, the two generals felt.

At 11:10 P.M., Wentzell reported to Colonel von Klinckowstroem, chief of staff of the LI Mountain Corps, that the Tenth Army "has had a run-in with the field marshal and the High Command."

A few hours later, at 2 A.M., May 27, Kesselring, furious at his commanders for their reluctance to follow orders, sent them a "very urgent" message:

"The Führer has ordered that the Caesar position be defended at all costs. The object of our present fighting must not, however, be to reach the Caesar Line soon; rather, while stubbornly holding the sectors designated from time to time, to inflict such heavy casualties on the enemy that his fighting potential will be broken even before the Caesar Line is reached."

A few hours later on May 27, the full Hermann Göring Panzer Division began launching vicious massed tank assaults against the enemy. It fought the Americans to a bloody stalemate in the Artena area—while German troops of the Tenth Army who would not simply stand and die poured past Valmontone on Highway 6, squeezing through the trap that had not quite closed.

Once more Kesselring had been proved "right" by the Allies. The Hermann Göring Panzer Division had been able to hold virtually alone —because Clark had permitted it to do so by splitting his forces.

A later German report of the battle stated: "If the Allies, as in previous days, had directed their [main] attack in the direction of Valmontone, the initially weak forces of the Hermann Göring Panzer Division would not have been able to prevent a breakthrough. The fall of Rome, the separation of both German armies, and the bottling up of the bulk of their units would have been unavoidable."[18]

General Clark helped to improve General von Mackensen's image also. Mackensen had predicted that Truscott's force would head directly for Rome from the Anzio beachhead, but it had instead attacked toward Cisterna. If the whole force had continued on to Valmontone he would have been the "goat." Now, however, Truscott, after reaching Cisterna, had switched his main attack toward Rome after all, and the excellent troops of the German I Parachute Corps who had been guarding this direct route were still in place. Mackensen's prediction had in the end been right—thanks to Clark's decision.

Mackensen took full advantage of his unexpected luck. His forces, entrenched in the Caesar Line that ran in this western sector along the base of the Alban Hills from the Tyrrhenian coast to Velletri in the east, repulsed every Allied attack and inflicted enormous casualties. The 1st Armored Division was stopped at Velletri and withdrawn into reserve to lick its severe wounds on the first day, May 26. The 34th Division was held before Lanuvio on May 27. And the 45th Division was stalled east of Campoleone the same day. Then the 1st Armored Division attacked again, this time west of Campoleone, only to fail once more.

On May 30 General Clark wrote in his diary: "I am throwing everything I have into the battle [for the Caesar Line], hoping to crack this key position, which will make it necessary for Kesselring to withdraw both his armies to the north of Rome."

This, Clark said later, was an understatement. He was actually committing "all of my reserves, every single man . . ."

Still he made no headway.

Nor were Allied efforts to pierce the Caesar Line, or to capture Valmontone, helped by confused American pilots. At 3:05 P.M., May 26, tough-minded General Harmon of the 1st Armored Division, warned in a report to VI Corps headquarters:

"Friendly planes have strafed our troops three times in the last two hours. Tell the Air Corps to get the hell out of the air, as we can get along better without the SOB's. If they don't stop strafing our troops we are going to shoot hell out of them.[19]

From May 26, General Clark was living a nightmare. He had split his forces and both had been stopped cold. And time was ticking away. The Allies were about to cross the English Channel. Moreover, the longer his Fifth Army was stalled, the more time Kesselring had to strengthen his defenses and to extract the German Tenth Army from the pincers trap before it could be sprung shut—if, as Alexander claimed, it could be.

And then there was the British Eighth Army. It was creeping up the Liri Valley, if at a snail's pace, and should it reach Valmontone before his own troops, Clark was sure, it would sweep on to Rome in its greed for "undeserved" glory—no matter what Alexander had said about the British bypassing it.

In fact, Alexander was making the most of the situation. The Germans were so busy blocking Clark's Fifth Army that they were offering less resistance to the British Eighth Army. Alexander now apparently hoped that Kesselring would so overcommit his forces against Clark's troops that the Eighth Army would be able to make a decisive breakthrough and exploit it by attacking the rear of both German armies. It *would* be difficult to ignore Rome in his plans for "exploitation."

On May 28, in the middle of Clark's nightmare, General Juin, during a visit to Fifth Army headquarters, suddenly came to his rescue. He offered Clark a possible solution to his double-pronged problem of breaking the Fifth Army stalemate and making sure the British would not get to Rome first.

Juin was being squeezed out, as originally planned, by the two forces converging on Valmontone. The Anzio troops had cut across his path of advance. And the British Eighth Army, though far behind the French on their northern flank, still had the exclusive right to use Highway 6. Alexander had finally permitted the French to advance north of Pico *toward* Highway 6 in support of the Eighth Army, but they were forbidden to use the road itself.

The French were thus left dangling in the Lepini Mountains south of Valmontone, in the vertex between the Americans and British—at a time when both were stalled. But Juin and his generals were not prepared to accept military oblivion—not after so brilliantly clearing the way for the others. As they stood upon the crests of hills bloodily conquered and gazed northwestward into the distance, their eyes reflected the glitter of Rome. Might it be possible for them to be first in Rome after all—at least ahead of the British? . . .

"In a very short while," Juin told Clark on May 28 during his visit to Fifth Army headquarters, "should we continue on the same axes, a large number of divisions will find themselves massed in front of Rome . . . on an extremely narrow front with poor communications. Therefore, it is important that from now on everyone's mission be clearly determined within the framework of the Army and the Army Group's over-all maneuver. Otherwise, there would be the risk of a terrible congestion of itineraries which would cause a complete lack of power against an enemy whose only aim is to gain time."

In other words, Juin pleaded, would Clark please see that the French be allowed to break out of their narrowing sector onto Highway 6—which, of course, just happened to lead to Rome.

Clark was sympathetic. After all, the French had sparked the drive toward Rome in the first place. It was unfair to squeeze them out now . . . And besides, if the French got astride Highway 6 in front of the British Eighth Army, they could make sure that this army would not reach Valmontone before the Americans and at the same time hasten the retreat of the Germans at Valmontone who stood between the Americans and Rome.

The following day, May 29, Clark went to see Alexander and proposed that the French advance on Ferentino, which straddled Highway 6 southeast of Valmontone but considerably northwest of the British Eighth Army's forward positions, and then continue along the highway to Valmontone. Alexander agreed, according to Clark. If he did, it was apparently because he felt that the French could help clear the way for the British Eighth Army. Shortly after the conference, unless Clark misinterpreted the agreement, Alexander had second thoughts. Once the French got on Highway 6, would they step aside to let the British Eighth Army pass them? It was more likely that they would clear the way for the Americans stalled before Valmontone.

Later in the day, General Harding, Alexander's chief of staff, called General Gruenther and told him that Alexander wanted to be certain that the strip of Highway 6 from Ferentino to Valmontone was kept open for the British Eighth Army. Gruenther was irritated. Such an order, he replied, nullified the earlier agreement.

"No," Harding said, "that is not true. He [Alexander] will be glad to have the French advance on Ferentino, which would have the effect of helping the Eighth Army along. But he insists that the road [from Ferentino] to Valmontone must remain clear for the Eighth Army. Otherwise, it might be impossible to bring the Eighth Army to bear in the battle for Rome."

So that was it! Alexander wanted, after all, to sneak the British into Rome ahead of Clark. Gruenther protested vigorously, and finally Clark and Alexander themselves were brought into the argument. On May 30 Clark dejectedly entered in his diary:

"My French corps is being pinched out. A more gallant fighting organization never existed; yet my offer to have it attack Ferentino was promptly turned down, unless the French then agreed to withdraw to the south over the roads they had come forward on."

Finally the generals hammered out a compromise. The French would advance to Ferentino, but would halt there as Alexander demanded and *not* use Highway 6. However, if Truscott's force captured Valmontone before the British Eighth Army did, these American troops *could* use Highway 6 to attack toward Rome. In that case, Alexander would send the Eighth Army northward from Valmontone to pursue the Germans escaping over the mountain roads. The British Eighth Army, in effect, would be diverted from Rome.

Clark was unhappy with this compromise. After all, he had intended to turn Truscott's force northwest toward Rome on Highway 6 *anyway* as soon as it captured Valmontone—with or without Alexander's approval. What Clark had wanted was to have the French block the path of the British Eighth Army on Highway 6 to *make sure* the British could not capture Valmontone before Truscott's men did. And Juin, understandably, was unhappier yet about this new decision to squeeze his troops off from any approach to Rome.

That day, May 30, Juin cabled General de Gaulle that the "increasingly sharp competition between the English and the Americans in the final race for Rome threatens to have painful repercussions on the utilization of the FEC [French Expeditionary Corps] . . ."

In a follow-up letter dispatched the same day, Juin stated that "it is a question of prestige . . . each wanting to enter Rome. History will not fail to judge them severely . . . With this northern limit which is imposed on it, the FEC's zone of action is reduced in proportion to British progress and will certainly disappear completely before Valmontone . . ."

But Juin, a fierce competitor himself who was not entirely contemptuous of the honor of being first in Rome, added with cheerful cynicism: "General Clark and I are hurrying things by disobeying orders."

Juin was apparently referring to a new meeting he had had that day, May 30, with Clark. No, they agreed, there was no point in the French heading for Ferentino just to help the British Eighth Army along. Clark suggested that there might be another way to outwit Alexander. Though the British general had forbidden the French to use the stretch of highway between Ferentino and Valmontone, he had said nothing about the portion from Valmontone to Rome—since Juin was to be squeezed out before reaching Valmontone.

Now, what if Juin simply bypassed Ferentino and fought through the

Lepini Mountains all the way to Valmontone, avoiding Highway 6? Then, from Valmontone, he could advance on the highway toward Rome. Technically he would not be disobeying Alexander's orders.

A pity that the French would have to lose so much time and suffer so many casualties by continuing to fight from one mountaintop to another along this hazardous route, when Highway 6 would be within sight on their flank. But such a plan seemed the only way to get the deserving French to Rome—and, incidentally, to use the French to help the Americans get there even sooner.

Juin agreed, and Clark promised him that "by hook or crook" he would see to it that the French took part in the attack toward Rome. Of course, he made it clear, he did not expect the French to show ingratitude by beating the Americans there.[20]

Clark did not have to depend entirely on Juin's trustworthiness. While he was quietly making his deal with the French general, he was contemplating another new plan that would further assure American entry into Rome first.

Major General Geoffrey Keyes's II Corps, which had ground its way up the Tyrrhenian coast, had already been squeezed out of the battlefront—after linking up with Truscott's VI Corps. Clark had ordered Keyes to turn over his Corps—comprising the 85th and 88th Divisions—to Lieutenant General Willis D. Crittenberger, commander of a newly formed IV Corps, which would clean up the areas it occupied behind the lines.

Keyes was deeply chagrined. After the magnificent advance of his corps, he was left at the moment glory beckoned with nothing more than a corps headquarters, without troops, territory, or even a band. Meanwhile, his colleague Truscott was about to thrust into Rome. Not that he begrudged Truscott the honor. But there was no reason why he, Keyes, and his brave men shouldn't have it. Besides, he felt, since the Fifth Army was stalemated, the 85th and 88th Divisions should be used in the breakthrough to Rome rather than wasted as cleanup units. And as he had commanded these troops, *he* obviously should lead them into Rome.

Keyes was close to Clark. Though a protégé of the flamboyant General Patton, he was a gentle-mannered, soft-spoken, modest man who seldom smiled or joked. His thoughtful demeanor and low-keyed agressiveness inspired confidence in both subordinates and superiors. Now he would tap that confidence in a plea to Clark.

Armed with a plan hastily drawn up by his staff, Keyes flew to Clark's headquarters at Anzio, hopeful that Clark would let *him* lead the way in to Rome. The Fifth Army commander listened with interest as Keyes proposed that the 85th and 88th Divisions join the force halted before Valmontone—and that *he* take over this expanded force. Truscott, after all, had problems enough with the troops stopped at the Caesar Line.

Clark had long felt that Truscott, after the difficult siege at Anzio, deserved the honor of taking Rome. But Keyes's plan made sense. It looked now as if the force at Valmontone had the best chance of smashing through to Rome. And the American flank at Valmontone, under the plan, would stretch far enough to the right to pinch off the British—as well as the French—heading for Valmontone from the southeast. The French would move in front of the British, and the Americans would move in front of the French. So who could beat the Americans to Rome?

Clark approved Keyes's plan and Truscott was left the leavings of Clark's Roman policy. Truscott's VI Corps would now include only those divisions attacking the Caesar Line in the Alban Hills. Keyes, with a reconstituted II Corps composed of the force before Valmontone as well as the 85th and 88th Divisions, would take Valmontone, wheel northwest on Highway 6, and smash on to Rome. Crittenberger's new IV Corps would have to remain a headquarters without divisions for the time being.

Ironically, in view of this plan, if Clark had permitted Truscott to plow ahead to Valmontone with his whole Anzio breakout force after Cisterna, he might have made it to Rome days earlier—after trapping many Germans on Highway 6 who had by now escaped.

Clark began to fear that even the new plan might fail. The Hermann Göring Panzer Division had won the race to Valmontone and might be joined by other divisions by the time Keyes attacked. For the 85th and 88th Divisions needed time to accomplish the cross-country trek from the Tyrrhenian coast to the Valmontone front, and the French needed time to trudge through the mountains to cover Keyes's right flank.

Moreover, D-Day for the cross-channel invasion was only a few days away, while the British Eighth Army might yet push to Valmontone during the delay. Clark could not depend on Keyes alone. Truscott's men must continue battering their heads against the Caesar Line with even greater determination.

On May 30, the day Keyes took over command of the Valmontone force from Truscott, Clark, preparing for the worst, lamented in his diary: "If I do not crack this position [the Caesar Line] in three or four days, I may have to reorganize, wait for the Eighth Army, and go at it with a co-ordinated attack by both armies."

Alexander, it seemed, might still have the last laugh—especially since Truscott's only remaining reserve force was Major General Fred L. Walker's 36th Division, which had just arrived by sea from Naples. Its past record, Clark felt, was not exactly distinguished.[21]

❖ ❖ ❖

General Walker seemed to be thinking aloud as he bent over the dusty road outside his headquarters, a dairy farm building northeast of Cisterna, drawing a rough map in the dirt with a stick.

"Now, if we could climb this mountain and get behind the defenses of Velletri," he said, bringing his tall, rangy physique erect, "we would have a good chance of breaking the defenses and taking all the enemy now holding it."

Lieutenant Colonel Oran C. Stovall, Walker's chief engineer, studied the map and then looked toward heavily forested Monte Artemisio, which swept three thousand feet into the sky behind the German-held town of Velletri sprawled along Highway 7.

"The key to this maneuver," Walker continued, "would be the possibility of your engineers building a road that would permit tanks, tank destroyers, and supply trains to support the operation. Can you do it?"

Stovall looked at the map once more and replied: "I'll make a detailed reconnaissance, General, and let you know tomorrow."

Tomorrow could not be too soon for General Walker. He had heard that morning, May 27, that General Clark was planning to have his 36th Division relieve the 34th Division, which had been pounding fruitlessly at the Caesar Line. Bad news. No wonder the 36th had earned a reputation as a "hard-luck" outfit. Clark always gave it impossible assignments and then blamed him and his division for any failures.

Perhaps Clark could be persuaded to change his mind—if Walker presented a plan that would permit his division to outflank the Germans rather than to crash hopelessly into a stone wall.

Walker was not optimistic. He knew Clark had no confidence in him and never took his suggestions seriously. When his troops had stormed ashore at Salerno in September 1943 under heavy fire, Clark was disgruntled with their performance, maintaining that they had very nearly been driven into the sea—a criticism that Walker found unjust. He felt that such a disaster had never really threatened, that his men had won a glorious victory.

Then, in January 1944, Clark had ordered the 36th to thrust across the Rapido River to keep German troops away from Anzio during the landings there, though almost all of his commanders—including Walker —argued that such an attack by a single division would be foolhardy. Walker, indeed, watched his division torn to shreds, with some 2,900 men lost in twenty hours as boatload after boatload vanished in the holocaust.

According to Walker, Clark admitted afterwards that he had made a mistake. Following the disaster, he says, Clark and Keyes—who had supported Clark—came to his headquarters. From the information available at the time, Keyes argued, the attack had seemed worthwhile. Clark, who has since claimed that the operation helped to save the Anzio beachhead, then interjected:

"It was as much my fault as yours."

At any rate, the complex question of "guilt" poisoned the relationship between Walker on the one hand and Clark and Keyes on the other. And when Clark ordered Walker to replace some of his favorite officers, Walker was convinced that they were just being made scapegoats for Clark's own blunder.

Clark, however, insisted that the officers were simply not good enough, that they—and Walker himself—had not adequately prepared and executed the attack (a view held by some other, but by no means all other, military experts). He was troubled, moreover, by Walker's "nepotism." One of Walker's sons was the division G-3, concerned with operations and planning, and another, his father's aide. And this situation did not change even after Clark, reluctant to issue a direct order on such a sensitive matter, gently told Walker in regard to the G-3 position:

"Fred, gosh, I just don't think it's right."

Walker, a graying fifty-seven, at one time had hoped Clark would give him a corps to command. Now, as his troops were about to attack the Caesar Line, he expected to be fired soon himself. He had ridden with General Pershing in Mexico. He had been wounded and decorated for his courageous leadership in the Second Battle of the Marne in World War I. And now it seemed that this "arrogant young general," who had been his pupil at the Army War College, was planning to relieve him of his command.

Walker was convinced that Clark was prejudiced against the 36th, at least in part because it had been a National Guard rather than regular army outfit until 1940—an all-Texan organization, though Walker himself was an Ohioan. Well, it was not all-Texan any longer. Most of the original members had been killed or wounded—sacrifices to what he felt was Clark's insatiable hunger for glory.

Now there would be more head-smashing against an impenetrable enemy barrier, more unnecessary casualties, more failures to blame on the 36th Division—unless he, Walker, could by some miracle sell Clark, and Truscott, on a more imaginative approach. Walker had studied Monte Artemisio from an artillery observer's aircraft and from forward observation posts, and he had scrutinized aerial photographs. Just that morning, May 27, he had sent a force to reconnoiter the area. All the evidence indicated that the mountain was undefended; apparently all German units in the area were committed against other American divisions attacking on less difficult terrain.

Now if only he could send a force through what seemed like a two-mile gap in the Caesar Line—as Juin had penetrated the Petrella-Revole gap in the Adolf Hitler Line. The Germans, outflanked, would have to retreat from Velletri, which guarded Highway 7 at the southern foot of Monte Artemisio as Valmontone, ten miles northeast, guarded Highway 6. The direct route to Rome would be open.

The hazards, of course, would be great. Walker's troops could be surrounded behind the German lines and wiped out. And this was one reason, Walker guessed, why Clark would certainly question the plan. Nevertheless, Walker felt that Clark's desperation was a hopeful sign. Clark might be ready to try anything that could conceivably get him to Rome before D-Day and the British.

He might even be willing to let the 36th Division gain the glory of unlocking the last door to Rome.[22]

On May 28, the day after General Walker conferred with his chief engineer about Monte Artemisio, Major General Schmalz, commander of the Hermann Göring Panzer Division, crouched behind some foliage and raised his binoculars to his eyes. He focused on a frightening sight: an American patrol. It had found the gap separating his own division on the east from the 362nd Infantry Division—the one routed at Cisterna—on the west.

Unfortunately, the Hermann Göring, barely holding at Valmontone, was already stretched to the breaking point from that town to the northwest through some of the Alban Hills. It simply could not fill the gap. But Schmalz had to do something. He rushed to his headquarters and ordered a patrol to the undefended area. He then requested General von Mackensen to instruct the 362nd Infantry Division to send a similar patrol to lock hands with his own.

Mackensen, however, apparently neglected to give such an order to the 362nd, but simply informed its commander, General Greiner, that Schmalz had sent out a patrol. Greiner therefore assumed that the gap had been filled. And he did not require much persuasion: his own division was busy enough elsewhere.

Meanwhile, on May 29, as Field Marshal Kesselring was driving to the front in his jeep, he noticed the gap. He called Mackensen and angrily ordered him to close it at once. Mackensen contacted Greiner, who said that the gap had now been closed—a conclusion he apparently based on what Mackensen had himself told him the day before!

The following day, May 30, Kesselring checked and was shocked to find the gap still unfilled. In a rage he telephoned Mackensen again and called his failure to take action "inexcusable." What one battalion could easily do today, he warned, a division might not be able to do tomorrow.[23]

At 9:00 A.M. on the same day, May 30, General Walker stood before his commanders seated on the floor of his headquarters and began tracing his finger on a giant wall map. This, he explained, was how the 36th Division would move up to replace the 34th Division and crack the Caesar Line at Lanuvio. Walker's open, toughly handsome face reflected his profound disappointment. The lines running from his flaring nostrils to the corners of his thin, determined lips were even deeper than usual.

Truscott had shown interest in his infiltration plan but Clark, as Walker had expected, found it unacceptable. The danger, Clark felt, was simply too great. Nor was he comforted by the report of the VI Corps chief engineer, who disputed the conclusion of Walker's engineer, Colonel Stovall, that constructing a supply road would be difficult but possible.

Clark remained adamant even when Walker's chief of staff, Brigadier General Robert I. Stack, breathlessly reported to him that he had found an old shrubbery-covered cart path leading up Monte Artemisio that could be broadened into an adequate support road.

Nevertheless, even while the division prepared for the move to Lanuvio, Walker and Stack continued to develop a plan for infiltrating Monte Artemisio. Walker would make a final plea to Truscott when the VI corps commander visited him toward noon to issue last-minute instructions. Perhaps Truscott could be persuaded to speak with Clark one more time.

When Truscott arrived, he quietly examined the new blueprint while Walker anxiously waited for his comment. Despite his own skepticism about the project, Truscott was as eager as Walker to find some alternative to more head-smashing against the Caesar Line. Clark, he felt, had not treated him (Truscott) fairly. First, Clark had made him shift direction away from Valmontone toward Rome; then he agreed to let General Keyes lead the way to Rome from Valmontone. The irony was that he, Truscott, might have been in Rome already if he had been permitted to continue on to Valmontone in the first place. Not that he cared that much about Rome, Truscott seemed to feel. It was a matter of principle.

Now if he could actually sneak through the Caesar Line . . .

"You may have something there," Truscott finally said in his gravel voice. "I'll call you back within the hour."

When Truscott departed, Walker, glowing with new hope, held up the movement of his troops toward Lanuvio. In his headquarters, he nervously paced back and forth. He refused to see or talk to anyone —until, uncharacteristically, he exploded to one officer:

"When I say I want a sector patrolled constantly, I mean *constantly!* I don't mean once a day or twice a day or when the mood strikes you. I mean every hour of the day and night. Now, get back up there and put those patrols out and report to me personally on everything they find! And I mean everything!"

Finally, at about 11 A.M., May 30, a half hour after Truscott departed, the telephone rang. It was Truscott. He had talked with Clark.

"Yes?"

Clark had approved the change and Walker should go ahead with his plan.

For a moment Walker was speechless. Then, just before hanging up, Truscott warned:

"And you had better get through!"

Walker's ecstatic reaction was tempered by what he regarded as a veiled threat. It was as though Truscott had said: If you don't succeed, you'll be on your way back to the States; the responsibility is all yours; although I approve of your plan and consider it better than mine, I assume none of the responsibility.

Walker was shocked and hurt. Truscott was apparently reflecting Clark's mood. He, Walker, was being given "another chance"—as if his 36th Division had not already proved itself one of the best in Italy. (Unknown to Walker, of course, top German officers who had fought against the 36th Division agreed with him that it had.*) Truscott's words continued to ring in his ears:

"*And you had better get through!*"[24]

On the evening of May 30, a single shot rang out and a young American lieutenant fell dead with a bullet in the heart. Within min-

* Colonel Rudolf Böhmler of the German 1st Parachute Division writes in his book, *Monte Cassino*, that the U.S. 36th Division was among the best Allied formations in the Italian campaign up to Rome. Others, he says, were the French Expeditionary Corps, the U.S. 3rd and 88th Divisions, and the II Polish Corps.

CRACKING THE CAESAR LINE

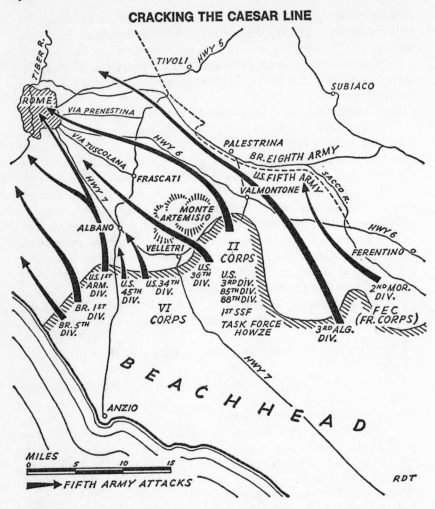

utes, his comrades had flushed out a German sniper from the forest
and dragged him to a regimental officer at his headquarters in a grove
of trees near Velletri.

"Surprised you brought him back," the officer said without expression.
"I don't care what you do with him. I just don't want to know about
it."

While the two men who had brought the sniper guided him back
into the woods, other officers gathered around the regimental commander under the trees, exchanged glances, and kept themselves busy
checking equipment, studying maps, and reading letters. No one said a
word. When the crack of a carbine shot finally echoed from deep in
the forest, they began talking again.

Colonel George E. Lynch, the ruddy, mustached commander of the 36th Division's 142nd Regiment, then called for silence. As he had been saying:

"This is the kind of job you know best how to do. You learned mountain fighting the hard way. This is the biggest infiltration job of this war and I want it done right."

Lynch, obviously tense, paused before giving instructions.

"There will be no rifle firing, regardless. Have your rifle magazines filled but I don't want a single cartridge in a gun chamber . . . If there's any killing, it must be done by bayonet or knife. If absolutely necessary, you may use a hand grenade. They may mistake it for an incoming mortar. But they know the sound of our small-arms fire and one single crazy shot can wreck the operation and get us all slaughtered. Once we cross that line, we're surrounded."

The men stared blankly at him and now understood why the sniper had to be executed. Some thought of the massacre of the Rangers in the first battle of Cisterna in January. At least the Rangers could fire back.

Lynch's executive officer, Lieutenant Colonel Sam S. Graham, an ex-college professor from Texas, tried to ease the tension: "Gentlemen," he drawled unacademically, "the general done personally promised me we won't meet more than one or two Germans at a time tonight. So who needs shootin' irons?"

After a few tentative chuckles, a company commander said: "What'll I tell my men? You tell a rifleman he can't use his rifle—no matter what —and it's the death sentence to him. He's naked. Knives? Sure, I gotta few knife guys, but not many. And that's close-in work. Real close in. Man, we'll tiptoe on rotten eggs tonight!"

As the briefing ended, about two hours before the advance would begin, one lieutenant requested, with a shaky voice, permission to join his own communications unit in the rear. But though he appeared to have valid military reasons, Lynch stared at him with contempt and refused. He looked again, however, and agreed. Then he silently contemplated the other officers and barked:

"Anybody else who wants out of this war better sound off now!"

After a moment of hushed silence, Graham piped: "I'll sound off. No damn mail again today. I'm mad as hell!"

Colonel Lynch grinned—but he wondered whether any of his men would ever receive mail again.[25]

"No more smoking. Pass it along . . . No more talking. Pass it along . . . Keep at five yard intervals. Pass it along . . ."

The midnight air vibrated with the chatter of German automatic fire on all sides. Then silence, except for the rustling of leaves and the crackle of twigs in the forests and terraced vineyards and fruit groves. Every gnarled tree and trembling shadow became a German soldier, every darkened house an enemy fortress. A dog barked, setting off a chain reaction of howls and the bray of a jackass. A peasant cursed. Silence again . . . The dog lay in the brush with its throat slashed.

Three A.M., May 31. Enemy aircraft engines rumbled in the sky and flares illuminated the shuddering greenery that cloaked prone men at prayer while antiaircraft guns coughed a fiery reply. Then forward again. Steeper and steeper. Knees bled on sharp-edged rocks and in thorny foliage. Eyes strained to see the black patch of humanity in front, flashing with panic at the lonely, horrifying moment it sometimes vanished in a mirage of night.

Private First Class Richard Kennedy tapped Associated Press correspondent Kenneth Dixon on the shoulder as he crept past him and pointed to the right, whispering:

"That guy must know you, reporter. He's smiling."

A German soldier propped up against a tree wore two grins in the moonlight—one of them a dark red gash across the neck.

The night suddenly exploded. The 141st Regiment was firing all it had on the left flank to divert any Germans in the area from the path of the silent 142nd.

"Medic! Aid man!"

A medic from the 142nd suddenly started toward the cry in the other regiment's sector but was stopped by his comrades. Was he insane? The cry grew louder and the medic sobbed. The others continued to scratch their way upward.

At dawn, a dirt trail began—only five hundred yards to the top of Monte Artemisio. One battalion branched off to the left, the other to the right; and at about 6:30 A.M., after capturing three German artillery observers, one while taking his morning bath, they reached the summit. Behind the 142nd Regiment came the 143rd, to be followed by three bulldozers which crawled up the mountain like monstrous beetles, hungrily consuming and then spitting out chunks of earth to pave the way for tanks, big guns, and supplies.[26]

An officer of the Hermann Göring Panzer Division atop the mountain observed the enemy force creeping forward, but, unaware of its size, reported to his battalion commander only that he had seen "some" Allied infantry. General Schmalz, if he was aware of this report at all, did nothing about it.

Field Marshal Kesselring, however, heard similar news that morning from an artillery commander in the area, and was distraught. He realized what this meant. But by the time he ordered Mackensen—from whom he had heard nothing—to counterattack and Mackensen relayed the order to Generals Schmalz and Greiner, the enemy was entrenched on the summit. Schmalz immediately threw a battalion into the breach, all he could spare from the Valmontone front, but it was no match for two American regiments. It was crushed.

Kesselring clearly saw that if the U.S. Fifth Army breakthrough troops, instead of heading northwest for Rome, swerved northeastward through the hills east of Rome between his two armies, they would probably cut off the whole retreating Tenth Army even more completely than if Clark had captured Valmontone earlier. Once this was done, these Fifth Army troops could swing westward toward the Tyrrhenian coast north of Rome and surround the crumbling Fourteenth Army as well. The war in Italy would then be over.

Yet even in this moment of catastrophe Kesselring was optimistic. Clark and the other Allied commanders, he sensed, were so obsessed with the promise of glory that they would attack toward Rome and let his armies escape to fight another day. The question now was: Should the Germans fight for Rome? A difficult prize to hold, but the Führer seemed determined to do it. And Kesselring himself had an enormous stake in the city.

While the field marshal wrestled with this question, Colonel Lynch stood at the western nose of the ridge atop Monte Artemisio and in the bright sunshine looked down upon the glaring white ruins of Velletri from its rear while his men shot up unsuspecting convoys on Highway 7.

The last door to Rome was open.[27]

12

The Threats

In the hills of Palestrina north of Highway 6, Carla Capponi, brandishing a pistol, approached the cave in which forty-seven Germans were being held prisoner and called out:

"Bring out a doctor!"

A German soldier emerged and accompanied Carla to where Rosario Bentivegna lay unconscious. The doctor felt Rosario's pulse, then slapped him about the face. The youth began to stir and soon his eyes opened. He was shocked to discover that a German was tending him, but Carla assured him that the German was their prisoner, not their captor.

When the doctor returned to the cave, the two partisans lay down again to conserve their remaining strength. They had not eaten for three days and had no idea when the men they had sent out might return with food. The Germans, moreover, could attempt to escape at any moment, being desperately hungry themselves and fully aware of their guards' feebleness. Rosario and Carla were armed only with pistols since the Russian escapers had deserted with all other weapons as well as the food and medicine.

Later that same day in late May, with the situation growing more ominous, a group of men emerged from some woods nearby.

"Look!" Carla exclaimed weakly, jostling Rosario. Their eyes brightened.

The partisans who had been sent out were returning, together with the Russians. Carla and Rosario greeted them with wan but joyous smiles, and one of the Russians apologized for their desertion.

"We doubted that you were really Communist partisans," he explained. "But now we know you are."

They had met another Communist leader in the area who had assured them that Carla and Rosario were indeed running partisan operations in the Palestrina zone. The Russians were thus persuaded to return—clearly fearful, it seemed to the Italians, that their desertion might be reported to officials back home in the Soviet Union. And they returned with the weapons, the medicine—and what remained of the food.

To further cheer Rosario and Carla, the news they had long been waiting for finally came through. On May 27, Radio London broadcast the message:

"Anna Maria has been promoted."

This was the signal for all-out partisan attacks in the Alban Hills south of Rome, including the Palestrina region. While the Americans attacked these hills frontally in the area between Highways 6 and 7, the partisans were to disrupt German operations behind the lines. In the Palestrina zone they would harass and cut off, if possible, German forces trying to escape from the British Eighth Army pursuing northward over the mountain road running through that town.

Carla and Rosario now led hit-and-run attacks on German vehicles that snaked along the road, blocking their passage and slowing up the enemy retreat with bombs, grenades, and gunfire—though the Eighth Army itself was too bogged down to take full advantage of this success. During one Allied air assault Carla was struck in the back by a piece of shrapnel, but she continued to lead raids despite the pain.

After a few days, Rosario and Carla were ordered by radio to return to Rome immediately, and Carla in her excitement almost forgot her wound, though she was growing weaker. Soon, she rejoiced, she would be helping to lead the insurrection that would finally cleanse Rome of the shame that had stained its name for so long—and perhaps produce a Communist-dominated government in the bargain.[1]

❖   ❖   ❖

While many CLN partisans prepared for an insurrection—the Clandestine Front still opposed one—German leaders in the city prepared to nip any such uprising in the bud. Field Marshal Kesselring, SS Colonel Kappler, and General Mälzer, Commandant of Rome, greatly feared a full-scale partisan attack and thought that even the Clandestine Front planned to participate. The havoc of Via Rasella would be multiplied many times, and the danger would be especially great because General von Mackensen's routed Fourteenth Army would have to retreat through Rome to escape encirclement by General Clark's U.S. Fifth Army.

Whether or not Hitler decided to defend Rome street by street, the partisan danger could prove fatal, the generals thought. In such a battle, the Germans would find themselves facing enemies in their midst as well as to their front. But even if the Germans withdrew without fighting, the partisans might slow up the withdrawal sufficiently to permit their entrapment.

To head off insurrection, the Germans pursued two tactics—kindness and terror. Mälzer distributed free stocks of rice, flour, and bread in the poorer areas of the city to stop the spread of hunger riots that threatened to explode into rebellion. And this time, he did not, as on previous occasions, retrieve the food after photographers had taken pictures to record his "humanitarianism."

Hunger in Rome was so great that even members of the middle class were crowding into soup kitchens the Vatican had set up. People waiting all day for a few soup ration tickets pushed and angrily shouted for food while mounted police charged them whenever it appeared they might spill violently into the streets. Some bakeries were, in fact, attacked, and inflammatory slogans crying for "Bread!" were being splashed on more and more walls all over the city.

While trying to diffuse public fury with handouts, the Germans were also greatly intensifying their crackdown on partisan leaders. And as they applied torture and threat ever more savagely, spies grew more numerous and so did the arrests—though many would-be victims were saved by counterspies . . .[2]

It was almost 9 P.M., curfew time, on May 25. Marchesa Fulvia Ripa di Meana, the murdered Colonel Montezemolo's energetic cousin, walked swiftly to the home of Commander Piero De Scalzi to pick up the list of people to be arrested that night. De Scalzi, a naval officer in the Clandestine Front, was in daily contact with a Fascist policeman, Celestino, or "Conte di Toledo," as he was sometimes called, who had access to Via Tasso reports. The commander had learned that a certain Delfino was daily denouncing partisan leaders to the SS.

"The list was late tonight," De Scalzi told her. "There's almost no time to warn the victims."

He telephoned Celestino and begged him to delay the police trucks somehow before they left on their rounds. Then Marchesa Ripa Di Meana rushed off to find people who could help her warn the potential victims by telephone or personal visit before it was too late. Among those who volunteered was Mariolina Odone, the tall, dark-haired daughter of General Angelo Odone, General Bencivenga's chief of staff and the top active Resistance leader after Bencivenga broke his leg while hiding in San Giovanni in Laterano.

Mariolina had spent the day daringly throwing thousands of fliers into the air on street corners and from streetcars, citing Nazi-Fascist atrocities and urging young men eligible for the Fascist army draft to ignore the enlistment deadline set for that day (May 25) despite the threatened penalty of death. Now, at night, she would continue her clandestine work.

The most wanted person on the day's arrest list was a military officer called Peppino, and he was also the most difficult to contact. Another officer, General Antonio Pizzuti, rushed to the apartment where Peppino was listed as hiding and rang the bell. The servant who came to the door said:

"There is no Signor Peppino here, and the people living here are away."

The general, however, peeked in and saw that smoke was still curling from a cigarette on the dining-room table. He surmised that whoever lived there was probably still at home.

"Please give me a piece of paper and an envelope," he said, "and be so kind as to have Signor Peppino read this note as soon as he returns. I am a friend and I have something urgent to tell him."

The general scribbled: "A friend advises you to escape immediately if you want to avoid arrest."

Two hours later the telephone rang at De Scalzi's house. The Fascist informer, Celestino, excitedly reported that the servant had brought the note to the Gestapo. And the SS trucks were already on their raids!

It was only a few minutes before the curfew, and General Pizzuti was now convinced that Peppino was in the apartment. Could he reach him in time? Suddenly an idea struck him. He remembered seeing the name of the apartment owner on the door. He raced to the home of a man he thought was a relative of the owner. Perhaps he would give him the telephone number, which was unlisted.

It turned out that he had identified the relative correctly. Quickly jotting down Peppino's number, the general picked up the telephone and dialed. After many rings, a voice finally answered:

"Hello."

"Hello. Am I speaking with Peppino?"

"Who wants him?"

"A friend. If you are Peppino, as I hope, get away as fast as possible or in a few minutes you will be arrested. Run, I beg you!"

Peppino hurriedly dressed and ran out of the apartment building just before an SS truck pulled up in front.

The following day, May 26, Celestino warned De Scalzi that the Gestapo was about to swoop down on top Resistance commanders, including General Odone. The Germans were determined to destroy the Resistance before it could stage an insurrection—though the Clandestine Front, at least, had no intention of staging one and would do all in its power to prevent the CLN from doing so.

Marchesa Ripa di Meana immediately told Mariolina Odone to warn her father to be especially careful and not to meet with others in any particular place more than once. Spies had told all.[3]

Signor X was more depressed than usual during this intensive crackdown. And his mood did not improve when he found that the Fascists had seized his car while it was parked in the street. He feared that they had learned he was working for the Clandestine Front.

Signor X, whose job was to contact spies in the Fascist police to gain information about future arrest plans, felt that he needed a car to make his rounds with minimum danger. Now he had lost even this small safeguard. He had joined the Resistance to play a personal role in ridding Italy of a disease that threatened his Jewish wife and had already stricken her aunt, who had been deported. But he had since concluded that the military on the Allied side were as foolish and insincere as the military on the German side. As a former professor and publisher, he could not understand the "illogic" of his superiors, who, in his view, spent more time fighting each other than the enemy and seemed interested only in clearing their own names.

Anyway, he was a civilian with no military training. What was he doing in a military organization? He had no desire to be a hero. The thought of arrest and torture tormented him day and night, and his fear was compounded by the threat to his wife, who was pregnant.

He had already prepared four pages of suggestions to be incorporated in the plan for taking over the city when the Germans withdrew—a plan which called for maintaining law and order but not for insurrection. His superior, Lieutenant Colonel Antonio Battisti, would present it to top leaders at an important Front meeting a few days later, on May 29, at the Fatebenefratelli Hospital on Isola Tiberina.

At the moment, however, his main concern was to get his car back.

Battisti suggested that he contact his cousin, a colonel in the Fascist Air Force who was collaborating with the Clandestine Front.

"Perhaps he can help you," Battisti said, giving Signor X the address of the *pensione* where his cousin lived.

Signor X went to the *pensione* and asked the *portiere* if the colonel was in.

"Yes," the *portiere* replied, "he's in the living room."

As Signor X entered the room he saw a man in civilian clothing sitting in an armchair.

"Who are you?" the man asked.

Signor X paled and mumbled a false name. Then the man rose and, flashing a police badge, searched him and removed some papers from his inside jacket pocket.

"What is this?"

"Just some private papers. Nothing important."

The man scanned the papers and then stared at Signor X. He had found the suggested plans for action when the Germans retreated.

"Come with me," said the policeman—who had been waiting for callers since Battisti's cousin had been arrested at the *pensione* two days earlier.

Captain Colombini, a *carabinieri* officer who had remained in the Fascists' service, smiled as he shuffled through the papers at the police station.

"What are these?" he asked in an almost sympathetic tone.

Signor X trembled. What was the use?

"I think they're self-explanatory."

Colombini continued reading, and in the sweaty silence Signor X mentally cursed Battisti, blaming him for his arrest, wondering if he had deliberately led him into a trap. Battisti could go to hell. And so could the other officers—on both sides. Who else mattered but his wife? He had suffered enough. And anyway, liberation was near. The Fascists would not dare act too rashly against the Resistance in these last days.

"If you let me go," Signor X said, "I'll co-operate. I'm only a little fish. I can help you catch the big fish."

The captain agreed, and when he had checked on his address, permitted Signor X to leave.

"We'll be in contact with you," he said, still smiling.

Signor X was relieved that they had released him without first grilling him. Those stupid Fascists! He decided that he and his wife, whom he feared might be arrested at any moment, would immediately seek refuge in the Vatican. His father-in-law had worked with Cardinal Tisserant in the Vatican Library, and Signor X hoped the cardinal could arrange for their internment. He rushed home to pick up his wife and took her to Café Greco near Piazza di Spagna. Signor X left his wife there while he went to make contact with Tisserant.

"Don't move from here," he instructed her. "I'll be back soon."

Unable to reach Tisserant immediately, Signor X returned to Café Greco, hoping to get in touch with the cardinal later, but found that his wife was no longer there. In a panic, he rushed out into the street and thought he saw in a passing car the man who had arrested him. He hurried inside the café again and phoned his home. The maid knew nothing. He phoned his sister-in-law. She also knew nothing.

He could draw only one conclusion. The police had arrested his wife as a hostage. In desperation, he returned to the police station where he had been taken earlier in the day. Captain Colombini looked surprised to see him.

"Why have you come back?" he asked.

"What have you done with my wife?" Signor X blurted.

"Your wife? I haven't seen her."

It then struck Signor X that perhaps the captain never really expected to see him again. After all, the Allies were about to arrive. As he started to leave, Colombini added:

"Since you're here, well, I want you back here later today."

And he added, according to Signor X, that perhaps his wife *could* be in danger.

Signor X returned to the café and there sat his wife. She had gone on a stroll and returned. Now there was no time to find a hiding place. Remembering Colombini's reference to his wife, Signor X went back to the police station as ordered. He had a friendly discussion with Colombini, he told the author, and tried to persuade him that his best interests lay in switching to the Resistance before the Allies arrived. He also gave information about his comrades.

The following day, Signor X met with several Clandestine Front members at the luxurious home of the brother of Colonel Carlo Scalera, General Odone's aide, on Piazza della Libertà. It was the favorite haunt of Front leaders because it was the only place in town where they could eat a thick steak; Scalera's brother was one of Rome's most important meat merchants. Time and again, they agreed to stop meeting there, since it was becoming too well known as a center of Resistance activity. But each time hunger drove them to break their vow.

Signor X's colleagues wondered why he had not shown up at another meeting held the day before.

"I was in an auto accident," he lied. "They took me to the hospital but fortunately I was not seriously hurt."

After the meeting Signor X warned several comrades: "We shouldn't meet here any more. I've heard that the police are on our tail."

"The police are always on our tail," replied one. "I'm used to it."

Several days passed without incident and Signor X breathed more easily, he says, feeling that his efforts to persuade Colombini not to act on his information had borne fruit.[4]

Late in the morning of May 29 General Odone met with Colonel Scalera on a street corner. They would lunch somewhere and then go to the meeting at the hospital on Isola Tiberina where final details would be worked out for taking over Rome when the Germans departed. It would probably be the most important meeting the Clandestine Front ever had—and the most dangerous. For most of the leaders would be there and could be wiped out in a single blow.

Where would they lunch? They considered various restaurants. But what rubbish they served. Once again they decided to eat at the home of Scalera's brother.

Within an hour they were sitting at the table together with the brother, the brother's wife, and his two young nieces ready to devour huge black-market steaks.

At about 1 P.M., the doorbell rang and one of the girls went to the door. Two men burst in with pistols drawn.

"Where are they?" demanded one.

Odone and Scalera, realizing the house was being raided, hid in a small room, but the two Fascists soon found them.

Meanwhile, firing broke out on the street. One of Odone's three bodyguards had fired at policemen surrounding the area, killing two, and he in turn was killed, while another bodyguard was wounded. The third bodyguard escaped around a corner and ran past a doorway where three men stood—Signor X and a policeman on either side of him.

According to Signor X, the police had picked him up on the street only some minutes earlier and taken him to the scene of arrest. He claims that he did not have the opportunity to telephone a warning to the victims and that he could not have known the two officers would drop in for lunch that particular day.[5]

At about the same time, three other Clandestine Front leaders were also having lunch—though a far more modest meal—before leaving for the Isola Tiberina meeting. General Filippo Caruso, the *carabinieri* chief, and two assistants, Colonel Caratti and Captain Geniola, had met in a restaurant on Via Attilio Regolo to discuss changes in the plan to be presented at the island meeting.

The three men were excited. The *carabinieri*, who had forsaken the Nazi-Fascists to follow the King into the Allied camp, would soon be playing a key role in Italian history. And Caruso was especially proud that he had been able to weld the various *carabinieri* bands that had deserted their former masters into a unified underground organization, true to its apolitical tradition—except for their absolute loyalty to the King. To Caruso and other *carabinieri*, belief in the King was almost as natural as belief in God—though the institutional question was the most explosive political issue dividing the anti-Fascist camp.

Caruso was proud of what his men had done so far. They had hidden Allied prisoners, gathered intelligence, shadowed enemy agents, escorted Resistance leaders, conducted sabotage. Those *carabinieri* captured had been brave.* Many had died—without talking—in the Ardeatine Caves.

Now Caruso's men would help to liberate Rome.

Suddenly two German soldiers entered the restaurant and walked over to Caruso's table.

"Your identity cards!" one demanded.

The three Italians reached into their inside jacket pockets, Caruso with his paper napkin. He drew out some papers, which were covered by the napkin, and shoved them into his mouth. One of the Germans immediately grabbed him by the throat with one hand to prevent him from swallowing the papers and, as Caruso struggled to his feet, placed a pistol at his head with the other. The general tripped the German and the pistol went off, barely missing his head. Both men fell, and with the German's grip on his throat loosened, Caruso swallowed the documents—the plan for the moment of German departure.

The two Germans then took their prisoners to Regina Coeli prison, the headquarters of General Caruso's Fascist namesake, from where they were transferred to Via Tasso.[6]

In the conference room at Fatebenefratelli Hospital, located on Isola Tiberina, a small island in the middle of the Tiber River, about thirty people sat around a large oval table or stood nearby, some

---

* One of the bravest of the *carabinieri* had been young Vice-Brigadier Salvo D'Acquisto. The Germans had taken D'Acquisto and twenty-two other Italians hostage in September 1943, after a bomb had killed several Nazis in the town of Torre, and were about to shoot them when the young officer claimed he alone was responsible for the bombing, though actually he knew nothing about it. And so he alone was shot.

speaking softly, others looking over documents, all obviously uneasy. The meeting was to have started at 3 P.M. and it was now after four. Why were so many people late, including important officers like Odone, Caruso, and Caratti?

One of the most nervous participants was Mariolina Odone. Earlier that day, when she had left the convent where she and her mother were staying, she had sensed that something would go wrong and had expressed this ominous thought to her mother. Her father was seldom late. What could have happened? As she stood thinking the worst, someone asked her:

"Have you any idea, Mariolina, where your father might be?"

She thought for a moment. "Perhaps at Scalera's house."

"Why don't you try calling there?"

"The telephone is just outside in the courtyard," said Father Maurizio, a partisan friar at the hospital.

As the girl started toward the door to the courtyard, someone rushed in, crying: "The police are here!"

The partisans scrambled into the corridors to hide in various rooms and wards, while Father Maurizio calmly gathered all the documents on the table and hid them behind heavy antique paintings on the walls. Then he disassembled a radio used to communicate with the U.S. Fifth Army and hurled the parts through a window and into the Tiber River.

Mariolina, frantic now about the fate of her father, ran outside to the telephone and called the Scalera home.

"Is my father there?" she asked the Scalera daughter who answered.

"They got sick and were taken to the hospital," came the reply.

That was the "conventional phrase." They had all been arrested.

Meanwhile, in an attempt to confuse the police, some of the partisans put on patients' pajamas and bathrobes and mingled with the sick. The police, in the confusion, let many people through the lines—including Mariolina Odone, who simply walked out arm in arm with another partisan, the two posing as happy lovers.

Thus only five men were captured—perhaps because Captain Colombini did not seem overenthusiastic about arresting people when Allied gunfire was echoing more loudly each hour.

Signor X admitted to the author that he informed the police about the Scalera house but denied giving information that might have led to the other two raids.[7]†

† Signor X told the author that the Fascists "took" him to Florence just before the Allies entered Rome. He said he was "locked" in a room in a luxury hotel but that he managed to elude his guards, leave the hotel, and make his way back to Rome a few days after the Allied arrival. He was arrested but was soon freed after his influential father persuaded merciful Resistance leaders not to press charges against him.

The arrests on May 29 did not satisfy the German leaders in Rome, but only made them fear that an insurrection was all the more likely. Why would all those Badoglio-Communists be holding so many meetings if they did not intend to rise up against the Germans? The documents that had been found, though incomplete, showed that the Resistance was planning something.

Rome's Gestapo chief, Colonel Kappler, decided he would find out more—particularly from General Caruso, since the *carabinieri* possessed the military means to attack the Germans. At first he had not known Caruso's true identity, but the general had proudly volunteered the information. And so, while Kappler looked on, his men began their torture of Caruso (described in the Prologue)—maiming his body but not his spirit.

Though Caruso refused to crack, Kappler would not relent in his effort to obtain new information. From one of the other arrested men he learned for the first time that the top Resistance leader was General Bencivenga and that Bencivenga was hiding in the Seminary of San Giovanni in Laterano. That made sense. Kappler had learned earlier that a radio hidden in the seminary was sending messages to the Allied command in the south. Now he decided that he would move against Bencivenga, regardless of official German policy toward the Vatican.

On May 30 he sent an ultimatum to the Vatican through Ambassador von Weizsäcker. Bencivenga must either leave the seminary or give up his command of the Roman Resistance. Otherwise, the Germans would raid San Giovanni and arrest everyone taking refuge there. The Vatican fearfully informed Monsignor Ronca at San Giovanni, instructing him to tell Bencivenga to leave the premises unless he promised to relinquish his command.

Though Bencivenga's broken leg had not completely healed and he had to walk with a cane, he said he was willing to leave the seminary. But, of course, he added, he would not permit himself to be arrested without a fight. He would shoot his way out if necessary.

Vatican officials were alarmed. Violence would breed violence and that was just what the Pope was trying to avoid. Bencivenga and Ronca argued the question fruitlessly on June 1, but the next day Monsignor Montini, undersecretary at the Vatican, came up with a suggestion. The Vatican would simply deny that Bencivenga was in San Giovanni —he was there under a false name anyway. At the same time, Ronca asked Colonel Ugo Musco, the head of Centro X, who was also living in San Giovanni, to persuade Bencivenga to leave the seminary secretly and take refuge in Velletri.

Maj. Gen. Geoffrey Keyes (with fingers in shirt pocket), General Clark, and Maj. Gen. Robert T. Frederick (extreme right) study a map as Allies close in on Rome.

Maj. Gen. Fred L. Walker, commander of the 36th Division.

Generals Clark and Keyes pose under ROMA sign at city limits of Rome.

Troops of the U.S. 88th Division fight their way into Rome.

General Clark, lost on entering Rome, asks an American priest how to get to the center of the city. Maj. Gen. Alfred Gruenther, his chief of staff, is seated directly behind General Clark.

A child salutes as crowds cheer American soldiers liberating Rome.

Partisans capture a Fascist leader on liberation day.

American Sgt. John A. Vita imitates Mussolini on the Duce's balcony during the liberation of Rome.

Romans read first newspapers announcing the liberation of their city.

"I promise you he will go there," Musco lied.

Montini thus assured Weizsäcker that Bencivenga was not in San Giovanni, and Kappler hesitated to carry out his threat. But now Kesselring took a hand in the desperate German attempt to thwart insurrection. If the partisans attacked the Germans, he informed the Vatican through Weizsäcker, he would "burn down" Rome.

Resistance leaders in San Giovanni, though some opposed insurrection themselves, reacted with a counterthreat. The wife of one Clandestine Front partisan went to Via Tasso and, posing as an informer, casually told Kappler as he sat stiffly at his desk:

"If the Germans sack Rome, the partisans will kill all the German wounded left in the hospitals of the city."

To further make their point, a group of partisans led by Colonel Gastone Pianella kidnapped one of Kappler's aides and drove him to the country, where Pianella told him: "Tell Colonel Kappler that if he destroys Rome we shall attack the Germans as they leave . . . If you leave Rome quietly we will permit you to go without trouble."

Kappler seemed unperturbed by these threats. Nor did he yet realize that a weak Clandestine Front would mean a weak defense against insurrection—which, in fact, even the Allies now opposed.

Reflecting the new Allied attitude, British Lieutenant General Sir Frank N. M. MacFarlane, who headed the Allied Advisory Council for Italy, had cabled General Wilson, the Mediterranean Supreme Commander, on May 6:

> It is essential to maintain order in Rome. Otherwise the resulting damage to Rome might well be worse than that inflicted by sporadic German attack from the air. When the Germans evacuate the city, its whole administration will be completely dislocated, since undoubtedly most of the capital's Republican Fascist Administration will flee, taking their forces of law and order with them. It is most doubtful that "Mr. X" [apparently General Bencivenga] and his organization can keep order with a large population which will be on the verge of starvation and in a highly excitable state. Inevitably there will be rioting, looting, reprisals.
>
> An AMG [Allied Military Government] will have to be provided, using Italian facilities, of course, as far as possible, since we cannot permit the possibility of such a state of affairs as that above mentioned. It will be essential to bring in our 2,500 *carabinieri* [from the south] as quickly as possible to maintain law and order. Moreover, we shall have to have troops available in the vicinity to handle major disturbances in the case of emergency . . .

What, then, of plans for insurrection? In another report, General Alexander explained to Wilson: "Resistance groups . . . can only function for a short space of time unless conditions are really favourable and dramatic news is being given them to encourage their efforts." He hoped, therefore, he said, to restrain them "until the news of OVER-LORD is announced, which we hope will coincide with success of DIADEM."

In other words, the Resistance would be held on a short leash until the Allies occupied Rome.

Bencivenga thus received an order *not* to launch an insurrection, an order welcome indeed to the Clandestine Front. The plan that was to be completed at the Isola Tiberina meeting on May 29—and which was approved by Bencivenga two days later—reflected the Front's attitude. It would not attack the Germans unless they tried to damage the city, but would simply maintain law and order in the period between German withdrawal and Allied arrival.

General Caruso and other military leaders told the author this meant they would prevent the leftists from fomenting insurrection, taking control of public buildings and facilities, and raising the red flag—even if preventive action sparked civil war. And though Bencivenga himself, as well as Ugo Musco and Felice Santini of Centro X, tended to be relatively moderate in their attitude toward the CLN political parties (the CLN had supported Bencivenga's candidacy for chief of the Resistance), the general assigned to the Communists, conventional and Red Flag, only a "reserve" role in the projected peaceful takeover of the city—despite their major military contribution to the Resistance and Togliatti's presence in the new Badoglio government.

In his order for mobilization, to be executed when the BBC transmitted the code word "Elephant," Bencivenga explained: "This is to permit more direct control inasmuch as the Communist party might create disorder . . ."

Kappler could hardly have asked for a plan geared more to tranquillity. Yet, ironically, he had jailed many of the men who could make it work and was trying to put the top man out of business.[8]

The question now was whether those leftists who were determined to detonate insurrection could be controlled. At a meeting of the CLN on May 30, De Gasperi of the Vatican-oriented Christian Democratic Party reported with emotion that a Vatican official had told him of Kesselring's warning that he would "burn down" Rome if an uprising took place. De Gasperi, evoking a horrifying image of the possible destruction—art masterpieces lying ripped and shattered on debris-filled streets, the Vatican in ruins, corpses everywhere—pleaded with his colleagues not to take the risk.

Some of the leftists, including the leaders of the Communist party, who were now supporting the King and Badoglio, agreed. But others did not. Ugo La Malfa and Emilio Lussu of the Action party brashly demanded insurrection at any cost, arguing that the Romans must participate in their own liberation if they were to regain their honor and dignity. And it was far from certain that all Communist party members—many were new and undisciplined—would obey their leaders after preparing so diligently for insurrection, even deliberately inviting reprisals with their Via Rasella action.

But most determined of all to rise up was the relatively large, ultra-revolutionary Red Flag party, which scorned the CLN. Its leaders felt that the regular Communist party, which they had long been feuding with, had betrayed the proletariat by making a deal with the monarchy. It had terrorized the Germans, as on Via Rasella, when terror could only backfire against the Resistance. But now when a co-ordinated attack might produce real revolution, the conventional Communists had "opportunistically" fallen in with the "reactionaries."

The Allies were so concerned about Red Flag plans that officers of the U.S. Fifth and British Eighth Armies arranged through liaison contacts for a meeting with Red Flag leader Antonio Poce on May 31 at a villa outside Rome.

"We want to know your intentions," one officer said.

"We are three thousand strong and ready to act," Poce replied.

"We don't want an insurrection in Rome," the officer responded crisply.

Poce, a large, squat man, resented his tone. He would not take orders from the Allies any more than he would from the conventional Communists, who had thrown him out of their party in 1928 for his pro-Trotsky tendencies.

"You cannot dictate the conduct of our party," he said.

"We shall hold you responsible if any of your men disobey our order," replied the officer, adding that General Bencivenga's force would fire on them. And if fighting broke out between the two groups, Allied soldiers would help Bencivenga.

Two days after this hostile encounter, on June 2, Bencivenga sent Poce a note requesting that he place himself at the service of the carabinieri. Poce replied that this order "can absolutely not be accepted by us for obvious reasons that you yourself know. Consequently, we will present ourselves at the [carabinieri] stations not merely for collaboration, but also to ascertain whether the chief himself deserves to remain in his position or to be removed."

Red Flag leaders then drew up plans for occupying and raising the party flag on key buildings and dealing with the enemy. "All comrades belonging to the movement," stated a party manifesto, "are absolutely forbidden to carry out individual actions for the purpose of avenging personal wrongs, whoever may have committed them . . . Traitors, spies, and corrupt men on our lists are not to be murdered but to be executed according to justice, and the verdict is to be given by a People's Court."

And, of course, such a court would have to function swiftly—during the insurrection that would precede the Allied entry into Rome.

Such Communist extremists—feared and threatened by the Pope, the Allies, the local Germans, the Clandestine Front, and even most Communists and others members of the CLN—could never imagine that the Nazi leadership was contemplating support for their cause.[9]

❖   ❖   ❖

Eitel Möllhausen was puzzled as he read a cable announcing that a special plane was being sent to take him to Foreign Minister von Ribbentrop's official residence in Fuschl, near Salzburg. A few weeks previously, in early May, Möllhausen had reluctantly moved from Rome to the North Italian town of Fasano, where Ambassador Rahn put him in charge of a new political section. Since Mussolini's rump government was not of primary importance to Hitler, Möllhausen wondered why he should suddenly be called home.

He departed immediately and when he arrived in Fuschl, a Ministry of Foreign Affairs official told him to prepare for an urgent meeting with Ribbentrop. He should contact two diplomats, Ambassador Gustav Hilger and Dr. Megerle, who would brief him on the subject. Möllhausen met with the two men and was shocked to hear the reason for his recall.

Ribbentrop wanted to consult with him on a secret plan submitted by Werner Naumann, Goebbel's deputy, to set up a Communist republic in Rome before the Allies arrived. Simultaneously, the long-prepared plan for destroying Rome would be implemented—and attributed to the Communists. This two-step scheme, Naumann had argued, would create chaos that the Allies would find difficult, if not impossible, to control and would also safeguard the Germans from the charge that *they* had destroyed Rome.

"This idea is totally idiotic!" Möllhausen exclaimed.

Neither Hilger nor Megerle appeared surprised by this outburst. Indeed, Megerle sighed with relief and Hilger said:

"Ah, just as well, just as well! That was our impression, too. But how can we tell the minister that?"

"Don't call it idiotic," Möllhausen replied. "Say it's impossible, impracticable, unfeasible."

"Unfeasible, that's the best word," Hilger said enthusiastically. "I'll go and tell him so right away."

He started for the door, then stopped and turned to Möllhausen: "Now we must all agree to the answer we give if he asks us why it is unfeasible."

Möllhausen replied: "Tell him, first of all, that there aren't any Communists in Rome, because they've been arrested or they're in hiding or they've gone away. Even if by chance we could lay our hands on one or two, it would not, in the circumstances, be easy to persuade them to create a republic bequeathed by the Germans. That the departure of the Germans will immediately be followed by the entry of the Allies. That even if this does not happen, there will already be Italian groups ready to take over, naturally not by agreement with us. That it would be impossible to make anyone believe that Italian Communists, real or presumed, would take to blowing up the vital structures and services of the city to celebrate the departure of the Germans."

When Hilger left the room, Möllhausen incredulously reflected on the proposal. Communists presiding over a Rome in ruins! . . .[10]

Field Marshal Kesselring meant every word of his threat to "burn down" Rome. Even before Möllhausen left for his meeting with Ribbentrop, a team of trained saboteurs had already arrived in Rome to organize and direct the destruction of the city's electric stations, industrial plants, telephone exchanges, railway nets, reservoirs, bakeries, bridges, luxury hotels, and ministries.

Since many of these installations and buildings were located amid private homes, offices, and historic monuments, a good part of Rome would go up in flames—as it almost did after the Anzio landing—though efforts would be made to spare the Vatican and the plants that served it.

With Kesselring's warning, as well as the sound of approaching artillery fire, echoing ominously, the Vatican frantically made three appeals: to the Resistance—avoid provoking the Germans; to the Germans—avoid provoking the Romans and leave Rome peacefully; and to the Allies—bypass Rome. The Eternal City, the Vatican feared, stood on the brink of catastrophe, its every structure threatened by sabotage or bombardment, its food supply completely cut off—a situation ideal for a Communist takeover.

Actually, it was no longer simply a question of monuments being destroyed, "but of avoiding that the Church be harmed in its vital center.

It is the very Catholic idea that seems to be now at stake." In their agony, Vatican officials began to suspect that some Protestant churches were influencing the Allies against an open-city policy in order to damage the prestige of the Catholic Church.

Perhaps General Wolff could help. He had promised the Pope to do what he could to avoid violence in Rome. But as luck would have it, Wolff had gone off to Karlsbad for a cure at just the wrong time. Meanwhile, it was Rome that needed the cure. With Vatican panic growing, Monsignor Domenico Tardini, who, like Monsignor Montini, was an assistant secretary of state, met on May 27 with Ambassador von Weizsäcker.

"Many times," Tardini said, "you have made statements concerning respect for the city and for its cultural values. Now is the moment to conduct yourselves accordingly and to take whatever measures are necessary to keep Rome from being damaged."

If Weizsäcker helped to save Rome, added Tardini, he would be serving Germany, civilization, and himself. The Holy See had already given instructions, and would renew them, to the vicars of Rome to recommend calm and discipline to believers.

Therefore, Tardini said, as if suggesting a deal, the Germans should avoid taking any action that might provoke the population. Already the Germans had acted too severely—under the very eyes of the Pope, Tardini asserted, using an expression that Cardinal Maglioni had used when appealing to Weizsäcker for cancellation of the October 16 round-up of Jews. Many arrests had taken place, even of priests, he complained. And the city was hungry . . .

Weizsäcker asked Tardini if the Vatican had a concrete plan for the safety of Rome.

"No," Tardini replied. "The plan of the Holy See is to say to one, 'Do not attack Rome,' and to the other, 'Do not make a defense stronghold of Rome.' More than this, I cannot say. Also, no one knows the plans of the military commands."

Tardini added, hoping to evoke an affirmative response, that he personally was sure that the German government wished, and that Field Marshal Kesselring's tactics were designed, to save Rome. Indeed, was not Kesselring withdrawing his troops eastward and not northward toward Rome? This showed that Kesselring intended to abandon Rome rather than defend it.

Weizsäcker shook his head and said: "No, I do not have that impresssion."

In his opinion, he added, Kesselring did not intend to abandon Rome.

Tardini grew pale. "But if he stays in Rome," he exclaimed, "he will only provoke assault and ruin!"

Weizsäcker replied enigmatically: "The assault will depend on the question of Roosevelt's re-election."

This ambiguous remark increased Tardini's fear. Did Weizsäcker mean, he wondered, that the Germans might force the Americans to damage Rome in order to provoke resentment among American Catholics and encourage them to vote against Roosevelt in the next election? The Germans might see salvation in the defeat of Roosevelt. Tardini apparently did not consider the possibility that Weizsäcker meant that Roosevelt, fearing defeat, might for that reason refrain from attacking the Germans in Rome.

Weizsäcker said nothing to Tardini that would tend to discredit an earlier observation by the officially neutral but pro-German Spanish ambassador that a new defense line, with Rome as the hinge, might be established.

It would be useless to approach the German government again on the question of saving Rome, Weizsäcker insisted. Nor, he added, was the moment ripe for making an appeal for peace since an unsuccessful attempt could obstruct future steps.

Tardini again stressed that a new cycle of terrorism and reprisal in Rome could do more to harm the Vatican's efforts for peace than anything else.

Weizsäcker agreed.

Actually, the ambassador knew, as is clear from his writings, that the Germans would soon be forced to leave Rome, with or without street fighting, though he apparently did not wish to risk saying so. For both Hitler and Kesselring felt that to admit in advance that a retreat might be necessary was defeatism, and even treachery—the main reason why the Germans were seldom prepared for an orderly withdrawal. Weizsäcker, moreover, silently agreed with Tardini that every measure should be taken to save Rome from damage, though their motives differed in emphasis.

While the Vatican cared mainly about protecting the seat of the Catholic Church and all the symbols that reflected its power, Weizsäcker's chief concern was how the fate of Rome was linked with opportunities for negotiating peace. Should the Germans destroy Rome or force the Allies to fight there, world reaction, particularly that of the Catholics, would reduce the chances for such a peace. On the other hand, if the Germans could convince the world that they alone had saved Rome from destruction, their "reasonableness" might make the Allies more receptive to something short of unconditional surrender.

The following day, May 28, Weizsäcker wrote a letter to his family, saying:

> It is the Vatican's desire again that I do something to save Rome and I am promised great honors. It is true that there can be heard

today . . . salvos of artillery resounding from the Alban Hills. But I do not really fear for Rome. Why should not the withdrawal of the Germans—if it ever happens—be as smooth as the one of the French from Paris in summer 1940? In any case, I am against talking now to our generals about this eventuality and forcing them to admit that it has already been decided to leave Rome.

Weizsäcker was apparently writing another of his coded messages —reporting that the Germans would have to withdraw by mentioning that possibility and that he was negotiating with the generals for the salvation of Rome by denying he had such an intention.[11]

The Pope's fervent pleas, as well as offers by neutral Ireland and Spain to mediate a plan for making Rome a nonbattle zone, stirred heated Allied debate. Washington was receptive and consulted with the British. Was an open city possible? The British, still pulling themselves out of the wreckage at home caused by German bombardment, scoffed. On May 19 General Wilson answered the State Department:

With German airpower shrinking, such a plan would be advantageous *only* to the Germans. They would have to retreat from Rome anyway, while the Allies, on occupying the city, would be unable to use it as a communications center for continuing their campaign northward. In short, the Allies should not tie their own hands.

In a note to the Vatican, the Allies then agreed that Rome would "be accorded the normal rights of a neutral and will be treated as an independent neutral state"—but that even the diplomatic immunity of Vatican property would "not be allowed to interfere with military operations."

In reply to a plea by Archbishop Edward Mooney of Detroit that Rome be spared from attack, Roosevelt wrote that the Eternal City's monuments, "unlike the spiritual principles at issue, are not eternal, and newer and greater monuments shall arise from the ruins in a world truly dedicated to the primacy of things of the spirit."[12]

❖   ❖   ❖

"If you trust me," Marchesa Ripa di Meana told Mariolina Odone, "I will make the attempt, but don't ask me anything."

The marchesa, after failing to free her cousin Colonel Montezemolo from Via Tasso, was doubtful that any plan to liberate Mariolina's father, General Odone, and other Resistance leaders from that in-

famous prison would be any more successful. But she would try anyway. She called Commander De Scalzi to her home and he agreed to
help. What was there to lose? The Germans would be forced to leave
Rome soon and would probably either kill the prisoners or take them
north, depending on how rapidly they would have to flee.

How could the prisoners be freed? De Scalzi decided the best plan
would be to capture several female German hostages. He and other
partisans gathered details on the layout of a number of German homes
and the schedules of their intended victims. One evening, they struck.
Four German women, including the wife of a German officer and the
mistress of SS Captain Kurt Schutz, Kappler's deputy, were seized and
carried away to Contessa Brambilla's house on Via Lorenzo Magalotti
and locked in a room.

Then De Scalzi boldly went to Via Tasso and told the guard on duty
in perfect German: "I wish to see Captain Schutz."

"Captain Schutz," the German replied brusquely, "can receive no
one."

"What is he afraid of?" De Scalzi asked in a firm tone, smashing his
fist on the table.

The guard stared at him in astonishment. Then, grimacing, he replied stiffly: "Captain Schutz is not afraid of anything. Follow me."

As they headed toward Schutz's office, De Scalzi wondered whether
he would leave Via Tasso alive."[18]

❖   ❖   ❖

Every day Kesselring had to listen to Weizsäcker's whining. The
ambassador sounded like Tardini himself—whether on the telephone
or at the field marshal's headquarters in Monte Soratte. The words
constantly jangled in the field marshal's ears:

There should be no battle in Rome . . . The plan for destruction
should be scrapped . . . Finally, still another plea: Don't permit the
Pope to be kidnapped! Weizäcker had received a new private warning
from Germany that Hitler had decided to seize the pontiff in order to
keep him out of Allied hands.

Kesselring was caught between two fires. Weizsäcker spoke rationally, but the Führer spoke fiercely. And his master's message was clear:
Don't give an inch *anywhere!* Nor did the young officers in the field
marshal's headquarters and many front-line commanders disagree.
Could he jeopardize his popularity among his men? More important,

could he jeopardize the security of the Fourteenth Army as it fled northward through Rome?

After carefully weighing all factors, Kesselring decided to support Weizsäcker. In the end, the destruction and desecration of Rome would so horrify Italy and the world that his military operations and those elsewhere as well might be gravely impeded. The Resistance would grow stronger and neutral nations such as Spain, which was strongly pro-Catholic, might turn against Germany. Even German Catholics would probably be resentful, affecting troop morale.

Kesselring was still uncertain about one point: Should he destroy Rome's historic Tiber bridges to slow up the Allied forces pursuing the Fourteenth Army? He ordered an army engineer to investigate how such destruction would affect nearby structures and utilities. The answer was that many historical sites, including St. Peter's Basilica, might suffer damage, while the gas and water conduits attached to the bridges would be destroyed. The bridges, except for one iron span, the field marshal concluded, should be saved together with the rest of Rome.

On June 2 Kesselring asked Hitler for permission to leave Rome without sabotage or battle and anxiously awaited the reply that would perhaps test the city's claim to eternity.[14]

13

The Decisions

Lt. Gen. M. W. Clark
Headquarters Fifth Army
A.P.O. 464, U.S. Army
June 1, 1944

Mother dearest,

Your V-mail of May 14th reached me in the midst of our desperate battle south of Rome. I know you have been pleased with the progress of the Fifth Army during the last three weeks. We have achieved glorious results. The fighting is severe now, but I am throwing everything in the world at him, but he is making a last-ditch stand before Rome. I pray for decisive results soon.

I am glad you gave nothing to the reporters with reference to my visit home [in April]. Again, by virtue of events of the Fifth Army, I am in the public eye, and we must be careful that I do not overdo. I have told Renie the same thing.

. . . I hope some day in the not-too-distant future I can come back and rest with you all.

Much love,
Wayne

P.S. Pal is fine and is with me all the time here in the Anzio area. He doesn't like to ride in cub planes and doesn't like the bombing either. I don't blame him.

Pal, the family cocker spaniel, was Mark Clark's link with home and with all the memories that nourished his spirit as he sat alone in his headquarters trailer in Anzio planning strategy. Things had been different when he had held lower rank. His staff officers would sometimes drop by in the evening to spin yarns or play cards. But recently he had written his wife: "The more stars a man gets, the more lonesome he becomes . . . They used to come around in the evening, but they don't any more."

Now, with Pal in his lap, Clark could look out of his trailer window at the summer flowers and, for a few moments, forget that Rome existed. Flowers had led to his marriage. He had taken Renie to his parents' home to see their superb garden—or so he had told her—and when she met his mother Renie asked almost immediately to come and help with the gardening as soon as spring began. Spring came, and so did Renie. And then, one night, in the middle of a card game, Clark suddenly asked her:

"You wouldn't think of marrying me, would you?"

"Will you say that again?" Renie replied as her cards fluttered to the floor.

He did, and she asked: "Is that to be taken in the form of a proposal?"

"It was intended as such."

Yes, he stammered, he loved her—deeply, in fact.

Well, that was better. She accepted . . .[1]

Clark's letter to his mother reflected the excitement he felt on June 1 as his troops launched an all-out attack on Rome following the breakthrough at Monte Artemisio. Only two significant barriers now stood in their way. Truscott had to take Velletri on Highway 7, which was already outflanked by the 36th Division atop the mountain, and Keyes had to capture Valmontone on Highway 6, which was still being defended strongly by the Hermann Göring Panzer Division.

One of the two American forces, it now seemed certain, would lead the way into Rome—unless Kesselring miraculously managed to hold on against both until the British Eighth Army reached Valmontone . . .

At 5:15 P.M., June 1, an American tank destroyer reached Highway 7 behind Velletri just as a German self-propelled 88-mm gun was crawling around a bend in the road. The German gunner fired two parting shots, narrowly missing the tank destroyer but killing Colonel Harold Reese and almost hitting Reese's superior—General Fred Walker.

Walker was personally leading the first troops into Velletri from the rear, and his euphoria dissolved in grief over the death of his close friend Reese, whom he had warned several times not to move ahead of the spearhead. As Walker came within sight of Velletri, snuggling white and crippled in the breast of Monte Artemisio, more enemy shells struck nearby and he and his men scrambled into a small culvert that ran under the road.

Walker's greatest worry was that they would come under attack from their own artillery. He had sent a messenger back with appropriate orders for his artillery commander—radio communications had been knocked out—but would the messenger make it safely through the enemy barrage?

"If my message to lift our artillery didn't get through," Walker quietly informed his officers as they lay in the culvert, "we are in for a barrage from our own guns in about four minutes."

The general kept glancing nervously at his wristwatch. The minutes ticked away—four, five, six. He finally crawled out of the culvert and shrugged:

"Looks like he got through in time."

Soon after 7 P.M., Walker's troops pushed into Velletri as the Germans fled toward the Eternal City through charred olive orchards before the Allies could trap them. What happened to two reserve Hermann Göring battalions that had been in the area? No one knew. Not even the German military police could find them.

While General Walker stood at the edge of the town, General Truscott drove up in his jeep and the two men exchanged smiles . . . *"And you had better get through!"* . . .

"You can go in now, General," Walker said casually. "The town is yours."[2]

Meanwhile, General Keyes attacked toward Valmontone on Highway 6, and Kesselring once more ordered the Hermann Göring Panzer Division to hold Valmontone at any cost. The field marshal knew the critical moment had come. If Keyes captured this town and, instead of heading northwest for Rome, pushed north and northeast into the hills, it could cut off the whole Tenth Army fleeing down Highway 6 and the mountain roads.

And if Truscott's men, who had already pierced the Caesar Line, also swung away from Rome and poured through the gap between the Tenth and Fourteenth Armies, it could help in the process. Then, with one army annihilated, the other—the Fourteenth—would be easy prey.

It seemed up to Clark. Would Rome so blind him, Kesselring wondered, that he would miss this extraordinary opportunity to crush two German armies? The field marshal remained optimistic. The Hermann

Göring, in any case, would have to hold at Valmontone, even though greatly outmanned.

It did.[3]

If this stalemate at Valmontone offered the British Eighth Army a final chance to at least share the big prize—Rome—its commanders seemed helpless to act. Trying to adjust to the new breakthrough situation, General Leese quickly shifted his troops and in the process produced the worst traffic jam to date. Infantry units moving in one direction collided with tank units moving in the other—while the Germans safely retreated.

Adding to British chagrin, the French, on June 2, reached Highway 6 in front of the Eighth Army at a point just south of Valmontone—as secretly planned by Clark and Juin after Alexander had refused to let the French use the stretch of highway from Ferentino to Valmontone. An advance Eighth Army infantry unit hurried forward to demand that the French get off the road, but the French commander threatened to fire if it tried to pass through his force.

When Alexander learned of the conflict he rushed to see Clark. The American supported the French position. He had to switch the French into British Eighth Army territory, he explained, because he needed the high ground there to protect Keyes's troops. And after all, he pointed out, the bulk of the Eighth Army was still far behind. Clark rather expected an argument, but Alexander responded pleasantly, even helpfully, referring to the stalemate at Valmontone:

"Wayne, if you can't do it, or if you feel that you're going to be tied down here, I'll direct the Eighth Army into Rome."

Alexander, Clark appears to have felt, had finally revealed his true intention. "Well," Clark replied testily, "you wait until I holler, because we're going to take it!"

Alexander was silent. The French were now firmly installed on Highway 6, blocking the way to the British Eighth Army. And this army was so far behind anyway, as Clark had stressed, that Alexander could no longer reasonably argue that it alone had the right to use it. Alexander took his defeat like a gentleman.

Very well, Clark's Fifth Army could head for Rome while the Eighth moved off Highway 6 onto the northern roads to chase the escaping Germans—even though the Fifth, being far ahead of the Eighth, would stand a better chance of cutting them off on these roads if it made the effort.

The two generals then drew up the text of a communiqué to be released when Rome fell, stating that "Fifth Army troops" entered Rome. No mention would be made of the British Eighth Army.

Alexander apparently chose not to inform his superiors yet of his bitter concession of defeat. At 7:20 P.M. that evening, June 2, he cabled General Wilson:

> I visited Clark today. He is confident that he can break the German front [in the Alban Hills]. His troops are fighting magnificently and I think he has a fair chance. A lot will depend on the arrival of fresh German divisions which are on their way. If Clark does not succeed within the next 48 hours we shall have to stage a combined attack by both Fifth and Eighth Armies when the latter gets up.

Alexander thus *still* clung tenaciously to the hope that Clark would, in the end, need the support of the British Eighth Army to break into Rome. But, in his cable to Wilson, he paved the way for a future explanation of the Eighth's failure:

> I saw Leese yesterday. His army is coming up well but is being seriously hampered in their advance by extensive demolitions and the extraordinarily enclosed nature of the country. I knew it would be difficult but was surprised to find it so broken and enclosed when I went over it yesterday.

Clark knew that it was too late for a miracle. He had beaten Alexander. Seldom had he felt such enormous satisfaction. Now all he had to do was beat the Germans.[4]

At about 11 P.M. that night, June 2, a patrol of the U.S. 3rd Division's 15th Infantry Regiment crept up to Highway 6 near Valmontone and dashed across the road to reconnoiter the area. The force edged through a lightly wooded area and started to cross a large clearing when it was suddenly ambushed. A hail of lead poured from enemy tanks, machine guns, and rifles, hitting the patrol from almost all sides and killing its leader instantly.

The survivors lay flat for several moments when suddenly two of them, Private Edlen Johnson, a BAR man, and Private First Class Herbert Christian, a submachine gunner, jumped up and began walking toward the enemy, motioning to the others to escape to the rear. As each of the two men headed toward an enemy machine gun, the Germans, hypnotized by such madness, momentarily forgot about the rest of the patrol.

Almost immediately, Christian was hit above the right knee by a 20-mm slug that completely severed his right leg. In the brightness of the flare-illumined sky, his comrades were sickened by the sight. Blood was gushing out of the stump, and shreds of flesh dangled from it. Instead of calling for aid, Christian, like an enraged wounded animal, hobbled forward on one knee and the bloody stump and blasted at least three Germans with his submachine gun.

Johnson raced to within five yards of a machine gun and liquidated its crew with one burst of fire. Then he reloaded his BAR and, wheeling toward the riflemen to his left, killed or wounded four of them. Struck by machine-gun bullets, he slumped forward—but managed to balance himself on his knees long enough to shoot another German before falling forward dead.

Christian crawled to within ten yards of the enemy and, after killing a German machine-pistol man, reloaded his weapon and sprayed one last burst. By now, the enemy, recovered from his shock, was concentrating fire on him. Dozens of machine-gun 20-mm, machine-pistol, and rifle bullets riddled his body before he fell dead. By this time, the remaining men in the patrol had escaped, and other 3rd Division troops had finally captured Valmontone—clearing Highway 6 for the last lap to Rome.[5]

Colonel Beelitz, Kesselring's chief of operations, excitedly informed General von Vietinghoff by phone in the afternoon of June 3:

"The enemy is advancing and is on Via Casilina [Highway 6]."

"No! . . . Where is the enemy?"

"Completely out of control!"

Kesselring's voice then came booming over Vietinghoff's phone: "I had to interrupt your telephone conversation with Beelitz because I have received more bad news from Mackensen that the enemy is very near the big city [Rome]."

"Meaning Schmalz and all are finished?"

"Not much will be left," Kesselring replied—unless Mackensen could somehow bring order to his Fourteenth Army troops, who were scurrying in panic down Highway 7 and several secondary roads toward Rome.

At one strongpoint near Lanuvio held by 130 Germans, two soldiers had persuaded their comrades to surrender, but were shot by officers who had learned of the plot. The remaining soldiers immediately killed the officers and gave up.

But Vietinghoff had problems of his own with his Tenth Army.

"Our main concern," he said, "is the road dilemma."

With Highway 6 now in Allied hands, all of his troops had to depend on the secondary mountain roads north of it to escape.

"How will we move on these roads," he groaned, "when they are continuously bombed?"

The situation seemed almost hopeless. Masses of men were tightly wedged into the narrow winding strips of mountain road. All planned time schedules had broken down and movement had to continue even in daylight, faltering spasmodically only until the smoke and dust from bombs settled over the corpses carpeting the stony routes.

Vietinghoff and Mackensen could only reflect with bitterness on their warnings to Kesselring to withdraw northward sooner when they could have moved along the major highways without great danger. Now Kesselring had become desperate. The fate of his two armies was no longer in his hands but in the hands of the Allied commanders.

Rome alone, it seemed, could save the Nazis in Italy.[6]

While the Germans fled northward, Clark read a message from Alexander's headquarters: The Polish commander in chief in London had requested that a detachment of Anders' troops take part in the triumphal entry into Rome. The Poles had, at Cassino, made the most terrible sacrifice of all, and Rome to them meant more than glory; it meant reminding the world of its debt to Poland. But Clark was ruffled. Apparently the idea had spread that there would be a formal parade into the capital.

"Please politely tell everybody, including the Swedes, if necessary," he said in a caustic message to General Gruenther, his chief of staff, "that I am not framing the tactical entrance of troops into Rome. God and the Boche are dictating that. I wouldn't know where to put everybody anyway and I concur in Alexander's idea of having a parade later, if necessary . . . So let everybody know that there will be no detachments of Greeks, Poles, Indians, or anybody else entering Rome until the formal parade is held. Also try to keep visiting firemen from running up here as soon as the capture of Rome is imminent."

But that same day, five Yugoslav officers arrived at Clark's headquarters with instructions from General Alexander that they were to tour the front. Hadn't he made himself clear to Gruenther? Clark angrily telephoned his chief of staff, but the connection was bad and Clark had to shout his message: Keep visitors away! Finally, somebody at a relay point along the line broke in and said he would pass on the message.

"All right," Clark said, "tell him that I've got five Yugoslavs here."

Hearing mumbled phrases on the line, Clark asked: "What did he say to that. What's he doing about my instructions?"

"General Gruenther," the voice answered, "says that he's a bit puzzled, but he guesses you want him to send you five Yugoslavs and he will try."

Clark yelled back: "Don't do that! I've got five I can't use now!"

He added irately: "Please make it clear to everybody that this was a most inappropriate time for them to come here. The first thing you know the claim will be that the Yugoslavs were the first to enter Rome."

Clark threw down the telephone in disgust, not realizing that the five Yugoslavs, who were standing nearby, had heard most of the conversation. They left in a huff.

Clark was now free to concentrate on taking Rome without interference from "foreigners." The "clumsy" British Eighth Army could chase the Germans through the mountains north of Valmontone. His own Fifth Army would do all its chasing through Rome. He still had one concern. Would the Germans defend Rome street by street? If they did, the city might not fall until after D-Day. He wired his commanders:

> We are now approaching Rome. Do not know if the Krauts are going to defend. It is urgently desired that private and public property in Rome not [be] damaged. Firing into Rome depends upon Krauts. If opposed, battalion commanders and higher commanders have power to eliminate same by fire and movement.

Clark sat back and contentedly watched the various units of his Fifth Army scramble along Highways 6 and 7 and subsidiary roads toward Rome, competing with each other for the coveted place in history that awaited the first man and unit in the city. His Americans couldn't lose now—unless, of course, the British or the French pulled a fast one.[7]

❖   ❖   ❖

As the Allies raced toward Rome, Pope Pius XII sat in angry splendor before the College of Cardinals on June 2 and solemnly warned the world that "whoever dared to raise a hand against Rome would be guilty of matricide in the eyes of the civilized world and in the eternal judgments of God." He charged that there were people "who scarcely dissimulate their program of violence or who openly espouse vengeance . . ."

To reduce the danger of violence and vengeance in Rome, the Pope had, the previous day, made an urgent request to the American and

British envoys to the Holy See: Send a small advance military force to the center of the city before the main one arrived and have food stocks ready to bring in immediately. Such action would demonstrate impending Allied control and administration. Otherwise, expect "Communist" disorders.*

But even if insurrection could be prevented, could street fighting between the Allies and Germans? On the morning of June 3 an Allied broadcast quoted General Wilson:

"The Allies have undertaken and will undertake military action against Rome only if the Germans use the city, its means of communications, and its streets for war purposes. If the Germans decide to defend Rome, the Allies will be compelled to take military measures to throw them out."

Even the Germans did not yet know whether they would defend Rome or whether they would destroy the city before leaving. Many public buildings, utilities, waterworks, bridges, and other installations had already been mined. More than two hundred pounds of nitroglycerine had been placed in the cellars of the telephone exchange in Palazzo del Viminale alone—enough to wreck the whole neighborhood.

Almost simultaneously with the Allied broadcast, General von Vietinghoff asked Colonel Beelitz by phone: "Nothing new on the great decision [on defending Rome]?"

"It has not yet been approved by headquarters," replied Beelitz. "The Führer himself will decide upon it. But I shall talk to Jodl again."

While waiting for Hitler's decision, Kesselring permitted the tattered remnants of Mackensen's Fourteenth Army to stream through the city toward the north. Even if the field marshal were to defend Rome, he would not need the whole army for this task. While fighting went on in the city, the bulk of the troops could form a new defense line north of it.[8]

John May, British Minister Osborne's butler, rushed to Major Sam Derry in the minister's Vatican apartment where the young officer was hiding and announced excitedly: "I've just had a message from the Vatican radio station. They are in contact with a British officer at Castel

---

* The Allies agreed to have food ready to move into Rome, but did not agree to send an advance force. At a meeting of the United States Joint Chiefs of Staff in Washington on May 30, 1944, Admiral Ernest J. King, the U.S. Navy Chief of Operations, argued that by dispatching such a force the Joint Chiefs would be mixing political with military matters and setting an unwise precedent for future military operations. Admiral William D. Leahy, chief of staff to President Roosevelt, disagreed, expressing the belief that it would be advantageous to make the friendly gesture to the Vatican, and London accepted this view in principle. But no action was taken on the proposal.

Gandolfo [eighteen miles from Rome] who wants to know if he can speak to somebody British."

"I'll deal with it," Derry said gleefully.

An operator set up some radio equipment and handed the receiver to Derry.

"Who are you?" a voice asked.

"Major Derry, First Field Regiment."

"Where the hell are you?"

"In the Vatican."

"Where did you say?"

"In the Vatican. Can I help you?"

"Yes—have you any idea what is going on in Rome?"

Derry looked out of a window and saw German vehicles and infantrymen crawling northward along Via Aurelia, which flanked the Vatican's high wall.

"The Jerries appear to be withdrawing from the city very nicely," he said.

"Is it orderly? Or are they going to do any street fighting?"

"They seem to be pulling back in an orderly manner. . . . When will you arrive?"

"Maybe tomorrow or the next day. I can't be sure. We are still pretty far ahead of our main forces."

Derry rejoiced as he put down the phone. Perhaps they would arrive before Bill Simpson and John Armstrong—who were still being held prisoner despite Pietro Koch's promise to release them—could be shot or taken north.[9]

In Via Tasso Commander De Scalzi fatalistically followed a German guard to the office of Colonel Kappler's deputy, Captain Schutz, to inform Schutz that the Resistance was holding his mistress, as well as three other German women, as hostages. Schutz stared at De Scalzi frozen-faced as the partisan officer calmly told him:

"We have four of your women in our hands. We will let them go only after you have opened the doors of this prison and liberated General Odone and the other officers you have arrested in these days. If that doesn't happen, your women will be killed, and if you arrest me now they will be killed by my friends."

As Schutz absorbed the threat in speechless dismay, the Italian continued: "My friends are awaiting my return at a precise time, and if I don't return my threat will be carried out."

Turning to leave, he said, "Goodbye," and walked out expecting to fall from a bullet in the back before he reached the street. But all he heard was the sound of his own footsteps. He was free.[10]

The same day, June 2, Kappler felt he must decide whether to honor General Wolff's pledge to the Pope to release the Socialist military leader, Giuliano Vassalli. The Gestapo chief had been stalling up to now, hoping to pressure the Vatican into letting him arrest General Bencivenga in the Seminary of San Giovanni in Laterano.

Vassalli had undergone the most horrible torture without breaking. His face was an unrecognizable mass of bloody welts and he was nearly blinded. He could barely stand after being cramped in a tiny, closetlike cell for weeks. His hands had been tied behind his back even during meals, and he had had to lap up his food from a bowl like a dog. But over and over again he repeated to the Germans:

"I am a Socialist. I fight Germans because they have invaded Italy. Do with me as you wish, but remember—I will always fight you. I have nothing more to say."

When now he saw a priest approach his cell, Vassalli's first thought was "The father-confessor—now it's come—you're going to be shot . . ."

Instead, Kappler shouted: "You are to go with Father Pfeiffer. I have received a promise that you will not leave the Salvatorian Monastery before the Allies arrive. You owe it entirely to the Pope that you leave here alive. Otherwise, you would be put against the wall and shot, as you deserve."

More dead than alive, Vassalli left with Father Pfeiffer.[11]

Michele Multedo, the painter whose life, unknown to him, General Wolff had spared because of the exhortations of the beautiful Lia T., calmly sketched each of the Gestapo men at Via Tasso. He worked slowly. He still had not got to the top commanders yet. While some Germans remained unsketched, he felt, he might be allowed to live. As he sat on the floor listening to the guns in the distance, he began to feel he might last until the Allies arrived after all.

Captain Schutz was Multedo's next model. Though the guns were growing louder and his own mistress was being held hostage by the Resistance, Schutz wanted his portrait completed. While sketching, Multedo felt a certain immunity. He could be frank.

"You tortured Montezemolo in this very room—probably while listening to Wagner," he mused.

"That's not your business!" Schutz replied.

"You have the eyes of a hyena!"

Schutz ignored the insult and sat quietly until his portrait was finally done—the last one Multedo completed before he was freed. His family had paid the guards eighty thousand lire.[12]

The fate of the other prisoners in Via Tasso, it seemed, would be less happy. Shortly after Vassalli and Multedo had been released, the "least dangerous" of them were piled in a truck to be sent, they were told, to northern Italy. Those remaining were vaguely envious, expecting immediate execution. And late that night, it appeared, the time had come.

A German officer read out the names of a group of prisoners while a secretary checked them off with a red pencil, and the men emerged from their cells and filed into the street with their hands tied behind them. SS men threw them into a truck like sacks of potatoes. But then, after some discussion, they pulled several out.

General Filippo Caruso, the *carabinieri* chief, was among these few. He was sorry. Now his suffering would be prolonged. The pain from the torture he had undergone was unbearable. He had not slept for days. When he lay down, he could not turn over, and he was barely able to stand. His ribs were fractured and his spine damaged. His left eye was blinded and his gums bled from the extraction of most of his teeth, making it impossible for him to chew food.

Yet his spirit remained unbroken. In a farewell message to his wife which he had smuggled out of prison, he wrote:

> Vidica of my heart, be strong and proud of your husband's sacrifice for his country. May the little girls grow up in the light of this great ideal which after that of God has formed the essence of all my life. Kiss them for me and give them my blessing. From Heaven where I hope to be received I will pray to the Lord for you and them . . . I embrace you tightly to my heart and I still hope that Saint Teresina will help me, too. I send you a long kiss . . .

Caruso and the others removed from the truck rejoined those prisoners, including General Odone and Carlo Salinari (leader of the Via Rasella attack), who had not yet been called and were waiting in a cell for another truck to come. After two hours a German officer leading several soldiers entered and ordered the men to stand and line up.

"It's all over," said one prisoner.

"*Viva* Italy!" shouted General Caruso, staring at each of the Germans.

The soldiers showed no reaction, but the officer walked out, avoiding Caruso's stare.

Eventually, the prisoners were permitted to sit down again and an officer explained: "Your truck has broken down and they are fixing it."

"But where will they shoot us?" asked a prisoner.

"What do you mean—shoot you?" the officer replied. "We're all going to Verona together and there Mussolini will see to everything."

Another lie, the prisoners were sure.

The sound of artillery grew still closer and the prisoners tried to calculate the distance. Probably less than three miles away. They discussed the speed of American artillery shells, the composition of the special types of steel used, the precision of the sighting instruments.

They also discussed politics. Each had fought for his own ideology, his own particular view. And now that they were about to die they realized that they were Italians above all. Communists, monarchists, republicans, leftists, rightists—all felt like brothers. They joined in singing the songs of each group, their voices tired and faint but throbbing with emotion, their eyes shining with tears. And the Germans listened silently.

The prisoners had no way of knowing that the partisans had taken several German women as hostages in a bargaining maneuver for the lives of at least some of them. Or that a group of *carabinieri* was at that moment preparing a lightning attack on Via Tasso in a desperate attempt to save them.[13]

The truck from which Caruso had been removed joined the long caravan of vehicles leaving Rome for the north and crawled less than ten miles along Via Cassia when traffic came to a complete halt. In exasperation the SS men in the truck instructed the driver to leave the main road and stop at a farmhouse nearby. The prisoners were then ordered out of the vehicle and shut in a barn, where they spent the night.

At dawn a soldier on a motorcycle drove up and spoke for a few minutes with the SS men, then continued on his way north. Several peasant women who were peering out of windows of the farmhouse observed the SS men nervously arguing with each other. The Germans dragged the prisoners out of the barn and pushed and kicked them into a little hollow. The women heard a burst of shots and saw the Germans run to their truck and resume their flight north.

Left behind in the hollow were the riddled bodies of fourteen men, including that of Socialist labor leader Bruno Buozzi; Eugenio and Enzo, the radio operators who had worked for Peter Tompkins; and Captain John Armstrong, the British prisoner of war. Armstrong had been transferred from Regina Coeli to Via Tasso just a few days earlier. He apparently had not realized that if, while in Regina Coeli, he had answered to his real name when it had been called out, Pietro Koch, who did not know his pseudonym, might have freed him.[14]

The panic reflected in the murder of the fourteen prisoners was spreading swiftly among the Germans in Rome. Up to June 3 even the highest German officials refused to concede that the Allies were about to enter the city, for Hitler had not yet agreed to withdraw. As a result, almost no preparations had been made for a retreat. Only on the morning of June 3 did Kesselring even permit the evacuation of army hospitals—prodded perhaps by threats from the Resistance that all wounded left behind would be killed.

Marianne von Weizsäcker, the German ambassador's tall, slender wife, hurried to the army hospital at Monte Mario in the new open car that the embassy had purchased only a few days earlier to deceive the Romans into thinking that the Germans meant to stay in Rome. In the chaos of evacuation, she found the head physician tending the most seriously wounded. The ambassador, she told him, requested that the house next to the hospital, which belonged to a cardinal and was being used by the nursing sisters as a dormitory, should be left in good condition. Weizsäcker was still determined to maintain good relations with the Vatican.

"To make sure the Americans get everything spick-and-span," the doctor grunted. "We are always dumbbells. I should like to see what a mess this will be afterward."

When he complained that the evacuation of wounded should have started three days sooner, Frau von Weizsäcker felt that he was thinking mainly of his own safety. And, in fact, he departed that same evening with the first available transport without bothering to inform anyone, followed by most of the other doctors and personnel. About a hundred severe casualties were left in the care of the few nuns and servants who remained.

An eighteen-year-old boy whimpered about his thickly swollen leg, which should have been amputated the previous day; now he would have to leave with the gangrene spreading. Others were being carried out to trucks with putrid bandages, which no one had time to change. Men screamed in agony; they were told not to worry, since they would soon be home.

But the roads and bridges were so jammed that the vehicles with the wounded could barely get out of Rome. Blocking the way were trucks loaded with troops and equipment, private cars, taxis, and even ox-drawn carts; and hordes of exhausted, frightened, beaten men, their uniforms ripped and filthy, their unit insignias a chaotic mixture.

All through the night of June 3 and the morning of June 4, disorganized groups of soldiers streamed northward through Rome, and gradually the Italians trickled from their homes, their faces mirroring hatred, relief, and, above all, pity. A few ran out to pour water from bottles into tin cups and cans.

But if the Germans were objects of pity, they were themselves pitiless whenever Fascist soldiers, afraid of being lynched by their own people, begged and pleaded for rides in the motley caravans. Two Fascists who tried to climb on a gun carriage in Piazza del Popolo were kicked off by German paratroops. And even a Fascist general, limping from an old war wound, was beaten when he protested the "confiscation" of his car.

Occasionally, the spectators would shout in joy—when they mistook retreating soldiers wearing Allied jackets and other abandoned enemy articles of clothing for their liberators.

Captain Erich Timm, who had led the Germans in the battle of Velletri, was wearing such a jacket as he plodded through the cobbled streets amid other soldiers he had never seen before and watched the brightening faces of the Italians lined up along the curbs. Suddenly, he saw small American flags waving in their ranks and heard the cries in English, "Welcome!" and "Hello!" He paused before one group of "welcomers" and said with an ironic smile:

"Be quiet for a little while. We're still Germans. The Americans will be coming soon."

The Italians stared at him in shock and hid their American flags. What else could one expect from the Italians, Timm thought. The Allies would bring food and other supplies. And for them, the war would be over. Rather strangely, he could understand their feeling, for he felt a sense of relief himself. The fall of Rome would symbolize the hopelessness of it all. Soon the war would be over for him, too.[15]

Among the people watching the German army disintegrate into a wretched mob was Eleanora Di Porto. The Di Portos, who had left the Convent of Notre Dame de Sion with their infant son in the wake of Fascist threats, were now hiding in separate places—she and the baby at the home of the obstetrician, and Giacomo at a Catholic uncle's.

On the afternoon of June 3 Eleanora had been shopping for food to take to her husband when, at Piazza di Venezia, she saw people lining the sidewalks as if at a parade.

"What's happening?" she asked someone.

"The Germans are leaving," was the reply. "The Americans are at the door of Rome!"

Almost dropping her precious parcels, Eleanora ran to her husband and excitedly reported the news.

"Maybe the family is safe, perhaps right here in Italy," she said hopefully. "In a few days, God willing, we will all be together again."

Giacomo did not dare tell her that he had heard a rumor from people who had escaped from German trucks on that nightmarish morning of October 16 the previous year that her whole family—eleven persons—had been deported to Germany.[16]

Eitel Möllhausen, the former German consul in Rome who had recently been transferred to Fasano, was growing more depressed each day as he languished in Foreign Minister von Ribbentrop's official residence at Fuschl. He felt his place at this moment of crisis was back in Italy with his collaborators, but Ribbentrop insisted that he remain until he had a chance to talk with him, though this chance would perhaps not come for days.

Möllhausen believed his colleagues had finally convinced Ribbentrop that the plan to set up a "Communist republic" in Rome was unfeasible. And since Möllhausen had been brought to Fuschl, ostensibly at least, to advise on this matter, there seemed little reason for him to remain any longer.

Finally, on the afternoon of June 3, Möllhausen saw an occasion to press for his return. Meeting Ribbentrop in a corridor of the ministry, he stopped him in violation of all rules of protocol and said:

"Your Excellency, Rome is about to fall. I must go back. Indeed, I hope you will lend me your plane. It is worth it as the matter is urgent."

Ribbentrop replied skeptically: "Rome is about to fall? Let's not exaggerate. It will be a long time yet before Rome falls—if it falls. Don't worry, and above all don't be defeatist. I still must talk with you. But not now; I haven't the time. I shall call you soon, perhaps tomorrow."

Möllhausen was now more bewildered than ever. What did Ribbentrop want to see him about?

That evening, June 3, he dined at a restaurant with two German officials, Karl Ritter, Ambassador for Special Assignments, and Colonel von Geldern, the liaison between the ministry and the army command. Suddenly he was called to the telephone. It was Ribbentrop.

"Listen, Möllhausen . . . in Rome . . . did you leave orders for the destruction of secret documents and codes in case of emergency?"

"Of course."

"Are you quite certain that your subordinates will obey the orders they have received?"

"Utterly certain, Your Excellency."

"But your subordinates are still in Rome?"

"They should be. Why, Your Excellency, would they not be?"

"Because they are already there. . . the others! But please tell no one!"

Stunned, Möllhausen returned to the table. His two colleagues looked at him curiously.

"Might one know," asked Ritter, "to what is owed the honor of this call?"

Möllhausen sat down slowly, paused, and said in a hushed voice: "Rome has fallen."

Geldern stuttered: "What? Who! When? I don't believe it! It must be Sonnleithner [a ministry official] who has been making it all up. Why, only this morning [Walter] Warlimont [a general on Hitler's staff] explained to me the situation of Rome. It is threatened, yes, but not seriously. We'll counterattack with divisions X and Y which are on their way down from Denmark, and this will upset the plans of the Allied K and Z divisions. Now I can show you . . ."

Geldern pulled a map from his jacket pocket with the gesture of a man unsheathing a sword. But Möllhausen interrupted. Unfortunately, he said, the situation Geldern was explaining was no longer of any interest. Ribbentrop himself had given him the news.

But the colonel would not accept the "truth." Certainly Rome could not have fallen after the assurances that the highest military authorities had given the Führer himself. He rose and left, in the hope, Möllhausen guessed, that he would soon be returning to say: "All is well. Just as I thought. Sonnleithner had been causing unnecessary alarm."

Möllhausen immediately telephoned Ambassador Rahn in Fasano. What was happening in Rome? Rahn knew nothing but said he would check with General Wolff, who had just returned from hospital treatment in Karlsbad. Rahn returned to the phone after a few moments. Wolff was also in the dark. As the ambassador was promising to put Möllhausen in contact with Kesselring, the conversation was suddenly interrupted despite Möllhausen's sharp protests.

"His Excellency the Foreign Minister is on the line," announced the switchboard operator impassively.

"Listen," said a familiar low-pitched voice, "did you tell anyone that Rome had fallen?"

"No, no one, Your Excellency."

"Good. Rome has not fallen. The Allies have entered the suburbs. But tell no one."

In the restaurant bar, Möllhausen found Geldern slumped in an armchair guzzling a whisky. Geldern had telephoned the army command and knew that, while Rome had not fallen yet, it had been written off. He looked up and said to Möllhausen:

"I can do nothing but tell the ministry what I am told myself by Warlimont, Jodl, and Keitel. Patience! By now we are used to setbacks. In any case, let us share this bottle. We shall drown our sorrow!"

Möllhausen now felt that he knew why Ribbentrop had wanted to talk with him. The Foreign Minister had supected earlier that Rome was about to fall, but, however exalted his position, he could not afford to admit the inevitable—to be a "defeatist." He had hoped to learn the true situation in a *secret* talk with Möllhausen. Möllhausen raged. Ribbentrop's fear of Hitler had jeopardized the safety of the diplomats in Rome, who could not burn papers or prepare to escape until the very last moment.[17]

Ribbentrop had apparently made his second call to Möllhausen a few hours after Kesselring, at about 4 P.M., June 3, personally briefed Hitler by phone. The field marshal contradicted other subordinates like Ribbentrop and Warlimont, who, as Möllhausen realized, found it a healthy policy to tell the Führer what he wanted to hear. The situation was hopeless, Kesselring made it clear. The Germans had to leave Rome, and he hoped he would not have to defend or destroy the city —the recommendation he had already made the day before.

According to Colonel Dollmann, the conversation was stormy. But after this talk the field marshal called General von Vietinghoff—at 4:15 P.M.—and revealed the Führer's grudging decision:

"Concerning the big city, the Führer has decided that no fighting is required within the city itself or in the surrounding area."

But though Kesselring himself had appealed for this decision, he apparently still harbored doubts about its military wisdom—or else he wanted his subordinates to think that it was not *he* who favored a retreat from Rome.

"This I regreat," he thus added, "because we shall lose valuable positions."

The field marshal then issued a memorandum on the morning of June 4, marked "For officers only," announcing: "The Führer has ordered that the city of Rome should not become a scene of battle because of its importance as a place of ancient culture . . ."

Kesselring felt that he should at least sweeten defeat with sugary artistic rationalization, the one kind of argument that could pacify even the most bloodthirsty Nazi.

Möllhausen writes in his memoirs that Hitler left it up to Kesselring to decide whether to implement the plan to destroy parts of Rome before evacuation. Ambassador Rahn, on a trip to Germany some days earlier, had influenced the Führer, Möllhausen claims, by arguing that if Rome were destroyed, the Allied troops would not suffer but the Romans would; as a result, Rahn reasoned, the growing partisan movement north of Rome would become even more dangerous.

Kesselring, in any case, ordered that only the Tiber bridges outside Rome—except for one iron bridge inside—be destroyed. Military storage dumps, supply depots, and repair shops would also be demolished.

In his talk with the field marshal on June 3, Hitler, it seems, did not bring up Ribbentrop's plan to set up a "Communist republic" or the plot against the Vatican, schemes which Kesselring opposed as threats to his military operations. But such silence did not necessarily reflect Hitler's intentions, since important SS and secret political projects were often undertaken without reference to military commanders.

The Führer's instinctive trust in Kesselring's judgment did not eliminate the danger of large-scale fighting in Rome. For he made it clear that the retreat must be a fighting one if the enemy—soldiers or partisans—tried to hinder it. Rome would be defended until the last German departed.

Fearing that the partisans would strike if they knew the Germans were about to abandon Rome, Kesselring ordered top German officers to attend the opera that night of June 3 to hide his intentions. Journalists had already been ordered to write at length on the forthcoming musical season. Even General Mälzer, the Commandant of Rome, showed up and, as usual, flirted with the women during intermission. And former Metropolitan Opera star Beniamino Gigli, performing in Verdi's *The Masked Ball*, had never been in better voice. It was a gala evening—unspoiled even by the sounds of bursting artillery, churning engines, and clopping boots that kept Rome joyously awake all night.[18]

In his conversation with Hitler, Kesselring suggested a plan he hoped might save the German Fourteenth Army retreating through Rome and, incidentally, the city itself. Hitler approved, and at about 8:30 that evening, June 3, Kesselring phoned Ambassador von Weizsäcker, who had himself proposed the plan to the field marshal much earlier. Would Weizsäcker please seek Vatican co-operation?

Two hours later, the ambassador's car zigzagged through the panicky remnants of the German Fourteenth Army to Monsignor Montini's residence, where Montini and Monsignor Tardini greeted him with nervous smiles, feeling that Rome's fate was in the balance. As the three men sat in the reception room sipping coffee, Weizsäcker spoke with thinly veiled casualness, as if this were a routine meeting.

Under the German plan, he said, both sides would agree to suspend hostilities for a limited time in a designated part of Rome. During this period, the Germans would leave the zone and the Allies would not enter until they had gone. In the interval between the departure of one and the arrival of the other, public order would be guaranteed by the Italian police. The Vatican itself would be in charge of securing food and administering the city.

The two monsignors listened grimly, obviously disappointed. Why, they inquired, should only a section of Rome—Vatican City and the German zones of retreat—be protected from battle? Such a limitation would virtually authorize the Allies to bomb the rest of the city. And in any event, the Allies would hardly agree to keep out of areas that the Germans themselves had occupied. Nor did the Vatican have the staff or means of administering Rome—an answer that would have surprised Mussolini and others who thought the Vatican would jump at the chance of extending its temporal power in the tradition of the old popes.

There was only one realistic way to negotiate the salvation of Rome at this point, the prelates concluded. Military representatives of the two sides would have to meet face to face. General Mälzer could remain behind to talk with an Allied general as the Allies entered the city. After negotiating, Mälzer would be free to leave Rome and catch up with his German comrades.

Perhaps, said the monsignors, this arrangement, made in the name of Rome, would be a good omen for future peace.

He would discuss these suggestions with the German commanders, Weizsäcker replied inscrutably. And despite his hurried air, he assured his hosts as he put down his coffee and departed that there was no real urgency. The ambassador, like his colleagues, was still reluctant to admit openly that Rome was lost and thus risk Hitler's wrath.

But within a few hours his action belied his words. At 4:30 the next morning, June 4, Montini's telephone rang, awakening him. It was Weizsäcker. The Germans, said the ambassador with controlled enthusiasm, had agreed to virtually all the Vatican suggestions.

Weizsäcker sent the final plan to Tardini at 7:30 A.M., and at 9:50 A.M. the Vatican delivered it to British Minister Osborne and American Representative Tittmann, who transmitted it to their repective capitals. The two diplomats, however, were skeptical about even this revised plan. It was a fine plan—for protecting the withdrawing German troops.[19]

Time was running out for the Germans—and for Rome. The Allies had virtually reached the city gates and the Resistance leaders threatened a bloodbath, though many were only bluffing. To frustrate their plans, Mälzer, in desperation, ordered the telephone lines cut, but had to rescind this order when he found that it caused even greater confusion among the departing Germans.

Late in the morning of June 4 Mälzer phoned Weizsäcker and in a nervous voice demanded: "What the hell am I supposed to do?"

Should he stay behind to meet the Allies or not? Nobody had given him any instructions.

He did not know yet, Weizsäcker replied. The ambassador then telephoned Kesselring. Would it not be a good idea for the field marshal personally to wire the enemy about a front-line meeting? No time remained for diplomatic intervention. The fate of the Fourteenth Army was at stake, the ambassador stressed, knowing that this argument would strike a deeper chord than the danger to Rome. He would think it over, replied Kesselring, and call back later.

The field marshal was optimistic even as Rome began slipping from his grasp. By his lights, Rome, in fact, had saved his two armies. If Clark's Fifth Army had driven northeast to join the British Eighth Army in cutting off his own Tenth Army, disaster would probably have been total, since the shattered Fourteenth Army would be unable to fight alone. But the Fifth was now chasing the Fourteenth northwestward through Rome. The Allied commanders, in their lust for the city, had split their forces as he had hoped, and both German armies had a good chance to escape and form a new defense line further north.

With his two armies separated by the Tiber River, which wound northward from Rome, the whole question now hinged, it seemed, on whether the Tenth could cross the first undestroyed bridges beyond Rome—at Orte and Orvieto—and link up with the Fourteenth before the Allies could reach them. Ironically, the Germans had blown all the bridges between Rome and Orte.

At least Kesselring would have a Fourteenth Army commander he could trust for this race. He had asked Hitler to choose between General von Mackensen and himself, and so Lieutenant General Joachim Lemelsen would replace the "insubordinate" Mackensen on June 6.

The field marshal's optimism now influenced even his most realistic staff officers, who clung to every reed of survival. When General von

Vietinghoff told Colonel Beelitz on the phone at 11:45 P.M., June 3, that "we hear the wildest rumors on the one hand and the most reassuring information on the other," Beelitz replied:

"The news is mixed. They [the enemy] have launched many attacks . . . which have been substantially repelled. So things are going pretty well in general . . . If we get through the night without trouble, things ought to go all right."

And the next morning, June 4, even after Weizsäcker's urgent call, Kesselring still thought that "things ought to go all right."

But not Weizsäcker, as he drove through the crowded streets in his new limousine and gazed in agony upon the mobs of silent, bitter men stumbling northward in pathetic disorder. He could see the death of Germany in their faces.[20]

"Elephant!"

The BBC announced this word repeatedly on the morning of June 2. It was a word that sent waves of excitement through most of the partisans; it meant "be ready to act!" But their leaders were less excited, for the Allies had already told them that they desired no insurrection; that the Roman partisans would never, in fact, be ordered to act—except to prevent the fleeing Germans from sabotaging bridges and other installations that would be valuable to the Allied forces.

Or to keep the leftists from taking over the city and perhaps proclaiming a Marxist republic.

The Allies, ironically, still depended in large degree on Communist leader Palmiro Togliatti, now in Naples, to keep the leftists in check, and he obligingly sent a last-minute message to his military representatives in Rome that no party members were to attack without the party's express authority. In many cases, word, however, never reached the small, far-flung groups operating in and around the city. And even Rosario Bentivegna and Carla Capponi, on returning to Rome from the Palestrina hills, expectantly awaited orders to attack.

Leaders of the Action party, on the other hand, were still split on the question, and some members were determined to strike whatever the decision.

The undisciplined Red Flag party, it appeared, could not be controlled. True, its top leader, Antonio Poce, had finally been pressured by the Allies, General Bencivenga, and Communist party leaders to issue a circular to his officers stating that "the behavior of the [Red Flag] movement's members must be such as to avoid wherever possible situations [open fighting] in which the population is placed in serious danger."

But Poce added, to give his subordinates authority to act on their own: "Where they do occur, intervene in a most determined manner, attempting to involve with you all those who are able to fight, appropriating weapons also wherever they might be."

Poce also warned that "for as long as the present state of tension lasts all comrades belonging to the [Red Flag] Movement are to consider themselves mobilized. Those who do not respond to the call, whatever their excuse, will be considered unworthy of belonging to the ranks of Communism and will be judged by special disciplinary councils."

Many Red Flag leaders, including such activists as Orfeo Mucci, saw in these words a loophole for revolution. They were ready to risk civil war to plant the seeds of a Communist state before the Allies arrived.[21]

General Bencivenga, on the morning of June 4, was lying in bed in the San Giovanni seminary compound, his leg still not entirely healed, when Ugo Musco burst in with news that the Allies had just requested by radio that he, Musco, meet advance troops that afternoon south of Rome to co-ordinate military and partisan activities.

Almost at that moment, a great blast shook the room and a window shattered. The Germans had fired a parting shell, barely missing the room.

Kappler still did not realize that Bencivenga's mobilization order was mainly intended to prevent the very Communist chaos he, Kappler, so dreaded—prevent it even at the risk of civil war.[22]

14

The Racers

In the green countryside within the acute angle formed by Highways 6 and 7, the air was electric as Allied soldiers raced the final lap to the magnetic apex—Rome.

Speeding past stalled and charred German vehicles, past twisted bodies shrouded in dust, past raggedly dressed Italian refugees weighted down with their pitiful belongings, the troops were oblivious of death, scornful of life. War had become a macabre game, the more exhilarating for the lack of rules, control, or firm opposition.

A refugee child kicked viciously at a German corpse while his mother pulled off the dead man's boots. A reporter, Eric Sevareid, of the Columbia Broadcasting System, ran blindly down the road, his eyes watering, his nostrils inflamed, his throat clogged with vomit from the terrible stench of human flesh decomposing under the hot summer sun. And Americans who had jumped from their vehicles during an enemy rear-guard barrage and were hugging the dry, scrubby earth exuberantly shouted questions to each other about the progress of the race.

The progress was spasmodic, often slowed by clusters of retreating German troops. A German staff car erroneously joined one American tank column and, while the driver frantically honked his horn, an officer rose in the front seat and waved angrily at the tanks, shouting with guttural authority for them to make way. He was still shouting while being hauled off to the rear.

One German emerged from a side road pulling a cart crammed with chocolate bars, probably looted from his post exchange. When he was stopped and relieved of his treasure, he sat down on the roadside and wept. Other Germans, lost to reality as they slouched along, simply ignored the Allied armored columns grinding past them.

General Keyes's II Corps, surging up Highway 6, had the advantage over General Truscott's VI Corps, blasting along Highway 7. For though Highway 7 was the shorter route to Rome, it wound through rugged, easily defended hills before reaching the Roman plain, while Highway 6 was relatively flat almost all the way from Valmontone.

That was why Highway 6, the venerable Via Casilina, had seen far more military traffic in its twenty-five centuries. Roman legions had done battle with the Samnites along this road in the fourth century B.C. Hannibal had used it in his unsuccessful assault on Rome some hundred years later. And Belisarius had stormed over it when he became the first conqueror of Rome from the south in the sixth century A.D.

On the other hand, Highway 7, the fabled Appian Way, was the ceremonious route of Roman heroes returning from battle in gilded chariots. It was too difficult a path for most invaders. Built more than two thousand years ago by slaves of the blind censor Appius Claudius Caecus, it was, in a sense, a road of peace. Ancient clans lined it with their tombs. St. Paul was greeted by his comrades at an Appian inn after surviving a shipwreck on the shores of Malta. And St. Peter, who had fled Rome to escape persecution by the Emperor Nero, turned back to suffer a martyr's fate after Christ appeared before him on this road; he had asked Christ: "*Domini, quo vadis?*" and Christ had replied: "To Rome, to be crucified again."

In addition to Highways 6 and 7, three other less important but relatively good roads were being used in the race for Rome: Via Prenestina running between those two highways; Highway 5 linking Tivoli and Rome; and Via Tuscolana connecting Frascati with Rome.[1]

The race was not simply between the two American army corps. Individual divisions, regiments, battalions, companies, and even platoons were also struggling to beat each other into Rome, barreling along every road and pathway. New York *Times* Correspondent Herbert L. Matthews overheard two platoon leaders on a walkie-talkie:

"We are on the way to Rome. We'll see you there."

"Damn you, we'll beat you there. Have your reporters ready."

In Keyes's II Corps, a unit of 3rd Division troops, which had been waiting on trucks for days to sprint into Rome, sped down Highway 6, head to head with an 88th Division reconnaissance patrol racing along Via Prenestina. An 85th Division force churned cross-country and threatened to cut in front of Truscott's VI Corps troops on Highway 7 —to Truscott's great annoyance. If the 85th succeeded in this maneuver, Keyes would almost certainly win, since his men would be leading the way along both major highways.

Colonel Hamilton Howze's task force (which had cleared the path to Artena several days earlier and might have gone all the way to Valmontone in the first thrust if Howze's tank had not developed engine trouble) stormed out in front on Highway 6. Howze, whose armor was now attached to the 1st Special Service Force, was still an angry man. He felt that he could long since have been first in Rome if Clark, instead of splitting the Anzio force at Cisterna, had sent the whole force to Valmontone. But he was still determined to be first in the Eternal City.

Howze soon faced new frustration when an officer drove up with an order transferring one of Howze's tank battalions to the 88th Division. As a result, the transferred battalion, no longer under Howze's orders, competed with his remaining force for road space, creating a traffic jam that stopped all movement on Highway 6.

General Keyes flew over the scene in a small plane and radioed a message: "Howze—get these tanks moving!"

Disgusted, Howze went to find the commander of the detached battalion, Colonel Glenn Rogers, a good friend. Howze would certainly get to Rome first. Didn't Rogers want to share this honor? Besides, weren't they old buddies? Rogers reflected for a moment, smiled, and agreed to put himself back under Howze's command—to hell with the transfer order. Howze then moved the battalion onto another road and the race resumed.

Howze was still dissatisfied with his speed. His tanks, which were meeting considerable rear-guard opposition, lost time by sizing up each bit of terrain before grinding ahead. So, though his flanks were wide open, he ordered an armored platoon to plow forward and clear the way for the rest of the force. When he saw that every several minutes the lead tank would burst into flame, Howze found himself in a painful dilemma.

"It was difficult and unpleasant to dispatch an element on what amounted to a suicide mission," he later wrote in a report, "but on the other hand such a maneuver frequently resulted in our gaining one or two thousand yards in ten minutes, at the cost of a single tank."

He added: "I hated to see the dead men, but I think nevertheless that the system paid off."[2]

Whatever human sacrifices were being made in the name of Rome, Keyes still feared Truscott would beat him there. He thus organized an elite patrol of sixty men in eighteen jeeps, representing every II Corps unit. Keyes's single, crisply given order: "Get into Rome in any way possible!" The patrol was to post blue-colored II Corps signs along the main streets and squares ("Follow the blue to speedy II"). And to make sure the world knew who got to Rome first, a movie cameramen, two still photographers, and a newspaperman would go along.

Selected to command this patrol was Captain Taylor Radcliffe of the 1st Special Service Force, who had a reputation for courage and ingenuity. Two months earlier the Germans had captured him, but though they beat him savagely with a rubber hose, he refused to answer questions. When an Allied shell hit the house in which he was being held, he escaped and made his way back to the Allied lines.

Radcliffe's patrol, starting well to the rear of the various spearheads converging on Rome, was to streak ahead on Via Tuscolana and join up with one of them, the Ellis Task Force, until it was time to break out in front. The patrol set out and eventually passed a convoy of tanks and troops that had been held up by concentrated sniper fire. As Radcliffe, in the lead jeep, raced past the lead tank, he noticed a bewildered expression on the commander's face.

The patrol then ran into new fire from cannons and machine guns, and the lead tank of the convoy it had passed came up and helped to knock out the defenders. The captain in that tank, still bewildered, then shouted at Radcliffe:

"What in hell are you doing here? Are you crazy or are you lost?"

He was trying, replied Radcliffe, to catch up with the Ellis Task Force.

"Hell, man," the tank commander exclaimed, "that's me!"

Radcliffe had been leading the task force for several miles without knowing it. He zoomed forward toward Rome.[3]

Despite the advantages enjoyed by Keyes's II Corps, Truscott was not prepared to concede that Keyes would beat his VI Corps into Rome. He made this clear to Michael Chinigo, a correspondent of the International News Service attached to the VI Corps, when Chinigo returned at about 11 P.M., June 3, to Truscott's command post from a press conference called by Keyes.

Keyes had announced that his II Corps would march into Rome the following morning and that Clark would join in the triumphal entry. Chinigo was about to pack up to join Keyes's troops when Truscott growled:

"If you want to be the first reporter in Rome, you better stay here, since my men are going to be the first to enter."

Chinigo elected to stay.

Truscott felt that General Harmon's 1st Armored Division represented his best chance for winning the race and relentlessly prodded it along Highway 7. But General Walker, whose troops were pushing down the northern slopes of the Alban Hills toward that highway, had other ideas. His 36th Division had opened the way to Rome; *it* deserved to enter the city first. He would show Mark Clark—even if Clark was still determined to deprive his division of the glory it deserved . . .

After the magnificent operation at Monte Artemisio and Velletri, Clark had finally come to Walker, all smiles, and said: "I am going to see to it that you and the 36th Division get credit for this in the newspapers back home. You have done a marvelous job."

Walker was overjoyed. At last Clark had been forced to recognize his worth. To avoid wasting time, he sent for Wick Fowler of the Dallas *Morning News*, told him what Clark had said, and let him use a reconnaissance plane to get his story back to Fifth Army headquarters for censorship. When Fowler shortly returned, Walker asked him if he had sent his story off promptly.

"No, General," Fowler replied. "By the time I arrived at Army headquarters, Clark had changed his mind, and my story did not get by the censor."

Walker was outraged. Clark had "lied." He was trying to take credit for Walker's military masterpiece. What could Clark say if the 36th got to Rome first? . . .

As his troops, after sporadic fighting, emerged from the mountains and were about to swing onto Highway 7, Walker met Colonel Hightower of the 1st Armored Division who had just arrived at this point, leading a column of tanks. The 1st Armored had the right of way on Highway 7, the colonel insisted. The 36th could follow. His eyes reflecting cold contempt, Walker imperiously placed his hands on his hips. Since when did a colonel give orders to a general? The 36th would *not* follow—though Walker knew very well that Hightower's orders were valid. The 36th would take the right half of the road and the 1st Armored could take the left. Hightower was furious but, outranked, reluctantly agreed.

As the two forces moved toward Rome side by side, they nearly pushed each other off the road, and the confusion compounded when the 85th Division, sent by General Keyes, threatened to cut in front of both of them. If it could do this, Keyes's men would be leading the way on both major highways—6 *and* 7. Truscott's chief of staff urgently telephoned Keyes's chief of staff: If Keyes's troops tried to cross *Truscott's* highway they might be greeted with gunfire.

Truscott then personally drove to the head of the VI Corps forces that chaos had brought to a halt on Highway 7.

"Fred," he gruffly asked Walker, "what are you doing outside your sector boundary?"

Walker had no reply. He had deliberately disobeyed orders so that his troops might reach Rome more swiftly. With bitter resignation, he moved his column north and advanced toward Rome along a secondary road.

Truscott turned to Colonel Hightower and asked if he knew what his orders were. Hightower replied that he was to secure the bridges over the Tiber.

"Well, Colonel, what are you waiting for?" Truscott rasped.

As Colonel Hightower's tanks roared off down Highway 7, Truscott told Mike Chinigo, who had accompanied him: "Mike, if you still want to be the first correspondent in Rome, you had better follow that leading tank."

General Harmon, the 1st Armored Division commander, joined Truscott and as the two generals straightened out the folds of a war map, a machine gun suddenly cut loose from a stone outhouse in the fields. A Sherman tank immediately smashed into the privy, and the two generals, who had thrown themselves to the ground, rose with somewhat injured dignity. With glory so near, they had barely missed going down in history as the victims of a "shithouse" sniper.[4]

While the Americans competed among themselves for eternal glory, the French had by no means dropped out of the race—though they knew they could only win surreptitiously since General Juin could not appear to betray Clark.

Captain Pierre Planès, in particular, was no man to be thwarted by formality. Most French forces were swinging toward Rome in a wide arc via the mountains to the east, but Planès' armor sped over Highway 6, challenging every American unit in sight. Orders or no orders, he, too, was determined to be the first in Rome. About fifteen miles from the city, however, the traffic congestion brought him to a complete halt.

He ordered his force to swerve off the highway and it continued on toward Rome along a dirt side road. At dawn, June 4, within a few miles of Rome, it was forced to stop again, this time by three American planes, which swooped down with guns blazing. As his men scrambled from their vehicles and dived behind roadside trees, Planès shook his fist at the sky and screamed:

"Ah, les cochons, les salauds!"

Since his vehicles were clearly marked, he was convinced that the planes—which also attacked advance *American* units on the roads to Rome, mistaking them for Germans—had deliberately tried to prevent him from beating the Americans into Rome.

He was now more determined than ever to beat them.[5]

Captain Taylor Radcliffe of the 1st Special Service Force awakened before dawn, June 4, in a movie studio on the outskirts of Rome. He and his sixty men of the II Corps, handpicked by General Keyes, had stayed the night in the Italian "Hollywood." It had been too dangerous to race through Rome's twisting, unfamiliar streets after dark. Hardly had one of his men informed him of the approach of another task force, accompanied by jeeploads of correspondents, when his own patrol was off again down Via Tuscolana.

With the first glimmer of daylight, Radcliffe, in the lead jeep, saw before him an overpass that led directly into Rome proper. He suspected that it was mined for demolition. As the overpass drew closer Radcliffe waited expectantly for the explosion that would deprive him of a unique place in history, if not, incidentally, of his life.

The patrol halted just before crossing and sappers cut the wires on demolition charges that had indeed been laid. Then, bolting across, the force passed through Porta San Giovanni and found itself in Rome. Radcliffe glanced at his watch—6 A.M., June 4. His cameramen had barely starting snapping pictures of this historic moment when the patrol came under heavy fire that forced it back across the overpass and tied it down all day.

Not exactly a triumphant entry, but, apparently, Radcliffe was the first Allied soldier to set foot in Rome.[6]

Twenty-five minutes later, at 6:25 A.M., another officer of the 1st Special Service Force led a regular patrol of that force into the railroad yards of Pietralata, inside Rome, though it, too, was forced by machine-gun fire to retreat swiftly. This patrol was part of a spearhead consisting of 1st Special Service Force units mounted on tanks of Task Force Howze—the competition that had worried Radcliffe.

Colonel Howze, who had personally led the pack down Highway 6, pushing his tanks forward at whatever cost, ironically was not with this spearhead at the moment of destiny. Major General Robert T. Frederick, the commander of the 1st Special Service Force to which Task Force Howze was temporarily attached, had sent his own men ahead with Howze's tanks—but without Howze, who was left behind in the suburbs to await further orders. After all, Howze was simply on loan from the 1st Armored Division. There was no point muddying the waters of glory.

In the next two or three hours a number of other units poked across the city limits, though not into Rome proper. Patrols of the 88th, the 3rd, and the 1st Armored Divisions all claimed to have entered between 8 and 9 A.M. In the confusion, word was sent to Generals Marshall and Eisenhower that the 88th had arrived first. Radcliffe's feat had apparently not yet been reported.[7]

Major Sam Derry rose before dawn on June 4 in the Vatican hospice housing the British Legation, brimming with excitement at the likelihood that this would be the day of liberation. He dressed quickly and joined Minister Osborne and other members of the Legation at a large window overlooking Rome. All eyes focused on the wide road along which so many thousands of Germans had fled northward in the past few days. Now the road—indeed, it seemed, the whole city—was utterly deserted.

They waited tensely, silently, their reflections a mixture of agonized memory and joyous anticipation. Suddenly a blur of dots, like ants crawling out of the horizon, materialized in the distance. As Derry and his colleagues strained their eyes to see if the moment had finally come, the tension burst. Ecstatic cheers echoed through the building as normally cool, dignified diplomats, officers, and clergymen clapped, shook hands, laughed wildly, and slapped each other on the back in an orgy of glee.

The "Americans" had arrived! . . .[8]

Unreported, and perhaps unknown, to the Allied command, Captain Pierre Planès' French tank destroyer unit entered Rome at about 9 A.M., June 4, and was apparently the first Allied force to reach the heart of the city and the one, it seems, spotted by Derry and his companions. Leaving his armored vehicles outside the city limits on the dirt road he had taken, Planès led a procession of jeeps past the Vatican and through the eerily deserted cobbled alleys of old Rome. Almost every window was shuttered, but through the slits of each green panel, it seemed, a pair of eyes watched. Apparently the Romans thought the patrol was a German one.

The jeeps finally emerged into the frightening openness of Piazza di Venezia where once crowds had gathered to enjoy Mussolini's theatrics on the balcony of his Fascist empire. Now, in this pause of fear and expectancy, the *piazza* was lifeless. The whole city, it seemed, had been struck dead a thousand years before. And there, vulgarly symbolizing its "demise," stood the pretentious Victor Emmanuel II monument with its great white "typewriter" columns.

Planès blew his obstructed nose, dabbed at it delicately with his handkerchief, and gave the order for his force to turn around and return by the same route to the position outside Rome where his tanks would be waiting.

On arriving shortly after noon, Planès was informed by the officer left in command of the tanks that General Monsabert, the commander of the 3rd Algerian Division, had come and was furious on learning that Planès, whose unit belonged to that division, had entered Rome without orders.

"He wants to see you immediately, Captain," said the officer.

Planès, his joy suddenly evaporated, drove to Monsabert's headquarters. He was nervous and uncomfortable as he saluted the frowning general.

"Planès," barked Monsabert, "you deserve sixty days in prison."

What, after all, would Clark say?

Planès stared silently at the ground.

The general then walked up and embraced him, kissing both cheeks.

"You also deserve my embrace," he said, smiling under his white mustache.

Yes, what the hell *would* Clark say?[9]

At about that time, General Frederick of the 1st Special Service Force was standing on Highway 6 watching a battle in progress when General Keyes drew up in a jeep, descended, and asked:

"General Frederick, what's holding you up here?"

"The Germans, sir," Frederick replied succinctly.

"How long will it take you to get across the city limits?"

"The rest of the day. There are a couple of SP [self-propelled] guns up there."

"That will not do. General Clark must be across the city limits by four o'clock."

"Why?"

"Because he has to have a photograph taken."

Frederick stared at Keyes, apparently wondering if he was serious, and replied: "Tell the general to give me an hour."

A few minutes later, Clark arrived by jeep from his headquarters in Anzio via Valmontone. Together the three generals would make their triumphant entry into Rome behind the force chosen to strike first to its heart—the 1st Special Service troops supported by Colonel Howze's armor (but without Colonel Howze). And the whole press corps had been invited along to record every glorious detail of this momentous event.

The newsmen had felt like conquering heroes that morning as they raced down the highway in several jeeps, greeted, the closer they got to Rome, by more and more Italians willing to leave their homes despite sporadic fire to throw flowers and kisses and scream, "*Viva Americani!*" The reporters whipped past infantry and tanks and past columns of Germans being marched back by their captors. As a blue and white sign crying "ROMA" loomed ahead, nothing seemed to stand between the press and Rome but an armored scout car some distance in front.

In one jeep, Dan De Luce of the Associated Press cautiously suggested to the driver: "Let's stay close to it for protection."

His competitor, Reynolds Packard of the United Press, grunted, "Let's not. It's a Kraut!"

The line of press jeeps, which was inadvertently spearheading the Fifth Army, screeched to a halt, nearly telescoping, and the reporters leaped into ditches along the road—almost simultaneously with the frightened occupants of the *German* armored car!

When De Luce had then bravely approached these Germans and taken them prisoner, allied tanks moved ahead. But as the tank in the lead chugged past the sign announcing the city limits of Rome—at 7:15 A.M.—it burst into flame, struck by a German shell. A machine gun immediately began firing from the flank next to a white church whose bells were ringing for early mass. The Allies on Highway 6 had thus ground to a halt as guns of the Hermann Göring Armored Division peppered the area.

General Frederick told Clark that he was reluctant to use artillery himself for fear of hitting civilian homes in this heavily built-up area. His men, however battle-hardened, were not eager to turn Rome into a cemetery, especially after sharing with the Italians moments of tenderness as well as terror . . .

There had been the woman who kept running out to pour wine for them; the youth who smiled and waved as he rode his rickety bicycle down the road; the man who crouched behind a soldier firing a bazooka, like an umpire behind a batter, waiting expectantly for the missile to strike the target for a deadly home run; the young couple who got married . . .

Casually, aloofly, the wedding party, eight young people in rows of two, had sauntered up the road from the little white church during a lull in the fighting. The groom wore polished shoes and a neat blue suit, and the bride, who clung to his arm, a gray suit adorned with a bright nosegay. He carried a pair of yellow gloves, she a bouquet of roses and green leaves.

Onward they strode through the no-man's land separating the two armies, like ghosts untouched by the carnage of war, immune to the threat of guns pointed in their direction. They walked past the big blue and white ROMA sign and seemed not to see the figures sprawled in the ditches, who watched them with startled, wistful looks. Slowing up when they came to a pile of German dead blocking the road, the couples held hands, tiptoed around, and continued on.

Then firing broke out again, and the scene, like an apparition, dissolved in a haze of dust . . .

Clark knew that he had come up against the central problem of capturing Rome: to take it without destroying it or its people. Were his men facing only rear-guard action to permit the Germans to escape through Rome to the north? Or would they have to fight for every house and street? In any event, there was no time to lose, civilian casualties or not.

"I wouldn't hold up too long," Clark told Frederick. "We've got to get in there."

Photographers then suggested that the three generals pose in front of the ROMA sign, which stood a short distance away at the top of an incline, and, when firing in the vicinity died down, they obligingly crawled to it through a ditch. On arriving, they stood up and, when the photographers had finished taking their historic pictures, Clark remarked to Frederick;

"Golly, Bob—I'd like to have that sign in my command post."

At that moment, sniper bullets whizzed by, one of them piercing the sign inches from Clark. The generals hit the ground, and as they crawled back through the ditch to safety, Frederick breathlessly explained to Clark:

"*That* is what's holding up the 1st Special Service Force!"

Later, when Clark was convinced that he could not feasibly drive into Rome until the following day, he flew back to his command post in his Piper Cub, which had been standing by for him. Frederick then ordered one of his men to take down the sign, which he would present to Clark as a perpetual reminder of his honored niche in history.

But why, Frederick asked Keyes, was Clark so impatient.

"Well," Keyes replied, "France is going to be invaded from England the day after tomorrow and we've got to get this in the paper before then."[10]

❖ ❖ ❖

The prisoners remaining in Via Tasso were asleep on the crowded floor of their single cell when suddenly, at about 7 A.M. on that day of June 4, they were awakened by shouts outside the building. At first they were convinced that a truck had finally come to take them to their death. But then the cries grew more coherent.

"Brothers," yelled a feminine voice, "come out. You are free!"

The prisoners ran to the barred windows and peered down into the street. A crowd of women had gathered outside the entrance—their wives and sweethearts!

"The guards have fled!" one prisoner yelled.

Pandemonium broke out. Some prisoners smashed into offices and with sticks and pipes began to destroy the furniture and all other items they could find, as if hoping to avenge the horrors they had suffered with one monstrous fit of rage. They grabbed all the files and papers in the drawers, ripped some into shreds, and threw the rest out of the windows.

Others dashed downstairs and into the arms of their loved ones amid sobs and cries and embraces, showered by the "confetti" hurled from the windows by their comrades.

Colonel Kappler and the German guards had that morning joined the throngs of fleeing Nazi soldiers choking the streets that led northward out of Rome—just before a group of *carabinieri* were about to attack the prison to free the remaining prisoners. The Germans had apparently decided to leave these prisoners behind rather than kill them or take them north, at least in part, it seems, because of Commander

De Scalzi's threat to kill the four German women—including the mistress of Captain Schutz, Kappler's assistant—whom the partisans had captured as hostages. The women were released shortly afterward.

Generals Caruso and Odone, Colonel Caratti, and other military chiefs hurried to the seminary compound of San Giovanni a few blocks away to place themselves at the service of General Bencivenga. The rest started home on foot or in whatever transportation was available. Carlo Salinari, the commander at Via Rasella, climbed into a streetcar and was immediately surrounded by the other passengers, who, shocked by his skeletal, bloody condition, offered him bread and ordered the driver to continue on nonstop to Salinari's destination.[11]

At about the same time, the doorbell rang in Renzo Lucidi's flat. Lucidi and his visitor, the British escaper Lieutenant John Furman, who were discussing the possible fate of their captured colleague, Bill Simpson, froze. It was the secret signal that Pasqualino Perfetti, the traitor, had revealed to the enemy—and had long since been discarded. Was this a Gestapo trick? Had Pietro Koch betrayed Monsignor O'Flaherty after making a deal with him for the release of Simpson and Captain John Armstrong?

Lucidi and Furman listened tensely as Peppina, the maid, went to open the door. Suddenly, they heard her scream. Trapped! But a moment later, fear turned into elation. For in walked Bill Simpson, Peppina hanging joyously from his shoulders.

Simpson was among the prisoners at Regina Coeli prison who, like those in Via Tasso, found themselves unguarded that morning and free to leave. Koch had apparently come through after all. In return for O'Flaherty's promise to protect his wife and mother, he had talked the Germans into leaving Simpson, whom he knew only by his pseudonym, alive in Rome.

Otherwise, Simpson might have met the fate of Captain John Armstrong, who had been transferred to Via Tasso and then murdered with thirteen fellow prisoners on their way north. (Ignorant of Armstrong's pseudonym, O'Flaherty could not pass it on to Koch so that he could save him, too.)[12]

Colonel Kappler was followed out of town by other Nazi and Fascist leaders, who left in such a hurry that Ambassador Rahn in Fasano compared them to "rats abandoning a sinking ship."

Among the most reluctant to leave was Colonel Eugen Dollmann, who had a double attachment to Rome: the power and glory it had conferred on him and the artistic beauty it had seduced him with. Before leaving, Dollmann asked Virginia Agnelli to take his "girl friend" and secretary, Signorina Bibi (Marie Celeste Rossi), north with her. But Bibi, who had earlier been engaged to Dollmann's nephew, had become attached to Prince Francesco Ruspoli, the colonel's close friend, and since Ruspoli was staying, she decided to remain, too. (Shortly after the war, she became Ruspoli's princess.)

Escorted by his Roman chauffeur, Mario, and his Alsatian wolf-hound—Koch later said that he went along, too—the SS colonel drove up to the peak of Monte Soratte, the hill celebrated in verse by Horace and Vergil, to bid goodbye to Kesselring. As he gazed upon Rome for the last time, he recalled that the youthful Emperor Otto III, son of the Greek Empress Theophano, had died at the foot of the hill. He had also been making his way north after being driven out of Rome.

By noon, June 4, only one important German military leader remained in Rome—General Mälzer. Kesselring, who would remain at his headquarters on Monte Soratte until eight that night, had not replied to Weizsäcker's suggestion that the Germans contact the Allies directly to arrange for the unobstructed departure of all German troops. But Mälzer, thinking he might still be needed as the German contact man, informed Kesselring's headquarters that he intended to stay in Rome "as long as possible." He then proceded to drink away his fear and sorrow.[13]

Lieutenant Ottorino Borin, Peter Tompkins' spy in the open-city government, hurried into Tompkins' headquarters at eight A.M., June 4, and reported the latest rumor. Under an accord mediated by the Vatican, Kesselring had ordered Mälzer to stay and turn over the city intact to the Allies. Until now Tompkins had not heard of any plans for Rome in the period between German departure and Allied arrival and had thought of taking charge himself.

To get more information he sent Borin to Mälzer's headquarters in the Excelsior Hotel, and Borin found the place in complete confusion. Mälzer was "stinking drunk" and shouting orders to everyone around in "lamentable French." Nor could Borin find any evidence that a deal had been made or that the CLN, the Clandestine Front, or any Allied authority had taken the initiative. Well, thought Tompkins, at least now he could be useful.

In the previous weeks he had continued to wallow helplessly in frustration, still unable to re-establish radio contact with his OSS base. After the arrest of Eugenio and the seizure of his radio equipment, he had written in his diary:

To risk one's neck and go through continual nervous tension and be absolutely of no use to anyone is the most demoralizing position in the world!

Adding to his chagrin, a new Italian OSS agent who had come to town with signal plans and crystals—Tompkins still had a radio but not this equipment—turned out to be a close collaborator of Captain Bourgouin and Mino Menicanti, Tompkins' mortal foes. The new agent, Prince Raimondo Lanza di Travia, who had been aide to General Carboni, the officer charged by Badoglio with the hopeless task of defending Rome in September 1943, was, in Tompkins' eyes, a drug addict, a Fascist, and a gambler.

Tompkins was enraged when Lanza and Menicanti asked him through a contact to turn over his radio to them, even though they assured him that all transmissions would take place in the presence of them all. Tompkins not only distrusted both of them, but viewed such gatherings as an absurd breach of security. Nor would he, as an American, take orders from an Italian agent.

Tompkins therefore replied through a courier that, on the contrary, Lanza should turn over his plans and crystals to him. Lanza threw the courier out of his apartment, screaming that he'd be damned if he would turn over any plans or crystals. Menicanti then began spreading a rumor among other agents: Tompkins had been sent to Rome simply to requisition houses for the OSS!

At last, by using parts of other radios, an operator working for Tompkins managed to make contact with the base. Peter was ecstatic —until headquarters replied to his offer of military information with a two-word message: "Not interested."

He was shattered. Was the contact a phony? A German plant? After all, Borin had reported that six clandestine radio stations of the Fifth Army were being used by German counterespionage to feed the Allies false information. Or had his own people disowned him for some reason? He had so much valuable information to send. Why would they not want it? Why wouldn't they believe him?

Whatever the answer, Peter was determined to do his duty. He would take over command of Rome.

On paper headed "United States Office of Strategic Services," Tompkins wrote out official orders to General Presti, chief of all Italian police groups, and to General Chirieleison, commander of the open city, to place themselves under General Bencivenga's command and take charge of public order. They were to prevent sabotage of buildings and public utilities, arrest and intern German and Fascist deserters, and keep civilians from leaving the city. Tompkins signed these orders "OSS O.C. Rome Area," and affixed the special OSS rubber stamp he had prepared for just such an occasion.

Borin delivered the orders to the two generals. Don't worry, they promised. They would carry out the orders to the letter. Actually, General Bencivenga, who commanded the Resistance, had already issued them similar orders, and CLN chief Bonomi was to meet with Chirielei-son that day to co-ordinate plans. But apparently neither Chirieleison nor Presti bothered to tell Borin about these communications. By making Tompkins think that he alone had given orders they could better keep him to his pledge that, if they co-operated with him, they would not be prosecuted by the Allies for collaborating with the Germans.

In the afternoon Tompkins emerged into the streets and watched the final pathetic scenes of retreat—blond, blue-eyed "supermen" reduced to hawking typewriters and stolen cars along the way; an endless stream of trucks piled high with goods; broken-down automobiles often without hoods or even tires; a motorcyclist bouncing along on a flat tire.

Suddenly, three PAI policemen came up and ordered Tompkins to go home. He noted that they had taken off their "MM" (Mussolini Militia) insignia and replaced them with the army *stellette*, or five-pointed star. How ironic it would be, he thought, if they recognized him as a "deserter" from their force and arrested him under the instructions he had himself issued. He was amused to think that they were responding to his command; that Peter Tompkins, who had been the lowliest "corporal" in the police, was now, in reality, their chief.

Yes, he would personally turn Rome over to the Allies.[14]

The PAI, the Financial Police, and the *carabinieri* had been fully mobilized early in the day according to plan, even though Kappler had captured almost all their top leaders recently in a desperate effort to prevent the very insurrection the leaders themselves hoped to frustrate. These forces now guarded public buildings, utilities, and the principal streets. And while they did not attack the departing Germans, they strongly defended against Nazi efforts to confiscate police vehicles, suffering a number of casualties in pitched fights that broke out in transport centers.

Nor was the police task complicated by serious attempts at insurrection. That morning, General Alexander, in a radio message, had helped to dampen partisan ardor by proclaiming:

> Citizens of Rome, this is not the time for demonstrations. Do what we tell you and continue with your daily work. Rome is yours. Your job is to save the city . . . Ours is the destruction of the enemy.

The Communist party leaders, as directed by Togliatti, kept the lid on their fighters; the Action party failed to move because its military leader, Riccardo Bauer, refused to lead an attack as demanded by its political chiefs; the Socialist party had been too weakened by the capture of its leaders, even though the militant Giuliano Vassalli had been released from Via Tasso on the eve of liberation; and Antonio Poce of the Red Flag party had finally concluded that his men would be uselessly slaughtered—by the police and the Allies if not by the Germans—should it launch an insurrection on its own.

Poce had been under great pressure from some of his subordinates to attack the Germans regardless. One of them, Orfeo Mucci, met with him on a street corner early on June 4 and pleaded for an insurrection.

"We can trap the Germans inside the city," Mucci argued, joining the fingers of both hands at their tips to illustrate his point. "We have lost so many men already, we have risked so much. Why not a little more? Even if we shorten the war only by minutes it will be worth it. Even if we can't set up a revolutionary government, the people will know who their liberators are."

But Poce had made up his mind. He had no choice, he replied. The Allies had threatened him. Bencivenga had pleaded with him. When Rome was liberated, Poce promised, the Red Flag party could become the nucleus of a Red Army that would lead the partisan battle in the north. Poce then ordered Mucci to take his force immediately to the southeast outskirts of Rome on Highway 6 and guide Allied troops into the city. With heavy heart, Mucci gathered his men and departed.

The revolution would have to wait.

Although partisan plans for organized insurrection were thus finally abandoned, sporadic fighting broke out all over Rome as individual groups fired on the Germans and the Germans fired at anyone they thought might try to block their retreat. To the despair of many partisans, however, not nearly enough blood was spilled to wash away the stain of collaboration with Fascism and Nazism for so many brutal, shameful years.

Rome was still Rome.[15]

While Orfeo Mucci went to greet the Americans on Highway 6, Ugo Musco, the Centro X chief and adviser to General Bencivenga, raced through Rome toward the Highway 7 approach as the Allies had instructed by radio. Still dazed from the shelling of Bencivenga's quarters in the San Giovanni seminary compound, he was further shaken when a group of Germans started firing at the several speeding jeeps in his party, which were being escorted by the now openly pro-Allied police. Musco jumped out of the lead jeep, followed by his comrades, and, as they lay on the street, shot it out for ten minutes with the Germans.

The Nazis finally fled and Musco's party continued on to a point several miles outside of Rome—near the place where Musco had met an American detachment on the morning of the Anzio landing when it also appeared that the Allies would soon be in Rome. Now, at 3:45 P.M., June 4, he met another group. Climbing out of his jeep, the pistol he had fired at the Germans still in his hand, he called out: "Elephant!"

An American officer in the first jeep replied with a smile: "Elephant!"

"Welcome to Rome," said Musco with deep emotion. "*Viva Italia! Viva* America!"[16]

❖ ❖ ❖

At approximately the same time, a single jeep streaked down Highway 7 toward Rome and sneaked past American MP's trying to clear the way for tank-led U.S forces. The jeep followed a Sherman tank to a bridge leading into Rome proper, then passed it and scurried across to be swallowed by a wild crowd in Piazza San Giovanni, the giant square overlooked by the seminary compound still sheltering General Bencivenga and many political leaders.

The Romans had finally summoned the courage to come out and celebrate their liberation. Young girls and bearded men embraced, kissed, almost smothered the men in the jeep, while someone attached an Italian flag to the hood and others threw flowers and waved tiny American flags.

"*Viva* America!" the welcomers shouted.

"But we're not American!" said one of the happy passengers in bad Italian.

Suddenly silence. Not more Germans!

"We're French."

The silence cracked like ice.

"*Viva la France!*"

The leader of the three men in the jeep was Major François de Panafieu whom General Juin had sent into Rome on a special mission. General de Gaulle, determined that history would not forget France on this memorable day, had ordered Juin to deliver by any means possible a personal letter he had written to the Pope before the other Allies could contact him.

De Gaulle had an additional reason for rushing to the Pope. The Vatican had excellent relations with the pro-Nazi Vichy government, which regarded the Church with far greater awe than had the previous leftist governments of France. De Gaulle now wanted to assure the Pope that he was a true and devoted son of the Church, hoping that His Holiness would switch at least his moral support to him.

"We're heading for the Vatican," Panafieu told one ecstatic young Italian. "Will you show us the way?"

Without hesitation, the youth climbed in, his rear protruding over the side of the vehicle, which then lurched forward through the throbbing wall of humanity. As it slowly advanced, Panafieu saw people at every window shouting and applauding, though they stayed behind their balconies, still apprehensive lest the Germans start firing.

Turning a corner, the Frenchmen found themselves face to face with a group of German soldiers. The vehicle trembled to a halt and Panafieu stood up and fired his rifle. A German fell, apparently dead. The jeep spurted through a hail of fire, then shook along on flat tires to the home of the young Italian guide, where the Frenchmen decided to remain until the danger diminished.

As the boy descended, he said, holding his buttocks: "Major, I'm wounded."

"Stop joking," Panafieu grinned. "You Italians have a great sense of humor."

But as the youth limped into his house, the Frenchman realized that he had, in fact, been hit—in the *derrière*. The young man's family embraced the visitors and soon all the neighbors in the building had crowded into the small apartment, grabbing at them and joyously serving wine. The young host, after being bandaged by his wife, joined the crowd dressed only in his shorts and proudly showed off his wound.

The Frenchmen stayed the night with an Italian nobleman Panafieu knew, and early the next morning French Cardinal Tisserant agreed to deliver De Gaulle's message to the Pope immediately.

Panafieu was to receive the Croix de Guerre later for risking his life to make sure that the Pope—and history—knew that the French were among the first to liberate Rome.[17]

As General Truscott had advised, Michael Chinigo of the International News Service followed in his jeep the lead tank of the 1st Armored Division spearhead barreling down Highway 7 to the outskirts of Rome. Suddenly, Chinigo relates, he saw a German soldier setting up a machine gun behind a bush. He ordered his driver to halt, jumped out and, waving a submachine gun, ran toward the man, shouting in German:

"Don't shoot! The war is over! Come with me and you will be safe!"

The German immediately raised his hands and meekly climbed into the rear of the jeep. By this time the tank had disappeared, but Chinigo instructed his driver to whip into Rome regardless.

Chinigo was not at all surprised by his capture of the prisoner. Though a thirty-six-year-old correspondent and not a soldier, few soldiers in the U.S. Army had taken more prisoners . . .

It had all started in Sicily where Chinigo became convinced that the Italians would surrender if given the opportunity. While an American battalion was firing on one Sicilian village, Chinigo says, he asked the commander to order a cease-fire, then calmly walked into the village waving a white handkerchief. Italian civilians took him to an Italian officer and, in excellent Italian, the American persuaded the enemy to give up. In two days Chinigo worked the same miracle in other villages, leading dozens of prisoners into the Allied lines.

Finally, General Truscott, who was then commander of the 3rd Division, asked to see the civilian who had performed this extraordinary, if entirely unauthorized, feat. Truscott admonished him roughly in his headquarters tent:

"I won't permit you to fight your own war. I don't happen to like newspaper people anyway."

Chinigo says he replied that he was trying to get assigned to another division anyway since Truscott's men were "lousy soldiers."

Truscott burst into laughter and ordered food and drink, and Chinigo thereupon moved in with the general. He was even permitted to send dispatches via official channels. This privilege guaranteed him a beat on all other reporters, though sometimes his colorful copy would be changed at Allied headquarters in Algiers to read like a dry army communiqué—to the despair of his office.

Against orders Chinigo entered Palermo with the first U.S. troops, appeasing the angry brass with a new catch—two truckloads of Italians whom he had simply flagged down. He then helped in the capture of Messina by talking an Italian commander into surrender—he gallantly refused to accept the commander's weapon—and turning him over personally to General Patton! He was awarded the Silver Star.

Shortly before the Anzio landing, Chinigo asked himself: Why not Rome? Once the troops were ashore, he could infiltrate into Rome with some tanks and take the city. Would Truscott agree? According to Chinigo, the general did. But Clark apparently heard about the deal, and as Chinigo was about to board a landing craft in Naples to take part in the landing, military police arrested him. He finally arrived at the beachhead a week later in a plane provided by Truscott, who explained to him on arrival:

"Clark disapproved of your plan. He said it was too dangerous and foolhardy, and that this is no Hollywood war." . . .

But now that the Allies were finally going into Rome, Chinigo would still be, he was determined, the first reporter in the city. And he apparently *was* the first—bursting into Rome shortly after 4 P.M., June 4.

"Head for the Plaza Hotel on Corso Umberto Primo," he ordered his driver, referring to the hotel where the Allied correspondents were to be housed. The jeep sped through what seemed to be a deserted city, passing the Colosseum and the Forum, and then crossing Piazza di Venezia into Corso Umberto Primo, where it was suddenly blocked by a streetful of people—German soldiers in retreat.

Barely slowing down, the vehicle wove its way through their dazed ranks; not a German appeared to notice, or to care, that the enemy had overtaken them. Nor did the docile German prisoner in the back seat utter a word.

When the jeep finally arrived at the Plaza Hotel, Chinigo walked to the entrance and, finding it locked, knocked on the glass door. A clerk inside waved his forefinger: Chinigo could not enter. The newsman pointed to the American insignia on his cap and silently mouthed the word: "*Americano!*"

With a startled look, the clerk motioned the visitor to go to the rear of the hotel. Within minutes, Chinigo, his submachine gun cradled in his arm, entered through the back door, informed the clerk that the hotel would be Allied press headquarters, signed the hotel register, and reserved the royal suite for himself and his "entourage."

Chinigo had one problem—the prisoner. He could not turn him over to the American forces since they had still not entered the city, at least this sector.

"Find an Italian policeman," he ordered the clerk.

But none could be found. The streets were still deserted, except for clusters of Germans in retreat. After temporarily housing the prisoner in a room of the royal suite, Chinigo decided to look for a policeman himself.

Back in the jeep with the driver and the German, he stopped off at a police station near Via Veneto and asked the policeman on duty to kindly keep the German for the night. But the Italian, fearing involvement in a war between foreigners, politely refused. Chinigo returned to the jeep and continued on, determined to find *someone* who would take the prisoner.

As he passed the Excelsior Hotel, the sudden realization that it was German headquarters stirred his journalistic instincts. He ordered the driver to stop at the entrance, and casually walked in past four German guards armed with burp guns. In the lobby he told a soldier behind the desk in English:

"I am an American reporter and I would like to see General Mälzer."

Obviously unnerved, the soldier replied in German: "Wait a minute."

He disappeared, returning in a few minutes to say: "General Mälzer regrets that he is unable to see any Americans. He is getting ready to leave. His advice to you is that you had better get out of the hotel unless you wish to leave with the Germans."*

With a shrug of disappointment, Chinigo climbed back into the jeep, in which the German prisoner still calmly sat—though, with his armed comrades standing nearby, he might easily have escaped—and headed back for the Plaza Hotel. He relaxed over dinner with a group of jubilant Italian refugees who had been hiding in the hotel—while the prisoner ate in his own luxurious room where he would await the Allies.

After dinner Chinigo, exhausted from the day's activities, went straight to bed. It was too bad he didn't have the facilities yet to file a story from Rome, but he was certainly not going to abandon his royal suite to return to field headquarters.

He had just fallen asleep in his king-sized bed when, shortly after 10 P.M., he was abruptly awakened by noise outside.

"*Viva* America! *Viva* America!"

Chinigo stumbled to the window and saw a large, cheering crowd welcoming the troops. Damn it! Waking him up like that. These troops should have arrived hours ago.[18]

Reynolds Packard, the paunchy, excitable United Press correspondent, still felt rather humiliated that afternoon as the result of the incident at the ROMA sign on Highway 6 earlier that day. How silly to have leaped from his jeep while the Germans were jumping from their armored car.

Packard was now driving alone toward Rome on another road, sure

---

* From the moment General Mälzer surrendered the magnificent favors of Rome, misfortune dogged him. First, according to Colonel Dollmann, his trusted orderly, Corporal Hoffmann, deserted him, staying behind in Rome and turning himself over to the Allies. Then, on his arrival at the Po River, Mälzer made the mistake of holding up traffic on a main bridge so that one of his messengers could get through. The messenger was the bearer of a cake for his favorite opera singer in Milan. The cake was intercepted by one of Kesselring's adjutants and presumably eaten by Mälzer's superiors. Mälzer was exiled to some insignificant post.

that he would be the first reporter in Rome. Suddenly, a group of civilians on the road flagged him down. There were mines ahead, they warned. As Packard stood on the road discussing the danger with them, another jeep drove past. He automatically waved . . . Oh, no, not his wife!

Yes, his wife! Eleanor Packard would not be scooped by her husband. She ran the United Press bureau in Naples, but she had flown to Anzio that morning to be in on the kill. Sometimes Reynolds wondered why he had ever helped her get a job with UP. Together they had covered the Italian invasion of Ethiopia and the Spanish Civil War and they had jointly written a best-selling book about Mussolini, *Balcony Empire.*

But the more they collaborated, the more competitive they became—though let anybody try to cross either and they reacted as one. After the Anzio landing, another UP reporter who dared claim that he headed the Anzio bureau found himself not only pummeled by Reynolds' beefy fists but bashed over the head with a bottle by tall, strong Eleanor.

The colonel driving Eleanor halted a short distance in front of Packard, just before reaching the suspected mine field. Husband and wife decided that the gamble was too great. They grumpily returned together to press headquarters and dined in the correspondents' mess.

"I think we can still make it into Rome tonight," Eleanor mused over dessert.

But the mine field . . . Well, thought Reynolds, he couldn't be less daring than his wife. Anyway, it was better to be blown up than henpecked to death. With a driver, they started out again in a jeep at 6:30 P.M. and sped down the road behind a Sherman tank, passing it when it ground to a halt.

"Why did the tank stop?" Packard asked the driver.

"Probably afraid of mines. They want to see if we get blown up before they continue on."

"*Stop! Stop Immediately!*" Packard shouted. And the driver lurched to a halt.

The tank finally passed them but then slowed up. The Packards' driver started following again but soon grew impatient with this game of leapfrog.

"If we drive fast as hell we got a good chance," he said.

When Eleanor agreed, he zoomed in front of the tank again before Reynolds could react. "Just think," said Eleanor, "if we make it we'll be the first to file copy on Rome."

Reynolds groaned.

At 8:30 P.M., the Packards drove over a bridge together with some of the first American troops and careened into Piazza dell'Esreda, then

headed for the Grand Hotel. It seemed strange to be returning. They
had been interned in that hotel during the Mussolini era before being
released in an exchange arrangement.

They stopped in front of the hotel and, as they entered, passed two
astonished German officers who were rushing out. In the bar off the
lobby they sat down and ordered a drink and offered drinks to several
Italians. But, thinking the offer some kind of German trick, the Italians
declined—until Pietro, the barman, suddenly recognized the two strangers.

"Signor Packard! Signora Packard!" he cried.

There were embraces and free drinks and shouts of "Viva America!"

The Italians, mostly noblemen, joined in the festivity, and Allied
flags were soon fluttering at the entrance. The Packards had their
scoop: "We drank to the fall of Rome tonight at the bar in the Grand
Hotel . . ."

Now they had to get back to press headquarters to file their story in
time to make the morning papers. As they stepped outside they found
themselves caught in a whirlpool of delirium. Men and women grabbed
them and showered them with kisses, pausing only when, with startled
cries of "Donna Americana!" they suddenly realized that Eleanor,
dressed in khaki and steel helmet, was a woman. In deference to Italian
tradition, the men, somewhat embarrassed, stopped kissing her face and
concentrated on her hands, and, to Reynolds' annoyance, on *his* face.

The Packards almost panicked when they noted that their jeep had
vanished. But some minutes later the driver returned with it, explaining that he had driven a sick woman to the hospital.

"There are people dying all over the place," Packard angrily replied.
"We're covering a story. Let's get the hell back to camp!"

The jeep raced back to press headquarters, and the Packards, who had
largely composed their story en route, ran to a typewriter. Eleanor
hammered out three quick takes. As soon as they were cabled—they just
did make the morning papers in the United States—shelling caused the
communications center to shut down and no further reports could be
sent immediately.

While other reporters, on learning of the Packards' scoop, scrambled
toward Rome, the couple contentedly went to bed. Nobody else, it
seemed, would be able to send a word about the liberation of Rome
until the next day.[19]

Toward evening, Peter Tompkins, in a triumphant mood after watching the Germans retreat and the police follow *his* orders, was about to

enter his headquarters building when he heard children shouting excitedly about a block away. A young girl then ran past crying:

"They're at San Paolo!"

"How do you know?" Peter asked.

"Because one of them gave a man a can of meat and beans!"

Was this a German trick to get the partisans out in the open? Tompkins decided it couldn't be. Only an American would have the audacity to distribute inedible C-rations to unsuspecting people.

Followed by Malfatti, Baldo, and Lele, Tompkins feverishly leaped up the stairs four at a time. They grabbed guns, rushed down the stairs again, and headed for the Tiber, passing civilians clustered at corners, apparently no longer afraid to violate the 7:30 P.M. curfew. It was now about eight. Tompkins was relieved to find the bridges unguarded and undamaged, but no Americans were in sight.

Uncertain which entry routes they would be taking, he and his agents decided to climb to the top of Palatine Hill, overlooking the Forum, from where they could see all the roads leading into Rome. En route, they noted the suspicious stares of people behind their windows, but once they pulled out their red, white, and green partisan arm bands a great cheer went up along the streets:

"*Viva Americani!*"

As they reached the path leading to the top of the hill, Tompkins thought of the moments he had spent there with L., his girl friend—until machine-gun fire interrupted his reverie. They had been climbing directly toward a nest of forty German paratroopers entrenched on top! Dashing down the hill, they found the street at the bottom exploding with shell fire, and in the confusion Tompkins and Lele got separated from Malfatti and Baldo. Under fire, Peter and his comrade ducked into a cave that penetrated the foot of Capitoline Hill.

They found themselves in what seemed like a chamber of horrors. Dozens of half-starved, lice-infested refugees who had been living in the dank, smelly cave for months were growing panicky, and the women and children began to scream and wail prayers. Then several men guarding the cave pulled a great iron gate shut, refusing to let anybody leave.

Tompkins feared that these desperate people might take him and Lele for Fascists and tear them to pieces—or discover they were partisans and do likewise, since many thought the partisans were shooting at them (though Fascists actually were). Besides, it was his duty to greet the Allies—before some "pretender" like Menicanti beat him to it.

Finally managing to slip out of the cave, the two spies, bent almost double, dashed across a *piazza* and jumped on the running board of a car loaded with armed partisans, who dropped them at Tompkins' headquarters. Peter just missed Ottorino Borin, who had urgently been looking for him so that they, together with General Presti, could turn over Rome to the Allies.

Tompkins ran through streets blacked out by a power failure to Piazza di Venezia, where he was sure the troops would head, and in the dim light emanating from the monument to the Unknown Soldier he saw a long row of American half-tracks and jeeps strung across the square, each surrounded by excited civilians.

Suddenly the idea of walking up to the troops in dirty, misfitting civvies, unshaven and unkempt, and formally announcing that he was handing over the city of Rome to them seemed rather ridiculous. Still, he could not resist speaking with a young lieutenant.

"Hello, Lieutenant," he stammered. "Could I . . . could I bum a cigarette? I haven't had an American cigarette in almost five months."

The lieutenant removed a pack of Lucky Strikes from his shirt pocket and offered him one. Then, as the officer reached for his pistol, or seemed to, Tompkins vanished in the crowd.

Puffing greedily on the cigarette, Peter felt like the "bum" he was sure the lieutenant had taken him for. He wondered how it could happen that after all the months of hiding from the Germans he was still hiding—now from his own countrymen.

He returned to his headquarters and started to telephone dear L., but as he dialed the number he heard a shot and the phone went dead. A partisan in the room had accidentally fired his rifle and the bullet cut the wire of the phone in his hand. The two men stared at each other and burst into laughter. What a way—and time—to die!

Peter finally made his call, and revealed to L. for the first time that he was really an American spy. There was silence for a moment. And all the time she had thought he was a Jewish refugee. Was he not circumcised? She nearly fainted.

As soon as he had calmed her down and hung up, Malfatti appeared, a candle in one hand, a bottle of brandy in the other. The hell with it, Tompkins sighed. For one day, he had been the absolute commander of Rome. Let someone else turn over the goddam city to the Allies.

Malfatti winked and poured Tompkins a big swig of brandy, which the American happily, yet rather sadly, gulped down.[20]

Captain Pierre Planès, after being kissed by General Monsabert for being the "first in Rome," even though he had disobeyed orders, proudly headed for medical headquarters to find his wife's ambulance unit.

"*Bouchon*," he jubilantly greeted Colette when he had found her,

"I was the first Frenchman in Rome, but you shall be the first French girl."

Yes, that night they would fulfill their dream of a second honeymoon. They would dine and *faire amour* in Rome. Again he would be acting against orders. French forces had by now reached the bridges leading into Rome and dismantled mines that had never been detonated. But they were forbidden to cross into the city proper. This was the wish of General Clark, who wanted to make sure that no non-American force could ever claim to be the first, or apparently even among the first, to enter Rome. The French, therefore, sat on the far bank of the Tiber, bitterly watching the tantalizing lights of Rome wink a gay welcome.

But Pierre Planès, the "conqueror" of Rome, would not be deprived of his spoils. With his wife, he climbed back in his jeep and ordered the driver to speed into Rome. Passing for Americans in the darkness of evening, they threaded their way into the city through crowds of cheering people and stopped at a hotel that the first American troops had occupied a little earlier.

They entered the bustling hotel restaurant, which was jammed with American officers, found a table, and had just begun to eat when their driver rushed in with the news that their jeep had been stolen. Planès nearly choked on his food.

"*Mon Dieu,*" he exclaimed, "we're in the soup now!"

Since they had entered Rome against orders, how could they ask the American command for transportation? The Planèses could barely finish the meal they had looked forward to for so long. After dinner they registered in the hotel and went immediately to bed.

At last the treasured moment.

"What are we going to do?" sighed Colette. "The Americans will certainly report us."

Why think of things like that *now?*

"Maybe we'll be court-martialed," she persisted.

"*Merde, alors!*"

What a climax to their second honeymoon!

In the morning the couple, with little choice, went to an American command post and asked for a vehicle to take them back to their division area. The Americans lent them a car, but, as expected, reported their unauthorized presence in Rome. When the couple later went to see their commander, they were greeted with cold fury.

"First," shouted the colonel, "you had your jeep stolen. Second, you didn't have perimssion to leave your unit. Third, the French are not supposed to be in Rome."

Planès apologized, agreeing idiomatically: *"Nous avons fait le con!"* ("We fucked up!")

The Planèses were in disgrace, but escaped punishment. After all, they *had* put one over on Mark Clark. And what Frenchman would penalize another for stealing away to a love tryst—even with one's own wife in a forbidden city?[21]

15

The Winners

Guided by partisans, the main Allied forces began entering Rome proper late in the afternoon of June 4 after fierce fighting in some areas, especially on Highway 6 near the ROMA sign.* General Frederick's men finally crashed through, leaving enemy armor aflame at intersections en route to the heart of the city.

Passing through Porto San Paolo, they immediately headed for the bridges in their sector to capture them if possible before they were blown up, but were delayed less by German tanks than by Italian crowds.

When Colonel Howze, who had reassumed command of the spearhead, nosed into the center of town in his jeep at about 6:30 P.M., the streets were still deserted and windows were shuttered tight. Then one darkened window opened and a scream echoed weirdly: "*Americani!*"

Immediately, hundreds of people rushed from their homes and, throwing themselves upon Howze and his men with shrieks of joy, grabbed hands, arms, and legs, and almost dragged the Americans out of their jeeps and tanks. Though Howze had in the past fought off whole battalions of enemy, he was unprepared for this onslaught by frenzied civilians, who suddenly realized that the Germans were gone and that it was safe to show their pleasure. A new conqueror had driven out the

* A battalion of the U.S. 3rd Division, which outflanked the Germans who were holding up General Frederick's 1st Special Service Force at the ROMA sign, claims to have been the first full Allied combat unit into the city.

old, and the cynical Romans were happy because the new one could hardly be worse than the old.

Howze's men, on the other hand, did not experience any great immediate compulsion to seek battle in paradise. Many apparently felt, as CBS reporter Eric Sevareid did, "wonderfully good, generous, and important." They are representatives of "strength, decency, and success, and it was impossible at this moment to recollect that Germans or Fascists had also once received the same outpouring of gratitude."

Finally, one officer who recalled that the war was not over, drew a revolver to keep the people away so that he could find those goddam bridges on a city map.

Still, the crowds grew, and their cheers rose in thunderous crescendo at each street crossing as the vehicles crawled along Via Nazionale in the shadow of Trajan's Column. Suddenly, a German flak-wagon—an antiaircraft gun mounted on a half-track—skidded around a bend firing red tracers. Exultation chilled into cold fear as the crowd gaped in shock for a moment, then scurried for cover while an Allied tank poured shells into the flak-wagon, converting it into a blackened shell.

The last German resistance had been crushed in the center of Rome.[1]

A small group of engineers and special troops under General Frederick's personal command escaped the clutches of the welcomers and dashed through the dark, narrow streets in jeeps to a bridge as the German guards fled. The force began inspecting the bridge for demolition charges, when Frederick saw some shadowy figures file out of a nearby alley and shouted, "Halt!"

A burst of fire was the reply, and one of Frederick's men fell dead while Frederick himself and two others were wounded. As the survivors returned the fire, the general, lying in the street, shouted: "Cease fire! Cease fire!"

The shooting stopped, and from the shadows emerged several men wearing the blue clover leaf of the 88th Division.

"Look what you did to us," moaned Frederick, only lightly wounded. "Aren't there enough Krauts around here to shoot at?"

"Mighty sorry, General," replied General Kendall, second in command of the 88th. "We were told there were no Americans here—figured you were Krauts."

And this *was* 88th territory.[2]

Early in the morning of June 5 German soldiers were still holding a key iron railway bridge on Via Salaria at the northern edge of Rome after having protected the retreat of the last Nazis still in the city. They apparently intended to blow up this bridge, but were coming under heavy attack from partisans determined to prevent its demolition.

Hearing the battle from his home nearby, twelve-year-old Ugo Forno ran to the hut of a peasant who lived near the bridge, and the peasant, a partisan himself, handed him a rifle and the two began firing at the Germans. Raised in an atmosphere of fear and anxiety, perpetually hungry, Ugo somehow sensed that his suffering and that of his family was the fault of those men lurking in the shadows of the structure. His partisan friends had briefed him well.

Shortly, the Germans responded with mortar shells, and three exploded near the hut. The peasant was hit and Ugo found himself defending an entire flank of the battle front all alone. He fired bullet after bullet, preventing the Germans from approaching the bridge, but finally a shell ripped the hut apart.

The firing soon stopped and several partisans approached carrying a tattered Italian flag tied to a broom handle. Ugo stared at the flag and whispered:

"*Viva Italia!*"

Then he died—without knowing that his steady fire had kept the Germans away from the bridge long enough to permit other partisans to kill them before they could demolish it and thereby hold up the Allied advance for perhaps hours.[3]

Colonel Carlton, the chief of staff of General Truscott's VI Corps, called General Walker, the 36th Division commander, at about 10 P.M., June 4, and asked:

"Where are you?"

"On the edge of Rome."

"Which edge?"

"Southeast edge."

"Well, everybody is on the near edge of Rome. Nobody is on the far edge. The general [Truscott] wants somebody on the far side of Rome, but everybody is sitting on this side of Rome. He wants to report that the VI has taken Rome. Do you understand?"

"Yes, sir."

Walker understood indeed. His 36th Division was to risk the dangers of a night march through Rome without even a compensatory taste of its pleasures and chase the Germans northward—another typical "hard-luck" assignment. He had tried desperately to get his troops into Rome before nightfall, and he was sure he could have if Truscott had not ordered him off Highway 7 to make way for the 1st Armored Division.

Shuttled onto a narrower, more defensible road, his division had suffered greatly as it advanced to the city's western outskirts, from house to German-fortified house.

His men, moreover, had been shaken by the sight of an American tank burning with the crew inside. The lieutenant who commanded the tanks became hysterical, shouting and weeping, wringing his hands, cursing the war and Walker. Then, to add to the agony, shells poured down on the troops—from the poorly aimed guns of the 1st Armored Division that was leisurely marching up Highway 7! Only at dusk did peace come, permitting the Italian women to come into the streets and cover the bodies with flowers from their gardens.

The 1st Armored Division, its tanks draped with ecstatic Romans, was winding its way through the city at that moment under a rain of Italian confetti, occasionally mixed with German shrapnel, and the 36th would follow. But Walker did not know what was happening. Would the Germans fight for the city? Were the streets blocked by defended barricades? Nobody had told him anything. And from what he *had* heard, there were no Italian policemen, no directional signs, no street lights, and no lights in any of the buildings.

At a conference of his commanders, one of them asked: "How am I going to get my combat team through Rome when I have no route or boundary?"

Walker could only answer: "You will be free to go where the situation demands."

He dismissed the conference and lay down on his bunk.

At about 2 A.M., the 36th, with infantrymen clinging like flies to everything that had tracks or wheels, began its march, crawling toward the Tiber through deserted, moonlit streets bordered by trees ballooning with summer foliage. As the orange beams of sunrise spilled light on the buildings, some people in the residential areas emerged in their bathrobes and pajamas to cheer, shout, and wave, but toward the center of the city not a soul could be seen.

A part of the division then started to cross the Tiber but found the way blocked by troops of the 85th Division. Angrily, General Stack, Walker's chief of staff, strode over to a colonel of the 85th and demanded:

"What the hell are you doing here?"

He was doing, said the colonel, what his orders directed him to do—and to prove it he showed his orders.

Stack gulped. Someone had screwed up at higher headquarters.

As Stack began looking for General Walker, who was leading another part of the 36th over another bridge, he found himself drawn, almost hypnotically, it seemed, by the glow of the golden dome of St. Peter's

Basilica. He led his force into the splendidly pillared embrace of the great square stretching before it. The lead tank clanked to a halt on the cobblestones and the force, strung for blocks through the city, whined gradually into silence like a great steel accordion.

Stack climbed out of his jeep, looked around at Vatican City, and cried: "We can't go in here. We'll create an international incident!"

He walked up to the Italians who had guided the division and they heatedly tried to explain something in their language, but he could not understand them. He looked at his map and, pointing to a street leading out of the square, yelled at the tank commander:

"Go that way!"

"Yes, sir!"

As the tank commander maneuvered in the designated direction, the Italian guides began to protest, but Stack cut them off. It soon became clear, however, that the division was heading in the wrong direction, and it had to turn back toward the Vatican. By now the sun was shining brightly and the streets were full of people, so full that the convoy could barely move. Romans threw flowers, offered wine to the soldiers, jumped on the tank turrets, and one man with a Luger at his waist leaped onto a jeep and exhorted his comrades to join him in pursuing the Germans.

The division ground to a complete halt as wild crowds swirled around every vehicle. Stack could only stare at them numbly—until he saw Walker's jeep inching toward him through the wall of humanity. The general was furious. Here the Germans were escaping to the north and his troops were having the time of their lives carousing with the women of Rome!

Finally, the division found the right route out of the city and were on the corpse-littered trail of the fleeing Germans.

And somehow, everybody in the "hard-luck" 36th was glad that they had taken the wrong street.[4]

As the message flew from radio to British radio that "our big cousins have entered the city," the Eighth Army desperately lunged for the crumbs of glory. Plagued by its own ponderous inefficiency as much as by General Clark's highly personalized sense of history, the British Eighth Army, lagging behind on Highway 6, had been squeezed out of the kill. And General Alexander, accepting reality, had some days before given up hope that a British unit would be among the first in Rome.

Still, the British and other nationalities in the Eighth Army wanted at least token recognition of their considerable contribution to the fall of Rome. The Eighth had made enormous sacrifices in finally capturing

Cassino, whatever assistance the Fifth Army had given it. Though the Eighth was now supposed to bypass Rome and advance east of the Tiber while chasing the German Tenth Army northward, it seemed only right to its disappointed commanders that some units should enter Rome on June 5, the day after its fall, and take part in ceremonies honoring that great event.

With this in mind, Captain William Philip Sidney, a distinguished Member of Parliament in civilian life, was ordered early on June 5 to race up Highway 6 with a battalion of Grenadier Guards, supported by South African tanks, to capture a Tiber bridge just to the east of Rome. But Sidney's flying column was soon halted by an American military policeman.

"I have orders from General Clark," said the MP, "not to permit any troops to advance along this route."

"Well, I have orders from General Leese," growled Sidney, who had jumped from his jeep, "to advance along this route."

The American then drew a pistol and aimed it at Sidney's deputy, who had been leading the way. Sidney was furious. He had won the Victoria Cross, Britain's highest decoration for valor, a few months previously, and he was not about to let some "stupid little policeman" hold up the British army. Perhaps he should whip out his own pistol and fire. No, there was another solution.

Calmly, he walked back down the road and ordered his tank commander to move one of his tanks to the head of the column. When the tank had come up, he told the MP, who was still aiming his pistol at the deputy commander:

"If you don't get out of the way, we'll have to run over you."

The MP looked at Sidney, then at the tank. He reholstered his pistol and moved out of the way.

Sidney ordered his column to advance and soon it reached its assigned bridge—only to find that the Germans had blown it up.

The British commanders did not seem overly shocked or depressed by this. They now had an excellent excuse to move westward into Rome— the kind of excuse that the Fifth Army commanders had suspected the Eighth of planning long before it was clear that the Fifth would win the race to Rome. General Kirkman, the British XIII Corps commander, rushed to General Keyes's headquarters before dawn on June 5 and requested permission from Keyes's chief of staff, Colonel John L. Willems, to use the bridges *inside* Rome, which were intact, for the British thrust northward.

Willems woke Keyes to ask him and Keyes rejected the request, though he said he "might make some kind of deal to give it to him part-time." His experience with the British showed that when they set a foot or a wheel on any road, they would not easily give the road back. Anyway, the British Eighth Army was supposed to advance *east* of the Tiber, not to cross it.

During the crucial hours of June 5, at any rate, the answer was "no." When the British began heading toward Rome regardless, Keyes's provost marshal, Lieutenant Colonel Michael Mabardi, organized an intricately tangled traffic jam at a vulnerable position on Highway 6, thus blocking the way.

In desperation, Kirkman took the matter to General Alexander. Alexander, it appears, took it to General Wilson, Wilson to Foreign Minister Anthony Eden, and Eden to Prime Minister Winston Churchill— who had insisted on the capture of Rome in the first place when American leaders were far less passionate about such an operation.

The question was whether sufficient pressure could ripple back again to end what was probably history's most controversial traffic jam and permit the British to enter Rome before the world forgot that the city had fallen.[5]

❖   ❖   ❖

Although it was only 7:30 A.M. on June 5, hundreds of people started gathering in Piazza di Venezia under the balcony of the brown-walled building to watch the man with the jutting jaw as he strutted, saluted with arm outstretched, clamped his hands on his hips, gazed arrogantly upon the adoring crowd, and shouted:

"*Vinceri! Vinceri! Vinceri!*"

The throngs cheered and applauded, and the speaker continued in pidgin Italian:

"Not for Mussolini, the Fascists, or the Germans, but for the Allies! Instead of castor oil, we bring you candy and food!"

Another roar of approval shook the plaza. U.S. Sergeant John A. Vita saluted and strutted again, pushing his bearded jaw out a little further.

Vita, a signal corps cameraman and an artist in civilian life, was keeping a vow he had made to his Italian-born mother.

"I am going to be one of the first American soliders in Rome," he had said. "And when I get there, I'm going to climb on Mussolini's balcony and outdo him."

His mother had laughed.

As the crowd grew, waiting for more amusingly garbled words, Vita regretted that he had not prepared a speech. Well, they wouldn't know the difference anyway. He harangued them anew—with Italian double-talk—pausing occasionally to acknowledge cheers.

Finally, Vita shouted "Death to Mussolini!" saluted once more, turned stiffly around, and re-entered the Duce's abandoned office, while the people in a gay mood, turned their attention to new troops pouring into the *piazza*, throwing more flowers, waving more flags and shouting their welcome in whatever English they knew. One old man simply kept yelling, "Weekend! Weekend!"

The welcomers then began snake-dancing around the *piazza*, some playing real musical instruments, others pumping imaginary trombones. They separated only to make room for an American soldier who was marching off a German sniper he had captured in the Colosseum.

Other GIs joined in the weaving parade, some in their jeeps and many wearing looted medieval helmets, eighteenth-century tricornes, and New Year's Eve paper hats. They let out great "Whoops!" clumsily reiterated by the Italians, and one soldier grabbed the reins of a passing fiacre from a driver and galloped the horse through the square. And in the midst of the frenzied celebration, Private Edward Savino of New York City met an aunt and cousin he had not seen in years.

Many of these GIs had "somehow" got separated from their units on the way out of Rome and were happily, tipsily "lost," though some were a bit concerned.

"I don't wanna lose my outfit," Private Abraham Goldstein of Brooklyn assured a *Stars and Stripes* reporter, Sergeant Paul Green. "It's a damn good outfit."

"Same with me," said Private First Class Victor Rossi of Los Angeles. "Wonder what my captain's gonna say?"

"Everybody got lost," explained Goldstein. "There must be a thousand guys wandering around Rome. I know Brooklyn, but I just can't figure out Rome. It's hell to get lost."

In other parts of Rome the people demonstrated in other parades, some led by partisans wearing either the red, white, and green armbands of the joint CLN-Clandestine Front or the red hammer-and-sickle armbands of the Red Flag party, whose members roved around lustily singing the party anthem, "Bandiera Rossa." Many pro-Allied Italians were missing; almost ten thousand had been executed during the nine months of German occupation.

The partisans had played an important, though hardly a decisive, role in the capture of Rome, taking prisoner many Germans and Fascists after bloody local battles and eliminating Fascist sharpshooters from the roofs of key buildings. Some were still smashing into Fascist headquarters located in stores and apartments, making arrests, and wrecking everything in these places.

In general, even the most ardent revolutionaries had taken pride in directing the various police groups, who eagerly obeyed their new masters, in the maintenance of "law and order." The Red Flag leader, Antonio Poce, had become an assistant police chief—though some weeks later he would himself be arrested by the Allies and thrown into Regina Coeli prison, where so many of his comrades had suffered and died. His crime: He would not halt efforts to recruit the "Red Army" he had hoped would fight in the north and eventually take over the country.

Soon afterward, the Red Flag party, isolated and pilloried by other political groups, most vehemently by the Communist party, would sadly disband itself, its dreams of revolution shattered.[6]

Driving a large black Lancia confiscated from the enemy, Peter Tompkins wove his way through the wild crowds to Excelsior Hotel, where, in a state of euphoria, he ordered a plush room for the night. The lobby buzzed with excitement. Fifth Army officers were drinking to their victory over the Nazis—and the British Eighth Army—while beautiful women, from contessas to prostitutes, all fashionably dressed in short, tight skirts, blouses with padded shoulders, and wedge-heel shoes, wooed them, as some had only recently wooed the Germans, with smiles and promises of a heady night.†

A heady night indeed! But for the moment duty called. Tompkins left to look for his OSS colleagues whom he knew must have arrived in an advance spearhead called "S-force," which was to capture enemy archives and records. When he found them at another hotel, an OSS captain, staring at him as if at a ghost, exclaimed:

"Everyone at the base thought you were dead!"

Since Tompkins wasn't, the OSS chief he then met agreed that he should make himself useful. He could start rounding up Fascists who had remained in Rome. As he left on this mission, Tompkins found that several of his men waiting for him outside had been arrested by *carabinieri* who had taken them for Fascists. He angrily walked over and whipped out a card that he thought would settle matters. It did. Instead of the *laizzer-passer* he had just been issued, he had produced a false document identifying himself as a Fascist officer!

"Oh, no!" Tompkins cried.

† An OSS security summary dated June 5–30 reported: "Various leave centers have been opened up within the city, and it has been reported that these are being frequented by women who in the past have worked as informers for the Germans . . . They constitute a potential danger, as a source of information to the enemy. The Excelsior Hotel has been particularly mentioned in this respect, and a full investigation is being made."

Before he could utter another word he, too, was arrested and hauled off to the police station.[7]

Carla Capponi could barely read the first proofs of the Communist newspaper *Unità*, so great was her pain, so high her fever. She had been guarding the offices of the confiscated Fascist newspaper *Il Tevere* on Via 4 Novembre since early that morning, June 5, despite her need of treatment for the shrapnel wound she had suffered some days earlier in Palestrina.

Carla and Rosario Bentivegna had rushed to Rome to take part in the insurrection that never materialized. Although she had spit blood all the way back, she—and Bentivegna—immediately volunteered for a new assignment. They were to bicycle to Tivoli with giant reflectors that would be used to signal Allied planes where to drop arms for the partisans, but they had been forced to turn back because of the heavy German traffic along the road. Their next assignment was to help occupy this Fascist newspaper building so that the first "above-ground" issue of *Unità* could be published immediately.

Other political groups had taken over other Fascist newspaper facilities and were also rushing out liberation-day editions. Even reporters for the American army newspaper, *Stars and Stripes*, had confiscated a newspaper plant, that of *Il Messaggero*. They found the linotypers only too glad to print a chronicle of the liberation, to be banner-headed: "WE'RE IN ROME."‡

Carla thus had not found the time yet to go home to her mother or to see a doctor. But despite the pain, the fever, the paralyzing fatigue, this was the happiest day of her life. Somehow, all the horror of the past few months now made sense. Rome was at last liberated from the physical grasp of a monstrous enemy. Of course, it was disappointing that the Romans had not been permitted to play a more important role in the final stage of their own liberation. And that social and economic "liberation" was still a thing of the future. But the first blow for freedom, as she saw it, had been struck.

This was the meaning of that moment months before when the young blond German messenger gasped quietly as he fell dead from her bullet; when hundreds of other young men, her comrades and co-fighters, fell dead from German bullets triggered by a plot she had

‡ On May 29 Sergeant Gregory Duncan, a well-known *Stars and Stripes* artist, was killed by a shellburst while driving a jeep near Cori, twenty-five miles from Rome—only a few days after his wife, Janice, a Red Cross nurse, had joined him in Naples for a joyful reunion. For months their friends had been rooting for them to be stationed together at the same base. When this had finally been arranged, Duncan had gone off on a "short assignment"—his last.

helped to conceive and execute. This was the meaning of the hunger, the frustration, the tears that would not come.

Now, at about 2 P.M., Rosario, also a guard in the building, implored her to go home for rest and treatment. Yes, home. She could rest at last, and in her mother's arms the tears would come again. Carla and Rosario walked out together.

What a beautiful, sunny day!

At almost that same moment, Lieutenant Giorgio Barbarisi was embracing *his* mother.

"*Mammina*," he said, "look what a sunny day! Keep the newspapers for me. These are exciting days!"

Barbarisi was an officer in the Guardia di Finanza, the Financial Police which "served" the Fascist administration but secretly worked for the Clandestine Front. He was leaving to meet an Allied officer whom he would help in keeping order. His mother had never seen him so joyous, so filled with dreams and hopes. How different had been his mood when he said farewell on another occasion. He had written her on March 9 before leaving on a mission which, in the end, was canceled:

> Adored *Mammina*,
> When you receive this letter I shall be far away. I wanted it to be this way because I could not bear the pain of a farewell. You do not know how much I love you . . . And on my knees before you I beg forgiveness for any fault of mine which has in any way brought to your most gentle heart a tear of sorrow.
> Adored *Mammina*, the thought of leaving you alone, with no one to help you, is the only thing that has tormented me these last few days, and this torment will be infinitely greater until once more I shall rest in your arms, near to you, the only person in the world who has always given without seeking anything in return . . .
> My resolution is the fruit of two considerations. The nation and the flag which represents its unity and honor are the true, living, moral symbols which one cannot betray. To this nation and its flag I swore to be faithful, trembling with pride and with my eyes wet with tears, at the age of seventeen! Mother! I cannot deny this oath without denying myself . . . Before such a great, deeply felt idea there can be no resistance.
> The atmosphere in Rome has become unbearable for me. As for me, only the thought of leaving you alone will cause me suffering, together with the sadness of leaving this unfortunate Italy of ours still divided, torn apart. Mother, forgive me if I pierce your heart with painful thorns. But do not cry. Pray!—Giorgio.

Barbarisi had joined the Resistance wholeheartedly. He had gathered information for the Fifth Army, hidden refugee officers, stored weapons in secret hideouts. Once he had been caught hiding weapons, but was released through the intervention of his superiors. Though he deplored Communism, he immediately warned a Communist partisan, Andrea Arena, about whom he had been questioned, that he was in danger.

On June 4, just before the Allies arrived in Rome, Barbarisi had led a group of men in fighting off a desperate German effort to confiscate vehicles from the garage of the Viole 21 Aprile police barracks. That evening, as the Allies began to penetrate the city, he commanded a Financial Police detachment that occupied the *municipio*, or city hall, in the Piazza del Campidoglio, and was ready to fight, if necessary, any of his Communist comrades who might try to occupy it. When Allied troops arrived, he turned it over to them and, in conflict with their plans, insisted—successfully—that the Italian flag be raised alongside the Allied flags on Capitoline Hill.

At noon, on this beautiful, sunny day of June 5, he had lunched at an Allied officers' mess and had returned home for a few minutes to bring his mother two loaves of bread. Now he was leaving again.

Still burning with fever as she walked beside Rosario Bentivegna on Via delle Tre Cannelle, Carla Capponi stopped to drink at a water fountain. Suddenly her eyes focused on a uniformed man carrying his jacket in one hand and tearing a poster from a wall with the other. The poster, one of many she and her comrades had plastered on walls shouting the praises of Communism, read VIVA L'UNITÀ! referring to the newspaper she had just helped to put out.

"Paolo!" Carla shouted, calling Rosario by his code name. "Look!"

Both ran to the man ripping down the poster and, they claim, this exchange took place between Rosario and the stranger—who, they say, was accompanied by a uniformed companion:

Bentivegna: "Stop that! What are you doing?"

Stranger: "I'm doing what I please."

Bentivegna: "You were doing what pleased you until a few hours ago. Now you're under arrest."

A few seconds later the stranger slumped to earth fatally shot. According to Bentivegna, he, Bentivegna, had drawn his own pistol only after the man's companion had fired first and the victim had reached for his weapon. The second man "escaped."

Immediately afterward, Carla says, a jeep stopped at the scene and an American officer, a Colonel Green, stepped out and asked what had happened. They had just killed a Fascist officer in self-defense, the two partisans replied. Green, according to Carla, kissed her on the cheek and congratulated both of them.

The couple then walked away and Carla went home, her physical pain no longer relieved by the joy of liberation. Even on liberation day her fingers dripped with blood.

A few days later, Rosario, after reading about the killing in the newspapers, reported to the Allied authorities and said that he had shot the man in self-defense. He was tried, convicted, and given an eighteen-months' suspended sentence.

The threatened civil war between the leftist and rightist segments of the Roman Resistance had, with tragic irony, boiled down to a trivial but fatal misunderstanding between two proud and brave men intoxicated with a victory they shared—Rosario Bentivegna and Lieutenant Giorgio Barbarisi.[8]

Michael Stern, a reporter for the North American Newspaper Alliance, climbed the steep hill winding from Piazza di Spagna to the Pincio in Villa Borghese until he found Pensione Jaselli-Owen. He examined the name plates in the lobby but could not find Colonel Eugen Dollmann's. When he asked a man coming out if he knew which room Dollmann had rented, the man personally led him to the top floor and knocked on a door.

The American secret police, the man excitedly told the maid, had come to check up on Colonel Dollmann. Almost immediately, a middle-aged woman (apparently the proprietor and the mother of Dollmann's "girl friend" Bibi) greeted Stern, who said that he would like to question her about the SS colonel.

"He fled yesterday," the woman replied.

Stern, who had done preliminary research on Dollmann before coming, asked: "Where is the Italian chauffeur who worked for him?"

"He fled with the colonel."

"And the blond mistress?"

Stern was stabbing in the dark, knowing of no mistress. He had struck a rather sore point.

"Blond mistress?" exclaimed the woman. "I don't understand what you mean."

"You know very well what I mean," said Stern, continuing his bluff.

"Oh no," replied the woman. "That is quite impossible. Let me show you."

She led him to the colonel's bedroom and patted one side of the large double bed.

"Here slept the colonel," she said.

Then, patting the other side of the bed, she added: "And here slept the chauffeur."[9]

Ambassador von Weizsäcker and his wife, out of sheer curiosity, emerged from their Embassy for a stroll on the morning of June 5. They had spent the evening before listening to the radio for news of the Allied arrival. At about 9:30 P.M. they had heard calls and shouts and applause from the direction of Via 20 Settembre, and they knew the moment had come. Though it had long been inevitable, their hearts sank. And their depression was deepened by the recollection of their proud soldiers retreating like desperate, wounded animals. They themselves, together with other members of the German mission to the Vatican and their families, would remain in Rome, enjoying diplomatic immunity, as Allied diplomats to the Vatican had done when the Germans first occupied the city. But they would move into the Vatican as soon as possible.

Now, on the first morning under enemy rule, the Weizsäckers wandered through the streets, watching the parades, the flutter of enemy flags, the Italian girls walking arm in arm with enemy soldiers. Yesterday the Romans had at least pretended friendship with the Germans. Today they loved the Americans and British. They had shifted their affection as easily as they might change their clothes. After all, while the Germans had nothing to offer them, Allied trucks were bulging with cigarettes, food, plenty of everything. Well, it was no secret, the Weizsäckers felt, that the Italians lacked the sturdy character of the Germans.

As the couple approached the Embassy after their stroll, they saw several boys pull the swastika from a flagpole and then drag it down the street to lead a new parade.

On entering, the Weizsäckers learned from the diplomats gathered there that two men were missing; Ludwig Wemmer and Albrecht von Kessel had been arrested despite their diplomatic immunity. Weizsäcker was almost thankful that Wemmer, whom he knew had been sent by Martin Bormann to observe him, was at least temporarily out of the way (Wemmer was soon repatriated by the Allies to Germany), especially since he suspected that Wemmer hoped to replace him after Rome's fall.* Weizsäcker felt that now, more than ever, he was needed in Rome.

* Hoffmann Günther, a former diplomat in the German Embassy to the Holy See, testified at the Nuremberg trial of Ambassador von Weizsäcker (doc. n. 287) that Martin Bormann intended to replace Weizsäcker with Wemmer. In May 1944, Günther said, Wemmer made a last attempt to oust Weizsäcker with a lengthy report to the SS, but this effort was frustrated by the Allied entry in Rome on June 4. Weizsäcker implies as much in his memoirs—though without mentioning Wemmer by name. After the war, Wemmer entered West German politics and became an aide of Franz Josef Strauss of the right-wing Christian Socialist Union party.

So, he apparently thought, was Kessel, whom the Allies were to detain for about six weeks. Kessel was the one man he could trust completely. Because of their relationship, it is likely that Kessel told Weizsäcker about the plot to assassinate Hitler planned for the near future, and, if so, this knowledge would have increased the ambassador's concern about his friend's arrest. Kessel was needed to play his role in the plot. If the plot succeeded, Weizsäcker's own diplomatic efforts in Rome might be amply rewarded. He was in a position to obtain the immediate co-operation of the Pope in mediating a negotiated peace between a post-Hitler Germany and the Anglo-Americans. And his moment of destiny might even come before the Russians set foot in Europe.

Nor did the "miracle" of Rome's salvation fail to comfort Weizsäcker. Without any agreement, the two sides had spared the city, and, aside from the railroad yards, about 95 per cent of it had come through the nightmare unscathed.

Weizsäcker liked to think that Rome's salvation had made possible the salvation of Germany.[10]

The Allies immediately began to arrest Germans and Fascists, even ignoring in some cases, as in those of Wemmer and Kessel, the diplomatic status of their prisoners. Unfortunately, many of the people arrested as Fascists had actually been among the most active Resistance leaders.

Before dawn on June 5 Ettore Basevi, who published the Clandestine Front's underground news sheet, met Colonel John Pollack, British chief of the military police for Rome, on Capitoline Hill as prearranged through Centro X radio. In a jeep taking them to the Allied MP barracks, Pollack showed Basevi a list of people whom he was to arrest for collaborating with the enemy.

"We must find all these people immediately," Pollack said.

Basevi read the list, name by name, and remained speechless for several seconds.

"But you can't arrest these people!" he exclaimed.

"Why not?"

"Because they have been working for the Resistance. You have the wrong list."

"But that is our official list."

Basevi insisted that the men and women on the list deserved to be honored, not arrested. Perhaps, he suggested, the German intelligence service had somehow switched lists on him. As he spoke, MPs were knocking on doors dragging off to jail many of the people on the list.

The appropriate list was finally produced, but not before many a Resistance hero spent the first exciting hours he had been so impatiently awaiting in a prison cell that, the day before, had been occupied by a comrade in arms who had been captured and perhaps tortured by the Nazis and Fascists.

Some of the worst criminals, however, were also arrested, though a number considerably after the fall of Rome. General Pietro Caruso, the Fascist police chief, was a prize catch. Caruso had fled Rome on the morning of June 4 at the head of a column of cars carrying Fascist collaborators and policemen. Allied planes began strafing them, and, when one policeman fell wounded off his motorcycle, Caruso loyally stopped to give him first aid—while the vehicles that had been following continued on, leaving him and the others in his car alone.

Trying to escape the planes, the car raced down a side road and crashed into a tree, and Caruso suffered a serious leg injury. His colleagues rushed him to a nearby hospital and then abandoned him. Local partisans soon found him and turned him over to the Allies, who remanded him to a cell in the same Regina Coeli prison which he had so ruthlessly operated.

Caruso's fellow police chief, Pietro Koch, was luckier—at least for a while. He escaped to Milan, still under German control, where he set up a new torture house. But his feud with the Fascist naval leader Captain Valerio Borghese and other leading Fascists soon had him reserving cells for colleagues as well as partisans.

In the end Koch lost this contest for power. His competitors arrested *him*. He was freed two months later, however—only to be captured by the Allies. He had heard that his mother and his first mistress, Tamara Cerri—he had since abandoned Daisy Marchi, the show girl—had been arrested, though his mother, who had fled south (thereby releasing Monsignor O'Flaherty from his pledge to protect her), had apparently only been questioned. Allied police did not arrest Koch's estranged wife.

Koch inquired about Tamara and his mother at a police station in Florence after the Allies had captured that city, and when his identity was suspected he finally admitted that he was Koch. For all his Germanic qualities, he had been trapped by a typically Italian characteristic: an extraordinary attachment to his mother.

Two women who had enjoyed the protection of top Nazi leaders reacted dramatically when the Allies arrived. The blond foreigner whom General Wolff was courting at the time of his meeting with the Pope committed suicide by cutting her wrists. And the Dutch girl who had been Colonel Kappler's mistress, and whom Colonel Dollmann had so greatly mistrusted, immediately began working with Allied authorities.

Another young woman, Celeste (Stella) Di Porto, the Black Panther, who had betrayed so many of her fellow Jews, hitched a ride to Naples with American soldiers and became a prostitute serving the troops. She was finally discovered and brought back to Rome, where police were barely able to keep a crowd of bereaved Jews from lynching her as she was entering a police station.[11]

As late as June 2 Mussolini had written to Hitler pleading that the Germans fight for Rome. For the next two days, nervous and depressed, he set at his desk in Salò like a wax mummy, ignoring the clutter of papers, too demoralized even to shave. Finally, on June 4, Ambassador Rahn informed him that the German military command had decided to spare Rome the horrors of war and withdraw from the city.

Though Rome's fall had been inevitable, the Duce felt a sense of shock. He ordered three days of national mourning and bitterly proclaimed to the people:

"Soldiers to arms, workers and farmers to work! The Republic is threatened by the plutocracies and their mercenaries of every race. Defend it."

Mussolini then vented his desperation in an article for *Corrispondensa Repubblicana*, hoping to win popular support by stirring racial emotions. How deplorable, he wrote, that black troops were passing under the arches and on the streets which had been built to exalt the ancient and modern glory of Rome. He added: "Garibaldi's cry, 'Rome or death,' will now become the order of the day, the supreme duty of all true Italians."

Count Mazzolini, one of the Duce's collaborators, commented: "How many people will listen to him? The bitter cup is not yet empty. We shall have to drain it drop by drop."[12]†

Giacomo and Eleanora Di Porto, with their baby, returned from their respective hiding places to the Convent of Notre Dame de Sion early in the morning of June 5 to thank and bid goodbye to the nuns who had protected and befriended them for the many terrible months. They found the convent bristling with excitement as their fellow refugees, so long penned up in terror, suddenly realized that the men marching past

† In August 1944, two months after the fall of Rome, Mussolini and Kesselring discussed in Salò the German retreat from the Eternal City. When the field marshal said it had been necessary to save the Tiber bridges because of their historical and artistic value, the Duce brusquely replied: "Field Marshal, you have made a mistake. You should have blown up all the Tiber bridges and, if necessary, the whole of Rome."

were not Nazis or Fascists but Americans. People wept, shouted with joy, hugged the nuns.

Among the happiest was the wife of Aldo Cava, one of the two Jews who had been captured by the Fascists as they fled the convent some days before. The Germans were about to deport Cava, but he managed to bribe a Fascist guard just before the death train departed. Only the previous day he had telephoned his wife that he was safe and that he would be returning to the convent today.

However, the wife of Angelo Di Veroli, the second man who had been captured, was unmoved by the gaiety. No word had come from him and it appeared that he had been put on the last train to leave Rome for Germany.

In the midst of the pandemonium, Sister Katharine, the convent cook who had learned to prepare kosher delicacies, left to go shopping for a festive meal and was just closing the front gate behind her when a familiar figure approached.

"Signor Di Veroli!" she cried.

The man ran to her and, sobbing, fell into her arms. Sister Katharine helped the enfeebled Di Veroli into the convent, shouting:

"Signor Di Veroli has returned!"

Seconds later, a crowd rushed to the entrance from every room on every floor. Among the first to appear were Di Veroli's wife and four children who smothered him with kisses and embraces.

With a strangely mixed feeling of joy and dread, the Di Portos left to visit the house of Eleanora's family. Perhaps someone in the building would know what happened to her parents, brothers and sisters, and relatives. Perhaps there was still hope. The neighbors offered none. They told them that when the Germans had come, knocking on all the doors in the building, many families had refused to answer and managed to escape. But Eleanora's family *had* answered and was herded into trucks waiting on the street. And the neighbors repeated the report that Giacomo had heard earlier but had kept from his wife: The whole family had been deported to Germany and presumably killed.

The young couple, silent and pale, made their way to their own apartment through streets crowded with cheering, laughing people. Her whole family . . . ? Eleanora pressed the infant asleep in her arms to her bosom as a new wave of delirium greeted American tanks and jeeps groaning by.[13]

Newsman Michael Stern, accompanied by Frank Caniff, editor of the Hearst newspaper chain, continued his search for feature stories, deciding now to try the Ghetto. They drove through the teeming alleys and stopped in front of the great temple. A crowd of Jews, almost hysterical in these first hours of liberation, swarmed over the jeep, and some, wearing *mezuzahs* on strings around their necks, dangled them before the two reporters to kiss.

With difficulty, the two Americans got out and worked their way to the entrance of the temple. Standing at the doorway was a white-goat-eed man trembling with excitement. Former Chief Rabbi Zolli grabbed Stern's hand and kissed it. He muttered:

"The truth about the tragedy of my people must be made known."

Suddenly, another man wriggled through the crowd and quietly but imperiously charged: "This man deserted his people in the time of need. He is no longer our rabbi."

Zolli stared with anger at Ugo Foa, then looked pleadingly at Stern. "He knows that my name was on the top of the Gestapo list of Jews to be liquidated. Dead, what good would I have been to my people?"

"No matter what might have happened to him," Foa replied, "his place was here."

Foa thus signaled the beginning of a new, bitter fratricidal struggle that was to virtually shatter the remains of the Jewish community of Rome. The Americans, as part of their anti-Fascist clean-up campaign, threw out Foa and his council (as well as Dante Almansi, who headed the Jewish community on the national level) on the grounds that they were "elected during the Fascist regime and during the racial per-secution period, and therefore cannot be considered as the expression of the will of the Jews . . ." They installed a new president of the Roman community and resurrected Zolli as Chief Rabbi.

If many Jews blamed Foa for not doing more to protect them from the Nazis, Zolli found even fewer friends within his flock, which, by and large, agreed, rightly or wrongly, that he had abandoned them. Zolli brooded over his isolation, and his spirits seemed wounded irreparably when, during a liberation ceremony at the temple, his assistant, Rabbi David Pancieri, pulled him from his seat on the pulpit and declared that it no longer belonged to him.

I began to feel, Zolli later wrote, more and more keenly the desire to find someone who would speak to me of the God of Love, the God who loves all without distinction and desires that the bonds which unite men should be those of love.

Was this Utopia? That might be, but I told myself: A novelist dreamed of the submarine long before it was ever invented; an artist likewise conceived the airplane. And I began to realize that I had a con-crete desire for something like that utopia: I dared to say, the Utopia itself.

And I inquired of myself: Surely the realization of my dreams of

Jesus is not to be merely at the "end of the days," in the prophets' language? Is the sea of love entered only at the end of life? Has not God created us for love? And shall we ascend to God, if we have not loved everyone and everything? This is the path I was treading as I approached the promised land of Christianity.

This was the path Zolli was treading as his people continued to reject his "love" for them and to withhold their own from him. He found himself falling back ever more on Jesus, who loved him as He did all men. And besides, was not Jesus Himself a Jew? By returning His love, therefore, he was not betraying the Jews. Zolli was rational even in his mysticism.

Just one simple step into Utopia and he would expunge the sore festering in his soul. Should he take it? Such a step would make those who had unseated him from the chair of honor most unhappy, but let them find their own peace.[14]

❖ ❖ ❖

General Clark, accompanied by staff officers in a convoy of jeeps, passed through Porta Maggiore into Rome at about 8 A.M., June 5, the third conqueror in history to enter from the south. After all the agony, horror, and uncertainty, he had finally succeeded where even Hannibal had failed—despite the firm prediction of his commander at Fort Benning, where he had trained, that he would never be an effective leader! . . .

The colonel had assigned Clark to lead an eight-man reconnaissance patrol over a five-mile route and report back anything they saw of military significance. But it was a lovely summer day and the violets were in bloom—and Renie had given birth to a child only two days before. So Clark began picking violets for her and the eight men with him decided to help since picking violets was more fun than scouting.

But the colonel, who greeted them stonily as they returned with their posies, was not a fun-loving type. What significant things had Clark observed on his leisurely stroll—when he wasn't picking violets? Well . . . well, after all, his first son was only two days old.

"It's a wonderful feeling, Colonel. Do you have children?"

The colonel did not. He wasn't even married. As for Clark, God help the army! . . .

God had helped the army—the Fifth Army. And now Clark and his staff were heading for the Piazza del Campidoglio and the *municipio*, on Capitoline Hill, appropriately the historic seat of Roman power, for a meeting with his corps commanders and the Italian Resistance leaders, who would officially turn over the city to him. But the column of jeeps got lost, though nobody would admit it, and wandered through the streets while Clark and his officers craned their necks looking at the sights, not much caring where they were.

Eventually, the conquerors found themselves in St. Peter's Square, and as they stopped to admire the great golden dome of the basilica, a priest strolling by paused and said in English: "Welcome to Rome. Is there any way in which I can help you?"

"Well," replied Clark with some embarrassment, "we'd like to get to Capitoline Hill."

After giving directions, the priest said: "We are certainly proud of the American Fifth Army. May I introduce myself?"

He told Clark his name and said he was from Detroit.

"My name's Clark," the general responded with a smile.

As the priest started to move on, he stopped, turned around, and stared at Clark: "What did you say your name is?"

Many Italians had by now gathered around and when the priest told them who the tall, lean man was, a youth on a bicycle shouted that he would show the way to Capitoline Hill. As the boy pedaled along, followed by jeeploads of brass, he proudly yelled: "Make way for General Clark!"

This cry only fueled the mounting excitement and by the time the party reached Piazza di Venezia the road was completely blocked by surging, screaming mobs. After a monumental effort, the jeeps finally broke a path through to Capitoline Hill and wound their way up to Piazza del Campidoglio.

Clark and the others descended from their jeeps, radiant from the welcome, and approached the front of the *municipio* with the dignified aplomb appropriate to the conqueror. But the door was locked and nobody was around to greet them. Clark knocked. No answer. Who ever heard of a conqueror who couldn't even get into the *municipio*? They all stood around sheepishly—until a caretaker finally came and apologetically let them in.

Other principals in the drama trickled in—General Truscott, General Keyes, General Juin, and Resistance leaders led by General Bencivenga, who proudly hobbled along on a cane and, for all his joy, bluntly told Clark that he had wounded Roman pride by occupying the *municipio*, which only Romans should control. Most of the Italians had come from San Giovanni where they had been taking refuge, some after brief, emotional visits with their families at home . . .[15]

General Filippo Caruso, the *carabinieri* leader who had been freed from Via Tasso only the day before and had stayed the night at San Giovanni, was driven home early that morning by two subordinates. But he found that his wife, on hearing of his liberation a few hours earlier, had rushed out like a madwoman to look for him, leaving the children with a neighbor. When she returned, she found her husband surrounded by friends who were embracing him and shouting their welcome.

She stared at him as if he were a stranger—this scrawny, crippled man with one bluish eye shut, with swollen jaws and a face scarred and horribly discolored. Then he smiled, showing raw, toothless gums. His wife took him gently by the arm and wanted to put him to bed, but he insisted on going to the *municipo* to meet General Clark. And so she helped him to change into his dress uniform. He must look his best.

Fate was to rob Caruso not only of his health but, at least for the moment, of deserved glory. The Allies and Badoglio, ill-informed about the Resistance in Rome, distrusted the *carabinieri* of this city. They had sent up from the south that day several units of *carabinieri* who had proven themselves loyal to the King, undercutting Caruso's authority.[16]

Actually, Badoglio—and the King—needed more than a few loyal troops to guarantee that Rome would return to business as usual. The King desired to be in Rome on this historic day, promising, as he had earlier agreed, to turn over his powers to his son, Humbert—who would become lieutenant general of the realm—on arrival; but the Allies did not trust the King and feared, in any case, for his life. They demanded that he vacate his throne immediately—without going to Rome. This he reluctantly did, while Badoglio, under American pressure, simultaneously dissolved his government.

Badoglio expected to form a new regime on his arrival in Rome the following day, June 6, but the CLN parties in that city—except, ironically, for the Communists, who still preferred the compromised Badoglio to a more liberal and untainted leadership that might compete more effectively with them for popularity—demanded that their own leader, Ivanoe Bonomi, head a new government composed entirely of CLN people.

Backed by Italian public opinion and the Roosevelt administration, the CLN proves irresistible. Bonomi would take over on June 10, though Churchill, wild with fury that his puppets had been ousted in favor of the unpredictable party politicians, tried his best to thwart this move.‡

General Bencivenga, for all his dignity, appeared a rather pathetic character as he welcomed Clark and the other Fifth Army generals to Rome. Badoglio had expected him to run the city in the period between German departure and Allied arrival, to keep order and make sure the leftists would not grab power. But since the Allies entered on the very heels of the Germans, the general had not had the opportunity to discharge this function. He now hoped to remain in power under the Allies, but the leftists were in fact about to take over, albeit democratically.*

Nevertheless, at this moment of triumph, the *municipio* resounded with cheers and laughter and deeply emotional messages as men who had suffered, bled, and prayed for this day came together as brothers to celebrate.[17]

In the Stampa Estera, the foreign press building, pandemonium reigned as correspondents rattled out stories, rushed to the censor, demanded to know how their copy was being sent. Suddenly, a public relations officer burst in with the announcement that General Clark had just called a press conference.

‡ On June 12, 1944, shortly before he agreed to accept the new Italian government, according to United States diplomatic records, Prime Minister Churchill sent the following message to President Roosevelt: "Badoglio's replacement by this group of aged and hungry politicians is, I think, a great disaster. From the time when, in spite of the enemy, Badoglio safely delivered the fleet into our hands, he has been a useful instrument to us. It was understood, I thought, that he was to carry on, at least until the democratic north could be brought in and a thoroughly sound Italian government could be formed. We are confronted, instead, with this absolutely unrepresentative crew . . . At the present time, I was not aware that we had given the Italians, who have cost us so dearly in life and material, the right to form any government they chose without reference to the victorious powers, and without even the slightest pretense of a popular mandate."

* An OSS report (85720) dated July 8, 1944, read as follows: "Two reports regarding Badoglio have gained currency in political circles. 1. It is reported that General MacFarlane [chief of the Allied Commission in Italy] was misled by Badoglio regarding latter's calculations that he was acceptable to Rome Committee of Liberation into declaring that it was almost a certainty that a fourth Badoglio cabinet would be formed at Rome. Fact is that from very outset of negotiations Badoglio was unacceptable to Rome Committee. 2. It is also reported that at Badoglio's suggestion General Alexander issued orders to Rome patriot bands to stay out of Rome and not go into action; that Rome, if free of patriot troops, was distinctly in favor of Badoglio's political position, and against him—perhaps personally dangerous—if armed patriots were present in the city. 3. It is also reported that General Bencivenga . . . joined with Badoglio in plans to keep armed bands out of Rome for political reasons."

The reporters stormed out and, as they approached the *municipio*, saw Clark casually leaning against the balustrade overlooking the square below, relaxed and happy. They ran up a stone stairway and found newsreel men and photographers already grinding and clicking away, silhouetting Clark's gangling figure against the panorama of the Rome he had so passionately sought. Surrounded by his commanders, Clark drawled:

"Well, gentlemen, I didn't really expect to have a press conference here—I just called a little meeting with my corps commanders to discuss the situation. However, I'll be glad to answer your questions. This is a great day for the Fifth Army and for the French, British, and American troops of the Fifth Army who made this victory possible."

Eric Sevareid, who was present, later wrote: "That was the immortal remark of Rome's modern-day conqueror. It was not, apparently, a great day for the world, for the Allies, for all the suffering people who had desperately looked toward the time of peace. It was a great day for the Fifth Army."

It was certainly not a great day for the Eighth Army—which, for all the fury of everyone from Churchill and Alexander to the lowliest soldier who had survived the lunacy of Cassino, had not yet broken through the skillfully organized Fifth Army traffic jam blocking its way to Rome.

Clark pointed to some places on a map spread on the balustrade, explaining something to his commanders, who kept stealing self-conscious glances at the cameras recording this moment for posterity.

Yes, it was a great day for the Fifth Army.[18]

❖ ❖ ❖

At 5 P.M. that day, June 5, the great bell of St. Peter's pealed and a roar of acclamation greeted the appearance of the slender, white-robed figure behind the ceremonial drapery decorating the parapet of the basilica's central balcony. People waved and applauded and held their children up and cried *"Viva Papa!"* And many carried flags—Italian, American, British, French, even the red flag—while an American Piper Cub overhead showered the area with flowers.

Pope Pius XII gazed down with smiling benevolence upon his children, who formed a massive mosaic of color, including large patches of khaki, as they stood bathed in the glow of sunset. Twice in the morning people had gathered in Saint Peter's Square to cheer him, and once he had appeared to extend his blessing. But he had been a bit piqued by the sight of an armored car at the edge of the square. He had telephoned his Secretary of State three times to demand that the car be sent away, but as soon as that one left, another appeared. If the Germans could respect Vatican neutrality, why could not the Allies?

Now he was in a subdued mood. The people of Rome still loved him. They knew that he had helped to save their sacred city, the center and symbol of Christian civilization. He raised his hand and his half-million listeners grew quiet as he began to speak:

"We must give thanks to God for the favors we have received. Rome has been spared. This day will go down in the annals of Rome."

After further references to Rome's "salvation," the Pope, frequently interrupted by applause, concluded his brief talk and blessed the kneeling crowd. Even after he had left the balcony the throngs continued to acclaim him. Then, while the military departed in their jeeps and trucks, the Italians, without public transportation because of the lack of fuel and electricity, walked back to their homes. It didn't matter. Rome was saved.

Actually, it seemed to many at the moment more important that Rome had been *liberated*—though the Pope had not mentioned liberation and *Osservatore Romano* had, in fact, neglected so far even to report that the Allies had arrived. But the people, however aroused by their sudden freedom, understood the Pope because they were Romans.

Conquerors and liberators had come and gone for centuries. They were but men, who eventually died, the good and evil alike, their deeds obscured in the infinity of history. But Rome—and the Church—were Eternal. And did not the Pope have the duty to make sure they remained so, whatever the price?[19]

Three days later, on June 8, the two most powerful men in Rome met. General Clark and his staff drove to the Vatican in jeeps, wearing battle dress, and were escorted to the Pope's chambers by Swiss Guards in their colorful uniforms. Pius invited Clark to talk with him alone before the regular audience and proved to be very well informed on military developments.

"I understand your headquarters are now in Rome," the Pope said. "How long will you be here? I am fearful that your presence may bring retaliation from the Germans."

Clark replied that he did not believe the Germans were in a position to retaliate but that in any event he would be in Rome only a few days longer.

The Pope then asked whether Clark had had any contact with the

Russians and expressed fear about the possible effects of Communism in Central Europe.

Much of the conversation sounded like those which the Pope had often conducted with the Nazis, except that now Pius was speaking in English rather than in German. This was nevertheless a historic moment. The Pope was meeting for the first time with the latest conqueror of Rome.†

The news of their meeting, however, was buried in the back pages of the world press, like all other reports from Italy—even those on the escape of the two battered German armies from the Allied trap that never closed.

For on June 6, hardly more than a day after the fall of Rome, the Allies crossed the English Channel.

Mark Clark had finally realized his dream. From the pinnacle of glory he had received the thunderous acclaim of the Allied peoples.

For one day.[20]

† The Pope expressed regret to General Clark that "your American soldiers do not like me." He said that while Italians or other Europeans attending audiences broke "into cheers and shouts of greeting and similar expressions of enthusiasm . . . your American soldiers . . . do not utter a sound. They do not say one word." Clark explained that the Americans were less demonstrative and that their background prompted them to maintain a reverent silence in the presence of the Pope. Pius XII seemed pleased by this explanation, but it is not clear what he thought when Eleanor Packard, the United Press correspondent who, with her husband Reynolds, had filed the first story on the liberation of Rome, attended an audience dressed in a uniform with slacks.

Epilogue

Deeply disappointed that the British—except for those who played a minor role in the U.S. Fifth Army—had not shared in the capture of Rome, Winston Churchill played down the event in a letter he wrote to Stalin on June 5:

> What we have always regarded as more important is the cutting off of as many enemy divisions as possible. General Alexander is now ordering strong armoured forces northward . . . which should largely complete the cutting off of all the divisions which were sent by Hitler to fight south of Rome.

The Prime Minister would be disappointed once again. As Field Marshal Kesselring was to write after the war about the Allied pursuit of the German Tenth and Fourteenth Armies north of Rome: "The even distribution of [the Allied] forces over the whole front . . . lessened the peril of a concentration at the seam of our two armies."

The Allied forces had dispersed their power. Instead of jointly punching through the gap between the two German armies so that each could be surrounded, Clark's Fifth Army pursued the German Fourteenth through Rome west of the Tiber River, while the British Eighth Army shadowed the German Tenth east of the Tiber.

With the two Allied armies thus stretched across a broad front, they were unable to concentrate on the "seam." It was easier, therefore, for the two German armies to stay ahead of the Allies until they could close the gap between them. Their problem was, as indicated earlier, to beat the two Allied armies to the first undestroyed Tiber bridges north of Rome—at Orte and Orvieto—so that they could link up before the Allies were able to isolate each.

Alexander himself hinted at the likely outcome of this race in a report to Churchill (dispatch 2928) on the night Rome fell, June 4: "If only the country were more open we would make hay of the lot. However, you may rest assured that both [Allied] armies will drive forward as fast as is physically possible."

They were not quite fast enough. The German Tenth Army, scrambling desperately through the hills, arrived at the Tiber bridges first—only a few hours before the Allies—and crossed to link up with the Fourteenth Army.

"If the enemy had not been prevented from seizing the crossings," writes General von Senger und Etterlin in his memoirs, "the results might have been incalculable. The Tenth Army would have been separated from the Fourteenth, and either army could have been crushed separately."

Ironically, Rome, by influencing the Allies to split their forces, had helped to save both of Kesselring's armies and thus assure new bloody battles in a theater that might have been eliminated from the war in summer 1944. For with their link-up at the two bridges north of Rome, these two German armies, buttressed by reinforcements from Western Europe, were able to form and hold a new powerful defense belt, the Gothic Line, in the Apennines north of Florence.

Nor could the Germans believe their good fortune when they discovered that the overwhelming Allied force that had almost devoured them had suddenly been reduced to manageable strength. Churchill had pleaded with the American command to let the entire force follow up the Rome rout with a relentless push into northern Italy. From there it could smash through the Ljubljana Gap and into the Balkans and Eastern Europe. And he was supported by every leading commander in the Mediterranean—Wilson, Alexander, Juin, Anders, and even the top American, Clark.

But on June 14, only ten days after the fall of Rome and while the Germans were still in full flight, Alexander was ordered to withdraw from the battle almost immediately a major part of Clark's Fifth Army (the 3rd, 26th, and 45th Divisions and the four divisions of the French Expeditionary Corps), many aircraft, and other units. These forces were to be incorporated in a new U.S. Seventh Army that was to invade southern France. While American leaders (though not Clark) insisted that General Eisenhower needed a large southern French port to support his cross-channel operation and pointed out that the only troops available to capture one were in Italy, Alexander cabled one final plea:

> I cannot overemphasize my conviction that if my tried and experienced commanders and troops are taken away for operations elsewhere, we shall certainly miss a golden opportunity of scoring a really decisive victory, and we shall never be able to reap the full benefits of the efforts and gains we have made during the last few weeks. I feel strongly that it is of the greatest importance not to let go the chance that has been so hard won.

The Americans, however, would not back down this time. In August 1944, shortly before the invasion of southern France, General Wilson, reflecting Churchill's bitter feeling, commented in a report to the Combined Chiefs of Staff:

> . . . A shift of our operations [from Italy] for [an invasion of southern France] seemed to me to imply a strategy aimed at defeating Germany during the first half of 1945 at the cost of an opportunity to defeat him [sic] before the end of 1944 . . .

Churchill, however, was not thinking simply in military terms. He now saw Eastern Europe lost to the Soviet Union.

Thus, the lust for Rome plus the shift of troops to southern France reconverted the battle for Italy into a savage slugging match, with each side using this theater simply to keep enemy forces that might otherwise be utilized in Western Europe tied down in relatively static positions.

The Allies finally breached the Gothic Line in the Apennines in autumn 1944, and by year's end reached a point south of Bologna, where they dug in for the winter.

Late in 1944 the top Allied commanders in the Mediterranean area all moved up a notch. Wilson became the permanent representative in Washington of the British Chiefs of Staff; Alexander, the Supreme Commander in the Mediterranean; Clark (who had been selected to lead the invasion of southern France, but forfeited this opportunity when he chose to capture Rome), the commander of the 15th Army Group—which embraced the Fifth and Eighth Armies; Truscott, the commander of the Fifth Army; and McCreery, the commander of the Eighth Army.*

---

* After the war, Alexander, by now a field marshal, served as Governor-General of Canada from 1946 to 1952, and as British Minister of Defence from 1952 to 1954. Clark became Commander in Chief of the United Nations Command in Korea and Commanding General of the U.S. Army Forces in the Far East in 1952. He retired in 1953 without having been appointed U.S. Army Chief of Staff, a position his friends thought he deserved but one which was denied him apparently in part because of accusations by members of General Walker's 36th Division that Clark had needlessly sacrificed a large part of the division in its abortive attempt to cross the

Less than a week after Rome fell, General Walker of the 36th Division (which was to take part in the invasion of southern France) received a note from Clark praising him highly—and asking about his "availability for assignment as the Commandant of the Infantry School."

Walker scribbled in his diary: "He just wants to get rid of me . . . Well! I have bellyached enough."

Although unhappy, he accepted the post.

On the German side, in March 1945 Hitler transferred Kesselring to the Western Front where, as supreme commander, the field marshal made a futile effort to halt the Allies in Germany. Characteristically, even after Hitler's suicide he continued, in his blind loyalty and bottomless optimism, to defend every inch of scorched earth until his only option, finally, was surrender. Vietinghoff, meanwhile, had replaced Kesselring as the Commander in Chief of the Southwest Command and of Army Group C.[1]

SS General Wolff continued to hope until early 1945 for a compromise peace between a Hitler-run Germany and the Western Allies, the "solution" he had apparently had in mind when he told the Pope that he would seek peace if the opportunity arose. Either German scientists might perfect a "secret weapon" in time, or the United States and Britain, to keep Russia out of Eastern Europe, might be willing to make a separate peace with Hitler. Both possibilities, he rationalized, would give the Nazis substantial bargaining power.

On February 6, 1945, however, Wolff visited Hitler's headquarters and learned from colleagues that no "secret weapon" was likely to be produced in time. He now saw little choice but to make peace on whatever terms possible—and, incidentally, to lay the groundwork for saving himself. He shrewdly suggested to the Führer that *something* be done to extricate Germany from its untenable situation—a proposition too vague to shock even Hitler, who was noncommittal. Wolff took the liberty of interpreting this ambivalence as a go-ahead to seek a channel for peace, at least in Italy where he was the SS boss.

He easily found other important Germans in Italy with a similar view—and instinct for self-preservation. Among them were Colonel

Rapido River in January 1944—though a congressional investigation of the charges did not establish their validity. General Juin, later marshal, served as Chief of Staff, French Armed Forces, from 1944 to 1947, as Resident General of Morocco from 1947 to 1951, and as Commander in Chief, Allied Land Forces, Central Europe, from 1951 to 1953 and of all Allied forces in that area from 1953 to 1956. He became a controversial figure in France, supporting rightist efforts, in conflict with General de Gaulle, to maintain France's African empire.

Dollmann and Ambassador Rahn. Dollmann records in his memoirs that he remembered the words of Father Pfeiffer, the Vatican liaison with the Germans, just before, he, Dollmann, had fled Rome:

"You have a mission, my dear Dollmann, and people trust you . . . Use this opportunity to do everything in your power to mitigate the horrors of the Italian civil war which, unbeknown to you, is raging in the north. One more thing: bear in mind that Germany has lost the war and that you must therefore do all you can to shorten it. Only the will of God can bring it to an end."

Dollmann indicates that he was also influenced by what he saw during his retreat from Rome:

"Looking into the weary, sweat-stained faces of the soldiers who shared my ditch by the roadside, I heard them tell of the latest battles . . . of their longing—their grim and desperate longing—to bid the war a last farewell and go home. To them, if not to me, every kilometre they retreated was a kilometre nearer their goal. Suddenly, in the course of that harrowing journey, I realized what I had to do, or at least what I had to try to do.

"Although it had been clear . . . that the final phase of the Second World War had arrived, I had always shut my eyes to this not over-brilliant piece of deduction and dismissed it from my mind as far as possible. The time for self-deception was now past."

The war had to end because it could not be won. Wolff, Dollmann, and Rahn, without Hitler's knowledge, contacted OSS representatives led by Allen Dulles, General Donovan's assistant, and after intense and dramatic negotiation the German forces in Italy, now under General von Vietinghoff, surrendered on May 2, 1945†—almost immediately after the Führer's suicide and several days before Kesselring, loyal to his master unto, indeed beyond, death, finally gave up in the West.

After the war, the Allies did not press war criminal charges against any of the three men—though Wolff was sentenced by a West German court in 1946 to four years' imprisonment for his involvement in high-altitude experiments on human beings for the Luftwaffe, and in 1964, to fifteen years for being "continuously engaged and deeply entangled in guilt." He was freed from his second imprisonment in 1971, however, on grounds of poor health.

† Details of the surrender were arranged on May 4 by General von Senger und Etterlin, who had come to General Clark's headquarters in Florence after a hazardous trip through partisan-controlled territory from Bolzano via the Brenner Pass. Saved from ambush by several American officers who were escorting him, he suffered a final blow to his dignity as he entered Clark's office. He inadvertently stepped on Clark's dog, Pal, and the canine bit into his booted leg. Senger was so flustered that he had to be reminded by Clark to remove his pistol, which Clark kept as a souvenir.

In an interview at his home in Darmstadt the author asked Wolff whether, if he could relive his life, he would join the SS again. He replied wistfully—while denying, despite ample evidence to the contrary, that he had any knowledge about the "Final Solution" to the Jewish problem:‡

"I lived a very good life. I was so young and I was a general. I had everything I wanted."

Dollmann "escaped" from an American internment camp in Rimini, Italy—with the help of OSS officers who furnished him false papers, the kind of help that might have saved the lives of Italians like Colonel Montezemolo if Dollmann had been willing—or able—to grant it. Dollmann eventually settled in Munich, where he has spent his time writing. Rahn became an executive in the German Coca-Cola company.[2]

Other German officers who played a role in Rome were not as fortunate. Mackensen and Mälzer in 1947 and Kesselring in 1948 were tried by British courts for their parts in the Ardeatine Caves massacre. The field marshal was also charged with "inciting and commanding . . . forces . . . under his command to kill Italian civilians . . ." All were sentenced to death, but the sentences were commuted to life imprisonment, and, in 1952, Kesselring and Mackensen were freed. Mälzer by this time had died in prison. Kesselring, shortly before his death in 1960, admonished his people to "keep our national character and respect our traditions," as he apparently felt he himself had done.

SS Colonel Kappler was tried by an Italian court in 1948 for his part in the Ardeatine massacre and for the extortion of fifty kilograms of gold from the Jews. He was sentenced to life imprisonment, largely on the grounds that he had ordered five more men killed at the caves than Hitler had officially authorized under the ten-for-one order.

The only person who has ever come regularly to see Kappler in prison was, ironically, Monsignor Hugh O'Flaherty, the man he had tried so hard to capture. In 1959 O'Flaherty, who had just been appointed chief notary at the Holy Office, baptized Kappler into the Catholic Church. The monsignor died a few years later, and Kappler is still in an Italian prison. In 1972 he married a German woman whom he had courted through correspondence.[3]

Ambassador von Weizäcker's personal mission at the Vatican—to arrange for the Pope to mediate a negotiated peace—was dealt a final

‡ In 1952 Wolff testified at the trial of another Nazi that he did not believe that even Hitler knew about the massacre of the Jews.

blow when the attempt by dissident German officers to assassinate Hitler on July 20, 1944, failed. Many of Weizsäcker's diplomatic associates were tortured and killed, including Adam von Trott zu Solz, who claimed at his trial that Weizäcker had been the leader of the plot in Rome, a statement never substantiated. Albrecht von Kessel, who had been an active participant, remained in Rome and therefore escaped arrest.

Weizsäcker realized that it was now too late for a negotiated peace, since no such peace was possible while Hitler remained in power. In helpless frustration, he sat out the war in the Vatican after moving there upon Rome's fall, remaining until mid-1946 when he returned to Germany. The Allies arrested him and tried him before a Nuremberg court for instigating war, taking part in the plunder of France, and participating in SS crimes, including the deportation of Jews.

Many of the documents used against him were messages he claimed were intended either to "limit" particular crimes or to give the impression he was co-operating with government policy so he would be in a position to sabotage it. In his final plea he stood before the court a broken man, though with his usual haughty, defiant bearing, and asserted:

"What does a sailor do when the weather and the captain have brought the ship into danger? Does he go below deck in order not to have any responsibility? Or does he set to and do all he can to help, with all his strength and all the means at his disposal. I did not attempt to leave the danger spot but tried to stick it out and fight. Such was my decision. My goal was peace."

Weizsäcker was convicted and sent to prison in 1948. He was released in 1950 and died the following year.[4]

In Rome the long cowed and terrorized inhabitants cried for Fascist blood—especially for the blood of Pietro Koch and Pietro Caruso, the two police chiefs.

Koch, at his trial in June 1945, was his usual cynical self, telling the judge at one point, while raising an eyebrow sardonically: "I wish to be confronted with those who were *supposedly* tortured."

The judge exploded: "But how do you expect me to confront you with dead people?"

In his cell, Koch told a priest—now Cardinal Mario Nasalli Rocca: "I am German in name and blood, and, like all good Germans, I may be a murderer but not a traitor."

He was fatalistic, pretentiously viewing himself as a man pushed by historical circumstance: "Danton killed and was killed; Robespierre killed and was killed. So it went for them all up to Pietro Koch, who killed and will be killed."

But as the hour of death approached, he grew more humble, and even penitent, telling the priest: "After being an unwilling student and a second-rate officer, I was suddenly given great power. Power excited in me the most intense ambition. At the age of twenty-eight, to be head of the police . . . ! I lost my head. Justice found that head again, but to nail it to a wall for me."

On the morning he was to be executed, the Pope sent for Rocca and showed him a letter he had just received from the condemned man. Guilty of the most atrocious crimes against the Resistance and the Jews, Koch now asked that the Pope forgive him—for having violated the sanctity of the Basilica of San Paolo.

"Hurry, go to Lieutenant Koch and bring him my forgiveness immediately," the Pope urged, handing the priest a rosary. "Give him my blessing and this rosary."

Koch was so moved on hearing the Pope's words that he said to the priest, with tears in his eyes: "Father, I, with these bloodstained hands, am not worthy. I cannot touch the Holy Father's rosary. Bring it to my lips yourself."

Rocca inquired if there was anything else he could do for him, and Koch asked that the Pope bless his mother, from whom he had not heard. Rocca rushed to the Pope, who, the priest notes in his memoirs, "raised his eyes to the heavens and made a great sign of the cross." Rocca hurried back to the prison to inform Koch, but the prisoner had left twenty minutes earlier for Forte Bravetta, the place of execution.

Impeccably dressed, his hair, as usual, carefully slicked back, Koch, standing before a firing squad, asked an official: "My mother . . . ?"

"Nothing . . ."

He was then tied to a chair with his back to the firing squad, and, in a moment, the Pope's rosary slipped from his stiffened fingers.[5]

On the day that Pietro Caruso's trial was to begin, in September 1944, an angry crowd stormed the Palace of Justice screaming: "We want Caruso!"

He had not yet arrived, but one woman, sighting a short, rather innocuous looking man in the courtroom, cried hysterically: "It's the jailer! He sent my son to his death!"

The mob lunged at Donato Carretta, Caruso's deputy at Regina Coeli, who had often secretly co-operated with the Resistance and was to be a prosecution witness. *Carabinieri* policemen finally broke through and saved him, but a little later the crowd caught sight of Carretta in another room, grabbed him, and hauled him out by the heels, beating and kicking him as they dragged him toward the Tiber.

The *carabinieri* once more rescued him and threw him into a truck, but the vehicle would not start, and when the driver got out to crank it he was overwhelmed by rioters. They tore the crank from his hands and struck Carretta over the head with it. Then they literally ripped the prisoner's hair from his scalp and pinned him to a streetcar track, ordering a tram operator to run over him.

When the horrified operator jumped out and fled, the crowd dragged Carretta to the Tiber and tossed him in, and while he struggled to swim youngsters in rowboats beat him on the head with their oars until he drowned. The body was pulled out and carried triumphantly to Regina Coeli where it was hanged by the feet from the entrance.

Two days later the postponed Caruso trial was held, and the following day Caruso, repenting for the San Paolo raid but denying other charges to the end, died, like Koch, with a papal rosary in his hand.[6]

Celeste (Stella) Di Porto stood trial in 1945, but, through the good offices of the Church, was simply sent to a convent to meditate on her crimes—a punishment that outraged the Jewish community. She soon left the convent, as a Catholic, and was not seen until 1948 when several Jews recognized her in a bar. A woman walked up to her table and hissed:

"Drink with me, Celeste!"

Shortly, a crowd, hearing of her presence, gathered outside and, when she came out, nearly lynched her (as another crowd had tried to do when she was first arrested) before police managed to carry her to safety.

Today no one knows where Celeste is, but she has not been forgotten. Still scratched on the wall of a cell in Regina Coeli prison are the words of one of her victims:

"Avenge me!"[7]

Many Romans, while thankful that the Allies had come, grew increasingly disillusioned with Allied rule after liberation. The new CLN government itself felt greatly restrained by the controls of the Allied Commission.* For one thing, Churchill in finally granting recognition

* The word "control" in "Allied Control Commission" was dropped earlier when Italian leaders persuaded Allied officials that, while the Commission, in reality, controlled Allied-occupied Italy, it was unnecessarily humiliating to stress that fact in its name.

to the new Bonomi cabinet, imposed a humiliating condition—that each member take an oath to observe terms of the armistice agreement and to make no attempt to overthrow the monarchy. A great Allied bureaucracy had to approve the government's every move and appointment.

Though electricity, in severely short supply, was always available in Allied billets, offices, and even dance halls, little was apportioned to the Italians. Bureaucratic Allied officials even refused a legless Italian ex-officer who had come to beg for a little electric stove to keep his stagnant blood circulating, as well as olive-mill operators who needed enough electricity to save the olive crop. But there were apparently no complaints from the wealthy set that had once entertained Fascist and German officials and who now invited Allied generals and colonels to their lavish drawing rooms.

The Romans thus began falling back on their traditional source of psychological comfort—apathy toward the transient conqueror. Like all the others, this one, even if better than most, would not survive long in this heartland of Eternity.[8]

Nevertheless, north of Rome, the Resistance grew rapidly after the liberation of the capital. And with Rome no longer threatened by destruction or "Communist revolution," Vatican pressure on the Allies to keep the partisans under control receded. On June 6, two days after Rome fell, the Allies instructed the Resistance by radio and leaflet:

> To those who have arms, all over Italy, use them and go on using them. Avoid battles, but make raids and ambushes . . . To all those who have explosives, blow up bridges and railway crossings, telegraph and telephone installations . . . To workers and clerks, leave your work. If that is not possible, work slowly and sabotage the workshops. To peasants who have no arms, do all you can to help the patriots in your districts . . . The Allies are supplying patriot groups with thousands of automatic weapons. Find out whether there is one for you . . .

Encouraged by this new Allied policy, Resistance groups throughout Nazi-occupied Italy set up a new Corps of Freedom Volunteers under a supreme military command in which all military formations were represented—the first attempt to unite the various underground groups under a single strong leadership.

Certainly this effort did not eliminate all the distrust between the CLN and royalist partisans—as the continuing bitter conflict between Peter Tompkins and Mino Menicanti tended to show. Tompkins (who was forced to spend the morning of June 5 in the police station persuading his wardens that he was not really a Fascist after all) and his

CLN friends were more convinced than ever of Menicanti's "disloyalty" to the Allies when they visited Via Tasso and saw scratched on the wall of one cell a drawing of two long ears with a grim warning scrawled over it: BEWARE OF CONIGLIO!

"Coniglio," meaning "rabbit," was Menicanti's code name.

Tompkins demanded that the OSS investigate Menicanti, and his superiors finally agreed—selecting Captain Bourgouin, Menicanti's French boss, as the investigator!

Menicanti's absolution nearly caused Tompkins' dissolution—in the Excelsior Hotel bar.

Despite disruptive partisan disputes, Kesselring felt it necessary on June 19, 1944, to issue an order to his forces from his new mountain headquarters north of Rome, saying:

> The partisan situation in the Italian theater, particularly Central Italy . . . , constitutes a serious danger to the fighting troops and their supply lines as well as to the war industry and economic potential. The fight against the partisans must be carried on with all the means at our disposal and with the utmost severity.
>
> I will protect any commander who exceeds our usual restraint in the choice of severity of the methods he adopts against partisans. In this connection the old principle holds good that a mistake in the choice of methods in executing one's orders is better than failure or neglect to act.

A few days later, on June 29, after partisans had killed two Germans in the village of Civitella, Kesselring's troops acted accordingly. They massacred 212 men, women, and children and burned down about a hundred houses, some with people in them—one of the Germans' many acts of atrocity as the Allies gradually pushed north. But the Resistance only grew, and so did its rage, with Communists especially showing no mercy for Fascists they captured.

Among the Fascist victims were Mussolini and his mistress who, while fleeing the Allied tide, were discovered and gunned down in a northern town on April 28, 1945.[9]

After the war, most of the men who led Italy were CLN Resistance leaders. And they finally achieved, peacefully and democratically, what some had been willing to risk civil war to accomplish before the fall of Rome; in 1947 the Italians voted to replace the monarchy with a republican form of government.

One of the most influential postwar CLN leaders was Palmiro Togliatti. He firmly continued his policy of co-operation with the other anti-Fascist parties and the monarchy (as long as it lasted) initiated before the liberation of Rome. After the city's fall, with the Allies removing the shackles on Resistance activity, he ordered, as he had not for Rome, Communist participation in insurrections throughout the part of Italy still under German control. But he nevertheless made clear to his party, in line with Moscow's global "national front" strategy, that this permission to fight the Germans did not extend to political and social *revolution*. Shortly after Rome's liberation, he issued a directive to his cadres saying:

> The insurrection which we wish does not have the aim of imposing social and political transformations in a socialist or Communist sense, but has as its aim national liberation and the destruction of Fascism. All other problems will be resolved by the people tomorrow, once all Italy is liberated, by means of free popular consultation and the election of a Constituent Assembly.

Togliatti's aim was the establishment of a mass Communist party that, after the war, would win control of the government, not through violence but through votes. The party became, in fact, a popular one, far less ideologically rigid than most Communist parties. It has never been able to govern Italy, but has consistently won about one third of the nation's votes—despite a decree issued by Pope Pius XII in 1959 (revoked later by Pope John XXIII) prescribing excommunication for those who joined or collaborated with the Communists or their allies.

Still among the party's staunchest supporters are Carla Capponi and Rosario Bentivegna, who were married shortly after the war. They have received medals for their roles in the Resistance but even today are sometimes denounced by Romans who cannot forget that Via Rasella sealed the death of their sons in the Ardeatine Caves. Carla was a Communist deputy in Parliament for several years and today, though suffering from ill health as a result of deprivation in her underground days, spends much of her time campaigning for the party cause. Bentivenga is a leading physician in Rome.

Other Resistance fighters who have been politically active include Giuliano Vassalli, long an influential Socialist deputy in Parliament, and Franco Malfatti (Peter Tompkins' assistant), who was for several years the Italian ambassador to Paris.[10]

The Jewish community in Rome continued to suffer under the curse of the holocaust long after the war was over. Israel Zolli, after being returned by Allied authorities to his position of Chief Rabbi, presided over a largely hostile congregation. He was clearly a source of division within the community, and even his supporters began to think that he should resign.

Zolli was deeply depressed—until, by his account, Yom Kippur, the Day of Atonement, in autumn 1944. While conducting services in the temple on that holiest of Jewish holy days, he recounts in his memoirs:

> I felt so far withdrawn from the ritual that I let others recite the prayers and sing. I was conscious of neither joy nor sorrow; I was devoid of thought and feeling. My heart lay as though dead in my breast. And just then I saw with my mind's eye a meadow sweeping upward, with bright grass but with no flower. In this meadow I saw Jesus Christ clad in a white mantle, and beyond His head the blue sky. I experienced the greatest interior peace.
>
> If I were to give an image of the state of my soul at that moment I should say: a crystal-clear lake amid high mountains. Within my heart I found the words:
>
> "You are here for the last time."
>
> I considered them with the greatest serenity of soul and without any particular emotion. The reply of my heart was: So it is, so it shall be, so it must be.

That evening at home, his wife, according to Zolli, told him: "Today while you were before the Ark of the Torah, it seemed to me as if the white figure of Jesus put His hands on your head as if He were blessing you."

Zolli writes that he was "amazed but still very calm. I pretended not to have understood." Then his youngest daughter Miriam called him to her room, he claims—though Miriam says today that she does not recall this episode—and said:

"You are talking about Jesus Christ. You know, Papa, tonight I have been dreaming that I saw a very tall, white Jesus, but I don't remember what came next."

What came next was that Zolli secretly began to take Catholic instruction while remaining in his position of Chief Rabbi. Under pressure from fellow Jewish leaders—who did not, however, suspect his plans—he resigned on February 1, 1945, and rejected an offer to head the Rabbinical College. Nevertheless, he continued to perform the duties of a rabbi—even presiding at divorce cases between sessions of Catholic instruction.

Finally, on February 13, Israel Zolli and his wife received the sacrament of baptism in the Basilica of Santa Maria degli Angeli and entered the Catholic Church.

The Jews were shocked and incredulous on reading in the newspapers of what the Jews termed Zolli's "treachery" and "deceit," convinced that he had converted not out of conviction but out of sheer spite. Otherwise, they asked, why would he keep his intention a secret? Why would he perform rabbinical functions until the very last day? Whatever the answers, Catholic priests who knew him insist that he was sincere.

Some Jews feared that a cascade of conversions would follow and precipitate still another disaster to the already shredded community. But on the following Sabbath eve, hundreds of Jews jammed, as seldom before, the temple where Zolli had conducted services so recently. They filed in solemnly, silently, as if for a funeral.

In a somber, quietly forceful voice, Rabbi Pancieri declared in a sermon that in the long history of the Jewish people many had deserted the fold and betrayed Israel but that their names had been forgotten. He did not even mention the name of Zolli. Zolli no longer existed. He was dead.

After services, the Jews of Rome walked out as silently as they had entered. A branch was lost but the tree would grow stronger. They were, it seemed, united at last.

Zolli, who changed his first name from "Israel" to "Eugenio" in honor of the Pope, began working for a small salary in the Vatican Library (the Jewish community refused to pay him the pension he claimed). At least one Jewish official concedes that during the reign of Pope John XXIII he helped to influence the historic revision of certain passages in the New Testament that had reflected unfavorably on the Jews. If this report is true, Zolli, ironically, performed as a Christian a service for the Jews far more important than any he might have performed as a Jew.

The former rabbi died in 1956 a lonely and impoverished man. The Jews despised him and many Catholics did not quite accept him, despite the Church's ill-concealed pleasure over its extraordinary conquest. Zolli told visitors on his deathbed that a feeling of peace had at last filled his soul. But no one will ever know the feeling that filled his heart.[11]†

† Bitterly hostile toward the Jewish community for what she regarded as its unfair treatment of her father, Miriam Zolli converted to Catholicism shortly after her parents did. She says today that she is only a nominal Catholic, having failed to find the satisfaction her father found in their new religion. But she is nevertheless bringing her children up as Catholics. Zolli's elder daughter, Dora, has remained Jewish.

Notes

The following notes indicate the principal sources of the facts presented in this book. Each note applies either to a single section or to two or more consecutive sections if they deal with the same subject. Included are the sources of all dialogue. The identities of interviewees named here (including the ranks of high military officers) are indicated in the lists of the *Acknowledgments* section. Further details on publications and documents mentioned here can be found in the *Bibliography*.

Prologue

1. Clark's trip home—Mark W. Clark's *Calculated Risk;* Maurine Clark's *Captain's Bride, General's Lady;* interview with Mark W. Clark.
2. Zolli flees into hiding—Eugenio (Israel) Zolli's *Before the Dawn* (dialogue); interview with Miriam Zolli (De Bernart).
3. Hitler-Wolff meeting—Karl Wolff's personal papers (dialogue); interviews with Eugen Dollmann, Karl Wolff.
4. Princess Pignatelli meets the Pope—Interviews with Princess Enza Pignatelli Aragona (dialogue), Father Robert A. Graham.
5. Mussolini-Dollmann meeting—Eugen Dollmann's *The Interpreter* (dialogue); interview with Dollmann.
6. Chilanti Red Flag mission—Interviews with Felice, Viviana, and Gloria Chilanti (dialogue reconstructed by all three), Antonio Poce.
7. General Filippo Caruso's ordeal—Filippo Caruso's *L'Arma dei Carabinieri in Roma durante l'occupazione tedesca;* interview with Filippo Caruso. (Dialogue from both sources.)

1   *The Plans*

1. Platt brothers lead attack—George Molesworth's *The History of the Somerset Light, Infantry, 1919–1945*; Hugh Williamson's *The Fourth Division, 1939–1945*; interviews with John and Humphry Platt.
2. Lieutenant Mahorowski's dream—Charles Connell's *Monte Cassino: The Historic Battle*.
3. Planès' departure—Interview with Pierre and Colette Planès.
4. Shea's eardrums—Interview with Charles W. Shea.
5. Weck and the monastery—Interview with Hans-Joachim Weck.
6. Churchill and Rome—Martin Blumenson's *Anzio: The Gamble that Failed*; Winston Churchill's *Closing the Ring* (dialogue); Herbert Feis' *Churchill, Roosevelt, Stalin*; Trumbull Higgins' *Winston Churchill and the Second Front*; Lord Moran's *Churchill: Taken from His Diaries— The Struggle for Survival, 1940–1965*; Robert Payne's *The Marshall Story*; Forrest C. Pogue's *George C. Marshall: Ordeal and Hope*; Henry L. Stimson and McGeorge Bundy's *On Active Service in Peace and War*; Albert C. Wedemeyer's *Wedemeyer Reports!*; World War II files, Washington National Records Center (WNRC), U.S. National Archives, Washington, D.C.
7. Alexander and Rome—Earl Alexander of Tunis' *The Alexander Memoirs, 1940–1945*; Clark's *Calculated Risk*; W. G. F. Jackson's *Alexander as Military Commander* and *The Battle for Rome*; Wilson report (*Report by the Supreme Allied Commander Mediterranean to the Combined Chiefs of Staff on the Italian Campaign, 8th January to 10th May, 1944*); *London Gazette*, June 12, 1950 ("The Dispatches of Field Marshal the Earl Alexander of Tunis: The Allied Armies in Italy"); *Newsweek*, September 6, 1943; *Time*, June 5, 12, 1944; Allied Forces Hq. records (WNRC); interviews with Clark, Alfred M. Gruenther, Sir John Harding, Sir Sidney Kirkman, Sir Oliver Leese, Lyman Lemnitzer, John North.
8. Clark and Rome—Alexander's *The Alexander Memoirs*; Stephen E. Ambrose's *The Supreme Commander* (Marshall quote about Clark; Eisenhower memo); Blumenson's *Anzio*; Clark's *Calculated Risk*; M. Clark's *Captain's Bride, General's Lady*; Ladislas Farago's *Patton: Ordeal and Triumph* (Patton's aborted assignment to Anzio); Lucian Truscott's *Command Missions* (quote by Clark–"The capture of Rome is the only important objective"); New York *Times Magazine*, September 19, 1943; *Time*, October 4, 1943 (dialogue—Clark and baseball game); Fifth Army records (WNRC); interviews with Clark, Gruenther, Harding, Lemnitzer, North.
9. Juin and Rome—René Chambé's *L'Épopée française d'Italie*; Clark's *Calculated Risk* (dialogue taking place in North Africa); Charles de Gaulle's *The Complete War Memoirs of Charles de Gaulle*; Robert Jars' *La Campagne d'Italie, 1943–1945*; Alphonse Juin's *Memoirs, L'Armée Française en Italie, Décembre, 1943–Juillet, 1944*; *La Participation Française à la Campagne d'Italie* (including April 27 mes-

sage from Juin to De Gaulle); *Hommes et Mondes* (Paris), January 1954 ("La Bataille de Rome en 1944," by Maréchal Juin); *The Contemporary Review*, December, 1944; *Miroire de l'Histoire* (Paris), April, 1966 ("Le Drame de Cassino," by Maréchal Juin); *Newsweek*, May 29, 1944; *La Revue des Deux Mondes* (Paris), May 1, 1952 ("La Bataille du Garigliano," by René Chambé); *Revue Historique de l'Armée* (Paris), May, 1967 ("Hommage au Maréchal Juin"); *Time*, May 29, 1944; interviews with Albert Bonhouré, Clark, Augustin Guillaume, Pierre Lyautey.

10. Anders and Rome—Wladyslaw Anders' *An Army in Exile* (dialogue taking place in Russia); Clark's *Calculated Risk*; Connell's *Monte Cassino: The Historic Battle*; *Collier's*, April 4, 1942; *Newsweek*, March 12, 1945; interviews with Tadeusz Anders, Zygmunt Bohusz-Szyszko, Clark, Bronislaw Duch, Kirkman, Leese, Eugene Lubomirski (dialogue involving Polish reserves).

11. Kesselring and Rome—Rudolf Böhmler's *Monte Cassino*; Dollmann's *The Interpreter*; Albert Kesselring's *A Soldier's Story*; Louis P. Lochner's (ed.) *The Goebbels Diaries, 1942–43*; Frido von Senger und Etterlin's *Neither Fear Nor Hope*; Canadian Army Report No. 24 (*The Italian Campaign*); captured German records, including verbatim telephone conversations (WNRC); postwar military reports by Kesselring, Heinrich von Vietinghoff, Eberhard von Mackensen, and other German generals; interviews with Dietrich Beelitz, Walter Warlimont, Siegfried Westphal.

12. Artillery barrage—Frank S. Praino's *Direct Support*; New York *Herald-Tribune*, May 13, 1944; New York *Times*, May 13, 1944; *Stars and Stripes*, May 13, 1944.

2   The Plots

1. Dollmann, Hitler, and Rome—Dollmann's *The Interpreter* and *Roma Nazista* (dialogue); Siegfried Westphal's *German Army in the West*; interview with Dollmann.

2. Wolff and kidnap plot—Wolff's private papers (dialogue); Constantine, Prince of Bavaria's *The Pope*; Allen Dulles' *The Secret Surrender*; Lochner's *The Goebbels Diaries*, *Foreign Relations of the United States, 1943*, Vol. 2 (section on Vatican); *Domenica del Corriere* (Rome), March 14, 1972; *Stern* (Hamburg), April 16, 1972; interviews with Dollmann, Rahn, Wolff.

3. Weizsäcker's background; his meeting with Pope—Carl Burckhardt's *Meine Danziger Mission, 1937–1939*; Constantine's *The Pope*; Harold Deutsch's *The German Conspiracy in the Twilight War*; Sir Nevile Henderson's *Failure of a Mission, Berlin, 1937–1939*; Erich Kordt's *Nicht aus den Akten*; Lewis B. Namier's *In the Nazi Era*; Ernst von Weizsäcker's *Memoirs*; *Journal of Contemporary History*, January 1968 ("Three Crises," by Leonidas Hill); *Journal of Modern History*, June, 1967 ("The Vatican Embassy of Ernst von Weizsäcker, 1943–1945,"

by Leonidas Hill); *Rundbriefe aus Rom* (collection of unpublished letters sent by Weizsäcker from Rome to his family, furnished the author by Marianne von Weizsäcker); Official Record, United States Military Tribunals, Nuremberg (Case No. 11, Tribunal IV [IVA], U.S. vs. Ernst von Weizsäcker et al., Vol. 28), 1948: pistol story from a defense affidavit written, but not used, by Weizsäcker's daughter-in-law Gundalena, to whom he told it; interviews with Leonidas Hill and Marianne, Adelheid (Gräfin zu Eulenburg), and Richard von Weizsäcker.

4. History of Vatican raid plot—*Domenica del Corriere* (Rome), March 14, 1972; interviews with Father Graham, other Vatican officials.

5. Weizsäcker's meeting with Pope—See Note 3.

6. Pope's family background—Constantine's *The Pope*; O. Halecki and J. Murray's *Pius XII: Eugenio Pacelli, Pope of Peace*; Alden Hatch and Seamus Walshe's *Crown of Glory* (includes dialogue on Munich confrontation); John P. McKnight's *The Papacy*; Nazareno Padellaro's *Portrait of Pius XII*; Corrado Pallenberg's *Inside the Vatican*.

7. Germans and Vatican raid plot—Eitel Möllhausen's *La carta perdente*; Rudolf Rahn's *Ruheloses Leben*; Weizsäcker's *Memoirs*; interviews with Dollmann, Möllhausen, Rahn, Wolff.

3 *The Jews*

1. Zolli's visit to Vatican—Zolli's *Before the Dawn* (dialogue).

2. Kappler's meeting with Foa and Almansi—Dante Almansi report (*Prima relazione al governo italiano circa le persecuzioni nazi-fasciste degli ebrei in Roma [settembre 1943–giugno 1944]*, August 15, 1944); Ugo Foa's *Relazione del presidente della comunità israelitica di Roma Foa Ugo circa le misure razziali adottate in Roma dopo 18 settembre a diretta opera delle autorità tedesche di occupazione*, November 15, 1943, and June 20, 1944 (booklet); Testimony, Herbert Kappler trial, (Foa, June 11, 1948; Kappler, June 1, 11, 1948).

3. Collection of gold—Giacomo Debenedetti's *16 ottobre 1943*; Renzo de Felice's *Storia degli ebrei italiani sotto il fascismo*; Robert Katz's *Black Sabbath*; C. Lizzani's *L'oro di Roma*; *L'Espresso* (Rome), December 3, 1961 ("Perchè non si difesero"); diary of Rosina Sorani (*Appunti personali di Rosina Sorani del periodo di occupazione tedesca in Roma*); interviews with Renzo Levi, Goffredo Roccas, M. Zolli.

4. Zolli's background—Louis I. Newman's *A "Chief Rabbi" of Rome Becomes a Catholic*; Zolli's *Antisemitismo, Before the Dawn*, and *The Nazarene*; *The Catholic Digest*, September, 1945 ("The Chief Rabbi's Conversion," by A. B. Klyber); *The Churchman*, June 1, 1945 ("The Conversion of a 'Chief Rabbi,'" by A. S. E. Yahuda); *The Congress Weekly*, March 2, 1945 ("The Case of Rabbi Zolli," by G. Bertel); Fifth Army chaplain's report on Zolli; Maurice Neufeld's collection of material on Zolli; interviews with Father Pietro Boccaccio, Sophia

Cavaletti, Ettore Dell'Ariccia, Father Dezza, Levi, Rabbi Alfred Ravenna, Roccas, Bernard Solomon, Elena Sonnino-Finzi, Settimio Sorani,
Rabbi Elio Toaff, M. Zolli.

5. Zolli's talks with Almansi and Foa—Zolli's *Before the Dawn* (dialogue); Neufeld papers; interview with M. Zolli.

6. Zolli at the Vatican—Zolli's *Before the Dawn*.

7. Collection of gold—See Note 3.

8. Foa and Zolli—Debenedetti's *16 ottobre 1943*; Newman's *A "Chief
Rabbi" of Rome Becomes a Catholic*; Zolli's *Before the Dawn*; Foa
report; interviews with Dell'Ariccia, Levi, Sonnino-Finzi, S. Sorani, Toaff,
M. Zolli.

9. Jews and Fascism—De Felice's *Storia degli ebrei italiani sotto il fas-
cismo*; Lochner's *The Goebbels Diaries*; Attilio Milano's *Il ghetto di
Roma* and *Storia degli ebrei in Italia*; Newman's *A "Chief Rabbi" of
Rome Becomes a Catholic*; Cecil Roth's *The History of the Jews of
Italy*; Zolli's *Before the Dawn*; *On the Jewish Question in Fascist
Italy*, Yad Vashem Studies, Vol. IV; *The Menorah Journal*, Winter
1940 ("The Role of the Jews in Modern Italy," by Marcel Grilli).

10. Collection of gold—See Note 3.

11. The Di Portos and the Ghetto—F. Gregorovius' *The Ghetto and the
Jews of Rome*; H. Vogelstein's *Rome*; *Commentary*, February, 1958
("An Outsider Visits the Roman Ghetto," by S. P. Dunn); *Scientific
American*, March, 1957 ("The Jewish Community of Rome," by L. C.
and S. P. Dunn); *The Influence of Ideology on Cultural Change*,
doctoral dissertation by S. P. Dunn, Columbia University, 1959; Foa
report, interviews with Giacomo and Eleanora Di Porto.

12. Weizsäcker and the Pope—Paul Duclos' *Le Vatican et la seconde
guerre mondiale*; Saul Friedlander's *Pius XII and the Third Reich*;
Rolf Hochhuth's *Sidelights on History* (appendix to *The Deputy*);
Gunther Lewy's *The Catholic Church and Nazi Germany*; Möll-
hausen's *La carta perdente*; Weizsäcker's *Memoirs*; articles in Eric
Bentley's (ed.) *The Storm over the Deputy*, including: "The Pope
and the Jews" by Albrecht von Kessel, "Pius XII" by Robert Leiber,
"Pope Pius XII and the Nazis" by L. Poliakov (also *Commentary*,
November, 1950); *American Historical Review*, October, 1964 ("Pope
Pius XII and Germany," by George O. Kent); Leonidas Hill's articles
in *Journal of Contemporary History* and *Journal of Modern History*
(see Note 3, Chap. 2); *Rundbriefe aus Rom*; diary of Marianne von
Weizsäcker, who permitted the author to read parts of it; interviews:
see Note 3, Chap. 2.

13. History of Vatican-Jewish relations—Gregorovius' *The Ghetto and the
Jews of Rome*; Roth's *The History of the Jews of Italy*; Vogelstein's
Rome.

14. Weizsäcker-Maglione meeting—Secret memorandum written by Maglione after meeting (dialogue; Hochhuth and other writers on the
Vatican-Jewish theme apparently were unaware of this vital conversation

and its contents when they wrote their reports); interviews with Father Graham, Father Burkhart Schneider, other Vatican officials.

15. Weizsäcker, Kessel, and the Jews—Weizsäcker's *Memoirs*; Kessel's article in Bentley's *The Storm over the Deputy* (dialogue); *Law Reports of Trials of War Criminals*, Vol. VIII, Kessel's testimony at Weizsäcker trial, June 21, 1948; interviews with Albrecht von Kessel, Möllhausen.

16. Meetings involving Kappler, Kesselring, Möllhausen, and Stahel—Duclos' *Le Vatican et la seconde guerre mondiale*; Möllhausen's *La carta perdente* (dialogue); interview with Möllhausen.

17. Efforts to prevent Jewish round-up—Möllhausen's *La carta perdente*; Kessel's article in Bentley's *The Storm over the Deputy* (dialogue); German Embassy, Rome, diplomatic dispatches; interviews with Kessel, Möllhausen, Rahn.

18. Kessel-Gumpert-Weizsäcker plot—See Note 17; Hochhuth's *Sidelights on History*; Katz's *Black Sabbath*; interview with Gerhard Gumpert.

19. Deportation of Jews—S. Bertoldi's *I tedeschi in Italia*; Debenedetti's *16 ottobre 1943*; Katz's *Black Sabbath*; R. Sorani's diary; interviews with Di Portos, Levi, Ravenna, S. Sorani, Roccas.

20. Di Portos and Convent of Notre Dame de Sion—Diary of convent; interviews with Di Portos, Sister Katharine.

21. Weizsäcker and Pope after round-up—Friedländer's *Pius XII and the Third Reich*, Hochhuth's *Sidelights on History*; Weizsäcker's *Memoirs*; *Foreign Relations of the United States*, 1943, Vol. II (section on Vatican—Tittmann audience, October 19), *Osservatore Romano* (October 25–26, 1943); interviews: see Note 3.

22. Hitler-Wolff meeting—See Note 3, Prologue.

4   The Escapers

1. Pius XII and the bombing of Rome—Constantine's *The Pope*; Halecki and Murray's *Pius XII*; Hatch and Walshe's *Crown of Glory* (dialogue); Padellaro's *Portrait of Pius XII*; Myron C. Taylor's *Wartime Correspondence Between President Roosevelt and Pius XII*; *Foreign Relations of the United States*, 1943, Vol. II (Tittmann audience, October 19); interviews with Vatican officials and bombing survivors, including Angela Maria Romano.

2. Monsignor O'Flaherty's escape—Sam L. Derry's *The Rome Escape Line*; J. P. Gallagher's *Scarlet Pimpernel of the Vatican* (dialogue); interview with Cardinal Alfredo Ottaviani.

3. Derry joins O'Flaherty—Derry's *The Rome Escape Line* (dialogue); Gallagher's *Scarlet Pimpernel of the Vatican*; interviews with Renzo Lucidi, Lily Marx, Ottaviani, Princess Nini Pallavicini (dialogue concerning spies in Vatican).

4. Princess Pallavicini's story—interview with Pallavicini.

5. Furman, Simpson, and Pollak arrive—Derry's *The Rome Escape Line*

(dialogue); John Furman's *Be Not Fearful;* Gallagher's *Scarlet Pimpernel of the Vatican;* interview with Lucidi.

6. French escapers and the Jews—Derry's *The Rome Escape Line;* Fernande Leboucher's *Incredible Mission* (story of Father Benoît; dialogue involving Gestapo agents); *Gestion Financière du Comité Français d'Entraide à Rome* (unpublished report of French Mutual Aid Committee activities); interviews with Father Benoît (statement of Pope and note from Vatican official), Jacques de Blesson, François de Vial.

7. Arvay and French deserters—*Commonweal,* June 8, 1945 ("The Italian People and the Jews," by Richard Arvay); unpublished report of French Mutual Aid Committee activities; interviews with Richard Arvay, De Blesson, De Vial, Levi, S. Sorani.

8. Derry moves further underground—Derry's *The Rome Escape Line;* interview with Lucidi.

5 *The Partisans*

1. The Pope and the Communists—*Foreign Relations of the United States, 1943,* Vol. II (Tittmann audience, October 19).

2. Bentivegna, Capponi, and Communism—Giorgio Amendola's *Il sole e sorto a Roma;* Roberto Battaglia's *The Story of the Italian Resistance;* Donald Blackmer's *Unity in Diversity;* Benedetto Croce's *The King and the Allies;* Robert Katz's *Death in Rome;* Luigi Longo's *Un popolo alla macchia;* Renato Perrone Capano's *La Resistenza in Roma;* E. Piscitelli's *Storia della Resistenza romana;* Carlo Trabucco's *La prigionia di Roma;* thesis on history of Italian Communism by Joan B. Urban, Catholic University, Washington, D.C.; Office of Strategic Services (OSS) reports; New York *Times Magazine,* June 18, 1944 ("A New Chapter in Eternal Rome," by Herbert L. Matthews); interviews with Giorgio Amendola, Rosario Bentivegna, Carla Capponi, Giorgio Caputo, Mario Fiorentini, Pietro Griffoni, Carlo Salinari, Antonello Trombadori.

3. The anti-Fascist parties—See Note 2; C. F. Delzell's *Mussolini's Enemies: The Italian Anti-Fascist Resistance;* Max Salvadori's *Brief History of the Patriot Movement in Italy, 1943–1945;* interviews with Luigi Barzini, Ugo La Malfa, Pietro Nenni, Sandro Pertini, Giuliano Vassalli.

4. The King and Badoglio flee Rome—Pietro Badoglio's *Italy in the Second World War;* Giacomo Carboni's *Più che il dovere;* Melvin Davis' *Who Defends Rome?;* Peter Tompkins' *Italy Betrayed;* R. Zangrandi's *1943: 25 luglio–8 settembre* (dialogue involving King, Mussolini, and Badoglio); *Collier's,* June 10, 1944 ("The Guilty—Victor Emmanuel III"); interviews with Giacomo Carboni, Giuseppe Cosmelli.

5. CLN formed—See Notes 2 and 3.

6. The Red Flag party and the Chilantis—Amendola's *Il sole e sorto a Roma; Bandiera Rossa;* interviews with Felice, Viviana, and Gloria

Chilanti (dialogue from all three), Roberto Guzzo, Orfeo Mucci, Antonio Poce.

7. Centro X formed—Interviews with Ottorino Borin, Arturo Musco, Ugo Musco, Felice Santini.

8. Calvi and Montezemolo—Dollmann's *The Interpreter*; Fulvia Ripa di Meana's *Roma clandestina* (dialogue); interview with Marchesa Fulvia Ripa di Meana.

9. Clandestine Front formed—F. Caruso's *L'arma dei carabinieri in Roma durante l'occupazione tedesca*; Gabrio Lombardi's *Montezemolo e il fronte militare clandestino di Roma*; Franco Maugeri's *From the Ashes of Disgrace*; Ripa di Meana's *Roma clandestina*; Trabucco's *La prigionia di Roma*; interviews with Ernesto Argenziano, Ettore Basevi, Alfredo Bernardini, Mario Buentempi, Emilio Ferreri, F. Caruso, Marx, A. Musco, U. Musco, Ripa di Meana, Carlo Resio, Santini.

10. German labor draft—Dollmann's *Roma nazista*; Möllhausen's *La carta perdente* (dialogue); interviews with Dollmann, Möllhausen.

11. Basevi's press and forgery service—Trabucco's *La prigionia di Roma*; interviews with Basevi, Buentempi, Marx, A. Musco.

12. "Divide and conquer"—Interviews with Basevi, Capponi.

13. Tompkins arrives in Rome—Peter Tompkins' *A Spy in Rome*; interviews with Donald Downes, Peter Tompkins.

14. Tompkins meets partisans—Tompkins' *A Spy in Rome* (dialogue); interview with Franco Malfatti, Tompkins.

15. Kesselring and Anzio—Interview with Wolfgang Hagemann (dialogue).

16. Clandestine Front and Anzio—F. Caruso's *L'arma dei carabinieri in Roma durante l'occupazione tedesca*; Jo Di Benigno's *Occasioni mancate*; interviews with Argenziano, Basevi, Bernardini, Buentempi, U. Musco (dialogue).

17. Communists and Anzio—Interviews with Bentivegna, Capponi.

18. Coppola and Anzio—Dollmann's *Roma nazista* (dialogue with Kesselring); Möllhausen's *La carta perdente*; Maugeri's *From the Ashes of Disgrace* (dialogue involving Coppola); interviews with Dollmann, Möllhausen, Resio.

19. Tompkins and insurrection—Tompkins' *A Spy in Rome* (dialogue); interviews with Riccardo Bauer, Tompkins, Vassalli.

6 *The Traps*

1. Coppola's mission—Maugeri's *From the Ashes of Disgrace* (dialogue); interview with Resio.

2. Koch's gang—Aldo Lualdi's *La banda Koch*; *Storia Illustrata* (Milan), February, 1972 ("La banda Koch"); Goffredo Roccas' collection of material on Fascist criminals, Rome; Koch trial records; interviews with Maria Denise, Nicola Onorati.

3. Daisy and Onorati—Roccas material; interview with Onorati.

4. Father Morosini captured—Trabucco's *La prigionia di Roma*; Don Morosini (pamphlet) and other material available in Via Tasso Library.

5. Maugeri's men captured—Maugeri's *From the Ashes of Disgrace* (dialogue); *Storia Illustrata* article; interview with Resio.

6. Montezemolo captured—Ripa di Meana's *Roma clandestina*; interviews with Michele Multedo, Pallavicini (dialogue).

7. Raid on San Paolo—Constantine's *The Pope*; *L'Azione dei Lavoratori* (Rome-underground), February 10, 1944 (dialogue); *La punta* (Rome-underground), February 23, 1944; interviews with Roberto Sermoneta, Vatican officials.

8. San Paolo and the Germans—Lualdi's *La banda Koch*; Möllhausen's *La carta perdente* (dialogue); *Storia Illustrata* article; interviews with Kessel, Möllhausen.

9. Fear in San Giovanni—Di Benigno's *Occasioni mancate* (dialogue); interviews with U. Musco, Nenni, Msgr. Pietro Palazzini.

10. Perfetti's betrayal—Derry's *The Rome Escape Line* (dialogue); Gallagher's *Scarlet Pimpernel of the Vatican*; interview with De Vial.

11. Garry's escape—Derry's *The Rome Escape Line*; *News of the World* (London), December 19, 26, 1954, and January 2, 9, 1945 (his own story by E. Garrad-Cole) (dialogue); interview with Lucidi.

12. O'Flaherty, Grossi, Simpson, Dukate, and Koch—Derry's *The Rome Escape Line* (dialogue); Gallagher's *Scarlet Pimpernel of the Vatican*; interview with Lucidi.

13. Arvay's escape—*Commonweal* article; interview with Arvay.

14. The Black Panther—Roccas material (dialogue); Celeste Di Porto trial records; interviews with many Roman Jews.

15. Giglio's arrest and Tompkins' party—See Note 14, Chap. 5; interview with Vassalli.

16. Dollmann and the marchesa—Di Benigno's *Occasioni mancate*; Dollmann's *Roma nazista*; Ripa di Meana's *Roma clandestina* (dialogue); interviews with Dollmann and Ripa di Meana.

17. The Pope and the marchesa—Ripa di Meana's *Roma clandestina* (dialogue); interview with Ripa di Meana.

18. Gloria and the Russians—Mauro Galleni's *I partigiani sovietici nella Resistenza italiana*; *Bandiera Rossa* (dialogue on shooting of partisans); interviews with the Chilantis.

19. Tompkins in hiding—See Note 14, Chap. 5.

20. Montezemolo fails to escape—Ripa di Meana's *Roma clandestina*; interview with Ripa di Meana.

7 *The Corpses*

1. Bentivegna and Caronia—Interviews with both.

2. Fascist anniversary meeting—Möllhausen's *La carta perdente*; *Giornale d'Italia*, March 25, 1944; interviews with Dollmann, Möllhausen.

3. Communists plot to provoke revolt—See Note 2, Chap. 5.

4. Explosion on Via Rasella—Amendola's *Il sole sorto a Roma*; Attilo Ascarelli's *Le Fosse Ardeatine*; Katz's *Death in Rome*; *L'Europeo*

(Milan), April 12, 1964 ("Morire a Roma") (dialogue); interviews: see Note 2, Chapter V.

5. German plans for retaliation—Dollmann's *Roma nazista*; Vincenzo Florio's *Quattro giorni a Via Tasso*; Katz's *Death in Rome*; Möllhausen's *La carta perdente* (dialogue); Paolo Monelli's *Roma 1943*; Ardeatine Caves Commission, inquest (*Sommario dell'incidente del 23 marzo 1944* [Rome]); Guido Stendardo's *Via Tasso*; testimony, Pietro Caruso trial, March 1944; testimony, Kappler trial, June 1948 (dialogue when Möllhausen not present); interviews with Dollmann, Möllhausen.

6. Black Panther hunts Jews—Roccas material (dialogue); interviews with many Roman Jews.

7. Baldo's tea party and Giglio—See Note 14, Chap. 5.

8. Kappler supervises torture—Stendardo's *Via Tasso*.

9. Ardeatine Caves massacre—See Note 4 for written material; testimony, P. Caruso and Kappler trials (dialogue from latter).

10. Romans shocked by Ardeatine massacre—Amendola's *Il sole e sorto a Roma*; *L'Europeo* article; *Il Messaggero*, March 25, 1944; interviews with Bentivegna, Capponi.

11. Tompkins learns of Giglio's death—See Note 14, Chap. 5.

12. Dollmann and Wolff visit Kesselring—Dollmann's *Roma nazista* (dialogue); interviews with Dollmann, Wolff.

13. The Pope and the Ardeatine massacre—Bertoldi's *I tedeschi in Italia*; Constantine's *The Pope*; Dollmann's *Roma nazista*; Alberto Giovannetti's *Il Vaticano e la guerra* (1939–40); Katz's *Death in Rome*; *Lo Speccio* (Rome), August 13, September 24, 1972 (Dollmann on Pope's attitude); *Osservatore Romano*, March 26, 1944; interviews with Dollmann, Kessel.

14. Execution of Father Morosini—See Note 4, Chap. 6.

15. Plan to evacuate Romans—Dollmann's *Roma nazista*; Möllhausen's *La carta perdente* (dialogue); testimony, Kappler trial; interviews with Dollmann, Möllhausen.

16. Dollman seeks way to "save" Rome—Dollmann's *The Interpreter*; Giovannetti's *Roma, città aperta* (Giovannetti was Vatican official and is today Holy See observer to the United Nations); Alberto Mellini's *Guerra diplomatica a Salò*; interview with Dollmann.

17. Multedo in Via Tasso—Interviews with Basevi, Buentempi, Multedo, Lia T.

18. Dollmann and Virginia Agnelli—See Note 16; interviews with Giovanni Agnelli, Jolanda Berardi, Carla Colli, Dollmann, Susanna Agnelli (Contessa Pattazzi), Lydia Redmond (Princess San Faustino).

19. A baby born to Di Portos—Interviews with Di Portos, Sister Katharine.

20. Wolff meets the Pope—Interviews with Dollmann, Wolff (dialogue, both).

8 *The Rippers*

1. Monte Cassino monastery embattled—Interview with Weck.
2. Platt brothers cross the Gari—J. J. Burke-Gaffney's *The Story of the King's Regiment, 1914–48*; Eric Linklater's *The Campaign in Italy*; Molesworth's *The History of the Somerset Light Infantry*; G. A. Shepperd's *The Italian Campaign, 1943–45*; Williamson's *The Fourth Division*; report by John Platt (*Early Days with the 2nd Battalion in Italy*); interviews with Platts.
3. The Indians cross the Gari—Dharm Pal's *The Campaign in Italy, 1943–45*; D. K. Palit's *The Italian Campaign*; John Frayn Turner's *The V.C.'s of the Army, 1939–1951* (Ram); *The Tiger Triumphs*; *The Victoria Cross* (Ram).
4. Mahorowski and the Poles—Anders' *An Army in Exile*; Jana Bielatowicza's *Ulani Karpaccy*; Connell's *Monte Cassino* (about Mahorowski, including dialogue); Melchior Wankowicz's *Bitwa Monte Cassino*; Adam Wargos' *Monte Cassino: The Battle of Six Nations*; Pawla Zaremby's *Dzieje: 15 Pulku Ulanow Poznanskich*; interviews: see Note 10, Chap. 1.
5. Platts are saved—Interviews with Platts.
6. Leese visits Anders—Interviews with Leese, Kirkman, Lubomirski.
7. Planès and Castelforte—Chambé's *L'Épopée française d'Italie*; interview with Planès.
8. Conquest of Monte Faito—Chambé's *L'Épopeé française d'Italie* (dialogue); Pierre Ichac's *Nous marchons vers la France*.
9. Juin's vow—Chambé's *L'Épopée française d'Italie* (dialogue); Chambé's *Le Maréchal Juin*; Juin's *Memoirs*.
10. Shea attacks Monte Damiano—John P. Delaney's *The Blue Devils in Italy*; James C. Fry's *Combat Soldier*; interview with Shea.
11. Attack on Santa Maria Infante—Clark's *Calculated Risk*; Delaney's *The Blue Devils in Italy*; Historical Division, War Department, *Small Unit Actions*; *Fifth Army History*, Vol. V, *1 April–4 June 1944*; *Newsweek*, May 29, 1944; *Saturday Evening Post*, September 7, 1945 ("The Blue Devils Stumped the Experts," by Sid Feder); interviews with Joseph Crawford, Walter Guntharp.
12. What had gone wrong?—Alexander's *The Alexander Memoirs*; Clark's *Calculated Risk*; Allied Forces Hq. records; interviews: see Note 7, Chap. 1.
13. Kesselring's dilemma—See Note 11, Chap. 1; XIV Panzer Corps Intelligence Diary; XIV Army intelligence reports; LI Mountain Corps War Diary (all these German records in WNRC).
14. Juin visits front; Majo falls—See Note 9.
15. Germans panic after Majo falls—See Note 11, Chap. 1; Note 13, above.
16. The *goumiers* attack—See Note 9; Bernard Simiot's *Soldats d'Italie 1944*; Pierre Lyautey's *La campagne d'Italie* (dialogue with Kendall);

Carl Mydans' *More Than Meets the Eye*; Jouin report, *goumier* attack in Aurunci mts.; interviews with Guillaume, Kendall, Lyautey.

9 *The Squabbles*

1. Under Cassino's rubble—Richard McMillan's *Twenty Angels over Rome*; P. Forbes and N. Nicolson's *The Grenadier Guards in the War of 1939–45*, Vol. II; interview with Hermann Voelck-Unsin.

2. Building Amazon Bridge—Jackson's *The Battle for Rome*; Williamson's *The Fourth Division*.

3. Decision on second Polish attack—Senger und Etterlin's *Neither Fear Nor Hope*; interviews with Harding, Kirkman, Leese.

4. German desperation on Monte Cassino—Böhmler's *Monte Cassino*; Valentin Feurstein's *Irrwege der Pflicht*; Kesselring's *A Soldier's Story*; Canadian Army report; German Tenth Army records (telephone conversations); LI Mountain Corps War Diary; postwar reports by Kesselring and Vietinghoff; interviews with Beelitz, Hermann Berlin, Karl-Heinrich Graf von Klinckowstroem, Westphal.

5. British 78th Division waits for battle—Jackson's *The Battle for Rome*; Fred Majdalany's *The Monastery*; Cyril Ray's *Algiers to Austria*; interviews with Harding, Kirkman, Leese.

6. Bobinski's triumph—See Note 10, Chap. 1, Note 4. Chap. 8; transcript of radiophone conversation provided by Colonel Wladyslaw Bobinski; interview with Bobinski.

7. Dobrowolski attacks—Connell's *Monte Cassino*; interview with Tomasz Dobrowolski.

8. The intercepted message—Anders' *An Army in Exile*; Connell's *Monte Cassino* (Rudnicki-Anders dialogue); interviews with Bohusz-Szyszko, Lubomirski, Josef Minski.

9. Kesselring decides to withdraw from Cassino—Tenth Army records (telephone conversation) (WNRC); Canadian Army report; interviews: see Note 4.

10. Anders and German bombing—Interview with Lubomirski.

11. Germans withdraw from Monte Cassino—Connell's *Monte Cassino*; interview with Weck.

12. Germans withdraw from Cassino town—Williamson's *The Fourth Division*; interview with Voelck-Unsin.

13. Anders sends patrol to monastery—Interviews with Kirkman, Leese, Lubomirski.

14. Thomas climbs to monastery—Williamson's *The Fourth Division* (dialogue).

15. Poles capture monastery—Anders' *An Army in Exile*; Wilhelm Berthold's *Vom Himmel zu Hölle*; Connell's *Monte Cassino*; interviews with Bohusz-Szyszko, Leon Hrynkiewicz, Lubomirski.

16. Germans praise French—Tenth Army records (telephone conversation).

17. *Goumiers* wipe out German force—See Notes 9 and 16, Chap. 8; dialogue from Guillaume interview.

18. Kesselring's telephone conversation with Wentzell—Tenth Army records.
19. The Planèses meet on battlefield—*Vie et psychologie des combattants et gens de guerre* (Gaullists and former Vichyites link up); interviews with Planèses.
20. *Goumiers* spread terror—Fifth Army records.
21. Clark-Alexander controversy over breakout—See Note 7, Chap. 1; Churchill's *Closing the Ring*; Truscott's *Command Missions*; *Life*, October 2, 1944 (article on Truscott).
22. Kesselring's controversy with his commanders—See Note 11, Chap. 1; Fourteenth Army records, including report: *Rückzug und Verfolgung nach der Einnahme von Rom* (WNRC).
23. Clark and Anzio—Robert Aldeman and George Walton's *Rome Fell Today*; Blumenson's *Anzio*; Clark's *Calculated Risk*; Christopher Hibbert's *Anzio: Bid for Rome*; Eric Sevareid's *Not So Wild a Dream*; Fred Sheehan's *Anzio—Epic of Bravery*; Truscott's *Command Missions*; W. Vaughan-Thomas' *Anzio*; John Bowditch's (ed.) *Anzio Beachhead*; interviews with Clark, Graham Heilman.

10   *The Survivors*

1. Planes attack Bentivegna and Capponi—Interviews with both.
2. Rome after Ardeatine massacre—See Note 2, Chap. 5; *Bandiera Rossa*.
3. Planes attack Bentivegna and Capponi—Interviews with both.
4. Tompkins in the PAI—See Note 14, Chap. 5.
5. Zolli in hiding—See Note 4, Chap. 3; Zolli's *Before the Dawn* (dialogue).
6. Pancieri and the Fascists—Interviews with Olympia Pancieri, Ravenna.
7. Fascist attack on convent—Interviews with Aldo Cava, Di Portos, Sister Katharine.
8. O'Flaherty's deal to free Simpson—See Note 12, Chap. 6.
9. Tompkins meets Menicanti—See Note 14, Chap. 5.
10. New government formed—Badoglio's *Italy in the Second World War*; Croce's *The King and the Allies*; Churchill's *Closing the Ring*; Agostino Degli's *Il regno del sud*; Delzell's *Mussolini's Enemies*; Cordell Hull's *Memoirs*, Vol. II; Longo's *Un Popolo alla macchia*; Robert Murphy's *Diplomat Among Warriors* (dialogue with King); New York *Times Magazine*, March 21, 1948 ("Italy in the Shadow of the Hammer and Sickle," by C. L. Sulzberger); *Time*, May 5, 1947 (Togliatti and Italian Communists); OSS reports; interview with Falcone Lucifero.
11. Bentivegna, Capponi, and the Russians—Galleni's *I partigiani sovietici nella Resistenza italiana*; interviews with Bentivegna, Capponi.

11   *The Breakthroughs*

1. Allies start breakout from Anzio—See Note 23, Chap. 9.
2. Attack toward Cisterna—Adleman and Walton's *The Devil's Brigade*; James Altieri's *The Spearheaders* (Rangers); Robert Burhans' *The*

First Special Service Force; George Howe's *The Battle History of the
1st Armored Division;* Linklater's *The Campaign in Italy;* Shepperd's
The Italian Campaign, 1943–45; Donald Taggart's (ed.) *History of
the Third Infantry Division in World War II; History of the 7th Infantry Regiment, World War II* (3rd Division); *History of the 30th
Infantry Regiment, World War II* (3rd Division); *Newsweek,* June 12,
1944 (Rangers); Allied Forces Hq. records.

3. Germans in confusion—Kesselring's *A Soldier's Story;* 14th Army records, including *Rückzug* report (telephone dialogue); postwar reports
by Greiner, Kesselring, Mackensen.

4. Truscott meets with Clark—Clark's *Calculated Risk;* Truscott's *Command Missions;* Greenfield (ed.), *Command Decisions* ("General
Clark's Decision to Drive on Rome" by Sidney T. Mathews); interview with Clark.

5. Battle for Cisterna—Taggart (ed.), *History of the Third Infantry Division in World War II; History of the 7th Infantry Regiment, World
War II;* Fourteenth Army records, including *Rückzug* report; postwar
report by Greiner.

6. Anzio link-up—Clark's *Calculated Risk;* New York *Herald-Tribune,*
May 26, 1944 (article by Homer Bigart, including dialogue); New
York *Times,* May 26, 1944; interview with Clark.

7. Voelck-Unsin and the Canadians—Jackson's *The Battle for Rome;* Ross
Munro's *Gauntlet to Overlord;* Gerald Nicholson's *The Canadians in
Italy, 1943–45; The Canadians at War, 1939–45;* Canadian Army
report; interview with Voelck-Unsin.

8. Thrust to Melfa River—See Note 7 (except interview).

9. Westphal calls Vietinghoff—Tenth Army records.

10. Mahoney crosses Melfa—See Note 7; Turner's *The V.C.'s of the Army*
(Mahoney); *The Victoria Cross* (Mahoney).

11. Kesselring refuses to withdraw—Feurstein's *Irrwege der Pflicht;* Kesselring's *A Soldier's Story;* Canadian Army report; Tenth Army records
(telephone and radio messages); interviews: see Note 4, Chap. 9.

12. Eighth Army unable to move—Jackson's *Battle for Rome;* interviews
with Harding, Kirkman, Leese.

13. Kesselring optimistic—Kesselring's *A Soldier's Story;* Canadian Army
report; Tenth Army records (dialogue).

14. Truscott ordered to change direction—See Note 4; from Truscott's
Command Missions (quote by Brann); statement by Truscott to
Brann from telephone conversation, VI Corps War Room Journal,
May 25, 1944, cited by Mathews in *Command Decisions;* interviews:
see Note 7, Chap. 1.

15. Gruenther sees Alexander—Alexander's *The Alexander Memoirs;*
Clark's *Calculated Risk; Command Decisions* (Mathews chapter); interviews: see Note 7, Chap. 1.

16. The Germans try to hold at Valmontone—Kesselring's *A Soldier's
Story;* Senger's *Neither Fear nor Hope;* postwar report by Vietinghoff;
interviews: see Note 4, Chap. 9.

17. Race to Valmontone—Taggart (ed.), *History of the Third Infantry Division in World War II*; Howze report; interview with Hamilton Howze.

18. The Germans hold at Valmontone—See Note 16.

19. Mackensen holds Caesar Line—See Note 3; Clark's *Calculated Risk*; Howze report (complaint about friendly bombing of Allied troops).

20. Clark's nightmare—Chambé's *L'Épopée française d'Italie*; Chambé's *Le Maréchal Juin*; Clark's *Calculated Risk* (dialogue); De Gaulle's *The Complete War Memoirs of Charles de Gaulle*; Juin's *Memoirs*; Jackson's *Battle for Rome*; *La Participation française à la campagne d'Italie*; interviews with Bonhouré, Clark, Gruenther, Guillaume, Harding, Lemnitzer.

21. Clark approves Keyes's plan—Adleman and Walton's *Rome Fell Today*; Clark's *Calculated Risk*; interviews with Clark, Gruenther, Robert W. Porter.

22. Walker's plan to infiltrate Caesar Line—See Note 23, Chap. 9; Adleman and Walton's *Rome Fell Today* (including Clark's quote on Walker's "nepotism"); Blumenson's *Bloody River*; Fred Walker's *From Texas to Rome* (including Clark's quote on Rapido responsibility); United States Congress, 79th Cong., 2 Sess., House Committee on Military Affairs: *Rapido River Crossing*; *Military Review*, February 1963 ("A Classic Stratagem on Monte Artemisio," by Ernest F. Fisher); *Southwestern Historical Quarterly*, July 1968 (article by Walker); Oran Stovall's collection of Walker letters and other documents relating to 36th Division Rapido and Monte Artemisio operations (including dialogue on feasibility of infiltration); interviews with Clark, Gruenther, Robert Ives, George E. Lynch, Robert Stack, Stovall, Mrs. Fred Walker.

23. Germans fail to fill gap—Kesselring's *A Soldier's Story*; Fourteenth Army records, including *Rückzug* report; postwar reports by Kesselring, Greiner, and Mackensen.

24. Walker's plan approved—Harold Bond's *Return to Cassino*; Clark's *Calculated Risk*; Truscott's *Command Missions*; Walker's *From Texas to Rome* (including dialogue with Truscott); *Argosy*, September, 1964 ("The Night of the Knife," by Kenneth Dixon, including Walker's angry order to officer); interviews with Ives, Lynch, Stack, Stovall.

25. Briefing before attack—Walker's *From Texas to Rome*; *Argosy* article; New York *Herald-Tribune*, June 1, 1944 (article by Homer Bigart); interview with Lynch. (Dialogue from *Argosy* and *Herald-Tribune* articles.)

26. Advance up Artemisio—See Note 23; George E. Lynch's *History of the 142nd Infantry, 36th Division, September 3, 1943–May 8, 1945*, Vol. I, *Italy* (unpublished); *Military Review* article; reports by Alden Williams and John Bob Parks, 36th Division Engineers; interviews with Elliot Amick, Richard Burrage, Ives, Lynch, Stack, Robert Wagner.

27. Kesselring comprehends danger—See Note 22.

12   *The Threats*

1. Bentivegna and Capponi in Palestrina—Amendola's *Il sole e sorto a Roma*; Galleni's *I partigiani sovietici nella Resistenza italiana*; interviews with Amendola, Bentivegna, Capponi.

2. Germans try to calm Romans—J. Patrick Carroll-Abbing's *But for the Grace of God*; Piscitelli's *Storia della Resistenza romana*; Jane Scrivener's *Inside Rome with the Germans*; postwar report by General Mälzer (January 1948).

3. Spies tell all—Ripa di Meana's *Roma clandestina* (dialogue); *Visto* (Milan), September 1, 1960 (article on Mariolina Odone); interviews with Ripa di Meana, Mariolina Odone.

4. Signor X denounces comrades—Interviews with Signor X, other former members of the Resistance. (All dialogue is from Signor X, though that concerning his warning to comrades is from another Resistance officer.)

5. Odone captured—Piscitelli's *Storia della Resistenza romana*; Ripa di Meana's *Roma clandestina*; *Il Momento* (Rome), November 30, 1945; interviews with Ripa di Meana, M. Odone, Signor X.

6. Filippo Caruso captured—Caruso's *L'Arma dei carabinieri in Roma durante l'occupazione tedesca*; Piscitelli's *Storia della Resistenza romana*; interview with F. Caruso.

7. Hospital meeting raided—See Note 5; interview with Giovanni Di Lorenzo, M. Odone (dialogue).

8. German effort to prevent insurrection—See Note 6; Di Benigno's *Occasioni mancatea*; Trabucco's *La prigionia di Roma*; *Rivista Diocesana di Roma* ("Il clero romano durante il periodo dell Resistenza"); OSS reports; interviews with Bernardini, Harding, La Malfa, U. Musco, Palazzini.

9. A Communist insurrection?—Amendola's *Il sole e sorto a Roma*; Piscitelli's *Storia della Resistenza romana*; *Bandiera Rossa*; interviews with Amendola, Guido Gannella, Aldo Garosci, La Malfa, Mucci, Pertini, Poce (including dialogue with Allied officers).

10. Nazi plan to "communize" Rome—Möllhausen's *La carta perdente* (dialogue); interview with Möllhausen.

11. Vatican effort to save Rome—Giovannetti's *Roma, città aperta* (including dialogue between Weizsäcker and Tardini and statement about Catholic idea being "at stake"); Möllhausen's *La carta perdente*; Weizsäcker's *Memoirs* and *Rundbriefe aus Rom* (including letter to his family).

12. Allies reject open-city plan—Giovannetti's *Roma, città aperta*; *Foreign Relations of the United States, 1944*, Vol. IV (section on Vatican); *Military Review*, August 1965 ("Rome: An Open City," by Ernest F. Fisher); German Embassy, diplomatic dispatches, Fasano, Foreign Ministry archives, Bonn; OSS files; World War II files (WNRC).

13. German women taken by Resistance as hostages—Ripa di Meana's

Roma clandestina (dialogue); interviews with M. Odone, Ripa di Meana.

14. Kesselring's decision—Dollmann's *The Interpreter* and *Roma nazista*; Kesselring's *A Soldier's Story*; Weizsäcker's *Memoirs*; interviews with Beelitz, Dollmann, Möllhausen, Westphal.

13 *The Decisions*

1. Clark's letter to his mother; memories of Renie—M. Clark's *Captain's Bride, General's Lady*; Clark files in Citadel, Charleston, S.C. (letter).
2. Walker captures Velletri—Walker's *From Texas to Rome* (dialogue); Sevareid's *Not So Wild a Dream*; Dallas *Morning News*, June 2, 1944 (article by Wick Fowler); interview with Stack.
3. Germans continue to hold at Valmontone—Kesselring's *A Soldier's Story*; postwar reports by Kesselring and Mackensen; interviews with Beelitz, Westphal.
4. Alexander bows to Clark—Alexander's *The Alexander Memoirs*; Clark's *Calculated Risk* (dialogue); Juin's *Memoirs*; Fifth Army records, interviews with Clark, Gruenther, Harding, Lemnitzer, North.
5. Christian and Johnson's double suicide attack—Taggart (ed.), *History of the Third Infantry Division in World War II.*
6. Kesselring orders swift retreat—Feurstein's *Irrwege der Pflicht*; Kesselring's *A Soldier's Story*; Tenth Army records (telephone dialogue); postwar reports by Kesselring and Vietinghoff, interviews with Beelitz, Berlin, Klinckowstroem.
7. Clark blocks non-Americans—Clark's *Calculated Risk* (dialogue); interviews with Clark, Gruenther.
8. Would Rome be defended?—*Foreign Relations of the United States, 1944,* Vol. IV (section on Vatican); Tenth Army records (telephone dialogue); Allied Forces Hq. records; interviews with Beelitz, Dollmann, Westphal.
9. British officer phones Derry—Derry's *The Rome Escape Line* (dialogue).
10. Scalzi's ultimatum—Ripa di Meana's *Roma clandestina*; interviews with M. Odone, Ripa di Meana.
11. Kappler frees Vassalli—Constantine's *The Pope* (dialogue); Ripa di Meana's *Roma clandestina*; unpublished report by Vassalli on his imprisonment; interview with Vassalli.
12. Multedo freed—Interview with Multedo.
13. Via Tasso prisoners prepare to die—F. Caruso's *L'arma dei carabinieri in Roma durante l'occupazione tedesca* (dialogue); Stendardo's *Via Tasso*; Angelo Joppi's *Report on Via Tasso*; interviews with F. Caruso, Salinari.
14. Fourteen prisoners killed—Derry's *The Rome Escape Line* (killing of Armstrong); *Avanti, Riscostruzione,* and *Tempo* (Rome periodical), June 8 to 11, 1944; *Il Corriere,* December 4 and 5, 1945; OSS files; interview with Vassalli.
15. Germans flee Rome—Carroll-Abbing's *But for the Grace of God;*

Scrivener's *Inside Rome with the Germans*; M. de Wyss's *Rome Under the Terror*; diary of M. von Weizsäcker (dialogue in hospital); interviews with Erich Timm, M. von Weizäcker, many Romans.

16. Eleanora Di Porto sees Germans leave—Interview with Di Portos.
17. Ribbentrop's premature report—Möllhausen's *La carta perdente* (dialogue); interview with Möllhausen.
18. Hitler's decision to spare Rome—Dollmann's *Roma nazista*; Möllhausen's *La carta perdente*; Tenth Army records (telephone dialogue); interviews with Beelitz, Dollmann, Giuseppe Dosi, Möllhausen.
19. German plan for open city—Giovannetti's *Roma, città aperta*; diary of M. von Weizsäcker; interview with M. von Weizsäcker.
20. Time running out for Germans—Kesselring's *A Soldier's Story*; Tompkins' *A Spy in Rome*; Weizsäcker's *Memoirs* and *Rundbriefe aus Rom*; diary of M. von Weizsacker; Tenth Army records (telephone dialogue); postwar reports by Kesselring and Mackensen; interviews with Beelitz, M. von Weizsäcker.
21. "Elephant"—*Bandiera Rossa*; interviews with Amendola, Mucci, Poce.
22. Germans fire on Bencivenga—*Rivista Diocesana di Roma* ("Il clero romano durante il periodo della Resistenza" [account by Bencivenga]); interview with U. Musco.

14 *The Racers*

1. Roads to Rome—See Note 23, Chap. 9, for published and unpublished sources; Christopher Buckley's *Road to Rome*; Jackson's *Battle for Rome*; Herbert L. Matthews' *The Education of a Correspondent*; McMillan's *Twenty Angels over Rome*.
2. Howze leads the way—Howze report; interview with Howze.
3. Radcliffe's patrol—Adleman and Walton's *The Devil's Brigade* and *Rome Fell Today*; Burhans' *The First Special Service Force*; report by Taylor Radcliffe (dialogue); U. S. Fifth Army records, 1st Special Service Force intelligence report.
4. Truscott and Walker push toward Rome—Ernest Harmon's *Combat Commander*; Truscott's *Command Missions* (dialogue with Chinigo and Hightower); Walker's *From Texas to Rome* (dialogue with Clark and Fowler); interviews with Michael Chinigo, Stack.
5. Planès heads for Rome—J. M. A. Lassale's *Panaches Rouges*; interviews with Jean Courtois, Planès (quotation).
6. Radcliffe first in Rome—See Note 3.
7. Other units enter Rome—Burhans' *The First Special Service Force*; Harmon's *Combat Commander*; Taggart's *History of the Third Infantry Division in World War II*; U.S. Fifth Army records, 88th Cavalry Rcn. Troop Journal; Allied Forces Hq. records; interviews with Howze, John T. Rielly (88th Div.).
8. Derry sees "Americans" arrive—Derry's *The Rome Escape Line*.
9. Planès reaches center of Rome—See Note 5; dialogue from interview with Planès.
10. At the ROMA sign—Adleman and Walton's *Rome Fell Today* (dia-

logue between Frederick and Clark and Keyes's remark—based on authors' interview with him—that "France is going to be invaded . . ."); Burhans' *The First Special Service Force*; Clark's *Calculated Risk*; Carl Mydans' *More Than Meets the Eye*; Sevareid's *Not So Wild a Dream* (including dialogue between Frederick and Keyes, starting: "General Frederick, what's holding you up here?"); New York *Times*, June 4, 1944 (Associated Press report by Dan De Luce); interview with Clark, Reynolds Packard.

11. Via Tasso prisoners freed—See Note 13, Chap. 13; Piscitelli's *Storia della Resistenza romana*; Ripa di Meana's *Roma clandestina*; interviews with Dosi, Ripa di Meana.

12. Simpson returns—Derry's *The Rome Escape Line*; Furman's *Be Not Fearful*; interview with Lucidi.

13. Nazis and Fascists leave Rome—Dollmann's *The Interpreter* and *Roma nazista*; Kesselring's *A Soldier's Story*; Tompkins' *A Spy in Rome*; Tenth Army records; interview with Dollmann.

14. Tompkins "commands" Rome—See Note 14, Chap. 5; interview with Ottorino Borin.

15. Insurrection plans abandoned—See Note 9, Chap. 12; interviews with Bauer, Vassalli.

16. Musco meets Americans—Interview with U. Musco.

17. Panafieu enters Rome—Interview with François de Panafieu.

18. Chinigo's feats—Truscott's *Command Missions*; interview with Chinigo.

19. The Packards' victory—*Stars and Stripes*, June 5, 1944 (article by Reynolds Packard); interview with Reynolds Packard.

20. Tompkins meets Americans—See Note 14, Chap. 5.

21. The Planèses' "second honeymoon"—Interviews with Planèses.

15   *The Winners*

1. Last German resistance crushed in Rome—Sevareid's *Not So Wild a Dream*; Howze report; New York *Herald-Tribune*, June 5, 1944 (article by Homer Bigart); interview with Howze.

2. Americans exchange fire—Interview with Paul W. Kendall. (Books reporting incident indicate, inaccurately, that Frederick was wounded by the *enemy*.)

3. Twelve-year-old boy dies fighting—*Il Popolo* (Rome), June 4, 1948.

4. 36th Division crosses Rome—Bond's *Return to Cassino* (dialogue in Vatican); Walker's *From Texas to Rome* (dialogue before march); interviews with Stack, Stovall.

5. Traffic jam halts British—Adleman and Walton's *Rome Fell Today*; Forbes and Nicolson's *The Grenadier Guards in the War of 1939–45*; Turner's *V.C.'s of the Army* (Sidney); *The Victoria Cross* (Sidney); interviews with James W. Holsinger, Kirkman, William Philip Sidney (dialogue).

6. Allies and Italians celebrate—Trabucco's *La prigionia di Roma*; Bandi-

era Rossa; New York *Times,* June 6, 1944 (article on John Vita); *The New Yorker,* June 17 and 24, 1944 ("Letter from Rome," by Daniel Lang); *Stars and Stripes* (Rome), June 5 to 12, 1944 (varied articles on Allied welcome); interviews with Mucci, Poce, John Vita, many Romans.

7. Tompkins arrested—See Note 14, Chap. 5.

8. Death of a policeman—*Il Risorgimento Liberale* (Rome-underground), July 15 to 23, 1944 (Bentivegna trial); *Il Tempo* (Rome), same dates and subject; testimony, Rosario Bentivegna trial; interviews with Bentivegna, Capponi.

9. A visit to Dollmann's *pensione*—Michael Stern's *An American in Rome* (dialogue); interview with Stern.

10. Weizsäcker's lingering hope—Weizsäcker's *Memoirs* and *Rundbriefe aus Rom;* diary of M. von Weizsäcker; interviews with Kessel and M. and R. von Weizsäcker.

11. Allied arrests—Di Benigno's *Occasioni Mancate;* Dollman's *Roma nazista* (about girl friends of Kappler and Wolff); Katz's *Death in Rome;* Lualdi's *La banda Koch; Storia Illustrata* article on Koch; Roccas material (Celeste Di Porto); interview with Basevi (dialogue), Marx.

12. Mussolini and the fall of Rome—Alberto Mellini Ponce de Leon's *Guerra diplomatica a Salò* (Mazzolini quote); *Corrispondensa Repubblicana,* June 1944; interviews with Dollmann, Rahn, Wolff.

13. The Di Portos and liberation—Interviews with Cava, Di Portos, Sister Katharine.

14. Zolli's path—See Note 4, Chap. 3; Stern's *An American in Rome* (including dialogue at synagogue); interview with Stern. (Zolli's quotes about path he was following are from his *Before the Dawn.*)

15. Clark arrives in Rome—Chambé's *L'Épopée française d'Italie;* Clark's *Calculated Risk* (including dialogue that takes place in Rome); M. Clark's *Captain's Bride, General's Lady* (flashback, including dialogue); Juin's *Memoirs;* Sevareid's *Not So Wild a Dream;* Truscott's *Command Missions; Rivista Diocesana di Roma* ("Il clero romano durante il periodo della Resistenza"); interviews with Bonhouré, Clark, Gruenther, U. Musco.

16. Filippo Caruso goes home—F. Caruso's *L'arma dei carabinieri in Roma durante l'occupazione tedesca;* interview with F. Caruso.

17. Badoglio and Bencivenga fade out—See Note 10, Chap. 10.

18. Clark's press conference—Adleman and Walton's *Rome Fell Today;* Clark's *Calculated Risk;* Jackson's *Battle for Rome;* Sevareid's *Not So Wild a Dream;* Truscott's *Command Missions;* interviews with F. Caruso, Clark, U. Musco.

19. Pope speaks to Romans—Halecki and Murray's *Pius XII;* Hatch and Walshe's *Crown of Glory;* New York *Herald-Tribune,* New York *Times,* and *Stars and Stripes,* June 6, 1944; interviews with many Romans.

20. Clark meets Pope—Clark's *Calculated Risk* (dialogue); interview with Clark.

Epilogue

1. To the Gothic Line—Alexander's *The Alexander Memoirs*; Churchill's *Closing the Ring*; Clark's *Calculated Risk*; Juin's *Memoirs*; Kesselring's *A Soldier's Story*; Senger's *Neither Fear Nor Hope*; Walker's *From Texas to Rome*; Wilson report; *London Gazette*, June 12, 1950 (Alexander dispatches); Allied Forces Hq. records; interviews: see Notes 7 and 11, Chap. 1.

2. Wolff, Rahn, and Dollmann seek peace—Constantine's *The Pope*; Dollmann's *The Interpreter* and *Call Me Coward* (detention and "escape"); Dulles' *The Secret Surrender*; Rahn's *Ruheloses Leben*; OSS reports; interviews with Dollmann, Donald Pryce-Jones, Rahn, Wolff.

3. The fate of Kesselring, Mackensen, Mälzer, and Kappler—Gallagher's *Scarlet Pimpernel of the Vatican*; Kesselring's *A Soldier's Story*; trial records for above four commanders.

4. Weizsäcker's fate—Weizsäcker's *Memoirs*; testimony, Weizsäcker trial; interview with Hill, Kessel, and A., M., and R. von Weizsäcker.

5. Koch's fate—See Note 2, Chap. VI for written material; Cardinal Mario Nasalli Rocca's *Accanto ai condannati a morte* (Koch's and Pope's statements to Rocca); testimony, Koch trial; interview with Msgr. Giovanni Battista Mocata.

6. The fate of Donato Carretta and Pietro Caruso—Katz's *Death in Rome*; Stern's *An American in Rome*; testimony, P. Caruso trial; interview with Mocata.

7. Celeste Di Porto's fate—*Il Paese* (Rome), December 27, 1948 (Celeste attacked at restaurant); Roccas material; testimony, Di Porto trial. (Few Roman Jews would even discuss Celeste, reluctant both to relive the horror and to express their bitter feelings toward the Vatican for protecting her from punishment.)

8. Romans disillusioned—Many Roman newspaper articles and interviews.

9. Resistance grows north of Rome—Delzell's *Mussolini's Enemies*; Kesselring's *A Soldier's Story*; Longo's *Un popolo alla macchia*; Salvadori's *Brief History of the Patriot Movement in Italy*; Tompkins' *A Spy in Rome*; OSS reports; German diplomatic reports; interviews with Beelitz, Rahn, Tompkins, Wolff.

10. CLN leaders run postwar government—Blackmer's *Unity in Diversity*; New York *Times Magazine*, March 21, 1948 ("Italy in the Shadow of the Hammer and Sickle," by C. L. Sulzberger); Urban thesis on history of Italian Communism; interviews with Amendola, Bentivegna, Capponi, Malfatti, Vassalli.

11. Zolli converts to Catholicism—See Note 4, Chap. 3 (all quoted material from Zolli's *Before the Dawn*); *Israel* (Roman Jewish newspaper), February 14, 1945 (Jewish account and reaction).

Bibliography

The following is a partial list of published and unpublished books, periodicals, and documents consulted by the author.

Books

Adleman, Robert H., and George Walton, *The Devil's Brigade*, Philadelphia, Chilton, 1966.

——, *Rome Fell Today*, Boston, Little, Brown, 1968.

Alexander of Tunis, Harold Alexander, Earl, *The Alexander Memoirs, 1940–1945*, New York, McGraw-Hill, 1962.

Alfieri, Dino, *Dictators Face to Face*, London, Elek, 1954.

Algardi, Z., ed., *Il processo Caruso*, Rome, Darsena, 1945.

——, *Processi ai fascisti*, Florence, Parenti, 1958.

Allied Commission, *A Review of AMG and AC in Italy*, Rome, Allied Commission, 1945.

Ambrose, Stephen E., *The Supreme Commander*, Garden City, N.Y., Doubleday, 1970.

Ame, Cesare, *Guerra segreta in Italia*, Rome, Casini, 1954.

Amendola, Giorgio (Associazione Nazionale Partigiani d'Italia, Comitato Provinciale di Roma), *Il Sole e Sorto a Roma*, Rome, n.d.

Amicucci, Ermanno, *Il 600 giorni di Mussolini*, Rome, Faro, 1948.

Anders, Wladyslaw, *An Army in Exile*, London, Macmillan, 1949.

Anfuso, Filippo, *Roma Berlino Salò*, Milan, Garzanti, 1950.

Arendt, Hannah, *Eichmann in Jerusalem*, New York, Viking, 1965.

Aris, George, *The British Fifth Division, 1939 to 1945*, London, Trustees of Fifth Division Benevolent Fund, 1959.

L'Armée française en Italie, Decembre 1943–Juillet 1944, Paris Commissariat à la Guerre, Direction des Services de Presse, n.d.

Ascarelli, A., *Le fosse ardeatine*, Rome, Palombi, 1945.

Associazione Nazionale delle Famiglie Italiane dei Martiri, *Roma onora i martiri del il risorgimento*, Rome, privately printed, 1957.

Associazione Nationale dei Partigiani d'Italia, *I crimini della Wehrmacht*, Rome, privately printed, 1955.

Augarde, Jacques, *Tabor*, Paris, France-Empire, 1952.

Bacino, Ezio, *Roma prima e dopo*, Rome, Atlantica, 1950.

Badoglio, Marshal Pietro, *Italy in the Second World War*, New York, Oxford, 1948.

Baldwin, Hanson W., *Great Mistakes of the War*, New York, Harper, 1949.

Ball, Edmund F., *Staff Officer with the Fifth Army*, New York, Exposition Press, 1958.

Bandiera Rossa, Rome, n.d.

Barclay, C. N., *The History of The Duke of Wellington's Regiment, 1919–1952*, London, Clowes, 1953.

———, *The History of the Sherwood Foresters (Nottingham and Derbyshire Regiment), 1919–1957*, London, Clowes, 1959.

Barkai, M., ed., *The Fighting Ghettos*, Philadelphia, Lippincott, 1962.

Bartoli, Domenico, *La fine della monarchia*, Milan, Mondadori, 1947.

Barzini, Luigi, *The Italians*, New York, Atheneum, 1964.

Battaglia, Roberto, *The Story of the Italian Resistance*, London, Odhams, 1956.

Bauer, Riccardo, *Alla recerca della libertà*, Florence, Parenti, 1957.

Bedarida, Guido, *Ebrei d'Italia*, Leghorn, Terrona, 1950.

Bedarride, J., *Les Juifs en France, en Italie et en Espagne*, Paris, Michel Levy, 1891.

Bellomo, Bino, *Sotto il segno di s. michele arcan gelo*, Bologna, Alfa, n.d.

Belot, Raymond de, *The Struggle for the Mediterranean, 1939–1945*, Princeton, Princeton University Press, 1951.

Bentley, Eric, ed., *The Storm over the Deputy*, New York, Grove, 1964. (Includes following articles: "The Pope and the Jews" by Albrecht von Kessel; "Pius XII" by Robert Leiber; "Pius XII and the Jews" by G. B. Montini; and "Pope Pius XII and the Nazis," by L. Poliakov.)

Berenson, Bernard, *Rumor and Reflection*, London, Constable, 1952.

Berliner, Dr. Abraham, *Geschichte der Juden in Rom*, Frankfurt, Kauffmann, 1893.

———, *Aus den letzten Tagen des römischen Ghetto*, Berlin, Rosenstein & Hildesheimer, 1886.

Berthold, Wilhelm, *Von Himmel zu Hölle*, Munich, Süddeutscher, 1957.

Bertoldi, Silvio, *I tedeschi in Italia*, Milan, Rizzoli, 1964.

Bielatowicza, Jana, *Ulani Karpaccy*, London, Nakladem Zwiazku Ulanow Karpackich, 1966.

————, *Laur Kapitolu I Wianek Ruty*, London, Nakladem Katolickiego Osrodka Wydawniczego "Veritas," 1954.

Blackmer, Donald L. M., *United in Diversity*, Cambridge, Mass., MIT Press, 1968.

Blumenson, Martin, *Anzio: The Gamble That Failed*, Philadelphia, Lippincott, 1963.

————, *Bloody River*, Boston, Houghton Mifflin, 1970.

Blustein, G., *Storia degli ebrei in Roma*, Rome, Maglione and Strini, 1921.

Böhmler, Rudolf, *Monte Cassino*, London, Cassel, 1964.

Bolla, Nino, *Dieci mesi di governo Badoglio*, Rome, Nuova Epoca, 1945.

Bonciani, Carlo, *F Squadron*, London, Dent, 1947.

Bond, Harold L., *Return to Cassino*, Garden City, N.Y., Doubleday, 1964.

Bonomi, Ivanoe, *Diario di un anno*, Milan, Garzanti, 1947.

Bowditch, John, III, ed., *The Anzio Beachhead* (American Forces in Action Series, Vol. XIV), Washington, D.C., Dept. of the Army, 1947.

Bradley, Omar N., *A Soldier's Story*, New York, Holt, 1951.

Brown, David, and Alfred Wagg, *No Spaghetti for Breakfast*, Nicholson and Watson, London, 1943.

Bryant, Arthur, *Triumph in the West*, Garden City, N.Y., Doubleday, 1959.

Buckley, Christopher, *The Road to Rome*, London, Hodder & Stoughton, 1945.

Bullock, Alan, *Hitler: A Study in Tyranny*, New York, Harper, 1953.

Burckhardt, Carl J., *Meine Danziger Mission, 1937–1939*, Munich, 1940.

Burhans, Robert D., *The First Special Service Force*, Washington, D.C., Infantry Journal Press, 1947.

Burke-Gaffney, J. J., *The Story of the King's Regiment, 1914–48*, Liverpool, Sharpe and Kellet, for the King's Regiment, 1954.

Butcher, Harry C., *My Three Years with Eisenhower*, New York, Simon and Schuster, 1946.

Cadorna, Raffaele, *Riscossa dal 25 luglio alla liberazione*, Milan, Rizzoli, 1948.

Calamandrei, Piero, *Uomini e città della resistenza*, Bari, Laterza, 1955.

The Canadians at War, 1939–1945, Ottawa.

Capano, Renato Perrone, *La Resistenza in Roma*, 2 vols., Naples, Macchiaroli, 1963.

Carboni, Giacomo, *Italia tradita dall'armistizie alla pace*, Rome, EDA, 1947.

————, *L'armistizio e la difesa di Roma*, Rome, De Luigi, 1945.

————, *Più che il dovere*, Rome, Danesi, 1952.

Carli-Bollola, R., *Storia della resistenza*, Milan, Avanti, 1957.

Carpentier, Marcel, *Les Forces Alliées en Italie*, Paris, Levrault, 1949.

Carpi, Daniel, *The Catholic Church and Italian Jewry under the Fascists*, Yad Vashem Studies IV, Jerusalem, Yad Vashem, 1960.

Carroll-Abbing, J. Patrick, *But for the Grace of God*, New York, Delacorte, 1965.

Carter, Barbara B., *Italy Speaks*, London, Gollancz, 1947.

Carter, Bruce, *The Other Side of the Fence*, New York, Carlton, 1963.

Caruso, Filippo, *L'Arma dei carabinieri in Roma durante l'occupazione tedesca*, Rome, Il Poligrafico (Italian Government printing office), 1949.

Cascioli, Ferruccio, *Roma 1943–1944*, Florence, Genzius, n.d.

Castellano, Giuseppe, *La guerra continua*, Milan, Rizzoli, 1963.

Castelli, Giulio, *La storia segreta di Roma Città Aperta*, Rome, Quatrucci, 1953.

Cavallari, Oreste, *La Guerra continua*, Milan, Gastaldi, 1958.

Chambé, René, *L'Épopée française d'Italie*, Paris, Flammarion.

———, *Le Marechal Juin*, Paris, Presse de ka Cité, 1968.

Chandler, David, ed., *A Guide to the Battlefields of Europe*, Vol. II, Philadelphia, Chilton, 1965.

Chandos, Viscount, and Oliver Lyttleton, *The Memoirs of Lord Chandos*, New York, New American Library, 1963.

Chaplin, H. D., *The Queen's Own Royal West Kent Regiment, 1920–1950*, London, Michael Joseph, 1954.

Churchill, Winston, *Closing the Ring* (*The Second World War*, Vol. 5), Boston, Houghton Mifflin, 1951.

Cianferro, Camille, *The Vatican and the War*, New York, Dutton, 1954.

Ciano, Galeazzo, *Ciano's Hidden Diary, 1937–1938*, New York, Dutton, 1953.

———, *Diaries, 1939–1943*, New York, Doubleday, 1946.

Cione, Edmondo, *Storia della Republica Sociale*, Caserta, Cenacolo, 1948.

Ciulla, C. C., *L'Attività criminosa della banda Koch coi particolari di villa triste a Milano* (pamphlet), Milan, privately printed, 1945.

Clark, Mark W., *Calculated Risk*, New York, Harper 1950.

Clark, Maurine, *Captain's Bride, General's Lady*, New York, McGraw-Hill, 1956.

Colvin, Ian, *Chief of Intelligence*, London, Gollancz, 1951.

Commager, Henry Steele, ed., *The Pocket History of the Second World War*, New York, Pocket Books, 1945.

Connell, Charles, *Monte Cassino: The Historic Battle*, London, Elek, 1963.

Consiglio, Alberto, *Vita de Vittorio Emanuele III*, Milan, Rizzoli, 1950.

Constantine, Prince of Bavaria, *The Pope*, New York, Roy, 1956.

Conway, John S., *Nazi Persecution of the Churches, 1933–1945*, New York, Basic Books, 1969.

Corpo Volontari della Libertà, *La Resistenza Italiana*, n.d.

Courtney, Godfrey, *100 Best True Stories of World War II* ("General Clark's Secret Mission"), Union City, N.J., Wise, 1945.

Crankshaw, Edward, *Gestapo*, New York, Viking, 1956.

Craven, Wesley Frank, ed., *The Army Air Forces in World War II*, Chicago, University of Chicago Press, 1948–52.

Croce, Benedetto, *The King and the Allies*, London, Allen and Unwin, 1950.

———, *Che cosa e il liberalismo*, Bari, Laterza, 1943.

———, *Il partito liberale*, Bari, Laterza, 1944.

————, *Pagine politiche*, Bari, Laterza, 1944.

————, *Pensiero politico*, Bari, Laterza, 1945.

————, *Per la nuova vita dell'Italia*, Bari, Laterza, 1944.

————, *Riposta a Badoglio*, Naples, Facsimile, 1943.

————, *Quando l'Italia era tagliata in due*, Bari, Laterza, 1948.

Czuchnowski, Marian, *The Polish Troops in Italy*, London, Library of Fighting Poland, 1944.

D'Agostini, L., and R. Forti, *Il sole è sorto a Roma*, Rome, Associazione Nazionale Partigiani d'Italia, 1965.

Daniell, David Scott, *History of the East Surrey Regiment*, Vol. IV: 1920–1952, London, Benn, 1957.

Davis, Kenneth S., *Experience of War: The United States in World War II*, Garden City, N.Y., Doubleday, 1965.

Davis, Melton, *Who Defends Rome?*, New York, Dial, 1972.

D'Azeglio, Massimo, *Gli ebrei sono uomini!*, Rome, Roma Organizzazione Editoriale Tipografica, 1945.

Deakin, F. W., *The Brutal Friendship*, London, Weidenfeld & Nicolson, 1962.

Dean, C. G. T., *The Loyal Regiment (North Lancashire)*, 1919–1953, Lancashire, Regimental Headquarters, The Loyal Regiment, 1955.

Debenedetti, Giacomo, *16 ottobre 1943*, Rome, O.E.T., 1944 (originally printed in *Mercurio* [Rome], December 1944).

De Felice, Renzo, *Storia degli ebrei italiani sotto il fascismo*, Turin, Einaudi, 1961.

De Gaulle, Charles, *The Complete War Memoirs of Charles de Gaulle*, New York, Simon and Schuster, 1964.

Delaney, John P., *The Blue Devils in Italy*, Washington, Infantry Journal Press, 1947.

Delzell, Charles F., *Mussolini's Enemies*, Princeton, Princeton University Press, 1961.

Derry, Sam, *The Rome Escape Line*, New York, Norton, 1960.

Deutsch, Harold, *The German Conspiracy in the Twilight War*, Minneapolis, University of Minnesota Press, 1968.

Di Benigno, J., *Occasioni mancate*, Rome, S.E.I., 1945.

Dineen, Joseph F., *Pius XII, Pope of Peace*, New York, McBride, 1951.

Di Rajata, Brando, *Humanity Face to Face*, New York, "La Voce d'Italia," 1949.

Di Santella, Mella, *Istantaneo inedite degli ultimi 4 papi*, Roma, n.d.

Dollmann, Eugen, *Call Me Coward*, London, Kimber, 1956.

————, *The Interpreter*, London, Hutchinson, 1967.

————, *Roma Nazista*, Milan, Longanesi, 1949.

Downes, Donald, *The Scarlet Thread*, London, Verschoyle, 1953.

Doyle, Charles Hugo, *Life of Pius XII*, New York, Didier, 1945.

Duclos, Paul, *Le Vatican et la seconde guerre mondiale*, Paris, Pedone, 1955.

Dulles, Allen, *Germany's Underground*, New York, Macmillan, 1947.

——, *The Secret Surrender*, New York, Harper & Row, 1966.

Dupuy, Trevor Nevitt, *Combat Leaders of World War II* (*The Military History of World War II*, Vol. XVII), *European Land Battles* (Vol. II), *Land Battles: North Africa, Sicily and Italy* (Vol. III), *Strategic Direction of World War II* (Vol. XVIII), New York, Watts, 1962.

Durant, Will, *The Age of Faith*, New York, Simon and Schuster, 1950.

Duroc-Danner, Jean, *Face aux Marocains*, Paris, Mappus, 1946.

Ebrei (Gli,) in Italia durante il fascismo, Milan, 1962.

Ehrman, John, *Grand Strategy*, Vol. V, London, HMSO, 1956–64.

Eisenhower, Dwight D., *Crusade in Europe*, Garden City, N.Y., Doubleday, 1948.

Enciclopedia Cattolica, Vol. 10, Vatican City, Vatican, 1939–1954.

Enciclopedia Italiana, Seconda Appendice, Vol. 2, Rome, Istituto della Enciclopedia Italiana, 1949.

L'Épopée de la 3e Division d'Infanterie Algérienne, Novembre 1942–Mai 1945, Algiers, n.d.

Espinosa, Agostino Degli, *Il regno del sud*, Rome, Migliaresi, 1946.

Fajans, Roman, *Italie 1944*, Cairo, Schindler, 1944.

Falconi, Carlo, *The Silence of Pius XII*, Boston, Little, Brown, 1970.

Faldella, Emilio, *L'Italia e la seconda guerra mondiale*, Bologna, Cappelli, 1959.

Fano, Enzo, *Brief Historical Survey of the Jewish Community of Rome*, Rome, B'nai B'rith Association of Rome, 1961.

Farago, Ladislas, *Patton: Ordeal and Triumph*, New York, Obolensky, 1964.

——, *Burn after Reading*, New York, Walker, 1961.

Farinacci, Roberto, *La Chiesa e gli ebrei*, Cremona, Cremona Nuova, 1938.

Feis, Herbert, *Churchill, Roosevelt, Stalin*, Princeton, Princeton University Press, 1957.

Feltrinelli, Istituto, *La resistenza in Italia 25 luglio 1945–25 aprile 1945*, Milan, Feltrinelli, 1961.

Fergusson, Bernard, *The Black Watch and the King's Enemies*, London, Collins, 1950.

——, *The Watery Maze*, New York, Holt, 1961.

Feurstein, Valentin, *Irrwege der Pflicht 1938–1945* Munich, Welsermühl, 1963.

Fifth Army History, Vol. V, 1 April–4 June 1944, Washington, Dept. of the Army, n.d.

Fighting 45th, Baton Rouge, 1946.

The First Armored Division, San Antonio, 1951.

Fisher, Desmond, *Pope Pius XII and the Jews*, Glen Rock, N.J., 1963.

Florio, Vincenzo, *Quattro giorni a Via Tasso*, Palermo, Industrie Riunite, 1947.

Foa, Ugo, *Relazione del presidente della comunità israelitica di Roma Foa Ugo circa le misure razziali adottate in Roma dopo 18 settembre a diretta opera delle autorita tedesche di occupazione*, Nov. 15, 1943, and June 20, 1944, Rome (booklet).

Forbes, P., and N. Nicolson, *The Grenadier Guards in the War of 1939–45*, London, Gale & Polden, 1949.

Foreign Relations of the United States, 1943, Vol. II; *1944*, Vol. IV, Washington, D.C., GPO.

Fornaro, V., *Il servizio informazioni Montezemolo*, Milan, Domus, 1946.

Forrest, Alan, *Italian Interlude*, Cape Town, Timmins, 1964.

La France et son Empire dans la Guerre, Paris, Editions Litteraires de France, n.d.

Friedländer, Saul, *Pius XII and the Third Reich*, New York, Knopf, 1966.

Fry, James C., *Combat Soldier*, Washington, D.C., National Press, 1968.

Fuller, J. F. C., *The Second World War 1939–45*, New York, Duell, Sloan and Pearce, 1948.

Furman, John, *Be Not Fearful*, London, Blond, 1959.

Gabrieli, Giuseppe, *Italia Judaica*, Rome, Fond, Leonardo, 1924.

Gallagher, J. P., *Scarlet Pimpernel of the Vatican*, New York, Coward-McCann, 1967.

Galleni, Mauro, *I partigiani sovietici nella Resistenza italiana*, Rome, Riuniti, 1967.

Garland, Albert N., *Sicily and the Surrender of Italy*, Washington, D.C., Office of the Chief of Military History, Dept. of the Army, 1965.

Giovannetti, Alberto, *Roma, città aperta*, Milan, Ancora, 1962.

———, *Il Vaticano e la guerra* (1939–40), Vatican City, Vatican, 1960.

Godfrey, E. G., and R. T. K. Goldsmith, *The History of The Duke of Cornwall's Light Infantry, 1939–1945*, Regimental History Committee, The Duke of Cornwall's Light Infantry, 1966.

Goutard, Adolf, *Le Corps Expéditionnaire Français dans la campagne d'Italie*, Paris, Charles-Lavauzelle, n.d.

Graham, Robert A., *Vatican Diplomacy*, Princeton, Princeton University Press, 1959.

Greenfield, Kent Roberts, ed., *Command Decisions*, Washington, D.C., Office of the Chief of Military History, Dept. of the Army, 1960.

Gregorovius, F., *The Ghetto and the Jews of Rome*, New York, Schocken, 1948.

Hagen, Walter (Wilhelm Hoettl), *The Secret Front*, New York, Praeger, 1954.

Halecki, Oscar, *Pius XII: Eugenio Pacelli, Pope of Peace*, New York, Farrar, Straus and Giroux, 1954.

Halperin, S. W., *Mussolini and Italian Fascism*, Princeton, Princeton University Press, 1954.

Harmon, E. N., *Combat Commander*, Englewood Cliffs, N.J., Prentice-Hall, 1970.

Harr, Bill, *Combat Boots*, New York, Exposition Press, 1952.

Harris, C., *Allied Military Administration of Italy, 1943–1945*, London, HMSO, 1957.

Hatch, Alden, and Seamus Walshe, *Crown of Glory*, New York, Hawthorn, 1957.
——, *Pope Paul VI*, New York, Random House, 1966.
Henderson, Sir Nevile, *Failure of a Mission, Berlin, 1937–39*, London, Hodder and Stoughton, 1940.
Hibbert, Christopher, *Anzio: Bid for Rome*, New York, Ballantine, 1971.
——, *Il Duce*, Boston, Little, Brown, 1962.
Higgins, Trumbull, *Winston Churchill and the Second Front*, New York, Oxford, 1957.
Hilberg, R., *The Destruction of the European Jews*, Chicago, Quadrangle, 1967.
Historical Division, War Department, U.S.A., *Small Unit Actions*, Washington, D.C., GPO, 1946.
Historical Record, VI Corps, 1944.
History of the First Division: Anzio Campaign, January–June, 1944, Jerusalem, "Ahva" Printing Press, n.d.
History of the 7th Infantry Regiment, World War II (3rd Division), n.d.
History of the 30th Infantry Regiment, World War II (3rd Division), n.d.
Hitler, A., and B. Mussolini, *Les lettres secretes échangées par Hitler et Mussolini*, Paris, Pavois, 1946.
Hitler Directs His Army, Germany, Wehrmacht, Oberkommando, n.d.
Hochhuth, Rolf, "Sidelights on History," Appendix to *The Deputy*, New York, Grove, 1964.
Hougen, John H., *History of the Famous 34th Infantry Division*, 1949.
Howe, George F., *The Battle History of the 1st Armored Division*, Washington, Combat Forces Press, 1954.
Hughes, H. S., *The United States and Italy*, Cambridge, Mass., Harvard University Press, 1953, 1965.
Hugot, Pierre, *Baroud en Italie*, Paris, n.d.
Hull, Cordell, *Memoirs*, 2 vols., New York, Macmillan, 1957–58.
Ichac, Pierre, *Nous marchons vers la France*, Paris, Amiot-Dumont, 1954.
International Military Tribunal, *Trial of the Major War Criminals*, Vol. 14 (May 22, 1946), London, HMSO, 1946.
Ismay, Lord, *The Memoirs of General Lord Ismay*, New York, Viking, 1960.
Italy's Struggle for Liberation, London, International, 1944.
Jackson, W. G. F., *Alexander of Tunis as Military Commander*, London, Batsford, 1971.
——, *The Battle for Italy*, New York, Harper & Row, 1967.
——, *The Battle for Rome*, London, Batsford, 1969.
Jacobsen, H. A., and J. Rohwer, *Decisive Battles of World War II: The German View*, New York, Putnam, 1965.
Jars, Robert, *La Campagne d'Italie, 1943–1945*, Paris, Payot, 1953.
Johnson, Charles Monroe, *Action with the Seaforths*, New York, Vantage, 1944.
Joppi, Angelo, *Report on Via Tasso*, privately printed, Rome, n.d.

Juin, Alphonse, *La Campagne d'Italie*, Paris, Guy Victor, 1962.
——, *Memoirs*, Paris.
Katz, Robert, *Black Sabbath*, New York, Macmillan, 1969.
——, *Death in Rome*, New York, Macmillan, 1967.
Keitel, Wilhelm, *The Memoirs of Field Marshal Keitel*, New York, Stein and Day, 1966.
Kennedy, Sir John, *The Business of War*, New York, Morrow, 1951.
Kesselring, Albert, *A Soldier's Story*, New York, Morrow, 1954.
Kirkpatrick, Ivone, *Mussolini—A Study in Power*, Englewood Cliffs, N.J., Hawthorn, 1964.
Kordt, Erich, *Nicht aus den Akten*, Stuttgart, 1950.
La Gorce, Paul-Marie de, *The French Army*, New York, Braziller, 1963.
Lassale, J. M. A., *Panaches Rouges: Historique du 3me régiment de Spahis Algériens de Reconnaissance*, Boppard am Rhein, 1947.
Laternser, H., *Verteidigung Deutsche Soldaten*, Bonn, Bohnemeier, 1950.
Launay, Jacques de, *Secret Diplomacy of World War II*, New York, Simmons-Boardman, 1963.
Law Reports of Trials of War Criminals, Vol. VIII (*Trials of Generals von Mackensen and Mälzer*), London, HMSO, n.d.
Leboucher, Fernande, *Incredible Mission*, Garden City, N.Y., Doubleday, 1969.
Lerecouvreux, *Résurrection de l'armée française de Weygand à Giraud*, Paris, Nouvelles Éditions Latines, 1955.
Lettres de Pie XII aux éveques Allemands, 1939–1944, Rome, Libreria Editrice Vaticana, 1966.
Lewy, Gunther, *The Catholic Church and Nazi Germany*, New York, McGraw-Hill, 1964.
Lichten, Joseph, *A Question of Judgment*, Washington, D.C., 1963.
Liddell Hart, B. H., *The Rommel Papers*, New York, Harcourt, Brace, 1953.
——, *Strategy*, New York, Praeger, 1954.
Linklater, Eric, *The Campaign in Italy*, London, HMSO, 1951.
Lizzadri, Oreste, *Il regno di Badoglio*, Rome, Avanti, 1963.
Lizzani, C., *L'oro di Roma*, Bologna, Cappelli, 1961.
Lochner, Louis P., ed., *The Goebbels Diaries, 1942–43*, Garden City, N.Y., Doubleday, 1948.
Lombardi, Gabrio, *Montezemolo e il fronte militare clandeste di Roma*, Rome, Edizioni del Lavoro, 1947.
Longo, Luigi, *Un popolo alla macchia*, Rome, Mondadori, 1947.
Lualdi, Aldo, *La banda Koch*, Milan, 1972.
Lussu, Joyce, *Freedom Has No Frontier*, London, Michael Joseph, 1969.
Lussu, Emilio, *Marcia su Roma e d'intorni*, Turin, Einaudi, 1945.
Luzzato, R., *Unknown War in Italy*, London, New Europe, 1946.
Lyautey, Pierre, *La Campagne d'Italie 1944*, Paris, Plon, 1945.
Mack-Smith, D., Italy, *A Modern History*, Ann Arbor, University of Michigan Press, 1959.

Majdalaney, Fred, *Cassino: Portrait of a Battle*, London, Longmans, 1957.

————, *The Monastery*, London, Lane, 1945.

Malaparte, Curzio, *Kaputt*, New York, Dutton, 1946.

Malvestiti, Piero, *25 luglio alla costituzione*, Milan, Bernabo, 1948.

Malvezzi, P., and G. Pirelli, *Lettere di condannati a morte della Resistenza italiana*, Turin, Einaudi, 1954.

Manhattan, A., *The Catholic Church Against the Twentieth Century*, London, Watts, 1947.

Martin, Ralph G., *The G. I. War*, Boston, Little, Brown, 1967.

Matthews, Herbert L., *The Education of a Correspondent*, New York, Harcourt, Brace & World, 1946.

Maugeri, Franco, *From the Ashes of Disgrace*, New York, Reynal and Hitchcock, 1948.

Mauldin, Bill, *Up Front*, New York, Holt, 1945.

McDermott, Thomas, *Keeper of the Keys: Life of Pope Pius XII*, Milwaukee, Bruce, 1946.

McKnight, John P., *The Papacy*, London, McGraw-Hill, 1953.

McMillan, Richard, *Twenty Angels over Rome*, London, Jarrolds, 1945.

Melling, Leonard, *With the Eighth in Italy*, Manchester, Eng., Torch, 1955.

Mellini Ponce de Leon, A., *Guerra diplomatica a Salò*, Bologna, Capelli, 1950.

Meneghini, M., *Roma, Città Aperta*, Rome, Magi-Spinetti, 1946.

Meyer, Robert, Jr., ed., *The Stars and Stripes Story of World War II*, New York, McKay, 1960.

Michaelis, Meir, *On the Jewish Question in Fascist Italy* (Yad Vashem Studies IV), Jerusalem, Yad Vashem, 1960.

Milan, M., and F. Vighi, eds., *La Resistenza al fascismo*, Milan, Feltrinelli, 1955.

Milano, Attilio, *Storia degli ebrei in Italia*, Turin, Einaudi, 1963.

Miles, Wilfrid, *The Life of a Regiment: The History of the Gordon Highlanders, 1919–45*, Vol. V, Aberdeen, Aberdeen University Press, 1961.

Misuri, Alfredo, *Con la monarchia o verso la republica*, Rome, Quadrifoglio, 1945.

Möllhausen, Eitel, *La carta perdente*, Rome, Sestante, 1948.

Molesworth, George, *The History of The Somerset Light Infantry, 1919–1945*, Regimental Committee, Somerset Light Infantry, 1951.

Momigliano, Eucardio, *Storia tragica e grottesca del razzismo fascista*, Milan, Mondadori, 1946.

Monelli, Paolo, *Roma 1945*, Pescara, Alternine, 1959.

Montgomery, Bernard Law, *El Alamein to the Sangro*, London, Hutchinson, 1948.

————, *Memoirs: Montgomery of Alamein*, Cleveland, World, 1958.

Moran, Lord, *Churchill: Taken from His Diaries—The Struggle for Survival, 1940–1965*, Boston, Houghton Mifflin, 1966.

Mordal, Jacques, *Cassino*, Paris, Amiot-Dumont, 1952.

Morison, Samuel Eliot, *Sicily-Salerno-Anzio, January 1943–June 1944* (History of U. S. Naval Operations in World War II, Vol. IX), Boston, Little, Brown, 1954.

Morpurgo, Luciano, *Caccia all'uomo*, Rome, Dalmatia, 1946.

Mowat, Farley, *The Regiment*, Toronto, McClelland and Stewart, 1955.

Muir, Augustus, *The First of Foot: The History of the Royal Scots*, Edinburgh, Royal Scots History Committee, 1961.

Munro, Ross, *Gauntlet to Overlord*, Toronto, Macmillan, 1946.

Munsell, Warren P., Jr., *The Story of a Regiment*, San Angelo, Tex., Newsfoto, 1946.

Murphy, Robert, *Diplomat Among Warriors*, Garden City, N.Y., Doubleday, 1964.

Murphy, Thomas D., *Ambassadors in Arms*, Honolulu, University of Hawaii Press, 1954.

Mydans, Carl, *More Than Meets the Eye*, New York, Harper, 1959.

Namier, Lewis B., *In the Nazi Era*, London, Macmillan. 1952.

Nenni, Pietro, *Sei anni di guerra civile*, Milan, Rizzoli, 1945.

———, *Vingt ans de fascisme*, Paris, Maspero, 1960.

Newman, Louis I., *A "Chief Rabbi" of Rome Becomes a Catholic*, New York, Renaissance Press, 1945.

Nicholson, G. W. L., *The Canadians in Italy 1943–45* (The Official History of the Canadian Army in the Second World War, Vol. II), Ottawa, Roger Duhamel, Queen's Printer.

Official Record, United States Military Tribunals, Nürnberg (Case No. 11, Tribunal IV [IVA], U.S. vs. Ernst Von Weizsäcker et al.), Vol. 28, 1948.

Omodeo, Adolfo, *La situatzione political*, Naples, Macchiaroli, 1944.

———, *Per la riconquista della libertà*, Naples, Macchiaroli, 1944.

———, *Il problema istituzionale*, Naples, Macchiaroli, 1943.

Orgill, Douglas, *The Gothic Line*, New York, Norton, 1967.

Ottobre 1943: Cronaca di un'infamia, Rome, Comunità Israelitica di Roma, 1961.

Padellaro, Nazareno, *Portrait of Pius XII*, London, Dent, 1956.

Pal, Dharm, *The Campaign in Italy, 1943–45*, London, Longmans, 1960.

Palit, D. K., *The Italian Campaign*, Ferozepore, India, English Book Depot, 1956.

Pallenberg, Corrado, *Inside the Vatican*, Englewood Cliffs, N.J., Hawthorn, 1960.

———, *The Making of a Pope*, New York, Macfadden-Bartel, 1964.

Parkinson, C. Northcote, *Always a Fusilier*, London, n.d.

La Participation Française à la Campagne d'Italie, Paris, n.d.

Payne, Robert, *The Marshall Story*, Englewood Cliffs, N.J., Prentice-Hall, 1951.

Peek, Clifford H., Jr., ed., *Five Years, Five Countries, Five Campaigns*, Munich, 141st Infantry Regiment Association, 1945.

Peters, G. W. H., *The Bedfordshire and Hertfordshire Regiment*, London, Leo Cooper, 1970.

Pietra, I., and R. Muratore, *La Resistance italienne*, Milan, Archivio storico del C.V.L., 1949.

Pisano, G., *Mussolini e gli ebrei*, Milan, FPE, 1967.

Piscitelli, E., *Storia della Resistenza romano*, Bari, Laterza, 1965.

Pleheve, Friedrich-Karl, *Schicksalsstunden in Rom, ende eines Bündnisses*, Berlin, Propyläen, 1967.

Pogue, Forrest C., *George C. Marshall: Ordeal and Hope*, New York, Viking, 1966.

Poliakov, Léon, *Il nazismo e lo sterminio degli ebrei*, Turin, Einaudi, 1955.

Pond, Hugh, *Salerno*, Boston, Little, Brown, 1961.

Praino, Frank S., *Direct Support*, Milan, Historical Section, 838th Field Artillery, 1945.

Prohme, Rupert, *History of the 30th Infantry Regiment*, n.d.

Puntoni, Paolo, *Parla Vittorio Emanuele III*, Milan, Palazzi, 1958.

Pyle, Ernie, *Brave Men*, New York, Holt, 1943.

Quigley, M., *Roman Notes*, New York, privately printed, 1946.

Rahn, Rudolf, *Ruheloses Leben*, Dusseldorf, Diederichs, 1949.

Ray, Cyril, *Algiers to Austria*, London, Eyre and Spottiswoode, 1952.

Reitlinger, Gerald, *The Final Solution*, New York, Beechhurst, 1953.

Reynolds, Robert L., *Story of the Pope*, New York, Dell, 1957.

Ribbentrop, Joachim von, *The Ribbentrop Memoirs*, London, Weidenfeld & Nicolson, 1954.

Riess, Curt, *Underground Europe*, New York, Dial, 1942.

————, *The Self-Betrayed*, New York, Putnam, 1942.

Ripa di Meana, Fulvia, *Roma clandestina*, Rome, O.E.T., 1945.

Robinson, Jacob, *And the Crooked Shall Be Made Straight*, New York, Macmillan, 1965.

Rocca, Mario Nasalli, *Accanto ai condannati a morte*, Rome, Libreria Editrice Vaticana, n.d.

Roe, F. Gordon, *The Bronze Cross*, London, Gawthorn, n.d.

Roma città aperta, Rome, Comune di Roma, 1964.

Rommel, Erwin, *The Rommel Papers*, London, Collins, 1953.

Rossini, G., *Il fascismo e la Resistenza*, Rome, Cinque Lune, 1955.

Roth, Cecil, *The History of the Jews of Italy*, Philadelphia, Jewish Publication Society of America, 1946.

Roy, Édouard, *Les Chemins d'Italie*, Paris, 1970.

The Royal Air Force 1939–1945, Vol. II, London, HMSO, 1954.

The Royal Fusiliers (City of London Regiment): History of the 2nd Battalion in North Africa, Italy and Greece, March 1943–May 1945, Aldershot, Eng., Wellington Press, 1946.

Le Saint Siège et la guerre en Europe, mars 1939–août 1940, Juin 1940–Juin 1941, Rome, Libreria Editrice Vaticana, 1965, 1967.

Salvadori, Max, *Brief History of the Patriot Movement in Italy, 1943–1945*, Chicago, Clemente, 1954.

Scaroni, Silvio, *Con Vittorio Emanuele III*, Milan, Mondadori, 1954.

Schellenberg, Walter, *The Labyrinth*, New York, Harper, 1956.

Schotland, A. P., *Der Fall Kesselring* (bilingual German-English text), Bonn, Leellen, 1952.

Schramm, Percy Ernst, ed., *Kriegstagebuch des Oberkommandos der Wehrmacht, 1940–1945*, Frankfurt am Main, Bernard and Graefe Verlag für Wehrwesen, 1961.

Schroder, Josef, *Italiens Kriegsaustritt 1943: Die Deutschen Gegenmassnahmen im Italienischen Raum: Fall "Alarich" und "Achse,"* Berlin, Frankfurt, 1969.

Schultz, Paul L., *The 85th Infantry Division in World War II*, Washington, D.C., Infantry Journal Press, n.d.

Scrivener, Jane, *Inside Rome with the Germans*, New York, Macmillan, 1945.

Secchia P., and F. Frassati, *La Resistenza e gli Alleati*, Milan, Feltrinelli, 1962.

Selsey, G. Valentine, *Italy Works Her Passage*, London, British-Italian Society, 1945.

Senger und Etterlin, Frido von, *Neither Fear nor Hope*, New York, Dutton, 1964.,

Sevareid, Eric, *Not So Wild a Dream*, New York, Knopf, 1946.

Sexton, Winton K., *We Fought for Freedom*, Kansas City, Burton, n.d.

Sforza, Carlo, *L'Italia dal 1914 al 1944*, Milan, Mondadori, 1946.

———, *Monarchia o repubblica*, Milan, Mondadori, 1946.

Sheehan, Fred, *Anzio—Epic of Bravery*, Norman, Okla., University of Oklahoma Press, 1964.

Shepperd, G. A., *The Italian Campaign, 1943–45*, New York, Praeger, 1968.

Sherwood, Robert E., *Roosevelt and Hopkins*, Vol. II, New York, Harper, 1948.

Silva, Pietro, *Io difendo la monarchia*, Rome, De Fonseca, 1946.

Simiot, Bernard, *Une Épopée Française, Soldats d'Italie 1944*, Paris, Spes, 1949.

Skorzeny, Otto, *Skorzeny's Secret Missions*, New York, Dutton, 1950.

Spataro, Giuseppe, *I democratici cristiani dalla dittatura alla repubblica*, Milan, Mondadori, 1968.

Starr, Chester G., ed., *From Salerno to the Alps*, Washington, D.C., Infantry Journal Press, 1948.

Stendardo, Guido, *Via Tasso*, Rome, privately printed, 1965.

Stern, Michael, *An American in Rome*, New York, Geis, 1964.

Stevens, G. R., *Fourth Indian Division*, London, Maclaren, n.d.

Stimson, Henry L., and McGeorge Bundy, *On Active Service in Peace and War*, New York, Harper, 1947.

Story of the 36th Infantry Division, Washington, D.C., U.S. Army Information Service, 1945.

Taggart, Donald G., ed., *History of the Third Infantry Division in World War II*, Washington, D.C., Infantry Journal Press, 1947.

Tamaro, A., *Due anni di storia, 1943-45*, 3 Vols., Rome, Tosi, 1948–1950.

Taylor, Myron C., *Wartime Correspondence between President Roosevelt and Pius XII*, New York, Macmillan, 1947.

Tedeschi, Paolo, *I communisti Italiani e l'unità nazionale contro gli invasori*, Naples, 1943.

Thruelsen, Richard, and Elliot Arnold, *Mediterranean Sweep*, New York, Duell, Sloan and Pearce, 1944.

Tidyman, Ernest, *The Anzio Death Trap*, New York, Belmont, 1968.

The Tiger Triumphs, London, HMSO (for the Government of India), 1946.

Togliatti, Palmiro, *Linea d'una politica*, Milan, 1948.

——, *Per la libertà*, Rome, L'Unità, 1944.

——, *Per la salvezza*, Rome, L'Unità, 1945.

Tompkins, Peter, *A Spy in Rome*, New York, Simon and Schuster, 1962.

——, *Italy Betrayed*, New York, Simon and Schuster, 1966.

——, *Shaw and Molly Tompkins*, New York, Potter, 1961.

——, *The Murder of Admiral Darlan*, New York, Simon and Schuster, 1965.

Tormento e gloria, Florence, Guzzo, 1964.

Tosti, Amedeo, *Pietro Badoglio*, Milan, Mondadori, 1956.

Trabucco, Carlo, *La prigionia di Roma*, Rome, S.E.L.I., 1945.

Trevelyan, Raleigh, *The Fortress*, London, Collins, 1956.

Trials of War Criminals before the Nuremberg Military Tribunals, Vols. XII–XIV, Washington, D.C., GPO, 1951–52.

La Troisième Division d'Infanterie Algérienne en Italie, Paris, n.d.

Le Troisième Regiment de Tirailleurs Algériens en Italie, Paris, Les Éditions de la Nouvelle France, 1945.

Troisio, A., *Roma sotto il terrore*, Rome, Mondini, 1944.

Truscott, Lucian King, *Command Missions*, New York, Dutton, 1954.

Turner, Frayne, *The V.C.'s of the Army, 1939–1951*, London, n.d.

United States Army, Fifth Army, *Road to Rome*, n.d.

United States Congress, *79th Cong., 2 Sess., House Committee on Military Affairs: Rapido River Crossing*, Washington, D.C., GPO, 1946.

Valabrega, G., ed., *Gli ebrei in Italia durante il fascismo*, Milan, Centro di Documentazione Ebraica Contemporanea, 1963.

Valiani, Leo, *Tutte le strade conducano a Roma*, Rome, La Nuova Italia, 1947.

Vaughan-Thomas, W., *Anzio*, New York, Holt, 1961.

The Victoria Cross (Centenary Exhibition), 15th June–7th July, London, Marlborough House, 1956.

Vie et psychologie des combattants et gens de guerre (Service Historique de l'Armée de Terre), Paris, Imprimerie Nationale, 1970.

Villari, Luigi, *The Liberation of Italy, 1943–47*, Appleton, Wis., Nelson, 1959.

Vincenzo, Fornari, *Il servizio informazioni nella lotta clandestina: "Gruppo Montezemolo,"* Milan, 1946.

Vogelstein, Herman, *Rome*, Philadelphia, Jewish Publication Society, 1941.

Waagenaar, Sam, *Il Ghetto sul tevere*, Milan, Mondadori, 1972.

Wall, B., *The Vatican Story*, London, Weidenfeld & Nicolson, 1956.

Wankowicz, Melchior, *Bitwa O Monte Cassino*, Vols. I, II, Rome, Wydawnictwo Oddz. Kultury i Prasy 2 Polskiego Korpusu, 1946.

Wargos, Adam, *Monte Cassino: The Battle of Six Nations*, London.

The War Reports of General of the Army George C. Marshall, General of the Army H. H. Arnold, Fleet Admiral Ernest J. King, Philadelphia, Lippincott, 1947.

Warlimont, Gen. Walter, *Inside Hitler's Headquarters*, New York, Praeger, 1964.

We Were There, U.S. 88th Infantry Division, Information and Education Section, n.d.

Wedemeyer, Albert C., *Wedemeyer Reports!* New York, Holt, 1958.

Weizsäcker, Ernst von, *Memoirs*, Chicago, Regnery, 1951.

Westphal, Siegfried, *German Army in the West*, London, Cassell, 1951.

Wheeler-Bennett, J. W., *The Nemesis of Power*, London, Macmillan, 1953.

Williamson, Hugh, *The Fourth Division, 1939 to 1945*, London, Newman Neame, 1951.

Wilson, Gen. Sir H. Maitland, *Report by the Supreme Allied Commander Mediterranean to the Combined Chiefs of Staff on the Italian Campaign, 8th Jan. to 10th May, 1944*, London, HMSO, 1946.

Wiskemann, Elizabeth, *The Rome-Berlin Axis*, London and New York, Oxford University Press, 1949.

Wyss, M. de, *Rome Under the Terror*, London, Hale, 1945.

Young, Gordon, ed., *The Army Almanac*, Harrisburg, Pa., Stackpole, 1959.

Zangrandi, Ruggero, *1943: 25 luglio–8 settembre*, Milan, Feltrinelli, 1964.

Zaremby, Pawla, *Dzieje: 15 Pulku Ulanow Poznanskich*, London, Nakladem Kola Ulanow Poznanskich, 1962.

Zolli, Eugenio (Israel), *Antisemitismo*, Rome, A.V.E., 1945.

———, *Before the Dawn*, New York, Sheed and Ward, 1954.

———, *The Nazarene*, Binghamton, N.Y., Herder, 1950.

Periodicals and Newspapers

L'Amitie Judeo-Chrétienne (Paris), Dec. 1949 ("Le Clergé et les Juifs à Rome sous l'Occupation Allemande," by M. Montefiore).

Argosy, Sept. 1964 ("The Night of the Knife," by Kenneth L. Dixon).

Aufbau (German language, New York), Aug. 23, 1946 (article on Himmler and Wolff witnessing shooting of Jews).

Catholic World, Sept. 1943 ("Vatican City Bombed," by J. L. Malloy); Dec. 1943 ("Holy Father on Bombing of Rome," by J. L. Malloy).

Christian Century, July 28, 1943 ("Bombs Rain on Rome"); Sept. 15, 1943 ("Behind the Pope's Peace Plea"); June 7, 1944 ("Vatican Fascism").

Christian Science Monitor Magazine, Oct. 9, 1943 ("Diplomat-Prisoner in the Vatican," by Oswald G. Villard).

The Churchman, June 1, 1945 ("The Conversion of a 'Chief Rabbi', by A. S. E. Yahuda).

La Civiltà Cattolica, Mar. 4, 1961 ("Pio XII e gli ebrei di Roma"); 1972, I, 319–327, 454–461, in booklet form ("Voleva Hitler allentare da Roma Pio XII?" by Robert A. Graham).

Collier's, Apr. 4, 1942 ("General Anders"); Feb. 28, 1943 ("While Rome Burned," by Quentin Reynolds); Dec. 4, 1943 ("Letters from a General"); Feb. 12, 1944 ("Alexander the Modest," by Frank Gervasi); Feb. 26, 1944 ("The French Fight for Rome," by Frank Gervasi); June 10, 1944 ("The Guilty—King Victor Emmanuel III"); Sept. 9, 1944 ("Rome Lives Again," by Frank Gervasi); Oct. 23, 1944 ("Rome's Black Monday," by J. A. Bishop).

Commentary, Nov. 1950 ("The Vatican and the Jewish Question"); Feb. 1958 ("An Outsider Visits the Roman Ghetto," by S. P. Dunn).

Commonweal, Dec. 17, 1943 ("The Vatican and Fascism," by Luigi Sturzo); June 8, 1945 ("The Italian People and the Jews," by Richard Arvay).

The Congress Weekly, Mar. 2, 1945 ("The Case of Rabbi Zolli," by G. Bertel).

Contemporary History, Jan. 1968 ("Three Crises, 1938–39," by Leonidas E. Hill).

The Contemporary Review, Dec. 1944 ("Alphonse Juin").

Il Corriere (Rome), Dec. 4, 5, 1945 (articles on murder of fourteen Via Tasso prisoners).

Corrispondensa Répubblicana, June 1944 (article by Mussolini deploring Allied capture of Rome).

Critica Marxista (Rome), Mar–Apr. 1965 ("Documenti inediti sulle posizione del PCI e del PSIUP dall' ottobre 1943 all' aprile 1944," ed. by Giorgio Amendola and F. Frassati).

Current History, May 1944 ("From Calabria to Cassino: Analysis of Allied Military Mistakes in Italy," by Donald W. Mitchell).

Dallas *Morning News,* June 2, 1944 (article by Wick Fowler on U.S. 36th Div.).

Department of State Bulletin, Oct. 20, Dec. 8, 1946 (Hitler-Mussolini meetings on April 22–23, 1944).

Domenica del Corriere (Rome), Mar. 14, 1972 (article by Robert A. Graham on papal kidnap threat).

Emilia (Bologna), Aug.–Sept. 1955 ("Gli ebrei nella lotta antifascista," by G. Volli).

L'Espresso (Rome), Dec. 3, 1961 ("Perchè non si difesero").

L'Europeo (Milan), Apr. 12, 1964 ("Morire a Roma," ed. by L. Tornabuoni).

Fortnightly, Nov. 6, 1943 ("Russia and Italy," by Sir Charles Gwynn).

Giornale d'Italia (Rome), Mar. 25, 1944 (article on Fascist anniversary meeting).

Harper's, July, Aug. 1966 ("The Secret Surrender," by Allen W. Dulles).

Hommes et Mondes (Paris), Jan. 1954 ("La Bataille de Rome en 1944," by Maréchal Juin).

Incom (Rome), Mar. 1959 (article by Herbert Kappler).

Israel (Rome), Feb. 14, 1945 (report on Zolli's conversion).

Jewish Journal of Sociology (London), Nov. 1960 ("The Roman Jewish Community: A Study in Historical Causation").

The Journal of Modern History, June 1967 ("The Vatican Embassy of Ernst von Weizsäcker, 1943–1945," by Leonidas E. Hill).

Life, Aug. 9, 1943 ("The Bombing of Rome"); May 29, 1944 ("First Attack: Italy"); June 19, 1944 ("The Fall of Rome"); June 26, 1944 ("Americans Take over Rome"); June 26, 1944 ("Pope Greets Americans in Vatican); July 3, 1944 ("Gestapo in Rome"); Aug. 14, 1944 ("The Fall of Esperia"); Oct. 2, 1944 ("Truscott, Lucian King, Jr."); Nov. 28, December 5, 1960 ("Eichmann Tells His Own Damning Story," by Adolf Eichmann).

London Gazette, June 12, 1950 ("The Dispatches of Field Marshal the Earl Alexander of Tunis: The Allied Armies in Italy").

Look, May 1, 1966 ("Comments on [Friedländer's] 'Pius XII and the Third Reich,'" by Father Leiber).

Menorah Journal (New York), autumn, winter 1940; spring 1941 ("The Role of the Jews in Modern Italy," by Marcel Grilli); autumn, 1945 ("Zionism Reconsidered," by Hannah Arendt).

Mercurio (Rome), Dec. 1944 ("Tre eroi [Montezemolo, Giglio, Di Pillo]"); Dec. 1944 ("Vita nella stalla," by A. Moravia).

Il Messaggero (Rome), Mar. 25, 1944 (German announcement of Ardeatine reprisal).

Military Review, Feb. 1963 ("A Classic Stratagem on Monte Cassino," by Ernest F. Fisher); Aug. 1965 ("Rome—An Open City," by Ernest F. Fisher); Feb. 1966 ("Sicily and Italy," by Martin Blumenson).

Miroire de l'Histoire (Paris), Apr. 1966 ("Le Drame de Cassino," by Marshal Juin).

Movimento di Liberazione in Italia (Milan), Sept. 1950 ("Alcuni documenti sull'attrività della banda Koch"); Apr.–June 1963 ("La Resistenza della scuola romana, by Giorgio Caputo); Apr.–June 1966 ("Documenti sull'attività del Sicherheitsdienst nell'Italia," by E. Collotti).

Nation, Nov. 6, 1943 ("Roads to Rome"); Mar. 31, 1945 ("Hitler's Last General," by Joachim Joesten).

New English Review, Apr. 1949 ("Monte Cassino," by Frido von Senger und Etterlin).

The New Republic, Mar. 8, 1943 ("The Pope and Fascism").

Newsweek, Aug. 2, 1943 ("Raids on Eternal City Stir Prelate and Laymen but Catholics Are Split"); Aug. 22, 1943 ("Open City"); Sept. 6,

1943 ("Master Strategist of the Year–General Sir Harold Alexander"); Sept. 27, 1943 ("Holy Hostage"); Oct. 4, 1943 ("Italy as an Air Base," by Peter Masefield); Feb. 14, 1944 ("Ferocity of Nazi Defense Shows Importance of Rome Beachheads"); Feb. 14, 1944 ("The Battle for Rome," by Paul B. Malone); Feb. 21, 1944 ("Smiling Albert"); Mar. 13, 1944 ("The 'Second Hand' Front in Italy," by J. F. C. Fuller); Apr. 3, 1944 ("Alexander's Rocket"); May 22, 1944 ("Kesselring: Soft Soap"); May 22, 1944 ("Report on Italy," by John Lardner); May 29, 1944 ("Allies Supply Missing Pieces for Jigsaw Puzzle of Attack"); June 7, 1944 ("The Why and Wherefore of the Italian Offensive"); June 12, 1944 ("Pope's Fears for Rome Take New Turn as City Becomes a German Target"); June 12, 1944 ("World Greets the Fall of Rome with Relief that City Is Safe"; "Rangers' Fate"); Mar. 12, 1945 (Anders and Poland).

New York *Herald-Tribune*, May 12–June 10, 1944 (daily reportage, particularly articles by Homer Bigart).

New York *Times*, May 12–June 10, 1944 (daily reportage, particularly articles by Milton Bracker and Herbert L. Matthews).

New York *Times Magazine*, June 20, 1943 ("Men of Destiny–Leaders in North Africa," by Hanson W. Baldwin); Aug. 8, 1943 ("Attack–Attack Again Is Alexander's Motto," by Frank L. Kluckhohn"); Sept. 19, 1943 (Mark Clark); Oct. 17, 1943 ("The Appian Road to Rome," by P. W. Wilson); June 18, 1944 ("A New Chapter in Eternal Rome," by Herbert L. Matthews); Mar. 21, 1948 ("Italy in the Shadow of the Hammer and Sickle,") C. L. Sulzberger; June 19, 1953 ("General Mark Clark Gets the Tough Jobs," by Milton Bracker).

The New Yorker, June 17, 24, July 15, 1944 ("Letter from Rome," by Daniel Lang); July 7, 1945 ("Letter from Rome," by Philip Hamburger); Nov. 21, 1945 ("Letter from Rome," by Genêt).

Odra (monthly, Wroclaw, Poland), Apr. 1972–Feb. 1974 ("Rozmowy z Katem" ["Conversations with an Executioner"] by Kazimierz Moczarski).

Osservatore Romano (Rome), Oct. 25–26, 1943 (editorial on Jewish question); Mar. 26, 1944 (editorial on Via Rasella and Ardeatine massacres).

Il Paese (Rome), Dec. 27, 1948 (Celeste Di Porto attacked at restaurant).

Il Ponte (Florence), Nos. 7, 8, 11, 1952; No. 7, 1953 ("Le persecuzioni razziali in Italia," by A. Spinosa).

Il Popolo (Rome), June 4, 1948 (twelve-year-old boy died fighting in Rome).

La Rassegna Mensile di Israel (Rome), Jan. 1957 ("La Chiesa cattolica e il problema ebraico durante gli anni dell'antisemitismo fascista"); 1962 ("Gli ebrei Italiani sotto il regime fascista," by M. Michaelis; "Una testimonanza sul capitolò italiano al processo Eichmann," by G. Romano).

La Revue des Deux Mondes (Paris), May 1, 1952 ("La Bataille du Garigliano," by René Chambé); Mar. 15, 1968 ("La 2e D.I.M. au
Garigliano," by Olivier Poydenot).

Revue Historique de l'Armée (Paris), Jan.–Mar. 1949 ("Le 5e R.T.M. en
Italie," by Colonel Piatte); Special Issue, 1954 ("The French in the
Drive on Rome," by Sidney T. Mathews); May 1967 ("Hommage au
Maréchal Juin").

Rinascita (Rome), No. 4, 1945 ("GAP di zona," by F. Onofri); Mar.
1954 ("Le condizioni della Resistenza romana," by Giorgio Amendola).

Rivista Diocesana di Roma ("Il clero romano durante il periodo della Resistenza").

Rome Daily American, June 4, 1969 (25 years after liberation—anniversary
issue).

Saturday Evening Post, Sept. 7, 1945 ("The Blue Devils Stumped the
Experts," by Sid Feder); May 18, 1946 ("They'll Never Forget Mark
Clark," by Sid Feder).

Scientific American, Mar. 1957 ("The Jewish Community of Rome," by
L. C. and S. P. Dunn).

Southwestern Historical Quarterly, July 1968 (article by Gen. Fred Walker
on the U.S. 36th Division).

Lo Speccio (Rome), Aug. 13, Sept. 24, 1972 (Dollmann on Pope's attitude).

Stars and Stripes (Algiers), May 12–June 4, 1944; (Rome), June 5–10,
1944; daily reportage.

Storia Illustrata (Milan), Feb. 1972 ("La Banda Koch").

Studi Storici, No. 4, 1962 ("I rapporti italo-tedeschi dopo 1'8 settembre").

Il Tempo (Rome, July 15 to 23, 1944 (trial of Rosario Bentivegna).

Il Tempo (Milan), February–March 1951 ("Ecco la Verità," series of five
articles by Karl Wolff).

Texas Parade, Aug. 1968 ("High Road to Rome," by Robert L. Wagner).

Time, July 26, 1943 ("The Arsenal City"); May 29, 1944 ("Juin and the
French"); June 5, 1944 ("Nightmare's End"); June 12, 1944 ("The
Man Who Paved the Way"); June 19, 1944 ("Sunshine and Scars");
Dec. 4, 1944 ("Field Marshal No. 8"); Jan. 28, 1946 ("Murder at the
Rapido").

Visto (Milan), Sept. 1, 1960 (story of Mariolina Odone).

Vital Speeches of the Day, June 15, 1944 (Pres. Roosevelt on fall of
Rome).

Yad Vashem Bulletin (Jerusalem), Oct. 1963 ("Criminal State vs. Moral
Society," by A. L. Kubovy); Mar. 1964 ("Eichmann in New York," by
M. Mushkat).

Unpublished Documents

(EXCEPT OFFICIAL MILITARY COMMUNICATIONS)

Almansi, Dante, *Prima relazione al governo italiano circa le persecuzioni nazi-fasciste degli ebrei in Roma* [*settembre 1943–guigno 1944*], report to Italian government, Rome, Aug. 15, 1944.

Almansi, Renato J., notes on Dante Almansi, New York.

Ardeatine Caves Commission, inquest, *sommario dell'incidente del 23 marzo 1944*, Rome.

Bobinski, Wladyslaw, some records of 3rd Carpathian Division, II Polish Corps, in final battle for Cassino, Paris.

Canadian Forces Headquarters, Dept. of National Defence, Report No. 24, *The Italian Campaign*, Ottawa.

Clark, Mark Wayne, Clark papers, The Citadel, Charleston, S.C.

Comité Français d'Entraide à Rome (French Mutual Aid Committee in Rome), *Gestion Financière*, Paris.

Dunn, S. P., *The Influence of Ideology on Culture Change*, doctoral dissertation, Columbia University, New York, 1959.

German Embassy, Rome and Fasano, diplomatic dispatches, Foreign Ministry archives, Bonn.

Graham, Robert A., *Pius XII and the Axis in World War II*, lecture, Rome.

Green, Paul S., notes on meeting between Prime Minister Pietro Badoglio and General Maxwell Taylor and planned American air drop on Rome, Washington, D.C.

Greiner, Heinrich, ed., *Battle for Rome and Retreat Northward* (report dated May 28, 1944, [German] 362nd Infantry Division), Washington National Records Center (WNRC), National Archives, Washington, D.C.; *War Diary of the Armed Forces Operations Staff*, WNRC.

Howze, Hamilton, lecture prepared for Army War College, Dallas, Tex.

Huesinger, Adolf, *Strategic Turning Points in German Operations in the Second World War*, WNRC.

Ives, Robert M., written reports (36th Division), Dallas, Tex.

Jodl, Alfred, *Estimate of American Operations and Commanders*, WNRC.

Jouin, Col., report on attack by *goumiers* on Aurunci mountains, furnished author by General Guillaume, Paris.

Kesselring, Albert K., *Operations from the Start of the Major Allied Attack up to the Evacuation of Rome, Inclusive*, WNRC; *Rapido River Crossing*, WNRC; *Special Report of the Events in Italy Between 25 July and 8 September 1943*, WNRC.

Kirkman, Sir Sidney, diary of events in battle for Rome, London.

Klinckowstroem, Karl-Heinrich Graf von, *Italy's Breakaway and the Fighting Around Rome, According to the Viewpoint of OB South* (dated Sept. 16, 1947, Neustadt, Germany), WNRC.

Lucas, John P., *The John P. Lucas Papers*, U.S. Army Military History Research Collections, Carlisle Barracks, Pa.

Lynch, George E., *History of the 142nd Infantry, 36th Division, September 3, 1943–May 8, 1945*, Vol. 1, *Italy*, Columbus, Ga.

Mälzer, Kurt, *The Problem of Rome During the Period of the Fighting near Anzio-Nettuno Until the Evacuation of Rome on 4 June 1944,* WNRC.

Neufeld, Maurice, collection of material on Zolli, copies in Library of Congress, Wash., D.C.

Notre Dame de Sion, convent diary, entries during German occupation, Rome.

Office of Strategic Services, Research and Analysis Branch, No. 2993, *The Contributions of the Italian Partisans to the Allied War Effort,* Library of Congress, Washington, D.C.

Planès, Pierre, memoirs of battle for Rome, Paris.

Platt, John, *Early Days with the 2nd Battalion in Italy [Somerset Light Infantry],* London.

Roccas, Goffredo, collection of material on Fascist criminals, Rome.

Sorani, Rosina, *Appunti personali di Rosina Sorani del periodo di occupazione tedesca in Roma,* personal diary, Centro di Documentazione Ebraica Contemporanea, Milan.

Stovall, Oran, personal diary, Walker letters, and other documents relating to 36th Division Rapido and Monte Artemisio operations, Bowie, Tex.

Testimony, trials, Rosario Bentivegna, Pietro Caruso, Celeste Di Porto, Herbert Kappler, Pietro Koch, Rome.

Urban, Joan B., thesis on history of Italian Communism, Catholic University, Wash., D.C.

Vassalli, Giuliano, report on his experience in Via Tasso prison, Rome.

Vietinghoff, Heinrich von, *The Campaign in Italy—The Operations of the 71st German Infantry Division During the Month of May 1944* (dated September 28, 1948), WNRC.

Weizsäcker, Ernst von, *Rundbriefe aus Rom,* collection of letters to his family from Rome, made available to the author by Frau Marianne von Weizsäcker.

Weizsäcker, Marianne von, personal diary from period of German occupation of Rome, Munich.

Wentzell, Fritz, *The Third Battle for Monte Cassino, 11 May 1944–22 May 1944,* WNRC.

Unpublished Official Military Communications

Allied Forces Headquarters, Italy, 1943–44, records, WNRC.

British Eighth Army, records, Ministry of Defense Library, London.

Commander in Chief, Southeast, Army Group C (Kesselring's hq.), records, WNRC.

German Tenth Army, records, WNRC.

German Fourteenth Army, records (including report: *Rückzug und Verfolgung nach der Einnahme von Rom),* WNRC.

German XIV Panzer Corps, war diary, WNRC.

German LI Mountain Corps, war diary, WNRC.

German 26th Panzer Division, records, WNRC.

German 44th Infantry Division, records, WNRC.
German 71st Infantry Division, records, WNRC.
German 94th Infantry Division, records, WNRC.
Hume, Edgar Erskine, *Allied Military Government of Rome under the 5th Army, 5–15 June 1944*, WNRC.
Italian Army, records, WNRC.
Office of Strategic Services, records, WNRC.
U.S. Fifth Army, records, WNRC.

German Military Publications

(AVAILABLE IN BIBLIOTHEK FÜR ZEITGESCHICHTE,
STUTTGART, WEST GERMANY)

Allgemeine Schweizerische Militärzeitshrift, Jahrgang 127, 1961, Nummer 1, Seite 24–26 ("Der Angriff des 2 Karpatischen Schützenbataillons vom 12 Mai 1944 auf die Höhe 593, NE Monte Cassino," by A. Zajac).

Alte Kameraden, Jg. 9, 1961. Nr. 2, S. 14–15 ("Landekopf Anzio-Nettuno," by Karl Hetschel); Jg. 10, 1962, Nr. 12, S. 22–23 ("Vor dem Generalangriff . . . aus dem Landekopf Nettuno," by R. Oehler); Jg. 11, 1963, Nr. 9, S. 28–30, Kt. ("Die 3/576 in der Schlacht von Cassino: Ihr Kampf und Untergang im Mai 1944"); Jg. 12, 1964, Nr. 12, S. 30–31 ("Schwerpunkt—Einsätze an der Via Emilia," by R. Oehler; Jg. 12, 1964, Nr. 5, S. 24–25 ("Das Werferregiment 71 bei Cassino"); Jg. 12, 1964, Nr. 5; S. 14–15 ("Durchbruch bei Cassino," by Rudolf Böhmler); Jg. 13, 1965, Heft 1, S. 26–27 ("Harte Kämpfe um die Stadt Cassino. Grenadierregiment 211 verteidigt verbissen die Ruinen"); Jg. 14, 1966, Nr. 11, S. 27 ("Hartes Ringen um den Monte Pantano. 577er und 578er Bringen die Amerikaner zum Stehen," by F. W. Hauck); Jg. 17, 1969, H. 4, S. 26–27 ("Es Stand auf des Messers Schneide. Rückzugskämpfe im Liri und Saccotal, Mai 1944," by F. W. Hauck).

Der Deutsche Fallschirmjäger, Nr. 9, Sept. 1954, S. 2–4 ("Feind bei Anzio-Nettuno Gelandet," by Walter Gericke); Jg. 1958, H. 2, S. 7–9 ("War die Verteidigung Sinnlos? Eine Antwort zur Frage des Widerstandes am Monte Cassino by Arno"); Jg. 1961, Nr. 7, S. 8n–9, Kt. ("Im Brennpunkt der Cassinofront: Der Polnische Angriff Gegen die Höhe 593," by Rudolf Böhmler; Jg. 1959, Nr. 5, S. 11–12 and Nr. 6, S. 12 ("Alarm bei Anzio-Nettuno" by Ernst Hermann); Jg. 1965, Nr. 5, S. 11 ("Rückzug durch Rom," by Höge).

Der Frontsoldat Erzählt, Jg. 16, 1952, Nr. 1, 2, 3, 5, 7 ("Am Monte Cassino," by W. Stahl); Jg. 17, 1953, Nr. 9, S. 229–231 ("Werfer-'Feuerwehr' der Südfront. Die Harten Kämpfe um den Monte Cassino. Erlebnisse u. Erfahrungen des Werferregiments 71," by Johannes Timke).

Der Gebirgstrupp, Jg. 15, 1966, H. 1. S. 17–20 ("Episoden aus der Schlacht um Monte Cassino," by Emil Boes).

Mitteilungsblatt . . . 44. *Infanterie Division,* Jg. 1964, Folge 16, S. 2–7, Folge 17, S. 2–7, Ktn. ("In Memoriam Oberstleutnant Schlegel: Die Rettung der Kunstschätze von Monte Cassino," by Otto Jans); Jg. 1964, Folge 16, S. 2–7, Folge 17, S. 2–7, Ktn. ("Vor 20 Jahren—Kriegsschauplatz Italien").

Die Österreichische Furche, Jg. 7, 1951, Nr. 45–50, ("Mein Wagnis in Monte Cassino," by Julius Schlegel); Jg. 8, Nr. 27, 1952 ("Neun Jahre Später . . . Mein Wiedersehen mit Monte Cassino," by Julius Schlegel).

Ringel: Hurra die Gams (Graz), Jg. 1956, S. 285–316 ("Monte Cassino," by Julius Ringel).

Rückzug und Verfolgung (Stuttgart), Jg. 1960, S. 197–231 ("Nach dem Ausbruch der Aliierten aus dem Landekopf Anzio-Nettuno 1944").

Schweiz. Militärztschr., Jg. 117, 1951, Nr. 5, S. 312–326 ("Die Angriffsschlachten Gegen Cassino," by Ernst Schuler); Jg. 117, 1951, Nr. 8, S. 545–558 ("Die Kämpfe am Monte Maio vom 10–13 Mai 1944," by Meister).

Staiger: 26. Panzer Division (Bad Nauheim), Jg. 1957 ("Brückenkopf 'Anzio-Nettuno'," by Georg Staiger).

Die Wildente, Nr. 8, Dec. 1954 ("Deutsche Soldaten beim Papst—Mar. 1944," by Al Altmeyer); Folge 10, Aug. 1955, S. 22–25 ("Der Traum der Schönen Crocerossina. Die Letzten Tage von Rom," by Al Altmeyer).

Underground Newspapers in Rome During German Occupation

(AVAILABLE IN VIA TASSO LIBRARY)

L'Azione dei Lavoratori, Feb. 10, 1944 ("L'eroica impresa di S. Paolo").

Fronte Unico, Nov. 23, 1943 ("Sette giorni fra i partigiani").

Giovani, Mar. 1, 1944 ("Notiziario").

Italia Nuova, Apr. 4, 1944 ("Via Rasella e il Germanesimo").

La Punta, Feb. 23, 1944 ("L'aggressione e le rapine").

Il Risorgimento Liberale, June 5, 1944 ("La strage del 24 marzo nel racconto di chi vide e ude"); June 15, 1944 ("Il Generale Mälzer trafficara in borsa nera"; "Storia segreta di Regina Coeli"); June 24, 1944 ("225 milioni asportati da Tamburini e 10 dall' 'alto commisario' Zerbino"); July 13, 1944 ("Documenti—Fosse Ardeatine"); July 15 to 23, 1944 (Rosario Bentivegna trial).

Libraries and Archives Used

UNITED STATES

The Citadel Library, Charleston, S.C.

Columbia University Library, New York, N.Y.

Library of Congress, Washington, D.C.

New York Public Library, New York, N.Y.

Stanford University Library, Stanford, Cal.
University of Texas Library, Austin, Tex.
U.S. Army Military History Research Collection, Carlisle Barracks, Pa.
Washington National Records Center, National Archives, Washington,
    D.C., and Suitland, Md.

ITALY

Archivio Centrale della Stato, Rome.
Associazione Nazionale Partigiani d'Italia, Rome.
Centro di Documentazione Ebraica Contemporanea, Milan.
Istituto Luce, Rome.
Istituto Nazionale Liberazione, Milan.
Il Messaggero archives, Rome.
Via Tasso Library, Rome.

GREAT BRITAIN

Imperial War Museum, London.
Ministry of Defence Library, London.
Polish Institute and Sikorski Museum, London.

FRANCE

Bibliothèque du Ministère des Armées, Paris.
Service Historique de l'Armée, Paris.

WEST GERMANY

Bibliothek für Zeitgeschichte, Stuttgart.
Foreign Ministry archives, Bonn.
Institut für Zeitgeschichte, Munich.
Militärgeschichtliches Forschungsamt, Freiburg.

Index

ABOUT THE AUTHOR

DAN KURZMAN, an award-winning foreign correspondent formerly with the Washington *Post,* is the author of four previous books.

His last one, the internationally acclaimed *Genesis 1948,* published in 1970, was described by Rod MacLeish in the Washington *Post* as "the best thing on the 1948 [Arab-Israeli] war that the reviewer has ever read—or is likely to read"; by James A. Michener as "brilliant"; and by *The Catholic World* as comparable in "sweep and intensity" to *War and Peace.*

Kurzman's first book, *Kishi and Japan,* which appeared in 1960, was viewed by the New York *Times* as "one of the most important biographies of the year" and by the San Francisco *Chronicle* as "probably the best book on the Japanese point of view yet written in English."

Kurzman won the Overseas Press Club Award in 1963 for that year's best book on foreign affairs, *Subversion of the Innocents,* a country-by-country study of the underdeveloped world.

His next book, *Santo Domingo: Revolt of the Damned,* was an expansion of reports appearing in the Washington *Post* on the 1965 Dominican revolution—reports that earned him Long Island University's George Polk Memorial Award for "insight, courage, and resourcefulness."

In 1964, Kurzman won the Newspaper Guild's Front Page Award for a series of articles he wrote for the Washington *Post* from Cuba.

Kurzman has written or broadcast from almost every country in Europe, Asia (including the Middle East), Africa, and Latin America, reporting on international politics and more than two dozen wars, revolutions, and riots.

He started his career as an International News Service correspondent in Paris, then served as the National Broadcasting Company's correspondent in the Middle East. He later became Tokyo bureau chief for the McGraw-Hill World News Service and joined the Washington *Post* in 1962.

Important events that Kurzman has covered include the assassination of Jordan's King Abdullah in 1951, the Tunisian anti-French riots and the Egyptian anti-British riots of 1952, the French Indochinese War in 1953, the U.S. Marine landings in Lebanon in 1958, the Congo massacres of 1961, the Peruvian *coup* in 1962, the U.S.-Haiti confrontation and the Panama Canal Zone riots in 1963, the Vietnam War and Brazilian revolution in 1964, and the Six-Day Middle East War in 1967.

While pursuing news, Kurzman has weathered a locust storm and a bandit attack on his bus in the Ethiopian wilderness; been expelled from South Africa for contacting the African underground; been arrested and threatened by the late "Papa Doc" Duvalier's strongmen in Haiti; been caught in the middle of a tribal battle in the primitive interior of Afghanistan; and ducked bullets and poisoned arrows loosed by dissident tribesmen while with Moise Tshombe's troops in Katanga.

Boston University has established a Dan Kurzman Collection in recognition of his "important contribution to twentieth-century journalism and historical literature."